The Second Battle of
WINCHESTER

The Confederate Victory that Opened
the Door to Gettysburg

Eric J. Wittenberg
and Scott L. Mingus Sr.

SB

Savas Beatie

California

First Edition, first printing

Library of Congress Cataloging-in-Publication Data

Names: Wittenberg, Eric J., 1961- author. | Mingus, Scott L., Author.
Title: The Second Battle of Winchester : the Confederate victory that opened the door to Gettysburg / Eric J. Wittenberg and Scott L. Mingus Sr.
Description: First edition. | El Dorado Hills, California : Savas Beatie LLC, 2016. | Includes bibliographical references and index.
Identifiers: LCCN 2016010383| ISBN 9781611212884 (hardcover : alk. paper) | ISBN 9781611212891 (ebk. : alk. Paper)
Subjects: LCSH: Winchester, 2nd Battle of, Winchester, Va., 1863.
Classification: LCC E475.5 .W58 2016 | DDC 973.7/349--dc23
LC record available at http://lccn.loc.gov/2016010383

SB

Published by
Savas Beatie LLC
989 Governor Drive, Suite 102
El Dorado Hills, CA 95762

Phone: 916-941-6896
(web) www.savasbeatie.com
(E-mail) sales@savasbeatie.com

Savas Beatie titles are available at special discounts for bulk purchases in the United States by corporations, institutions, and other organizations. For more details, please contact Savas Beatie, P.O. Box 4527, El Dorado Hills, CA 95762, or you may e-mail us at sales@savasbeatie.com, or visit our website at www.savasbeatie.com for additional information.

Proudly published, printed, and warehoused in the United States of America.

"To many of us this was a new and strange scene, and will live in our memories as long as reason occupies her throne."

— Cpl. George K. Campbell, Co. B, 116th Ohio Volunteer Infantry

This book is respectfully dedicated to the memory of those Civil War soldiers, blue and gray, who fought at the Second Battle of Winchester, and to the many civilians living or visiting there, whose lives were disrupted during the occupation and subsequent fighting.

Lt. Gen.
Richard S. Ewell

LOC

Maj. Gen.
Robert Milroy

LOC

Table of Contents

Table of Contents (continued)

Foreword

As former Union general Robert H. Milroy lay on his deathbed in Olympia, Washington, in late March 1890, friends and family surrounded and comforted him. While his wife Mary and three sons lamented his impending death, Milroy grieved that he had not done enough during his final 27 years to remove the tarnish his legacy received—despite his exoneration by a court of inquiry—from his disastrous defeat at the Second Battle of Winchester in mid-June 1863. Strong enough to speak barely above a whisper, Milroy implored his family to have a judge visit him so he could give one last statement in his final hours that he bore none of the blame for what happened at Winchester—"the supreme occasion of his life."[1]

Inspired by the statement Milroy gave to a judge, identified in Milroy's obituary as "Justice Austin," newspaper reporters in Olympia covering Milroy's failing health did what they could to not only further exonerate him, but to resurrect an idea held by some of Milroy's veterans who fought at Winchester in 1863: If Milroy had not made such a stubborn resistance against Lt. Gen. Richard Ewell's Second Corps, the Army of the Potomac would not have had the opportunity to defeat Gen. Robert E. Lee at Gettysburg. The Union defeat at Winchester, mused a journalist for Olympia's *Republican Partizan* after Milroy's death, "so detained Lee's army that Meade was enabled to fight more advantageously at Gettysburg."[2]

General Milroy wanted historians to write a detailed chronicle of the Second Battle of Winchester, and in a historical utopia remember his role therein from the *Partizan's* perspective. Alas, the battle faded into the historical shadows and remained there for decades. Early histories gave it only scant attention, and when it did get a nod from historians, the battle and its context were generalized. Popular historian Bruce

1 *Republican Partizan* (Olympia, Washington), April 5, 1890.

2 Ibid.

Catton—who condemned Civil War historians for often oversimplifying the conflict's battles—made the same mistake in his 1952 classic *Glory Road* when he described Second Winchester's complexities in a single sentence: "Off beyond the Blue Ridge Lee's army was moving, and Federal outposts in the Shenandoah Valley collapsed before a tidal wave of Rebel soldiers."[3]

Even some of the earliest studies of the Gettysburg Campaign, of which Second Battle of Winchester played an important part, treated it as a sideshow to the story of Lee's invasion into Pennsylvania. In fact, Edward J. Stackpole, in his once popular *They Met at Gettysburg* (1956) subtitled his two-paragraph treatment of the battle as "The Winchester Sideshow." Glenn Tucker offered similar scant attention to Winchester in his highly touted *High Tide at Gettysburg: The Campaign in Pennsylvania* two years later by devoting only one slim paragraph to the clash between Milroy and Ewell.[4]

Douglas Southall Freeman, in his early 1940s magisterial three-volume study *Lee's Lieutenants: A Study in Command*, and Edwin Coddington in his classic 1968 *The Gettysburg Campaign: A Study in Command*, offered more space to the battle, but failed to fully examine the intricacies of Ewell's victory and the combat's significance.[5] After all, Milroy's defeat had not only opened the door for the Army of Northern Virginia's invasion of the Keystone State, but brought relief to Winchester's Confederate civilian population, which had been enduring Milroy's somewhat harsh occupation for nearly six months. Ewell's success also ended the active enforcement of the Emancipation Proclamation in the Shenandoah Valley, which would not resume until Union forces under Maj. Gen. Philip H. Sheridan wrested the region once more from the Confederacy's grasp in the autumn of 1864.

Ultimately, it was not until 1989 that this crucial engagement received its first stand-alone study in *The Second Battle of Winchester: June 12-15, 1863*, by Charles S. Grunder and Brandon H. Beck. Although a short monograph of fewer than 100 pages, Grunder's and Beck's *The Second Battle of Winchester* laid the intellectual

---

3   Catton wrote of the problem of oversimplification of Civil War history: "We take what we know of the war… as it recedes in the distance… and… we tend to oversimplify it." See John Leekley, ed., *Bruce Catton: Reflections on the Civil War* (New York: Berkeley, 1982), 4; Bruce Catton, *Glory Road* (New York: Doubleday, 1952), 251.

4   Edward J. Stackpole, *They Met at Gettysburg* (Harrisburg, PA: Eagle Books, 1956), 15; Glenn Tucker, *High Tide at Gettysburg: The Campaign in Pennsylvania* (Gettysburg, PA: Stan Clark Military Books, 1995), iv, 22.

5   Douglas Southall Freeman, *Lee's Lieutenants* (New York: Charles Scribner's Sons, 1944), 3: 20-26; Edwin B. Coddington, *The Gettysburg Campaign: A Study in Command* (New York: Charles Scribner's Sons, 1968), 80-91.

foundation for future scholarship on the battle as it not only gave a more complete treatment of the engagement, but offered the first-ever driving tour of the battle's sites not yet lost to development.[6] It certainly laid the cornerstone for my study of General Milroy published in 2006.

Despite my previous work on Milroy, and Grunder's and Beck's *The Second Battle of Winchester*, one thing that serious historians always understand is that no work is truly ever definitive because new research material will always surface from some dusty box in an attic, and historical perspectives change with each generation—hence Voltaire's wise counsel proffered centuries ago that each new generation needs to reexamine the past as each one ponders new historical questions. With the passing of a generation since the publication of Grunder's and Beck's monograph the time has indeed come for a fresh, updated, and more thorough examination of the Second Battle of Winchester.

Seasoned Civil War authors Eric Wittenberg and Scott Mingus—no strangers to writing about events in the Shenandoah Valley or the Gettysburg Campaign—have amassed a significant amount of new material in this study, and through clear prose offer an objective examination of the Second Battle of Winchester sure to become not only the final word on the battle for another generation, but a fitting tribute to the veterans of Milroy's and Ewell's commands who engaged in deadly combat for four days in and around the Shenandoah Valley's most important city, one which witnessed unspeakable horrors and incessant conflict throughout four years of hard war.

Jonathan A. Noyalas

Assistant Professor of History & Director,

Center for Civil War History, Lord Fairfax Community College

---

6   Charles S. Grunder and Brandon H. Beck, *The Second Battle of Winchester: June 12-15, 1863* (Lynchburg, VA: H.E. Howard, 1989).

Acknowledgments

"I consider Winchester about as unsafe a combat as I saw anywhere,
yet the historians say nothing about it."

— R. H. McElhinny, 13th Pennsylvania Cavalry

That innocuous 1909 observation from the pen of an obscure Civil War veteran is exactly why, more than 150 years after the battle, we decided to present the results of years of our combined research on the Second Battle of Winchester.

Only two full-length studies of the battle have made their way into print: *The Second Battle of Winchester, June 12 - 15, 1863*, by Brandon Beck and Charles S. Grunder (Lynchburg, VA, 1989) and *Gateway to Gettysburg: The Second Battle of Winchester*, by Larry Maier (Shippensburg, PA, 2002). For a variety of reasons, including timing, neither monograph utilized the majority of contemporary accounts from the participants. We are blessed to live in the digital age, where thousands of old newspapers, diaries, journals, and other primary sources are now available online. Catalogs of historical societies, local and national archives, libraries, army records, and other collections are now easily accessible. Our efforts to extensively mine these repositories uncovered more than 100 rarely seen (and largely unpublished) accounts of the fighting that add significant depth and insight to the previous historiography of Second Winchester.

So many people have been helpful on this journey. Robert J. Wynstra, the expert on Robert Rodes' division in the Gettysburg Campaign, provided countless leads on original material and shared files from his own collection. We are indebted to him for his contribution, as well as Steve Zerbe, who sent piles of excellent material to sort through. Likewise, Jerry Holsworth of the Stewart Bell Jr. Archives at Handley Library in Winchester pored through the documents, books, maps, and photographs in their collection and made many useful and appreciated suggestions. Lila Fourhman-Shaull provided considerable assistance in locating accounts at the York County Heritage Trust, where researcher and award-winning author Dennis W. Brandt freely shared his voluminous files on the 87th Pennsylvania, as well as his exhaustive database of York and Adams County soldiers' records. Terry Lowry, the dean of all things Civil War West Virginia, provided us with some useful material on the 12th West Virginia Infantry's role in the battle.

Rich Baker and Tom Buffenberger at the U. S. Army Heritage and Education Center in Carlisle, Pennsylvania, did their usual yeoman assistance in digging out old records and letters, as did the folks at the Miami University Archives with the Robert C. Schenck Papers. Eric Burke kindly searched the records at Ohio University for information on Dr. Josiah L. Brown, the assistant surgeon of the 116th Ohio, and for accounts by other members of that regiment. Iren Snavely, the Rare Books Librarian for the State Library of Pennsylvania, graciously scanned and sent old newspaper clippings for us. Carol Poole at the Franklin County (NY) Historical and Museum Society copied the pertinent pages of the diary of the 106th New York's William Hubbard. Amanda Smith at the Meserve-Kunhardt Foundation licensed us to use a seldom-seen photograph of Bower's Hill taken from Fort Milroy late in the 19th century. Jonathan Noyalas, Ronn Palm, Chester Urban, Chris Buckingham, Ben Ritter, and Ken Turner provided images from their collections, as did Jerry Holsworth and Rebecca Ebert at the Handley Regional Library in Winchester.

Karen Mason and Janet Weaver at the University of Iowa Womens' Archives cheerfully provided scanned copies of a letter from Pvt. Albert Miller of the 67th Pennsylvania. Fellow author Linda Fluharty shared information from her vast knowledge of Carlin's Wheeling Battery and sent a signed copy of her interesting book on the letters of Lt. Milton Campbell of the 12th West Virginia. Debbie Harner and Lara Westwood gave gracious assistance in pulling various Civil War documents and files at the Maryland Historical Society. Daryl Poe, Bob Moore, and several others, some wishing to remain anonymous, granted us permission to quote letters from their private collections. Alan Crane shared photos and files from his collection on the 18th Connecticut Infantry. Michael Smith graciously sent us a copy of his ancestor James Mason Smith's unpublished wartime diary.

We also thank our great group of proofreaders and early reviewers who made many contributions and helped steer us on the right path. They include, but are not limited to, our good friend Scott C. Patchan (an expert on the Shenandoah Valley whose book on *Last Battle of Winchester: Phil Sheridan, Jubal Early, and the Shenandoah Valley Campaign, August 7 – September 19, 1864* is a must-read), longtime Ohio Civil War expert and living historian Phil Spaugy, Craig S. Breneiser, Prof. Jonathan Noyalas, Dr. Bradley Gottfried, Rob Wynstra, and Sherry Nay. Martinsburg, WV, historians and writers Jim Droegemeyer and Steve French provided invaluable assistance and commentary on the June 14, 1863, fighting in that vicinity. Charlie Downs painstakingly proofread the final text and made many excellent suggestions to improve the book.

The maps in this book are from California-based artist Hal Jespersen, whose talents have recently been seen in several other Savas Beatie books, including Scott Patchan's Winchester study and Scott Mingus's 2013 award-winning biography of charismatic Confederate General William "Extra Billy" Smith. Hal's painstaking research and attention to detail are evident in his work. Terry Heder of the Shenandoah Valley Battlefield Foundation graciously granted us permission to reuse the text from that organization's brochure outlining a driving tour of Second

Winchester, a permission echoed by its author, Jonathan Noyalas. Judy Kanne, the historian of Jasper County, Indiana, graciously provided photographs of the impressive statue of General Milroy which stands in Rennsselaer.

We certainly cannot overlook nor praise enough the wonderful help from our good friend and managing director Ted Savas, who offered guidance on the writing and editing of this study, and his staff at Savas Beatie, most notably production manager Lee W. Merideth, marketing director Sarah Keeney, and author liaison Michele Sams. Their professionalism and enthusiasm are among the many reasons why Savas Beatie has become one of the premier publishers of military history books in the country and why many authors keep coming back to them to publish their books.

Finally we would like to thank our respective families and support networks. Without their patience, support, and love, this work would have not been possible.

Eric J. Wittenberg,
Columbus, Ohio

Scott Mingus,
York, Pennsylvania

Introduction

Major General Robert Huston Milroy fretted. A large force of Confederates—about one-third of Lee's vaunted Army of Northern Virginia—was bearing down on his garrison in Winchester, Virginia. Milroy had only about 8,200 men available to hold the important Shenandoah Valley town, but he was convinced its extensive network of earthworks would provide an adequate defense. Still, the restless Milroy was worried.

Robert Milroy had an excitable nature. Born on a farm near Salem, Indiana, on June 11, 1816, he had long sought glory. The family moved to Carroll County, Indiana, in 1826, where the young Milroy worked on the family farm. In 1840, at the age of 24, Milroy enrolled in Captain Partridge's Academy in Norwich, Vermont. Now known as Norwich University, Captain Partridge's Academy was a military institute along the lines of South Carolina's The Citadel or the Virginia Military Institute.[7] Milroy graduated first in his class of ten cadets, earning a Bachelor of Arts, a Master of Military Science, and a Master of Civil Engineering in just three years. He tried to obtain a commission in the U. S. Army, but was rebuffed at every turn. The failure to obtain a commission seeded in him an institutional bias against what he labeled the

---

7 For an excellent full-length biography of Milroy, see Jonathan A. Noyalas, *"My Will is Absolute Law": A Biography of Union General Robert H. Milroy* (Jefferson, NC: McFarland & Co., 2006). The authors recommend this fine work to anyone wanting a detailed look at the life of this controversial figure. For a detailed discussion of the important role played by Norwich alumni during the Civil War, see Robert G. Poirier, *By The Blood Of Our Alumni: Norwich University Citizen Soldiers In The Army Of The Potomac, 1861-1865* (Mason City, IA: Savas Publishing, 1999).

"royal priesthood of West Point." This bitterness would only grow as the years passed.[8]

Milroy enrolled in law school at Indiana State University. Craving adventure rather than a desk job, however, he dropped out after one year and went to Texas to try and obtain a commission in the fledgling army of his cousin Sam Houston's Texas Republic. However, when his father and older brother died in the fall of 1845, Milroy was called home to take over the operation of the family farm in Indiana. Still, Milroy dreamed of somehow utilizing the military training he had received at Captain Partridge's Academy.[9] Little did he realize the opportunity to embark on the great military adventure for which he so longed was about to present itself.

When the Mexican War broke out in 1846, he eagerly pitched into recruiting and training a company of Indiana volunteer infantry. The effort paid off when Milroy was elected captain of the company.[10] Although he and his troops were sent to Mexico, they never saw combat. Instead, they spent their time performing guard and garrison duty at Matamoros and Monterey. Rather than battlefield glory, Milroy found boredom and misery. When their term of enlistment expired in 1847, Milroy recruited another company, this time of mounted infantry, and returned to Mexico with his new command. He offered his troops to Gen. Zachary Taylor, who would only accept them as regular—and not as mounted—infantry. Taylor suggested Milroy offer his troops to the government of Texas, which also declined to accept them.[11]

Frustrated, and without any other viable options, Milroy returned to Indiana and resumed his legal education at Indiana State University. He graduated in 1850, married, and was admitted to the bar. He also became involved with politics, attending Indiana's 1850 constitutional convention as a delegate. An ardent abolitionist, he enthusiastically supported the state's fledgling Republican Party in the late 1850s. After briefly serving as a judge, Milroy resigned to open what would become a prosperous law office in Rensselaer, Indiana, in 1854. The busy lawyer was still engaged in the practice of law when the secession crisis broke out.

A devoted patriot, Milroy personally recruited a company of infantry in Rensselaer before President Abraham Lincoln's inauguration in 1861. Two weeks after South Carolina forces fired on Fort Sumter in April, Milroy was commissioned

---

8 Milroy to Gen. Robert Schenck, January 18, 1863, Robert Schenck Papers, Miami University, Oxford, Ohio.

9 Noyalas, *My Will is Absolute Law*, 10-11.

10 Ezra J. Warner, *Generals in Blue: Lives of the Union Commanders* (Baton Rouge: Louisiana State University Press, 1964), 326.

11 Noyalas, *My Will is Absolute Law*, 12-13.

colonel of the 9th Indiana Infantry, a three-month regiment. He reenlisted for three years after the regiment's initial 90-day term of service, and took part in Maj. Gen. George B. McClellan's campaign in western Virginia.

Milroy's shock of wild gray hair and thick beard prompted his men to call him "the Grey Eagle." His looks and attitude made him the subject of numerous pen portraits. "Gen. Milroy is a tolerably large man about 50 years old," wrote one of his soldiers in 1862. "His hair is quite gray, sandy whiskers. Rides a white horse puts me very much in mind of pictures of Gen. [Zachary] Taylor." David Hunter Strother, a Union cavalry officer, left a vivid description of the Hoosier: "Milroy is a man of fifty, tall and well made, florid complexion with red beard, sharp features crowned with stiff, grey hair which rose from his forehead like a porcupine's quills."[12]

A kinder contemporary, Maj. Gen. Oliver O. Howard in a postwar account described Milroy as having silvery white hair, with "a clear eye and a fine face." Howard believed "there never was a man more loyal to his country," but "he was brave to rashness. Of course Milroy would not run unless he received orders to do so." Howard added that the general's "ardor for the Union made him severe towards disloyal inhabitants."[13] Major General Carl Schurz, who served under Howard, left his own vivid postwar description. "When [Milroy] met the enemy he would gallop up and down his front, fiercely shaking his first at the 'rebel scoundrels over there,' and calling them all sorts of outrageous names," wrote Schurz, "he would 'pitch in' at the head of his men, exposing himself with the utmost recklessness. He was a man of intense patriotism. He did not fight as one who merely likes fighting. The cause for which he was fighting—his country . . . was constantly present to his mind . . . he did good service, was respected and liked by all." Another accurately described Milroy as "a zealous patriot, but patience was not one of his virtues."[14]

An enlisted man of the 116th Ohio Volunteer Infantry who admired Milroy even after the debacle that would befall him at Winchester, left this description: "Gen. Milroy is a noble, generous man, would just as soon talk with a private as a colonel; he

12 Garber A. Davidson, ed., *The Civil War Letters of the Late 1st Lieut. James J. Hartley, 122nd Ohio Infantry Regiment* (Jefferson, NC: McFarland & Co., 1998), 15; Cecil D. Eby, Jr., ed., *A Virginia Yankee in the Civil War: The Diaries of David Hunter Strother* (Chapel Hill: University of North Carolina Press, 1961), 194-95. David Hunter Strother, aka "Porte Crayon," was one of the foremost illustrators of the day. The Martinsburg, Virginia (now West Virginia) native was a cousin of Union Gen. "Black Dave" Hunter.

13 Oliver O. Howard, "Gen'l. O. O. Howard's Personal Reminiscences of the War of the Rebellion," *National Tribune*, June 19, 1884.

14 Carl Schurz, *The Reminiscences of Carl Schurz*, 2 vols. (New York: Doubleday, Page & Co., 1907-1908), 2:387-88; *Buffalo Evening News*, February 17, 1913.

is a genuine hater of red tape and its influence, he is animated by a lofty patriotism, influenced by a fearless bravery and high daring, that very few possess; his whole soul is in the work in which he is engaged; he says, he just wants to live to see the old flag floating over every inch of soil of the 'Old Union' and he is satisfied. He is beloved by his command."[15] This Buckeye's opinion echoed that of many others who served under the Grey Eagle's command.

Another ardent Milroy admirer was the Reverend Charles C. McCabe, who served as the chaplain of the 122nd Ohio Infantry. According to the Methodist minister, the male citizens of the Lower Valley had fled, leaving their towns virtually deserted: "They think our General is the most heartless of mankind—They don't know him. I did what I could to correct this impression. He is one of the most tenderhearted men that ever led a battalion" (an opinion not shared by the locals). "To him treason appears to be the blackest, the basest of crimes. To the rich, aristocratic traitor he carries an iron front, and holds the scale of retributive justice with an even hand." He testified that Milroy would reach into the bottom of his own pockets when he saw a brother soldier in want, no matter his rank, "provided there was a necessity for such generosity."[16]

Other colleagues were not so kind in their assessment of General Milroy. "He was brave, but his bravery was of the excitable kind that made him unbalanced and nearly wild on the battlefield," recalled Maj. Gen. Jacob D. Cox. "His impulsiveness made him erratic in all performances of duty, and negligent of the system without with the business of an army cannot go on. . . . Under the immediate control of a firm and steady hand he could do good service, but was wholly unfit for independent responsibility." Many who served under Milroy's command did not quite know what to make of him. "He had energy enough, but it was of the extremely nervous, excitable kind," wrote one of his officers. "He was generally out of patience with something or other, and when in such a mood it seemed difficult for him to treat one civilly."[17]

Milroy's bombast endeared him to his enlisted men. They appreciated his concern for their well-being, and they loved his enthusiastic rejection of the army's stuffy conventions. In the spring of 1863, the wife of Pvt. Josiah Staley, a member of the 123rd Ohio Infantry, was expecting a baby. "What do you think of R. H. Milroy for a

---

15 "Letter from the 116th O.V.I," *Athens Messenger*, July 16, 1863.

16 Charles C. McCabe, "From the 122nd Ohio, *Zanesville (Ohio) Daily Courier*, May 20, 1863.

17 Jacob Dolson Cox, *Military Reminiscences of the Civil War*, 2 vols. (New York: Charles Scribner's Sons, 1900), 1:405-406; William H. Beach, *The First New York (Lincoln) Cavalry* (New York: Lincoln Cavalry Association, 1902), 220.

name for that boy?" he asked.[18] Despite Milroy's mercurial nature, his men loved him and were prepared to follow him anywhere he asked them to go.

Milroy was promoted to brigadier general on September 3, 1861, and appointed to command the Cheat Mountain District in what would become West Virginia. He had the unfortunate luck of leading his brigade against Maj. Gen. Thomas J. "Stonewall" Jackson's forces at McDowell during Valley Campaign of 1862. Later that summer, Milroy's independent brigade joined Maj. Gen. John Pope's Army of Virginia. Milroy despised West Pointers. "Scientific West Point generals and their Science is proving as detrimental to the Nation as Treason," he sneered.[19] His constant conflict with the army's institutionalized command structure undoubtedly hindered his career.

Milroy's troops found themselves on Henry House Hill in the eye of a vortex at the climax of the Second Battle of Bull Run on the afternoon of August 30, 1862. Extremely agitated and by some accounts out of control, Milroy tried to stem the tide of routed Union soldiers streaming off the field in the wake of the sledgehammer blow delivered by Maj. Gen. James Longstreet. "I saw that a *Second Bull Run* was commencing and thought I would stop a great tide of cowardly runaways," was how he described it in a letter to his wife after the battle. He tried to rally the fleeing Union soldiers with the point of his sword. When that failed, he ordered his brigade to fix bayonets. The effort succeeded in rallying some of the routed soldiers, and Milroy plugged a hole in the Union line on Henry House Hill.[20]

Shifting troops to shore up the faltering Federal front, Milroy begged for reinforcements. None were forthcoming. His demeanor while doing so, however, persuaded other officers that he was unstable and disturbed, "shouting like a crazy man" according to one account. Eventually, the overwhelming majority of Longstreet's forces drove the Union soldiers from the field. Bowing to the inevitable, General Pope ordered a retreat. The order horrified Milroy. "Up to this time I was buoyed with confidence in our glorious case, but now I was entirely cast down [and] all appeared to be lost and the glorious inheritance won and transmitted to us by our fathers [was] gone forever," he lamented to his wife. Once again, the mercurial Milroy

---

18 Nancy K. Stout, ed., *The Blue Soldier: Letters of the Civil War* (Brush Prairie, WA: privately published, 1998), 72.

19 Warner, *Generals in Blue*, 326; Robert H. Milroy to Mary Milroy, August 2, 1862, Margaret B. Paulus, comp., *Papers of General Robert Huston Milroy*, 2 vols. (n.p., n.d.), 1:60.

20 Milroy to Mary Milroy, September 4, 1862, Robert H. Milroy Papers, Jasper County Public Library, Rensselaer, Indiana (hereinafter "Milroy Papers"). For more on the Chinn Ridge and Henry House Hill fighting at Second Bull Run, see Scott C. Patchan, *Second Manassas: Longstreet's Attack and the Struggle for Chinn Ridge* (Dulles, VA: Potomac Books, 2011).

blamed professional soldiers for the devastating defeat. "All this has been brought about by *West Pointers*—Soulless, brainless, Selfish Villains who have made their *Profession*—Care nothing for the country, so that they can be hoisted into high places."

Shortly after the debacle Milroy met with Lincoln, Secretary of War Edwin M. Stanton, and General-in-Chief Henry W. Halleck and denigrated Pope's generalship to the men who had personally plucked Pope from the West and ordered him to command the new Virginia army thrown together for him. Milroy told the president that if he "continued to let *West Point* rule in our armies that it would ensure the destruction of the Union beyond doubt." The chief executive made no response beyond a silent glare at the bold and presumptuous officer. However, Milroy did get the satisfaction of seeing Pope relieved of command and exiled to Minnesota. The episode marked the abrasive Hoosier as a man who might be trouble.[21]

Not long after, Milroy and his brigade were sent to western Virginia, where he again assumed command of the Cheat Mountain District. He soon became notorious for his righteous heavy-handedness against civilians, whom he viewed to be in rebellion against the United States. Milroy was promoted to major general of volunteers (dating from November 1862), assumed command of the 2nd Division, 8th Corps, and was assigned to the Baltimore-based Middle Military District helmed by Maj. Gen. Robert C. Schenck. That same month Confederate troops evacuated Winchester, and the strategic crossroads town returned to Union control.[22] In January 1863, Schenck ordered Milroy and his division to occupy Winchester.

And so the mercurial, controversial, and outspoken Robert Huston Milroy mounted the stage as the central figure in what many would see as a Greek tragedy.

Author's Note

At the time of Second Winchester, West Virginia was still formally part of Virginia and would not become a separate state until later in the month. However, for clarity's sake, we use West Virginia for the various Union military units from that region (12th West Virginia Infantry, 1st West Virginia Artillery, etc.). We believe this is easier to follow than 12th Virginia (Union). During the Civil War, modern Charles Town, West Virginia, was usually spelled Charlestown. To avoid confusion for the modern reader with the state capital of the similar name, we use "Charles Town."

---

21 Charles F. Walcott, *History of the Twenty-First Regiment Massachusetts Volunteers* (Boston: Houghton-Mifflin, 1882), 148-49;.Milroy to Mary Milroy, September 1862, included in Margaret B. Paulus, comp., *Papers of General Robert Huston Milroy*, 2 vols. (n.p.), 1:98 and 1:122.

22 Noyalas, *"My Will is Absolute Law"*, 1-218.

Chapter 1

December 1862 - June 1863

"The devil ne'er hated holy water with half the bitterness
that these lovely young Winchester girls hated us."

— *James M. Dalzell, 116th Ohio Infantry*

The town of Winchester, Virginia, occupied a strategic place in the Lower Shenandoah Valley. The macadamized Valley Pike—a major north-south route of commerce—ran through the historic town north from Staunton down the scenic valley to the Potomac River and beyond into rural Maryland and, eventually, Pennsylvania. The fertile region was once home to many Indian tribes, including the Shawnee nation, and witnessed bloody intertribal wars with the Iroquois, as well as conflicts with the Catawba and others. In the mid-1700s, white settlers, mostly Quakers, Germans, and Scots-Irish from New York and Pennsylvania, supplanted the Indians and spent the next century establishing farms, mills, and light industry. The rich soil enabled farmers to prosper. Orchards produced a wide variety of fruit, most notably apples, and the fields sprouted a host of crops. Therapeutic mineral springs abounded, and several became popular resorts.[1]

By the middle of the 19th century, Winchester featured gas lights, sidewalks, dozens of tidy brick storefronts, popular hotels and taverns, and a handsome iron-fenced county courthouse built in the Greek Revival style. Stately brick or stone homes lined the main streets, indicative of the town's prewar wealth. Since the late

---

1 Files of the Stewart Bell, Jr. Archives, Handley Regional Library, Winchester, VA. Scottish engineer John L. McAdam pioneered in 1820 the concept of building roads with successive layers of finer stones (usually limestone) to establish a smooth and compacted surface. In 1822, the first macadam road in America opened between Hagerstown and Boonsboro, Maryland.

Panoramic view of downtown Winchester taken in 1894 by an unknown photographer; looking southeast from the Main Fort. *Handley Regional Library*

1830s, the Winchester & Potomac Railroad had offered a convenient outlet for farmers and merchants to ship their wares north 31.5 miles through Summit Point and Charles Town to Harpers Ferry, where the standard gauge tracks intersected the extensive Baltimore & Ohio system. From there, the goods moved in every direction.[2]

Winchester had developed into an important center of regional commerce and the seat of Frederick County. Good roads radiated out of the town (clockwise) north to Martinsburg, [West] Virginia, Berryville to the east, Millwood to the southeast, Front Royal to the south, Strasburg to the southwest, Romney to the west, and finally, Pughtown to the northwest leading to Berkeley Springs, [West] Virginia, and on to Hancock, Maryland. Several secondary roads also fed Winchester, including the Senseny Road to the east and the old Front Royal Road (also known as Paper Mill Road) to the south. Several meandering watercourses cut across the hilly terrain forming steep ravines and ditches. The most important of these streams included Opequon Creek to the south, and closer to town, Abram's (also called Abraham's) Creek, Town Run, and Red Bud Run.[3]

---

2   Ibid. Charles Town was known as Charlestown in 1863. We use the modern spelling throughout his book to avoid confusion with Charlestown WV.

3   United States Department of War, *Atlas to Accompany the Official Records of the Union and Confederate Armies* (New York: B&N Books, 1983), Plate 39:4, Capt. W. Alonzo Powell map. The Pughtown Road (modern VA Route 522) was also called the North Frederick Turnpike, and the Romney Road was also known as the Northwestern Turnpike (1885 Frederick County map by D. J. Lake & Co.) Abram's (Abraham's) Creek flows southeasterly around Winchester's hills before turning east to empty into Opequon Creek. The creek took its name from prominent early Quaker businessman Abraham Hollingsworth, who constructed a large stone grist mill along its banks in the mid-1700s (Winchester-Frederick County Historical Society).

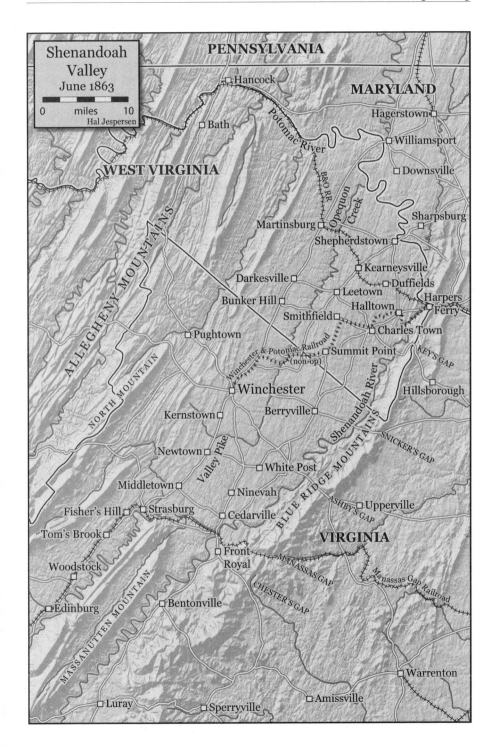

Shenandoah
Valley
June 1863

0   miles   10
Hal Jespersen

PENNSYLVANIA

Hancock

MARYLAND

Hagerstown

Bath

Potomac River

Williamsport

WEST VIRGINIA

Downsville

B&O RR

Opequon Creek

Sharpsburg

Martinsburg

Shepherdstown

Kearneysville

Darkesville

Duffields

Leetown

Harpers Ferry

Bunker Hill

Halltown

Smithfield

Pughtown

Charles Town

ALLEGHENY MOUNTAINS

NORTH MOUNTAIN

Winchester & Potomac Railroad (non-op)

Summit Point

KEY'S GAP

Winchester

Hillsborough

Kernstown

Berryville

Shenandoah River

SNICKER'S GAP

Newtown

Valley Pike

White Post

BLUE RIDGE MOUNTAINS

Middletown

Ninevah

ASHBY'S GAP

Upperville

Fisher's Hill

Strasburg

Cedarville

Tom's Brook

VIRGINIA

Woodstock

Front Royal

MANASSAS GAP

Manassas Gap Railroad

MASSANUTTEN MOUNTAIN

Edinburg

Bentonville

CHESTER'S GAP

Warrenton

Luray

Sperryville

Amissville

A series of roughly parallel ridges and low mountains dominated the landscape, the most prominent being pine-covered Little North Mountain west and northwest of Winchester. Northeast of this high ground was the lower Apple Pie Ridge, named for the abundant orchards populating the area. A low extension of Apple Pie Ridge known as Flint Ridge lay between the Pughtown and Romney roads. Closer in toward town on its immediate southwestern side was the broad plateau of Bower's Hill (sometimes called Potato Hill for its most notable early crop), with the Valley Pike bordering much of its eastern slope. The southern extremity of this ridge was often called Milltown Heights after several nearby woolen, paper, and flour mills. The most notable of these was a three-story, triple-pillared stone mill along Abram's Creek, near the Valley Pike, which was owned by Issac Hollingsworth. A two-mile wooden mill race provided water power for the old mills, several of which dated from the turn of the century. The creek and race continued eastward across the Valley Pike before winding north past the Front Royal Road, where the race terminated at another of the prolific Hollingsworth family's string of mills. The stream continued on from there, taking an abrupt easterly turn before emptying into Opequon Creek.[4]

South of town, at the intersection of the Valley Pike and Millwood Pike, was Camp Hill, so named because of the troops who pitched their tents there during times of war. Near it, Cemetery Hill sported multiple adjacent graveyards—including separate ones for fallen Union and Confederate soldiers—as well as the town's main civilian cemetery. Well to the southwest toward the village of Kernstown, the terrain was highlighted by the low tree-covered Sandy Ridge and a broad and relatively open hill on the Samuel R. Pritchard farm, crisscrossed by numerous old stone walls. In recalling the March 1862 battle of Kernstown, a soldier wrote, "the country was level and cultivated, with patches of woodland. . . . In our center and just to the right [west] of the turnpike was a high, conical elevation, called Pritchard's Hill. This hill was under cultivation. From its slopes and summit there was a fine view of the entire field. It furnished good positions for some of our batteries," he added, "and an admirable screen for troops and maneuvers."[5]

---

4 Ibid.; *The War of the Rebellion: A Compilation of the Official Records of the Union and Confederate Armies*, 128 vols. (Washington, DC: Government Printing Office, 1889), Series 1, vol. 27, Part 2, 44, hereinafter cited as *OR*. All references are to Series 1 unless otherwise noted). Quaker businessman Isaac Parkins constructed a large house known as "Milltown" (later "Willow Lawn") on the site. Some accounts and maps spell Bower's as Bowers' and Bowers.

5 Ibid.; George K. Johnson, *The Battle of Kernstown, March 23, 1862: A Paper Prepared and Read before the Michigan Commandery of the Military Order of the Loyal Legion* (Detroit: Winn A. Hammond, 1890), 6. Sandy Ridge is no more than 100 feet high at its tallest point. Relatively open stands of pine and oak trees covered part of it in 1863. The Middle Road generally follows its eastern slope.

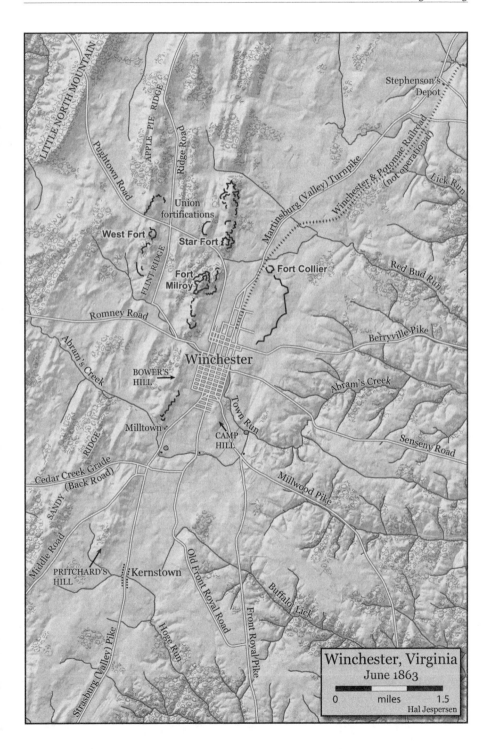

Winchester, Virginia
June 1863

0   miles   1.5
Hal Jespersen

According to the 1860 census, Winchester boasted 4,403 inhabitants, including 655 free blacks and 708 slaves. The early years of the war sparked a mass exodus of young white men into the Confederate army, and more than a few nervous residents fled to escape the conflict. Anyone who could read a map or even a newspaper had fair warning that war would come often to the important Lower Shenandoah Valley community. More than half of the populace had departed by the end of the war's second year. Control of the Valley, its critical transportation network, and vast food supplies was of great strategic importance to both North and South. As a result, Winchester changed hands more than 70 times during the Civil War, and had thus far witnessed considerable fighting during the 1862 Valley Campaign. The town's two newspapers, the *Republican* and the *Virginian*, ceased operation in early 1862. Soldiers of the occupying 5th Connecticut Infantry used the *Virginian's* printing press in March to produce their own paper.[6]

The hard hand of war first paid Winchester a visit in the spring of 1862, when Maj. Gen. Nathaniel P. Banks and 6,500 Union soldiers marched in to occupy the strategic town. Banks was an influential Republican politician from Massachusetts, his high rank more the result of his political clout than his military prowess. On May 25, 1862, Maj. Gen. Thomas J. "Stonewall" Jackson and some 17,000 Confederates marched north from Front Royal and attacked Banks on Bower's Hill in what would eventually come to be known as the First Battle of Winchester. Banks was unable to defend the town and was driven out in a wild rout. Jackson, who had no political clout at all, owed his rank to his experience and military prowess, which he would demonstrate time and again over the coming months. The beaten Unionists retreated nearly 40 miles to the Potomac River and crossed to the far bank at Williamsport, Maryland. Banks suffered more than 2,000 casualties to Jackson's 400. The Winchester fighting was Stonewall's first major victory in his Shenandoah Valley Campaign, a success that siphoned away thousands of Union soldiers from Maj. Gen. George B. McClellan's Peninsula Campaign opposite Richmond, Virginia, and the defenses of Washington. The Rebels' subsequent plundering of the massive Union supply depot at Winchester earned for Banks the unflattering sobriquet "Commissary Banks." Banks' defeat raised the question of whether a small force of infantry could hold Winchester against a numerically superior enemy force. By the early summer of

---

6   Thomas E. Pope, *The Weary Boys: Colonel J. Warren Keifer and the 110th Ohio Volunteer Infantry* (Kent, OH, Kent State University Press, 2002), 35. Perhaps 1,500 residents remained in Winchester by the start of 1863; *The Eighth Census of the United States* (Washington, DC: United States Government, 1860); "Chronicling America: Historic American Newspapers" website, Library of Congress, http://chroniclingamerica.loc.gov/lccn/sn85025369/, last accessed December 5, 2013.

1863 the issue was about to be put to the test once more: thousands of Union soldiers were once again garrisoned in and around Winchester.[7]

After the occupying Confederates departed in late November 1862, Brig. Gen. John Geary marched his Federals into town on December 3, only to march back out soon thereafter when reports of smallpox crossed his desk. Rebel cavalry returned for a short time, only to ride out on the 15th. Meanwhile, Union Brig. Gen. Robert H. Milroy had directed his French-born subordinate, Brig. Gen. Gustave Paul Cluseret, to lead a 3,000-man force of infantry, artillery, and cavalry into the city. Cluseret arrived on Christmas Eve to the consternation of much of the populace. One young lady named Laura Lee bemoaned, "The wretched, horrible Yankees are here again!" Indeed they were, and many more were on the way. On New Year's Day, 1863, Milroy marched the rest of his division into downtown Winchester.[8]

Milroy's command, a division of the Eighth Corps, came under the jurisdiction of the Middle Department, which had been created earlier in the war to oversee and handle troops within the Mid-Atlantic States. Milroy reported to Maj. Gen. Robert C. Schenck, a former Ohio congressman, diplomat, and veteran of the disastrous 1862 Valley Campaign. Badly wounded in the right arm at Second Bull Run in late August, Schenck was now in charge of the Middle Department with his headquarters in Baltimore, Maryland. It was Milroy's job to protect the Lower Shenandoah Valley from Winchester while Brig. Gen. Benjamin F. Kelley controlled the Union defenses of the upper Potomac River from his headquarters at Harpers Ferry. The composition of Milroy's force fluctuated throughout his time in Winchester, but it usually consisted of three brigades under General Cluseret (and his eventual successor Brig. Gen. Washington L. Elliott), Col. Andrew T. McReynolds, and Col. William G. Ely.[9]

Those citizens of Winchester of the Confederate persuasion felt Milroy's iron fist. Soon after his arrival, his policies prompted the exit of another round of refugees when he strictly enforced the provisions of President Abraham Lincoln's Emancipation Proclamation and establish firm Federal control over what Milroy perceived to be an unruly and rebellious populace. On January 1, 1863, the general

---

7   As of the writing of this study, there is no detailed tactical monograph on the First Battle of Winchester. The only published monograph on the battle is Brandon H. Beck and Charles S. Grunder, *The First Battle of Winchester: May 25, 1862* (Lynchburg, VA: H. E. Howard, 1992).

8   Laura Lee Diary, entry for December 24, 1863, Manuscripts and Rare Books Department, Swem Library, College of William & Mary, Williamsburg, VA.

9   Jonathan A. Noyalas, *My Will is Absolute Law: General Robert H. Milroy and Winchester, Virginia* (Blacksburg, VA, master's thesis, Virginia Tech, 2003), 21. Although abolished in July 1862 when it was re-designated the Eighth Corps, the name Middle Department was still employed in reference to this corps and the general administrative district it encompassed.

assembled his entire command, galloped along the lines of his reunited division brandishing his sword above his head, and cried out, "This is Emancipation Day!" According to a soldier in the 122nd Ohio Infantry, "The whole division responded with resounding cheers. I looked, and the sun was just rising to usher in the first day of real liberty this republic ever saw." Most of Winchester's citizens did not share the Buckeye soldier's enthusiasm for emancipation.[10]

On January 5, Milroy issued a bold proclamation of his own emblazoned with the provocative headline "Freedom to Slaves!" and announced that he intended to "maintain and enforce" Lincoln's Emancipation Proclamation. Anyone who resisted its peaceful enforcement would be "regarded as rebels in arms against the lawful authority of the Federal government and dealt with accordingly." Typical of Milroy's early targets was Berkeley County plantation owner Philip De Catesby Jones, a member of a prominent long-time Shenandoah Valley family. Union Generals Robert Patterson and Nathaniel Banks had earlier deported several of Jones' slaves from Virginia. Milroy now finished the task by sending the rest of them under army escort north across the Potomac. In total, the pro-Confederate Jones lost seventeen slaves in this manner.[11]

Milroy proved to be an equal opportunity squabbler. In addition to the Virginians, he argued with some of his senior officers, including a public spat with General Cluseret that caught the attention of the townspeople. Mary Greenhow Lee reported that Cluseret was upset with Milroy's emancipation policy and that "he did not come here to fight for negroes, & to arrest women, & that is contrary to the usages of war to refuse to feed prisoners." The determined Milroy forced Cluseret to relinquish his command and leave Winchester in mid-January, but the distraught Frenchman did not officially resign his commission until March.[12]

---

10 *The Rome (NY) Daily Sentinel,* April 12, 1899.

11 U.S. Brigadier General R. H. Milroy's Order to Citizens of Winchester and Frederick County, Virginia, in Reference to the Emancipation Proclamation of President Abraham Lincoln, January 5, 1863, National Archives and Records Administration (NARA), Washington, DC.; List, 1861-1863, of African-American slaves of Philip De Catesby Jones of Berkeley County, VA (now WV) who were removed from Virginia by the U.S. Army between 1861 and 1863, Philip De Catesby Jones Papers, Virginia Historical Society, Richmond. The 71-year-old General Robert Patterson, a Mexican War veteran, commanded the Army of the Shenandoah in mid-1861. His lack of aggression in the Valley made it easier for Confederate Gen. Joseph E. Johnston to move his command from Winchester east to Manassas to reinforce the army fighting there under Gen. P. G. T. Beauregard along Bull Run. Nathaniel Banks assumed command after Patterson was mustered out of the army in late July. Banks lost the First Battle of Winchester on May 25, 1862, and was driven from the Lower Valley.

12 Mary Greenhow Lee Diary, entry for January 10, 1863, Handley Library, Winchester, VA; Noyalas, *"My Will is Absolute Law,"* 26. Cluseret returned to New York City and co-founded a

"My will is absolute law," Milroy bragged to his wife Mary on January 18. "None dare contradict or dispute my slightest word or wish. The secesh here have heard many terrible stories about me before I came and supposed me to be a perfect Nero for cruelty and blood, and many of them both male and female tremble when they come into my presence to ask for small privileges, but the favors I grant them are slight and few for I confess I feel a strong disposition to play the tyrant among these traitors." He did so uniformly, incurring the hatred of anyone not an ardent Unionist. "Hell is not full enough," he later scorned. "There must be more of these Secession women of Winchester to fill it up."[13]

The saucy tongue of one young secessionist woman became almost mythical. During the winter, Milroy directed his men to seize hay, fodder, corn, and other forage from Confederate sympathizers in the region, and to deny the sale of such items to anyone judged disloyal to the Union. When a party of soldiers visited the farm of a poor man named John Arnold and carried off a small hayrick, the man's daughter, Laura, went to the general to beg for its return, or for a permit to obtain forage for the family's cow, whose milk was the chief support for the family. "You shall not have it, unless your father will take the oath," demanded Milroy. "Are *you* loyal?" he supposedly asked her. "Yes," she replied. He began to write the permit before inquiring, "To the United States?" "To the Confederacy, of course," Laura replied. After conversation concerning how the cow would starve over the winter without the hay, Milroy finally denied her request, exclaiming, "You all brought on this devilish rebellion and ought to be crushed and starved with the cows." "Well, General Milroy," the girl is said to have retorted, "if you wish to crush this devilish rebellion by starving John Arnold's cow, you can do that and be drat!" Milroy relented and gave orders for his men to not molest her further, but the incident left lingering bitterness among the residents.[14]

Not all of Winchester's women were ardent secessionists; some accounts suggest perhaps 10-12% of the residents remained loyal to the Union. Over the winter, the 87th Pennsylvania Infantry's 22-year-old quartermaster, Lt. Lewis Maish, courted

---

Radical Republican newspaper with his former commander, John C. Frémont. The two later had an acrimonious dispute which led to a lawsuit. Cluseret lost and had to pay Frémont more than $1,000, but he retained control of the *New Nation*.

13 Robert Milroy to Mary Milroy, January 18, 1863, Milroy Papers.

14 D. H. Hill, ed., "The Haversack," *The Land We Love*, vol. 5, no. 3, July 1886, 276-77; *The Diary of Margaretta "Gettie" Sperry Miller, March 23, 1863-September 19, 1863* (Winchester, VA: Godfrey Miller Historic Home and Fellowship Center Board of Directors, 2008), copy in Stewart Bell Jr. Archives, Handley Memorial Library, Winchester, VA. Several slightly different versions of the dialogue exist. See also the *Atlanta Daily Intelligencer*, September 20, 1866, and Laura V. Brown's obituary notice in the *Alexandria* (VA) *Gazette*, January 12, 1903.

Jennie E. Gaensler, the daughter of a pro-Union man from Maish's hometown of York, Pennsylvania. They married in late March. However, loyal men and women comprised a minority of residents. Milroy allowed his soldiers to bring their wives and sweethearts (as well as laundresses, sutlers, and miscellaneous civilians). However, some of the secessionist ladies, many reduced to wearing homespun and old-fashioned clothing, grew to resent the officers' wives as they paraded around town in their finery. They openly scorned the Yankee women, some of whom the Southerners suspected of being consorts, common-law wives, and other tawdry camp followers.[15]

As a result, pro-Confederate townspeople, their civilian opposites, and the Union soldiers maintained an uneasy relationship at best. "Winchester is a town pleasantly situated and had many good-looking young women," admitted Prussian-born Cpl. John C. Keses of the 87th Pennsylvania, before adding they were also "the most rabid Rebels I have ever seen." Several women diarists, mostly secessionist, kept detailed accounts of the occupation. One of them, Kate Sperry, likened Milroy to infamous Maj. Gen. Benjamin F. "Beast" Butler whose oppressions after occupying New Orleans garnered widespread coverage in the Southern press: "He's a second Butler and $100,000 is the price the Confederacy [some people in the Confederacy] has placed on his head—I wish I could get it."[16]

Milroy, often called the "Grey Eagle of the Army" because of gray hair and conspicuous facial features, forced several pro-Confederate residents to turn over their homes to quarter his soldiers. "Milroy was placed in command of the post of Winchester and our troubles reached their height," wrote resident Mary Tucker Magill. "He was a low, Western Yankee, with all the will to emulate Butler in New Orleans, with none of Butler's ability. He furnished his headquarters on Main street by pressing furniture from the different residences in the town, giving a certificate that it should be paid for at the close of the war, if the owners should be found to have sustained the characters of 'loyal citizens' during the struggle. Of course this was the

---

15 Jonathan A. Noyalas, "The War Returns to the Valley," a lecture presented at the Virginia Museum of the Civil War, New Market, VA, on March 8, 2014; George R. Prowell, *History of the Eighty-seventh Regiment, Pennsylvania Volunteers* (York, PA: Press of the Daily Record, 1903); Kate McVicar Collection, Handley Regional Library, Winchester, VA. Maish fell ill over the winter and was taken to the Gaensler house to recover, according to researcher Dennis Brandt. Lewis, soon to be a captain, fell in love with Jennie. After the war, they moved to Minneapolis, MN. He died at a soldier's home there in 1917.

16 John C. Keses [Kesses] Papers, Civil War Times Illustrated Collection, United States Army Heritage and Education Center, Carlisle, PA, as well as in the York County Heritage Trust, York, PA; Kate Sperry diary entry as cited by Noyalas, *"My Will Is Absolute Law,"* 26.

most useless form," she continued, "as they did not take the property of 'loyal citizens,' so-called."[17]

While Milroy enjoyed the town's luxuries, most of his men did not. In the first week of February, a trooper in the 13th Pennsylvania Cavalry escorting a newly arrived wagon train complained that the Federal government had neglected the Winchester post in more ways than one. The men and horses had to remain on the streets in the bitter snowy cold because of insufficient billets and stable space. They troopers eventually pitched their tents south of town along the Front Royal Road. "Winchester is desolate," declared the frustrated soldier. Its store shelves were empty, and few merchants remained open. Flour fetched $20.00 a barrel and whiskey retailed for twice that much per gallon. Tavern landlords demanded $10.00 a week for board, and the remaining hotels had mostly been converted into military hospitals. The only public transportation was an old Troy stagecoach that arrived about eight o'clock each night carrying passengers and baggage from the Baltimore & Ohio Railroad depot in Martinsburg, an area of the state that would soon break off and become part of West Virginia. On one side of the turnpike, the fence rails were missing and nearby homes were largely abandoned. The soldier looked on as a solitary black man worked in the fields, breaking up wood for the family of a nearby mansion, outside of which grazed a few sheep. "The cattle had been driven off," he continued, "and even chickens are scarce." Such was the state of affairs for much of the populace, particularly the secessionists.[18]

In addition to monotony, illness, and saucy-tongued females, the Federal soldiers endured the fear of Rebel incursions. Periodically, guerillas or Confederate cavalry under Brig. Gens. William E. "Grumble" Jones and John D. Imboden harassed Milroy's forward outposts. In one particular incident in early February, rumors spread that Jones and Imboden were approaching with 12,000 men. Milroy issued strict orders for all troops to remain in their quarters, to refrain from going into town, or to be away from their camps for any reason because he expected the enemy to attack in the morning. "It all proved to be a false alarm," the 12th West Virginia's Sgt. Milton B. Campbell wrote to his sister. "We have not been attacked, nor do we fear one. They can have no object in attacking us here, and if they do, they will meet with a warm

17 Mary Tucker Magill, "The Old Red House on Fort Hill," in *"Our Women in the War": The Lives They Lived, The Deaths They Died* (Charleston, SC: The Weekly News and Courier, 1885), 397.

18 "A Winchester Letter," *Philadelphia Inquirer*, reprinted in the *Alexandria* (VA) *Gazette*, February 13, 1863.

reception. The old 'Grey Eagle' has sent them word to come whenever they feel like it."[19]

The general belief that helped swell such confidence was that any incursion would consist of nothing more than a cavalry raid. According to Sergeant Campbell, on February 11 there were no Rebels within 30 miles except deserters who arrived daily "in considerable numbers." Milroy demanded they take the oath of allegiance. When the deserters asked whether that meant they had to enlist, the general emphatically declared that he did not want "such d—d men as them in our army." If they failed to swear the oath, he sent them back to the Confederate lines. "He cares very little for the feelings of a rebel," Campbell recorded, "and gives them cool comfort when they are brought before him." Bushwhackers, in particular, received harsh treatment; the homes of anyone associated with ambushing Union soldiers were often burned to the ground.[20]

Such tactics continued to drive a wedge between the Indiana general and the Southern-leaning populace. The secessionist ladies, still smarting over Milroy's emancipation edicts, soon had a good laugh at his expense. On February 14, the general received an ornate hand-painted valentine from a woman who simply signed herself "She Reb." The valentine showed a fair likeness of Milroy waving his hands at two black women with the request, "Be seated, ladies." A published description sniffed, "The pair certainly were not very prepossessing as painted." The valentine, from the hand of Mrs. Cornelia Peake McDonald, also depicted a pretty young Southern maiden, handsomely dressed "and as charming as the artist could paint her," sneering at a Milroy declaring, "Out, you d—d rebel!" The same published description noted, "With a look calculated to freeze anything into an iceberg, she responds, 'Jackson will avenge us.'"[21]

The civilian Unionists of Winchester, by contrast, enjoyed a strong relationship with Milroy and his soldiers. "If I could have [a] choice," wrote Capt. Clark Barnes of the 116th Ohio Infantry, "I would prefer staying here in preference to any place I have been since I have been in the service. Our nearest neighbors are all loyal. Treat us very

---

19 Milton Campbell to dear sister, February 3, 1863, in Linda Cunningham Fluharty, *Civil War Letters of Lt. Milton B. Campbell, 12th West Virginia Infantry* (Baton Rouge, LA: self-published, 2004), 21. At Winchester, Campbell was a sergeant in Company I. He was belatedly promoted to lieutenant in January 1864 to fill a role created by a fatality at Second Winchester.

20 Ibid., Milton Campbell to dear sister, February 11, 1863; *Mifflinburg* (PA) *Telegraph*, May 5, 1863.

21 "A Hand Made Comic," *Morning Olympian* (Olympia, WA), February 14, 1904. This treasured keepsake remained in the hands of the Milroy family well into the 20th century, and is now in the collection of the Handley Library in Winchester.

kindly."[22] Other soldiers agreed with the prewar Buckeye attorney. "I don't care how long they keep us here," declared the 12th West Virginia's Sergeant Campbell. "We are all getting pretty well acquainted and the citizens say we suit them better than any soldiers that have ever been here. Although we are very strict with them," he added. While out on the picket line one day in mid-March, the young sergeant searched a woman to make sure she was not carrying dispatches, quinine, or other contraband intended for the Rebels. "We tell them they will have to be searched if they go out but it makes no difference," he explained in a letter to his sister. "I suppose they would suffer for the necessities of life if they could not get into our lines to get them, and they have to do it."[23]

In mid-March, the 6th Maryland (Union) Infantry force-marched its way to Winchester with concerns of bushwhackers and partisans dogging the column throughout the miserably cold night. Fear kept the Federal soldiers stumbling through the darkness with few breaks to alleviate their aches and exhaustion. "I was hardly able to walk part of the time and would have laid down along the road," Pvt. George Hamilton admitted, "but we were in the enemies country and if I had I should have been captured by the Rebel guerillas as there was a body of them followed us all night and picked up two men from the 67 Pa Regt." The danger increased whenever the soldiers found themselves isolated or straggling. A few weeks later, the 6th Maryland's Lt. Mellville R. Small, an aide-de-camp to Col. J. Warren Keifer, was riding alone a short distance from a camp in Loudoun County when some of John Mosby's rangers surrounded him. After being robbed, Small eventually wound up in Libby Prison in Richmond.[24]

Some observers continued to fear a major Confederate attack in the Lower Shenandoah Valley, believing the increased partisan and cavalry activity foreshadowed a significant advance. The 6th Maryland's chaplain, Joseph Brown, had remained at headquarters in Harpers Ferry. He had watched his own regiment and several others depart for Winchester and other locations believed to be under threat. "Thousands of troops have [moved] through here in the last 48 hours westward," he wrote his wife on

22 Clark Barnes to Milton Barnes, May 13, 1863, Winchester, Mason Archival Repository Service, George Mason University, Fairfax, VA

23 Milton Campbell to dear sister, February 3, 1863, in Fluharty, *Civil War Letters of Lt. Milton B. Campbell*, 34.

24 George Hamilton to his niece Anna, March 18, 1863, Winchester, VA, private collection; 6th Maryland Company H Descriptive Book, Jim Fisher's Sixth Regiment of Maryland Infantry Descendants Association website, http://www.6thmarylandinfantry.org/DescriptiveCoH. htm; last accessed February 15, 2014. Small was mortally wounded in October 1864 at the battle of Cedar Creek.

March 24. Worried that this foretold an approaching battle, he forecast, "The world would be shocked at the terrible destruction of human life . . . the Battle of Antietam was a terrible struggle and slaughter of men—but it was nothing when compared with what it is to come in Winchester."[25]

The Winchester region continued to attract martial attention from both sides. On April 6, 1863, Milroy sent Capt. Hamilton L. Karr's Company G of the 116th Ohio Infantry about nine miles out on the Romney Road to break up and if possible capture a band of Rebel horse thieves infesting that section. The Buckeyes captured two notorious thieves and a local militia captain. The latter told Karr that Union forces had made 18 attempts to capture him, and he had always eluded them until now. The Buckeye retorted, "Yes, but this is the first time Company G of the 116th Ohio has been after you."[26]

Milroy had received a belated promotion to major general dating back to March 31, 1863, an honor most of his men and the pro-Union residents of Winchester loudly hailed. With his new rank in hand, and the coming of spring and likelihood of fighting, Milroy tightened his grip on the secessionist populace. "General Milroy was a man of violent temper and the least thing ruffled it," declared a teenager named Emma Cassandra Riely. "He was a rough, backwoods western man, with a great shock of grey hair which stood up like porcupine bristles, yet we heard he had a soft side to his nature." When her family tried to find that characteristic in an effort to save their home, they managed to receive somewhat better treatment than many of their neighbors. They were allowed more freedom in coming and going, and additional privileges.[27]

Milroy's heavy-handedness further soured Southern-leaning civilians, who chafed under his strict rules and policies. The arrival of Mary, the general's wife, did not help things. Mrs. Milroy shared her husband's haughty attitude, and she did not hesitate to show her disdain for the local citizens. "She was a woman not above but below the stamp of a servant," sneered Mary Tucker Magill. "We amused ourselves very much with her general appearance and manners. When she arrived she was much disappointed that her appearance created no military enthusiasm. Putting her head out of the carriage she said: 'I'm the wife of *Gener'l* Milroy, why don't you hurrah?' But they still refused to hurrah. Mrs. Milroy," continued Magill, "was much dissatisfied with the

---

25 The Rev. Joseph Brown to his wife, March 24, 1863, Harper's Ferry, Historical Society of Cecil County (MD).

26 Thomas F. Wildes, *Record of the One Hundred and Sixteenth Regiment Ohio Infantry Volunteers in the War of the Rebellion* (Sandusky, OH: I. F. Mack & Bro., 1884), 22.

27 Emma Cassandra Riely Macon, *Reminiscences of the Civil War* (Cedar Rapids, IA: The Torch Press, 1911), 67-68.

quarters provided for her. With all the fine houses the 'Rebels' had she did not see why she should be stuck down on Main street in the dust."[28]

Mary Milroy's stay along Main Street proved short-lived. Winchester resident Lloyd Logan had struck it rich as a tobacco trader, and he and his family owned a handsome mansion on the north side of town. When war came he joined the Confederate army, leaving his wife and children behind in Winchester. Logan's beautiful daughters hated the Yankees, and when Milroy occupied the town, several cavalry officers took up quarters in their home. This gave the Logan girls the opportunity to pump them for information, which they passed on to others. When Milroy finally ordered the family's home searched, letters to Richmond containing valuable intelligence and a box of Confederate uniforms were found hidden in the house.[29]

The news infuriated Milroy, who gave the family 24 hours to vacate. Mrs. Milroy arrived while the family was preparing to leave on April 7, clapped her hands, and exclaimed, "Go, ye secesh rebels. I hope you may be made to starve." Union soldiers escorted the Logans from their home at the point of the bayonet. "Imagination can but faintly picture the painful parting—a rebel family leaving household goods, a home adorned by wealth's unstinted profusion, friends, relatives, everything," reported a trooper of the 1st New York (Lincoln) Cavalry. He continued:

> It was very natural for the young ladies to weep when their friends (and they had a host of them) crowded around them to say adieu; but I cannot call to mind a scene from memory like this, where the penance of tears was compelled without giving relief. So, the beautiful young ladies, who had but yesterday, in a home delightful as a dream, pointed the finger of scorn at the 'low-born Yankees,' took one long agonizing look at the wide open door of their mansion and its glittering furniture, and then the cavalcade passed out of Winchester toward Dixie.

The girls and their mother were placed in an ambulance and driven beyond the lines, followed by a wagon containing a single trunk of clothing—all Milroy permitted them to take. With the Logans gone, the Milroys seized their mansion for their quarters, a move that further infuriated the local citizenry, which did not easily or quickly forgive such horrific treatment. "Of course the community was terribly

---

28 Magill, "The Old Red House on Fort Hill," 397.

29 For more on Milroy and the Logans, see Macon, *Reminiscences of the Civil War*, 67-68. Their efforts led to the capture of a portion of the 13th Pennsylvania Cavalry on February 26 in a series of skirmishes with Jenkins's cavalry at Winchester, Fisher's Hill and Woodstock. For more, see Noyalas, *"My Will is Absolute Law,"* 30-31.

excited at the outrage," Mary Tucker Magill wrote, "for which there was not even the pretence of an excuse."[30]

"Old Milroy has come back again," 13-year-old Margaretta "Gettie" Sperry Miller complained after the Union general returned from a trip to western Virginia. "I am very sorry of it. I wish he would stay away and let the other General take command. Maybe he would be more lenient toward us and give us a pass to go out to Mrs. Baker's again." A few days later, in early April, she claimed some of the Yankee officers resigned in protest over Milroy. The one who lost his billet at the Logan house when Milroy ejected the family supposedly ripped off his shoulder straps and threw them at his feet. Milroy subsequently court-martialed him. "He is so hateful," Gettie added, "I mean old Milroy."[31]

A Richmond reporter visiting Winchester in mid-April saw firsthand the effects of war. "The Yankees have laid waste to that once beautiful old town," he rued, "and there is said to be scarcely a house or building in the place that does not bear marks of their depredation and vandalism." The Federals had their flag flapping from the house of the Sherrard family and had also appropriated several other private homes. The Farmer's Bank now housed military supplies, reported to include an immense quantity of ammunition. "Sorrow and desolation mark the place," he added, "and our people are anxiously looking forward to a day of deliverance, when they will be freed from the cruel and merciless invaders. Milroy still continues his terrorism over the people, and hunts them down like a wild beast does his prey. There is no such thing as mercy with him."[32]

The 1st New York Cavalry spent the winter and spring of 1863 in Winchester. Private James Suydam was attending church one Sunday morning when he noticed an odd phenomenon among the town's women, who remained determined to resist Milroy's tyranny in any way they could. "Two young ladies I noticed had little gloves turned up at the finger, i.e., inside out," he wrote. "At first I thought it was done to expose the white hand or the bracelet, but on examination I discovered a little SECESH flag painted which they make visible to expose to public eye." Fascinated by

---

30 Sixty Union cavalrymen escorted the Logan family to Milltown and left them there, without the means to go farther and without any of of their possessions but the single trunk of clothing. "Lehigh," "From Captain Bennett's Company," *Syracuse Daily Standard*, May 17, 1863; "Milroy in Winchester—A Family Driven from Their Home," *Staunton (VA) Spectator*, April 21, 1863; Magill, "The Old Red House on Fort Hill," 397.

31 *The Diary of Margaretta "Gettie" Sperry Miller*. The "other General" was Milroy's new second-in-command, Brig. Gen. Washington L. Elliott, who had arrived in March to replace the departed Cluseret. There were a few Bakers in and around Winchester. Gettie may have been referring to Portia Baldwin Baker, a neighbor.

32 "From Winchester—Atrocities of Milroy," *Richmond Examiner*, April 18, 1863.

this practice, he concluded with a wry sense of humor, "I would like to have captured the glove but not the hand."[33]

In some cases Milroy resorted to expulsion. His clerks read the townspeople's mail in search of disloyal sentiments. Anyone uttering public statements or aiding suspected Confederates could expect to be arrested and expelled from Winchester. "It is done by escorting guilty parties beyond the lines South, with one change of clothing, to seek the sunny air of that (to them) delightful land, the fraternity and equality they ignore here," recounted a trooper of the 1st New York Cavalry, "their property thereafter confiscated." Milroy enforced the strong-armed tactic repeatedly in late May 1863 when some residents dared to wear mourning pins and ribbons for the late Stonewall Jackson, a figure much beloved in Winchester. Just a few weeks later, Milroy expelled Dr. Robert S. Baldwin and his wife Katie in their carriage, escorted out of town by a wagonload of armed infantry.[34]

"Every day our enemies were becoming harder and harder for us," Katie complained once the couple arrived safely in Woodville, Virginia. "There is only one prayer in Winchester, and that is, 'Oh God, how long, how long?' breathed from hearts filled with suffering and misery. God only knows what the people of Winchester had to bear and suffer from those fiends in human face. . . . Soldiers have been camped about in town all winter," she added, "and such a dirty place you never saw. The church opposite was taken for a stable, and we had the horses quartered all around us." She ridiculed Milroy's children as "ugly little red-headed things." The soldiers told her they would take all the blacks with them whenever they departed. Another lady called on Milroy to ask for a pass to cross through the lines. "I will give you a pass to Hell," he supposedly sneered. She retorted that she didn't know his lines extended that far; she had often heard it, but now had it from his own lips.[35]

Captain Frederick W. Alexander's Baltimore Artillery arrived in Berryville in late April after a rain-soaked march of 23 miles. After a good night's rest, the men reached Winchester the next day and took quarters before moving to their camp site "in a beautiful place," as Pvt. William H. Moffett Jr. recounted in a letter to his father. Parts of Winchester reminded him of Baltimore. There was an air of expectation in the troops who went out scouting every day. "I guess our turn will come sometime this week," he penned. "They have a skirmish most every day and always end with bringing

33 Daniel P. Black, ed., *A Lincoln Cavalry: The Civil War Letters of Henry Suydam, 1st New York Lincoln Cavalry* (Hampstead, MD: Old Line Publishing, 2011), 119.

34 "Lehigh," "From Captain Bennett's Company"; Gettie Miller diary entries for June 10, 1863.

35 *Richmond Examiner*, June 18, 1863.

in some of the rebels. We were ordered to be ready last night, as they expected the rebels to attack us, but everything passed off quiet."[36]

Not far from the camps, doctors treated more than 2,000 sick or wounded soldiers, including many who were not from Milroy's division, scattered throughout downtown Winchester. The largest concentration stayed in the columned three-story Taylor Hotel along Loudoun Street. On December 28, 1862, the quartermaster and surgeon of Milroy's lead brigade under the French-born General Cluseret had contracted the hotel for $4,000 annually for use as a military hospital. The Federals established other hospitals in the York House and Union Hotel, and began rousting private citizens from their homes and converting the dwellings for official use. Two relatively new military cemeteries just east of town—one Confederate and one Union—ominously served to remind the soldiers of their potential fate. The graveyards contained re-interred bodies from the 1862 battles of Winchester and Kernstown, as well as men who had died of disease, particularly typhoid fever. Eventually the army spread absorbent lime on the streets and walkways and, by the end of spring, other than a few lingering cases among the townspeople the fever had largely abated.[37]

Milroy's persistent cruelty, coupled with a severe outbreak of typhoid that struck soldiers and civilians alike, had a telling effect. Fever victims included Dr. Walter R. Gilkey, the surgeon of the 116th Ohio Infantry, who died on June 4, and Lt. James H. Gilliam of the 123rd Ohio Infantry, who expired six days later. At one point, Winchester endured eight funerals in a single week. By early June, few residents remained in the town except women, children, and old men, according to the 18th Connecticut's chaplain, William C. Walker, and most of them looked daily for the Confederates to appear and drive away the hated Yankees. In his opinion, it was not surprising that many residents detested the Yankees or, at the least, found their presence annoying. Although they acquiesced to Milroy's rule, they did so with bitter animosity. Milroy's harsh measures included a rule that no one, male or female, could

---

36 William H. Moffitt Jr. to Dear Father, April 27, 1863, Winchester, VA, Moffett Papers, MS 1373, Maryland Historical Society, Baltimore.

37 *Richmond Daily Dispatch*, June 18, 1863; Milton Campbell to Dear sister, June 11, 1863, in Fluharty, *Civil War Letters of Lt. Milton B. Campbell*, 47. The Taylor Hotel is at 129 N. Loudoun Street. Edward McGuire opened the first hotel on the site in 1755. After it burned down, Bushrod Taylor constructed a new and larger hotel in 1836. Guests included Andrew Jackson, Henry Clay, and Stephen Douglas. The hotel closed in 1911 and was sold to J. G. McCrory Co. for use as a dime store. The Union military cemetery is now the Winchester National Cemetery at 401 National Avenue. Cluseret, a former officer in the French army, resigned his commission in March 1863 and left Winchester. He was replaced by Brig. Gen. Washington L. Elliott, who transferred from the Department of the Northwest in Wisconsin.

purchase anything from the local stores without a written permit. And, to get that document, he forced the townspeople to swear an ironclad oath of allegiance. Company D of the 18th Connecticut spent considerable time trying to compel the citizens to "have proper respect for the Federal government and an acknowledgement of its rights."[38]

Winchester did not present many attractions and plainly showed the marks of war, thought the abolitionist-minded Chaplain Walker. His regiment had reached the city on May 25 after a long journey from Baltimore. Few of the buildings were attractive, he added, and most seemed at least a half-century out of date. The old houses with their clay-filled cracks and the seeming absence of churches and schoolhouses became popular topics among many of the soldiers. "Everything indicated a lack of intelligence and enterprise," penned the chaplain. "The curse of slavery was everywhere visible, and the degradation and humiliation of the poor whites and blacks was a sad sight to men who had been blessed with a home of intelligence, and plenty in New England."[39]

James M. Dalzell, the sergeant-major of the 116th Ohio Infantry, disagreed with Walker's dismal assessment. He thought Winchester a "beautiful place in spring-time and early summer, one of the loveliest spots I ever saw. Its long ridges of hills roll back grandly from the sweet little city in the valley, hill rising upon hill higher and higher on either hand until at length they tower into the shadowy outline of the Blue Ridge in full view afar off." Dalzell continued his vivid description of the northern Shenandoah city: "Its well-kept gardens, fine residences, well paved streets, and still more its air of literary and moral refinement make it one of the most desirable little cities in all Virginia." He also observed that "its girls were intensely beautiful and intensely disloyal. The devil ne'er hated holy water with half the bitterness that these lovely young Winchester girls hated us."[40]

Throughout the spring of 1863, General Milroy, described by a Virginia cavalryman as nothing more than a "bombastic coward and cow stealer," dispatched several of reconnaissance patrols to watch for significant Rebel threats. The extensive highway network surrounding Winchester presented a series of defensive problems. There were several principal roads to monitor, each of which offered an artery of

38 *Official Army Register of the Volunteer Force of the United States Army for the Years 1861, '62, '63, '64, '65* (Washington, DC, Adjutant General's Office, 1865), Part 5, 213, 220; *Richmond Whig*, June 23, 1863; Gettie Miller diary entry for April 24, 1863; William C. Walker, *History of the Eighteenth Regiment Conn. Volunteers in the War for the Union* (Norwich, CT: Veterans Committee of the Eighteenth Connecticut, 1885), 104; *Richmond Daily Dispatch*, June 18, 1863.

39 Walker, *History of the Eighteenth Regiment*, 97.

40 James M. Dalzell, "A Lucky Blunder," in *Lovell's Library*, vol. 20, no. 967, May 9, 1887.

advance for enemy raiders, particularly the toll roads to Strasburg and to Front Royal.[41]

Milroy's task was made all the more difficult because a series of crossroads intersected and connected the main arteries. Milroy responded by strengthening his defenses and spreading his 8,200 soldiers in a wide arc to protect his supply and communication lines, using strong detachments to garrison Berryville and Bunker Hill, which was farther north in what would become the new state of West Virginia on June 20. "Our men are busily employed throwing up breastworks," the 87th Pennsylvania's Pvt. Thomas O. Crowl informed a friend, "and therefore I suppose the intention is of our men to hold this place that is if they can." Not a fan of Milroy, Private Crowl wrote to his sister, "Our old General says that he thinks more of the Blacks than his soldiers, but if we get into Battle he will stand a good chance of getting his infernal old gray head shot off."[42]

Whatever his difficulties, Milroy intended to hold Winchester. He believed his extensive network of fortifications would deter any Rebel attack. Confederate Pvt. George Michael Neese of James Ewell Brown (Jeb) Stuart's horse artillery visited the defenses on November 30, 1862, during a period when the Rebels controlled the area. "This afternoon I went through the fortifications, or rather earthworks, situated on the hills west and northwest of Winchester," he wrote long after the war. Neese continued:

> The earthworks were constructed by the Yankees and are about half a mile from town, and thoroughly command the town and all the surrounding country. There are five or six separate works, all of an octagonal form, surrounded by a ditch ten feet wide and twelve feet deep. One of the works is constructed of bags filled with clay, and I suppose that there are about two hundred thousand bags in the one work. The walls are thick and built with a careful precision as to proportions and angles, and all of them are perfectly

41 See, for instance, the letter by Sgt. H. E. Gutelius of the 12th Pennsylvania Cavalry regarding a sortie by the blue-clad horsemen chasing after Confederate interlopers in early May, about which Gutelius wrote, "we fired on them, and away they went as fast as they could, without firing half a dozen shots. A great many of them threw away their arms without firing them off." *Mifflinburg Telegraph*, May 26, 1863.

42 *OR* 27, pt. 2, 47; Thomas O. Crowl to My Dear and Obedient Friend, March 4, 1863, Winchester, Virginia, Civil War Documents Collection, USAHEC; *Atlas to Accompany the Official Records*, 119. The Martinsburg Road and the Strasburg Road comprised what is known as the Valley Pike (today's U.S. Route 11) north and south of Winchester, respectively. Pughtown, which was about nine miles northwest of Winchester, was renamed Gainesboro well after the end of the Civil War.

Edwin Forbes' sketch of Winchester looking northeast from the Main Fort. *Library of Congress*

shell-proof—at least against field guns. In the center of each work is an earth-covered magazine for ammunition storage, and in one of the works is a cistern for water.[43]

Milroy spent the spring expanding these old defenses. "We are building strong fortifications, have them very nearly completed, and when done they will be very hard to take by storm or in any other way," boasted the 12th West Virginia's Sergeant Campbell. "Our soldiers are in good spirits, and are confident of ultimate success, and that at no distant day." The perceived strength of this extensive network of earthworks, coupled with the persistent and widespread belief that the Rebels would only send cavalry raiders and not risk an infantry attack, created a sense of security for the Grey Eagle and his men. Whether that was warranted remained to be seen.[44]

An open ridge northwest of Winchester sported the largest of the defensive works. A deep ravine with a stream divided the heights, with a small artillery redoubt on the narrow southern crest and the Main Fort, or Battery #2, on a broader plateau to the north.[45] Confederates constructed the Main Fort early in the war on the

43 George M. Neese, *Three Years in the Confederate Horse Artillery* (New York and Washington: Neale Publishing Co., 1911), 136-37. Neese, who served in R. Preston Chew's Battery, Army of Northern Virginia, wrote one of the best artillery memoirs of the war.

44 Milton Campbell to dear sister, February 3, 1863, in Fluharty, *Civil War Letters of Lt. Milton B. Campbell*, 22. Milroy and his troops adopted the same mentality as the 20-century French, who believed static defenses like the Maginot Line could withstand any invaders. The Maginot Line, of course, was never tested, but Winchester's defenses would be later in June 1863.

45 The construction of these fortifications imposed upon and angered even the most loyal local citizens. William Fahnestock, an ardent Unionist, watched in frustration while his woods were chopped down to expand the Main Fort and the Star Fort. After the war, he filed a 49-page reparations claim seeking $3,000 for the timber (about $50,000 in today's dollars). Fahnestock's neighbor, elderly Quaker Abner Bond, claimed Milroy cut his 20-acre woodlot

Fahnestock farm above the Pughtown Road. In early 1863, Federals under engineer Capt. W. Alonzo Powell expanded and strengthened the "Fort Garibaldi" works and rechristened it Fort Milroy. They also added significant infantry flank entrenchments. Some observers called it the Flag Fort because of the huge banner flying from a tall wooden pole. Commanding the western and northern approaches to Winchester, the Main Fort and its flanks could hold some 2,000 defenders. The bastion boasted four 20-pounder iron Parrott Rifles and a pair of 24-pounder bronze smoothbore howitzers. On the evening of June 11, Capt. William F. Martins' Company I of the 1st [14th] Massachusetts Heavy Artillery arrived from Harpers Ferry, some 20 miles to the north, and reported to Captain Powell to take charge of the big guns.[46]

Just to the north on Strine's Hill, a low rise above the Pughtown Road, sat Battery #3. More commonly known as the Star Fort, some soldiers derisively called it "Fort Forage Sack" for the mountains of supplies housed therein. Built on the site of earlier Confederate gun emplacements known as Fort Alabama, Union troops began constructing the irregular eight-sided earthwork late in 1862. It featured sturdy stone and wooden gun platforms, with much of the materials coming privately owned buildings (including Winchester Academy and the Market House) ripped apart for that purpose. In late January 1863, the staunchly abolitionist Milroy ordered his men to use stone from the nearby burned home of former U. S. Senator James Mason, who had been instrumental in the passage of the controversial 1850 Fugitive Slave Law. Federal soldiers pulled down the walls of "Selma" and hauled the usable stone to the construction site. Flanked by rifle trenches, the Star Fort theoretically could hold more than 1,500 defenders and up to eight guns. The fort was about 1.5 miles due north of Winchester and a one-half mile west of the Valley Pike-Martinsburg Road.[47]

On Flint Ridge, a little less than one mile west of the Main Fort and about 2,000 yards southwest of the Star Fort, was the smaller West Fort. Several tributaries of Red

---

and confiscated a large amounts of hay and straw. The government approved their claims. See Union Provost Marshals' File of Papers Relating to Individual Civilians, Publication M-345.

46 *OR* 27, pt. 2, 43-44; Rhodes, Robert M., "Fortifications in Frederick County," in Sam Lehman, ed., *The Story of Frederick County* (Winchester, VA: Frederick County Board of Supervisors, 1984). In some Union accounts, this ridge is considered an extension of Apple Pie Ridge, which was northwest across the Pughtown Road. The battery was formed from the 14th Massachusetts Infantry, so the 14th designation remained in popular usage. The site of many of the Main Fort's old entrenchments is now part of the Whittier Acres subdivision.

47 Ibid.; *Wheeling* (WV) *Sunday Register*, April 26, 1891; Cornelia Peake McDonald, *A Woman's Civil War: A Diary with Reminiscences of the War, from March 1862*, ed. Minrose C. Gwin (Madison: University of Wisconsin Press, 1992). Selma had been burned during the 1862 fighting at Winchester. A disgusted townswoman, Portia Baldwin Baker, complained: "They are foot by foot and plank by plank destroying our property." Portia Baldwin Baker Diary, Handley Library.

The Star Fort as it appeared in 1920. *Jonathan A. Noyalas*

Bud Run meandered in the meadows and pastures between these fortifications. Also known as the West Lunette or Battery #5, this unfinished west-facing redan was open to the rear, allowing easy access and retreat. It could hold three light guns and up to 2,000 men in its considerable line of hillside rifle pits. Ditches and *abatis* [sharpened felled trees] protected the western approaches. Work parties were still busy finishing traverses and a flanking entrenchment, and chopping down trees to clear fields of fire. Nearby was Battery #6, a three-gun lunette on a slightly higher elevation near the Pughtown Road, with a larger unmanned and unfinished earthwork, Battery #7, across the road on Apple Pie Ridge. Battery #7 could hold eight guns. Immediately east of Battery #7 was another small and unmanned irregularly shaped redoubt called Battery #8, supported by a single-gun lunette facing Apple Pie Ridge Road.[48]

Milroy's other prepared defenses included the unmanned, Vauban-style Fort Collier to the northeast on the Winchester & Potomac Railroad near Red Bud Run.[49]

48 *Atlas to Accompany the OR*, 119; Notes on the West Lunette, Allan Tischler Collection, Handley Library, Winchester, VA. Traces of some the earthworks near the West Fort still exist today on private property off Pondview Drive. James Woods High School occupies the site of Battery #7.

49 Sébastien Le Prestre de Vauban, Seigneur de Vauban and later Marquis de Vauban, was a sixteenth-century French military engineer famous for his fortifications. Simply put, a Vauban-style fort is a "star fort," often of irregular shape. The theory underlying the Vauban-style of fortification is that no attacker can approach such a fort without coming under fire from two directions, from two different bastions of the fort. Fort Monroe at the tip of the Virginia peninsula, with its seven sides, landward and seaward, offers the classic example of a Vauban-style fort in America. For more detail, see Thomas A. Kimber, *Construction of Vauban's*

Maj. Gen. Henry W. Halleck, the Union general-in-chief and Milroy's chief antagonist.
Library of Congress

This long crescent-shaped line of rifle pits extended southward from the Confederate-built fort through several fields on the "Smithfield" farm down to the Frederick W. Kohlhousen property along the Berryville Road. Less than two miles south of the Main Fort, another series of works lined the southern crest of Milltown Heights and the eastern side of Bower's Hill. However, the broad expanse of ground Milroy was forced to man meant his front was discontinuous, leaving a skillful opponent to potentially pick off the widespread fortifications one by one. To guard the southern approaches, he deployed five relatively inexperienced infantry regiments along with cavalry and artillery. This, he believed, was enough men in his estimation to fend off small raiding parties.[50]

Throughout the spring Milroy further antagonized the locals with his seemingly endless demands. He occasionally ordered work crews to tear down private buildings, fences, barns, and outbuildings for firewood and construction materials. His obsession with fortifying Winchester exasperated the Union high command. "As I have often repeated to you verbally & in writing, that is no place to fight a battle," Maj. Gen. Henry W. Halleck, the army's general-in-chief, scolded Milroy's superior General Schenck in late April. "It is merely an outpost, which should not be exposed to an attack in force." Halleck had spent the last six months trying to convince Schenck to pull Milroy's command out of Winchester on his own accord. For his part,

First System, Consisting of Six Drawings as Executed at Sandhurst and Addiscombe (London: Parker, Furnival, and Parker, 1851).

50 The Main Fort was separated from the crest of Bower's Hill by about 1.4 miles; Milltown Heights was another half-mile to the south. Kohlhousen was a farmer and vinter, and vineyards and orchards abounded in this area. The site of Milltown is near where the modern Valley Pike (Rt. 11) crosses the railroad tracks south of Winchester.

Schenck disregarded his superior's suggestions. For reasons known only to Halleck, he refused to give Schenck a peremptory order to abandon Winchester.[51]

Criticism of the decision to defend Winchester dated back as far the previous November when Halleck's chief-of-staff, Brig. Gen. George Washington Cullum, inspected the works and declared that their location rendered them indefensible. Winchester was of limited military value and did not warrant a heavy garrison, being merely "an eye of the National army looking up the Shenandoah Valley." Cullum recommended that all the infantry be withdrawn and only a cavalry picket retained. Schenck ignored the suggestion and instead sent Milroy and his men to reinforce the place.[52]

Milroy remained confident, determined to make a stand behind the ramparts of his precious fortifications, regardless of what Washington or the men of his command thought about it. "They are now repairing the larger fort and are putting in large guns and next week we will have to move outside and have ours repaired also and are going to put in five field pieces in it. So I think we will be in a safe place," recounted Pvt. Henry Kauffman of the 110th Ohio on April 19. A few days later, he declared, "Our fort has been fixed up a little and I suppose there will be some siege and field pieces put in soon and there is a strong talk of our Company being detached from the regiment to man those guns and we are all hoping that it may come true."[53]

Confederate cavalry made several feints toward Winchester throughout the spring of 1863, but they were little more than mounted probes that included nothing more than limited skirmishing. "In fact, these feints had become so frequent and amounted to so little that the commanders of the Federal forces had almost ceased to apprehend any serious demonstration by the enemy," recalled Lt. Col. Robert S. Northcutt of the 12th West Virginia. "It was thought that the Confederates would not try during that summer to repossess the lower Shenandoah Valley." When his wife told him that she was worried about his being involved in combat, Pvt. Josiah Staley of the 123rd Ohio declared, "I think you can rest easy for the rebs have got no men they want killed bad enough to attempt driving us out of this place even if they would force

51 Halleck to Schenck, April 29, 1863, Robert C. Schenck Papers, Miami University Archives, Oxford, OH; Wilbur S. Nye, *Here Come the Rebels!* (Baton Rouge: Louisiana State University Press, 1975), 70. Schenck commanded the Middle Department from his office in Baltimore. His force included the troops of the Eighth Army Corps, which included Milroy's division.

52 W. A. Croffut and John M. Morris, *The Military and Civil History of Connecticut During the War of 1861-65* (New York: Ledyard Bill, 1868). 350.

53 David McCordick, ed., *The Civil War Letters of Private Henry Kauffman: The Harmony Boys are All Well* (Lewiston, NY: E. Mellen Press, 1991), 24, 28. Kauffman was captured at West Fort on June 14 and wounded in 1864 at Cedar Creek. He survived the war.

us out they would suffer great loss and then they could not spare men enough to hold the place any length of time."[54]

Milroy, however, recognized the potential threat of a more serious attack and sent his wife and family away from Winchester in early May. However, he allowed his subordinate officers to bring their wives to join them in their garrison. Ironically, he did not take any steps to ensure that these women would be able to safely leave should a serious Confederate attack be launched upon Winchester.

If an attack was in fact launched, Milroy ordered that one of the Main Fort's massive siege guns be fired as a general signal to the defenders. One night about midnight, the old gun let loose with a terrific roar which, according to the 110th Ohio's Lt. Charles M. Gross, "caused the earth to tremble beneath us, so as a matter of course we were not long falling in line." Just as the officers formed their companies into line at their respective quarters, Quartermaster Sergeant David J. Martin came hustling along with musket in hand. The 34-year-old German fell at the foot of one group and exclaimed, "I fights mit Company G." The Buckeyes of the 110th admired Martin's patriotism and pluck, especially from a comrade whose supply role would normally make him a noncombatant. Instead of a major attack, however, the signal gun's boom heralded only a slight Rebel probe against the outer pickets.[55]

Occasionally, Milroy's far-flung scouting patrols encountered small bands of Confederates. In mid-May, a one brief bloodless encounter served to raise the morale of the 123rd Ohio. "We got a shot at the rebels the last time out," wrote a teenage private named Ambrose Ingerson to his mother back home in Sycamore, Ohio. "I tell you it made the boys feel good." The cavalry seized more than 100 horses, and a flag now flew over the expanded fortifications. Many of the Buckeyes itched for a bigger fight—the one rumored by so many to be coming soon.[56]

On June 1, Sgt. Jefferson O. McMillen of the 122nd Ohio told his father, "If I do not miss my apprehensions you will hear some stirring news from the east in the next two weeks to come. For General Lee is concentrating his forces for an attack on

54 Robert S. Northcott, "Milroy at Winchester," *Philadelphia Weekly Times*, December 4, 1880; Stout, ed., *The Blue Soldier*, 76-77. Staley was captured at New Market, Virginia, in May 1864, and sent to Andersonville Prison. He survived his stint there and in a weak state was paroled at Charleston, South Carolina, on December 13, 1864. He died in a Federal hospital in Annapolis, Maryland, that year on Christmas Day.

55 Charles M. Gross, "Sketch of Army and Prison Life from the Diary of Charles Milford Gross 1823-1909," Cathy Coplen collection, http://www.latinamericanstudies.orgcavada/charles-gross.htm, last accessed on February 15, 2014

56 Ambrose Ingerson to his Mother, May 16, 1863, Winchester, Va., privately owned.

General Hooker and there will be one of the greatest battles fought that this continent ever witnessed."[57]

Three days later, Josiah Staley of the 123rd Ohio wrote on rumors that his brigade was going to Washington to join Maj. Gen. Joseph Hooker's Army of the Potomac. "I don't know how true it is," he penned. "There is a good many troops coming here. I don't know whether it is to relieve us or whether they expect an attack or whether they are going to make a raid up the valley but it looks as if we were going to be attacked for the cavalry is scouring the country all the time especially at night and the pickets are doubled every night." He concluded, with some foresight, "Last night the troops were out in line all night or at least part of them. The rebs will not come here unless they come in large force to get into Maryland and if they do, some of them will get hurt before they get past Winchester." The next day the private added, "The rebs have not bothered us yet. I guess they have plenty to attend to at other points without trying to drive us out. There can be no use of their coming with less than 25,000 men and I don't think they can send that many and take care of other places more valuable to them and what is more, Milroy has no notion of letting them get this place."[58]

Staley and his comrades in the 123rd Ohio were relative newcomers to Winchester, having spent much of the spring in Romney, [West] Virginia. They claimed to be ready and anxious for a fight if the Rebels came near. In mid-March, they had drafted a series of resolutions for publication in newspapers back home: "Resolved, That we, officers and soldiers of the 123rd O. V. I., are still, and ever shall be loyal to the flag of our country, no matter whether it is assailed by Southern Rebels in arms; and we will carry it aloft with stout hearts and strong arms, ready to sacrifice our lives if need be in defense of the Union of which that flag, with its stars and stripes, is symbolical." Other resolutions denounced Northerners who were against the war effort. Signed by Col. William T. Wilson and almost all of his field and line officers, the document asked fellow citizens to refrain from partisan politics until after the war.[59]

"Not until the Union is saved should patriots disagree," urged the author, Maj. A. Baldwin Norton, a Democrat who had voted for John Breckinridge in the presidential election of 1860. "The peace offerings of rebel sympathizers in the North, like the peace offerings of the Greeks to the Trojans, are filled with hypocrisy, deceit and trickery, and are only calculated and intended to aid and assist our enemies to

---

57 Wilfred Black, ed., "Civil War Letters of George Washington McMillen and Jefferson McMillen, 122nd Regiment O.V.I.," *West Virginia History*, vol. 32, no. 3 (April 1972), 177. McMillen was promoted to 1st lieutenant of Co. K. in June 1864 and mortally wounded on July 9, 1864 at Monocacy.

58 Stout, *The Blue Soldier*, 88-89.

59 "Resolution of the 123rd Ohio," *Tiffin* (OH) *Weekly Tribune*, April 3, 1863.

overthrow our Government." The fiery Norton added, "we are in favor of using every beast of burden, every grade of intellect, every engine of power, all of God's creation and all of man's invention, known and recognized in civilized warfare, and within our power, for the overthrow of this hellish rebellion." He urged that peace could only come when a decisive victory on the battlefield brought "utter and complete defeat" to the Rebels. Their naïve confidence that they would win a decisive victory over the enemy would soon be put to the test.[60]

Indeed, a major battle was drawing closer, as many of the rumors suggested. "As early as June 1, it had been observed that the enemy in the vicinity of Winchester was becoming bolder," observed Milroy's chief of staff, Maj. J. Lowry McGee of the 3rd West Virginia Cavalry. This activity added fuel to the soldiers' overconfidence. That same day, Pvt. James M. Smith of the newly arrived 18th Connecticut recorded smugly in his diary, "There is a report that Lee is coming up the Shenandoah Valley again. Let him come." The next night, rumors spread of an impending attack some time after 9:00 p.m. The men got up, loaded their weapons, and slept on their arms, but no Confederates came. On June 3, Smith manned a picket post at Union Mills, a task that required a lieutenant and a sergeant, three corporals, and 23 privates. Expecting an attack at any hour, General Milroy dispatched more than 200 cavalry scouts and reinforced the pickets with six full companies of the 18th Connecticut. Word later arrived of that an insignificant cavalry skirmish had been fought near Newtown. "And back we went to bed, like a pack of fools," grumbled Smith. "Nothing occurred during the night."[61]

Five days later on June 8, a company of the 1st Michigan Cavalry clattered into Winchester. The blue troopers brought with them the news that a large force of Southern horsemen had gathered in Culpeper County preparatory to a raid against the Baltimore & Ohio Railroad that could also target Winchester. "They cut their way thru at Front Royal," recounted a musician named James B. Willoughby of the 123rd Ohio. "This caused little apprehension of danger, for the reason that the Federal position was deemed impregnable against a cavalry attack," recounted the 12th West Virginia's

60 Ibid. Rarely in good health, Norton had resigned in early March 1863 and was preparing to head home to Ohio to recuperate. He never fully regained his health. After the war, Norton moved to Santa Fe, New Mexico, to work as Superintendent of Indian Affairs. He died there in January 1868 before he could implement many of his ideas to help the Navajo and other Indian tribes.

61 J. L. McGee, "Milroy at Winchester: Gen. Milroy Remained in Obedience to Orders and Against his Judgment," *National Tribune*, May 29, 1913; James Mason Smith diary entries for June 1, 2, and 3, 1863, Winchester, VA, private collection of his descendant Michael Smith.

Lieutenant Colonel Northcott. "General Milroy, in order to prevent surprise, kept the surrounding country well scouted."[62]

That same day, concerned about the state of Milroy's command, General Schenck sent his chief of staff, Lt. Col. Donn Piatt, a 44-year-old Ohio lawyer, former judge, and diplomat, to Winchester to get a better sense of the state of affairs there. Piatt had *carte blanche* to allow Milroy to remain at Winchester or order him back to Harpers Ferry. Piatt's reconnaissance led him to conclude that "Winchester, as a fortified place, was a military blunder. It covered nothing, while a force there was in constant peril. I had learned enough in the service to know that a subordinate should take no chances, and I ordered Milroy back to Harper's Ferry." Milroy, still believing his force was not in imminent danger and that the Rebel activity did not signal a major incursion, took no action and remained put. Schenck, though riled, did not enforce his instructions.[63]

Milroy also was embroiled in battles with his subordinates, taking some of his focus off of the Rebels. Colonel Andrew T. McReynolds of the 1st New York (Lincoln) Cavalry commanded one of Milroy's three brigades. McReynolds, a 44-year-old Irish immigrant and a veteran of the Mexican War, was a successful lawyer and politician in Michigan before war broke out in the spring of 1861. In early June, Milroy sought permission from Schenck to remove McReynolds from brigade command because the Irishman "drinks too much whisky and permits it to be drank freely in his command." Milroy and McReynolds also disagreed on occupation policy and emancipation. On June 9, Milroy resumed his complaints, telling Schenck that McReynolds "is very popular with the . . . rebels and furnishes many of them with guards at their houses and allows them to pass in and out of his lines and purchase goods [from] his sutlers without oath of allegiance in violation of my orders." Milroy added, "He allows slaveholders in and around his lines to hold and enforce slavery."[64]

In addition to the threat of Rebel cavalry and the internal senior command squabbling, Confederate guerrillas also made life miserable for the Union garrison at Winchester. Major John S. Mosby's 43rd Battalion, Virginia Cavalry regularly buzzed around the Union edges, the partisan troopers wreaking havoc whenever and

---

62 J. B. Willoughby diary, entry for June 9, 1863, West Virginia State Archives, Charleston, WV. Willoughby survived the war.

63 Donn Piatt, *Memories of the Men Who Saved the Union* (New York: Belford, Clarke & Co., 1887), 39. Piatt had an interesting life, serving as a diplomat, poet, writer, general, world traveler, and newspaperman, among other pursuits. He was well known for his attacks on government corruption using a variety of media. For a full-length biography, see Peter Bridges, *Donn Piatt: Gadfly of the Gilded Age* (Kent, OH: Kent State University Press, 2012).

64 Roger D. Hunt, *Colonels in Blue: Union Army Colonels of the Civil War, New York* (Atglen, PA: Schiffer Military History, 2003), 196-97; Milroy to Schenck, June 9, 1863, Schenck Papers.

Col. Andrew T. McReynolds of the 1st New York (Lincoln) Cavalry, the influential Irish immigrant who commanded a brigade under Milroy. *Library of Congress*

wherever they could. Although the damage was slight, their presence added to the anxiety Milroy's men felt about the rumors of a pending movement by Lee's army. "We have been doubling the picket every night for a week or two expecting to be attacked by a heavy force," reported Jefferson McMillen to his sister on June 9, "but we have never seen any of them yet."[65]

"Nothing of special interest occurred on the 9th and 10th save that there was more trouble with the pickets," observed a member of the 18th Connecticut Infantry. "It was growing daily more apparent that the rumors of Lee's advance were only too true." On June 10, rumors of the approach of a large force of the enemy filtered into Winchester. Milroy's men spent all their time either doing picket duty or working on strengthening the town's network of fortifications. Nevertheless, "we feel confident that if the Rebels attack us we will give them their fill of Milroy's Yankees, as they call us," declared Pvt. Charles H. Berry of the 110th Ohio. The 18th Connecticut's Lt. George Kies echoed the sentiment, telling his wife he doubted the Rebels would come that way, but they would be repulsed if they did. He cited the strong earthen forts and Milroy's confidence in holding them.[66]

At 2:00 a.m. the next day, the 11th, the alarm sounded. Tents were struck and the men formed into line with arms stacked. However, at 8:00 a.m. that morning, the orders were countermanded and the men instructed to unload the wagons, pitch their tents again, "and in a short time the camp of the [18th Connecticut] assumed its usual appearance." A flurry of rumors reported "the force of the enemy approaching Winchester was small and it was supposed had entered the Shenandoah Valley for the purpose of foraging." Milroy stubbornly accepted these rumors as the truth.

---

65 Black, "Civil War Letters," 178.

66 Walker, *History of the Eighteenth Regiment*, 103; Charles Berry to his wife, June 10, 1863, Charles Berry correspondence, Clark County Historical Society, Springfield, OH; George Kies to Fannie Kies, George Kies Letters, Connecticut Historical Society, Hartford.

Maj. Gen. Robert C. Schenck, commander of the Middle Military District, who was Milroy's immediate superior. *Library of Congress*

Milroy's stubborn belief found support in Colonel Piatt, the officer sent by Schenck to evaluate the situation. Piatt had a change of heart after spending more time with Milroy. The Ohioan wired Schenck on June 11, "Just in from inspection of fortifications and troops. All works fine. Can whip anything the rebels can fetch here."[67]

That same day, Schenck bowed to Halleck's pressure (and ignored Piatt's observations) and gave Milroy a direct order to withdraw his forces from Winchester. "In accordance with orders received from Halleck, received today, you will immediately take steps to remove your command from Winchester to Harpers Ferry. You will, without delay, call in Colonel McReynolds and such other outposts not necessary for observation from the front." The telegram stunned Milroy, who refused to seriously consider abandoning his prized fortifications at Winchester. The general responded a few minutes later, arguing that he could "hold it against any force the Rebels could afford to bring against it," and that it would be "cruel to abandon the loyal people in this country to the rebel fiends again."

Taking a broader view of the conflict, the War Department considered Harpers Ferry, not Winchester, to be the important military position to hold in that region. On June 12, Milroy telegraphed Schenck in Baltimore that his advance had fought "a splendid little skirmish. The enemy are probably approaching in some force," he added. "I am entirely ready for them: I can hold this place." Schenck ignored Milroy's plea and ordered him to prepare to withdraw—but to maintain his position until further orders arrived. "Give constant information," he added. Milroy had sufficient transportation to remove all the supplies from town in six hours if the Rebels did not cut him off from Martinsburg. Keeping the Valley Pike open was critical.[68]

67 Walker, *History of the Eighteenth Regiment*, 103; Northcott, "Milroy at Winchester"; Crofutt and Morris, *The Military and Civil History of Connecticut*, 350; OR 27, pt. 1, 161.

68 *OR* 27, pt. 2, 50, 188, 547.

Chapter 2

The Confederate Advance on Winchester, June 3 - 11, 1863

"The dust is almost intolerable & that together with the heat
make the marching very severe."

— *Pvt. Samuel Pickens, 5th Alabama Infantry[1]*

The battle of Chancellorsville (May 1-5, 1863) was one of Gen. Robert E. Lee's greatest victories. With only part of his Army of Northern Virginia present (two of Lt. Gen. James Longstreet's three First Corps divisions were on detached foraging duty around Suffolk, Virginia), Lee's 61,000 troops thrashed Joseph Hooker's significantly larger Army of the Potomac.

Hooker's campaign began well enough when he stole a march on Lee, crossed the Rappahannock and Rapidan rivers, and turned the Confederate left flank. Lee defied conventional military wisdom by dividing his army in two, one part to hold the Yankees in place before Fredericksburg while the balance raced west to confront Hooker's turning movement. Instead of falling back, Lee was calling Hooker's bluff. The next day he divided his inferior army yet again leaving only about 15,000 men to hold the bulk of the Yankee army in place around Chancellorsville while sending the rest under Lt. Gen. Thomas J. "Stonewall" Jackson on a daring 7-mile flank march to turn and crush the exposed Union right. Jackson's massive May 2 assault rolled up the Army of the Potomac's right flank. One of the bloodiest days of the war followed on the 3rd, during which Hooker was knocked unconscious when an artillery shell struck

---

1   Hubbs, G. Ward, ed., *Voices from Company D, Diaries by the Greensboro Guards, Fifth Alabama…* (Atlanta: University of Georgia Press, 2003), 175.

a pillar of the portico next to where he was standing. The Union army began pulling out the next day, and by the end of May 6 it was all over.[2]

As great as this victory was, the cost to the Confederacy in general, and to Lee's army in particular, was tremendous. Stonewall Jackson was mortally wounded on the night of May 2, accidentally shot by his own men in a confused encounter in a heavily wooded area. Jackson's senior division commander, Maj. Gen. A. P. Hill, was also wounded in the same friendly fire episode. Lee had his reliable cavalry commander, Maj. Gen. J. E. B. Stuart, assume command of Jackson's corps and continue the offensive. Stuart performed admirably in an unfamiliar role, but Lee needed the gifted cavalryman to continue to serve as the eyes and ears of the army. Stuart was not a permanent solution to the problem posed by Jackson's wounding and subsequent death from pneumonia on May 10.

Jackson's death cast a pall over the entire South and left Lee without a commander of fully one-half of his army. Who could step up and lead that many men and divisions? Lee had long fretted that employing such huge corps commanded by only two subordinates in wooded terrain meant that these units were "always beyond the range of his vision and frequently beyond his reach." Simply put, the structure of his army—only two corps, including the 30,000 or so men of Jackson's corps—was unwieldy and had to change. Lee decided to reorganize his army from two corps to three, with each corps now comprised of three divisions.[3]

Longstreet would continue to lead his First Corps, with one of its divisions spun off to form a portion of the new Third Corps. Jackson's Second Corps also provided a division for use in the new Third Corps. A. P. Hill, arguably Lee's most aggressive and successful division commander, was the logical choice to command one of the two leaderless corps. He was promoted to lieutenant general and assigned command of the newly formed Third Corps. The question of who would command Jackson's former corps remained an open question.[4]

---

2   A detailed discussion of the Chancellorsville campaign is beyond the scope of this book. For the best single-volume treatment of this campaign, see Stephen W. Sears, *Chancellorsville* (Boston: Houghton-Mifflin, 1996). The overlooked but critical fighting at Salem Church on May 3 is the subject of an excellent recent book by Chris Mackowski and Kristopher D. White entitled *Chancellorsville's Forgotten Front: The Battles of Second Fredericksburg and Salem Church, May 3, 1863* (El Dorado Hills, CA: Savas Beatie, 2013).

3   *OR* 25, pt. 2, 810.

4   For a detailed discussion of the reorganization of the Army of Northern Virginia and the selection of the new corps commanders after following Jackson's death, see Douglas Southall Freeman, *Lee's Lieutenants: A Study in Command*, 3 vols. (New York: Charles Scribner's Sons, 1946), 2:683-714.

Major General Richard S. Ewell had performed exceptionally well in command of a division of infantry during Jackson's 1862 Shenandoah Valley Campaign, but a severe wound cost him a leg at the Second Battle of Manassas nearly nine months earlier. He had not been with the army since. Whether the terrible wound had changed him, or whether Ewell still had the stamina to serve in the field after such an injury, remained to be seen.

Born in the District of Columbia on February 8, 1817, Ewell came from good stock. His paternal grandfather was the colonel of a Virginia infantry regiment during the Revolutionary War, and his maternal grandfather, Benjamin Stoddert, served as the first secretary of the navy. Ewell's father died when he was just nine years old, leaving the family in poverty. Unable to pay for her son's education, his mother arranged for young Dick to receive an appointment to West Point. He graduated 13th out of 42 in the Class of 1840, which included William T. Sherman and George H. Thomas.[5]

The newly minted army lieutenant was commissioned into the 1st Dragoons. He spent the rest of his Regular Army career in the mounted service. Ewell served against Indians on the western plains and fought in the Mexican War the Mexican War, where he earned a promotion to captain. When that conflict ended, he served at various frontier outposts in Arizona and New Mexico. The arrival of the Civil War convinced him to resign his commission and accept a commission as lieutenant colonel of cavalry in the Provisional Army of the Confederate States. On June 17, 1861, he was promoted to brigadier general and assumed command of a brigade holding the right end of the Confederate line at near Manassas. He served well in that battle and on January 24, 1862, was promoted to major general and assumed command of an infantry division in Jackson's army operating in the Shenandoah Valley. He performed good service in the Valley and again during the Peninsula Campaign. By the close of the Seven Days' Battles around Richmond, Ewell was one of the mainstays of Jackson's command and considered a reliable and aggressive officer.[6]

During the intense fighting at Groveton (Gainesville) on August 28, 1862, part of the Second Manassas campaign, a Union bullet shattered Ewell's left knee, requiring the amputation of the leg just above that joint. A bad fall on Christmas Day, however, tore open his imperfectly healed stump and the hemorrhaging that followed raised

---

5 Donald C. Pfanz, "Richard Stoddert Ewell," included in William C. Davis and Julie Hoffman, eds., *The Confederate General*, 6 vols. (New York: National Historical Society, 1991), 2:111; Cullum's Register of West Point Graduates, http://digital-library.usma.edu/libmedia/archives/cullum/VOL9_PART0001.PDF, accessed January 15, 2014.

6 Pfanz, "Richard Stoddert Ewell," 2:111-12.

serious questions about whether Ewell was ready to take the field.[7] He recuperated in Richmond under the care of his first cousin and fiancée, a widow named Lizinka Campbell Brown. The recovery was a long and difficult one, requiring months in bed. "My leg is nearly healed over," he happily wrote Maj. Gen. Jubal A. Early, one of his former brigade commanders, in March 1863, "but I am unable to use a wooden leg yet or to keep it long in a vertical position." By early May, the old cavalryman had made dramatic progress. "I have been in the saddle several times since my leg healed and find that I have so little trouble keeping my seat that I have offered my services to resume duty in the field professing my willingness to take a small division in view of my short comings in the way of legs," he joked in a letter to Gen. P. G. T. Beauregard on May 9.

Lee, who had never worked directly with Ewell, nonetheless selected him to lead the Second Corps rather than the small division he perhaps preferred. He was promoted to lieutenant general on May 23, 1863, and three days later married Mrs. Brown. He and the new Mrs. Ewell took a train from Richmond to meet the men of his former division (now commanded by Jubal Early) and the men of Jackson's old division (now commanded by Maj. Gen. Edward "Allegheny" Johnson). They greeted him with what one eyewitness called "an enthusiastic reception." Ewell formally assumed command of the Second Corps on June 1, and met with Robert E. Lee to discuss the commanding general's plans for the upcoming campaigning season.[8]

Ewell was an odd-looking fellow. He stood 5'8" tall, had grey eyes, a large nose, a bushy brown beard, and a nearly hairless dome that earned him the nickname "Old Bald Head." "Bright prominent eyes, a bomb shaped, bald head and a nose like that of Francis of Valois, gave him a striking resemblance to a woodcock, and this was increased by a birdlike habit of putting his head on one side to utter his quaint speeches," recalled Lt. Gen. Richard Taylor, who served with Ewell in the Shenandoah Valley in 1862. "He fancied he had some mysterious internal malady, and would eat nothing but frumenty. . . . His nervousness prevented him from taking regular sleep, and he passed nights curled around a campstool, in positions to dislocate an ordinary person's joints." Known for his cranky nature and prodigious swearing, Ewell also had a wry sense of humor and was well-liked. He was also a strict

---

7   Richard S. Ewell to Jubal A. Early, March 8, 1863, included in Donald C. Pfanz, ed., *The Letters of General Richard S. Ewell: Stonewall's Successor* (Knoxville: University of Tennessee Press, 2012), 235; Ewell to Beauregard, May 9, 1863, 238; Nye, *Here Come the Rebels!*, 41.

8   Jedediah Hotchkiss, *Make Me a Map of the Valley: The Civil War Journal of Stonewall Jackson's Topographer*, Ed. by Archie P. McDonald (Dallas: Southern Methodist University Press, 1983), 146; Pfanz, "Richard Stoddert Ewell, 2:112. Johnson received his nickname (also sometimes spelled Alleghany) from his fine performance at the small fight of Camp Allegheny in December 1861.

Maj. Gen. Jubal A. Early, commander of a division of Ewell's corps. *Library of Congress*

disciplinarian and a capable subordinate whose ability to function well on his own initiative in independent command remained an unknown.[9]

Brigadier General John B. Gordon, who served under Ewell for much of the war, left behind a vivid description of his commander and friend. "General Ewell . . . had in many respects the most unique personality I have ever known," Gordon declared. "He was a compound of anomalies, the oddest, most eccentric genius in the Confederate army. . . . No man had a better heart or a worse manner of showing it. He was in truth as tender and sympathetic as a woman, but, even under slight provocation, he became externally as rough as a polar bear, and the needles with which he pricked sensibilities were more numerous and keener than porcupines' quills."[10]

Ewell's Second Corps consisted of approximately 20,000 men organized into three divisions under Maj. Gens. Jubal A. Early, Edward Johnson, and Robert E. Rodes. Early led Ewell's old division, while Johnson assumed command of Jackson's former division, and Rodes oversaw Hill's old command. These solid and dependable fighters were veterans of the Valley, the Seven Days' Battles, Second Manassas, Sharpsburg, Fredericksburg, and Chancellorsville, and many knew of and respected Dick Ewell. Indeed, for all his eccentricities and physical infirmities, Ewell appeared to be the right man to command them. Still, he was untried in leading anything larger than a division, and was used to operating within a tight system dictated by Stonewall Jackson's precise orders. Lee, however, rarely gave detailed instructions to his corps commanders, relying instead on their initiative and judgment. Only a test in the field would determine whether Ewell could adapt to such a system.

9   Richard Taylor, *Destruction and Reconstruction: Personal Experiences of the Late War* (New York: D. Appleton & Co., 1879), 37. Frumenty is a dish of hulled wheat boiled in milk and sweetened with sugar.

10 John B. Gordon, *Reminiscences of the Civil War* (New York: Charles Scribner's Sons, 1903), 38.

Hooker's defeat at Chancellorsville offered General Lee a chance to seize the initiative for the summer campaigning season. Before him beckoned an opportunity to launch another invasion of the North—a second thrust northward through Maryland and into Pennsylvania. It was something Lee had wanted to do since his repulse in Maryland the previous fall. Once Maj. Gen. Ulysses S. Grant's army crossed the Mississippi River and surrounded Lt. Gen. John C. Pemberton's Confederate army at Vicksburg, President Jefferson Davis invited Lee on May 26 to present his plan for that summer's operations to the Confederate cabinet. Three days of intense discussion followed. Davis expressed doubts about invading Pennsylvania instead of detaching troops from the Army of Northern Virginia to reinforce a relief army in Mississippi being formed under Gen. Joseph E. Johnston to save Pemberton. Ultimately, a majority of the cabinet supported Lee's proposal, as did Davis. Lee's considered opinion, explained Confederate Secretary of War James A. Seddon, "naturally had great effect in the decisions of the Executive."[11]

Lee and Davis hoped the large scale movement north would serve a variety of purposes. First, it would draw Hooker away from its base at Falmouth, giving Lee an opportunity to defeat the Army of the Potomac in the open field. Another decisive Union defeat, this time on Northern soil, might bring about sufficient pressure from the Democratic Party and the war-weary citizenry to force the Lincoln administration to negotiate a peace with the Confederacy. Second, the strategic offensive held the potential of relieving Federal pressure on the beleaguered Southern garrison at Vicksburg without having to send troops all the way to Mississippi. Third, it would provide the people of Virginia an opportunity to recover from "the ravages of war and a chance to harvest their crops free from interruption by military operation." Finally, Lee wanted to spend the summer months in Pennsylvania in the hope of leveraging the political gain such an invasion naturally offered the Confederacy. With any success Lee could threaten the state capital of Pennsylvania at Harrisburg and perhaps even Philadelphia. After the war, President Davis claimed that "the main purpose of the movement across the Potomac was to free Virginia from the presence of the enemy. If this could be done by maneuvering merely, a most important result would be cheaply obtained."[12]

---

11 Jeffry D. Wert, *Cavalryman of the Lost Cause: A Biography of J.E.B. Stuart* (New York: Simon & Schuster, 2008), 234.

12 Jefferson Davis, *Rise and Fall of the Confederate Government*, 2 vols. (New York: D. Appleton & Co., 1881), 1:437-38. For a detailed discussion of the process by which the invasion of the North was approved by the Confederate high command, see Edwin B. Coddington, *The Gettysburg Campaign: A Study in Command* (New York: Macmillan, 1968), 1-9. See also Armistead L. Long, *Memoirs of Robert E. Lee* (New York: J. M. Stoddart & Co., 1886), 267-69.

Lee was a gambler by nature. He understood that if he did not seize the initiative and defeat the enemy, sooner or later Hooker (or some other general Lincoln installed to defeat him) would make another move against Richmond. The industrial might and population of the Northern states meant time was not Lee's friend. Union armies would only grow larger and more powerful while the South's manpower pool and resources shrank. As Brig. Gen. John B. Gordon later put it, "In the logistics of defensive war, offensives are often the wisest strategy." As Lee's military secretary, Col. Charles C. Marshall, put it, "If General Lee remained inactive, both Vicksburg and Richmond would be imperiled, whereas if he were successful north of the Potomac, both would be saved."[13]

The best way to reach Pennsylvania, and one that would shield his movement from prying Union eyes, was for Lee to march west and north out of Fredericksburg into the Shenandoah Valley, north to the Potomac River, and then cross into Maryland and points beyond. The obvious potential snag in this plan was waiting for the Confederates at Winchester, where Robert Milroy's garrison sat squarely across Lee's route. A well-armed enemy of some 8,000 men could not be left unmolested in the rear of the army's advance athwart Lee's lines of supply and communication. As one of Lee's artillerists assigned to Early's division put it after the war, "The town of Winchester and the surrounding country were dominated by a strong closed earthwork, heavily armed and manned, which it would have been madness to assault, yet folly to neglect." Unless Milroy evacuated Winchester during Lee's approach (a very real possibility), the Confederates would have to forcibly evict the Union force.[14]

Lee's entire army (including Longstreet's other two divisions, which had returned from southern Virginia) remained around Fredericksburg along the Rappahannock River, the waterway that marked the general dividing line between the Union and Confederate armies for much of 1863. Lee and his lieutenants spent a number of days perfecting their operational plan while the logistics were put in place to support it. Ewell's corps would lead the Confederate advance and sweep the Lower Valley clear of Union troops. These veterans of Stonewall Jackson's 1862 Valley Campaign knew the ground well, for they had marched and fought over much of it. They had taken Winchester during the spring of 1862, and were prepared to take it again. On May 27, Lee reviewed Early's and Johnson's divisions outside Fredericksburg. "After the

---

13 Gordon, *Reminiscences*, 137; Sir Frederick Maurice, ed., *An Aide-de-Camp of Lee, Being the Papers of Colonel Charles Marshall, Sometime Aide-de-Camp, Military Secretary, and Assistant Adjutant General on the Staff of Robert E. Lee, 1862-1865* (Boston: Little, Brown & Co., 1927), 186.

14 Robert M. Stiles, *Four Years Under Marse Robert* (New York: Neale Publishing Co., 1910), 192-93.

review we returned to camp much exhausted from standing so long in the sun," groused Lt. John H. Stone of the 2nd Maryland (CSA) Battalion.[15]

Colonel George H. Sharpe, who headed the Army of the Potomac's Bureau of Military Information, was also watching. Reviews of large bodies of troops often preceded a large scale movement, and on May 27 Sharpe reached a chilling conclusion: the Confederates were planning to commence a summer campaign of "long marches and hard fighting in a part of the country where they would have no railroad transportation," and that they would move in a northwesterly direction so as to fall upon the right flank of the Union army, or, worse, somewhere to the north of it. Sharpe was absolutely correct in his assessment; Lee intended to begin moving on June 3 with part of Longstreet's First Corps leading the way, trailed by Ewell's Second Corps. The rest of Longstreet's First Corps eventually would follow suit, while A. P. Hill's Third Corps remained in the lines at Fredericksburg to freeze Hooker's army in position while the rest of the Army of Northern Virginia gained a march on its opponent. Once that had occurred, Hill would bring up the rear. Lee's plan was not without risk, for an aggressive response by Hooker could force Hill to fight alone.[16]

Jeb Stuart arrived in Culpeper on May 20 and established his headquarters there to oversee the concentration of the Confederate cavalry in preparation for the coming invasion. Within a few days, three brigades of Southern horse soldiers had established their camps in the lush fields of Culpeper County. By the beginning of June another two brigades arrived. On June 5, Stuart held a noisy, day-long review of his troopers. The large concentration of mounted units did not pass undetected. Vigilant Union cavalry scouts reported the gathering. Joe Hooker grew concerned that Stuart was planning another ride around the Army of the Potomac, this time at his expense. The more troopers that joined Stuart's command, the more nervous Hooker became.

A local citizen of Culpeper County named G. S. Smith, known as a reliable source of intelligence, reported to the Army of the Potomac's Cavalry Corps commander, Brig. Gen. Alfred Pleasonton, that "this movement of General Lee's is not intended to menace Washington, but to try his hand again toward Maryland, or to call off your attention while General Stuart goes there. I have every reason for believing that Stuart is on his way toward Maryland. I do not positively know it, but have the very best of reasons for believing it." These reports convinced Hooker to "send all my cavalry

15 Henry Kyd Douglas, *I Rode with Stonewall* (Chapel Hill: University of North Carolina Press, 1948), 241; Thomas G. Clemens, ed., "The 'Diary' of John H. Stone, First Lieutenant, Company B, 2nd Maryland Infantry, C.S.A.," *Maryland Historical Magazine*, No. 83 (Summer 1990), 130.

16 *OR* 27, pt. 2, 528.

against" the assembling mass of Confederate horse in an attempt "to break . . . up [this offensive] in its incipiency."[17]

The movement of the main body of the Southern army began on June 3, when Maj. Gen. Lafayette McLaws' division of Longstreet's Corps marched out of the lines at Fredericksburg heading for Culpeper, 35 miles to the northwest. McLaws' men had no way of knowing it, but they had just kicked off the Gettysburg campaign. Behind them, Dick Ewell also prepared his men to move out. Ewell's Corps already had orders to prepare three days' rations and be ready to move at a moment's notice. Rodes' division marched at 2:00 a.m. the next morning and covered 14 miles before halting for the night near Spotsylvania Court House. "Gen. Rodes Division had just passed," one of Early's staff officers noted in his diary, "and some of his men having imbibed pretty freely from 'mountain dew' were in a happy state." Early's and Johnson's divisions left the next day, June 5, with Johnson's men also moving out about 2:00 a.m. "This unusually early start being intended, I suppose, to prevent our movement being discovered by the gentleman who daily ascended in the balloon to spy upon us and report to General Hooker," speculated Lt. Randolph H. McKim whose Maryland brigade was part of Johnson's division.[18]

Ewell, who rode in a carriage rather than on horseback, rolled through the Chancellorsville battlefield. "I gave General Ewell an account of the fight as we went along," recalled cartographer Jedediah Hotchkiss, "pointing out to him the localities of incidents as we passed them. He was much interested and asked many questions. Spoke of the fine positions of the enemy and was surprised they had not held them longer." Everyone who passed through the thickets recalled the horrible sights along the way, including dead men and horses left unburied, and parts of skeletons rooted up by animals.[19]

Despite the efforts to mask the Army of Northern Virginia's movement away from Fredericksburg, alert Union pickets picked it up. On June 5, Hooker ordered a probing attack by Maj. Gen. John Sedgwick's Sixth Corps to determine whether the Army of Northern Virginia still occupied their lines at Fredericksburg. "Evening before last the enemy began a furious cannonade just below Fredericksburg," wrote Brig. Gen. William N. Pendleton, the Army of Northern Virginia's chief of artillery, on June 7. "They succeeded in driving off our sharpshooters, laid down their bridge, and

---

17 Ibid., pt. 3, 33.

18 George Greer diary, entry for June 5, 1863, CWTI Collection, USAHEC; Randolph McKim, *A Soldier's Recollections: Leaves from the Diary of a Confederate* (New York: Longman, Green & Co., 1911), 138. For a more detailed examination of these events, see Bradley M. Gottfried, *Roads to Gettysburg: Lee's Invasion of the North, 1863* (Shippensburg, PA: White Mane, 2001), 9.

19 Hotchkiss, *Make Me a Map of the Valley*, 148.

crossed. This kept me up till late that night hard at work preparing for them." It rained hard that night, soaking the men to the skin and adding to their discomfort.[20]

Hooker ordered further probes the next day in an effort to more fully flesh out Lee's intentions. This time, however, the Confederates were ready for them and Pendleton's batteries responded in kind to Hooker's guns. The noisy probing attacks brought about the halt of Ewell's column in case it had to turn around and return to Fredericksburg to help A. P. Hill. "We are near the enemy & expect to be much nearer," declared the 2nd Maryland (CSA) Battalion's Lt. John Stone.[21]

Pendleton and Lee himself remained just behind the firing lines until about 1:00 p.m., watching the action to determine whether Hooker was preparing to launch a full-scale thrust across the river or merely conducting a probe. When Lee concluded it was the latter, he ordered Ewell's troops to resume their westward march.[22] "Last night rumors reached [us] that a portion of the enemy crossed the river near Fredericksburg and were driven back across the river again," wrote a lieutenant in the 12th Georgia of Brig. Gen. George Doles' brigade, part of Rodes' division. "It is said that was the reason of our stopping yesterday. We are now on the direct road to Culpeper and I heard this morning that we would go there tonight."[23]

Many of Ewell's veterans who had served under Stonewall Jackson were used to hard marching, a trait that had earned them the moniker "Jackson's Foot Cavalry" earlier in the war. A few weeks later in Pennsylvania, James Gall of the U. S. Sanitary Commission set down a valuable description of Gordon's brigade as it tramped into York, Pennsylvania. The description could have applied to any brigade in the Second Corps:

Physically, the men looked about equal to the generality of our own troops, and there were fewer boys among them. Their dress was a wretched mixture of all cuts and colors. There was not the slightest attempt at uniformity in this respect. Every man seemed to have put on whatever he could get ahold of, without regard to shape or color. Their shoes, as a general thing, were poor; some of the men were entirely barefooted. Their equipments

---

20 Susan P. Lee, ed., *Memoirs of William Nelson Pendleton, D.D., Rector of Latimer Parish, Lexington, Virginia, Brigadier-General C.S.A.; Chief of Artillery, Army of Northern Virginia* (Philadelphia: J. B. Lippincott, 1893), 276; Diary of Jacob Lemley, entry for June 6, 1863, Civil War Diaries and Letters Collection, Handley Regional Library, Winchester, VA.

21 Clemens, "The 'Diary' of John H. Stone," 130.

22 Lee, *Memoirs of William Nelson Pendleton*, 276.

23 Johnnie Perry Pearson, ed., *Lee and Jackson's Bloody Twelfth: The Letters of Irby Goodwin Scott, First Lieutenant, Company G, Putnam Light Infantry, Twelfth Georgia Volunteer Infantry* (Knoxville: University of Tennessee Press, 2010), 126.

were light as compared with those of our men. They consisted of a thin woolen blanket, coiled up and slung from the shoulder in the form of a sash, a haversack slung from the opposite shoulder, and a cartridge-box. The whole cannot weigh more than twelve or fourteen pounds. Is it strange then, that with such light loads they should be able to make longer and more rapid marches than our men? The marching of the men was irregular and ill-kept. Their whole appearance was greatly inferior to that of our soldiers.[24]

When Ewell's carriage rolled up to Somerville Ford on the Rapidan River on June 7, the men of the Second Corps spotted their new commander and raised a lusty cheer, just as they had done for Jackson. In truth, he despised having to ride in a carriage, which the one-legged warrior deemed unseemly and inappropriate for a soldier of any rank. Nevertheless, Ewell doffed his cap and ordered the driver to guide the wheeled vehicle along their lines so that the men could see him. Ewell didn't attempt to stand, for his tender stump at the bottom of his amputated leg was bothering him. Once the short review ended, Ewell rode on to Culpeper Court House for a meeting there with Lee and Longstreet.[25]

Ewell's men marched again on June 6. Longstreet's troops were also on the move. A. P. Hill's Third Corps, meanwhile, continued making sure the Yankees did not realize that two-thirds of Lee's Army of Northern Virginia had withdrawn. "We marched till night . . . and we were overtaken by a violent rainstorm," recalled Randolph McKim, a staff officer in Ed Johnson's division. "The woods is full of locusts one cannot sleep on account of their perpetual singing," complained another Marylander.[26]

They moved out again at 4:30 a.m. the next morning, marching toward Raccoon Ford on the Rapidan River via Verdiersville and Orange Court House. "The weather was fine, the roads excellent, the men in good spirits, but *they had no rations* (emphasis in original)," observed McKim. "One of them remarked good-humoredly, 'They put a fellow in the guard-house now for taking a drink of water; and as to *eating*—that's out of the question.' The same day we crossed the Rapidan, not at Raccoon, but at Somerville Ford, in the usual Confederate way," continued McKim. "No pontoons for us!" Despite the lack of food and water there were few stragglers. Thankfully Ewell's wagon trains kept pace with the snaking gray column as it wound its way

---

24 J. H. Douglas, "Report of the Operations of the Sanitary Commission during and after the Battles at Gettysburg," in *Documents of the U. S. Sanitary Commission* (New York: 1866), 2:78. Gall's description on June 29, 1863, came on the heels of the skirmish at Wrightsville.

25 Hotchkiss, *Make Me a Map of the Valley*, 149.

26 Clemens, "The 'Diary' of John H. Stone," 130.

across the Virginia countryside, so provisions were available if the opportunity to stop and eat them presented itself.[27]

Alfred M. Edgar was a lieutenant in the 27th Virginia, part of the Stonewall Brigade now under Brig. Gen. James Walker. A veteran of "Jackson's foot cavalry," Edgar was long accustomed to exhausting marches and hard fighting. "Our marching is different from what it was when Stonewall Jackson was leading us," wrote Edgar many years after the war. "We now march quietly along, no hurried order. We of his old corps cannot but not note the difference and whilst we are eager for more victories, we do not feel that we can do the efficient work we were to do under him."[28]

None of the men knew where they were headed. "I have no idea where we are going to," admitted a Georgian on June 7. "I think it is a flank movement it may be the enemy are changing their base of operations higher up the river. Time will soon reveal all." In the meantime, the men trudged on through the thick dust, their feet suffering from bad shoes and worse roads. They rested for ten minutes each hour in the hope that doing so would prevent them from wearing out too quickly. The heat and humidity wore the soldiers down. "The first three days were the hottest weather I have ever felt and I reckon I saw more than a hundred men who had fallen in the road perfectly helpless. It is reported that several died," recounted a Virginia infantryman. Part of Longstreet's corps and Rodes' division of Ewell's command arrived in Culpeper on the afternoon of June 7, with the balance of both corps reaching that place the next day. Tens of thousands of men spread their camps in the lush fields surrounding the base of Pony Mountain.[29]

"We passed through Culpeper Court House this morning about 8 o'clock a.m.," reported Col. Clement A. Evans of the 31st Georgia of Gordon's brigade in a letter to his wife Allie on June 8. "Like all the Virginia towns in this section it is built on rocky uneven ground and can make no claim to beauty. Many of the houses appear old, and the town wears a desolate appearance. Much of this is attributable to the war." Ominously, Evans observed that the men had had no news of the movements of the enemy. "I suppose they move on the other side of the Rappahannock so as to

---

27 McKim, *A Soldier's Recollections*, 139; G.W. Nichols, *A Soldier's Story of His Regiment (61st Georgia) and Incidentally of the Lawton-Gordon-Evans Brigade, Army of Northern Virginia* (Jesup, GA: privately published, 1898), 113. Somerville Ford is a few miles above Raccoon Ford on the Rapidan River.

28 Alfred M. Edgar, *My Reminiscences of the Civil War with the Stonewall Brigade and the Immortal 600* (Charleston, WV: 35th Star Publishing, 2011), 129.

29 Pearson, *Lee and Jackson's Bloody Twelfth*, 126; Ross Family Correspondence, Fluvanna County Confederate Soldiers Letters, Letter of June 21, 1863, State Library of Virginia, Richmond.

confront us. I do not know whether we are to fight or not, the probability is that a battle will take place at no distant day."[30]

While Ewell's men were marching into Culpeper, Hooker and his intelligence officers were collating all the raw data pouring in from the field. It was Colonel Sharpe's conclusion that the Confederates intended to launch a massive cavalry raid, "the most important expedition ever attempted in this country" he insisted with some exaggeration. He estimated the size of Stuart's command at 12,000 to 15,000 troopers. "There were strong indications that the enemy's entire Infantry will fall back upon Richmond and thence reinforce their armies in the west." Although Sharpe's conclusions about Stuart's ultimate objective were wrong, and he inaccurately thought that only the Confederate cavalry would be involved, his analysis that there would be a large expedition into the North was absolutely correct. He also did not know that Lee had ordered the march northward to resume on June 10 or that Stuart had concentrated his cavalry in Culpeper County to cover the advance of the infantry of Longstreet and Ewell.[31]

While Lee reviewed his cavalry and horse artillery in anticipation of the upcoming campaign on June 8, Hooker—in response to Sharpe's analysis—ordered General Pleasonton to fall upon this large concentration of Confederate cavalry with his entire command, in an effort to "destroy or disperse" it before it could commence raiding operations. With 12,000 troopers and 3,000 select infantrymen, Pleasonton did just that on June 9 in a move that triggered the largest cavalry battle ever waged on the North American continent. The fighting encompassed 14 hours and included 21,000 Union and Confederate horse soldiers and 3,000 Union infantry, all of whom slugged it out on the hills and fields around Brandy Station. The initial Union thrust caught Stuart completely by surprise, but he gained control of the situation and fought a masterful battle under very difficult and fluid circumstances. At the end of the day, the Federal horsemen withdrew, leaving the battlefield in Stuart's hands. The Union mission to destroy or at least disperse the large concentration of Confederate cavalry had failed.[32]

---

30 Robert Grier Stephens, Jr., ed., *Intrepid Warrior: Clement Anselm Evans* (Dayton, OH: Morningside, 1992), 189.

31 Edwin C. Fishel, *The Secret War for the Union: The Untold Story of Military Intelligence in the Civil War* (Boston: Houghton-Mifflin, 1996), 426-28; Heros von Borcke and Justus Scheibert, *The Great Cavalry Battle of Brandy Station*, trans. Stuart T. Wright and F.D. Bridgewater (1893; reprint, Gaithersburg, MD: Olde Soldier Books, 1976), 35.

32 OR 27, pt. 3, 27-28. The specifics of the battle of Brandy Station are beyond the scope of this study. For a detailed discussion of Brandy Station, see Eric J. Wittenberg, *The Battle of Brandy Station: North America's Largest Cavalry Battle* (Charleston, SC: The History Press, 2010).

When Lee learned about the large-scale cavalry battle raging nearby, he mounted his horse Traveler, and rode to the sound of the guns to watch the action unfold. Ewell joined him, and together they watched the climax of the fighting. When he learned a significant force of Union infantry was involved, Lee sent a message to inform Stuart that two of Ewell's infantry divisions were nearby and could quickly reinforce the cavalier. Concerned about the situation, Lee had Ewell send reinforcements closer to the action so they would be there to support Stuart if called upon.

Ewell moved Rodes' division to within a mile or so of the fighting. "Got here in a roundabout way and formed in line of battle with two lines of skirmishers in front," a North Carolina infantryman recorded in his diary. "We reached the field in time to see the fight close," recalled Lt. Irby Scott of the 12th Georgia. "My Regt. were down in sight of the river when they crossed but none of the infantry were engaged."[33]

Lee personally ordered Brig. Gen. Junius Daniel and Col. Edward A. O'Neal, two of Rodes' brigade commanders, to keep their infantry concealed from Union observation, and cautioned them to only bring the foot soldiers forward in an emergency. Elements of Johnson's division were also ordered closer to the action, but once Daniel's brigade took position the orders to Johnson were countermanded and his command returned to camp.[34]

Major Alexander S. "Sandie" Pendleton, the son of the army's chief of artillery, served on Ewell's staff. Referring to the Battle of Brandy Station, Pendleton wrote to his mother that day that he hoped the Union thrust across the Rappahannock was "an armed reconnaissance in force," and that "I hope it will soon be over and let us move on. I am anxious to get over into the valley and thence to Maryland." Jedediah Hotchkiss, one of the army's premier cartographers, remembered, "At one time we thought the enemy's cavalry would come to our headquarters and General Ewell said that we could gather into the house and defend it to the last." Fortunately, the threat never developed to test the defensive capabilities of that structure.[35]

As Ewell's chief of staff, Sandie Pendleton had ample opportunity to observe the new corps commander. After several days in the field with the one-legged general, he

---

33 Louis Leon, *Diary of a Tar Heel Confederate Soldier* (Charlotte, NC: Stone Publishing Co., 1913), 29-30; Pearson, *Lee and Jackson's Bloody Twelfth*, 126.

34 Von Borcke and Scheibert, *The Great Cavalry Battle at Brandy Station*, 98; Lemley diary, entry for June 9, 1863.

35 Lee, *William Nelson Pendleton*, 277; Hotchkiss, *Make Me a Map of the Valley*, 150. Sandie Pendleton, just 23 years old, had ably served as Stonewall Jackson's chief of staff, and assumed that same role for Ewell after Jackson's death in May. In 1864, when Jubal Early assumed command of the Second Corps, he arranged for Pendleton's promotion to lieutenant colonel, and the capable young man served as Old Jube's chief of staff until he was mortally wounded at Fisher's Hill on September 22, 1864, dying the following day.

reported to his mother on the same day as the Brandy Station fighting, "General Ewell is in fine health and fine spirits—rides on horseback as well as any one need to. The more I see of him the more I am pleased with him. In some of his traits of character he is very much like General Jackson, especially in his total disregard of his own comfort and safety, and his inflexibility of purpose." Sandie continued: "He is so thoroughly honest, too, and has only the one desire, to conquer the Yankees. I look for great things from him, and am glad to say that our troops have for him a good deal of the same feeling they had towards General Jackson."[36]

After the last of the Union troops withdrew across the Rappahannock River about 6:00 p.m. and the threat around Brandy Station subsided, Rodes returned his men to their camp near Pony Mountain, where they remained for nearly 18 hours to see whether Union cavalry and infantry might launch a second thrust across the river. Ewell, meanwhile, called for a conference with his three division commanders to discuss the routes their respective commands would take when they resumed the march.

They did so about 3:00 p.m. that afternoon of June 10, when Ewell reformed his divisions and set out for Winchester. The northern Shenandoah town garrisoned by a strong enemy was still about 60 miles northwest. Early and Johnson marched their divisions along the Old Richmond Turnpike, while Rodes guided his men on a parallel road in an effort to hide his troops from the probing eyes of advance Union soldiers (though none were encountered along the way). After a brisk march of some 20 miles, Early and Johnson camped at Woodville and Rodes bivouacked at Gourd Vine Baptist Church near Rixeyville. The opening phase of the second invasion of the North by the Army of Northern Virginia was now well underway.[37]

Far in advance of the marching infantry column roamed two brigades of Confederate cavalry that had not been present at Brandy Station. The riders, led by Brig. Gens. Albert G. Jenkins and John D. Imboden, protected the head of Lee's army, scouring the Valley of any resistance, cutting telegraph wires, seizing supplies, and wreaking general havoc. "Every one was eager to participate in the advance on the enemy which everything indicated was the intention of our leaders," concluded Pvt. James H. Hodam of the 17th Virginia Cavalry. While the cavalry fanned out to do its job of screening the advance, Milroy's Union equivalent remained stationary about Winchester. The Union general had not sent out any detachments of cavalry to act as an early warning system should a Confederate force come sweeping down the

---

36 Lee, *William Nelson Pendleton*, 277.

37 Barrett Y. Malone, *Whipt 'Em Everytime: The Diary of Bartlett Yancey Malone* (Jackson, TN: McCowat-Mercer Press, 1960), 80-1; Leon, *Diary of a Tar Heel Confederate Soldier*, 30; and McKim, *A Soldier's Recollections*, 143.

Shenandoah. The unopposed Jenkins and Imboden, meanwhile, did a fine job covering Lee's advance and creating a large buffer zone in front of Ewell's foot soldiers.[38]

The Southerners had another important advantage. They were moving through friendly territory, which meant they received from civilians eager to help the cause plentiful and accurate information about the whereabouts and dispositions of any unfriendly forces. Between the reports of these friendly civilians and those being forwarded by Jenkins and Imboden, Dick Ewell and his division commanders had a very clear and accurate picture of the disposition of Milroy's forces as they headed toward their destination at Winchester.[39]

Ewell resumed his march about 4:30 a.m. on June 11. "The day was pleasant—dusty," noted Ewell's cartographer Jedediah Hotchkiss in his diary, "but a shower and a fresh breeze improved the day. We found the grass, clover, and timothy, perfectly luxuriant—a great change from the bare fields of Fredericksburg. The men marched well."[40]

Rodes' troops had a harder time this day. According to the division commander, his division on the way to Newby's Crossroads marched on "the worst road I have ever seen troops and trains pass over." A portion of that route was rendered completely impassable due to rutting and washouts. The hardscrabble marching demanded by the rough road conditions quickly wore out his men and horses. Exasperated, Rodes ordered his troops to detour to the Richmond Turnpike, which placed all three divisions of Ewell's corps on the same road. Rodes waited for Early's division to pass, but when Ewell's carriage rolled up the corps commander told him the other two divisions had been delayed and that he should proceed. Rodes eased his men onto the road and marched another 15 miles that day, camping for the night about two miles north of Flint Hill.[41]

---

38 Robert P. Hodam, ed., *The Journal of James H. Hodam: Sketches and Personal Reminiscences of the Civil War as Experienced by a Confederate Soldier* (Eugene, OR: privately published, 1995), 58; O. O. Howard, "Gen. O. O. Howard's Personal Reminiscences of the War of the Rebellion. Between Campaigns, Movements Preliminary to Lee's Second Invasion," *National Tribune*, June 19, 1884. Both Jenkins and Imboden were lawyers and not professional soldiers. Their men came from what is today West Virginia, and they lacked experience in the traditional roles of cavalry such as scouting, screening, and reconnaissance. The Gettysburg Campaign was the first campaign in which they performed these formal roles, and both brigades provided important service.

39 Ibid.

40 Hotchkiss, *Make Me a Map of the Valley*, 150.

41 *OR* 27, pt. 2, 546.

Johnson's division, meanwhile, passed through Sperryville about 11:00 a.m. and headed northward toward Little Washington with Early's division behind it. The men had a difficult day, for it was very warm and the thick dust churned into the air by thousands of marching feet and comping hooves made breathing difficult. "The dust is almost intolerable & that together with the heat make the marching very severe," the 5th Alabama's Pvt. Samuel Pickens scribbled into his diary. Johnson arrived at Little Washington about 1:30 p.m. and went into camp. The van of Early's column arrived about 90 minutes later. Lieutenant William Kincheloe of the 49th Virginia, part of Early's command, was pleased to find the small town "full of pretty ladies; they employed themselves in watering the soldiers, cheering them, etc." Early used the opportunity to chat with Ewell about what roles the various divisions would assume when the time came to attack Milroy's garrison.[42]

Unfortunately for Lieutenant Kincheloe and his comrades, Early's division only stayed put for a short rest before organizing itself on the road once more and marching a few more miles to a spot between Little Washington and Flint Hill, where it camped for the night after covering 16 miles that day. That evening, Colonel Evans of the 31st Georgia scribbled another quick letter to his wife. "From this point we can turn to the left, cross the mountains at Chester Gap by Front Royal on to Winchester and down [north] the Valley; or we can turn to the right and march toward Manassas, to drive Hooker back toward Washington," he explained to Allie. "The probability of either course being taken are so nearly equal that I cannot prophesy which will be the route taken. I said in a letter written a day or two since that I seriously doubted whether we would invade the North, but I begin to be somewhat shaken in that opinion. Our army is so well organized, disciplined, armed, and enthusiastic, enjoys such remarkable health & is encumbered with so little baggage, that it is a splendid instrument in the hands of such skillful generals as we have to punish the invasion of our country by a counter invasion."[43]

That night, Ewell convened a conference with his officers to plan the route of the next day's march. This far, the Confederate march had encountered no resistance, and everything was going as well as it had been scripted. The Union high command seemed unaware that the entire Second Corps had left its front at Fredericksburg and was now descending upon Winchester. Ewell's soldiers had already covered 60 miles

---

42 Diary of Samuel Pickens, entry for June 11, 1863, Robert Brake Collection, USAHEC; Laura V. Hale and Stanley S. Phillips, *History of the Forty-Ninth Virginia Infantry, C.S.A.: "Extra Billy Smith's Boys"* (Lanham, MD: S. S. Phillips, 1981), 68-69.

43 Stephens, *Intrepid Warrior*, 194-95. Early arrested at least one of his officers who permitted his men to fall out of the column and visit a local house.

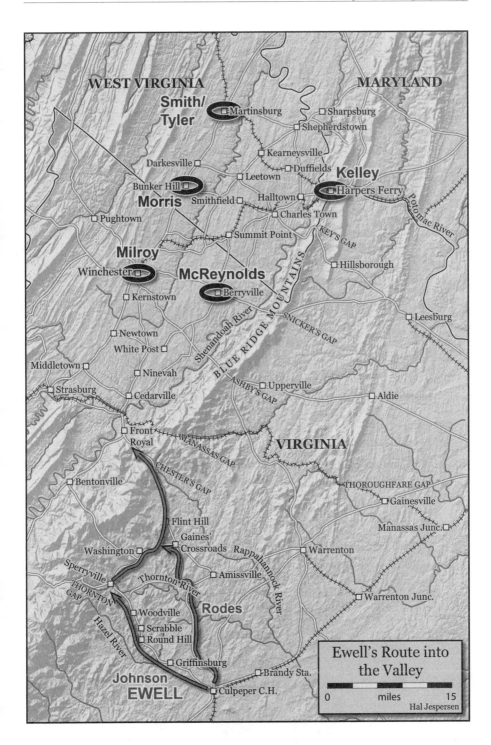

WEST VIRGINIA

Smith/
Tyler   Martinsburg

Darkesville

Bunker Hill
Morris   Smithfield

Pughtown

Milroy

Winchester   **McReynolds**

Kernstown   Berryville

Newtown
White Post

Middletown   Ninevah

Strasburg   Cedarville

Front
Royal

Bentonville

Flint Hill
Gaines'
Washington   Crossroads

Sperryville
THORNTON
GAP

Woodville   **Rodes**
Scrabble
Round Hill

Griffinsburg

Johnson
EWELL   Culpeper C.H.

MARYLAND

Sharpsburg
Shepherdstown

Kearneysville
Duffields   **Kelley**
Leetown
Halltown   Harpers Ferry
Charles Town

Summit Point   KEY'S GAP

Hillsborough

SNICKER'S GAP   Leesburg

Shenandoah River   BLUE RIDGE MOUNTAINS

ASHBY'S GAP   Upperville
Aldie

MANASSAS GAP   **VIRGINIA**

CHESTER'S GAP   THOROUGHFARE GAP
Gainesville

Manassas Junc.

Rappahannock River   Warrenton

Thornton River   Amissville

Hazel River   Warrenton Junc.

Brandy Sta.

Ewell's Route into
the Valley

0   miles   15
Hal Jespersen

Potomac River

since departing Fredericksburg, and Milroy's unsuspecting bastion at Winchester was nearly in sight.[44]

Rumors swirled throughout Winchester that a major force of Rebels was heading its way. "You no doubt hear daily that we are about having one of the most severe engagements of the war," the 12th West Virginia's Sgt. Milton Campbell wrote to his sister Mary the same night Colonel Evans wrote his wife. "Don't allow any such reports to have any weight with you. They are mere rumors without foundation." He continued in his attempt to reassure her: "There is not an enemy within forty miles of us, as reported by our cavalry scouts and Union people coming from the south, who are sent through to our lines by the rebels. We feel as safe here as we did in Clarksburg."[45]

44 Nye, *Here Come the Rebels!*, 73; A. J. Hertzog, who was 18 in 1863, served in the 13th Pennsylvania Cavalry. Years after the war, he claimed that after being sent to Leesburg under a flag of truce on June 11, he returned to the lines at Winchester that evening. Hertzog claimed that upon his return, Milroy asked him whether he had seen many of the enemy along the way. Hertzog claimed that he told Milroy that he had seen 15-20,000 of them and that he had counted 16 batteries. Supposedly, Milroy sniffed, "My boy, you are excited." This account cannot be corroborated and seems unlikely given that there were no Confederate troops of that force anywhere near Leesburg. A. J. Hertzog, "Milroy at Close Range," included in "All Stand Up for Milroy. Comrades Tell of Their Experiences with Milroy at Winchester and While He was in Alabama," The *National Tribune*, March 31, 1910.

45 Milton Campbell to Dear sister, June 11, 1863, in Fluharty, *Civil War Letters of Lt. Milton B. Campbell*, 46-47.

Chapter 3

Friday, June 12

"It began to look like as if there was going to be serious work on the morrow."

— *Lt. Col. James Stahle, 87th Pennsylvania Infantry*[1]

The Army of the Potomac remained largely inactive along the Rappahannock River around Fredericksburg while Robert E. Lee moved to transfer the war north into Pennsylvania; it was a dangerous gambit for the daring Southern general. By the second week of June Lee's lines of communications stretched nearly 100 miles and his army was dangerously divided. Hill's Third Corps still held the lengthy entrenchments near Fredericksburg to keep Hooker off balance and stationary. James Longstreet's First Corps, meanwhile, was camped some 30 miles to the northwest around Culpeper, while Richard Ewell's Second Corps was poised to enter the Valley another 20 miles to the northwest in their movement on Winchester. Shortly after the war ended, *New York Times* war correspondent William Swinton suggested Lee's audacity stemmed from a great contempt for his opponent.[2]

Ironically, just a week prior, General Hooker had predicted Lee would assume the strategy he was now undertaking. He had at that time considered pushing a couple infantry corps across the Rappahannock to interpose them between Hill and Longstreet, a move which, if properly executed, would have thoroughly disrupted Lee's plans and perhaps resulted in the isolation and destruction of Hill's exposed

---

1 *York (Pa.) Gazette,* June 13, 1893.

2 William Swinton, *Campaigns of the Army of the Potomac: A Critical History of Operations in Virginia, Maryland, and Pennsylvania from the Commencement to the Close of the War 1861-5* (New York: Charles B. Richardson, 1866), 315.

Brig. Gen. Albert G. Jenkins, commander of the cavalry brigade assigned to Ewell's corps for the invasion of Pennsylvania.
U.S. Army Heritage and Education Center

command. In Washington, General Halleck worried about the risks of such a plan and denied the request. President Lincoln sided with his general-in-chief. "If Lee should leave a rear force at Fredericksburg, tempting you to fall upon it," Lincoln informed Hooker on June 5, "he would fight you in intrenchments and have you at disadvantage; and so, man for man, worst you at that point, while his main force would in some way be getting an advantage of you northward." Lincoln added in his characteristic picturesque imagery, "In a word, I would not take any risk of being entangled upon the river, like an ox jumped half over a fence, and liable to be torn by dogs front and rear, without a fair chance to gore one way or to kick the other."[3]

Now, on June 12, with most of Hooker's infantry stationary along the Rappahannock River near Fredericksburg, Lee took the opportunity of Union inaction to attack Milroy's isolated command in the northern end of the Valley. General Rodes' division, the vanguard of Ewell's 19,000-man Second Corps, would cross the Blue Ridge at Chester Gap. Generals Johnson and Early would follow in behind Rodes. Longstreet's task was to screen the move from inquisitive Union eyes by marching on the eastern foothills. Once this was underway, A. P. Hill would slip away from Fredericksburg and follow Ewell and Longstreet into the Valley and the route north.

While Lee finalized his plans, 33-year-old Brig. Gen. Albert G. Jenkins' Rebel cavalry brigade, which had not arrived in time to participate in the Battle of Brandy Station, joined Ewell's column on June 12. It was an unusual command. Jenkins, who was born near Huntington in what is today West Virginia, was a Harvard-trained lawyer and politician leading an independent command of irregulars, and so his brigade was not formally part of Stuart's cavalry division. His nearly 1,100 troopers consisted of the 14th, 16th, and 17th Virginia cavalry regiments and the 34th and 36th

---

3 OR 27. pt. 2, 31; Basler, Pratt, and Dunlap, *The Collected Works of Abraham Lincoln*, 6:249-51.

battalions of Virginia cavalry. Traditional cavalry these were not. Generally speaking, Jenkins' troopers used their horses to move from one place to another in order to dismount and fight using infantry tactics. In addition to two-band Enfields, they carried a wide variety of muzzle-loading rifles and rifled muskets, including Model 1841 Mississippi rifles, Austrian Lorenz rifles, and Model 1855-61 Springfields. Only a few companies in each regiment carried sabres. Those who did were usually termed "flanking" or "charging" companies, and were employed to press home an attack on an enemy. These tough men hailed from the mountains of southwestern Virginia, and, until summoned to join the Army of Northern Virginia in May 1863, had spent the war engaged in bushwhacking and guerilla-style warfare in that region.[4]

Soon after they met up with Ewell's infantry, Jenkins' Virginians enjoyed quite a spectacle. "Late that evening we halted on the level bottom opposite the town of Front Royal and at the Junction of the two [branches of the] Shenandoah Rivers," recalled a trooper with the 17th Virginia Cavalry. "But the unexpected Sight we beheld filled us with wonder and amazement. The roads, the fields and town and the hills beyond, seemed to be a living mass of humanity. An Army with banners slowly marching dusty, dirty and determined towards Winchester. All night long we listened to the rumble of artillery, the rattle of wagons, the clatter of canteen and bayonet as the brigades of Gen. Early's veterans onward marched." The sight of multiple thousands of men thus engaged was utterly foreign to these irregulars.[5]

Ewell's plan to conquer the northern reaches of the Shenandoah Valley was both complex and ambitious. His design featured simultaneous attacks against Federal-held Winchester and Berryville, a small town some ten-and-a-half miles east of Milroy's main garrison, while also attacking the Union force stationed at Martinsburg about 25 miles north. General Rodes was to take his division through Millwood to Berryville,

---

4   OR 27, pt. 2, 440. Jenkins had served as a delegate to the 1856 Democratic convention that nominated James Buchanan for president and as a United States Congressman from 1857-1861. When Virginia seceded in April 1861, Jenkins embraced the Confederate cause and organized a company of so-called border rangers that formed the nucleus of the 8th Virginia Cavalry. After performing well in the early days of the war, he was eventually commissioned colonel of the 8th Virginia. In February 1862, Jenkins resigned that commission to take a seat in the Confederate Congress, but in August of that year accepted a commission as brigadier general with an assignment to serve in western Virginia. His troops conducted a 500-mile-long raid through western Virginia and into Ohio. In March 1863, he led another long raid, and in May, General Lee summoned his brigade to join the Army of Northern Virginia for the push northward. The Gettysburg Campaign was Jenkins's first campaign in the regular service. Unfortunately, Jenkins was badly wounded on July 2 at Gettysburg, and no report of his or his brigade's service in the campaign was filed. Jeffry D. Wert, "Albert Gallatin Jenkins," included in Davis, ed., *The Confederate Generals*, 3:161.

5   Hodam, *The Journal of James H. Hodam*, 59.

Maj. Gen. Robert E. Rodes. A rising star in the army, Rodes commanded the largest division in Ewell's Second Corps.

Library of Congress

attack and seize the town, and then advance without delay to Martinsburg. Once Ewell had taken Winchester, Rodes was to march immediately into Maryland via Williamsport or other convenient crossing point of the Potomac River. Once Rodes was safely in Maryland, he would wait for Ewell's other two divisions to join him. It was a bold plan, but one Ewell believed would be successful. He assigned Jenkins' brigade to assist Rodes in carrying out the plan and to forage for food and supplies after crossing the Potomac.[6]

At 33 years old, Robert E. Rodes was one of the youngest major generals in Lee's army. Trained at the Virginia Military Institute, the Lynchburg native possessed a keen sense of tactics and was a handsome, energetic, and charismatic leader of men. His work as a civil engineer in Alabama before the war developed within him a keen eye for terrain, a valuable trait he would put to good use in the Confederate army as the colonel of the 5th Alabama. Quickly developing a reputation as a brave, hard fighter, Rodes had been wounded in the arm at Seven Pines. He was again wounded while defending the "Sunken Road" at the battle of Sharpsburg (Antietam) in September 1862. He had commanded a division under Stonewall Jackson at Chancellorsville, leading a devastating flank attack on the Union Eleventh Corps on May 2, 1863. His performance earned him a subsequent promotion to major general. Rodes' division became part of Ewell's new corps when General Lee reorganized the Army of Northern Virginia after Jackson's death.[7]

Brigadier General George P. Doles' veteran brigade of Georgians comprised Rodes' vanguard, with the 12th Georgia in the forefront. Early on the morning of June 12, Rodes as planned crossed the Blue Ridge Mountains at Chester Gap and marched through Front Royal about 11:00 a.m., forded both forks of the Shenandoah River, and continued on through Cedarville along a lightly traveled country road toward Mill-

6   *OR* 27, pt. 2, 546.

7   For a detailed biography of Rodes, see Collins, Darrell L., *Major General Robert Rodes of the Army of Northern Virginia* (El Dorado Hills, CA: Savas Beatie, 2008).

Brig. Gen. George P. Doles, one of the brigade commanders in Robert Rodes' division.

U.S. Army Heritage and Education Center

wood. Once in the Shenandoah Valley, Rodes utilized the services of the "most excellent" John McCormack, a soldier-guide who had intimate knowledge of the terrain and road network.[8]

George Doles, the commander of Rodes' Georgia Brigade, was a prewar businessman and militia captain with little real military training. However, he quickly developed as a leader and earned a reputation for bravery and efficiency on the battlefield, particularly as colonel of the 4th Georgia during the Peninsula Campaign, where he suffered a painful wound at the battle of Malvern Hill. When Brig. Gen. Robert Ripley fell wounded at Antietam in September 1862, Doles as senior colonel assumed temporary command of the brigade, a role made permanent in November of that year with his promotion to brigadier general.[9]

"The people of this teeming valley were fairly mad with joy at our coming," wrote Capt. John C. Gorman of the 2nd North Carolina, part of Brig. Gen. Stephen D. Ramseur's brigade, to an influential friend and newspaper editor back home. They had endured oppression "almost beyond belief by the tyrant Milroy." The officer's belief was confirmed when Ramseur's North Carolina brigade was marching past the doorway of a small cottage and a gray-haired civilian tearfully thanked God that "Gray Backs were come, and they were free once more." Captain Gorman continued his description, which is worth setting forth in full:

> Maidens fairly paved our pathway with flowers, bright eyes beamed with unalloyed pleasure and delight on our tattered, dusty garments, matrons stood at the gates with pitchers and buckets of cool water and milk, offering freely to our thirsty soldiery whilst even the little children were happy in the general joy. I never felt so proud as a soldier

8 Henry W. Thomas, *History of the Doles-Cook Brigade, Army of Northern Virginia, C.S.A.* (Atlanta: Franklin Printing, 1903), 6; *OR* 27, pt. 2, 546. John McCormick, a Shenandoah Valley native transferred from Company C, 2nd Virginia to serve on Rodes' staff, was a frequent courier for the general during the Gettysburg campaign.

9 Ibid.

before. I felt I was no bare hireling in a doubtful cause, but as a hero who was battling for truth, justice and right, and could I feel always as I then felt, the trials, vicissitudes and dangers of the soldier life would be nothing, and I would be content to remain one for life.[10]

"This has been one of the bright days of my life," gloated Mattela Page (Cary) Harrison who lived near Millwood. "I was seated quietly in the porch when an alarm was given about the coming of Yankees." That thought struck fear into the hearts of most residents in the vicinity of Winchester. After hearing the clattering of hooves, Cary grabbed her pistol and "ran down to the door determined to resist their entrance if they attempted it." At the nursery door, several soldiers asked her "very respectfully for milk." Their gentle tone surprised her, and she "made several inquiries which proved they were Confederates. I exclaimed can it be possible gentlemen you are Confederates. They were quite shocked at the idea of being taken for anything else. I made them heartily welcome and they rode off, after giving me joyful news of the position and strength of our forces." The troops soon came thick and fast. "While in the woods," she added, "I heard a shout and looking behind saw my precious husband and dear Cousin John. My happiness was too great for words. Oh that I could feel as thankful as I ought, but my poor wicked heart is so hard, when prosperity comes, I am so prone to forget the giver."[11]

The road-toughened soldiers in Rodes' division had marched more than 100 miles in eight days by the time they passed through the old Warren County town of Front Royal. The town was a regional transportation hub at the confluence of the North and South Forks of the Shenandoah River. Its citizens, often the target of Milroy's frequent supply raids, heartily welcomed the Confederate arrivals. "The ladies treated us very handsomely," recalled Pvt. Louis Leon of the 53rd North Carolina. One of the ladies who has so pleased the private was young Lucy Buck, who rejoiced, "Oh how the gallant boys cheered and shouted. Ma and I went up on the house and when they saw us, they waved and hurrahed us. Oh! It was glorious!"

10 John C. Gorman to "Friend Holden," who was William W. Holden, editor of the *North Carolina Standard*, June 22, 1863, "Our Army Correspondence," unidentified newspaper clipping, North Carolina State Archives [hereafter cited as NCSA], Raleigh, copy in the library of the Gettysburg National Military Park.

11 Matthela Page Harrison Diary, John W. Daniel Collection, Box 25, Folder, June 14, 1863, Jubal Early Material, Battle of Winchester, Special Collections, Alderman Library, University of Virginia.

Several townspeople encouraged the gray-clad soldiers to catch Milroy soon and give him a good whipping.[12]

A spellbound boy named Thomas Ashby watched as thousands of Southern soldiers marched past his house. "The men were in splendid condition and in high spirits," he fondly remembered. "As they passed through the village, the soldiers closed up their ranks and the bands played as if on parade. The artillery and the wagons, interspersed between the different commands, added to the impressiveness of the occasion and gave a good idea of the details and appurtenances of war."[13]

The gala-like atmosphere sat well with the troops. The residents were "frantic with delight at seeing 'the boys in grey' once more," boasted staff officer Lt. Col. Wharton J. Green. He and Lt. Col. William Gaston Lewis of the 43rd North Carolina were riding near the head of Brig. Gen. Junius Daniel's brigade when they encountered two young ladies standing at their front gate. The women offered the officers a drink from pails of fresh buttermilk. "Every old soldier knows that such an invitation could not be refused," Green continued. While they drank buttermilk, their regiment marched past. "Come out of that, you know you have got a wife and baby at home, and if you don't, I'll tell on you," joked one wag. Much to Green's confusion, each passing man soon took up the "vile outcry" until the entire brigade had passed. "I need not ask which one of you it is, for your countenance has fastened it on you," teased one of the young ladies as she coyly pointed a finger in Green's direction. With their buttermilk cups soon empty, Green and Lewis rejoined the marching column. Shortly thereafter, Rodes' troops crossed Crooked Run and rendezvoused with Jenkins' cavalry.[14]

The 5th Alabama, part of Col. Edward O'Neal's brigade of Rodes' division, passed through Front Royal early that evening. One of its members, Pvt. Samuel Pickens, thought it "an old looking town—situated in the Valley & seems to be

---

12 "From Start to the Finish: Diary of a Confederate Soldier," *Charlotte Observer*, November 16, 1892; Louis Leon, *Diary of a Tar Heel Confederate Soldier* (Charlotte, NC: Stone Publishing, 1911), 30; Lucy Rebecca Buck diary entry for June 12, 1863, cited in Elizabeth R. Baer, ed., *Shadows on My Heart: The Civil War Diary of Lucy Rebecca Buck of Virginia* (Athens: University of Georgia Press, 1997), 212. Incorporated in 1788, Front Royal grew steadily in the seven decades before the Civil War. According to the 1860 Census, nearly a quarter of its population of 6,000 was slaves.

13 Thomas A. Ashby, *The Valley Campaigns: Being the Reminiscences of a Non-Combatant While between the Lines in the Shenandoah Valley during the War of the States* (New York: Neale Publishing Co., 1914), 240.

14 Wharton J. Green, *Recollections and Reflections: An Auto of Half a Century and More* (Raleigh, NC: Edwards and Broughton, 1906), 172. Green was taken captive at Gettysburg and spent the rest of the war in the Johnson's Island prison camp in Lake Erie. He later became a two-term U. S. congressman and a prominent vintner.

Brig. Gen. George H. Steuart commanded the Confederate Maryland Line, which was part of Maj. Gen. Ed. "Allegheny" Johnson's division. *U.S. Army Heritage and Education Center*

surrounded by mountains when you see it at a little distance. The people delighted to see us, & hoped we would be able to catch Milroy. His province extended only to the Shenandoah a mile above the town, but he frequently made raids on that side." Pickens marveled at the lush scenery, which included "a comfortable lookg. house in a thick shady grove & on one side there was one of the richest meadows I have ever seen—covd. with the most luxuriant hay grass of some kind & along a stream running though it there were 2 rows of weeping willows—the largest and most fluorishg I ever saw."[15]

Marcus Blakemore Buck tended a handsome farm just outside of Front Royal. That night he noted in his diary, "This morning at 10 o'clock, the head of the column of Ewell's Corps (formerly Jackson's) commenced poking through town and have continued to poke at a quick march during the entire day and till this hour." He also observed that another large column had passed through the Blue Ridge at Snicker's Gap, headed toward Winchester. "Milroy is known to have been still in Winchester yesterday morning. He will soon be made to feel the vengeance of an outraged people, if he is still there," Buck gloated. After noting that several officers from the 6th Alabama of O'Neal's brigade had visited his property that evening, he took in the scene around him and concluded with no little satisfaction, "Tonight the North is beautiful, illuminated with campfires."[16]

Like Rodes' men, the soldiers of Johnson's division also had hard a hard march on June 12. Reveille had sounded at 3:00 a.m. for Brig. Gen. George H. Steuart's mixed brigade of Virginians, Marylanders, and North Carolinians. Steuart, descended from a prominent Maryland family of planters and soldiers, had graduated from West Point

---

15 Hubbs, *Voices from Company D*, 176.

16 Marcus Blakemore Buck Diary and Farm Journal, entry for June 12, 1863, Special Collections, Alderman Library, University of Virginia, Charlottesville.

in 1848. He served in the 1862 Valley Campaign as commander of the 1st Maryland regiment and later was elevated to brigadier general following the battle of Chancellorsville. This would be his first campaign as a general. He and his Maryland regiments looked forward to returning to their home state during the summer campaign. After a hasty breakfast washed down with coffee, his men moved out at 4:30 a.m. and tramped through the hamlet of Flint Hill toward Front Royal in the Shenandoah Valley, a hike of nearly 23 miles that necessitated the ascent and descent of Chester Gap. Steuart's brigade crossed the Shenandoah River about 4:00 p.m. "on Confederate pontoons—that is by wading straight through in column of fours," joked Lt. Randolph H. McKim, a former college student from Virginia now serving as Steuart's aide-de-camp. "Forded both branches, the men cheering and in fine spirits. I never saw a ford so well made." Thus far the march had been steady, relatively enjoyable, and with scarcely any stragglers.[17]

One of Allegheny Johnson's Virginians left a vivid description of his passage over the Blue Ridge into the Shenandoah. "It was raining when we started and when we got to the top the clouds were all around us and so thick that you couldn't see a man fifty steps," he wrote. "After going about six miles we came down the mountain and crossed the Shenandoah River." As the men approached the river ford, they "pulled off there clothes, and I believe it was good for us, as we felt fine when we got our clothes on again."[18]

Meanwhile, Jubal Early's division moved from Little Washington into the Valley through Chester Gap and then marched toward Front Royal. "The weather was hot and the roads dry and dusty," complained Pvt. I. Gordon Bradwell of the 31st Georgia, part of Brig. Gen. John B. Gordon's brigade. "This dust, worked up by the wagon trains and artillery, settled on us until we were as brown as the dust itself." General Gordon rode past the regiment and called out, "Boys, if your mothers could see you now, they wouldn't know you!" When he noticed some of his men were limping along on blistered feet, according to Bradwell the general dismounted and helped a footsore private up into his saddle. Once he was in place, Gordon fell into the ranks with a gun slung over his shoulder and trudged along with his men, a shrewd move which endeared him to his troops.[19]

17 Randolph H. McKim, *A Soldier's Recollections: Leaves from the Diary of a Young Confederate* (New York: Longmans, Green, and Co., 1910), 143.

18 Ross Family Correspondence, letter of June 21, 1863.

19 John Gordon to Fanny Gordon, June 13, 1863, Hargrett Rare Book & Manuscript Library, University of Georgia Libraries, Athens; Bradwell, "Capture of Winchester," *Confederate Veteran*, vol. 30, September 1922, 330.

After passing through Front Royal about 5:00 p.m., Gordon's and Brig. Gen. Harry T. Hays' brigades, together with Lt. Col. Hilary P. Jones' sixteen-gun artillery battalion, camped along the Front Royal-Winchester Road on the eastern side of the South Fork of the Shenandoah River. The rest of Early's veteran divison was within supporting distance. Robert Hoke's brigade of North Carolinians, commanded by Col. Isaac E. Avery, following Hoke's wounding at Chancellorsville, and 65-year-old Brig. Gen. William "Extra Billy" Smith's Virginia brigade had crossed both forks of the Shenandoah farther north. Meanwhile, Johnson's division was camped beyond the streams around Cedarville, roughly a dozen miles south of Winchester. Rodes' division pitched camp at Stone Bridge five miles northeast of Front Royal. General Ewell called a meeting at Cedarville, where he explained his intended course of action to his three division leaders. The next day, he explained, the Second Corps would attack Winchester and Berryville, and thereafter, Martinsburg. Once the Valley was cleared, the corps would march to the Potomac and cross into Maryland at Boteler's Ford.[20]

Private William S. White of the 3rd Richmond Howitzers chafed at being so far back in the snaking miles-long column. As part of Ewell's rear guard, White was unsure his company would reach Winchester in time to fight. "[M]y impression," he explained to his diary, "is that we will have an easy job in cleaning out Milroy's forces." Wanting to get in on the upcoming scrap, White and some of his comrades hastened on toward Winchester once the quartermaster, commissary, and ordnance wagons halted for the night. Much too soon for their tastes, however, orders arrived for them to return and guard the wagon train, a mundane and thankless task. At least they now had time to get something to eat, White confessed, "even if we don't share in the glory of capturing Winchester."[21]

---

20 Early, *Autobiographical Sketch*, 238-39. Robert Hoke was still recovering from wounds suffered during the Chancellorsville campaign, which elevated Colonel Avery to command the brigade in his absence. William Smith was the oldest general in the Army of Northern Virginia. A five-term U. S. congressman and former governor of Virginia during the Mexican War, Smith received the nickname "Extra Billy" because of his prewar penchant as a Federal postal contractor to routinely use loopholes in his contracts to find ways to charge for extra services. For a detailed biography of Smith, see Scott L. Mingus Sr., *Confederate General William "Extra Billy" Smith: From Virginia's Statehouse to Gettysburg Scapegoat* (El Dorado Hills, CA: Savas Beatie, 2013).

21 William S. White, "A Diary of the War: What I Saw of It," in Carlton McCarthy, ed., *Contributions to a History of the Richmond Howitzers, Pamphlet No. 2* (Richmond, VA: Carlton McCarthy and Co., 1883), 186.

Opening Skirmish near Newtown and Middletown

While the Confederates marched into position throughout the day on June 12, the Union soldiers of Milroy's division of the Eighth Corps followed their normal routine, with many of the men toiling on the unfinished fortifications in the heat and dust. Everyone knew there were Rebels operating beyond their vision, but they were wholly unaware an entire corps of the Army of Northern Virginia was less than a day's march distant. The 18th Connecticut's Pvt. James M. Smith manned a picket post under an ash tree along a small creek near the 87th Pennsylvania's camp. "Have had a pleasant day, thus far," observed Smith, "though the wind blows very hard." Little did he know it would be his last pleasant day for some time to come. Reports trickled in of Rebel cavalry on the Valley Pike just a few miles southwest of Winchester. "We are in expectation of active work in the Valley and frequently sleep upon our arms," Maj. Harry L. White of the 67th Pennsylvania, stationed in Berryville, told his father. "I think we will have a cavalry dash through here. Our force is weak but we will do the best possible."[22]

Because of the persistent and credible rumors that Jeb Stuart was planning a major raid into the Shenandoah Valley, Milroy periodically sent out strong patrols to keep a close watch on the roads running south and southwest out of Winchester. During the afternoon of June 12, Albert Jenkins' Confederate horsemen charged a Union outpost at Nineveh some twelve miles south of Winchester on the road to Front Royal and lost a few men, including Lt. Charles Norvell, who was wounded and captured.[23]

That morning Milroy dispatched Col. John W. Schall and 700 men on a strong reconnaissance up the Valley Pike south toward Strasburg. The force consisted of 400 men of Schall's own 87th Pennsylvania infantry regiment, six companies of the 13th Pennsylvania Cavalry (popularly known as the "Irish Dragoons"), and a pair of 3-inch rifles from Battery L, 5th U. S. Light Artillery. The 13th had recently welcomed back almost 50 comrades who had been released and exchanged from Richmond's

---

22 James M. Smith diary entry for June 12, 1863. Harry L. White to Judge Thomas White, June 12, 1863, Berryville, VA, White Collection, Historical and Genealogical Society of Indiana County, PA.

23 OR 27, pt. 2, 548; "The Evacuation of Winchester," in *Baltimore American and Commercial Advertiser*, July 6, 1863; Henry S. Clapp, "With Milroy at Winchester: The Reminiscences of a Private," *The National Tribune Repository: Good Stories of Experience and Adventure*, vol. 1, no. 4 (Washington, DC, National Tribune, 1908), reprinted as "123rd Ohio: Recollections of a Private, 1863," in E. R. Hutchins, ed., *The War of the Sixties* (New York: Neale Publishing Co., 1912), 202-207.

notorious Libby Prison. They had been taken captive on February 26, 1863, in an ambush near Fisher's Hill and the subsequent retreat to Strasburg.[24]

The horse soldiers were not looked upon favorably by many of their comrades in the infantry. Some of the problem stemmed from the February ambush. The 12th West Virginia's Sgt. Milton Campbell was down on Loudon Street that cold and rainy winter day when he "saw the scared Pa. cavalry coming in, covered with mud, awful looking men, and so badly scared they could not tell which regt. they belonged to when Gen. Milroy asked them. They are a perfect laughing stock among the other soldiers," added Campbell, "and have so completely disgraced themselves that they will have to do an awful daring act to regain any kind of reputation."[25]

Still smarting from the snickers and jibes leveled at them by the infantrymen, the Irish troopers headed back out toward Strasburg with Schall's foot soldiers and the artillery trailing behind them. Few of the Keystone riders realized that today would be their chance for redemption. After an uneventful 10-mile march from Winchester, Schall's force passed through Newtown about noon. Early that afternoon, scouts spotted mounted enemy pickets in the distance beyond the colonial-era "Vaucluse" estate, a local landmark and springs southwest of Newtown. The Union patrol continued south on the turnpike within small arms range, triggering a brief but bloodless skirmish near the David Dinges farm. The Rebel advance was comprised of Capt. William I. Rasin's Company E of the 1st Maryland Cavalry Battalion, a few troopers from the 14th Virginia Cavalry, and eight of Maj. Harry W. Gilmor's Maryland rangers—in all about 60 riders. What neither the Union patrol nor Schall realized was that these men formed the vanguard of Brig. Gen. Albert G. Jenkins's brigade en route from Cedar Creek to report to Ewell. When he heard the intermittent gunfire, the charismatic Gilmor left his hospital bed in Middletown, donned a new yellow-braided uniform, and galloped north to join his rangers. After some additional skirmishing, the Union patrol withdrew with Gilmor and company following them.[26]

24 Michael Dougherty, *Prison Diary of Michael Dougherty, Late Co. B, 13th Pa. Cavalry* (Bristol, PA: Chas. A. Dougherty, 1908), introduction. It is uncertain which section of the battery accompanied Schall's expedition, although it may have been Lt. Edmund Spooner's two guns.

25 Milton Campbell to Dear sister, February 28, 1863, in Fluharty, *Civil War Letters of Lt. Milton B. Campbell*, 28.

26 William W. Goldsborough, *The Maryland Line in the Confederate Army, 1861-1865* (Baltimore: Guggenheimer, Weil, and Co., 1900), 174-76; Sarah Eliza Steele and John Magill Steele diary entry, June 12, 1863, cited in Garland R. Quarles, *Diaries, Letters, and Recollections of the War Between the States* (Winchester, VA: Winchester-Frederick County Historical Society, ca 1955), 3:75. Newtown is now Stephens City. Rasin survived the war and became a successful businessman in Baltimore. He died in 1916.

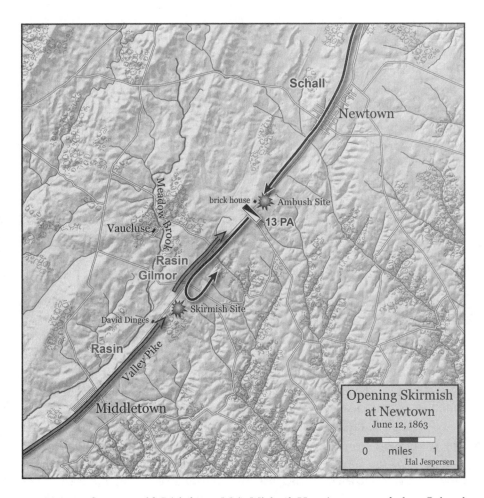

Opening Skirmish
at Newtown
June 12, 1863

0   miles   1

Hal Jespersen

Twenty-five-year-old Irish-born Maj. Michael Kerwin proposed that Colonel Schall ambush the advancing Rebels by pretending his cavalry was retreating in confusion.[27] Schall agreed, halting the column and deploying his men in a wide semicircle off the pike near the J. Chrisman farm. He concealed most of his infantry in a dense grove to the right (west) while his two artillery pieces unlimbered left (east) of the pike behind a low ridge. His other men hid in a wooded ravine lining a nearby pasture left of the road, and behind a stone wall along the road itself. With Enfield rifled muskets loaded, they awaited the arrival of the Confederates. "We took our positions flat down in a clover field a little out of sight while the cavalry pushed on to

27 Kerwin was a colorful character. For more on the young Irishman, see http://irishamericancivilwar.com/2012/01/05/irish-colonels-michael-kerwin-13th-pennsylvania-cavalry/, accessed on October 10, 2013.

draw on the rebs," Cpl. John C. Keses recalled. Kerwin launched a pair of feints and fell back in something mimicking confusion, but the Rebels refused to take the bait and aggressively pursue the Union troopers. His third attempt at the ruse, however, worked. "The disposition of our force had hardly been made," the 87th's Lt. William H. Lanius reminisced, "when the advance guard of cavalry made its appearance on the hill, coming in on the run, closely pursued by the enemy, who were howling like demons."[28]

Several women suddenly appeared in a top-floor window at the gable end of a nearby large brick house. When the Rebels dashed over the hill, the ladies gestured with their hands and frantically waved handkerchiefs as a warning. "We screamed and begged and waved them back, but it was too late," bemoaned Kate Sperry. The Winchester resident was visiting her friends and found herself watching combat unexpectedly unfolding before her eyes. Major Gilmor, yelling wildly and waving his sword, was leading the horsemen onward when the withdrawing Federal riders suddenly wheeled about. This, combined with a sudden and wholly unexpected broadside burst of canister fire from the pair of previously hidden iron tubes stunned the Confederates, as did the appearance of Union infantrymen, who rose and poured a volley into them. The deadly fire knocked riders off their mounts and sent frightened horses with empty saddles racing aimlessly hither and yon. While Gilmor and Rasin tried to rally their remaining troopers, the women watching the bloodshed screamed, "My god, they are killing all our men!" "It was a little like butchering," admitted the 87th Pennsylvania's Sgt. George Blotcher.[29]

"It was the best trap and the most successful that I saw during the war," gushed Pennsylvania cavalryman Pvt. R. H. McElhinny. The returning Irish cavalrymen slammed into the confused enemy horsemen, triggering individual hand-to-hand melees as the Confederates desperately tried to disengage. During the clash, Major Kerwin severely wounded Captain Rasin with a savage saber cut to his head. "That brave fellow Rasin came at me like a bullet," the fiery Kerwin later narrated, "but I was

---

28 York (Pa.) *Gazette*, June 13, 1895; OR 27, pt. 1, 42, 54; Prowell, *History of the Eighty-seventh Regiment*, 65-66; John C. Keses Papers, USAHEC; *Athens (Ohio) Messenger*, July 9, 1863; Harold Hand, Jr., *One Good Regiment: The 13th Pennsylvania Cavalry in the Civil War 1861-1865* (Victoria, BC: Trafford, 2000), 49. Keses is incorrectly spelled "Kesser" in the regimental history and in Bates' *History of Pennsylvania Volunteers*.

29 Kate Sperry Diary, Handley Regional Library, as cited in Brandon H. Beck and Charles S. Grunder, *The Second Battle of Winchester, June 12-15, 1863* (Lynchburg, VA: H.E. Howard, 1989), 25-26; Diary of George Blotcher, Sam and George Blotcher Papers, YCHT, York, Pennsylvania. This property is listed as the "J. M. Long" house on an 1885 map of Newtown. A stone house, the Jacob Chrisman place, was across the pike about 1,000 yards away according to Nye, *Here Come the Rebels!*, 76. Some accounts call this fight "the affair at J. Chrisman's."

the stronger and quicker and got in the first blow." A dismounted Rebel cavalryman struggled with Pvt. Frank T. C. Metzgar of the 87th's skirmish company. Metzgar, who had been detailed as the brigade's baker back in December, finally wounded his antagonist and took him prisoner. Once the shooting stopped, he bound his prisoner's injuries.[30]

"The rebel cavalry got such a warm reception that they fled with the 13th Pa. Cav. in hot pursuit," declared a Pennsylvania horse soldier. Years after the war, other Keystone State horse soldiers proudly recalled how their regiment and the 87th had set a trap for the approaching Confederates—quite an accomplishment considering the relative inexperience of the two regiments. According to member of the 12th West Virginia noted, "About 75 saddles were emptied, and among the first to fall was their leader. This threw them into confusion, and they retreated in great disorder. About 40 were killed or wounded and as many taken prisoner."[31]

Once disengaged, the Southerners raced back through Middletown with Kerwin's troopers in hot pursuit before the Federals finally gave up the chase after a half-hour or so. Gilmor tried to deflect the blame onto Rasin when he later reported the affair to General Jenkins. Kerwin and his triumphant cavaliers trotted back to Middletown, where they paused to rest and water their horses. The young major stopped at the Steele household, where he chatted with the family for some time, including 12-year-old Sarah Eliza and her 14-year-old brother John.[32]

Concurrent with Kerwin's successful ambuscade, several men from Lt. Col. Monroe Nichols' 18th Connecticut sat in their camp near Shawnee Springs off the Millwood Pike. They were relatively recent arrivals in the Valley, which they reached from Baltimore on May 25; few had combat experience. Being so close to the Rebels sobered 18-year-old Pvt. Charles F. Porter, who "like most young soldiers, [was] filled with exaggerated ideas of the adventurous life before me." Now, "we had got through playing soldier. Lively times were ahead." The low rumbling of gunfire to the southwest startled the soldiers, with one excitedly crying out, "They have found the rebels and the Eighty-Seventh Pennsylvania are giving them grape!" Several men expressed a desire to participate in the fray. "I wish we could only get one chance at

30 R. H. McElhinny, "Milroy at Winchester: A Very Unsafe Place Generally," *National Tribune*, May 20, 1909; Grunder and Beck, *The Second Battle of Winchester*, 26; Prowell, *History of the 87th Pennsylvania*, 87.

31 S. T. Linn, "The Cavalry at Winchester," included in "All Stand Up for Milroy;" S. R. Evril, "Gen. Milroy at Winchester," *National Tribune*, November 29, 1888. See also "J. W. S." (John W. Schall), "Letter from the Camp," *The Adams Sentinel and General Advertiser*, September 29, 1863; "H. C. H.", "From the 12th Virginia," *The Wellsburg Herald*, July 3, 1863.

32 Steele diary entry for June 16, 1863, Quarles, *Diaries, Letters, and Recollections*, 3:75.

them," one bemoaned. "They never give us anything to do." Twenty-year-old William Caruthers overheard the remark. "Don't be in a hurry, boys," the English-born veteran of First Bull Run muttered more to himself than anyone else. "You will have your full share of fighting at no distant day."[33]

Back at the skirmish site, recent German immigrant Sergeant Blotcher thought that Colonel Schall's equally inexperienced Keystoners had done a "great days work." And they had not lost a man. However, the heavy hand of war had become very personal for Kate Sperry and her friends. Blotcher assumed one of them had just lost a husband or a brother. A dead man was laying in the yard, he recalled, and "the way the women went out and screamed it was enough for a hard hearted man to sympathize in their bereavement." Schall reported his men killed or wounded 50 Rebels and seized 37 prisoners, whom they did not parole, and 30 fully accoutered horses. The Steele children recorded the numbers as substantially lower when they wrote in their joint diary that the Yankees "killed four, wounded several, and took about thirty prisoners." The 87th Pennsylvania's Lt. Col. James A. Stahle took note of two bodies lying side by side under an apple tree by the road. One was a rather large, fine-looking middle-aged man, and the other a beardless boy. According to a prisoner, the dead were father and son. The Federals remained on the scene for an hour tending to the wounded and carrying them to the brick house while Schall sent out cavalry patrols to ascertain if a larger enemy force was nearby. When the scouts returned to report there was no evidence of a major Confederate concentration in the area, Schall retired toward Winchester.[34]

Back in Winchester, meanwhile, Milroy received reports of enemy movement to the south on the Front Royal Road. If true, these Confederates might cross over to the Valley Pike and intercept and capture Schall's men. The general ordered Col. William H. Ball's 122nd Ohio Infantry of Brig. Gen. Washington Elliott's brigade to march out to support the column. After tramping a few miles, the Buckeyes encountered the victorious Pennsylvanians of the 87th returning in high spirits. "Considerable excitement prevailed," observed Pvt. James M. Smith of the 18th Connecticut, who,

33 OR 27, pt. 2, 75; Charles F. Porter, "Daring and Suffering: Three Chapters in the History of a Veteran," in *The Old Guard*, vol. 4, no. 1, February 5, 1889, 7; Walker, *History of the Eighteenth Regiment*, 105; J. H. Sawyer, "Sketches and Echoes: Abandoned at Winchester," *National Tribune*, April 6, 1916. The camps of the 6th Maryland and 12th West Virginia were also near Shawnee Springs, a popular pre-war picnic spot on the southeastern outskirts of Winchester near the road to Millwood.

34 OR 27, pt. 2, 42; Steele diary entry for June 16, 1863; Quarles, *Diaries, Letters, and Recollections*, 3:75; Nye, *Here Come the Rebels!*, 77. Schall's estimate of casualty figures appears in the *Official Records*, but he may well have exaggerated them. Confederate accounts on this skirmish and losses are sketchy.

along with most of the men of his regiment, was spending the day strengthening the fortifications.[35]

Schall's force and the Ohioans returned to their camp near Hollingsworth's Mills (off the Millwood Pike) about 7:00 p.m. "We marched back to Winchester shouting our victory," wrote the 87th's Cpl. Charles Z. Denues, "but when we arrived there we found Milroy and his whole force on duty. We were ordered not to make fires, but to prepare to get out of the way. We did not thirst for blood, but for coffee." "We skunked them," another soldier gloated. The wounded Rebels were taken to the Taylor Hotel for treatment, and a strong guard was stationed around the healthy captives. One of the prisoners complained about Harry Gilmor: "May I be eternally d—d if I ever foller that fellow with the spang-new yaller clothes again!" For most of the Pennsylvania infantrymen this small affair at Newtown marked their baptism of fire. "This is not the beginning of our hard and heavy work," Sgt. George W. Schriver penned in his diary. "But it is the beginning of our bloody work."[36]

Schall's reconnaissance and the information he relayed fell upon deaf ears at headquarters. The sharp engagement did not confirm a major enemy movement, nor was it the first such report. Lieutenant Colonel Joseph L. Moss and 400 men of the 12th Pennsylvania Cavalry had earlier encountered a large force of Confederate cavalry, infantry, and artillery near Cedarville twelve miles south of Winchester on the Front Royal Road. After skirmishing awhile and ascertaining their strength, Moss retired to Winchester with two wounded men and reported in at 3:00 p.m. Many of Milroy's officers, however, discredited the news because Moss's officers and scouts gave contradictory information. A force drawn from the 116th Ohio, 12th West Virginia, Carlin's Wheeling battery, and more of Moss's cavalry later marched out past Kernstown. They later claimed to have drawn some Rebels into an enfilading fire and sent them retiring "up the valley faster than they had come down," according to an Ohio officer. Despite these incidents, Milroy discounted Schall's fresh report because all the prisoners were from Confederate forces known to have been operating in the Valley for some time. However, according to Schall, some unnamed staff officers speculated that Confederate Brig. Gen. William Jones's and Brig. Gen. John

35 "The Winchester Fight: Graphic Particulars," in *Zanesville* (OH) *Courier*, July 22, 1863; "The Fight at Winchester, Va. and the Retreat of the Forces," in *Philadelphia Public Ledger*, June 24, 1863; *York* (PA) *Gazette*, June 13, 1893; James M. Smith diary entry for June 12, 1863, Winchester, Virginia.

36 Blotcher diary entry, YCHT; "Second Battle of Winchester," in *Philadelphia Inquirer*, July 4, 1897; OR 27, pt. 2, 42; John S. Apperson and John Herbert Roper, ed., *Repairing the March of Mars: The Civil War Diaries of John Samuel Apperson, Hospital Steward in the Stonewall Brigade* (Macon, GA: Mercer University Press, 2001), 463; George Schriver diary entry for June 12, 1863, George E. Schriver Diary, YCHT. The original Apperson diaries are in the collection of Virginia Tech.

Imboden's commands which had for some time been operating in the Valley had been consolidated and strengthened, and now planned to attack.[37]

Milroy and his second in command, General Elliott, concluded the enemy lurking out on the Front Royal Road and Valley Pike were these same Rebel horsemen or perhaps some of Jeb Stuart's men on a raid. As far as Milroy was concerned, his command was more than a match in either scenario, and he could easily hold his position at Winchester; how could it be anything else? It was unthinkable that Lee's army, with its immense artillery and baggage trains, could have slipped away from the Army of the Potomac around Fredericksburg and crossed the Blue Ridge through Ashby's, Chester, or Thornton gaps and entered the Shenandoah. A move of that distance and scope would consume five or six days—and General Hooker's headquarters would have surely wired him had the Rebels departed Fredericksburg and marched toward the Valley.[38] Milroy remained determined to stand at Winchester.

On the evening of June 12 , unconfirmed reports of significant Confederate movements circulated within the Army of the Potomac and the War Department in Washington. At 7:00 p.m. General Pleasonton, the commander of Hooker's cavalry, wired the army's assistant adjutant general, Seth Williams, at Warrenton Junction: "A colored boy just captured on the 9th, states Ewell's corps passed through Culpepper on Monday last, on their way to the Valley, and that Longstreet's had gone also. A second negro, just across the river, confirms the statement." The reports must have given Pleasonton an unpleasant pause. The general dispatched a reconnaissance to investigate the claims. Surely they could not be correct?[39]

As if the flood gates had opened, additional reports began to steadily arrive in Winchester. A detachment of the 1st New York (Lincoln) Cavalry lost two men in a lively skirmish near the crossroads hamlet of White Post in rural Clarke County, likely against Brig. Gen. Junius Daniel's Confederate infantry brigade, part of Rodes' division. The 67th Pennsylvania's Col. John F. Staunton, who had been in Winchester earlier that day, rode back to Berryville to tell brigade commander Col. Andrew T. McReynolds that the enemy was reported to be advancing on the Front Royal Road southeast of Winchester. Milroy sent his own messenger to order McReynolds to reconnoiter in that direction and be ready to move his entire brigade, if needed. In case of a serious attack, cautioned Milroy, McReynolds was to fall back on Winchester, but

37 C. M. Keyes, *The Military History of the 123rd Ohio Volunteer Infantry* (Sandusky, OH: Sandusky Steam Press, 1874), 44; James A. Stahle Papers, Harrisburg Civil War Round Table Collection, USAHEC; Keyes, The Military History of the 123rd Ohio, 44. For more on Schall's skirmish and Moss's reconnaissance, see Nye, *Here Come the Rebels!*, 77.

38 *OR* 27, pt. 2, 43.

39 Ibid., 184-85.

if he heard the Main Fort's heavy guns fire the predetermined signal announcing an attack, he was to march immediately.[40]

The 122nd Ohio's chaplain, the Rev. Charles C. McCabe, possessed a booming baritone voice that had helped popularize *The Battle Hymn of the Republic* within the Union army. Downtown that evening, McCabe and a group of fellow musicians sang a patriotic song for General Milroy, who enjoyed the impromptu serenade from an open window of the Logan mansion. The light mood disappeared when a scout galloped up to announce that the enemy was approaching in great force.[41]

Milroy immediately doubled the pickets around Winchester and dispatched strong cavalry patrols out on all the major roads. "Everything betokened activity," remembered the 18th Connecticut's Pvt. James M. Smith.[42] "All that night the Yankees were flying around at a great rate," one Winchester lady penned in her diary, "but we could hear nothing, though trying our best to do so. All their movements, which we watched closely, indicated great uneasiness." Well after dark, Company B of the 123rd Ohio, part of Colonel Ely's brigade, marched from Winchester three miles down the Front Royal Road. It was a beautiful moonlit night, 21-year-old Pvt. Henry S. Clapp recalled, and "our orders to move quietly put a glamour of mystery and adventure over the proceeding that appealed to our young blood." The company of Buckeyes bivouacked about 10:00 p.m. in a grove of small trees near the road. Fortunate to escape picket duty, they sank down upon the dewy grass and slept soundly. No one could light a campfire in case the Rebels were near.[43]

As these various bits and pieces of news filtered into Winchester and Union outfits of varying strength moved here and there in response, frustration mounted among the men who had encountered the Rebels that day. "I knew then—five thousand and more privates at Winchester knew—that Ewell and Rhodes with forty thousand men, the pick and choice of the Confederate Army, were within striking

---

40 Ibid., 67; James H. Stevenson, *Boots and Saddles: A History of the First Volunteer Cavalry of the War, Known as the First New York (Lincoln) Cavalry* (Harrisburg, PA: Patriot Publishing, 1879), 183; Anonymous, "The Defense and Evacuation of Winchester," *The Continental Monthly*, vol. 4, no. 5 (November 1863), 483. White Post, about 10 miles by road southeast of Winchester, was at the crossroads of White Post and Berry's Ferry roads off the Lord Fairfax Highway (modern-day U.S. Rt. 340).

41 Walker, *History of the Eighteenth Regiment*, 441. McCabe had admired The Battle Hymn of the Republic since reading the poem in *Atlantic Monthly*. He first heard it used as a song at a well-attended war rally in downtown Zanesville, Ohio, in the autumn of 1862 and began singing it after he joined the 122nd Ohio Volunteer Infantry as its chaplain.

42 James M. Smith diary entry for June 12, 1863.

43 Anonymous, "Leaves from a Diary Kept by a Lady," *Southern Bivouac*, vol. 1, no. 12, August 1883; Clapp, "With Milroy at Winchester."

distance of Milroy," Sgt.-Major James M. Dalzell of the 116th Ohio would write after the war. Headquarters "hooted as absurd and impossible" the regiment's report of engaging the Rebels. "We were there," he complained. "We knew better."[44]

Notwithstanding Milroy's brusque overconfidence, some of his officers and men were already quietly questioning his decision to stand and fight. After pushing back a strong line of enemy pickets near Kernstown south of Winchester earlier that day, the 116th Ohio's Lt. Col. Thomas F. Wildes fully expected hot work on the morrow, or so he wrote after the war. "While we wondered at our remaining there in the presence of so large a force," he explained, "it was only ours to obey such orders as were given us, ask no questions and cast no reflections."[45]

About 10:00 p.m. Milroy wired his superior, General Schenck, to report Schall's "splendid little skirmish." Milroy added, "The enemy is probably approaching in some force. Please state specifically whether I am to abandon this place or not." No timely reply was forthcoming, however, because Jenkins' Rebel troopers had severed several telegraph wires between Winchester and Harpers Ferry. Left on his own, Milroy concluded that, from all the information previously received, it was his duty to hold Winchester. He wanted to protect the Unionists in the area, as well as the routes to the Baltimore & Ohio Railroad skirting the Potomac River some 25 miles to the north. He believed the strengthened defenses around Winchester would be sufficient to withstand Rebel assaults, and he intended to deny the enemy access to the area's remaining crops and livestock.[46]

Winchester's pro-Confederate residents who had long chafed under Milroy's iron rule also remained unaware of Ewell's approach; however rumors had abounded since the battle of Brandy Station that at least part of the Army of Northern Virginia might be heading for the Valley. "Our life is so monotonous that there is nothing to record from day to day but the same oppressions and tyranny," penned Laura Lee. "It is still a mystery what has become of Gen. Lee's army, but all admit some great move is on hand." General Milroy, for his part, appears to have dismissed the possibility. Most of the Federal troops passed an anxious night, sleeping with their weapons at hand. No one could speak with any certainty what daylight might bring. Perhaps the 87th Pennsylvania's Lt. Col. James Stahle summed it up best when he wrote, "It began to look like as if there was going to be serious work on the morrow."[47]

---

44 Dalzell, "A Lucky Blunder," 95.

45 Wildes, *Record of the One Hundred and Sixteenth Regiment Ohio*, 54.

46 *OR* 27, pt. 2, 51, 178.

47 Michael G. Mahon, ed., *Winchester Divided: The Civil War Diaries of Julia Chase and Laura Lee* (Mechanicsburg, PA: Stackpole Books, 2002), 91; *York* (PA) *Gazette*, June 13, 1893.

Chapter 4

Saturday, June 13, Part I

"We wished we were at home."

— *Pvt. Lorenzo D. Barnhart, 110th Ohio*

As the morning sun slowly rose over the distant Blue Ridge Mountains and cast its first beckoning rays westward into the Shenandoah Valley, 20-year-old Pvt. Lorenzo D. Barnhart of the 110th Ohio grew wistful. It had been less than a year since he left his father's farm in Darke County to enlist in the army, slipping away early one September morning without getting a chance to say goodbye to his family. Now, he was a Union soldier in the West Fort. "The weather was fine and balmy," he commented. "We wished we were at home to help the farmers plant corn." Little did the homesick young Buckeye and his comrades stationed around Winchester realize how prophetic that statement would become in the next few days. The bright, cloudless day promised to be "unusually hot, and all nature seemed reposing in an ominous hush," according to the 110th's Lt. Henry Y. Rush, a pre-war preacher and Bible student. "Everything alive and off duty in camp had sought the shade of shanty or tent till the stillness was portentous and painful. I can never forget the feeling that something terrible was being foreshadowed."[1]

Off to the east, when the wind was right, the odor of decomposing dead horses occasionally wafted into the 18th Connecticut's camp near Shawnee Springs. The nauseating smell was "all that could be imagined," Pvt. James H. Sawyer complained.

---

1 Roger Barnhart, ed., *The Reminiscences of Private Lorenzo D. Barnhart, 110th Ohio Volunteer Infantry, Company B,* Library of Congress; Henry Y. Rush and B. F. Vaughan, ed., *Life and Writings of Rev. Henry Y. Rush, D. D.* (Dayton, OH: The Christian Publishing Association, 1911), 222. Rush's Civil War reminiscences were originally published as a series of articles in the *Franklin* (OH) *Chronicle.*

Camp of the 18th Connecticut near Shawnee Springs southeast of Winchester.
William C. Walker, History of the Eighteenth Regiment Conn. Volunteers

Recovering from a recent bout of typhoid fever, he and seven ill comrades shared a canvas wall tent about 100 yards west of the camp. On a low open hill south of the Millwood Pike stood two deserted brick buildings close together. Beyond them stretched the Front Royal Road, the most likely route of Confederate approach. Sawyer could see no signs of enemy presence in that direction despite repeated rumors that "the Johnnies are coming!" Lieutenant Colonel Robert Northcutt of the 12th West Virginia noted, "Officers and men began their usual routine of camp life, such as they were employed in when no enemy was near."[2]

However, the Johnnies indeed were coming. The soldiers of Lt. Gen. Richard S. Ewell's Second Corps looked forward to ending Milroy's six-month reign of terror. "The enemy was not aware of our approach at all," correctly observed Pvt. J. Peter Williams of the Chesapeake Artillery of Johnson's division. The "outlaw Milroy" did not know of the Rebels' arrival, boasted a member of the 1st Virginia Artillery Battalion, and had made no preparations to receive such formidable visitors. Other than sporadic Confederate cavalry patrols, Milroy apparently had no inkling a surprise party was on its way. "The old despot was venting his malice to his heart's content," the 1st Virginia artilleryman bemoaned, "on the defenseless women, children and old men of this section of the country, without hindrance, when we stepped in to interrupt

---

2 Sawyer, "Abandoned at Winchester," 9; *Atlas to Accompany the Official Records*, 119; Northcutt, "Milroy at Winchester."

his delightful occupation." However, conquering Winchester would not be a walk-over because the Grey Eagle indeed was prepared for a cavalry raid. A force, however, of the size and power of Ewell's oncoming columns was beyond Federal comprehension. No one suspected that a large portion of the Army of Northern Virginia was at hand. Most believed Lee was still idle in his defenses at Fredericksburg with the rest of his force near Culpeper.[3]

Despite the series of Union defenses, many Confederates remained determined to sweep Milroy from the Shenandoah Valley. "Winchester was Milroy's headquarters," the 2nd North Carolina's Capt. John Gorman explained. "Here he had extensive fortifications on almost impregnable hills, and there he issued his orders of oppression, while his minions permeated the valley, seizing, confiscating and destroying all they could lay their rife hands on. But a little longer procrastination on our part, and this prolific valley, whose whole surfaces was made glad with teeming fields, would have been a desert. Its proud people are as true as steel to the Confederacy and they have suffered immeasurably."[4]

Milroy's senior command remained unaware that thousands of Confederate infantry, artillery, and cavalry had entered the Lower Valley and taken aim at Winchester. After being awakened about 3:00 a.m., almost two hours before sunrise, Jubal Early's veteran division near Front Royal prepared to head for Winchester, as did Allegheny Johnson's division. The Second Corps' artillerymen also readied themselves and their horses. "Some time before day," Pvt. John William Ford Hatton of 1st Maryland Artillery, Dement's Battery, recorded, "we were very quietly roused from our sleep by the sergeants going around rousing their men. The drivers harnessed and hitched their horses. The cannoneers were at their posts, and all were ready for orders. Not a bugler or drum sounded, but quiet prevailed except the moving of troops."[5]

By first light the infantry had assembled in column formation. "At daybreak again took up our line of march," reported a soldier of the 2nd Maryland Battalion, "halting

---

3   J. Peter Williams to his wife, June 16, 1863, J. Peter Williams Papers, Special Collections, Alderman Library, University of Virginia, Charlottesville; "The Victory at Winchester – Capture of Martinsburg – More Artillery and Prisoners Taken," in *Charleston* (SC) *Mercury*, June 22, 1863, citing unnamed Richmond newspapers. Williams later noted that his battery (also known as the 4th Maryland Light Artillery) went into position at Winchester but was not engaged. "It is the first time we have ever been even in ten miles of a battle & not put right in the thickest of it."

4   John C. Gorman to Friend Holden, June 22, 1863, North Carolina State Archives, Raleigh (hereafter cited as NCSA) and GNMP.

5   *OR* 27, pt. 2, 520, 540; John William Ford Hatton Papers, Library of Congress. Sunrise on June 13, according to the U.S. Naval Observatory, came at 4:45 a.m.

frequently, as we have plenty of time." Crossing the Shenandoah River would be the first act of the day for the famed Louisiana Tigers, one which they did without any hesitation. The water was rather cool for wading, "but that was nothing," Sgt. Edmund L. Stephens of the 9th Louisiana boasted. The column halted to allow the men to put on their clothes and shoes before being called back into ranks.[6]

General Early used the 2nd Virginia's Lt. Strother Barton, a native of the region, as a guide. Colonel J. Thompson Brown's reserve artillery under Capt. Willis J. Dance trailed the long column as the soldiers tramped north from Front Royal through Ninevah and then took a side road that intersected the Valley Pike in Newtown. There, the Steele family fed Confederate soldiers all day, including thirty of Capt. "Hans" McNeil's partisans who called asking for bread and butter before picketing the Back Road (also known as the Cedar Creek Grade). Early's division then marched toward Kernstown, about 3½ miles southwest of Winchester.[7]

At the same time, most of "Allegheny" Johnson's division continued on the wood-planked Front Royal Road through Cedarville with most of Lt. Col. R. Snowden Andrews' artillery battalion in tow. Major James H. Nounnan's battalion of the 16th Virginia Cavalry, detached from Jenkins' brigade that had accompanied Rodes' division toward Martinsburg, screened the advance. The Stonewall Brigade and Carpenter's Allegheny artillery battery took Island Ford Mills Road before rejoining the division. Civilians coming down from Winchester mentioned that all was quiet there; the Federals did not have any inkling of the Rebel movement. About 7:00 a.m., Johnson reached the Double Tollgate at the intersection of the Front Royal Road and the dirt road from Newtown which continued on through White Post to Berry's Ferry.[8]

Meanwhile, scores of absent Confederate soldiers, individually or in small groups, hustled toward Winchester to catch up to Ewell. Some had recently been released from hospitals or were returning from detached duty. Others had been on furlough or were former prisoners of war. Color Sergeant Gabriel Shank of the 10th Virginia had

---

6 Thomas J. Williams diary, entry for June 13, 1863, Allen Tischler Collection, Handley Library, Winchester, Virginia; Edmund Stephens to Dear Parents, June 20, 1863, near Sharpsburg, Edmund Stephens Collection, Library of Northwestern State University of Louisiana, Natchitoches; M. H. Ackred, "Early's Brigade at Winchester," *Confederate Veteran*, vol. 29, February 1921, 264.

7 Nye, *Here Come the Rebels!*, 78; Steele diary entry for June 16, 1863.

8 *New York Herald*, June 22, 1863; Hotchkiss, *Make Me a Map*, 151; Nye, *Here Come the Rebels!*, 78; OR 27, pt. 2, 520, 540. Island Ford, east of Berryville on the Shenandoah River, was also known as Parker's Ford. It was near Cool Spring and Castleman's Ferry. The double tollgate location is at the intersection of modern Front Royal Pike (U.S. 522) and the Fairfax Pike (VA Route 277)/Lord Fairfax Highway (U.S. Route 340).

Col. William G. Ely of the 18th Connecticut Infantry, commander of Milroy's Second Brigade.
U.S. Army Heritage and Education Center

enjoyed a much-needed 13-day rest at home with his teenaged wife Annie. The 24-year-old was wounded and captured at Chancellorsville, paroled, and sent home to recuperate. He left his house on June 11 and headed for Culpeper, the army's last reported position. Learning it was on the march, he and a few others hastily passed through New Market and traveled through the night to Luray, arriving at daybreak on the 12th. After a brief rest, at 10:00 a.m. they climbed into a one-horse wagon and departed through the scenic Page Valley bound for Front Royal. They arrived there at nine o'clock that evening only to learn the army had already left. After a good night's sleep, they departed early on Saturday morning. Shank and his comrades finally overtook the Second Corps about three miles from Winchester just as Ewell deployed his troops into line of battle.[9]

Fighting Along the Front Royal and Millwood Pikes

The arrival of the Confederates did not pass unnoticed. General Milroy had posted a strong picket line about four miles south of Winchester at the Parkins' mill outpost, located on a hillock along the Front Royal Road overlooking the Opequon Creek crossing. This steep-banked watercourse, a small tributary of the Potomac River, presented a significant obstacle. The bridge was the only viable option for moving artillery and wagons across the creek. However, the few Union pickets on

---

9 Gabriel Shank, "Military Records, Articles, and Diary," compiled by his great-great-granddaughter Margaret S. Mohr Weaver. http://www.rootsweb.ancestry. Com/~varockin/shank/Gabriel Shank.htm, last accessed June 8, 2013. Shank was captured again in September 1864 at the battle of Fisher's Hill in the Shenandoah Valley. He died from smallpox in March 1865 while being held prisoner at Fort Delaware. He left behind his pregnant wife and infant daughter.

duty were not strong enough to defend the crossing against anything but a small raiding party or scouts.[10]

Milroy dispatched several cavalry patrols out the Valley Pike and Millwood Pike to ascertain the enemy's strength and current location. "This morning the cavalry were running in and out," 13-year-old Gettie Miller penned, "and they have been bringing in their wounded and sick and the sutlers have been moving." A few minutes before 8:00 a.m. scouts well out on the Front Royal Road reported the Rebels were approaching in force. Under the circumstances, Milroy believed his entire command should reunite at Winchester. He ordered the Main Fort to fire a four-gun signal to alert Col. Andrew McReynolds' Third Brigade at Berryville, as well as the other scattered outposts. He also shifted his command structure by transferring the 12th West Virginia to General Elliott and the 87th Pennsylvania to Col. William G. Ely's brigade.[11]

Very early that morning officers roused the soldiers of the 18th Connecticut in their camp at Shawnee Springs. The men quickly struck tents and marched south to the Front Royal Road. They stacked their arms and lay down along the stone fences lining the road awaiting further orders. Finally, about 8:00 a.m. instructions came to return to camp. Once there, they had pitched a few tents when an orderly came tearing down the road about ten o'clock. Private Charles Lynch was standing near Colonel Ely's quarters when he saw a "scout coming, almost flying," down the pike. The messenger effortlessly jumped his horse over the stone fence surrounding the campsite and headed straight for Ely's tent. Without any ceremony, he dismounted, rushed in, and breathlessly informed the colonel the enemy was almost upon them. "Fall in, fall in, double quick!" Ely immediately shouted. A long drum roll summoned the men to the ranks, and the regiment soon marched off in column of fours. They turned into a nearby field past the malodorous dead horses. After marching toward the Valley Pike, the 18th reversed course and double-quick-timed to the Front Royal Road. The men dropped their knapsacks and haversacks at the headquarters of the

---

10 In November 1864, Capt. Julian Weir of the 5th U. S. Artillery expanded these works into a small, crescent-shaped lunette for his horse artillery. This position was near a mill owned by Alfred Parkins, whose son the Rev. Alexander Parkins perished at First Manassas. This mill should not be confused with Nathan Parkins' three mills along Abram's Creek a few miles to the north. They operated under the collective name of Union Mills, and during Milroy's occupation Nathan Parkins did considerable business with the U. S. government. In 1864 Maj. Gen. David Hunter's Federal troops destroyed the largest of these mills.

11 Gettie Miller diary entry, June 13, 1863, Handley Library; OR 27, pt. 2, 44; Prowell, *History of the 87th Pennsylvania*, 70. Milroy frequently changed his organization structure, swapping units to meet specific needs. In this case, the 87th's camp was close to Ely's position, so it was opportune.

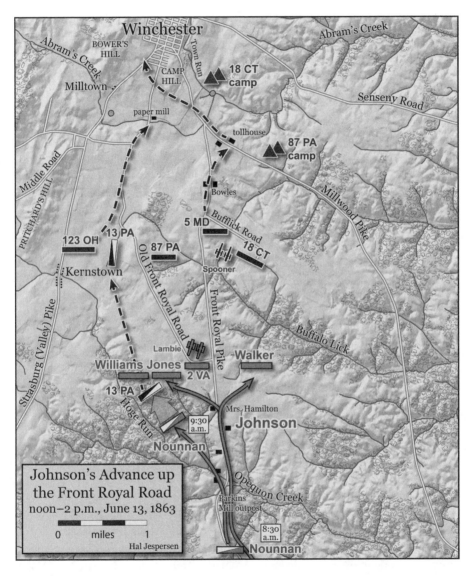

Johnson's Advance up
the Front Royal Road
noon–2 p.m., June 13, 1863

0   miles   1

Hal Jespersen

advance pickets. The 87th Pennsylvania and the 5th Maryland also left their camps along the Millwood Pike. Shortly Lt. Edmund D. Spooner's section of Battery L, 5th U. S. Light Artillery dashed past the 18th's camp and turned down the Front Royal Road following the infantry. General Milroy had ordered Ely to "feel for the enemy," but one of his soldiers later punned, "The feeling was mutual."[12]

12 Croffut and Morris, *The Military and Civil History of Connecticut*, 350.

Ely assumed battle positions past the Bowles farm within sight of his camp, and sent out advance skirmishers and cavalry scouts. His men nervously awaited their inaugural combat after months of mundane picket or bridge guard duty in various places. Critics later castigated Milroy for not being better prepared. "Why should he have been so completely surprised with the means of information at his command," Chaplain William Walker of the 18th Connecticut questioned, "being in a valley bounded both right and left by mountain ranges, so favorable for observation, has never been satisfactorily explained. 'Let the rebels come' was the cry on every hand, 'we will give them all they want.'" He reported intense excitement as the soldiers awaited developments. "Why don't the Rebels come on?" they cried as they scanned the meadows and woods to their front.[13]

They soon received their answer. About 8:30 a.m., Major Nounnan's battalion of the 16th Virginia Cavalry readily drove off the forward Union pickets near Alfred Parkins' mill. Johnson soon continued his methodical advance with General Ewell at his side. "You are the operator now," Ewell directed. "I am only a looker on." The one-legged Ewell traded his usual carriage for his favorite horse, "Rifle," but when he tried to jump a rail fence in a meadow just south of the Opequon, Rifle threw him heavily. With help, Ewell picked himself up, dusted off his uniform, and re-mounted his horse. Long columns of Southern infantry, artillery, wagons, and ambulances began crossing the bridge. They steadily marched northward at a pace of about two miles an hour through the countryside.[14]

Meanwhile, the pickets of Company B of the 123rd Ohio, stationed some three miles south of Winchester, kept their eyes peeled for any sign of the enemy. About 9:00 a.m., they spotted a suspicious rider. "We had been looking for rebels for months," Pvt. Henry S. Clapp mentioned, "and now our hopes or fears were about to be realized, but we only saw one, a cavalryman on a distant hillside." Because the scout was well beyond musket range, the Buckeyes made no effort to molest him and he soon disappeared. Clapp's detached company soon returned to their regimental camp in Winchester, but found it deserted except for sick men and a few guards.[15]

Half an hour later along Hoge Run, Major Nounnan initiated a series of relatively bloodless firefights between his battalion of the 16th Virginia Cavalry and Major

---

13 Lynch diary entry for June 13, 1863; Sawyer, "Abandoned at Winchester," 9-10; *National Tribune*, April 6, 1916; OR 27, pt. 2, 540; James M. Smith diary entry for June 13, 1863; Walker, *History of the Eighteenth Regiment*, 105. Companies G and H of the 87th were with McReynolds' brigade at Bunker Hill.

14 Donald C. Pfanz, *Richard S. Ewell: A Soldier's Life* (Chapel Hill: UNC Press, 1998), 283; Jedediah Hotchkiss Papers, Library of Congress; *Richmond Daily Dispatch*, February 5, 1864.

15 Clapp, "With Milroy at Winchester."

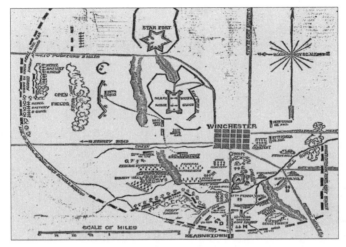

Map of the Second Winchester battlefield. *New York Herald, June 22, 1863*

Kerwin and the skirmishers of the 13th Pennsylvania Cavalry (also known as the Irish Dragoons). Nounnan, a lawyer in the Kansas Territory before the war, had a reputation of relishing any chance to kill Yankees. His personal hygiene also elicited commentary. One observer recorded that Nounnan "never washed, nor combed his hair nor put on clean garments," and that he frequently looked "dirty, haggard and worn." In the late morning, Nounnan's scouts discovered enemy infantry pickets about four miles south of Winchester near the junction of Front Royal and Buffalo Lick roads.[16]

The 18th Connecticut's Maj. Henry Peale had just deployed companies A and B as skirmishers in front in some woods. Well behind them, Lieutenant Spooner quickly wheeled his pair of 3-inch ordnance rifles onto a knoll east of the Front Royal Road. Colonel Ely deployed the bulk of the 18th lying in a field of high clover behind the knoll with 300 riflemen of the veteran 5th Maryland in close support. Many of the Marylanders had experienced the horrors of Antietam the previous September and knew what to expect. The relatively green 87th Pennsylvania was off to their right lining the northern edge of a stone-wall-bounded, 400-yard long pasture west of the

---

16 Jack L. Dickinson, *The 16th Virginia Cavalry* (Lynchburg, Va.: H. E. Howard, 1991), 19, 220; Robert L. Krick, *Lee's Colonels: A Biographical Register of the Field Officers of the Army of Northern Virginia* (Dayton, Ohio: Morningside Bookshop, 1992), 268. Hoge Run is alternatively termed Hogg's Run, Hogg's Creek, or Hogg Run in some accounts. It was named for an early 18th-century resident, Scotsman William Hoge, who built a log cabin along the narrow tributary to Opequon Creek. James W. Beeler of Carpenter's battery placed the first firing at 10:00 a.m.

Col. John Q. A. Nadenbousch, commander
of the 2nd Virginia Infantry of the
Stonewall Brigade. *Ben Ritter*

Front Royal Road. Buffalo Lick, a small
tributary of Opequon Creek, formed a deep
ravine between the Keystoners and the
guns.[17]

Upon receiving the report of the enemy
presence Johnson halted the Stonewall
Brigade and deployed Col. J. Q. A.
Nadenbousch's 2nd Virginia as skirmishers
west of the road. Behind them in John M.
Jones' brigade, Dr. Abram S. Miller of the
25th Virginia wanted to "see the fun," so he
headed to the front. He soon spotted the
grayclad skirmish line which had advanced to within 1,000 yards of the enemy.
Cautiously following the skirmishers, Miller believed he would have a fine view of the
impending fight.[18]

Major Beale and the 18th Connecticut's anxious skirmishers observed Rebels
filing out from the distant wooded eminence and slowly moving toward them. Men
who had itched to join the fray when they heard the Newtown ambuscade the night
before and who had decried that morning "where are the Johnnies" now anxiously
prepared to meet them. From the safety of the hill, Doctor Miller watched as
Nadenbousch's 2nd Virginia skirmishers slowly drove their Yankee counterparts out
of the woods. Spooner soon sent a pair of explosive shells arcing toward the timber. In
response, Confederate Lt. Col. R. Snowden Andrews positioned a pair of Lt. William
T. Lambie's 12-pound Napoleon smoothbores of Carpenter's battery behind a stone
fence in a meadow. They were in front of a dense timber thicket and about 200 yards
west of the road.[19]

17 OR 27, pt. 2, 75-76, 540; Walker, *History of the Eighteenth Regiment Connecticut Volunteers*, 106;
New York Herald map, June 22, 1863; *Gettysburg Star & Sentinel*, April 2, 1902. Buffalo Lick Road
is now Bufflick Road.

18 *New York Herald*, June 22, 1863; OR 27, pt. 2, 499-500, 520; A. S. Miller to Dear Julia, June
16, 1863, Handley Regional Library, cited in Quarles, *Diaries, Letters, and Recollections*, 3:27.

19 Abram Schultz Miller to Dear Julia, June 16, 1863, Winchester, Virginia, Handley Library;
OR 27, pt. 2, 76, 499-500; *Richmond Examiner*, July 4, 1863. Lambie, the son of a Scottish

The Stonewall Brigade's heavily laden supply wagons remained well in the rear. Ordnance Sergeant Watkins Kearns of the 27th Virginia's "Shriver Grays" (Company G) scrawled in his diary, "March along without interruption to within about 3 miles of town when the ordnance trains are parked in a clearing on the left of the road & the troops are formed in line of battle, our brigade in front, & move forward." The 25-year-old Wheeling resident added about 11:30 a.m., "Skirmishing has commenced and preparations appear to be made for a knock down fight . . . things look belligerent." Private Michael Hanley of Company A, 18th Connecticut fell early on with a severe wound to his left leg; the Irish-born teenager may have been the first Union soldier shot in the battle. Young Winchester resident Emma Riely was on the street when the first wounded Union soldiers came in shortly after noon. "We had heard an occasional volley of musketry," she wrote, "but did not suppose it amounted to much."[20]

The 13th Pennsylvania Cavalry was positioned well off the 87th Pennsylvania's right. "It was one of the most peculiar things to watch the countenance of the men who were entering their first battle," one of the Irish Dragoons recounted. "At the first shot, no matter whence it came or where it struck, you could see them tremble as they took a firmer grip on their guns. Their faces would often become the color of snow and oftentimes their mouths would open and their eyes actually bulge out as though they would leave their sockets. Yet few of them ever seemed to think of running away from the field."[21]

The Pennsylvania troopers sensed danger, a concern which increased when they saw several horses creeping over a hill only a few hundred yards from their line. They watched Lambie's cannoneers stop and unlimber two cannon pointed in their direction. The sight was unnerving, especially to the less experienced soldiers. "We could do nothing but keep our eyes pointed on those guns which seemed to be pointed directly at our individual heads," one wrote. Two minutes later, they saw a little cloud of smoke puff from one of the cannon, and almost instantly they heard a shell hissing overhead. Every man looked up and prepared to duck, but luckily

---

immigrant, became a civil engineer in Southern California after the war. He was killed in 1900 at the age of 60 in Los Angeles when a tunnel he was inspecting collapsed. In 1864 his brother Edward L. Lambie commanded a company of U.S. Colored Troops.

20 Watkins Kearns diary entry for June 13, 1863, Watkins Kearns Diaries, 1861–1864, 3 vols., Mss5:1K2143:1-3, Microfilm reel C598, Virginia Historical Society, Richmond; OR 27, pt. 2, 75-76; Walker, *History of the Eighteenth Regiment Connecticut Volunteers*, 107; Macon, *Reminiscences of the Civil War*, 79. Hanley's injury required amputation. He died March 15, 1866, and is buried in St Mary's & St Joseph's Cemetery in Norwich, Connecticut.

21 *Philadelphia Inquirer*, June 13, 1897. The 87th's position was near today's Paper Mill Road.

Lambie's initial aim was very bad. Even the soldiers new to war smiled when the shell burst well to the rear.[22]

To the north, James Sawyer and his ill comrades heard the muffled sound of Spooner's artillery from the direction of the toll road. As it turned out, the guns were much closer than they realized because of an intervening hill and the still, sultry air. "I guess the Johnnies have come now, sure," a convalescent commented. "It does sound so," another anxiously responded. They spotted movement on a distant hillside past the two deserted brick buildings Sawyer had earlier nervously eyed. He saw men congregated around a fieldpiece which had suddenly appeared on the slope. White smoke soon rose, followed by the deep boom of Lambie's first shot. The next instant Sawyer heard a "screaming, gushing, vindictive sound" overhead, followed by a crash in the field beyond the tent. War had finally come to the 18th Connecticut in its tenth month of service. Just then, regimental surgeon Dr. Charles M. Carleton rode up as shells began dropping closer to the campsite. He ordered his patients to retire to the hospital in the Taylor Hotel.[23]

Out on the front lines, the 18th Connecticut's Pvt. James M. Smith reported, "Just as we arrived the Rebs commenced shelling us from easy range, and the shells begun to whistle around our heads pretty lively. Our Guns replied as well as possible." Spooner and Lambie exchanged fire at a distance of 400 yards for about 90 minutes. At least four other Confederate guns arrived and opened. Colonel Ely immediately ordered the horse soldiers to fall back as the shells and solid shot increased. The retiring cavalrymen soon changed from a slow trot to a full gallop, racing up the Front Royal Road and turning left onto the Millwood Pike. They reformed near Abram's Creek, where they rested and watered their horses.[24]

Confederate shells burst above the 87th Pennsylvania's camp along the Millwood Pike, scattering the rear echelon soldiers left there to gather up odds and ends missed during the regiment's hasty evacuation earlier that morning. "Black Joe," the field officers' black cook, was busy filling a straw hat with a stash of cigars Lt. Col. James Stahle had left under the floor of his tent. Shell fragments narrowly missed him, and Joe hastily joined the exodus.[25]

Some of Spooner's overshots landed near Andrews' reserve artillery which Ewell had parked in a depression while bringing up Raine's Virginia battery to support

22 *Philadelphia Inquirer*, June 13, 1897.

23 Sawyer, "Abandoned at Winchester," 10.

24 James M. Smith diary entry for June 13, 1863, Winchester, Va.; *Philadelphia Inquirer*, June 13, 1897; *New York Herald* map, June 22, 1863.

25 James A. Stahle, "Around Winchester Town," *Gettysburg Compiler*, June 27, 1893.

Lambie. A shell exploded in a nearby infantry regiment scattering stacks of muskets and wounding some soldiers. Private Joseph Bailey, a driver in Dement's 1st Maryland (CSA) battery, laughingly said, "I'll get in a safer place." He led his horse to a ditch behind the slope and flattened out with his bridle reins tucked under his arm. His comrades continued lying on the slope while Pvt. J. W. F. Hatton peeked over the crest to watch the unfolding action. A shell passed a foot overhead and exploded near a caisson wheel, destroying it and hurling shell fragments into Bailey's shoulder and side. Comrades carried him to the rear where he soon died.[26]

Inside Winchester, a correspondent for the *Richmond Whig* named Lawson was fighting illness that day. However, the unexpected noise of battle revived his spirits. "The hearts of our oppressed and down-trodden people were made joyous by the sound of Southern cannon as it came booming upon their astonished ears;" he rejoiced, "gradually it advanced nearer and nearer, driving the accursed fiends, who for months back have been holding high carnival in our midst." During the prolonged cannonade, the 18th Connecticut's James Sawyer, his overcoat draped over his arm in the hot sunshine, joined a procession of teamsters and stragglers filling the road into Winchester. His seven tent mates had disappeared; he never saw them again. "The shells came at intervals," he recalled, "bursting overhead and on either side. Little jets of dust springing up in the road, and [the] thud of bullets striking the rocks and stone fences, indicated that our friends on the hillside were using shrapnel." Sawyer, under hostile fire for the first time, paused and thought, "Is it possible those fellows up there are trying to kill us?" He soon ceased his musings and hustled toward Winchester, only to find the roads near the town full of Union cavalry heading south toward the Valley Pike. He left the road and began traipsing through the nearby fields.[27]

South on the Front Royal Road, the sudden explosion of one of Spooner's limbers added to the developing noise and confusion. Several badly burned, blackened, and bleeding artillerists lay in agony around the destroyed limber. The regulars quickly limbered their field pieces and galloped off to the north, taking their injured men off with them. They raced past Dr. Lowell Holbrook of the 18th Connecticut and Dr. Charles E. Goldsborough of the 5th Maryland who happened to be retiring at a more leisurely pace with two ambulances filled with their own wounded. They quickly made way for the battery to pass and then continued on their journey. However, a Rebel solid shot struck under the hind wheel of one of the ambulances and sent a startled stretcher bearer, who was standing on the rear step, 15 feet into the air. That taught the doctors an important lesson. "From that to

---

26 John William Ford Hatton Papers, LOC.

27 *Raleigh* (NC) *Weekly State Journal*, July 2, 1863; Sawyer, "Abandoned at Winchester," 10.

Winchester," Goldsborough explained, "the battery had nothing to boast of in point of speed over the Medical Corps."[28]

The Confederate cannoneers, finally free of the counterbattery fire, turned their full attention against the Federal infantry. Major Salome Marsh, commanding the 5th Maryland, survived a close call when a shell took off his horse's head and splattered him with blood and brains as it fell to the ground. Lucky to be alive and to have escaped serious injury, the 34-year-old Baltimore resident regained his feet and ordered one of his aides to remove the saddle and secure another horse. Despite the sudden shock of the near-miss and hard tumble to the earth, and that he was not feeling well from excessive duty and exposure, Marsh remounted and continued to lead his veteran regiment.[29]

At least one battery focused on the 87th Pennsylvania whose pesky sharpshooters were annoying the gunners from behind a stone wall. At length the flying rock and shell fragments proved too much for several men who sought shelter in the nearby Buffalo Lick ravine. "It became so hot for us we left our stone fence," the 87th's Charles Z. Denues said, "for the fifteen guns of the Southerners disabled our two guns, five of the artillerymen being killed in a short time." The 87th suffered only one fatality, 17-year-old drummer Daniel H. Karnes. Colonel Ely eventually withdrew his force northward beyond Abram's Creek.[30]

The 87th's Pvt. Joseph H. Hines was scrambling over a stone wall when a solid shot struck it and a rock fragment badly bruised his left thigh. Private George Washington "Squaw" Flemming, his company's champion forager, injured his back while leaping over the wooden race near Hollingworth's Mill. Ely's exhausted soldiers began stumbling into position. Officers excitedly shouted orders, bugles blared above the cacophony, and soon the brigade had reformed into some semblance of military

---

28 Dr. Charles E. Goldsborough, "Fighting Them Over: What Our Old Veterans Have to Say about Their Old Campaigns: Winchester," *National Tribune*, December 18, 1884.

29 Dr. Charles E. Goldsborough, "Milroy's Fight at Winchester," *Gettysburg Star & Sentinel*, April 2, 1902. Marsh later testified at the trial of the Lincoln conspirators about his mistreatment at Libby Prison. He returned to Baltimore after the war and served as a city councilman.

30 OR 27, pt. 2, 499-500, 540; *New York Herald*, June 22, 1863; Kearns diary entry for June 13, 1863, VHS; Prowell, *History of the 87th Pennsylvania*, 71-72; James A. Stahle Papers, USAHEC. Karnes, an Adams County native from New Oxford, was the first soldier in the 87th Pennsylvania to perish in combat. When he died, he owed sutler Charles Thomas $8.00, which of course went uncollected. Spooner's section did not report having any guns disabled, and he did not report his losses in crew members. Lambie reported losing one man killed, one wounded, and three horses disabled during the day, all likely during the 90-minute engagement with Spooner.

order. They had been there a short time when the Confederates opened fire with canister.[31]

The 2nd Virginia shifted its attention to the 13th Pennsylvania Cavalry, whose troopers awaited the attack they all knew was coming. The largely Irish horsemen only had to wait a short time before a line of Rebels came at them, "yelling as though they would scare all of us to death," a trooper wrote. The Keystoners answered by yelling as loudly as their throats and "poorly fed lungs" would allow. In a few minutes, they were in a desperate firefight not 400 feet from the Stonewall Brigade's skirmishers. "Every shot seemed to tell," the trooper commented. A second volley brought down two men to his left, and soon men all around him tumbled to the ground. "Every minute or two the cracking sound of the rifles would be dimmed by the great roar of one or more cannons," he added, "and all the time we heard the continuous zip-plunk and whistles of the bullets as they sped on their passage of death." Surprisingly few cavalrymen died. The trooper estimated that 99 out of 100 musket balls passed fifty feet over their heads. "I have never seen or heard of such poor marksmanship as those Confederates were that day," he wrote. "It was the cannon that did the work." The bursting shells made the battlefield look as if it was on fire. Soon, thick clouds of white smoke obscured their vision, and all they could do was shoot low and aim where they could hear the crack of other rifles. "How many times I fired… no one will ever know," he admitted. "I shot and shot and shot with determination. I had murder in my heart. I wanted not only to kill one of the enemy, but I wanted to take ten thousand lives. No slaughter would have been too great… I simply longed to wade in the blood of the enemy." He believed every man in the regiment had the same feeling and would have endured torture at the stake to "have a chance to kill a few hundred of the boys in gray." However, the troopers soon retired north toward Winchester as the Rebel infantry pushed forward.[32]

Meanwhile, Lieutenant Spooner had unlimbered his two artillery pieces in an orchard on Camp Hill sandwiched between the intersection of the Valley Pike and Millwood Pike on the southern outskirts of Winchester. There, they joined Capt. Wallace F. Randolph's two reserve sections while Ely's infantry retired still farther northward from Abram's Creek. The colonel posted the 87th Pennsylvania along the turnpike with the 18th Connecticut guarding the Senseny and Berryville roads to prevent a flanking movement to the east. The 5th Maryland and the 13th Pennsylvania Cavalry protected Randolph's guns with the Marylanders posted in and around the

31 Dennis W. Brandt, Civil War Soldiers Database, YCHT, based upon post-war pension records at NARA.

32 *Philadelphia Inquirer*, June 13, 1897.

town's black cemetery. Occasionally, small detachments of Confederate cavalry approached the heights, but Ely's well-protected pickets and skirmishers easily drove them off. The six reunited guns "plied shot and shell with a vim, but it was not returned," recalled Pvt. James M. Smith of the 18th Connecticut.[33]

Dr. Charles Goldsborough and the 18th's assistant surgeon, Dr. Josiah B. Harrington, remained near Camp Hill to give immediate aid as needed, while the 5th Maryland's assistant surgeon, 23-year-old Dr. H. Lindsley Pierce, joined the 18th Connecticut's Dr. Lowell Holbrook in town to help establish a hospital in the Braddock Street Methodist Episcopal Church. The wounded began trickling into the small house of worship. A few of Lieutenant Spooner's cannoneers, horribly burned in the limber explosion, died soon after they arrived.[34]

Shortly before 2:00 p.m. Brig. Gen. James A. Walker began deploying the rest of the Stonewall Brigade behind the 2nd Virginia. Lieutenant Colonel Hazael J. Williams' 5th Virginia formed in a clover field east of the road with the 4th Virginia on its right and the 27th Virginia on its left. When all was ready, including skirmishers, Walker advanced the 4th toward the Yankees with Williams' 5th trailing in support. The Virginians moved easterly through Buffalo Lick ravine, halting at its head and reforming in line of battle before moving northeast. The last regiment to arrive, the 33rd Virginia, filed off to the right, caught up with the brigade, and formed in line with skirmishers out front.[35]

Farther to the south, Confederate teamsters and rear echelon troops spent the day listening to the sound of battle. "The firing grow[s] further & further off & at last appears to proceed from & beyond Winchester," the 27th Virginia's Sgt. Watkins Kearns scribbled in his diary. "Ordnance train moves back to a brick house on the left of the road without orders however. Conclude to remain here." Kearns got a better view of the Yankee position from a farmhouse just north of Opequon Creek. The

---

33 Ibid., 44; *New York Herald,* June 22, 1863; James M. Smith diary entry for June 13, 1863, Winchester, Virginia. Orrick Cemetery, named for its original land owner, is still in use. It is bounded today by the Valley Pike to the west, W. Southwerk Street to the north, S. Braddock Street to the east, and W. Whitlock Avenue to the south. The cavalrymen may have been Frank Bond's Marylanders who accompanied the 2nd Maryland to Hollingsworth's Mills east of the Millwood Pike.

34 *Gettysburg Star & Sentinel,* April 2, 1902. Goldsborough, who after the war lived in Hunterstown, Pennsylvania, did not record the whereabouts of the 18th's second assistant surgeon, Dr. William B. North, on June 13. The trustees of the Braddock Street Methodist Episcopal Church South filed an extensive claim for $4,800 in damages and rental fees after the war; Congress finally approved $2,560 in 1904 (Damage Claims, NARA).

35 *OR* 27, pt. 2, 524, 527-28. Many of the men in companies A and K of the 5th Virginia hailed from Winchester.

Miss Kate McVicar, one of Winchester's many female diarists. *Handley Regional Library*

clatter of hooves and harness drew his attention to the arriving corps commander and escort. General Ewell ordered the wagons to move back to the position they had recently vacated.[36]

The tumult of the shooting approaching Winchester threw the pro-Union civilians and the soldiers' wives and sweethearts into a well-deserved panic. Several hastily started packing vital possessions in case of an emergency evacuation. "The town is all in an uproar," diarist Julia Chase penned, "wagons lining the streets all day, cavalry & infantry passing by, the secessionists very joyful flocking to the sutlers, buying up all they can for their friends. God in his mercy, grant that Winchester may not be given up to the Rebels." She went on to question, "Oh how sad and dreadful the thought to think that these men who ought to be living on brotherly terms are arrayed against the other. When will the shedding of blood stop?" By contrast, Mary Greenhow Lee and other secessionists exulted at the prospects of another change in military control. Mary had "everything in nice order" for the Confederates. Rumors were the Union soldiers planned to burn the town, if necessary, as a "prudential measure," recalled Mary's sister-in-law Laura Lee, "we would bring down our trunks from upstairs where we keep them already packed."[37]

Scores of curious townspeople climbed onto their roofs to watch the action. "From the top of the house," a lady unnamed to history wrote, "we could, by the aid of a spy-glass, see our own dear gray coats, while with the naked eye we distinctly saw a long line of blue coats drawn up on the edge of town waiting the advance of the Confederates." The long rumored liberation from Milroy's tyranny finally appeared to be at hand.[38]

36 Kearns diary entry for June 13, 1863, VHS.

37 Mary Lee and Julia Chase diaries, both June 13, 1863; see also Quarles, *Diaries, Letters, and Recollections*, 3:93.

38 "Leaves from a Diary Kept by a Lady."

When the 2nd Virginia and Lambie's Napoleons came into range, the southeastern-facing guns of the 1st Massachusetts Heavy Artillery in the Main Fort opened fire. The thunderous roar added to the growing excitement inside Winchester. An old black woman called Aunt Judy lived off Market Street. When the big guns opened, she raced to the nearby McVicar house to seek shelter in the cellar. The devil on the hill was going to tear everyone to pieces with the shells, she exclaimed. "Lawd, Lawd save us," she cried to Miss Kate McVicar, "and kill dat old Milroy debbil."[39]

According to young Gettie Miller, the Yankees were "making a great to do" about firing their guns. "I was so glad," she rejoiced in her diary. "I thought the rebels were coming to town." A shell struck a house belonging to the Lutheran congregation and set it on ablaze. "I wish our men would see the smoke and make a rush in here and drive these wretches out," she added. At the Taylor Hotel, ill Connecticut soldier James Sawyer spent the remainder of a restless day listening to the heavy gunfire. The "wild idea" that they had destroyed the entire Rebel army entered his fever-wracked mind.[40]

In fact, Confederate casualties were still surprisingly slight, but the shelling unnerved some of the newer soldiers in J. M. Jones' Brigade. "This was my first taste of battle," the 25th Virginia's Pvt. John R. King admitted. The young carpenter had recently left his home in Upshur County, [West] Virginia, to join the Confederate army. "I wish you could have seen me dodge the first shell. If a hole had been near I would have disappeared. I would like to impress on your minds that I had a fine brave heart, and a pair of legs that had a wonderful inclination towards carrying my body out of danger, but I succeeded in coaxing them to stay with the crowd." Another private in King's 25th Virginia, Leonard H. Hammer, recalled suffering lingering headaches after shells exploded nearby. About 3:00 p.m. General Johnson began pulling his forward troops back while the Main Fort shelled the woods near Winchester for nearly half an hour without drawing return fire.[41]

---

39 "Echoes of the War," a collection of articles by Mary Katherine McVicar (using the pen name "Nemo," Latin for nobody) *Winchester Evening Star*, March 12-May 29, 1901, Handley Regional Library, Winchester; *Philadelphia Public Ledger*, June 24, 1863. She lived at the time of the battle with her parents, John M. and Catherine McVicar. Her father was a trusted secret service agent for Stonewall Jackson, and her brother also served briefly as a scout before joining Chew's Battery of the Stuart Horse Artillery.

40 Gettie Miller diary entry for June 13, 1863; Sawyer, "Abandoned at Winchester," 10-11.

41 John R. King, *My Experience in the Confederate Army and in Northern Prisons: Written from Memory* (Roanoke, VA, 1916); quoted in Richard L. Armstrong, *25th Virginia Infantry and 9th Battalion Virginia Infantry* (Lynchburg, VA: H.E. Howard, 1990), 61; OR 27, pt. 2, 500, 524; Elsie Byrd Boggs, *The Hammers and Allied Families, with Their Family Circles Centering in Pendleton County, West Virginia* (Harrisonburg, VA: Joseph K. Ruebush Co., 1950), 71.

During the cannonade, three terrified artillery horses dashed out of the fort and thundered more than a mile south toward Confederate lines. The men of the Rockbridge Artillery watched as the galloping steeds appeared and disappeared from their view as they galloped across the undulating terrain. The gunners soon captured the trio of wayward horses and kept them for their own use, derisively naming one of them "Milroy."[42]

The 2nd Virginia lay prone behind a stone fence near the Millwood Pike. Major G. Campbell Brown, General Ewell's stepson and chief-of-staff, watched a solid shot strike the wall. Fortunately, the shower of stones thrown skyward fell back to earth without hurting anyone. Ewell, however, instructed Colonel Nadenboush to find a new spot for his regiment with better shelter. The two officers were discussing the best place to move the infantry when a private called out, "Gen'l, there is a little hollow, in front of the wall. Wouldn't it be a good place?" Ewell warmly thanked him, complimented his judgment, and immediately ordered the position change. The ravine offered a perfect natural shelter and was fronted with turf so that at a distance it was imperceptible. Despite the prolonged heavy shelling, not a man in the 2nd Virginia suffered any serious injuries.[43]

When the guns fell silent after firing some 70 rounds, Johnson ordered his men to stack arms. Nicholls' Louisiana Brigade under Col. Jesse Williams and Brig. Gen. John M. Jones' brigade rested west of the Front Royal Road supporting the guns near the bend in the Old Front Royal Road while the Stonewall Brigade remained in and around the ravine near the Millwood Pike. Some of Johnson's soldiers ventured eastward across the pike and occupied the abandoned camp of the 87th Pennsylvania.[44]

Johnson's overall losses had been slight. He reported that his casualties were "happily few" at just two men killed and three horses disabled. The other troops which came to his support also experienced trifling losses. Dement's 1st Maryland Battery suffered a few crew and horse casualties and retired southward along with Lambie's Napoleons; both outfits went into park for the night.[45]

42 Edward A. Moore, *The Story of a Cannoneer under Stonewall Jackson* (New York: Neale Publishing Co., 1907), 187.

43 OR 27, pt. 2, 520; Terry L. Jones, *Campbell Brown's Civil War: With Ewell and the Army of Northern Virginia* (Baton Rouge: Louisiana State University Press, 2001), 191-92. Brown recorded the man's name in a memorandum, but lost it and never was able to remember his identity.

44 OR 27, pt. 2, 72, 524; *National Tribune*, December 18, 1884.

45 Jennings Cropper Wise, *The Long Arm of Lee, of the History of the Artillery of the Army of Northern Virginia*, 2 vols. (Lynchburg, VA: J.P. Bell Co., 1915), 2:601.

Action at Kernstown and Pritchard's Hill

While Snowden Andrews' artillery was dueling with Unionists manning the Main Fort, action heated up southwest of Winchester near Kernstown, an area bitterly contested during Stonewall Jackson's 1862 Valley Campaign. A key terrain feature was Sandy Ridge. The low, wooded elevation stretched from just beyond Winchester's western limits for several miles southwest of town before being bisected by Abram's Creek and ending in the valley of Opequon Creek. The Valley Pike, or the Strasburg Road as it was otherwise known in that section of Shawnee Township, ran from Winchester about two miles southwest to Hillman's Tollgate. There, a crowned dirt road known as the Cedar Creek Grade branched off to the west and crossed Sandy Ridge through a depression on the John N. Bell farm. Another dirt lane, the Middle Road or Old Cedar Creek Road, angled more to the southwest. The Valley Pike continued through the village of Kernstown up the Shenandoah Valley. Just northwest of Kernstown between the pike and Sandy Ridge lay a considerable elevation known as Pritchard's Hill which had proven in the past to be a good platform for artillery.[46]

Early settler William Hoge constructed a modest log cabin on the hill in 1735. In 1756, some of the land was granted to Rees Pritchard, whose grandson Samuel erected an impressive two-story brick house, "Brightside," on the southern portion in 1854. The somewhat conical-shaped hill featured three cleared knolls, each about 70 yards apart in a rough triangle with its peak pointing northward. Union guns had deployed there in the 1862 battle of Kernstown. Now, a year later, General Milroy intended to use the cultivated elevation once more.[47]

During the bitter fighting the previous year, Samuel and his much younger wife, the Northern-born Helen (Johnston) Pritchard—both strong Unionists—and their three small children had huddled in their cellar. When the shooting stopped, they emerged to find considerable damage to their property and crops. To make matters worse, Union Col. Nathan Kimball appropriated seven horses from Pritchard as replacements for artillery horses killed in the battle. Helen, who was pregnant at the

---

46 William Allan, *History of the Campaign of Gen. T. J. (Stonewall) Jackson in the Shenandoah Valley of Virginia from November 4, 1861, to June 17, 1862* (Philadelphia: J. B. Lippincott, 1880), 48-49; Jedediah Hotchkiss, "Sketch of the Second Battle of Winchester, June 13th, 14th, and 15th, 1863," Library of Congress. The J. N. Bell farmhouse ("Homespun") is at 949 Cedar Creek Grade (VA Route 622). At the time of the war, this 466-acre farm, part of the Second Battle of Kernstown in 1864, extended south to the Pritchard farm. The road bisected the property. Orchards covered about half the property according to an 1858 survey.

47 Gary L. Echelbarger, *"We are in for it!" The First Battle of Kernstown* (Shippensburg, PA: White Mane, 1997), 85.

Farmhouse of Samuel R. Pritchard north of Kernstown. *Scott Mingus*

time, spent the next few weeks tending to wounded Federal soldiers in her walnut-shaded house and saved the lives of several of them. Now the family was once more trapped in their home as hundreds of soldiers occupied their land preparing for battle.[48]

Earlier that morning, Milroy advanced a pair of large reconnaissance forces southward on the Valley Pike. The 123rd Ohio and parts of the 13th Pennsylvania Cavalry headed out on the turnpike to watch for any Rebel movement coming from the vicinity of Kernstown, a small village some two miles south of Winchester. About 6:00 a.m., the forward elements of the cavalry regiment, already in position near Kernstown, had heard the bugle call "Boots and Saddles." No one had any inkling of an impending battle, but the surprised soldiers turned out ready for whatever may happen. They were not kept in suspense very long, for within three minutes of forming they received orders to move out to reconnoiter. The troopers scarcely had ridden a mile south when they caught their first glimpse of distant Rebels strung out in a long line of battle south of Kernstown. The Pennsylvanians halted and finally

---

48 Samuel R. Pritchard damage claim, Union Provost Marshals' File of Papers Relating to Individual Civilians, Publication M-345, NARA.

withdrew northward. Several troopers breathed a good deal easier riding away from the enemy than they did while moving toward them. After retiring half a mile, the column halted while the officers conferred.[49]

Milroy's other main probing column consisted of Lt. Col. Joseph L. Moss and the 12th Pennsylvania Cavalry and Col. J. Warren Keifer's 110th Ohio Infantry. Buckeye Lt. Henry Rush was studying the New Testament in the officers' wall tent when the long roll sounded. "In that rapid, rattling, continuous drum-beat there seemed the hurrying of footman and horse, the rattle of light arms, and the mandatory meaning of war," he penned. "Though frequently heard before, it had never sounded just as it did that day—so real, so significant, so ominous." Colonel Keifer, Lieutenant Rush, and the rest of the anxious Buckeyes were soon marching south out of Winchester to Milltown (also known as Union Mills). About 7:00 a.m., the Keystone troopers trotted down the Valley Pike and soon rode past Keifer's regiment. They made a right turn onto the Cedar Creek Grade and rode three more miles before halting. They kept watch for about an hour, but saw no signs of enemy activity southwest of town. The horsemen relaxed as their scouts probed a little bit farther south and west.[50]

Milroy dispatched Brig. Gen. Washington L. Elliott to take command of all of the troops on the Valley Pike with orders to feel out for the enemy. The 38-year-old Elliott, son of a U. S. Navy commodore who had had fought the British on Lake Erie during the War of 1812, was an experienced career officer. The Pennsylvanian withdrew from West Point in 1844 to study medicine, but later served as a lieutenant in the Mexican War. He fought at Wilson's Creek in Missouri in August 1861, and rose to the rank of colonel of the 2nd Iowa Cavalry under Maj. Gen. John Pope in the battle for Island Number Ten along the Mississippi River. Elliott received a promotion to brigadier general on June 11, 1862, served on Pope's staff, and transferred east to command the cavalry when Pope assumed command of the Army of Virginia. Elliott was wounded at Second Bull Run, and after an administrative stint in Wisconsin, returned to the field as a brigade commander under Milroy in March 1863.[51]

---

49 OR 27, pt. 2, 69. See also Larry B. Maier, *Leather & Steel: The 12th Pennsylvania Cavalry in the Civil War* (Shippensburg, PA: Burd Street Press, 2002).

50 Rush, *Life and Writings*, 222; OR 27, pt. 2, 69.

51 Ibid., 57; Mark A. Chance, "Prelude to Invasion: Lee's Preparations and the Second Battle of Winchester," *Gettysburg Magazine*, No. 19, Jan. 1999, 14; Ezra J. Warner, *Generals in Blue: Lives of the Union Commanders* (Baton Rouge: LSU Press, 2006), 141-42; OR 51, pt. 1, 1098. Commodore Jesse D. Elliott won a Congressional Gold Medal for his actions on Lake Erie while commanding the USS *Niagara*. He feuded for years with Oliver Hazard Perry who accused Elliott of deliberately holding back *Niagara* while the British pummeled Perry's USS *Lawrence*.

Brig. Gen. Washington L. Elliott, commander of Milroy's First Brigade.

U.S. Army Heritage and Education Center

Despite his pedigree and experience, the West Pointer's battlefield prowess failed to impress many observers. He was "amiable and capable in all that pertained to military discipline," believed the 110th Ohio's Col. J. Warren Keifer, "but timid and un-enterprising. He performed all duty faithfully, but no further." Elliott's lackluster energy sharply contrasted with General Milroy's style, an officer Keifer believed to be "restless and always on the alert . . . eager to achieve all it was possible for his command to accomplish."[52]

In mid-morning, while Colonel Keifer and his 110th Ohio regiment were at Milltown, "it was soon ascertained that the enemy had massed a heavy force upon that road [the Valley Pike] about three miles from Winchester." General Elliott dispatched Lt. Charles C. Theaker's section of two 3-inch Ordnance Rifles from Carlin's Battery D, 1st West Virginia Light Artillery to strengthen Keifer's force small force. When the guns arrived, Keifer moved his combined force about one mile southward (likely on the Middle Road), "keeping well on the ridge between the pike and the Cedar Creek road." Once there, Keifer did not spot any Rebels and assumed "the enemy kept under cover." Lacking orders to bring on an engagement, he pulled back to the intersection of the Valley Pike and the Cedar Creek Grade to await further instructions.[53]

Reinforcements arrived in the form of Col. John Klunk and his 12th West Virginia Infantry, temporarily detached from Colonel Ely's brigade. Although in the service for almost ten months, the majority of Klunk's men had little real combat experience. The morning started in frustrating fashion when they struck their tents near Shawnee Springs and packed them into wagons, only to be told to repitch the tents, and a short time later, pull them down once more and prepare for battle. The West Virginians filled their canteens, stuffed a day's rations in their haversacks, and

---

52 J. Warren Keifer, *Slavery and Four Years of War*, 2 vols. (New York: G. P. Putnam's Sons, 1900), 1:322.

53 Ibid., 2:8.

about 11:00 a.m. marched out the Valley Pike and then some side roads to take up a position on Elliott's right flank.[54]

About midday, Milroy, concerned with General Johnson's movement on the Front Royal Road, ordered Elliott to withdraw his brigade from its widely scattered positions and concentrate behind Abram's Creek to better protect Carlin's two reserve sections near the old Quaker Centre Meeting House and cemetery. He formed his infantry regiments into a more compact line of battle and sent the 12th Pennsylvania Cavalry out to protect his extreme left flank near the Front Royal Road. Sometime about 2:00 p.m., General Milroy sent word for Elliott to advance Colonel Keifer's 110th Ohio, supported by the 12th Pennsylvania Cavalry, a squadron of the 13th Pennsylvania Cavalry, and Theaker's section of two 3-inch rifles, south toward Kernstown as a reconnaissance in force. "I moved forward promptly with the 12th on the left on the plain," recalled Keifer, "the infantry and artillery in the centre covering the Strasburg pike [Valley Pike], and the squadron on the ridge to my right, which extended parallel with the pike." He proceeded a mile in this formation before his skirmishers began to encounter resistance. Theaker's light guns rolled up Pritchard's Hill west of the pike and unlimbered. The road-weary 110th Ohio was off to the southeast deploying astride the turnpike immediately north of Kernstown while the cavalrymen of the 12th Pennsylvania edged farther south toward Newtown. To protect the right flank, Elliott sent the 12th West Virginia south of the Cedar Creek Grade, where they formed in line south of the J. N. Bell farm in some woods on Sandy Ridge. The Mountaineers and the Buckeyes piled their knapsacks in preparation for a battle that nearly everyone was expecting at any moment.[55]

Back in Winchester, meanwhile, Pvt. Henry Clapp and the 123rd Ohio's detached scouting party downed a hasty lunch after returning to their nearly deserted camp. They soon departed and followed the Valley Pike south toward Kernstown, where

---

54 William T. Wilson diary, entry for June 13, 1863, William T. Wilson Diary for 1863-1864, Ohio Historical Society, Columbus; OR 27, pt. 2, 57; William Hewitt, *The History of the 12th West Virginia Volunteer Infantry: The Part It Took in the War of the Rebellion, 1861-1865* (Twelfth West Virginia Infantry Association, 1892), 39-40; Hotchkiss map. This regiment is often mentioned by its older name, the 12th Virginia (Union). For convenience we will use the West Virginia designation although it did not formally become a separate state until June 20.

55 OR 27, pt. 2, 57; Keifer, *Slavery and Four Years of War*, 2:8-9. The Hollingsworth and Parkins families, early Quaker settlers, established the graveyard in the 1700s. It is just east of the Valley Pike immediately south of the intersection of W. Jubal Early Drive and Plaza Drive. In John Parkins' will, dated 1815, he directed that it be "Forever reserved for the purpose of burying ground for the use and to be at the disposal of the Society of Friends in general." (Text from the historical marker on one of the walls). Unfortunately, the old cemetery is now badly overgrown. Among those interred is miller Abraham Hollingsworth whose descendants still operated his nearby 3-story stone mill during Milroy's occupation in 1863.

Maj. William W. Goldsborough of the 2nd Maryland (CSA) Battalion, assigned to Ewell's Corps. *Maryland Historical Society*

they found the regiment resting in a small orchard just off of the road. "There was a quiet seriousness about the men that told us plainer than words that there was something doing," the young Buckeye added, "There is nothing more trying to a soldier's courage than the period of inaction which often precedes a battle. It is then that thots of home and loved ones make life seem a thing too precious to be wantonly thrown away; but when the time for action comes," he continued, "the words of command, the sound of the bugles, the cheers of the victors and the groans of the dying drive all thots of self away, and the soldier becomes again merely a part of a fighting machine called an army."[56]

Trouble was indeed lurking south out the Valley Pike. The previous night, General Ewell had ordered Lt. Col. James R. Herbert to move to the vicinity of Newtown and await the arrival of Early's division from Front Royal. Herbert's unattached command consisted of his own 2nd Maryland Battalion of infantry, Capt. Wiley H. Griffin's Baltimore Light Artillery, Capt. Frank A. Bond's Company A and 19-year-old Capt. George M. Emack's Company B of the 1st Maryland Cavalry. They had been in the Valley for several months as part of Brig. Gen. Alfred G. Jenkins' command. On the afternoon of June 12 Ewell sent a message to Jenkins that he was near Front Royal, and Jenkins was to report to him. The news surprised the Marylanders, who presumed Ewell was still on the Rappahannock with General Lee. Late that night, orders came for Herbert to move in the morning toward Newtown and await General Early's arrival.[57]

"The men were in high spirits and eager to encounter the enemy, who were believed to be in their immediate front," related the 2nd Maryland's Maj. William Goldsborough, the older brother of the 5th Maryland's surgeon. Being unfamiliar with the roads, Herbert requested the services of a local named Robert T. "Robbie" Barton. After crossing Opequon Creek, the youthful Herbert halted his force near

56 Clapp, "With Milroy at Winchester."

57 Goldsborough, *The Maryland Line*, 93.

Springdale, about five miles south of Winchester, to wait for Early's arrival. As a precaution, Herbert unlimbered his artillery and formed his infantry into a prone skirmish line along the edge of a field. He also sent out vedettes and flankers and advanced a six-man squad of Bond's cavalry as scouts.[58]

Soon after Herbert's command was in place, the vanguard of the 12th Pennsylvania Cavalry rode into sight, approaching "rapidly and rather incautiously" on the turnpike according to cavalryman Maj. Harry Gilmor. He and several Marylanders mounted and rode in front of the guns to mask them from enemy eyes. The vedettes fell slowly back as the Pennsylvanians trotted within a half-mile of Herbert's line and then charged in column of fours. When they were in easy range, Gilmor's masking horsemen wheeled to the sides and one of Griffin's Baltimore gunners yanked his lanyard. "The shot was a good one whether it did any execution or not, and had a magical effect," Major Goldsborough noted, "for the cavalry disappeared like the mist." One of Herbert's infantryman boasted, "A shot from [our] battery scattered them in all directions."[59]

North of Kernstown, the 123rd Ohio's Henry Clapp still sat in the roadside orchard with his regiment. When tired and dejected cavalrymen began coming in from the front along with occasional ambulances filled with wounded, the Buckeye foot-soldiers asked about the Rebels. The replies were disconcerting when the troopers confirmed they would find "plenty of them back there." The Ohioans braced for their first battle, and Colonel Wilson threw out a heavy line of skirmishers to better protect his front.[60]

---

58 Margaretta Barton Colt, ed., *Defend the Valley: A Shenandoah Family in the Civil War* (New York: Oxford University Press, 1999), 256-57; Frank A. Bond, "Company A, 1st Maryland Cavalry," in *Confederate Veteran*, Vol. 6, February 1898, 78; Goldsborough, *The Maryland Line*, 93-94; Harry Gilmor, *Four Years in the Saddle* (New York: Harper and Brothers, 1866), 83; Washington Hands, "Civil War Notebook 1860-1865," Manuscripts Division, Alderman Library, UVA, 90; copy also in the Maryland Historical Society, Baltimore. Griffin's first name is mistakenly listed as William in many accounts. According to horse artillery expert Robert Trout, his first name was Wiley. See Trout, *The Hoss: Officer Biographies and Rosters of the Stuart Horse Artillery Battalion*, (Myerstown, PA: JebFlo Press, 2003), 201-204. Robert Barton served in the Confederate army until tuberculosis forced his discharge in 1862. He then did some work for the CSA Dept. of Nitre and Mining. Springdale was the Barton family home, so he did knew the area well and looked for any way to support the Confederate war effort. For more on Barton, see Jonathan A. Noyalas, "Portrait of a Soldier: The Confederate Military Service of Robert T. Barton, 1861-1862," *Winchester-Frederick County Historical Society Journal*, 16 (2004), 73-94.

59 Gilmor, *Four Years in the Saddle*, 83; Goldsborough, *The Maryland Line*, 94; Washington Hands Civil War Notebook, 90, Special Collections, Alderman Library, University of Virginia, Charlottesville.

60 Clapp, "With Milroy at Winchester," Keyes, *The Military History of the 123rd Ohio*, 45.

The village of Kernstown as it appeared in 1864 to artist James E. Taylor.
Western Reserve Historical Society

Herbert's Marylanders, meanwhile, remained in place at Springdale awaiting the planned rendezvous with Early's division. "Allegheny" Johnson's guns boomed off to the northeast as he engaged Colonel Ely's brigade, and a more distant rumble soon could be heard farther in the same direction as Maj. Gen. Robert Rodes' division attacked Martinsburg more than 25 miles away. As time passed, Major Goldsborough wondered how long it would be before a large enemy force appeared to confront them. Much to his relief, a distant dust cloud off to the south finally heralded Early's approach. When he arrived, the general ordered Herbert to send Major Goldsborough and three companies of the 2nd Maryland forward as skirmishers to develop the Union position. The cavalry formed on their right and advanced at the same time. The adventurous Harry Gilmor, seeking redemption after the embarrassing Newtown ambush, tagged along with the skirmishers.[61]

After passing through Kernstown, Goldsborough spotted the 110th Ohio and some cavalrymen about half a mile away. At midday, Lieutenant Theaker's section of Union guns on Pritchard's Hill soon opened, "raining shell upon the little Maryland command," explained Goldsborough. "But the gallant Griffin, of the Baltimore Lights, soon got to work, and then occurred one of the prettiest artillery duels of the war." One of Herbert's infantrymen looked back on the event and boasted, "Our battalion behaved finely under the first firing." Theaker shelled the woods in all directions, but did little damage to the Confederates. Washington Hands, who served

---

61 Goldsborough, *The Maryland Line*, 94; Bond, "Company A, First Maryland Cavalry."

Brig. Gen. Harry T. Hays, the commander
of the famed "Louisiana Tigers"
brigade in Jubal Early's division.

U.S. Army Heritage and Education Center

in Herbert's 2nd Maryland Battalion, commented, "The enemy iron made his appearance in force, and opened a severe fire on Griffin from his batteries, which was vigorously responded to." Another Confederate reported, "Just here, our line was most severely shelled by a Yankee Battery at short range. Fortunately, no great injury was done."[62]

General Early consulted his maps to decide how best to position his oncoming division for an attack. After carefully reconnoitering the ground, he rode back up the Valley Pike and located Brig. Gen. Harry T. Hays. Early then conducted Hays' First Louisiana Brigade northward through a woodlot and meadow to reach a narrow country lane which led from the vicinity of Bartonsville northwesterly toward the Cedar Creek Grade. Hays led his column a half-mile north on the Middle Road toward the Pritchard farm before halting in mid-afternoon when he spotted a considerable infantry force on the ridge to his left. A courier galloped back to inform Early, who ordered Brig. Gen. John B. Gordon's brigade of Georgians to swing to the west and clear what would prove to be the 12th West Virginia from atop Sandy Ridge. "Old Jube" began deploying the 9th Louisiana into a line of battle east of the Middle Road, with Herbert's Marylanders well off to their right front. The rest of Hays' column remained stationary on the roadway.[63]

General Early met with Major Goldsborough, who requested permission to withdraw his infantrymen to avoid sacrificing them needlessly. The enemy, after all,

---

62 Goldsborough, *The Maryland Line*, 93-94; Gilmor, *Four Years in the Saddle*, 84; "The Capture of Winchester," *Richmond Whig*, June 23, 1863; Washington Hands Civil War Notebook, 91; Thomas S. McCullough diary, entry for June 14, 1863, Jedediah Hotchkiss Papers, UVA. Lt. H. E. Alexander believed the noisy artillery duel lasted about two hours.

63 OR 27, pt. 2, 476; Early, *Autobiographical Sketch*, 241-42; Gilmor, *Four Years in the Saddle*, 84. Bartonsville, a small community along the Opequon Creek, was also known as Barton's Mills or Bartonville.

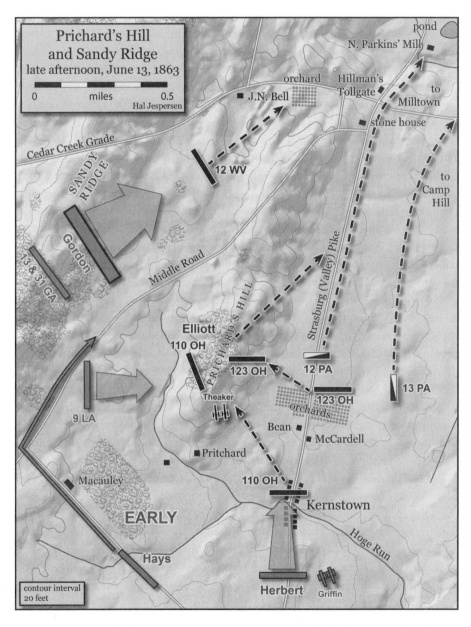

Prichard's Hill
and Sandy Ridge
late afternoon, June 13, 1863

0   miles   0.5
Hal Jespersen

contour interval
20 feet

had their range. "You have done your work thoroughly," Early responded with unusual positive candor. "You have a splendid body of men in your Maryland command, and I wish there were more of them." The division commander had just placed General Gordon in position to drive the enemy on Sandy Ridge back into Winchester, he reassured his subordinate. When Goldsborough heard their Rebel yell and the opening of their fight, he would be relieved. In the meantime, he was to stay put.[64]

All the while, Theaker's section of rifled cannon continued blasting away from Pritchard's Hill. Early's division artillery commander, Lt. Col. Hilary P. Jones, ordered his batteries forward to assist Griffin in silencing Theaker, but the range proved too far for the Southern long-arm. After Jones placed parts of three batteries in position to cover any emergency, one of Theaker's shots exploded amongst them, killing a man and two horses in Capt. Asher Garber's Staunton Artillery and a horse in Capt. James McD. Carrington's Charlottesville Artillery.[65]

The 110th Ohio's Colonel Keifer years later recalled the initial action against Herbert's Marylanders, "It was soon apparent to me that the enemy extended along a wide front, his advance being only a thin cover. But as my orders were to develop the enemy, I brought my whole command into action, drove in his advanced line and with the artillery shelled the woods behind this line. We suffered some loss, but pressed forward until the enemy fell back to a woods on the left of Kearnstown [sic]. My artillery opened with canister, and for a few moments our front seemed to be cleared."[66]

General Milroy, meanwhile, remained unaware of Early's approach. Winchester's commander was instead focused on Colonel Ely's precarious position protecting the Front Royal and Millwood pikes southeast of town, while Early was approached from the south and southwest. About 2:00 p.m. General Elliott sent a staff officer, Lt. William Alexander, riding north to find Milroy, who was on Milltown Heights just southwest of Winchester near Carlin's reserve sections. Elliott reported there were indications the enemy was massing forces off to the left near the Front Royal Road. Milroy directed the staff officer to instruct Elliott to retire his men on the Valley Pike to put them in position to support either Colonel Ely or the forts, as needed. Before Elliott could execute the order, however, two long lines of Rebel infantry he estimated at 2,000 strong appeared off to his right looking for all the world as if they intended to flank him and cut off his lines of retreat. This was no cavalry raiding party.[67]

What Elliott had no way of knowing was that these enemy troops were the cream of Jubal Early's veteran division. Harry Hays' famed Louisiana Tigers remained in a long line of battle east of the Middle Road, while John Gordon advanced his hard-fighting Georgians farther west to protect Hays' left and rear. They soon moved

64 Goldsborough, *The Maryland Line*, 94.

65 *OR* 27, pt. 2, 493-94.

66 Keifer, *Slavery and Four Years of War*, 2:8.

67 Ibid., 44-45.

into position to launch an attack on the 12th West Virginia on Sandy Ridge. Early placed his reserve brigades astride the Valley Pike south of Kernstown near Bartonsville, with Brig. Gen. William "Extra Billy" Smith's Virginians to the left or west of the road and Col. I. E. Avery's North Carolinians to the east. Hays dispatched Col. Leroy Stafford's 9th Louisiana into the fields in his front as a strong skirmish line using cedar and pine thickets, stone walls, and tree stumps as cover. Once in position, Stafford ordered his men to attack the 110th Ohio. As the Tigers began pressing forward, Colonel Keifer ordered his Buckeye skirmishers to fire a volley and retire into the center of the line. His men did not waver as they experienced their first combat. "We held them stubbornly and disputed every inch of ground," recalled Pvt. Lorenzo Barnhart. Griffin's Rebel guns "shot something at us," he continued, "we thought it was pieces of railroad iron. It screamed and whizzed over our heads, and made a deathly noise. Some of these missiles went over our heads, and some lit on the ground. We could hear them thump." A spent bullet fired from long range struck Keifer and left a painful bruise, but he continued leading his force.[68]

While the firing increased on Pritchard's Hill, General Milroy, now fully aware of the developing action, sent a brief telegram to Lt. Col. Donn Piatt, the Eighth Corps' Assistant Inspector General, at Harpers Ferry to inform him, "Enemy approaching in strong force. Infantry and artillery on Strasburg [Valley] pike. Elliott pitching into them. Any extra star very much in the way; ought to be there myself. Will get them, if Elliott falls back." Piatt forwarded the message to his superior, corps commander Maj. Gen. Robert Schenck, in Baltimore. At 2:55 p.m., Schenck responded and told Piatt to "instruct General Milroy to use great caution, risking nothing unnecessarily, and to be prepared for falling back, in good order, if overmatched. I relay on your having support afforded him as far as may be practical. In the meantime, go with your concentration of forces. Keep me advised of what is needed. What movement has been made from Romney? [concerning sending any relief force to Milroy's aid]."[69]

While Milroy, Piatt, and Schenck exchanged telegrams, on the battlefield Colonel Stafford's continued pressure and the clear threat of Hays' additional Louisiana regiments joining the fray forced the 110th Ohio to abandon its defensive position on southern Pritchard's Hill. Colonel Keifer explained, "But my flankers now reported the enemy turning my right with at least a brigade of infantry. I therefore withdrew slowly and in good order, embracing every possible opportunity to halt and open fire."[70]

68 Barnhart, *Reminiscences*.

69 *OR* 27, pt. 2, 173; pt. 3, 96.

70 Keifer, *Slavery and Four Years of War*, 2:8.

With the way now clear, General Hays advanced the rest of his Louisiana regiments past the Pritchard house where they halted on the slope and deployed into a lengthy battle line. He sent six companies, including his sharpshooters, into a woodlot on his right to contest any enemy advance on the turnpike. This new threat to Lieutenant Theaker's two guns prompted Col. William T. Wilson's 123rd Ohio to cross the pike and angle northwest to support the hard-pressed artillery, a move that drew sharp fire that killed or wounded several men. Once in position, the Buckeyes began shooting, slowing the Tigers and lessening their return fire. Despite their inexperience, Wilson's Ohio soldiers "behaved splendidly," Sgt. Charles M. Keyes bragged, "taking their position as coolly as veterans."[71]

Gordon's Attack on Sandy Ridge

While Hays was getting into position, General Gordon's Georgians approached the 12th West Virginia off Hays' left. In the mid-afternoon, Gordon deployed a heavy line of skirmishers in some open fields on Sandy Ridge west of the Middle Road, not far from the site of fighting back in the 1862 battle of Kernstown. Just to the northeast, Col. John Klunk and his West Virginians watched the Confederates from the shelter of some timber. His position for the last hour was, according to one of his infantrymen, on a "rather an elevated piece of ground, with cleared field beyond and then another wooded hill. From these woods the rebels debouched in very fine style, in perfect line, skirmishers in front." Captain Carlin's two sections of artillery on Milltown Heights to the northeast shelled them at long range, but with little effect. Gordon soon drove back some advanced 12th Pennsylvania Cavalry skirmishers and then engaged the West Virginia skirmish line. The Rebels soon doubled their line of skirmishers and, according to Klunk, "the action became quite warm." Gordon moved the 26th, 38th, 60th, and 61st Georgia in column formation toward the distant Yankee-held wooded rise, holding the 13th and 31st Georgia in reserve. After advancing several hundred yards, he brought the four attacking regiments into line of battle. The Mountaineers, despite their inexperience, did not panic at the sight and held their ground. They began hearing peculiar whistling sounds they could not readily identify. Some soldiers claimed it was the sound of flying bullets; others thought not. An officer overheard the discussion and exclaimed, "Boys, those are bullets as sure as you live."[72]

71 Keyes, *The Military History of the 123rd Ohio*, 45; OR 27, pt. 2, 44.

72 Ibid., 80 and 491; Bradwell, "Capture of Winchester," 331; Hewitt, *History of the 12th West Virginia*, 39-40. The exact order of Gordon's regiments in the battle line is uncertain. He

Klunk shouted "Fire!" and the 12th West Virginia unleashed its first hostile volley, temporarily checking the Rebels. The sound of the musketry signaled to Major Goldsborough near Kernstown that his 2nd Marylanders were now relieved and could now retire to the rear as Early had instructed. The Mountaineers and Georgians exchanged a steady and heavy fire for at least half an hour. One Rebel bullet broke off the hammer of Irish-born Pvt. Tommy Burke's musket. He instinctively reached for his knapsack which he had removed earlier. "Captain, captain," Burke bemoaned in his thick brogue to W. B. Curtis, "the bloody rebels have cut ahff my supplies." Before long, Adjutant George B. Caldwell reported to Colonel Klunk that the Rebels were flanking the position on the right. Klunk dispatched Lt. William Burley and Company A as skirmishers in an effort to protect that flank, but the solitary company proved insufficient to stop Gordon's maneuver. Klunk had but little choice other than to direct the entire regiment to fall back to a sheltering stone fence. Instead of simply about-facing in battle line, he employed the unusual tactic of filing his men to the left flank. The West Virginians turned to the left as ordered and marched successively along the line until they reached a designated spot. Once there, they turned 90 degrees to the left. The extreme right of the regiment had to march much farther than the left to reach the new position. The maneuver also left their knapsacks behind in the woods. "They, of course, fell into the hands of the Johnnys," bemoaned Sgt. William Hewitt, "who, no doubt, examined them with a good deal of interest." The bullets kept flying even during the retreat, and one of them found and killed Lt. Thomas I. Bradley of Company I. "When in danger of being cut off by a flanking party, we were compelled to fall back, which we did in good order," was how one of the Mountaineers recalled the movement. "We retreated to a strong position which we held with little difficulty until midnight."[73]

Klunk's withdrawal, however, exposed Lieutenant Theaker's repositioned guns to the oncoming Rebels. The cannoneers recognized the danger in time, limbered as quickly as possible, and made haste for the rear to rejoin Carlin's battery on Milltown Heights. General Gordon rued not capturing the field pieces, which were considered valuable prizes of war. The charge, claimed Gordon, was "executed with spirit and unchecked at any point." The "unchecked" attack, however, stripped 75 men from his ranks, including "some efficient officers," such as the 38th Georgia's Capt. Charles A. Hawkins, a son of a prominent Oglethorpe County judge. The tall blonde 22-year-old

---

claimed he started his advance at 4:00 p.m., but some Union accounts suggest it began an hour earlier.

73 Ibid., 41; *OR* 27, pt. 2, 53; Mark A. Miner, "First Fight, First Blood: The Twelfth West Virginia Infantry at the Second Battle of Winchester," http://www.markminer.com/ 12wv. htm, accessed December 26, 2013; "H.C.H.", "From the 12th Virginia."

captain was leading Company E, the Tom Cobb Infantry, toward the Yankee-held stone wall about 75 yards away when a Minié ball passed through his left side. The newlywed yelled as he collapsed, "Boys, they have killed me, but go on!" His men carried the position. Comrades carried Hawkins to a nearby farmhouse where he died the following evening.[74]

The Federals ran "in every direction, throwing away their guns and everything else," claimed the 38th Georgia's Lt. W. C. Mathews, although Union accounts suggest a more orderly withdrawal. "We shot at them as they ran, and poor devils, we slaughtered them like dogs," he added. "I never saw so much running and screaming in my life." Gordon's brigade reformed and advanced toward the sprawling J. N. Bell farm and adjacent properties to link with Hays' Louisiana Tigers. Colonel Clement A. Evans of the 31st Georgia put a fine point on the affair when scoffed, "Yankees acted cowardly."[75]

Fighting at Hillman's Tollgate and Milltown

While Gordon pushed the 12th West Virginia off of Sandy Ridge, Harry Hays' long line of battle slowly advanced northward on Pritchard's Hill and outflanked successive positions of Keifer's force and Colonel Wilson's 123rd Ohio along the Valley Pike. When the Louisianans pushed north toward the Cedar Creek Grade, Wilson's regiment retired to Milltown while Keifer tried to delay the Rebels. Carlin's two sections of West Virginia artillery on Milltown Heights, as soon as they had the range, opened on the distant Tigers and temporarily threw them into some confusion. Hays halted his advance, and his soldiers hunkered down behind a stone wall for cover.

With the reprieve caused by Hays' halt, Colonel Keifer withdrew his mixed force of infantry, cavalry, and artillery farther northward. He received word that reinforcements were on the way. He sent instructions that when the fresh troops arrived they should be posted on Milltown Heights in front of the Valley Pike bridge over Abram's Creek. That bridge was crucial; it was the best way for the retreating infantry and artillery to cross the steep-banked stream and adjacent mill race. The 12th

---

74 OR 27, pt. 2, 491; *Augusta* (GA) *Chronicle*, July 30, 1863. Charlie Hawkins had the year before survived a serious wound at Sharpsburg. He is buried in Plot 58 of the Georgia section of the Stonewall Cemetery in Winchester. His young widow, Hortense, never remarried. Younger brother John Milner Hawkins, a sergeant in Company E, survived the war and became a school teacher.

75 OR 27, pt. 2, 477; Early, *Autobiographical Sketch*, 242; *The Sunny South*, Jan. 10, 1891; Stephens, *Intrepid Warrior*, 189. Note that casualty figures from the 12th WV do not support such a "slaughter" as Mathews claimed.

Pennsylvania's Lieutenant Colonel Moss did not believe he could get his horses across the tail-race with its steep embankments or the creek, so he began moving his troopers toward the bridge. Keifer sternly turned Moss back "with imperative orders to cover the left flank as long as necessary or possible, then find a crossing below the Mills." As Lieutenant Theaker's guns arrived at the bridge, the artillerymen found it jammed with the soldiers of Colonel Wilson's 123rd Ohio. The Buckeyes had turned about and were now marching to Keifer's relief under the guidance of one of General Elliott's staff officers, Capt. W. L. Shaw. Keifer, in tactical command as the senior colonel, directed Wilson to deploy on his right after his regiment cleared the bridge.[76]

With the Rebels now stationary, General Elliott sensed an opportunity to extract Theaker and the cavalry safely. He moved the 110th and 123rd Ohio just south of Hillman's Tollgate where the turnpike intersects the Cedar Creek Grade, and prepared to counterattack. On Elliott's order, the two regiments moved forward, with Colonel Wilson's 123rd Ohio initially in column formation, toward the northern spur of Pritchard's Hill. Some of Lieutenant Colonel Moss's 12th Pennsylvania Cavalry moved to the left of the advancing Union line to protect Keifer's flank.[77]

The 110th Ohio promptly encountered some of Gordon's skirmishers sheltered in a stand of locust trees parallel to the Valley Pike. "The thoughtless fellows failed to salute our coming with blank cartridges," joked Buckeye Lt. Henry Rush about the bullets whizzing past they heads. "Their sudden volley emptied several saddles and took some fatal and disabling effect among the infantry. A slight pause, as if just a little surprised at rebel impudence, and we pushed forward. A few hundred yards farther on it became obvious that we had come squarely against business—that a huge contract was upon our hands," he continued, "Rebels to the right of us, rebels to the left of us, rebels to the front of us, and rebels behind and far beyond all these, rebels." As the Buckeyes moved forward firing at the long gray lines, "Rebels seemed to swarm on every swell of field and sweep of valley." As casualties mounted, Rush encouraged his comrades to closed rank and continue forward. They drove off Gordon's forward skirmishers, who fell back, reformed, and received reinforcements. "More and harder work yet awaits us," Rush realized as Colonel Keifer led the regiment south toward the main Rebel line.[78]

76 Keifer, *Slavery and Four Years of War*, 2:8.

77 *OR* 27, pt. 2, 45; Robert Knox Sneden, "Plan of the Battle of Kernstown, Va. March 23rd 1862," LOC; see also Robert Knox Sneden Scrapbook Mss5:7 Sn237:1, Virginia Historical Society, Richmond. In the May 1862 battle of Winchester, Robinson's Battery L, 1st Ohio Light Artillery, had used this same elevation as a platform to fire upon Confederates on Milltown Heights.

78 Rush, *Life and Writings*, 222-23.

Hillman's Tollgate and house along the Valley Pike south of Winchester. *Scott Mingus Collection*

Like the infantrymen of the 110th Ohio Infantry, most of the members of the 123rd Ohio were also green when it came to real combat. They were engaged before they could form into a proper line of battle. "That we were novices in the art of war," Pvt. Henry Clapp frankly commented, "is shown from the fact that we were moving towards an unseen foe in double ranks, close order, with no skirmish line in front of us." Colonel Wilson halted the Buckeyes of his 123rd regiment on the northern crest of Prichard's Hill and surveyed the scene before him.

At the far end of a field about 200 yards wide was the "most active and belligerent rebel skirmish line it was ever my misfortune to meet," observed Private Clapp, who together with his fellow Buckeyes stared south at the forward elements of Harry Hays' Louisiana Tigers. One glance indicated they were veterans. Clapp was so "charmed with their manner of doing business" that he gazed at them momentarily with open-mouthed admiration. Although mesmerized by the enemy's abilities, he also realized the danger they posed to he and his comrades. "They would take deliberate aim at us, fire, and then setting the butts of their guns on the ground move around them in a circle while loading," he later related, "and doing it all with a careless indifference to danger which was hard to comprehend by a tenderfoot who had not yet learned that a soldier's life is an incident, the closing of which is not worth a moment's thot." As the Buckeyes stayed stationary on the northern tip of Pritchard's Hill, Hays' main line continued to man the stone wall some distance behind his

The Valley Pike/Strasburg Road "one mile south of Winchester." This area played a prominent role in the fighting on June 13-14, 1863. *Handley Regional Library*

forward skirmishers. Soon, to the Buckeyes' consternation, the Tigers started advancing.[79]

Colonel Wilson ordered a series of volleys. "For one bloody half hour we stood in that unprotected spot, in double ranks, close order, a human wall, stopping every bullet that did not go over our heads," Private Clapp recounted. He recalled firing 25 rounds, and that "several of them went where they were aimed." Clapp's greatest fear, however, was not the Rebels but his comrades immediately behind him. The muzzles of their Austrian rifle muskets were uncomfortably close to the ears of the men manning the front rank, and some of their hands were rather unsteady. They anxiously loaded and fired as fast as possible. In frustration, Clapp turned around and admonished them to be careful when pulling the trigger. Casualties mounted, especially in Company B which lost 17 men. One musket ball shattered Pvt. Albert Nye's ankle. Nearby, Capt. John Randolph ordered another private named Irving Cole to load his gun. In response, Cole raised his blood-covered hand and said he couldn't do it. Hotly pressed, Clapp was unable to go to his friend and offer help; Cole would eventually lose his arm. The sights of his first battle made a lasting impression on Clapp, especially when it came to the expressions on the faces of mortally wounded comrades sinking down to the ground to die. One blood-soaked man, crazed by a

---

79 Clapp, "With Milroy at Winchester."

horrible wound to his face, staggered about before finally collapsing. "These are some of the scenes I would gladly forget," admitted Clapp.[80]

While Clapp and his comrades were fighting, bullets pierced the 123rd's flag and clipped off its tassel. A teenaged private named Edwin H. Forrester watched in horror when his friend, 21-year-old Pvt. William H. Gillard, suffered a gunshot to his back that pitched him violently to the ground. Gillard was able to partially raise himself using his arm and gasp to Cpl. William H. Lovering, "Tell my mother I died for my country." In an effort to find relief from the murderous fire, Colonel Wilson moved the 123rd Ohio, but did so by the flank because of terrain impediments. Lieutenant Theaker's two limbered guns and some retreating infantry, likely from the 12th West Virginia, dashed through his ranks about this time, adding to the already substantial confusion. Wilson and his officers restored order behind another stone wall. Once there, the Buckeyes fired a volley, loaded, and then fired at will. By this time more than 75 soldiers had been killed or wounded out of the 355 riflemen Colonel Wilson carried into the fight.[81]

As Hays pushed forward toward the 123rd Ohio, Gordon pressed the 110th Ohio and the remnants of Colonel Klunk's 12th West Virginia, which had reformed behind a stone wall not far from the Cedar Creek Grade. The Rebels attacked with a "quick and determined step," admitted Lt. David Powell of the Mountaineers' Company H. He later recalled that the enemy pushed their lines almost to the stone wall defended by the Mountaineers where the Georgians gave way and retired. The Georgians reformed and pushed forward, meeting even deadlier fire this time; once again they fell back. Gordon and Hays threw in their respective reserve regiments, which poured over the crest and advanced quickly to support the hard-pressed front lines. "Fresh troops that seemed to rise like locusts from the ground," was how the 110th's Lieutenant Rush described the swarming advance. The Rebels, he continued, "lengthened and deepened their long, strong lines of battle." The combined weight of Hays' and Gordon's Rebels, along with Capt. Wiley Griffin's effective long-range artillery fire from his Maryland gunners, proved too much. The heavily outnumbered

---

80 Ibid.; "Army Correspondence," *Norwalk* (Ohio) *Reflector*, June 30 and July 6, 1863. Clapp wrote two letters home, one from New Creek, West Virginia, on June 18 and another from Bloody Run, Pennsylvania, on June 26. The Peru, Ohio, resident later became a lieutenant in the 19th U. S. Colored Troops. Irving Cole had his right arm amputated.

81 Clapp, "With Milroy at Winchester"; Col. W. T. Wilson to My Dear Wife, November 1, 1863, Libby Prison, Richmond, cited in *Norwalk* (Ohio) *Reflector*, December 22, 1863; Keyes, *The Military History of the 123rd Ohio*, 46. Wilson had 355 rifles in line, but did not have all of his regiment with him. Company D was on provost duty guarding prisoners and about 100 men had picket duty.

Buckeyes and West Virginians, now facing two full brigades, "fell back, not in a panic but with a judicious speed," admitted Rush.[82]

Colonel Keifer admired Colonel Wilson's spirited work that afternoon and later declared, "A more gallant fight, under all the circumstances, was never made. It enabled me to safely take the artillery over the bridge, and to withdraw to a new position [near Milltown Heights] from which we could cover the bridge with our artillery and easily repulse the enemy. Colonels Wilson and Moss were each withdrawn in good order, the former above and the latter below the bridge." Kiefer's observation that the retirement was conducted in an orderly fashion did not agree with some Southern observers.[83]

About a mile to the east along the Front Royal Road, Allegheny Johnson and his left-most troops observed Keifer's withdrawal. "The Yanks broke and ran and our men ran after them. It was a splendid sight—the roaring of musketry and artillery," wrote Dr. Abram S. Miller of the 25th Virginia. The aggressive Johnson spotted an opportunity. Under the direction of 19-year-old Maj. Joseph W. Latimer, a pair of 3-inch rifles of Carpenter's battery under Lieutenant Lambie opened fire at long range, accelerating the Yankees' speed. James J. Hartley, a second lieutenant in Company K of the 122nd Ohio, wrote his wife that the Rebel guns fired "some pieces of railroad iron two feet long and spikes and everything that they thought they could do mischief with." The telltale puffs of white smoke followed a second or two later by the deep boom of cannon attracted the attention of Union gunners manning the Main Fort just west of Winchester, who opened a counter-battery fire. Lambie's crew suffered only light casualties in the ensuing exchange, but John M. Jones' Virginia brigade stationed behind them lost eight infantrymen.[84]

General Elliott's rallying position was Old Milltown, the complex of mills and outbuildings along Abram's Creek off the Valley Pike southwest of town. The marshy lowlands around the stream—along with stone fences, hedges, and the two-mile-long mill race—afforded strong protection. Milroy had wisely left infantry pickets in the trenches on Milltown Heights and now Elliott's beleaguered men were scrambling for

82 *Zanesville* (OH) *Courier,* July 22, 1863; Powell, "Shenandoah Valley," *National Tribune,* May 16, 1889; Rush, *Life and Writings,* 224. Powell mistakenly believed the second Union regiment was the 18th Connecticut.

83 Keifer, *Slavery and Four Years of War,* 2:9.

84 A. S. Miller to Dear Julia, June 16, 1863, Handley Regional Library; *OR* 27, pt. 2, 500; Wise, *The Long Arm of Lee,* 2:601. James J. Hartley and Garber A. Davidson, ed., *The Civil War Letters of the Late Lieut. James J. Hartley, 122nd Ohio Infantry Regiment* (Jefferson, NC: McFarland & Co., 1998), 42. Toward evening Latimer withdrew Carpenter's guns and placed them in a reserve park near the rest of Andrews' battalion leaving Lambie's section on the front line.

all they were worth across the broken terrain a half-mile or more to reach the position. The idea of spending time in a Dixie prison helped hurry them along.[85]

Immediately east of the Valley Pike, a willow-lined pond near Nathan Parkins' mill impeded the fleeing Federals. Just north of the pond, the pike bent to the northeast with a thick hedge fence lining its western side. On the heights behind this hedge, Captain Carlin's cannoneers loaded their quartet of 3-inch Ordnance Rifles and waited. They didn't wait long. Gordon's whooping and yelling infantry advanced, by now looking more like a dense mass than an ordered battle line. The Rebels crossed the pike a mile to the south and headed for the heavy woods beyond the 110th Ohio's right flank. Once he had a clear shot, Carlin opened at 800 yards. "The word 'fire' was given and crashing and crushing went grape and canister through the masses of men," recalled the 12th West Virginia's Lt. David Powell. "The cry of 'Oh Lord, Oh Lord, Oh Lord' came loud and plaintive, a full one-fourth of a mile away." At every explosion, the 110th Ohio's Lieutenant Rush could see men lifted literally into the air. Carlin's four guns each fired twice into the howling Rebels, halting their progress. The respite allowed Keifer's and Wilson's exhausted infantrymen to head for Milltown Heights to rejoin General Elliott's main body. By 4:30 p.m., nearly all of the Buckeyes had reassembled behind the mill race or on the heights. Their concentrated volley fire forced Gordon to retire.[86]

Confederate Captain Wiley Griffin repositioned his Baltimore battery on a knoll a few rods south of Abram's Creek east of the turnpike, and opened a raking, enfilading fire on the new Union defensive position. In response, Captain Carlin moved Lieutenant Theaker's section behind the millpond under the cover of a few old weeping willows. Martin's 1st Massachusetts Heavy Artillery in the Main Fort hurled counterbattery rounds at Griffin's guns. The third shot successfully "broke one of the brass cannon in two pieces," claimed Lieutenant Powell. "The remaining guns limbered up and fled to a more secure place . . . many thought the enemy was retiring."[87]

As the Federal guns pounded away, General Gordon's weary regiments reformed and went prone in the fields south of Abram's Creek to minimize their exposure. Jubal Early ordered Colonel Herbert's 2nd Maryland Battalion to swing around to Gordon's right to protect his flank. Herbert's young civilian guide, Robbie Barton, barely

---

85 OR 27, pt. 2, 44-45; Rush, *Life and Writings*, 225.

86 Powell, "Shenandoah Valley"; Shenandoah Valley Battlefields National Historic District, "Winchester at War"; Rush, *Life and Writings*, 226. This mill pond appears on an 1873 map, "Battlefield of Winchester, Va. (Opequon), Prepared by Bvt. Lt. Col. G. L. Gillespie, Major of Engineers," Library of Congress. It is just west of Paper Mill Road.

87 Rush, *Life and Writings*, 225-26; Powell, "Shenandoah Valley."

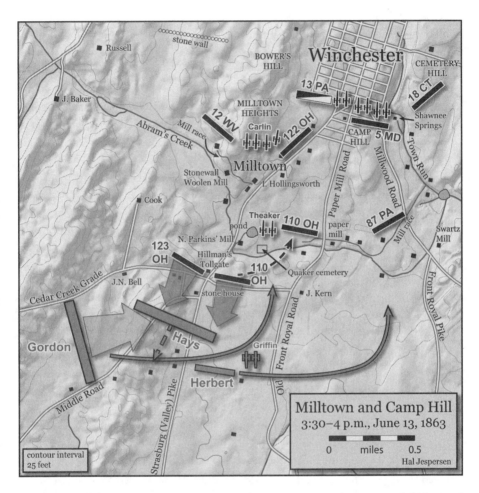

Milltown and Camp Hill
3:30–4 p.m., June 13, 1863

0   miles   0.5

Hal Jespersen

contour interval
25 feet

escaped death from a shell fired from the Main Fort as he rode across a field beyond Hillman's Tollgate.[88]

The repulse of Gordon's attack allowed Colonel Keifer to shift his 110th Ohio down into the valley and form a battle line just north of Abram's Creek. The Buckeyes were now only about 300 yards from a woodlot held by some of Gordon's advanced Georgians. Keifer sent Company E forward into an apple orchard as skirmishers with the right platoon protected by a low stone wall. Twigs and limbs rained upon the Buckeyes when enemy musketry raked their position. "The woods were literally alive with Confederates," recalled Lieutenant Rush, "and sharpshooters were behind

88 Early, *Autobiographical Sketch*, 243; Colt, *Defend the Valley*, 257; *Richmond Examiner*, July 4, 1863. Barton had been away for much of the day visiting his ailing father, who lived south of Kernstown. He had returned to Early's front lines just as the attack waned.

numerous scattering trees in the open pasture grounds to their point." One of these "saucy marksmen had ventured annoying close" to the skirmishers. So close, in fact, that Rush fired his revolver at him, clipping the bark from his sheltering tree and sending the Rebel running for his life. When another took his place and began taking aim at a mounted Ohio officer (perhaps Keifer). Rush ordered a marksman, George Search, to shoot him. Search fell with a wound, but soon returned to the ranks. Every man was needed as Milroy continued to move troops around to counter the serious threats closing in upon him that evening.[89]

Meanwhile, on Gordon's extreme left, the 31st Georgia's prone riflemen took note of increased activity at the distant Main Fort. According to Pvt. I. Gordon Bradwell, it was "one of the most splendid spectacles" he had ever witnesses. "The sally port was open and out of it rode squadron after squadron of well-mounted cavalry, with their shining swords drawn and other equipment reflecting the bright sunshine. They formed as if to occupy the entire width of the pike, intending to cut their way out by a sudden and overwhelming dash through our lines... The rattle of their steel scabbards, the clanking of their spurs, and the noise of the iron shoes of their horses as they struck the hard surface of the pike were awe-inspiring." The cavalrymen moved down the long slope toward the Rebels.[90]

In response, Colonel Stafford of the 9th Louisiana sent Company A forward 200-300 yards, where the Tigers crouched behind a low stone wall at an angle to the turnpike, ensuring a good field of fire. Captain Francis J. Montgomery walked up and down the line calmly remarking, "Now, boys, don't shoot until you hear the report of my pistol; then each man be sure he strips a saddle." However, when the unsuspecting enemy troopers rode within killing range Montgomery's men opened fire before he could give the signal. Private Bradwell of the 31st Georgia claimed the "few well directed shots" emptied half a dozen saddles. A few of the startled Yankee horsemen managed to return the fire and wound three Tigers, including Captain Montgomery whose serious leg injury later required amputation. According to Bradwell, the premature musketry drove the Federals back into the fort in a disorganized mass before the 31st Georgia could also open fire. "We were holding our guns in readiness for use at the proper time," Bradwell added, "but were disappointed by the too great haste of our Louisiana comrades."[91]

---

89 Rush, *Life and Writings*, 226-27.

90 Isaac G. Bradwell, "Second Winchester," *Confederate Veteran*, vol. 30, September 1922, 331.

91 Ibid.; Thomas Benton Reed, *A Private in Gray* (Camden, AR: s.n., 1902), 35-36. The other two casualties were Pvts. Saul D. Harrison and Manisco McGowen. After recovering, McGowen deserted and joined a Mississippi cavalry regiment.

Although Colonel Stafford did not identify this mounted enemy in his report, they may have been from the 12th Pennsylvania Cavalry. Major Titus Darius later said his regiment advanced on the Valley Pike to the vicinity of the mills and, from there, sent out skirmishers. They found Rebels in large force occupying the woods east of the road. Artillery fire soon supplanted the musketry when Federal guns shelled the woods. The Confederates fell back to a new position west of the roadway. One cavalryman was killed and two more wounded.[92]

Shortly after 5:00 p.m., some of the Louisiana Tigers advanced and captured a picket post, surrounded on three sides by a stone wall that commanded the Valley Pike. An hour later, Capt. Zebulon Baird and two companies of the 12th West Virginia dislodged Hays' forward picket line from behind the stone wall, capturing a prisoner who identified himself as a member of a Louisiana regiment. The information was relayed to Milroy, who correctly surmised that General Ewell's Second Corps and, incorrectly, that part of James Longstreet's First Corps were in the immediate vicinity. A deserter soon confirmed the men were indeed part of Ewell's command. This was Milroy's first solid information that a large part of General Lee's Army of Northern Virginia had slipped away from Fredericksburg and marched into and down the Valley all the way to Winchester. Ewell's Confederates were now in control of the roads south and southeast of Winchester. The Union garrison was in dire trouble.[93]

Meanwhile, the 87th Pennsylvania rested on Camp Hill until 6:00 p.m. when Col. John Schall received orders to report to Milroy on Bower's Hill with his regiment. The general directed Schall to march a mile south on the Valley Pike to confront some Rebel sharpshooters occupying one of Nathan Parkins' mills. The pesky Southern marksmen were firing at General Elliott's infantry line and Carlin's cannoneers up on Milltown Heights. After driving them off, Schall advanced his Pennsylvanians and encountered a line of enemy infantry. A brisk skirmish broke out and was maintained until the gathering darkness hid the enemy from view.[94]

By now it was about sunset. General Ewell rode over to the Valley Pike from his headquarters off of the Front Royal Road to meet with Jubal Early. Under a canopy of inky black thunderclouds, Early surveyed the formidable enemy positions on Milltown Heights through his field glasses and decided to call off

92 *OR* 27, pt. 2, 69.

93 Ibid., pt. 1, 1055; pt. 2, 45. Colonel Klunk of the 12th West Virginia reported losing one officer and six men killed, with sixteen wounded.

94 Prowell, *History of the 87th Pennsylvania*, 71; *Gettysburg Compiler*, June 27, 1893. After the firefight ended about 9:00 p.m., Milroy returned the 87th to Camp Hill, supporting Randolph's Battery L, 5th U. S.

further assaults. He had no suitable place for his guns to bombard the entrenchments without exposing them to a punishing cross-fire. Some of his infantrymen also took stock of the distant Yankees on the heights and in the Main Fort. "A brisk little skirmish drove the cowardly hounds back to their entrenchments, where they had been digging dirt for the last six months," the 5th Louisiana's Capt. Samuel H. Chisolm complained. "The hill held by them is a very high one and slopes off gradually, forming a beautiful plateau for several miles. They were strongly entrenched and had siege guns mounted, whose frowning mouths looked down on us in a threatening aspect. We could not bring our batteries to bear upon them at all."[95]

Minor skirmishing persisted in the dark woods and meadows flanking Abram's Creek (particularly west of the Valley Pike and extending almost to the Romney Road), but the main fighting was over for the day. Trigger-pulling activities finally "ceased on both sides as by mutual consent, until only once in five minutes could the crack of a rifle be heard," a 13th Pennsylvania cavalryman recalled. "The last shot was fired by some soldier who was so angry he did not want to stop." Jubal Early reformed Gordon's line across the Valley Pike near Hillman's Tollgate and moved the Louisiana Tigers to Gordon's left. General William "Extra Billy" Smith's Virginians took position off Hays' left flank. Early held Col. Isaac E. Avery's brigade in reserve to support any renewed advance, but soon ordered the North Carolinians back to Kernstown to guard the ambulances, ordnance wagons, and medical supply wagons and to protect his artillery from any Union flanking movement.[96]

Recriminations for being surprised that day started before the guns stopped firing at Winchester. Some of Milroy's men questioned why the War Department in Washington had not warned them that a large part of the Army of Northern Virginia was marching on Winchester. "All night…, the Confederates were so close to us we could hear them conversing and see them standing about their campfires cooking their supper," complained the 116th Ohio's Sgt.-Major James Dalzell, "while Hooker and Halleck and every newspaper writer north of the Potomac had no more knowledge of their whereabouts than if they were lost in the Sahara."[97]

General Elliott's exhausted troops on Milltown Heights celebrated their role in stopping the Rebels. Most of Milroy's staff, including aide-de-camp Capt. Fred A. Palmer, believed Ewell's twin attacks had failed. "Our forces had successfully engaged

95 Jones, *Campbell Brown's Diary*, 192; Rush, *Life and Writings*, 228; Samuel H. Chisolm to Capt. R. J. Chisolm, Winchester, Virginia, June 17, 1863, in "Forward the Louisiana Brigade," *Confederate Veteran*, vol. 27, December 1919, 449.

96 *Philadelphia Inquirer*, June 13, 1897; Early, *Autobiographical Sketch*, 243; *National Tribune*, December 18, 1884.

97 Dalzell, "A Lucky Blunder," 97.

them at all points," boasted Palmer. "They had everywhere been repulsed, and we were convinced that the worst was over, and that their attack on Winchester had proved a disastrous failure." Milroy shared this optimistic view. Charles Lynch of the 18th Connecticut, however, would have none of it. "The sudden appearance of so large a force was a surprise," he admitted. "It was plainly seen that a large force of Confederates were surrounding the town and that we were in a bad fix, as we could see the gray in all directions and knew that we were more than outnumbered."[98]

The doubters included at least two of Milroy's key subordinates. "It was now obvious Milroy's command could not hold Winchester," admitted the 110th Ohio's Colonel J. Warren Keifer. He assumed that Milroy would undertake a retreat during the night, but the commanding general said nothing of the sort to Keifer or General Elliott during a brief conversation that night. Keifer, still smarting over a rebuke from Milroy the previous evening, decided "to make no further suggestions to him with respect to his duty in this emergency." Elliott and Keifer sullenly rode back to Keifer's campsite on the heights northwest of Winchester. Elliott mentioned that he thought it was too late to retreat to Harpers Ferry. Keifer suggested that the Romney, Pughtown, and Apple Pie Ridge or Back Creek roads were still open, and that the division would be able to retire safely over one or more of them. Elliott agreed to call Milroy's attention to the suggestion, but, according to the Buckeye colonel, "if he did the suggestion was not favorably considered."[99]

It was about 9:00 p.m., when some Union troops were celebrating while others were less enthusiastic about their long-term prospects, that telegraphic communication with the outside world ceased. With the lines down, rumors spread in Winchester that Union Col. James A. Mulligan was advancing from Cumberland, Maryland, with a relief force. Milroy believed the rumor and dispatched Company F of the 13th Pennsylvania Cavalry north toward Bunker Hill to escort Mulligan's men into Winchester. Instead of meeting a relief column, the Irish Dragoons encountered some of Albert Jenkins' Rebel cavalry. "We realized then that Lee's army was around us," was how Pvt. R. H. McElhinny explained the depressing news.[100]

---

98 OR 27, pt. 2, 54; Charles H. Lynch, *The Civil War Diary, 1862–1865, of Charles H. Lynch, 18th Conn. Vol's* (Hartford, CT: Case, Lockwood and Brainard, 1915), 19.

99 Keifer, *Slavery and Four Years of War*, 2:10.

100 OR 27, pt. 2, 174; McElhinny, "Milroy at Winchester." Colonel Mulligan of the 23rd Illinois commanded the garrison in Cumberland. However, his men were not en route to relieve Milroy's beleaguered men. Ironically, Mulligan was mortally wounded in 1864 south of Winchester at Second Kernstown. The antebellum Chicago attorney died two days later in the Pritchard house. His pregnant wife Marian hastened from their temporary Cumberland home to Winchester, but arrived after Mulligan expired. (Kernstown Battlefield Preservation Society).

As night deepened, the long-threatened thunderstorm unleashed itself in full fury. "Continuous were the torrents, and the roar was unbroken and sublime," recalled the 110th Ohio's Lt. Henry Rush. "Hungry, drenched, weary—blind even to the armed soldier at one's side, and deaf to all sounds save echoing thunder and emptying clouds, we stood in ignorance of where and how we might pass the night." Rush claimed that almost simultaneously with the storm came the rockets—a series of signals sent arcing high into the sky by the Rebels.[101]

Across the fields, Early's and Johnson's soldiers settled down as best as they could. The idea of being defeated was not something that had crossed their minds. In fact, they fully expected the hostilities to renew in the morning. Relief parties set out in the inky darkness to collect the rain-soaked wounded. Several compassionate Kernstown residents opened their doors as temporary field hospitals. About 40 Georgians received treatment in Grandma Kern's orchard, lying in tents or out in the open with only a canopy of fruit trees above them. Another 20 injured soldiers quartered in Rebecca Hoover's home, where one severely wounded Rebel awaited death on her porch.[102]

The 21st North Carolina, part of Robert Hoke's brigade now under the command of Colonel Avery, had taken position around Kernstown to protect Early's wagon trains and reserve artillery. Its commander, Col. William W. Kirkland, an antebellum U. S. marine lieutenant, formed a heavy picket line on the outskirts of the village. The rest of the Tar Heels turned in for the night, sleeping with their weapons handy in case of trouble. To the northeast along the Front Royal Road, "Allegheny" Johnson took similar precautions and detailed troops to guard his division's supplies. Out on the front lines close to Winchester, pickets kept a sharp eye for any signs of Federal movement.[103]

Marcus Blakemore Buck, who the previous day had watched Ewell's powerful columns traipse past his prosperous estate near Front Royal, had then predicted that General Milroy "will soon be made to feel the vengeance of an outraged people, if he is still there." The heavy cannonading emanating from the vicinity of Kernstown

---

101 Rush, *Life and Writings*, 227. Accounts vary as to when the violent thunderstorm struck, but most suggest about 9:00 p.m.

102 Sarah and John Steele diary entry for June 14, 1863, in Quarles, *Diaries, Letters, and Recollections*, 3:76.

103 June 10, 1863, Field Return of Hoke's Brigade, Box 2, Jubal A. Early papers 1861-1865, Entry 118, RG 109, NARA. Kirkland had been shot in both thighs in the 1862 battle of Winchester, knocking him out of action for several months. After his recovery, he was Chief of Staff for Gen. Patrick Cleburne during the Murfreesboro campaign in Tennessee before returning to the 21st North Carolina early in 1863.

throughout June 13 had confirmed that Milroy and his hated Yankee invaders had not flown the coop. Buck, the uncle of noted pro-Confederate diarist Lucy Buck, ventured northward to see the sights. "I witnessed this evening some of the horrors of the battlefield, than I have yet done," he noted in his diary that night. "A good many killed and wounded brought out to Kernstown." Buck stayed nearby, hoping he could help quell the suffering of the wounded.[104]

It was not until long after dark that General Ewell returned to his headquarters, "in the midst of as hard a rain as I remember," was how his stepson and staff officer Maj. Campbell Brown put it. The two of them slept underneath his carriage that night, meager quarters for the commander of one of Lee's corps. The day's results buoyed Ewell's confidence as it did the morale of his men. Many expected to take Winchester on the morrow despite the heavy enemy presence on the heights south of town and the imposing forts. "Milroy is supposed to have between five and eight thousand troops there," Pvt. John Henry Vest of the 2nd Richmond Howitzers penned. "The place is well fortified on all sides but we are confident of success."[105]

The reaction of Winchester's residents to the day's surprising events ranged from glee within the ardent secessionist community to outright apprehension among the Unionists. Lawson, the correspondent for the *Richmond Whig*, was still under the weather and still in town. "By night, the Yankees had been driven in on all sides," he reported, "and we then felt certain that our deliverers had come in sufficient force, and that the town was indeed invested on all sides." His optimistic sentiment was shared by many pro-Confederate observers in and around Winchester that evening.[106]

General Milroy, penned Mary Greenhow Lee in her diary, "says he will see the town streaming with blood from one end to the other before he will give it up." "We did not go out to class this evening," wrote young Gettie Miller, "I did not get my lessons." She had watched the passing Yankees almost all day and thought they looked scared, a thought which made her happy. "I don't believe our men are coming in, I expect," she added with a slight touch of gloom. "I would have to cry [from] Joy if they would."[107]

104 Buck diary, entry for June 13, 1863.

105 Jones, *Campbell Brown's Diary*, 192; Diary entry for June 13, 1863, John Henry Vest Diary, Soldiers Diaries Collection, Museum of the Confederacy, Richmond. Vest was killed in action on October 19.

106 Reprinted in the *Raleigh Weekly State Journal*, July 2, 1863.

107 Mary Lee and Gettie Miller diary entries for June 13, 1863. Mrs. Lee (1819-1907), a widow since 1856, lived in a house on Market Street (now Cameron Street). She was a daughter of Robert Greenhow, a past mayor of Richmond and Virginia assemblyman.

With the telegraph cut and reports of Rebels from several directions, the initially confident Milroy finally began to realize that he did not have enough infantry to withstand a determined attack and his front was too long to hold. He began drawing his scattered commands closer to Winchester to shorten his front and man better ground. With Rebels reportedly advancing from Berryville, he redeployed the 18th Connecticut in the lower portion of the crescent-shaped line of rifle-pits between the Berryville Road and Martinsburg Pike, with the regiment's right stretching southward across Cemetery Hill. The men lacked blankets or shelter of any kind, and "were anything but comfortable," Chaplain William Walker recorded. "The emotions of the men during that scene can better be imagined than described. There was but little sleep if any that night, as the boys stood upright, the water streaming down their backs to their feet, and filling the trenches several inches deep, causing much discomfort if not actual suffering." "We were wet through," confirmed Pvt. Charles Lynch. "Not allowed fires as it might draw the enemy's fire." After midnight, the men of Company K were wet and cold enough to ignore orders and built a large bonfire to boil their coffee and warm their chilled bodies. Their efforts yielded but little success, at least initially, but they finally got enough of a fire going so that "we got dry in a measure," recalled Pvt. James M. Smith. He and his comrades tried to catch some much needed sleep, to little avail.[108]

Once the fighting ended, observed a 13th Pennsylvania cavalryman, "came the worst part of it all, a night on the battlefield. Even in our camp we could hear the cries of the men dying on the ground, where we dare not go to assist them." Milroy's medical officers dispatched search parties to locate any wounded close enough to save. "Here some men were yelling for water, others wanted food, others were calling for their wives, mothers and children, while others were calling upon their God," the trooper added. "Then the man who had his passions worked up to madness during the engagement became cool and calm. He saw his old comrades, perhaps his tent mate, lying cold in death or suffering mortal agonies from a wound of shot or shell."[109]

Several injured men crawled into the underbrush in an effort to find shelter. The 123rd Ohio's Cpl. George Buskirk and two mortally wounded comrades had been left behind when Colonel Wilson retreated that afternoon. One man soon died, but the 21-year-old Buskirk, badly shot in his right calf muscle, and his friend who had been shot in the bowels decided to try to reach a house about half a mile across the fields. Together they hobbled along as torrents of rain washed down upon them. Before

---

108 Walker, *History of the Eighteenth Regiment*, 108; James M. Smith diary entry for June 13, 1863, Winchester, Virginia.

109 *Philadelphia Inquirer*, June 13, 1897.

long, however, the friend had grown too weak to help Buskirk, so he staggered on alone. Buskirk crawled along on his own until he reached an eight-rail wooden fence. Somehow he managed to remove the top rail, but tumbled over it and landed in a ditch full of muddy water. The determined Buckeye private pulled himself out of the muck and crawled through the night until he finally arrived at the house about daylight—wet, muddy, and chilled to the marrow. Once inside he found his wounded friend, who was now close to death. The homeowner, an old black man, rendered what little assistance he could provide.[110]

The plight of the wounded touched the heart of the 5th Maryland's Dr. Charles Goldsborough. He and Assistant Surgeon H. Lindsley Pierce took an ambulance and some stewards to find them and bring them out of the rain. They were moving out the Front Royal Road when they encountered some cavalrymen who challenged, "Who come there?" When Goldsborough replied, "Medical Corps," the riders let them pass. A flash of lightning revealed they were Confederates. The doctors hastily turned to the east and passed between the picket lines. They reached the Berryville Road guided only by lightning flashes, where they turned to the left and headed back toward Winchester. As they neared the outskirts of town, several pickets hailed them. To Dr. Goldsborough's relief the men belonged to Capt. John Sachs' company—part of the doctor's own 5th Maryland. The exhausted Goldsborough uttered the password and Sachs gave the proper countersign, "New Orleans." Goldsborough and his small party returned to the Methodist church and fell asleep on the cold pews.[111]

While Dr. Goldsborough was on his mission of mercy, his brother William's 2nd Maryland Confederate skirmishers were slowly advancing in two lines through "impenetrable darkness" to within 600 yards of Winchester, just south of Isaac Hollingsworth's mill off of Millwood Pike. Major Goldsborough soon recalled his pickets and sheltered some of his men in a deserted barn. The rest remained exposed to the elements. J. William Thomas, his friend George Edelen, and several other comrades bivouacked on the north side of the road, where Thomas and Edelen covered themselves with the latter's shawl. "But soon the water came through in streams," Thomas complained. "Nevertheless we fell asleep and did not wake till morning, when I felt refreshed." When the rain finally stopped sometime before dawn, Thomas's body heat dried his clothes enough so that they were only damp by sunrise. Despite the miserable weather, the Marylanders rejoiced in their success.

---

110 Buskirk obituary, *Bryan* (OH) *News*, June 2, 1904. Buskirk's mother died of cholera when he was very young and his father was a soldier in the Mexican War and then a pioneer in the Washington Territory, so his maternal grandmother raised him. He left his farm, wife, son, and adopted daughter to join the army in August 1862.

111 *Gettysburg Compiler*, April 2, 1902.

"Today we had quite an engagement & we were quite fortunate having lost but 4 men," Lt. John H. Stone penned in his diary.[112]

The rain-soaked troopers of the 12th and 13th Pennsylvania Cavalry remained patiently in line of battle south of town keeping a wary eye out for any sign of Rebels. About midnight they received orders to return to their respective camps. The 12th mounted their horses and trotted to their base along the Martinsburg Pike near Fort Collier and Red Bud Creek. Once there, they packed almost everything except for their tents and relocated to a new position along the Pughtown Road a mile west of the Main Fort near the West Fort.[113]

The heavy bolts of lightning and deep rumbling were long recalled by the men who watched the sky's fireworks. "There came one long peal of thunder which was the most terrible of any I have heard since or before," wrote a trooper riding with the 13th Pennsylvania Cavalry. "The earth seemed to tremble and my horse, which was a half-broken colt, became terror-stricken. He leaped and galloped so that by the time I regained control over him I was outside the camp, and for all intents and purposes, lost." The forlorn cavalryman wandered around aimlessly in the pouring rain until he heard the command to move. He had fortunately located his regiment and accompanied them to the east of Winchester, where he and his comrades spent a sleepless night near Cemetery Hill.[114]

Late in the night, Capt. Murray S. Cross came into the Union lines with a bedraggled detachment of the 87th Pennsylvania. They had walked all the way from White Post (about 11 miles southeast of Winchester) where they had been reconnoitering the roads. Cross had heard the Main Fort's four-gun signal to withdraw to Winchester. Somehow he had avoided the roving Rebel patrols to lead his rain-soaked soldiers safely through the darkness to rejoin the regiment.[115]

By 2:00 a.m., Milroy was concentrating his forces inside a triangle loosely defined by the Main Fort west of town, the Star Fort to its immediate north, and the West Fort off to the west of the Star Fort. The general did so as quietly as possible, withdrawing

---

112 Goldsborough, *The Maryland Line*, 94; *Richmond Whig*, June 23, 1863; Thomas diary, entry for June 13, 1863; Thomas G. Clemens, ed., "The Diary of John S. Stone, First Lieutenant, Company B, 2nd Maryland Infantry, CSA," in *Maryland Historical Magazine*, vol. 85 (1990), 109-143. Lieutenant S. T. McCullough reported that his men of Company D slept in an "old and dilapidated church."

113 *OR* 27, pt. 2, 69-70.

114 *Philadelphia Inquirer*, June 13, 1897.

115 *Gettysburg Compiler*, June 27, 1893. Cross likely used the Millwood Pike for most of his route and then managed to keep away from Johnson's division which controlled that road closer to Winchester.

his artillery and most of his infantry, but leaving skirmishers to confront Ewell and help cover the movement. The bad weather helped shield the maneuver from Confederate eyes. Milroy kept the 122nd Ohio in its camp despite earlier having ordered the Buckeyes to pack everything onto wagons. He forbade campfires in the new positions to avoid tipping off the Rebels. Milroy believed he could withstand renewed Confederate assaults for 24 hours until relieved by the Army of the Potomac. For many, the march was miserable. "Had a taste of 'Virginia mud' which is quite deep," complained Pvt. James M. Smith of the 18th Connecticut. The regiment halted at the foot of the ridge below the Main Fort and remained there until daylight.[116]

Meanwhile, the soldiers of the 123rd Ohio rued their losses in their first taste of real combat. Few had ever seen a man be killed or maimed by the hand of another. The relentless downpour, flashing lightning, and dark night added to their misery. The Buckeyes pulled back into downtown Winchester, where they stood in formation on a dirty street. They were tired, hungry, wet and disheartened over the loss of comrades and their defeat. About 2:00 a.m., Colonel Wilson received orders to return to camp, pack the baggage and supplies, and proceed to the fortifications surrounding the Main Fort. He and his weary infantrymen did not arrive there until almost dawn. It had been a long day and an even longer night for Milroy's beleaguered division. Much worse was yet to come.[117]

---

116 OR 27, pt. 2, 45, 58; *Zanesville* (OH) *Courier*, July 22, 1863; James M. Smith diary entry for June 14, 1863.

117 Clapp, "With Milroy at Winchester"; *Norwalk* (OH) *Reflector*, December 22, 1863.

Chapter 5

Saturday, June 13, Part II

"Our coming was as a thunderbolt from a cloudless sky."

— *Captain John C. Gorman, 2nd North Carolina*

The early morning of June 13 was a busy one for Lieutenant General Ewell's Second Corps. While two-thirds of his veteran infantry under Maj. Gens. Jubal Early and Edward Johnson tramped their way toward the important city of Winchester from the south and pushed back General Robert Milroy's Union garrison closer toward town, Ewell's remaining division under Maj. Gen. Robert E. Rodes marched on Berryville, the seat of Clarke County, about eleven miles east of Winchester. "My division was ordered to take the Berryville road, via Millwood, to attack and seize Berryville," Rodes wrote in his report, "then to advance without delay on Martinsburg, and thence proceed to Maryland, there to await further orders; this while the other two divisions of the corps reduced Winchester."[1]

Berryville, a small hamlet at the intersection of the Charles Town Road and the Winchester-Snickersville Turnpike, was founded in the late 1700s. The land originally belonged to Lord Thomas Fairfax, who in 1750 hired George Washington to survey his five-million-acre estate. The village was initially called Battle Town, a name sometimes attributed to frontiersman Daniel Morgan and his frequent brawls with young toughs at the intersection, but more likely the result of a nearby rowdy tavern. After the American Revolution, Benjamin Berry bought a portion of the tract

---

1 Clarke County Historical Association, Berryville, VA. For more on the Confederate movement upon Berryville, see Robert J. Wynstra, *The Rashness of That Hour: Politics, Gettysburg, and the Downfall of Confederate Brigadier General Alfred Iverson* (El Dorado Hills, CA: Savas Beatie, 2010), 149.

including 20 acres around the site of the former crossroads tavern. He established a town there in January 1798. The early settlers, a mix of Scots-Irish and Germans, included a number of slave owners. By 1860, Berryville had swelled to almost 500 people and boasted a variety of shops and small businesses. Towering over the intersection was the 100-foot steeple of Grace Episcopal Church.

Most Berryville residents' sympathies were decidedly in favor of the Confederacy. The previous October, Jeb Stuart's Rebel cavalry had camped outside Berryville. The day was cold and rainy, and General Stuart and his staff, including Prussian-born aide Maj. Heros von Borcke, dined that evening with a prominent resident who provided "a warm cup of tea, a capital old Virginia ham, and afterward a pipe of Virginia tobacco before a roaring wood fire."[2]

In March 1863, Federal troops had occupied the town, much to the chagrin of most of its citizens. Milroy had advanced Col. Andrew T. McReynolds' brigade as a forward outpost, primarily to keep watch on the important mountain passes to the east, as well as Snicker's and Berry's fords on the Shenandoah River. McReynolds was also tasked with keeping the lines of communication open with Harpers Ferry. "It was a fertile and pleasant region, a land of fine farms and intelligent people," wrote Lt. William Beach of the 1st New York Cavalry. "It was full of places of historic interest. We enjoyed it."[3]

The commander holding this critical post was born on Christmas Day in 1808 in Tyrone County, Ireland. McReynolds immigrated to America in 1830 and settled three years later in Detroit, Michigan, where he eventually became an attorney. With the outbreak of the Mexican War he recruited a company of the 3rd U. S. Dragoons and became its captain. McReynolds received an honorary brevet promotion to major for gallantry in action, returned to his legal practice after the war, and moved to Grand Rapids, Michigan, in 1859. At the start of the Civil War, the Irishman received an appointment directly from President Lincoln as colonel of a regiment he raised in New York City. This resulted in the unit being popularly referred to as the "Lincoln Cavalry," or more formally, the 1st New York Cavalry.[4]

---

2   Heros von Borcke, *Memoirs of the Confederate War for Independence: A Prussian Officer with J.E.B. Stuart in Virginia* (Edinburgh, Scotland: W. Blackwood & Sons, 1866; reprint, Nashville: J. W. Sanders & Co., 1999), 227-28. Snickers' Gap was on the main east-west road into Berryville. To the south was Ashby's Gap. Both were possible routes into the Lower Valley for Rebel raiders.

3   Lt. William H. Beach, "Some Reminiscences of the First New York (Lincoln) Cavalry," in *War Papers Read Before the Commandery of the State of Wisconsin, Military Order of the Loyal Legion of the United States* (Milwaukee: Burdick, Armitage, & Allen, 1896), 2:283.

4   Albert Baxter, *History of the City of Grand Rapids, Michigan* (New York and Grand Rapids, Munsell & Company, 1891), Chapter 52.

A war-time sketch of Berryville by artist James E. Taylor. *Western Reserve Historical Society*

McReynolds' mixed command consisted of his own cavalry regiment, Col. John F. Staunton's 67th Pennsylvania Infantry, Col. John W. Horn's 6th Maryland Infantry, and Capt. Frederick W. Alexander's six-gun Baltimore battery. The latter outfit arrived at Berryville on April 27 and relieved two sections of Battery B, 1st West Virginia. Also in the Berryville area was Company F of the 2nd Potomac Home Brigade, an independent mounted infantry unit under Capt. George D. "Dent" Summers. Elements of Maj. Henry D. Cole's 1st Potomac Home Brigade Cavalry consisting of loyal Maryland men also helped patrol the roads in the region. McReynolds's Federals received a chilly reception from Berryville's residents. Sporadic Rebel raids—including a bold dash on the night of Wednesday, April 8, when three members of the 12th Virginia Cavalry assaulted a forward observation post and seized two Yankees and five horses, complete with saddles and trappings—kept the pickets on edge.[5]

A mile closer to Berryville was an outpost manned by Company I of the 12th West Virginia Infantry, on temporary assignment from its usual Winchester

5 William L. Wilson and Festus P. Summers, ed., *A Borderland Confederate* (Pittsburgh: University of Pittsburgh Press, 1962); L. Allison Wilmer, J. H. Jarrett, and George W. F. Vernon, *History and Roster of Maryland Volunteers, War of 1861-5*, (Baltimore: Press of Guggenheim, Weil & Co., 1898), 1:816; Jack Sanders, *Guarding the River, the Canal, and the Railroad: Papers of Captain Benjamin Brubridge Shaw, Commanding Officer, 2nd Regiment, Potomac Home Brigade, Maryland Volunteers* (New Creek, WV: J. Sanders, 1998). Lt. Milton Rouss, who led the Rebel raiders, was captured at Brandy Station on June 9.

Col. John W. Horn, commander of the 6th Maryland Infantry. *Library of Congress*

encampment. There, Sergeant Milton Campbell heard the distant firing as the Rebels attacked the observation post. The next morning, Campbell and his comrades were astonished when the two captured Yankee cavalrymen, minus their weapons and horses, walked into their outpost. The Rebels "told them they did not want them, and that they might return to camp. . . . I thought it very kind of the rebs to let them return," admitted Campbell. The main body of Rebel cavalry, camped some 25 miles to the south, had sent "these small squads out just to capture our cavalry pickets for their horses." Reports a couple of days later filtered in that a major Confederate advance was afoot, but Sergeant Campbell thought it "nothing but a false alarm. We look for such alarms," he wrote his sister, "some scouts get scared and come in and report an enemy advancing on us, when they have seen nothing at all. You need not believe any reports you hear," he assured her. "I know there are some tall stories written home from camp, most of them without any foundation whatever. We all feel as safe here as we would in New Cumberland [his hometown in Hancock County, West Virginia] for we know there is not more than two or three thousand rebels in this valley. We have that number here, and can have fifteen thousand more in two hours, such is the position we are now in, and you need not fear at all of our being attacked."[6]

While there were few Confederates operating in the Valley in April, it was not quite as safe as Campbell related to his sister. "You say in your letter that you hear the government wont trust the Maryland troops in the field," the 6th Maryland's Pvt. James F. Stepter penned. "The next person that you hear say so, tell them it is a damned lie. I am a Marylander myself and not ashamed of it and belong to a Maryland regiment and when our regiment does get into a battle it will do its part and we won't shoot our own men like the Pennsylvania 67th has done to the first New York Cavalry. They killed and wounded seven of them," he admitted. "I helped bring them across

6 Milton Campbell to Dear sister, April 13, 1863, in Fluharty, *Civil War Letters of Lt. Milton B. Campbell*, 37.

the river."[7] The friendly fire incident took place on May 6 near Upperville, Virginia, during what was supposed to be an ambush of Confederate Maj. John S. Mosby's men. The men of the 67th fired prematurely when they mistook oncoming New Yorkers for Mosby's Virginians. "This was the most criminal and inexcusable blunder that I ever heard of," exclaimed one of the cavalrymen. When the approaching Mosby heard the gunfire, he halted his raiders in time to lose only one man wounded in the aborted ambuscade.[8]

The excitement of the occasional enemy raids was a rare exception to the mind-numbing monotony of garrison duty. Prolonged boredom and a sense that Berryville was isolated in the war's backwaters plagued McReynolds' men. "The boys are beginning to make some fortifications near this place and I wish we would be drove away before tomorrow night because there is no use in such work that I can see and if we would move on to where we would have something to do it would be better," the 67th Pennsylvania's Pvt. Robert F. Templeton complained to his mother in a letter home on May 24. "I think there is very little danger of any rebels except bushwhackers coming here," he continued, "and this is the way that the war has been carried on all the time."[9] Some, however, thought their duty rather stimulating. "Scouting was continual and often exciting," claimed Lt. William H. Beach of the 1st New York Cavalry. "So desirous were the men to go on these scouts that they would ask, days beforehand, to be detailed on the next scout ordered." All of this changed by the second week of June, when "unusual activity" was uncovered, "and we were on the alert," wrote Beach.[10]

To prepare his men, many of whom had never experienced combat, McReynolds intensified drills. "It looks very much like the heads of this Brigade expect a fight soon," the Baltimore Battery's Pvt. William H. Moffett, Jr. observed. "We had an imaginary battle a few nights ago. We all was sleeping soundly (except the camp guard) in camp when the long roll startled us from our slumber. Which means turn out and face in line with guns & accoutrements which was done. I am glad to say without any

7   James F. Stepter letter, May 27, 1862 [incorrectly dated; the regiment first entered service in the fall of 1862 and did not arrive in Berryville until 1863], Berryville, Va., private collection. More than 20 of Stepter's other Civil War letters are in the collection of the University of Maryland. Captured at Stephenson's Depot on June 15, he died of disease in October 1864 in a prison in Richmond. He left a widow Amanda and three children. (Widow's Pension Claims, Mrs. James F. Stepter, NARA).

8   Jeffry D. Wert, *Mosby's Rangers* (New York: Simon & Shuster, 1991), 61.

9   Robert F. Templeton to Dear Mother, May 24, 1863, The Civil War Letters of Robert F. Templeton, Special Collections, Indiana University of Pennsylvania, Indiana, PA.

10 Beach, "Some Reminiscences of the First New York (Lincoln) Cavalry," 2:283.

confusion as it was reported that the Rebs in strong force was approaching and had but ½ hour march and be in sight." It turned out some guerillas had fired into some pickets of the 12th Pennsylvania Cavalry, "who got frighten[ed] and made for Headquarters and reported the whole Rebel Army was on us. We was under arms the whole night waiting for the Rebs," continued Moffett. "Not until daylight was the truth known."[11]

Colonel McReynolds believed he had sufficient troops to deter any Confederate raiding party, but he realized his men would not be able to withstand a large force of Rebels like that rumored to be approaching. In an effort to prepare against any contingency, he had his troops construct, and then strengthen, a line of low entrenchments and rifle pits along the major approaches to Berryville. Several residents later filed damage claims with the Federal government asking for compensation for personal property taken by McReynolds' men. A farmer named William F. Stolle requested $6 for 150 hickory boards which Captain Alexander used in the fortifications. The unfortunate Stolle, who had been victimized in March 1862 during the last significant Federal occupation of Berryville, also reported that Capt. John J. Bradshaw of the 6th Maryland appropriated his wagon (worth $175) and harness ($20). His horse ended up in the possession of the 1st New York Cavalry.[12]

On Friday, June 12, when the 67th Pennsylvania's Colonel Staunton rode from Winchester into Berryville to report that Rebels were indeed moving north down the Valley in strength, McReynolds and his subordinates began preparing to evacuate if they heard the signal guns from the Main Fort 11 miles west at Winchester. Colonel McReynolds sent an orderly to relay the news to Captain Alexander of the Baltimore Battery. The unfortunate courier galloped into a wire clothes line that swept him from his horse and temporarily stunned him. Once he regained his senses, he withdrew the message from under his belt and handed it to Alexander. The battery, explained McReynolds, was to be ready to move out at a moment's notice if so ordered. The Maryland cannoneers packed their knapsacks, but left their tents standing. They also kept their horses harnessed through the night, feeding them from nose bags and carrying water to them instead of leading them to a nearby stream as usual.[13]

That night, "We received orders to pack and be ready at a moment's notice for a move," Pvt. Henry Suydam of the Lincoln Cavalry wrote. Once finished, the troopers

11 W. H. Moffett to Dear Father, June 3, 1863, Berryville, Va., Maryland Historical Society.

12 Union Provost Marshals' File of Papers Relating to Individual Civilians, Publication M-345.

13 Frederick W. Wild, *Memoirs and History of Capt. F. W. Alexander's Baltimore Battery of Light Artillery, U. S. V.* (Loch Raven, MD: Press of the Maryland School for Boys, 1912), 51; *OR 27*, pt. 2, 87.

lay down to sleep with their arms within ready reach.[14] The quartermasters and their supports had more to do and so got little if any sleep. "I was up all night packing up the commissary goods," explained Pvt. William H. Moffett Jr., "as there was a report 15,000 Rebels advancing on Berryville. We were ready to move at a moment's notice."[15]

Earlier that day, McReynolds had sent 30 enlisted men and two lieutenants of the 6th Maryland to escort a wagon train from Berryville to Harpers Ferry to gather supplies. The wagon train arrived in Harpers Ferry, where work crews loaded the railcars. After starting back for Berryville, the wagons made it as far as Halltown, where the men bivouacked for the night. The men set out with the wagons early on the morning of June 13, blissfully unaware they were rolling directly into trouble.[16]

In Berryville that same Saturday morning, McReynolds' soldiers awoke in their canvas-walled Sibley tents, in full readiness to move if the guns in Main Fort opened fire. The gunners providing McReynolds' artillery support, the Baltimore Battery, had pots on their fires with beans half-cooked when he ordered them to move two guns into the breastworks on the high ground flanking the outskirts of the village. McReynolds also began evacuating the civilians. Early in the morning, a four-seated vehicle passed through the artillery camp on its way north to Harpers Ferry. The passengers included a gentleman escorting two officers' wives who had been visiting their husbands.[17]

The Maryland and Pennsylvania infantry had spent a restless night sleeping on their arms, uncertain what daylight would bring. The arrival of dawn arrived and they solemnly filed into the light works. Many of the men had not experienced significant combat, and their nerves were on edge with the prospect of a pitched fight with General Lee's veteran infantry and artillery. The pickets scanned the horizon for any enemy activity while reconnaissance patrols and individual scouts searched the nearby roads, paying particular attention to the Charles Town Road south of town. Thus far, there was no enemy to be seen. Perhaps the approaching gray storm would strike elsewhere.[18]

---

14 Daniel P. Black, ed., *A Lincoln Cavalryman: The Civil War Letters of Henry Suydam, 1st New York Lincoln Cavalry* (Hampstead, MD: Old Line Publishing, 2011), 126.

15 W. H. Moffett to Dear Father, June 16, 1863, Maryland Heights, Md., Maryland Historical Society.

16 William J. Grant, "Letter from Lieut. W. J. Grant," *The Cecil Whig*, June 27, 1863.

17 Wild, *History of Capt. F. W. Alexander's Battery*, 51.

18 Harry L. White to Judge Thomas White, June 12, 1863, Berryville, Va., White Collection, Historical and Genealogical Society of Indiana County, Pa.

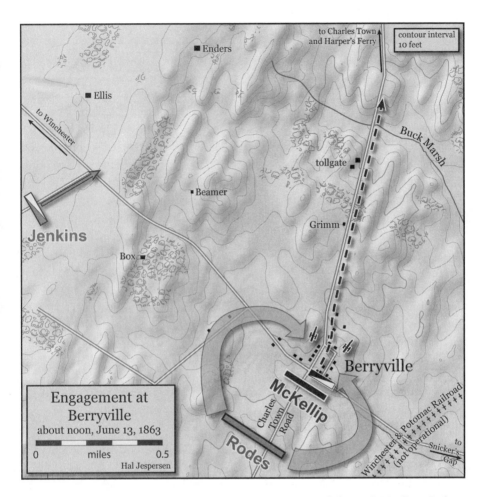

Engagement at
Berryville
about noon, June 13, 1863

0   miles   0.5

Hal Jespersen

Unbeknownst to the Berryville Union garrison, Confederate Maj. Gen. Robert Rodes had marched his veteran infantry division past the Double Tollgate, and was now moving in the morning sunshine through the verdant rolling countryside past the sprawling "Page Brook" plantation in rural Clarke County.[19] The scenery was spectacular and the region as of yet unspoiled by the hard and cruel hand of war. "On one side there was one of the richest meadows I have ever seen, covered with the most luxuriant hay grass of some kind, & running through it were 2 rows of weeping willows—the largest and most flourishing I ever saw," marveled Pvt. Samuel Pickens

19 Gold, *History of Clarke County, Virginia*, 113.

of the 5th Alabama Infantry. "[T]hey must swim in milk and butter all thro' this country."[20]

The mood was light and the pace steady until about 9:00 a.m., when a roving Union cavalry patrol discovered Rodes' vanguard as it approached the village of Millwood seven miles southwest of Berryville. A blue courier galloped back to McReynolds, who took pains to protect his baggage and stores. Quartermaster Lt. William H. Boyd Jr. and Commissary Frank McReynolds organized 42 brigade and regimental supply wagons into a lengthy train that was soon rolling its way north toward Bunker Hill. Lieutenant Franklin G. Martindale's Company H of the 1st New York Cavalry escorted the wagons once the loudly swearing teamsters finally got the procession underway. "About 9 o'clock our company was falling in expecting an attack," George W. Hamilton of the 6th Maryland nervously recorded in his diary.[21]

Rodes sent Albert Jenkins' brigade ahead to engage the Federals, although the cavalryman's persistent dawdling and failure to secure Millwood the previous night annoyed him. Rodes was concerned that the main body of Yankees might flee Berryville. He pushed his division with "the utmost celerity," hoping to get there in time to capture the enemy. Startled residents poured from their houses or peered out windows at the unexpected sight of thousands of Confederate infantrymen tramping rapidly through their hamlet. "They soon came thick and fast," observed Matella Page Harrison. "I ran down through the woods to feast my eyes and oh what a joyful array." One of Rodes' men told Harrison that Edward Johnson and Jubal Early were also marching on Winchester, and there was no escape for Milroy. It was, exclaimed Matella, "one of the brightest days of my life."[22]

As the Rebels comprising Brig. Gen. Stephen D. Ramseur's brigade tramped through Millwood, they learned enemy cavalry was less than one hour ahead of them. When the head of Rodes' division marched within seven miles of the town, evidence

---

20 Samuel Pickens diary entry for June 13, 1863, in G. Ward Hubbs, ed. *Voices From Company D: Diaries by the Greensboro Guards, Fifth Alabama Infantry Regiment, Army of Northern Virginia* (Athens: University of Georgia Press, 2003), 177.

21 OR 27, pt. 2, 442, 548; Thomas, *History of the Doles-Cook Brigade*, 6; Steve French, "Federals on 'Safe' Road to Trouble," *Washington Times*, Dec. 2, 2005. Berryville is in Clarke County about 10 miles east of Winchester off today's Va. Route 7 (the road to Leesburg). Although his namesake, Lieutenant Boyd was actually the nephew of Capt. William H. Boyd of the 1st New York Cavalry. People often confused them for father and son. George W. Hamilton diary, entry for June 13, 1863, Cecil County Historical Society, Elkton, Maryland.

22 OR 27, pt. 2, 442; Matella Page Harrison diary entry for June 13, 1863, in Richard C. Plater, Jr., ed., "Civil War Diary of Miss Mattella Page Harrison of Clarke County, Virginia, 1835-1898," *Proceedings of the Clarke County Historical Association*, Vol. 22 (1982-1983), 64. Rodes approached the town from the southwest using what today is the Bishop Meade Highway (Va. Route 255) and Lord Fairfax Highway (U.S. Route 340).

of a recent firefight with Federal cavalry came into view.[23] A portion of Cole's Maryland Cavalry had been operating in the Potomac region for some time. Company A, under Capt. George W. F. Vernon, boldly attacked a superior force of Jenkins' advance Confederate cavalry, but was compelled to retreat after losing several men. However, Vernon accomplished the purpose of the reconnaissance, and he dispatched a scout through Confederate lines to apprise General Milroy of the looming danger.[24]

Rodes' vanguard approached the outskirts of Berryville shortly after 11:00 a.m., catching the local farmers and their families by surprise. No one had expected any of Lee's army to be in the Lower (northern) Valley. Indeed, one resident observed, only a short time earlier Yankees had walked leisurely past his house toward Berryville. Now, he watched in amazement as a long line of Confederate skirmishers passed through his yard heading in the same direction. General Rodes rode past the man and supposedly commented that he expected to capture the entire Yankee force at Berryville.[25]

Unfortunately for Rodes, Union vedettes had already told Colonel McReynolds that the guns of the Main Fort had fired, signaling the recall. The Union commander hastily prepared to evacuate Berryville in an effort to rejoin the division at Winchester. The soldiers gathered what few belongings they could carry, but in their haste left most of the tents standing and food cooking on the campfires. One particular sutler possessed an extensive inventory, which he could not possibly pack in time. Rather than abandoning his goods to the Rebels, he threw open his quarters and told the Union men to help themselves. The announcement lifted their spirits and the soldiers stuffed their haversacks and pockets with as much as they could hold.[26] McReynolds, meanwhile, sent a courier to find and warn the wagon train coming in from Harpers Ferry so it could turn and head for Bunker Hill and on to Winchester via that route. "We at once turned the train and struck for Bunker Hill," recounted Lt. William J. Grant of the 6th Maryland. "When we had proceeded a few miles, we were joined by the balance of the train from Berryville, retreating in the same direction supported by a company of the 1st New York Cavalry."[27]

23 Michael Taylor, ed., "Ramseur's Brigade in the Gettysburg Campaign: A Newly Discovered Account by Capt. James I. Harris, Co. I, 30th Regt. N.C.T." in *Gettysburg Magazine*, No. 17, January 1997, 27-28. Harris was killed in May 1864 at Spotsylvania.

24 J. Thomas Scharf, *History of Western Maryland*, 2 vols. (Genealogical Publishing Co., 2003), 268.

25 *Charleston* (S. C.) *Mercury*, June 22, 1863, citing unnamed Richmond newspapers.

26 Beach, *History of the 1st New York (Lincoln) Cavalry*, 231.

27 Grant, "Letter from Lieut. W. J. Grant."

Brig. Gen. Stephen D. Ramseur, who
commanded a brigade in Rodes' division.
U.S. Army Heritage and Education Center

McReynolds left Captain Boyd's
cavalry company, Lt. H. Eugene
Alexander's section of the Baltimore
Battery, and some of the 6th Maryland as a
rear guard under command of Lt. Col.
William A. McKellip to slow down the
Rebels, if necessary. He took Lt. Charles H.
Evans' and 2nd Lt. Peter Leary, Jr.'s gun
sections to protect his main body,
interspersing them in the column. Fearing
that Confederate cavalry would block the
road to Winchester, McReynolds took the
Harpers Ferry Road in an effort to use a
circuitous route through Summit Point, a nondescript stop on the Winchester &
Potomac Railroad in West Virginia, before turning west to the Martinsburg Pike. This
route covered about 20 miles, almost double the direct road, but it offered a better
chance of avoiding Rebels. Behind him, Lieutenant Colonel McKellip and his rear
guard defenders prepared to buy as much time as possible for McReynolds'
evacuation. To do so, he placed Eugene Alexander's section in the southern
fortifications along the road and spread out his infantry, deploying two companies of
the 6th Maryland on either side of the guns and sending forward cavalry skirmishers.[28]

Shortly before noon, Rodes came up against this Union rear guard, studied the
situation, and decided to assault the works. The day had turned hot and sultry, with the
likelihood of a thunderstorm later in the afternoon. Under cover of the rolling terrain
and woods, Rodes deployed his division to attack the Yankees defending Berryville.
"The infantry," he later wrote, "save one brigade [O'Neal's] were ordered to move to
the right and left of the place, to unite in its rear." His plan was a classic
double-envelopment movement, with the columns to meet in the rear to surround the

---

28 Walker, *History of the Eighteenth Regiment*, 94; "The Defence and Evacuation of Winchester,"
484; Col. Wm. A. McKellip to John E. Smith, June 19, 1863, *Baltimore Sun*, April 19, 1904; "The
Fight at Berryville, Va.: Captain Alexander's Baltimore Battery," in *Baltimore Sun*, June 19, 1863.
Summit Point, W.V., is at the intersection of the Charles Town Road and the Leetown Road
(County Road 1). Leary's father was a former U. S. congressman.

enemy position. Within a short time, Southern scouts discovered the garrison evacuating the town. Jenkins' cavalry rode to the left (west) of Berryville to cut off any retreat on the Winchester-Snickersville Pike—the exact move McReynolds had anticipated and taken pains to avoid.[29]

Rodes ordered Col. Edward O'Neal to advance his Alabama brigade, closely followed by Capt. W. J. Reese's Jeff Davis artillery. As they moved forward, Lieutenant Eugene Alexander's two Union guns opened fire on them. "The artillery threw shells among their ranks with great rapidity," recalled a trooper of the 1st New York (Lincoln) Cavalry. Another shell buzzed through the air toward Ramseur's brigade. It exploded 200 or 300 yards away from the infantrymen and landed near some Confederate medical wagons and ambulances and sent the surgeons, stewards, litter bearers, and teamsters scrambling for cover, much to the Tar Heels' amusement. McKellip estimated that Alexander's two guns fired for 90 minutes while the Rebels deployed, giving McReynolds a good head start.[30] Captain F. W. Alexander later recorded that his brother's two guns had fired three percussion shells and 24 rounds of case shot in the defense of Berryville.[31]

With the Rebels coming on in force, Lt. Eugene Alexander's gunners and drivers hastily dumped their steaming pots of bean soup into the fire, packed some tents into the battery wagon, and burned the rest. Once the guns were limbered, the artillerists departed through the 67th Pennsylvania's abandoned camp and spotted the sutler's abandoned goods. The barrels of ginger cakes, boxes of lemons, jars of pickles, supplies of suspenders, shoe blacking, toilet soap, and other trade articles proved irresistible to Alexander's men. "It was fun," admitted a teenaged private named Frederick W. Wild, who eagerly stuffed his pockets with ginger cakes and lemons. Noting extra heavy blankets, heavy boots, half a dozen thick woolen shirts, and other winter garb, Wild assumed they must belong to troops from Maine, though none were operating in the region. McKellip's rear guard had scarcely cleared Berryville when, according to another Union eyewitness, Rodes' entire division came "rushing in like a

---

29 Stevenson, *Boots and Saddles*, 183.

30 John Purifoy, "With Jackson in the Valley," *Confederate Veteran*, Vol. 30, No. 10, October 1922, 384; Taylor, "Ramseur's Brigade in the Gettysburg Campaign," 27-28; *Baltimore Sun*, April 19, 1904; William D. Hall, "Milroy at Winchester. A Fight of Thirty Minutes That was One of the Most Desperate of the War," *Philadelphia Weekly Times*, March 5, 1881. The Jeff Davis Artillery was also known as Reese's Battery for Capt. Wm. J. Reese. The Mexican War veteran and antebellum dentist had recently served under Nathan B. Forrest in the 51st Alabama Partisan Rangers

31 1863 Monthly Returns, June 1863, Baltimore Battery of Light Artillery Records, 1862-1865, MS 176, Maryland Historical Society.

tidal-wave, foaming with rage because we had eluded them, when they had fully expected to 'bag' the whole brigade."[32]

The Tar Heels of Brig. Gen. Junius Daniel's brigade formed a battle line about half a mile south of town, threw out skirmishers, fixed bayonets, and double-quicked toward the distant breastworks, but the "blue-birds" had flown. Daniels' men took to looting nearby tents, as well as quartermaster and commissary stores.[33] One staple drew particular interest. "The great quantity of Yankee beans captured in this camp was a novel sight to the men of the Jeff Davis Artillery," Pvt. John Purifoy mused. "This was a new food to them, or to the majority of them, as few of the men had ever seen such beans before." The bean-gathering Rebels narrowly missed the opportunity of capturing the wife of Union Capt. Samuel C. Arthurs. Lydia Arthurs had been tending her sick husband when the Southerners swooped in and seized 67th Pennsylvania's camp. She barely escaped, but her husband fell captive.[34]

Ramseur's brigade also rushed into Berryville. "We took the enemy by surprise, and our coming was as a thunderbolt from a cloudless sky," gloated Lt. John C. Gorman of the 2nd North Carolina. The former journalist and printer had spent several years in "Bloody Kansas" in the 1850s before returning to the Tar Heel State and resuming his career. He noted that the Yankees "hardly got a glimpse of our battle flags across the open fields before they fled in confusion." His comrades captured "300 prisoners, all their stores, camp and garrison equipage, a good many horses, mules, wagons, etc. They left their tents . . . standing—their clothes and private effects intact, and their dinners cooked ready for eating. Our whole brigade partook of a hot dinner of beans and pork, baked beef and fresh loaf bread furnished ready for eating by our accommodating Yankee friends," Gorman added, "while every soldier filled his haversack with the pure bean coffee, sugar and other camp delicacies."[35]

"The cowards had deserted the place and given leg bail, leaving over 100 of their sick as prisoners," sneered the 30th North Carolina's Capt. James I. Harris. "There stood their tents just as they had left them a few minutes before—sutler tents filled with everything that luxurious living could call for, and officers and privates tents filled with everything that convenience could demand." Private William Alexander

---

32 Wild, *History of Capt. F. W. Alexander's Baltimore Battery*, 51-52; *Baltimore Sun*, April 19, 1904.

33 *Charlotte Observer*, Nov. 16, 1892; Leon, *Diary of a Tar Heel Confederate Soldier*, 30-31.

34 Purifoy, "With Jackson in the Valley," 383; Kate M. Scott, ed., *History of Jefferson County, Pennsylvania* (Syracuse, NY: D. Mason & Co., 1888), 169. A distraught Lydia Arthurs would eventually make her way to Baltimore where she worked in the military hospitals while seeking Samuel's release. They finally reunited in March 1865 after his parole.

35 John C. Gorman to Friend Holden, North Carolina State Archives and GNMP.

Smith of the 14th North Carolina agreed. "They were preparing a meal, not scant rations we were accustomed to but pots, plenty of pots, full of beef stew, loaf bread piled in stacks, with other edibles, condiments, etc.," he wrote with no little amazement. "The fires were still burning under the pots. We ate all we could, to our entire satisfaction, filled our haversacks and marched on greatly refreshed."[36]

Northeast of Berryville, meanwhile, Colonel McReynolds force-marched his retreating column on the Summit Point Road, stopping frequently to rest his men. Soldiers tossed out anything that would lighten their load. The same held true for McKellip's rear guard. "One would see a fellow with a good pair of boots in his hand, looking at his feet and not knowing which pair to discard," recalled artilleryman Fred Wild. "Another unslinging his knapsack and taking out a blanket to lighten his burden, wash basins, shoe brushes, razor strops, and many other articles that the older soldiers had learned to dispense with." Wild tossed twenty blankets into the battery wagon. They dared not dawdle because Jenkins' cavalry periodically harassed them. Wild likened the Virginians to "a pack of hungry wolves, kept at bay by the New York Cavalry." The artillerists "had a choice of three ways of marching," he noted, "riding on horseback, sitting on ammunition chests, or walking; but the poor Infantry had a hard time of it." After marching 15 miles from Berryville, McKellip dispatched a courier to ask McReynolds if his escape depended upon the rear guard engaging the enemy, but no answer was forthcoming.[37]

A middle-aged mulatto woman and four- or five-year-old girl struggled to keep up with the column, laden as they were with clothing, bedding, and other possessions. Her husband was a slave who had run away to the north several months ago, and she intended to follow the Union soldiers in the hope of finding him. During mid-afternoon, the child tired out and the mother tried to carry her in addition to her baggage. Moved by the heart-wrenching scene, young Fred Wild offered to let the girl ride in front of him on his horse. Wild's comrades teased him, but it was a humane act and he did not mind the joshing. The exhausted child quickly fell asleep. "I have often thought I would like to have a picture of myself with that little sleeping negro baby on my lap," he wrote many years later. "I can at this late day, sitting in a warm, comfortable home smoking my pipe, close my eyes and see it, as well as many more such pictures of the past, like a dream."[38]

36 James I. Harris to his friend Burton, August 24, 1863, Walter J. Bone Collection, State Archives of North Carolina; William Alexander Smith, *The Anson Guards: Company C, Fourteenth Regiment North Carolina Volunteers 1861-1865* (Charlotte: Stone Publishing, 1914), 198-99.

37 Wild, *Capt. F. W. Alexander's Baltimore Battery*, 53.

38 Ibid., 53-54; *Baltimore Sun*, April 19, 1904.

FREDERICK W. WILD
THE AUTHOR

Post-war image of Frederick Wild
of the Baltimore Battery.
*Memoirs and History of Cap. F. W. Alexander's
Baltimore Battery of Artillery*

In late afternoon, Lieutenant Colonel McKellip halted his column at Locke's Ford east of Brucetown. Weary soldiers bathed their feet or heads in Opequon Creek, while others filled canteens upstream. "It was a general refreshment for man and beast," Wild recalled. The teenager chewed on some hardtack and drank lukewarm water from his canteen while awaiting the order to resume the march.[39]

When the head of McReynolds' tired column finally reached the Martinsburg Pike, it turned south and moved toward Winchester. The men and wagons had already marched 25 hard miles that day and were not yet finished.[40] Earlier that morning, before beginning his retreat, McReynolds had ordered Maj. Alonzo Adams to send Company K of the 1st New York Cavalry to explore the roads near Millwood. At midday (concurrent with McReynolds' circuitous march), this isolated patrol captured a private of the 16th Virginia Cavalry of Jenkins' brigade about two miles from Millwood. The Rebel prisoner informed Capt. Ezra H. Bailey that the Federals had retreated from Berryville. This was the first news Bailey had that McReynolds had evacuated the town. Bailey dispatched couriers to relay the news to General Milroy in Winchester.[41]

Back in Berryville, meanwhile, the 5th Alabama's Maj. Henry A. White detailed Company D to guard the abandoned camps and prisoners. "We turned in & ran off all the Cavalry & stragglers that were plundering & Lt. Jones posted us around to keep them out," recalled Pvt. Sam Pickens. "It was as much as we could do to keep the men out; they'd slip in in spite of ourselves. In this way we were kept so busy that we had

---

39 Ibid., 54. Locke's Ford is about 4.5 miles north of the Berryville Road. It is off of today's Swimely Road (Rt. 672). George Armstrong Custer's cavalry crossed the Opequon there on Sept. 19, 1864, during the second Valley Campaign.

40 George W. Hamilton diary, entry for June 13, 1863.

41 Maj. A. W. Adams to Milroy, June 26, 1863, Milroy Collection, Jasper County Public Library.

but a poor chance to get anything ourselves." Luckily, the bounty was abundant. Private Pickens appropriated a good haversack and stationery. His comrades had to fight off several of Daniel's late-arriving North Carolinians who wanted a share of the spoils. The relative luxury of the Union camps stunned the Confederates, from the size of the tents, some of which boasted carpet, to the copious amounts of food and supplies. To Pickens' astonishment, the Yankees even "had martin boxes fixed up in their camp."[42]

Several townspeople emerged from their homes to greet the Rebels. "Great rejoicing by the citizens to be relieved from the ridicule and insults of our enemy," confirmed William E. Ardrey. The young lieutenant had left his studies at Davidson College to join the 30th North Carolina of Ramseur's brigade. Early in the evening, a bugler sounded the command to fall in. Rodes' well-rested and fed soldiers marched north toward Summit Point. Evidence of McReynolds' hasty retreat was everywhere. "Overcoats, blankets, etc. were cut to pieces and thrown away completely lining the roadside for many hundred yards," observed Captain Harris of the 30th North Carolina. A light rain that began falling about 6:30 p.m. Had turned the dirt road into a thick muddy gruel, but the mud only added to the general merriment coursing through the ranks. "Our boys hallooed—whooped and huzzaed, slipped, slided forward backward zigzag, up, down, well every way that the most fertile imagination could picture or pen describe," recalled Harris. Adding to the delight, they never failed to be "greeted at every house by any number of the fair sex who seemed much delighted to see us and who seemed as if they would lose their arms in waving their handkerchiefs."[43]

The column did not pause until it was six or seven miles past Berryville, when darkness and a heavier cold rain finally halted the pursuit. Reese's cannoneers of the Jeff Davis Artillery started campfires and dug into their haversacks for the captured Yankee beans. The pilfered food filled every available kettle, but their efforts to cook the beans proved to be dismal failures. They had not added enough water. As it evaporated, they refilled the kettles with cold water, but soon learned that chilled beans did not soften well. "Many of the men ate the hard beans," Pvt. John Purifoy explained, "and paid for their temerity in the pains which followed. Fortunately, nothing serious came of this indulgence."[44]

---

42 Hubbs, *Voices from Company D*, 177. This refers to birdhouses for purple martins.

43 William E. Ardrey diary entry for June 13, 1863, W. E. Ardrey Papers, Davidson College Archives, Davidson, NC; James I. Harris to his friend Burton, August 24, 1863, State Archives of North Carolina.

44 Purifoy, "With Jackson in the Valley," 384.

The weather worsened, the rain and wind intensified, and a lightning storm broke out above the resting troops. "It is raining very hard," Louis Leon wrote home to a local newspaper, "and of course, we have no shelter." "As had become usual," the 30th North Carolina's Captain Harris added, "a perfect hurricane came along." Meanwhile, some 8-9 miles west of Rodes' campsite, in Winchester, some of Edward Johnson's Confederate soldiers near Winchester were disappointed that Rodes' division had not arrived to assault the Union lines from the east, wholly unaware of Ewell's master plan. "Roads [Rodes] failed to get up in time to make an attack," was what the 10th Virginia's Pvt. Samuel A. Firebaugh of Brig. Gen. George Steuart's brigade penned in his diary.[45]

*   *   *

Near Brucetown, part of Lieutenant Colonel's McKellip's rear guard command—companies E and H of the 6th Maryland (about 60 men) and Maj. Alonzo W. Adams' 200-man "German battalion" of the 1st New York Cavalry—protected the eastern approach to Opequon Creek while the rest of the column crossed Locke's Ford and proceeded westward toward the turnpike. Unbeknownst to McKellip, between 5:00 and 6:00 p.m. Maj. James W. Sweeney and 350 men of the 36th Battalion, Virginia Cavalry approached the ford from the east-northeast. Sweeney decided to bypass the Yankee rear guard and strike the enemy column at the creek. The Brucetown Road made a sharp turn near the stream, so he led his column diagonally through the cover of some woods to the road, emerging just beyond the bend.[46]

As the Rebels trotted through the timber, a messenger galloped up to Major Adams to report that the Rebel cavalry was upon them. The major wheeled his troopers behind the bend and threw down the fences along the right flank intent on forming his squadrons in a field. He barely finished his deployment when Sweeney's shrieking horsemen charged him. The carbines wielded by the New Yorkers emptied several Rebel saddles and temporarily halted the Virginians. Taking advantage of the momentary confusion, Adams rode in front of the 1st Squadron and ordered his men

---

45 *Charlotte Observer*, November 16, 1892; Leon, *Diary of a Tar Heel*, 30-31; Lynch, *Civil War Diary*, 19-20; James I. Harris to his friend Burton, August 24, 1863, State Archives of North Carolina; Samuel Firebaugh diary entry for June 13, 1863, Samuel Angus Firebaugh Diary, Sept. 1862-March 1864; SHC.

46 Wild, *Capt. F. W. Alexander's Baltimore Battery*, 56. Major Adams, who came from a wealthy and influential New York City family and was a veteran of the mounted service in the Mexican War, was popular with many of the men of the 1st New York Cavalry, who thought him "an agreeable fellow" who was "social even to merriment. He is a true gentleman and a thorough soldier." "Lehigh," "From Capt. Bennett's Company."

to attack. For some reason, neither Capt. Lambert Simmons nor Lt. Franz Passager of Company I executed the directive, and the limp effort petered out. Blaming what he called the "criminal hesitation" of the two officers, Adams fell back toward the ford with Sweeney's screaming Rebels men in hot pursuit.[47] "The German battalion, which had been formed in line at an angle of the road, retreated before superior numbers in considerable confusion," recounted a trooper of the 1st New York. "Capts. Boyd, [Lambert I.] Simons and [Abram] Jones, and Lieut. [Charles] Woodruff, exerted every effort to rally them, but in vain."[48]

The cannoneers of Lt. Eugene Alexander's rearmost gun were crossing the creek when they heard hundreds of pounding hooves approaching. The enemy was closer than anyone had believed. Artilleryman Fred Wild still had the little black girl on his horse. "Here, Auntie, take your baby!" he shouted to the mulatto mother. "Oh Lawdy God, what is gwine to become of me now?" she pleaded as she reached for her child. "Kill the n———r stealer!" screamed one of the Rebel troopers. A smattering of bullets whistled past Wild. "They were bold, these Johnnies," he later admitted. After one Confederate had his horse killed, he scrambled down the embankment, confronted Capt. Frederick Alexander, and demanded his surrender. Alexander would have none of it, choosing instead to raise his pistol and put a ball squarely in the Virginian's forehead. The dead man's brother came to his sibling's rescue a few seconds too late and was taken prisoner, as were another half-dozen Virginians.[49]

The fighting was still swirling around them when Captain Alexander told Wild to ride ahead and tell the lieutenant [his brother Eugene] to get a gun in position to the right of the road. Wild took a potshot at a nearby Rebel before racing his horse up and out of the ford area, leaving the frightened woman and child standing helplessly in knee-deep in the stream. Wild clattered past an abandoned limber, its tongue broken, at another sharp bend in the road. Lieutenant Alexander had anticipated his sibling's order and his artillerists were already pulling a heavy ordnance rifle up the steep embankment to the right of the road. They paused at the top to tear down a fence before rolling the gun into a patch of spring onions behind a small cabin 150 yards

47 Adams to Milroy, June 26, 1863, Milroy Papers.

48 "Veritas," letter of July 24, 1863, Sharpsburg, Md., 1st Regiment Cavalry, NY Volunteers Civil War Newspaper Clippings, http://dmna.ny.gov/historic/reghist/civil/cavalry/1stCav/1stCavCWN.htm. Accessed June 11, 2014. "Veritas" was in Company F.

49 "Headquarters Co. F, 1st New York Cavalry to Messrs. Editors Standard," July 24, 1863, Sharpsburg, MD, quoted by the New York State Military Museum and Veterans Research Center, http://dmna.ny.gov/historic/reghist/civil/cavalry/1stCav/1stCavCWN.htm; accessed June 11, 2014; Stevenson, *Boots and Saddles*, 185-86; Wilmer, Jarrett, and Vernon, *History and Roster of Maryland Volunteers*, 1:817; Wild, *Capt. F. W. Alexander's Baltimore Battery*, 54-55; see also French, "Federals on 'Safe' Road to Trouble."

Maj. Alonzo Adams, commander of the 1st New York (Lincoln) Cavalry. Adams was not liked by the officers of his command.
U.S. Army Heritage and Education Center

west of the creek. Concurrently, McKellip posted a company of the 6th Maryland on each side of the road to protect the cannoneers.[50]

Taking advantage of the sharp turns in the country road, Alexander waited until the Rebels came within 50 yards before blasting double canister, temporarily throwing them into confusion and unhorsing several men. "The rebs gave the charge on our guns, howling at a fearful rate, and ran up to our guns," reported Henry Suydam of the 1st New York. "Our guns gave it to them hot and heavy, but as they came up to our muzzles, our company was ordered to charge, which saved the guns."[51] In a different letter home written a few days later, Suydam rather colorfully wrote, "But on they came horses without riders and many biting the dust, so desperate were they that one fellow rode past the guns and demanded a surrender but he was shot down and our cracking of revolvers were like packs of fire crackers."[52]

Several other horsemen from both sides fell in the ensuing melee. The 6th Maryland's bugler alerted McKellip to a Rebel taking aim at him. The bullet missed, and McKellip drew his revolver and fired twice, putting the second shot into his antagonist's brain. He emptied what remained in his cylinder at the swirling Rebels, wounding another. Once they had a clear shot, the Union infantrymen caught the remaining Confederates in a cross fire. Their coordinated rounds convinced the Southern horsemen to fall back across the creek.[53]

Meanwhile, Major Adams reformed his New York cavalrymen west of the creek behind a slight elevation near the bend and ordered another charge. Lieutenant

---

50 Wild, *Capt. F. W. Alexander's Baltimore Battery*, 54-55; Wilmer, Jarrett, and Vernon, *History and Roster of Maryland Volunteers*, 1:817; *Baltimore Sun*, June 19, 1863.

51 Black, *A Lincoln Cavalryman*, 126-27.

52 Ibid., 129.

53 *Baltimore Sun*, April 19, 1904; Stevenson, *Boots and Saddles*, 185-86.

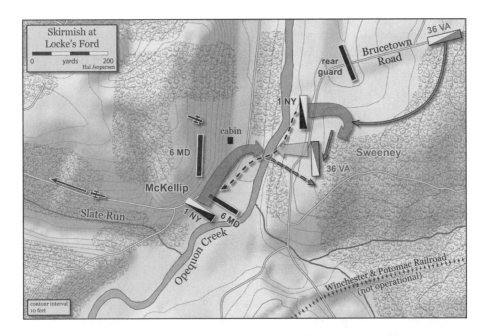

Woodruff with his own Company F and Company M (whose commanding officer, Lt. Richard G. Prendergast, had just been captured) drew sabers and impetuously galloped upon the advancing enemy column. "The spirited and determined onset of F and M," wrote one an unknown New Yorker, "repelled and checked the rebel advance, at which juncture Capt. Jones brought up a portion of the 1st Battalion, and completed the work so nobly begun." The fighting freed the fortunate Prendergast.[54] The entire fight, which lasted perhaps a quarter-hour, was unusually violent and often face-to face with men cutting and thrusting at one another and firing pistols at point blank range. The flashing steel was visible to the 1st New York's Capt. James Stevenson, McReynolds' adjutant, who had deployed up on the knoll with the reserves. He could distinctly hear the shouts of the combatants. "In this charge," New Yorker Lt. William H. Beach observed, "the men of both sides became so mixed up that in the dust that was raised, it was for a little while difficult for one to recognize his own comrades."[55]

Lieutenant William D. Hall of the Lincoln Cavalry left a vivid description of this nasty engagement. "A desperate hand to hand fight, which lasted some ten minutes, ensued, when the enemy were driven to the rear," he wrote. "They rapidly formed and made a second charge, which was met by a fierce fire from four companies of the Sixth

54 "Veritas," letter of July 24, 1863.

55 Ibid.

Maryland Infantry and grape and canister from the battery already mentioned, which the First New York Cavalry followed up by a thundering charge, completely routing the enemy."[56] The sharp combat left dozens of men bleeding or dying, including Confederate Major Sweeney, who sustained a severe arm wound and a lung injury. Hall later claimed "the fight lasted but thirty minutes, but was one of the most desperate I ever witnessed in my more than four years' service. In this little engagement," he continued, "the enemy lost two captains and twenty-eight killed, a colonel, major, and fifty-four men wounded and captured, while the loss on our side was two killed, five wounded, and two captured, all members of the First New York Cavalry."[57]

"The encounter they had was hand to hand, and blade to blade," recalled an unidentified trooper fighting with the Lincoln Cavalry. "Honorable mention is due Sergts. [Josiah H.] Barton, [John] Baughan and [Edward] Lake, and privates [Edward] Wright, [Christian F.] Williamson, [Morgan] Warren, [Peter] May and [Michael] Manhattan, all 'the bravest of the brave,' for meritorious conduct during the engagement." Williamson, Warren, May, and Manhattan were all wounded, and all but Warren fell into the hands of the enemy. Manhattan's captors disarmed him and assigned a single man to guard him. The guard held Manhattan's belt with his saber attached. The enterprising Empire Stater realized the possibility and, after patiently waiting for the right opportunity, grabbed his saber, ran the guard through, and made good his escape.[58]

By the time Maj. Timothy Quinn appeared on the scene with Lt. Erwin C. Watkins of Company K, the shooting had ended. The squabbling, however, had just begun. His appearance brought little joy to Major Adams, who was relishing "the moment of my victory over the enemy." Quinn, who disliked Adams, announced that Colonel McReynolds had sent him back to assist Adams, if required. Adams shot back that the fight was over and that the enemy had been defeated and driven back. Quinn surveyed the body-strewn ground and conversed with one or two of the senior officers who likewise detested Adams. Quinn observed that most of his officers were of the opinion that Adams had endangered his command by risking a battle at that place, and wanted him to take command because, in their opinion, Adams should

---

56 Hall, "Milroy at Winchester."

57 Ibid.; Walker, *History of the Eighteenth Regiment*, 94; Brian S. Kesterson, *Campaigning with the 17th Virginia Cavalry: Night Hawks at Monocacy* (Washington, WV: Night Hawk Press, 2005), 24. Sweeney spent most of the rest of the war on medical furlough. Several of Major Sweeney's men were early members of the "Shriver Grays," a volunteer unit from Wheeling that became Company G, 27th Virginia. They transferred to the cavalry in May 1863.

58 "Veritas," letter of July 24, 1863.

Modern view of Locke's Ford with the old road trace in the foreground. *Scott Mingus*

have fallen back to the main column and Alexander's other sections for mutual protection. When Adams angrily retorted that he would not permit such talk in the presence of the officers and men, Quinn dispatched Lieutenant Watkins to report the affair to Colonel McReynolds. The ugly affair was about to get even uglier. When Watkins returned, Quinn informed Adams that he was now in command, and that McReynolds had ordered Adams' arrest. The stunned major protested the "this irregular mode" of arrest, which did not in his opinion follow protocol. He had apparently assumed that once McReynolds heard the facts, he would resume command of the regiment.[59]

While the New York cavalry officers bickered, Lieutenant Colonel McKellip held his position near ford for an hour in case the Rebels returned. Now that the brigade had driven the enemy back, Chaplain Joseph F. Brown of the 6th Maryland turned his full attention to the wounded. One infantryman in Company E had a severe injury to his foot, while another in the some company had wounds to both of his

59 OR 27, pt. 2, 83-84.

hands. Brown assisted the doctors in amputating one of the latter man's fingers before dressing his wounds.[60]

While the Marylanders nursed their wounded and policed the battlefield, artilleryman Fred Wild oversaw a poignant scene when the brother of the Rebel shot by Captain Alexander knelt over the body and tenderly kissed him good-bye before being marched away as a prisoner. Wild scooped up a bunch of onions near the cannon to augment the purloined ginger cakes crammed into his pocket. Once McKellip thought it was safe, his column departed the Opequon crossing. Wild helped escort the captives before turning them over to the provost guard. He munched his cakes for dinner while on the march, musing throughout about the missing mulatto woman and her little girl. At one point McKellip formed a battle line on ground well adapted for defensive warfare, a place where it would have been "almost impossible for any force to have dislodged us." When no Rebels appeared to challenge his new position, he resumed the march with the Rebels keeping a respectable distance.[61] By now full night had fallen and hunger set in. Artilleryman W. H. Moffett, Jr. rued the separation from the supply wagons, "which contained all of our clothing, feed, and spare ammunition."[62] Elsewhere in the bedraggled column, Chaplain Brown alternately walked on foot and rode on a cannon carriage. "Very dark," he later complained, "can't see what is around me. No dinner. No supper."[63]

After the savage fight at Locke's Ford, General Jenkins dispatched the 36th Virginia Battalion to pursue the retiring Yankees, while he and his remaining horsemen trotted toward Bunker Hill in the gathering darkness. After their lengthy night march McKellip's Union column approached Winchester just as the long threatened thunderstorm hit, together with considerable lightning. Fred Wild and his fellow cannoneers became separated from the main body in the downpour. When a mounted officer approached and inquired about their command, Wild replied they were part of Alexander's battery. "Follow me," announced the officer. The situation seemed odd to the Marylanders, and one of the older more experienced artillerists asked the officer to identify himself. "Major Starr of General Milroy's staff," came the reply. The artillerist remained unconvinced. "But you might be some d——d rebel, and lead us into your lines." He told Wild to "cover him with your revolver on his

60 Chaplain Joseph F. Brown diary entry for June 13, 1863, Cecil County Historical Society, Elkton, Maryland.

61 Wild, *Capt. F. W. Alexander's Baltimore Battery*, 55-56; *Baltimore Sun*, April 19, 1904.

62 W. H. Moffett to Dear Father, June 16, 1863, Maryland Heights, Md., Maryland Historical Society.

63 J. F. Brown diary entry for June 13, 1863.

right, and I will his left, and if he takes us wrong, we will blow his brains out." The officer assured them all would be right, and continued leading them on a short distance. "Do you see that light moving up and down?" he asked. "That is the signal light to show the way to your battery. Just march up to it." Wild's comrade, still not satisfied with the circumstances, insisted otherwise. "No," he countered, "you go with us." One of the section's officers took charge and dismissed the unknown officer, who was in fact speaking the truth. Major Starr was visibly relieved to escape the collection of Union revolvers leveled at him. About midnight the cannoneers marched into the Star Fort. After attending to his horses, Wild lay down along the side of the parapet, covered himself with his rubber blanket, and using his saddle for a pillow fell asleep.[64]

Safe for the time being in Winchester, the bedraggled Federal commanders evaluated their Locke's Ford losses. Union casualties were surprisingly light considering the violence of the melee. A Baltimore artillerist suffered a severe wound to his kneecap which lamed him for life.[65] Captain Alexander had only fired two shots, one a deadly round of close-range canister and the other a longer-range case shot, but that was enough to inflict significant execution.[66] Major Adams reported Confederate casualties as 19 killed and 47 wounded. Of those, Lieutenant Alexander said a Rebel told him his canister killed a dozen men and wounded more than 30. Adams reported losing just two killed and 10 wounded. Adams regained command in Winchester, but would rail in his official report against the "ungentlemanly and mutinous conduct" of his contentious fellow cavalry officers. Major Quinn, he argued, "evince[ed] unmistakable signs of jealousy and envy."[67]

According to Lt. William Beach, "Some of us found an old hall where, in our drenched clothes, we lay down on the bare floor, packed in as close as we could lie, to sleep. At midnight, an officer came into the crowded, steaming room, and said we must get out of there, for the enemy was all around us." Shivering from the cold, they pulled back to the forts until daylight.[68]

---

64 Ibid., 57.

65 W. H. Moffett to Dear Father, June 16, 1863, Maryland Heights, Md., Maryland Historical Society.

66 Baltimore Battery of Light Artillery Records, 1862-1865, MS 176, Maryland Historical Society.

67 "The Defence and Evacuation of Winchester," 484; OR 27, pt. 2, 83-84, 442; Baltimore Sun, June 19, 1863. Adams' questionable performance in the Second Battle of Kernstown in 1864 drew the ire of division commander Alfred Duffié.

68 Beach, "Some Reminiscences of the First New York (Lincoln) Cavalry," 2:284.

The Defense of Bunker Hill

Throughout the long afternoon of June 13, Colonel McReynolds' reunited wagon train, escorted by Lt. Frank Martindale's company of the 1st New York Cavalry, continued its dash toward what they hoped would be safety. The hurried movement did not escape notice. Jenkins' Virginians spotted them near Summit Point and his troopers rode after them in pursuit. About 4:00 p.m. the first heavily laden wagons reached Bunker Hill, a popular turnpike stop in Berkeley County, West Virginia, ten miles north of Winchester and about equidistant from Martinsburg. War correspondent James E. Taylor remembered Bunker Hill as a "hamlet, pleasantly situated on high ground, comprising a mill, a hotel, two dozen dwellings or more, all located east of the [Valley Turnpike], while three churches constructed of brick, and a smith, made up the section of the village west of the pike."[69]

Needing rest and water for their exhausted horses and mules, the teamsters parked in an open field along the Smithfield Road near Opequon Creek just east of the turnpike. Couriers galloped off toward Winchester to find Colonel McReynolds. The train included a handful of nonmilitary conveyances including a few sutler wagons and the private carriage of Mrs. William H. Boyd, wife of the Canadian-born captain of the 1st New York Cavalry's Company C. Three miles farther east, Lieutenant Martindale and part of his company set up picket outposts near Smithfield to watch for Rebels.[70]

They were not the only Federal forces in Bunker Hill. Since the end of May, Maj. William T. Morris with two companies (A and I) of his 116th Ohio and two companies of the 87th Pennsylvania (G and H), in all a little more than 200 men, had guarded the crossroads. They constructed a heavy fence across the turnpike to impede any enemy movement, posted a series of lookouts, and turned their barracks at the Presbyterian and Methodist Episcopal churches into improvised fortresses, barricading the doors and windows and knocking out bricks for loopholes for their rifles. It was a formidable position for short-term defense, but could readily be flanked if an enemy had sufficient time to do so. Ironically, their regimental chaplain had twice conducted religious services there in more peaceful days. The men of the 116th Ohio had reason to be confident. They had received brand-new Springfield Model 1861 rifle muskets on April 3 to replace their inconsistent, older .54-caliber Austrian weapons. "Now we

---

69 James E. Taylor, *The James E. Taylor Sketchbook: With Sheridan Up the Shenandoah Valley in 1864* (Dayton, OH: Morningside, 1989), 175. The Welsh-born, doubly named Col. Morgan Morgan founded the first permanent settlement on Bunker Hill about 1726.

70 See French, "Federals on the 'Safe' Road to Trouble." Smithfield is now Middleway. This part of the old Smithfield Road is now Giles Mill Road (WV Route 26).

Two images of the village of Bunker Hill, as it appeared in 1864, by artist James E. Taylor.
Western Reserve Historical Society

felt, for the first time, that we had a serviceable and respectable arm." wrote one of its field officers.[71]

Shortly after 4:00 p.m. Jenkins' Virginia vanguard caught up with Martindale's rear guard near Smithfield. Jenkins ordered a saber-wielding squadron to charge, driving in the Union pickets. Martindale sent a courier galloping toward Bunker Hill with a warning and hastily withdrew his troops. Hoping to gain sufficient time to get the wagon train going, Martindale initiated a series of running fights over the next five miles hoping to delay the Rebels long enough to avoid losing any wagons. His messenger arrived at the wagon park and breathlessly reported that 1,500 Rebel

---

71 Ibid., Prowell, *History of the 87th Pennsylvania*, 59; Wildes, *Record of the One Hundred and Sixteenth Regiment Ohio Infantry*, 23. Prowell lists the strength as 300, while others put it at 200.

cavalry were on their way. The wagon master passed the word to hitch the horses and mules but, to maintain order and strength in numbers, "No teamster shall start until I give the orders." When he gave the requisite command, the drivers, sutlers, and civilians sprang into action, and the first wagons pulled out on the turnpike toward Martinsburg. Within minutes, a huge cloud of thick choking dust rose above the caravan careening northward toward presumed safety.[72]

The 87th Pennsylvania's Pvt. John C. Hoffman guarded the bridge over Opequon Creek as the wagon train rumbled across. Hoffman had strict orders to not allow anyone to pass except army teamsters. When the private halted a German sutler, the merchant cried, "Och, mine Got in Himmel! Lass mir ga, lass mir ga! All mine goots in das train. Hoffman, however, stubbornly refused to allow him passage until the last of the military wagons had crossed and moved up the nearby hill.[73]

Meanwhile, out on the Smithfield Road, Martindale's little force maintained its sharp fight with the Rebels for more than half an hour, buying enough time for the wagons to roll away. Quartermaster Lt. William H. Boyd Jr. ordered his drivers to lay on the whip and, having the luxury of a good turnpike, safely reached Martinsburg without losing a single wagon. However, his aunt and his cousins Andrew and Minnie had ridden in a buggy with the wagon train from Bunker Hill. When the fighting began, their horse ran away, upsetting the vehicle in a roadside ditch. Mrs. Boyd suffered a badly sprained ankle, and she and her party soon became prisoners.[74]

Back at Bunker Hill, and still assuming the enemy was only a small raiding party, Major Morris arranged his 200 infantry in an extended line 500 yards east of the village and the Martinsburg Pike. Two companies held the left of the line at the edge of a clover field, with the other two to the right. They barricaded the road to slow down any oncoming Rebels. "This afternoon about four Oclock, our pickets were driven in by the rebels," wrote the 87th Pennsylvania's Cpl. Jacob M. Herr, a 19-year-old Mennonite from Cumberland County. "Our little band of veterans was . . . drawn up in line to receive them. But they came to[o] slow for us. We went half way but then it commenced. Our line was as follows: Co. G, A, I, and H was on the extreme left."[75]

---

72 Kesterson, *Campaigning with the 17th Virginia Cavalry*, 25; Prowell, *History of the 87th Pennsylvania*, 67.

73 Prowell, 67-68. The Pennsylvania German phrase is loosely translated as "Oh, my God in Heaven! Let me go, let me go! All of my goods are in the train."

74 OR, pt. 2, 65; Stevenson, *Boots and Saddles*, 184-85.

75 Wildes, *Record of the One Hundred and Sixteenth Regiment Ohio Infantry*, 55; G. K. C. (George K. Campbell), "Letter from the 116th O.V.I.," *Athens* (OH) *Messenger*, July 9, 1863; Jacob M. Herr entry for June 13, 1863, courtesy of descendant Robert Moore; Prowell, *History of the 87th Pennsylvania*, 68-69.

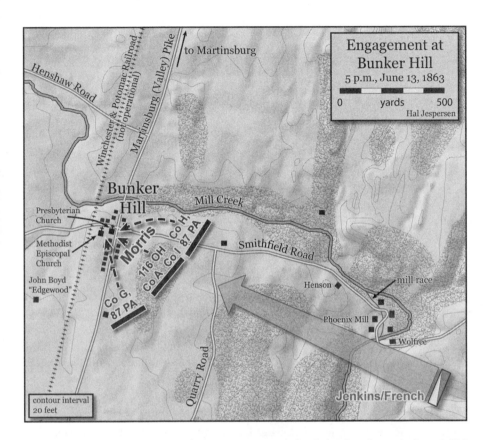

Morris had not anticipated the appearance of a brigade of more than 1,500 cavalry. About 5:00 p.m. he spotted horsemen on a high hill opposite Mill Creek coming from the direction of Berryville. He deployed skirmishers in a line extending obliquely from the Berryville Road toward the Martinsburg Pike. Jenkins in turn dismounted most of his men, and his skirmishers methodically began pushing downhill toward Morris's position. "We marched down to the creek, skirmishing as we went," the 17th Virginia's Lt. Addison Smith recalled. "This was the first fight many of us were ever in." Smith saw his first dead Yankee, a German, lying near the road. Sergeant Isaac H. Brisco's company also approached the enemy and then "charged two hundred of them lined up in a field."[76]

Morris's men were prone, and the only visible target was a lone Yankee making his way through a distant clover field. With his bridge duty at an end, the stubborn Private Hoffman was trying to rejoin the 87th Pennsylvania. Likely to his surprise, a series of bullets whistled past his ears and cut the clover at his feet. The flying lead

76 Kesterson, *Campaigning with the 17th Virginia Cavalry*, 24, 235.

prompted Hoffman to make a beeline for his comrades and dropped down beside them. There, he found men loading their rifle muskets while lying on the ground, and rising only to fire. Casualties slowly mounted over the course of the next 90 minutes. On the right side of the line, Pvt. William G. Irvin continued to fight despite gunshots to his right hip, left elbow, and left foot.[77]

Albert Jenkins brought up Capt. James S. A. Crawford's mounted Company F. The "Nighthawks" were the only company in the 17th Virginia Cavalry armed with pistols and sabers. Once they were in place, Jenkins led them across the creek toward the Federals. An initial volley staggered them, but the Nighthawks regrouped and pressed ahead while the dismounted companies rose and followed suit. "The boys let them have the saber freely," Addison Smith noted. They slashed the chronically unlucky thrice-wounded Private Irvin twice in his head before capturing him. Several other beleaguered Federals threw down their weapons and promptly surrendered. Not everyone participated in the attack, however. Lieutenant Smith found one of his men, Spencer Staats, cowering behind a large rock. When the officer demanded to know what he was doing, Staats adamantly responded that he would not come out to fight. Cowardice was in his constitution, he explained, and he could not help it.[78]

Realizing the hopelessness of remaining exposed in the fields, Major Morris withdrew westward across the Martinsburg Valley Pike toward the fortified churches. As the Pennsylvanians fell back, Lt. Henry Morningstar jumped his horse over a fence and narrowly escaped capture when his scabbard caught on the brush-choked obstacle. The father of five managed to extricate himself before the Rebels arrived. Other Keystoners were less fortunate. Lieutenant Michael S. Slothower and Cpl. Joseph T. Henry sustained mortal wounds. Slothower's cousin, Orderly Sgt. Andrew Bentz Smith, was among dozens of men seized as prisoners. Sergeant Major Joseph F. Welsh suffered a severe injury to his left thigh while on the skirmish line. Friends carried him to a nearby farmhouse, where they had to leave him to Rebel mercy. Other residents took in Sgt. John M. Griffith who, shot through the leg, fell bleeding in their

---

77 Prowell, *History of the 87th Pennsylvania*, 68; Herr diary entry for June 13, 1863; Brandt database, YCHT.

78 Kesterson, *Campaigning with the 17th Virginia Cavalry*, 24, 266. Spencer Staats later admitted that he was "no account as a soldier," and wanted to be allowed to go home, adding that his mother had told him to never desert. Noting his youth, Smith sat down and wrote out the discharge papers and sent Staats home. However, Yankee cavalry captured the young Confederate soldier, who would spend the rest of the war in Camp Chase prison near Columbus, Ohio.

yard. Despite being the family of a Confederate sergeant, they mercifully hid Griffith for more than a month.[79]

Just to the south, intense fire raked the 116th Ohio. Captain Alexander Cochran fell with a painful gunshot to his right arm. Youthful Lt. Adolphus B. Frame took command of Company I as it fell back, guns blazing, toward the churches. His calm demeanor steadied those around him. When he later heard the inspirational story, Maj. Gen. Abner Doubleday wrote, "Under a most galling fire, he covered the retreat to the church, keeping his men in hand as well and as coolly as on a parade ground and was among the last of the men to enter the church. . . . Mere boy, though he was," continued the general, "that day showed himself possessed of great courage, and superior soldierly qualities."[80]

Those soldiers not yet safely in the churches faced serious trouble. Jenkins ordered Company B of the 17th Virginia to advance. They steadily drove the Yankees back, and then Company C charged forward and killed two enemy soldiers, wounded four, and captured the remainder. The prisoners included most of the 116th Ohio's Company A, including musician Albert Gates.[81]

Once inside the improvised bastions with all doors barricaded, Morris's remaining men opened fire through the loopholes. The Rebels scattered and took cover, their initiative stifled. The fighting devolved into long-range sniping that remained heavy for quite some time. Safe inside the sturdy brick walls, Morris believed his men could hold out until nightfall without taking many additional casualties. He did not have time to take a roll call, but he had lost almost one-half of his command. His casualties included several officers, including Lt. R. O. Knowles of Company I

---

79 Wildes, *Record of the One Hundred and Sixteenth Regiment Ohio Infantry*, 24; Prowell, *History of the 87th Pennsylvania*, 68, 83; Brandt database, YCHT; J.M. Griffith, "Milroy at Winchester. The Commander was not Court-Martialed, but Given Another Command," *National Tribune*, February 11, 1909. Federal reports (*OR* 27, pt. 1, 193) place the 87th's losses at 2 killed and 17 wounded. Days later, on July 9, 1863, the *Athens* (Ohio) *Messenger* published a letter from George K. Campbell of the 116th OVI accusing the 87th of giving way, while the Buckeyes stood fast. As for Griffith, he stated, "I, however, never reached the church, being shot through the leg as I was running through a yard, and was taken into the house of a Confederate sergeant, and cared for over a month, passing for a paroled prisoner, with my arms hid in the house. Other wounded prisoners were quartered in an old house, except a member of the 116th Ohio, with a broken leg, I think, was cared for in another family." Griffith, "Milroy at Winchester."

80 *Athens* (OH) *Messenger*, July 9, 1863. See also French, "Federals on the 'Safe' Road to Trouble." A few days later Cochran, held prisoner at Winchester, befriended a citizen and fellow Mason, J. B. T. Reed, who helped him escape.

81 Kesterson, *Campaigning with the 17th Virginia Cavalry*, 25; Ohio Roster Commission, "116th Regiment Ohio Volunteer Infantry," in *Official Roster of the Soldiers of the State of Ohio in the War of the Rebellion, 1861-1866*, 12 vols. (Cincinnati: The Ohio Valley Press, 1888), 8:182-85.

and Lt. John S. Manning of Company A, both of the 116th Ohio.[82] According to Sgt. George A. Way, Company A took 67 men into the fight. Now, only 28 were left, with Manning and the balance presumably captured. Corporal Simpson Smith of Woodsfield and Pvt. John Welch of Lebanon lay dead in the open fields.[83]

Concerns grew inside the sanctuaries that the Rebels might bring up artillery to bombard them. As the evening wore on the worry proved unfounded. Unbeknownst to the trapped Unionists, Jenkins' horse artillery under Capt. Thomas E. Jackson was well to the south in Staunton. Despite his numeric superiority, Jenkins dared not risk a frontal assault, and he did not flank the crossroads. Finally, with darkness approaching, he sent a citizen named John Lemon forward under a flag of truce to ask the Federals to surrender. The defiant Morris refused: "We are not into that kind of business." Once Lemon delivered the denial to Jenkins the shooting resumed in earnest until it was too dark to see anything.[84]

The fighting finally ended about 9:00 p.m. when, under a cold rain falling, Jenkins broke off contact. He posted pickets around the two churches, severed the telegraph lines to Winchester, and camped about two miles from Bunker Hill. While grazing their horses, his men ate what little they had in their haversacks. "I tied my horse to my foot and lay down in the wet grass," the 17th Virginia Cavalry's Pvt. James Hodam recalled. "We did not sleep much as a matter of fact. I did not have a blanket and came near to chilling to death. No one will ever know how we suffered that night." Well into the night, as the downpour intensified, Major Morris decided it was safe to evacuate the fortified churches. About 2:00 a.m., his men silently slipped through a gap in Jenkins' picket line and rejoined their regiments near Winchester.[85] The survivors were happy to be on their way, but mourned the loss of their comrades. The 116th Ohio's Sgt. George A. Way wrote home that "our heroic little garrison stole forth from what had been a living tomb."[86]

---

82 Prowell, *History of the 87th Pennsylvania*, 68-69. One officer and an enlisted man in the 87th Pennsylvania were killed or mortally wounded at Bunker Hill, with three men wounded. The 116th Ohio lost 4 killed, 11 wounded, and 42 missing or captured.

83 *The Spirit of Democracy (Woodsfield, Ohio)*, July 1, 1863. Way reported that Pvt. Abel Hall of Graysville had been shot through both legs below the knee and Pvt. Hiram Shaffer of Woodsfield shot in the right groin.

84 Herr diary entry for June 13, 1863. See also French, "Federals on the 'Safe' Road to Trouble."

85 Kesterson, *Campaigning with the 17th Virginia Cavalry*, 25; *The Continental Monthly*, Vol. 4, No. 5, November 1863.

86 *The Spirit of Democracy (Woodsfield, Ohio)*, July 1, 1863.

Morris's survivors reflected on their accomplishment in delaying Jenkins for several hours, which allowed Martindale and Boyd to lead the wagon train northward without Rebel impediment. "Our little force held the churches until night and made their escape," recalled the 87th's Sergeant Griffith, "and marched 12 miles to Winchester to join their regiment." A few Keystone soldiers remained behind and hid for a while until they ultimately surrendered.[87] "We had to leave that [place] for their number was too great for us," youthful Pvt. Thomas O. Crowl recounted to his sister Mary. "We killed a great many of them and also they done the same with us. Our loss was 20 out of the co." Despite the intensity of the Union fire, Jenkins only lost a handful of men.[88] The 116th Ohio's Company I suffered three men wounded and listed 25 as missing. It had been a long emotional evening for the young Buckeyes and their major, one punctuated with the knowledge they had left half their men behind.[89]

The wagon train had its own ordeal. As it headed toward Martinsburg "our small force skirmishing briskly with the enemy, and holding him in check, with the loss of one killed and two wounded (one a Captain of cavalry) on our side and much greater loss to him," reported Lieutenant Grant of the 6th Maryland. "We succeeded in eluding their grasp at Bunker Hill, and keeping the advance we succeeded in reaching Martinsburg at 9 o'clock on Saturday night, being hotly pursued by the enemy, who seemed to be determined to capture our train and stores." When the wagon train arrived at Martinsburg, the soldiers found the town completely cut off from the rest of the Union garrison at Winchester because Jenkins' men had severed the telegraph wires at Bunker Hill. At Martinsburg, they found another wagon train in the same circumstances—stranded there without further instructions as to what to do next.[90]

Captain William H. Boyd's Company C of the 1st New York Cavalry joined the wagon train at Martinsburg. "When Milroy found he was surrounded by Lee's army, he sent for a bold officer and fifty men to carry a dispatch to Martinsburg, and [Captain] Boyd was detailed with his old company," recounted Capt. James H. Stevenson of the 1st New York. "They knew every cow-path in the Valley and succeeded in flanking the rebel force then between Winchester and Martinsburg." When Boyd arrived at Martinsburg, he used the telegraph to send the first intelligence

---

87 Griffith, "Milroy at Winchester." According to Griffith, one of these men made his way home to York County, Pennsylvania, but was ashamed to be seen because he might be considered to be a coward.

88 Thomas O. Crowl to Dear Sister, June 16, 1863, Harper's Ferry, WV, Civil War Documents Collection, USAHEC. Crowl, a pre-war shoemaker, was captured in July 1864 at Monocacy; he died two months later at Danville Prison in southern Virginia.

89 Wildes, *Record of the One Hundred and Sixteenth Regiment Ohio Infantry*, 27.

90 Grant, "Letter from Lieut. W. J. Grant.".

to Baltimore and Washington that Milroy's little army was under attack by a large portion of the Army of Northern Virginia. "That night," Stevenson continued, "a dispatch for Milroy arrived in Martinsburg, and three of Capt. William H. Boyd's sergeants—Oliver Lumphries, John V. Harvey, and George J. Pitman—volunteered to take it to Winchester. After several hairbreadth escapes, they arrived in the beleaguered town at midnight, and Milroy called a council of war."[91]

News of the fighting reached Col. Benjamin F. Smith's garrison at Martinsburg. "Tis very warm today. am on picket. can here firing all around. look for some work," an unnamed soldier of the 126th Ohio penned in his diary. "The wagon trane is retreating. They are having hevy fiting up at Berryville and Bunker Hill. [We] are looking for a fight to night." The Buckeyes spent a nervous evening awaiting an attack that never materialized. The morrow, however, would be a different story.[92]

91 James H. Stevenson, "The First Cavalry," in Alexander K. McClure, ed., *Annals of the War* (Philadelphia: Weekly Times Publishing Co., 1887), 638.

92 Anonymous, June 13, 1863, diary entry, Martinsburg, WV, in "Diary of a Civil War Soldier in Company F, 126th Ohio Volunteer Infantry, August 23, 1862 thru August 3, 1863," Stanley Scott Collection, Hancock County Museum, Findlay, OH. Transcribed by Richard F. Mann.

Chapter 6

Sunday, June 14

"Lee's army was gradually tightening its coils around us."

— *Pvt. Henry Clapp, 123rd Ohio*[1]

The torrential downpour finally let up late on the night of June 13-14. The horse soldiers of Confederate General Jenkins' brigade of cavalry and mounted infantry rose well before daylight, the men cold and wet after sleeping in the open. They mounted and quietly approached Bunker Hill at dawn, expecting to renew the fight with the stubborn Yankee infantry ensconced in the loop-holed, sturdy brick churches. To their relief, they discovered the enemy had fled.

"So we found only the dead and their camp with tents and plenty of provisions for man and horse, which we feasted on till satisfied," Pvt. James Hodam recalled. "We did not forget our poor horses, but fed them until they were full. We laid in a good supply of clothing and brand new blankets, both wool and gum [rubberized], and then put fire to their tents which they had left standing." Smoke filled the sky above Bunker Hill while the remaining residents hunkered inside their dwellings. "We did not tarry long here," Hodam added. "It was glory enough to fight the Battle of Bunker Hill again, so we moved out slowly. We knew that 12 miles distant was Martinsburg and were well satisfied that the place was well fortified and manned by a large force."[2]

Meanwhile, other elements of Jenkins' brigade had their hands full with running skirmishes that morning with Capt. George W. F. Vernon's company of Cole's

---

1 Clapp, "With Milroy at Winchester."

2 Kesterson, *Campaigning with the 17th Virginia Cavalry*, 25, 266.

Cavalry along several roads leading to the Potomac River from the Winchester region. "Dent" Summers' Company F of the 2nd Potomac Home Brigade ran into a large body of Rebel cavalry outside Berryville. After losing one man wounded and two captured in the ensuing brief melee, Captain Summers fell back to Charles Town and then to Halltown with the Confederates in hot pursuit. The Marylanders turned frequently to contest the ground, delaying the Rebels for a time and inflicting a few casualties.[3]

Morning Action at Winchester

Chaplain Joseph F. Brown of the 6th Maryland was not feeling well that morning. He had endured the long march in the rainstorm from Locke's Ford to Winchester, and was feeling the effects of exposure and exhaustion, coupled with the hard work of tending to wounded and the lack of substantial food the previous day. The Cecil County chaplain finally managed to consume some bread and coffee, but he and his comrades faced another long day as the Confederates showed no signs of leaving.[4]

"Breakfast over, the drum-beat brought every company again into line," the 110th Ohio's Lt. Henry Rush explained. "But fatalities of the preceding day had told sadly upon our ranks. The roll was called, but silence was the solemn answer to many a name." The same sadness permeated several other Union camps in the predawn Sabbath hours. For many regiments, this had been their first taste of combat and few of the men had any desire to repeat the horrifying experience. "This was a singular Sunday," the young minister- turned-officer, added. "Its ritual was the rites of war and its ceremonial was of clashing arms. . . . We were literally besieged, surrounded, shut in—the door bolted. It was but a question of a few hours when all must be prisoners, or when by dint of daring a remnant of the living may cut through a six-fold force and escape."[5]

The Confederates were also stirring that morning, but with considerably more optimism for the day's prospects. Privates Thomas Benton Reed and Jackson Dawkins of the 9th Louisiana, part of Harry Hays' brigade, rose well before dawn in the soggy meadows south of Abram's Creek below Winchester. They decided to hang their rain-drenched blankets over a nearby fence to air dry, but Dawkins worried they might have to leave them behind if the regiment was quickly marched away. Reed,

---

3 Scharf, *History of Western Maryland*, 268; OR 27, pt. 2, 203.

4 Brown diary entry for June 14, 1863.

5 Rush, *Life and Writings*, 230-31.

confident they would once again defeat the Yankees, predicted, "Well, we will get some dry ones tonight."[6]

Most of Milroy's forces anticipated renewed Confederate attacks, but when the first cracks of dawn appeared in the eastern sky, there was no sign of the enemy. That didn't mean much, thought an Ohioan who went on to express what most of the Federals probably believed: "Whatever officers may have thought, the men were convinced by this time of two things—namely that we were surrounded, and that the force was overwhelming." About 4:30 a.m. General Milroy ordered the 1st Massachusetts Heavy Artillery's Capt. William Martins to fire four shots from the Main Fort, one in each direction where the enemy had last been spotted. The shots drew no response, and everything remained quiet on every side. Milroy pondered the situation and ordered the army stores in Winchester packed and transported to the forts. After a delay of some while, Milroy also advanced skirmishers to feel for the enemy. They soon found them.[7]

The thunderous boom from a Federal light gun signaled the renewal of hostilities, and infantry skirmishers began popping off as the sun crept higher and targets became visible. "It was after 5:00 a.m.," Pvt. William B. Bailey of the Louisiana Guard Artillery penned, and "skirmishing is going on, the enemy having opened slow and deliberate fire from their batteries." Watching from a hill near the Star Fort, members of the 13th Pennsylvania Cavalry laughed at several distant Rebels frantically trying to get away from a shell streaking toward them. It landed right amongst them, but luckily for them it did not explode. "In my ears still ring the yells of the Southerners and the hurrahs of the Northern lads," wrote a trooper three decades later, "and then the peculiar sound as the two yells mingled."[8]

Some of the earliest fighting that Sabbath morning occurred in front of Milltown Heights along the Louisiana Tigers' line. As soon as it was daylight, the 123rd Ohio discovered a large force of Rebels lurking in woods 400 to 500 yards away. "We immediately commenced firing on them," Pvt. W. H. Bruder mentioned, "& they without any further ceremony returned the compliment." The 8th Louisiana's Capt. Albert Dejean, Jr., a popular and competent young officer, died of a gunshot not long after his regiment advanced to a stone wall just south of Abram's Creek. After the

6   Reed, *A Private in Gray*, 36.

7   J. M. D., "The Attack on Winchester–A Fresh and Graphic Account," in *Philadelphia Press*, June 26, 1863; *Zanesville* (Ohio) *Courier*, July 22, 1863; "Leaves from a Diary Kept by a Lady."

8   William B. Bailey diary entry for June 14, 1863, William Britton Bailey Memoirs, 1861-1864, Folder 54, Civil War Collection, Howard-Tilton Memorial Library, Tulane University, New Orleans; *Philadelphia Inquirer*, June 13, 1897.

Brig. Gen. William "Extra Billy" Smith, commander of a brigade in Early's division and the oldest general in the Army of Northern Virginia. *Library of Congress*

initial sharp exchange, the firing along the line became desultory but continued for more than an hour.[9]

A *Richmond Whig* correspondent watched the early action from a safe distance. "On Sunday morning (always the day of our deliverance, this being the third time)," Lawson later penned, "the firing commenced bright and early between the skirmishers on the edge of town, the Yankees making free use of their artillery, whilst we were unable to repay in kind for fear of destroying the town." Most residents stayed indoors and found shelter as best as they could in case of an artillery bombardment.[10]

As the opposing skirmishers dueled, and a few Union guns barked, Jubal Early recalled Col. W. W. Kirkland's 21st North Carolina from Kernstown, leaving Maj. Rufus W. Wharton's 1st North Carolina Battalion behind as a provost. The rest of Brig. General Robert Hoke's brigade, led north by Col. Isaac E. Avery, formed behind a low stone fence along the Valley Pike and awaited orders. About 7:00 a.m., Early instructed Generals Harry Hays and John Gordon to advance a regiment each toward the enemy skirmish line behind the long millrace and probe the Federal defenses. Hays sent forward Col. D. B. Penn's 7th Louisiana, coordinating its movements with Gordon's Georgians. To the Tigers' left, General "Extra Billy" Smith's Virginia skirmishers slogged across the marshy ground fronting Abram's Creek. The well-coordinated advance cleared the mills and millrace of Federal skirmishers. Howling Confederates swept up the steep hillside, driving back the remaining defenders and seizing the earthworks on Milltown Heights. Gordon ordered Griffin's

9   Bruder Journal, USAHEC; J. Warren Jackson to R. Stark Jackson, July 20, 1863, in Terry L. Jones, "Going Back in the Union at Last: A Louisiana Tiger's Account of the Gettysburg Campaign," *Civil War Times Illustrated*, vol. 29, no. 6, January/February 1991, 12.

10   Reprinted in the *Raleigh Weekly State Journal*, July 2, 1863.

battery and the Salem Artillery to roll to the hilltop, where the guns unlimbered in a position to bombard the Main Fort.[11]

Just before Smith's Virginians went into action, Early's adjutant general, Maj. John W. Daniel, rode toward the Virginia brigade to deliver the order to attack. He found the 65-year-old Smith at the head of his column holding his trademark blue umbrella to shield himself from the morning sunshine. His appearance was unusual, with his black beaver top hat and an old-fashioned standing collar that hearkened back to his days as governor of Virginia during the Mexican War. His horse carried civilian saddlebags. Smith, observed one eyewitness, "had nothing of the martial air about him." An amused Daniel commented,

> The general looked more like a Judge going to open court than like a Southern Brigadier, or fire-eater; and his smiling face and urbane manners gave little inkling of grim-visaged war. But in a twinkling the umbrella went down; forward— quickstep—ran down the column; the horse caught the fire of his rider, and if one had seen Smith's brigade as they came into line in front of Milroy, he would have recognized instinctively they were veterans who knew their business. And a glance at Gen. Smith would have shown that here was the born leader who could inspire men with his own calm but energetic and indomitable courage.[12]

In Winchester, meanwhile, the 110th Ohio's Col. J. Warren Keifer, a 27-year-old attorney from Clark County who evolved into one of the war's outstanding line officers, was presiding over a military commission in the dining room of the Sherrard home. His recorder, Lt. Hiram L. Sibley, left his sick bed that morning for the first time in a week. He walked into the room and was conversing with Keifer when the Rebel artillery opened fire. The colonel buckled on his sword belt, announced "I think there won't be any further use of this commission," and left to take command of his regiment. Another commission member, Capt. J. W. Chamberlain, returned to the 123rd Ohio's camp to get something to eat. He found the tents standing, but the camp deserted. The occasional musket shots reverberating south of town guided him in that direction, where he found his company on the front lines.[13]

11 William H. Mayo diary, entry for June 14, 1863, Huntington Library, San Marino, California; Jackson, "Going Back in the Union at Last," 12; Early, *Autobiographical Sketch*, 243.

12 John W. Bell, *Memoirs of Governor William Smith of Virginia: His Political, Military and Personal History* (New York: Moss Engraving, 1891), 117.

13 Macon, *Reminiscences of the Civil War*, 80; Wildes, *Record of the One Hundredth and Sixteenth Regiment, Ohio*; J. W. Chamberlain, "Scenes in Libby Prison," in Robert Hunter, ed., *Sketches of War History, 1861-1865: Papers Read Before the Ohio Commandery of the Military Order of the Loyal*

Col. J. Warren Keifer, commander of the 110th Ohio Volunteer Infantry. *Library of Congress*

The early morning movements of their regiment mystified the men of the 18th Connecticut. Since the previous evening, the regiment had manned the earthworks and rifle pits near the foot of the ridge below the Main Fort. The outfit was first ordered into the Main Fort but it did not remain there very long. A short time later, another order sent the men marching down the hill and into Winchester proper, "for what purpose I cannot tell," wondered Pvt. James M. Smith. After an hour of inactivity, and much grumbling within the ranks, the Connecticut men were ordered to return to the Main Fort.[14]

Milroy's scouts, Company K of the 1st West Virginia Cavalry, manned the rifle-pits south of the Main Fort. It was a bad place for dismounted troopers. The Rebels launched shells and railroad iron "pretty thick in amongst our company," recalled Pvt. Archibald H. Rowand, an 18-year-old Philadelphia native. The private had attended Quaker school for several years in Greenville, South Carolina, where his father worked as a bookbinder. Too young to join a Pennsylvania regiment at the start of the war, he traveled to Wheeling, Virginia (present-day West Virginia), where his uncle was raising a cavalry company. That decision put him squarely in the middle of this dangerous situation, where he was experiencing the terror of his first significant combat. "The shells would come over our heads causing the boys to dodge pretty often," he recounted in a letter to his mother. When he was made aware of this one-sided situation, Milroy ordered the troopers to move to the right of the fort to reduce their exposure to the enemy artillery.[15]

Legion of the United States (Cincinnati: Robert Clarke & Co., 1888), 2:342. Colonel Keifer lodged with the Sherrards in their home above the Farmer's Bank. Years later he was Speaker of the U. S. House of Representatives.

14 James M. Smith diary entry for June 14, 1863.

15 Arch Rowand to Mother, June 21, 1863, Harpers Ferry, WV, "Letters Home by Arch Rowand" website, Gauley River Book Company, http://www.jessiescouts.com/JS_Letters_1863_June_21.html, accessed December 8, 2013. Rowland later received the Medal of Honor

Bower's Hill, Winchester, Virginia, 1885. Photograph by William G. Reed (Boston).
Courtesy of the Meserve-Kunhardt Foundation

Almost directly under the path of the arcing shells on the elevated north side of the Romney Road sat the two-story "Hawthorn" house of Cornelia Peake McDonald and her absent Confederate husband, Col. Angus McDonald. As she and a female friend sat in the dining room, "it seemed perfectly strange to sit quietly in a rocking chair and watch the progress of a battle on that sweet June morning." As another Winchester woman noted, "Of course we were all in an intensely painful state of excitement. The Yankees had withdrawn all their forces to the fort and the town was entirely deserted by them, except now and then a stray scout, on horseback, would dash past." She watched the Yankee women "tearing round the streets in the most frantic manner; nobody could find out anything, there was no one of whom you could ask a question; all were ignorant and anxious alike."[16]

for his heroic actions on April 6, 1865, at Danville, Virginia. He was one of two men who succeeded in getting through the enemy's lines with dispatches to General Grant. Rowand was also active in the Jessie Scouts.

16 Cornelia Peake McDonald, "Battle at Winchester," in *Southern Bivouac*, vol. 2, no. 18, June 1884, 446-50; "Leaves from a Dairy Kept by a Lady." For more on Mrs. McDonald, see Brandon H. Beck and Charles S. Grunder, *The Three Battles of Winchester: A History and Guided*

After Gordon's Georgians cleared Milltown Heights, Ordnance Sgt. Watkins Kearns of the 27th Virginia, part of Walker's Stonewall Brigade, visited the site, "where a view can be had of the town about two miles distant." Kearns saw nothing of concern. "The Yankees have all left Winchester & are now in the fort the other side of town in the Pughtown Road. They are firing at long interval." "Our skirmishers", he added, referencing Gordon's men who had continued pushing forward, "are at work at the edge of town." Realizing they were on the eve of a full-scale battle, most of Winchester's residents remained behind closed doors in "breathless anxiety and anticipation," according to young Emma Riely.[17]

Milroy was willing to sacrifice Milltown Heights in order to concentrate his forces around Winchester and the forts. He placed pickets from the 12th Pennsylvania Cavalry on the ridge well north and west of the Main Fort, while other scattered outposts kept watch for enemy activity in other directions. Most of his pickets focused on the last known Rebel positions south and east of Winchester. Tensions remained high, morale by now had sagged, and many Federals were rapidly losing confidence in their senior leadership. The retreats and the miserable weather had done nothing to help their flagging spirits.[18]

Despite the very real issues of imperfect logistics and growing fatigue, Milroy remained hopeful the Rebels might break away and move toward Harpers Ferry. If not, he believed his men could hold out until reinforcements arrived. In order to determine whether Ewell had moved west, about 7:20 a.m. Milroy dispatched Capt. Charles B. Morgan and two companies of the 12th Pennsylvania Cavalry to reconnoiter on the Pughtown Road, returning via the Romney Road. He also sent out a detachment of cavalry on the Berryville Road, but Confederate skirmishers and sharpshooters soon drove these horsemen away. Company G of the 13th Pennsylvania Cavalry under a lieutenant with the unusual name of Aquilla Breech slipped through the Rebel lines and retired to Martinsburg, abandoning its stores and equipment as it did so. Rebels controlled every major road into and out of Winchester except for the Martinsburg Pike. Although the town's pro-Union citizens did not fully know all this, the enemy's obvious growing presence was bringing on a near-panic.

Tour (Berryville, VA: Civil War Foundation, 1997), 19. This part of the Romney Road is now Amherst Street. The McDonald house, once part of the "Glen Burnie" estate, was just west of James Mason's dismantled "Selma." Cornelia's husband, Col. Angus McDonald, was the first commander of the 7th Virginia Cavalry. Disabled by rheumatism, he was on post duty in 1863. Yankees captured him in 1864 and imprisoned him in Wheeling. After being released, his health broken, he died in Richmond in December of that year.

17 Kearns diary entry for June 14, 1863, VHS; Macon, *Reminiscences of the Civil War*, 79.

18 *OR* 27, pt. 2, 70.

Many of them, as well the soldiers' families and free blacks, sought refuge inside the forts or streamed north on the open turnpike toward Martinsburg and its presumed safety.[19]

Milroy, meanwhile, toured his fortifications and looked across the intervening terrain for signs of further movement. Using block and tackle, his men hauled him up a flagpole in a small wooden box. From that high perch, the general spent a considerable amount of time studying the enemy positions and pondering his next move. "All day Sunday Milroy was up on a look-out forty feet above the works with a field glass in hand watching Lee's veterans closing around our brave and devoted little army," the 87th Pennsylvania's Lt. Col. James A. Stahle penned. "What an uncomfortable time we had," he lamented. "No sleep, nor rest, for two days, rations getting short, everybody wet to the skin, all ready for immediate action, with the outlook anything but assuring. We knew we were being surrounded on all sides," he continued, "that rebel pickets were out on every road, is it any wonder that men became despondent and lost heart." By this time his soldiers were openly discussing why they had remained at Winchester at all when they could have escaped on Friday night and joined the forces at Harpers Ferry. Manning the works on Bolivar and Maryland heights, after all, would have given them at least a chance of holding the Rebels in check.[20]

Many other Union soldiers shared their growing concern. "Lee's army was gradually tightening its coils around us," explained the 123rd Ohio's Pvt. Henry Clapp. The 1st New York Cavalry's Capt. James H. Stevenson agreed: "It seemed strange that we should have been left at Winchester to be crushed by Lee's army, without some word from headquarters, but such was really the case, and somebody was to blame for such a blunder." To the 18th Connecticut's Chaplain Walker, the situation was "anything but encouraging to the Union army. All night the rebel commanders had been bringing up their forces, drawing in their lines and pressing us back, giving the boys 'another taste of Virginia mud,' which, owning to the pouring rain of the previous night, was quite deep. At this time the rebels were in full view," he added, "and were seen 'prowling about on the edge of town,' apparently in high glee over the success they had achieved. The rebel citizens of Winchester also were delighted with the situation, rejoicing at the prospect of the capture of the entire Yankee force within a few hours."[21]

---

19 Ibid., 45-46, 55, 96; *New York Herald*, June 22, 1863; *Philadelphia Public Ledger*, June 24, 1863.

20 OR 27, pt 2, 96; Stahle Papers, USAHEC.

21 Clapp, "With Milroy at Winchester"; Stevenson, *Boots and Saddles*, 188; Walker, *History of the Eighteenth Regiment*, 108-109.

Fighting on Bower's Hill and Near the Glen Burnie Stone Wall

During the morning, General Ewell and his staff met Jubal Early on Bower's Hill west of town, a prominent point from which they enjoyed a "very distinct view of the works about Winchester." Visibility by then was excellent, for the rain clouds and mist had departed. "There appeared to be no very heavy force in his [Ewell's] front," reported the corps commander's staff officer Campbell Brown, "the enemy evidently trusting to the fire of the large square fort (the 'flagstaff Fort') to repel any attempted advance along the top or by the base of this ridge." Early's attention soon turned to a higher ridge a half-mile west of the Main Fort and a little more than a mile northwest of his own position. Capturing the two gun positions there (West Fort and Battery #6) would give Early a good platform to attack Milroy's main bastion. A low orchard-covered ridge in front of Little North Mountain offered a good place from which to assault Flint Ridge and would screen the movement. Ewell agreed, and directed his division commander to move with his main force to the west and north and carry the works.[22]

Early decided to leave Gordon's brigade, Griffin's Baltimore Light Artillery, and the Salem Artillery on Bower's Hill to occupy the attention of the Yankees to his front and immediate left. The remainder of the division, some 3,600 men and 20 guns, would execute a wide flanking movement to gain control of the low ridge and enable his batteries to command the West Fort. Ewell instructed Early to conduct this movement in secrecy to avoid alerting the enemy, which might shift troops to the threatened area to confront him. Concurrently, General Johnson was ordered to make a ruckus and divert attention away from Early.[23]

Gordon's left wing and Smith's Virginians advanced toward the Romney Road, west of Bower's Hill, while Gordon's right wing knelt behind a stone wall on the hill proper. Milroy watched these moves with some alarm and dispatched General Elliott with the 122nd Ohio and Klunk's 12th West Virginia (temporarily detached from the Second Brigade), Carlin's Wheeling Battery, and Lt. Peter Leary, Jr.'s section of Alexander's battery to counter these movements. "We were sent about one mile from the fort . . . with orders to hold a stone wall and prevent if possible the advance of the rebels," noted one of Klunk's Mountaineers. The terrain west of Bower's Hill featured

---

22 Ibid., 440; "Diary of a Confederate Widow," *Milwaukee Journal*, May 24, 1935; Jones, *Campbell Brown's Diary*, 192.

23 Early, *Autobiographical Sketch*, 244. The Salem Artillery had two 3-inch rifles and two Napoleons. Captain Abraham Hupp had been away since October 1862 because of illness; he died of cancer in 1864. In his absence, Lt. Charles Peale Griffin commanded the guns at Second Winchester.

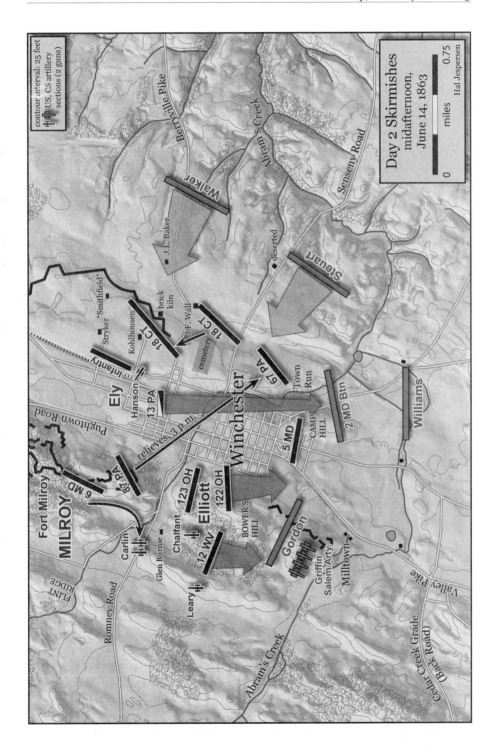

Day 2 Skirmishes
midafternoon,
June 14, 1863

0   miles   0.75

Hal Jespersen

contour interval: 25 feet
US, CS artillery
sections (2 guns)

several low narrow ridges with open fields and occasional belts of woods. Carlin unlimbered his guns on a rise to the left of the 12th West Virginia, with Leary's section to the Mountaineers' right. A squadron of cavalry protected Leary's flank. "Our section was ordered out to help the skirmishers," penned Pvt. William H. Moffett, Jr., one of Leary's men. "We fought them all day."[24]

The 122nd Ohio slowly advanced off Colonel Klunk's left flank, its progress hampered by the uneven terrain. Buckeye Sgt. David H. Danhauer had shouldered his musket and marched along with Company A even though he was on detached duty and did not have to do so. "But as I came out to fight," he stated, "I thought it a good opportunity to do so." Lieutenant Colonel Moses M. Granger deployed Companies A and E as skirmishers. They soon spied Rebels on the crest of Bower's Hill and opened a brisk round of skirmishing. "But I must confess," Danhauer added, "that is it not a very comfortable position to be in, to have men draw up and take aim at you, while the balls are whising all around you." The Buckeyes behaved well, despite advancing over open ground while the Southerners enjoyed the relative safety of a stone wall and woods. When Granger ordered the double-quick to take the crest, his men responded with alacrity and Gordon's Confederates there fell back. Their advance to the high ground had cost them several wounded and a few killed.[25]

During a brief lull in the fighting, principal musician John T. Patterson of the 122nd Ohio walked about in a desperate search to find his friend, 18-year-old drummer Price Worthing. Rebels spotted Patterson and opened fire, but he doggedly continued his search. The McConnellsville native eventually heard a low rhythmic beat coming from a hedge near the Romney Road. Ignoring the enemy gunfire, he investigated and found Worthing lying on the ground with both legs badly injured. He wielded a pair of twigs to tap a drum roll on his rifle stock to attract help. Patterson, with assistance from his hometown friend Pvt. Elbridge Robinson, picked up the wounded lad and carried him back to the Buckeyes' line, despite suffering his own painful wound in the process when one of the distant Rebel rounds finally found him.[26]

---

24 "H.C.H,." "With the 12th Virginia"; OR 27, pt. 2, 58; Hotchkiss map; Powell map; "War Sketches, Being Anecdotes and Experiences of West Virginia," in *Wheeling Sunday Register*, April 26, 1891; W. H. Moffett to Dear Father, June 16, 1863, Maryland Heights, MHS; April 26, 1891; "The Battle of Winchester: Authentic Details of the Contest," in *Philadelphia Public Ledger*, June 23, 1863.

25 *Zanesville* (OH) *Courier*, July 22, 1863.

26 *Juneau County Chronicle*, Mauston, Wisconsin, March 9, 1922; *Madison Capital Times*, Jan. 27, 1964. Drummer Worthing (in some accounts spelled Worthin) died from his wounds four days later on June 17. Both Patterson and Elbridge would receive the Medal of Honor for their

General Gordon's renewal of the fighting pushed back the Buckeyes, who retired in good order. Off to the east, a large force of Georgians advanced on an old Quaker church off of the Valley Pike and threatened the flank of the 87th Pennsylvania. Worried they would prove too much for the Keystoners, Captain Carlin brought his guns to bear and sent three or four shells plowing through the roof of the church. "The way those skirmishers left that church put me in mind of rats leaving a falling building," wrote George W. McClelland, a teenaged private working one of Carlin's guns.[27]

Some commotion in the grass off to their right caught the eye of Carlin's artillerists, but what was causing the commotion remained up for debate. When Carlin decided it was a man crawling toward the Wheeling battery, he ordered the No. 1 gun pointed in that direction. Sergeant Curran Mendel, the gunner, zeroed in on the target, recalled Private McClelland, and "whoever he was would have been torn to pieces" if Mendel was ordered to yank the lanyard. Just moments before the lanyard was to be pulled, however, a hand stuck up above the tall grass and waved at the Unionists. A pair of artillerists dispatched to get him discovered the man was a wounded soldier from the 122nd Ohio Infantry. The West Virginians brought him in and took him to the hospital.[28]

Meanwhile, Lieutenant Colonel Granger commanding the 122nd Ohio reformed and counterattacked, clearing once more the Rebels away from the stone wall and nearby woods on Bower's Hill. "Men, you must hold this position," he commanded. Further Confederate movements toward their line failed to dislodge the Buckeyes. Granger's valor and charisma helped hold his men in place as he rode up and down his line giving calm and cool orders as though nothing unusual was going on. Granger would pause occasionally, dismount to view the Rebels from some commanding spot, casually remount, and move on.[29]

Courage by itself, however, could not overcome lack of sleep, exhaustion, and dwindling rations. On Granger's flank, the 12th West Virginia had been subsisting for

---

heroic action. Patterson survived his wound and the war and died in 1922. He is buried in Oakwood Cemetery in Mauston, Wisconsin.

27 *Wheeling Sunday Register*, April 26, 1891. Major General Nathaniel Banks' Union troops took possession of the Centre Meeting House in March 1862 and the congregants relocated. By the end of the war, only the foundation of the building remained. The site is bounded by today's Washington, Monmouth, Stewart and Germain streets. For more information, see Garland Quarles, *The Churches of Winchester, Virginia: A Brief History of Those Established Prior to 1825* (Winchester, VA: n. p., 1960).

28 Ibid.

29 *Zanesville* (OH) *Courier*, July 22, 1863.

19th-century view of "Glen Burnie." *Scott Mingus*

some time primarily on hardtack and what little food the men had scrounged in their haversacks. Earlier that morning, the Mountaineers had marched out of the fortifications about 6:00 a.m. when Granger advanced and headed south. After crossing the Romney Road, the West Virginians tramped through the sprawling Glen Burnie estate, once the property of Winchester's founder, Col. James Wood, and now owned by Col. Thomas and Catherine Glass. Passing the stately two-story brick manor, the Mountaineers halted in a pasture a quarter-mile farther south and crouched behind a massive stone wall five feet tall and three feet thick marking the southern edge of the property. This sturdy wall ran east-west about 850 feet. Once there, Klunk's soldiers spotted some of Gordon's Georgians advancing on their position. A brisk exchange of skirmish fire erupted with Confederates 150 yards away behind a parallel stone wall. Klunk eventually withdrew part of his regiment, leaving behind a portion at the stone wall that he reinforced with a pair of fresh reserve companies while holding the left wing in reserve. Klunk's right battalion supported Carlin's guns, which unlimbered on high ground about 900 yards from the Confederate lines. However, with Klunk's men now to their front, Carlin no longer had a clear field of fire, and broken ground to his rear reduced his ability to maneuver.

Consequently, he withdrew his battery at 11:00 a.m. into the Main Fort's entrenchments.[30]

With orders to make a demonstration and hold the Union men in position while other Confederate brigades marched beyond their flank farther west, Gordon advanced skirmishers into the field between the gun positions, but Klunk's West Virginians easily pushed them back because the Rebel objective was not to drive them away but to hold their attention. Meanwhile, accurate fire from Lieutenant Leary's section knocked several holes in the Rebel-held stone wall and scattered the enemy in a "lively manner." The distant sport provided some amusement for the hot, hungry, and tired Mountaineers. Some of Klunk's men were so tired they stretched out and fell asleep despite the booming cannons and popping of small arms fire. Unfortunately for the resting Lt. John T. Ben Gough, a Rebel bullet struck him. Carried back to the Taylor Hotel, he died that night.[31]

East and a bit north of the 12th West Virginia, Pvt. W. H. Bruder's company of the 123rd Ohio manned a skirmish line near the northern part of Bower's Hill. These Buckeyes had been skirmishing all morning, but about 10:00 a.m. noticed Rebels advancing toward the left of their line in Winchester's extreme southwestern outskirts in an effort to flank the pickets. Bruder ordered the pickets to fall back. Once they were in place, the rest of the company reformed about 200 yards behind this new picket line. He had scarcely assumed this new position when Confederates, who outnumbered him about four to one, rushed across an open meadow. After firing a volley, the Buckeyes fell back to their camp, which they found deserted, the regiment having packed everything before moving to a new position.[32]

Several of the 123rd's wounded from the previous day's fighting remained on the field. The injured Cpl. George Buskirk, now incapacitated from his wounded right calf muscle, and his mortally wounded friend resting in the old black man's house near the

---

30 *New York Herald*, June 22, 1863; Wilmer, Jarrett, and Vernon, *History and Roster of Maryland Volunteers*, 1:817; *Gettysburg Compiler*, June 29, 1863; Hewitt, *History of the 12th West Virginia*, 42; *Philadelphia Public Ledger*, June 23, 1863; Miner, "First Fight, First Blood: The Twelfth West Virginia Infantry at the Second Battle of Winchester," *http://www.markminer.com /12wv.htm*, accessed December 8, 2013. The historic Glen Burnie estate, the location of the Museum of the Shenandoah Valley, is at 901 Amherst Street. Its owner, Colonel Glass of the 51st Virginia Militia, also owned the Rose Hill estate southwest of Winchester which played a role in the March 1863 fighting. Remains of the old stone wall the Mountaineers defended still exist along a chain link fence bordering John Kerr Elementary School north of Jefferson Street. The Rebel-held stone wall was likely between today's Jefferson and Seldon Drive.

31 Ibid.; J. N. Waddell, "Milroy at Winchester: A Veteran of the 12th Va. Gives His Experiences," *National Tribune*, January 14, 1909. Waddell was lying beside Gough when he was mortally wounded.

32 Bruder Journal, USAHEC.

Valley Pike experienced a tortured journey to medical care. A squad of Confederates found them in the house in the forenoon and loaded them into an ambulance. Inexplicably, the Rebels unloaded the two Buckeyes along the roadside just a mile or two away—and left them there. Later, a Confederate colonel found them there and ordered some of his men to care for the wounded enemy soldiers. Unfortunately, it was too late for Buskirk's comrade, who died before he could be picked up. Buskirk was taken to a hospital, but what little care he received there was poor indeed. One of his arteries ruptured and he nearly bled to death before someone was able to tie it off. During the operating procedure, however, the surgeon inadvertently severed a nerve that crippled Buskirk for life.[33]

The Defense of Camp Hill and Cemetery Hill

While the fluid fighting on and around Bower's Hill and Glen Burnie unfolded, action continued south and southeast of Winchester. As early as 7:00 a.m., the 5th Maryland under Colonel Ely's direction had begun skirmishing with Confederates on Cemetery Hill. The soldiers of the 18th Connecticut, back in the works near the Star Fort after their confusing early morning jaunt into Winchester, had just received their rations. They had yet to cook their food when orders arrived to move out and relieve the 5th Maryland. The Connecticut commander, Lt. Col. Monroe Nichols, was ill and Maj. Henry Peale was now in charge. With at least one company left behind in the earthworks until noon, the regiment once more marched through Winchester, where some of the men paused to protect workers who were busy removing quartermaster and commissary stores. During the march up to the rifle pits, Marylanders could be heard lustily singing *The Battle Cry of Freedom*.[34]

The right battalion of the 18th Connecticut's skirmishers took shelter behind a stone wall at the eastern base of Cemetery Hill. A limekiln and the John F. Wall home anchored the left side of this advanced line. Behind them up in Mount Hebron and the soldiers' cemeteries, another company or two backed them up. To the north, across the Berryville Road, other companies manned the rifle pits and light works on the F. W. Kohlhousen property not far from his extensive vineyards. The 5th Maryland

---

33 Buskirk obituary, *Bryan* (OH) *News*, June 2, 1904. Buskirk was exchanged and went home, using crutches for four years. He worked in the grocery business, sold sewing machines, was the city marshal of Bryan, farmed, and owned a candy store, overcoming his handicap for 41 years after his injury.

34 Walker, *History of the Eighteenth Connecticut*, 109, 112; James M. Smith diary entry for June 14, 1863.

moved southwest to Camp Hill, where the soldiers deployed behind a long stone wall and into the town's black cemetery.[35]

Jubal Early, meanwhile, sent a courier back to Lt. Col. James Herbert to send some of his 2nd Maryland Battalion, deployed southeast of Winchester, into the town. Herbert dispatched Maj. William Goldsborough with three companies, which advanced in line across the pike to within 200-300 yards of the town's southern outskirts. "This morning, a little after daybreak, we received orders to advance our skirmish line, which we did," wrote S. Thomas McCullough, a member of the Confederate 2nd Maryland Battalion, "coming upon the enemy so and dearly and unexpectedly that they were forced to abandon their breakfasts, which were on the fire—their clothing—camp accommodations, etc.—poking through their camp, we pursued them to the outskirts of Winchester, where they engaged us from behind the houses."[36]

The previous night, Confederate cavalryman Harry Gilmor spent the night with Goldsborough on the skirmish line. Before daylight, Gilmor bet his friend that unless he was killed, Gilmor would be the first man to enter Winchester. The dashing cavalier moved up along the Millwood Pike, which he reached at sunrise. When he did not see any Federals, he rode cautiously ahead near Swartz's Mill, where he began to find bodies, knapsacks, blankets, and guns strewn where Edward Johnson's infantry had engaged the 110th Ohio and 5th Maryland the previous afternoon. Feeling his way farther north, Gilmor entered the Marylanders' abandoned camp at the foot of Camp Hill, where he rummaged through a pile of knapsacks jammed with plunder of all varieties. While his horse munched on oats, Gilmor amused himself for a time by reading the letters scattered about, and then gathered up about 100 gum-cloths, carried them to a nearby house, and consigned them to a woman there until such time he and his men could come back for them.[37]

Gilmor had just gained the crest of Camp Hill when the whistling of two or three bullets indicated the presence of Yankees concealed behind a distant stone fence. He wisely turned back down the Front Royal Pike and came upon the remnants of Lieutenant Edmund Spooner's exploded caisson from Battery L, 5th U. S. Artillery. A dead man lay on his back, his uniform burned off and his body perfectly black. The lid of the ammunition chest was nearby, with several blankets and a large tent-fly strapped to it. Gilmor was gazing at the spectacle when Major Goldsborough hailed

35 Ibid.; Hotchkiss map. The 18th's rifle pits were along today's Battle Avenue. CSA Brigadier General Joseph Johnston's troops dug them in 1861.

36 McCullough diary, entry for June 14, 1863.

37 Gilmor, *Four Years in the Saddle*, 85.

him from the 5th Maryland's abandoned camp. The cavalry officer rode over and his friend, told him about the enemy skirmishers, and together they dashed up the hill after them. After surveying the scene, Goldsborough deployed his skirmishers. They began exchanging fire with the 5th Marylanders, some of whom returned fire from behind the gravestones in the black cemetery. The Yankees soon learned their opponents were from the 2nd Maryland Battalion, which included acquaintances, relatives, and even old schoolmates.[38]

Dr. Charles Goldsborough borrowed a field glass from a friend and scanned the Rebel lines hoping to glimpse his older brother. He thought he recognized William leading the advance atop a sorrel horse. The Rebel officer passed along his lines several times, and the Union Marylanders behind the tombstones took deliberate aim to bring him down. When the horse and rider tumbled to the ground, a shout went up along the entire line. Whoever he was, the fallen officer was neither Major Goldsborough nor Major Gilmor.[39]

Major Goldsborough and his three companies (B, C, and E) of Maryland Rebels charged, opening a hole in the 5th Maryland's line that allowed them to push into the southern outskirts of Winchester. The small tactical victory allowed Harry Gilmor to set spurs to his mount and ride into town just ahead of Major Goldsborough, winning their friendly bet (although Goldsborough also claimed the honor). Several women, "wild with joy and excitement," soon came out to converse with the dashing officer from Baltimore, who was still decked out in his new yellow-trimmed uniform. When a Union cavalryman approached, Gilmor drew his revolver and rode toward him. The surprised Yankee opened fire and ran off, still shooting as he made his escape. Gilmor gave chase on his fleet horse "Old Bill," but could not get his pistol caps to ignite. He chased the Federal four blocks but broke off the pursuit when he encountered what looked to be an enemy infantry regiment deployed in line of battle. Gilmore wheeled about and reversed course, but before he could round the nearest corner a bullet struck his horse in the muscle above its hock. The horse limped on three legs for a few steps, regained its strength, and carried Gilmor to safety. That regiment Gilmor stumbled into was the 87th Pennsylvania, which Milroy had dispatched to flush the advancing Rebels out of Winchester's southern outskirts.[40]

Corporal Charles Z. Denues of the 87th Pennsylvania had looked forward to going to church services that morning. Instead of sitting in a pew, however, he and his

---

38 Ibid., 85-86; Goldsborough, *The Maryland Line*, 117-18; *Gettysburg Star & Sentinel*, April 2, 1902.

39 *National Tribune*, December 18, 1884; Goldsborough, *The Maryland Line*, 117-18.

40 Gilmor, *Four Years in the Saddle*, 86.

Wartime view of the Taylor Hotel. *U.S. Army Heritage and Education Center*

comrades filed into marching column about 9:00 a.m. and tramped about half a mile through town to contest the encroaching Confederate Marylanders. Brisk encounters ensued over the next couple of hours on South Market, Main, and Braddock streets. According to the 87th's Lt. Col. James Stahle, his men were fired upon from windows and rooftops, and it was only with difficulty that he was able to prevent his men from setting fire to the buildings. According to a soldier in the Union 5th Maryland, he and his comrades captured Lt. James P. Quinn of Company E, 2nd Maryland Battalion "in a most unaccountable manner, in a house, where he could easily have fallen off." He also noted that during the rapid exchange of fire, Lt. W. R. Byus, also of Company E, took a painful round in the heel.[41]

41 *Philadelphia Inquirer*, July 4, 1897; Prowell, *History of the 87th Pennsylvania*, 72; Stahle Papers, USAHEC; McCullough diary, entry for June 15, 1863. Market Street is now Cameron Street, and Main is Loudoun.

The 2nd Maryland's Capt. Ferdinand C. Duval, commanding Company C, fell with a bullet wound to his right leg, just below his knee. Fortunately the round did not strike the bone, but the painful injury kept the 28-year-old Millersville farmer out of action for almost a year. S. Thomas McCullough of his company helped carry the injured officer from the field to a nearby home, where Duvall's wound was treated before he was sent to the rear. His company lost six men wounded, but none killed. Lieutenant John H. Stone deemed the street fight "quite an engagement." Company B, in which Stone served, suffered four casualties.[42]

The patients inside the Taylor House listened as the street firing approached them. Scores of wounded men streamed in throughout the morning from every direction of the compass. The 18th Connecticut's James Sawyer went from room to room looking for any comrades from his regiment. When he returned to his own room, he found the cot beside his own holding an Ohioan with a bullet in his side. The man's brother, a lieutenant, kept watch by the bedside. As Sawyer was wondering why the officer, who was not sick or wounded, was absent from his post, a "very fat boy, a drummer" from the same Buckeye regiment walked in and took another cot. Like the lieutenant, he too appeared able-bodied.[43]

While Sawyer worried about healthy men leaving the front, Jubal Early worried that the Union artillery in the Main Fort would shell the town to clear out the Confederates. He finally decided to retire and sent orders via General Gordon for Goldsborough to do just that. The Marylanders withdrew, leaving Captain Duval and other wounded men behind. With the Pennsylvanians and 5th Marylanders in pursuit, the 2nd Maryland took up a new position behind a stone wall 200 yards south of town, triggering another brisk skirmish with the 5th Maryland. Rebel William H. Lyons of Company E tabulated the Maryland Line's not insubstantial losses that day at "17 men wounded, some mortally."[44]

Colonel John Schall of the 87th Pennsylvania, meanwhile, detailed Company A to conduct mop-up operations to secure Winchester. Four men searched a house where a Rebel sharpshooter was supposedly holed up. The Union soldiers entered through the basement and carefully searched floor by floor without success. The quartet was

---

42 "The Capture of Winchester," in *Richmond Whig*, June 23, 1863; pension records, NARA; McCullough Diary, entry for June 15, 1863. Duval was wounded again at the battle of Peebles' Farm in Sept. 1864 and then in April 1865 was taken prisoner at Hatcher's Run. He spent the rest of the war in the Johnson's Island prison camp in Ohio.

43 Sawyer, "Abandoned at Winchester," 11.

44 Goldsborough, *The Maryland Line*, 118; Walker, *History of the Eighteenth Connecticut*, 109; William H. Lyons diary, entry for June 14, 1863; Diary of William H. Lyons, Company E, 2nd Maryland Infantry, C.S.A., MS 1860, MHS.

crossed the landing of the second floor stairs when distant Rebel Marylanders fired a handful of shots through the windows. One bullet, which would leave a scar several inches long, grazed Pvt. Charles E. Zimmerman's left temple and cut off two-thirds of the rim of his hat. Another Minié ball pierced Alfred Jameson's arm but did not break a bone.[45]

In mid-morning division commander Edward Johnson moved to obey Early's order to divert attention from Jubal Early's position on Bower's Hill. Johnson left a strong skirmish line south of Winchester to hold the Yankees in position and marched James Walker's Stonewall Brigade north across the Millwood Pike to a range of wooded hills east of town straddling the Berryville Road, with George Steuart's brigade moving behind it. Colonel William Ely spotted the lines of Rebels when they arrived on the heights. The quick-thinking Union brigade commander moved some of the 18th Connecticut to the crescent-shaped rifle pits northeast of town to block the move.[46]

Once in position, with the rest of the Stonewall Brigade and Steuart's brigade halted behind them in support, Lt. Col. H. J. Williams and four companies of the 5th Virginia, Walker's brigade, advanced as skirmishers toward Cemetery Hill, but quickly encountered Federals sheltered in houses and behind fences. The Virginians knelt behind a stone wall east of the hill, but were within easy musket range of much of the 87th Pennsylvania and 18th Connecticut, whose fire proved "brisk and continual." General "Allegheny" Johnson directed the fighting from the shelter of a stand of woods behind the right flank of his skirmish line. The rest of his division (Williams' Second Louisiana Brigade and John Jones' Virginians) remained idle south of Winchester along the Front Royal Pike throughout the morning, including his ordnance trains, which were still well in the rear also along the Front Royal Road. "We still occupied our position," bemoaned the 25th Virginia's adventure-seeking Dr. Abram S. Miller, "not having anything to do."[47]

---

45 Prowell, *History of the 87th Pennsylvania*, 86. Jameson became a railroad conductor after he mustered out in late 1864. The following June, he was found mortally injured on top of his railcar after he collided with a bridge support. His family buried him on what would have been his wedding day.

46 *OR*, 27, pt. 2, 500; Walker, *History of the Eighteenth Connecticut*, 109, Lynch diary entry for June 13, 1863.

47 *OR* 27, pt. 2, 500; *Richmond Daily Dispatch*, February 5, 1864; Miller to Dear Julia, June 16, 1863, Handley Library. This part of Senseny Road is E. Cork Street in modern Winchester while the roughly parallel Berryville Road is National Avenue. Mount Hebron Cemetery contains marked graves dating from 1769. Today the sprawling burial grounds encompass three other old graveyards, including a Lutheran Cemetery which dates from at least as far back

The J. W. Baker property on the Berryville Pike; the 18th Connecticut charged Virginia sharpshooters ensconced in this brick house. *Handley Regional Library*

As they had during the previous day, several daring residents watched the action from their top-floor windows or rooftops; most hoped for a Confederate victory. On what she described as "a glorious day for us," young Gettie Miller rejoiced in downtown Winchester, "our men are coming." She and her family went up in the garret (an attic floor) and peeked out the trap door. "We could see the yankees up by Mrs. Senseny's and our men come out of the wood and shoot."[48]

At one point, several Virginians entered Josiah L. Baker's large brick house along the Berryville Road about half a mile east of town. Surrounded by dense shrubbery, the property offered the riflemen a natural bastion. The skirmishers knocked out a few bricks in the second floor, and their ensuing fire made it hot for the 18th Connecticut's forward rifle pits just to the northwest. Once the Connecticut men determined they had had enough, Capt. Charles D. Bowen's Company H launched itself and carried the Rebel position, killing an enemy officer and five other Virginians, and seizing 19 prisoners. The captives soon revealed that indeed all of Ewell's corps was on hand, including an estimate of the force's approximate size.

The Connecticut troops were returning to their lines when a Minié ball drilled through the lower lobe of Englishman William Caruthers' liver, passed his stomach, and lodged in his back muscles near his spine. Two men helped the stricken Caruthers to the rear, where the 5th Maryland's Dr. Charles Goldsborough stopped his ambulance and loaded them inside. A short time later, as the ambulance was rolling toward a hospital, an artillery shell exploded in front of it, killing and wounding several unlucky men standing nearby. The vehicle stopped at the Lewis house along the Martinsburg Pike, where Goldsborough tried to save Caruthers by extracting the bullet, which came out with coffee grounds. The hideous wound appeared obviously mortal, and the doctor announced just that, and gave the Englishman only 30 minutes to live. A couple men started digging a grave in the Lewis yard, but Caruthers

as 1777; a public cemetery chartered in Feb. 1844; and the post-war Stonewall Confederate Cemetery dedicated in 1866.

48 Gettie Miller diary entry for June 14, 1863, Handley Library.

confounded everyone by surviving. He would live well into the 20th century and serve as postmaster of Norwich, Connecticut.[49]

Another Nutmeg boy shot that hot day was Pvt. Daniel B. Sullivan of Company A. Shot in his left side, he crawled down the hillside to find some relief under a tree from the unrelenting sun. Realizing he was in bad shape, a sympathetic comrade offered him a canteen of water. A young French-born surgeon later tended to Sullivan, but refused to probe for the bullet resting within a quarter-inch of his heart. Somehow Sullivan survived, and carried the flattened Minié ball in his body for nearly four decades before it eventually worked its way out by itself.[50]

Corporal William T. Ziegler of Gettysburg served in Company F of the 87th Pennsylvania. "After engaging the enemy for several hours and preventing them from entering the town, I was suddenly seized with the determination to leave my command and go to the skirmish line at the cemetery," he wrote. "The skirmish line is the one place where a soldier especially dislikes to go. You are very close to the enemy, and generally between two fires. But without a thought of the danger I was running into, I hurriedly left my command and followed up the street until I entered the cemetery gate, and instead of following the driveway around to where our line was, I took out across the graves." During this move Ziegler found a desperately wounded Union soldier amongst the gravestones. After staunching the bleeding, the former coach maker's assistant made his way back into town to secure a stretcher. With a detail of four men, Ziegler carried the stricken Buckeye back to the safety of a field hospital, where the surgeons saved the wounded man's life.[51]

As the morning wore on, and the Northerners stubbornly held onto Winchester, doubts began to creep into the minds of some Confederates whether they really could push the Yankees out of their network of artillery-studded forts, earthworks, and rifle pits. Robert H. Depriest, a veteran infantryman from the 2nd Virginia, later wrote his wife that the enemy "was so well fixt i thought we wold not get them out."[52]

"Sunday morning showed that we were invested entirely on the east also," observed a Federal soldier. The ongoing fighting now engulfing Winchester panicked

---

49 OR 27, pt. 2, 45-46; Lynch diary entry for June 14, 1863; "Great Civil War Record of Norwich Postmaster," in *New London* (CT) *The Day*, December 10, 1907; Dr. C. E. Goldsborough, "Reminiscences from an Army Surgeon," in *The National Tribune Scrapbook: Stories of the Camp, March, Battle, Hospital and Prison Told by Comrades* (Washington, DC: National Tribune), 42-43.

50 "Bullet Drops Out of His Breast," *Norwich* (CT) *Bulletin*, March 13, 1900.

51 W. T. Ziegler, "A Wartime Recollection of Hon. W. T. Ziegler at the Battle of Winchester," *Gettysburg Compiler*, July 2, 1913; Prowell, *History of the 87th Pennsylvania*, 85.

52 R. H. Depriest to Dear wife, June 15, 1863, Robert H. Depriest Letters, Library of Virginia.

Brig. Gen. John M. Jones, who commanded a brigade in Johnson's division. *Library of Congress*

loyal, pro-Union civilians. "A general alarm now prevailed: all classes of persons— soldiers and citizens, Union families and negroes—were either taking refuge in the fortifications which line the west by northwest suburb of the town, or were breaking out for Martinsburg," continued the Union man. "Brisk skirmishing taking place at every quarter, we were completely hemmed in," with exception of the turnpike northward. It was now obvious that the Confederates had arrived in overwhelming numbers, and everyone, soldiers and civilians alike, worried whether they would be able to escape.[53]

By this time the same thought was likely crossing the mind of General Milroy, who remained perched atop his improvised observation platform watching the enemy tentacles spread around Winchester. About 11:00 a.m., the 10th Virginia's Pvt. Samuel Firebaugh ascended Bower's Hill west of town to view the enemy's fortifications. He caught sight of the Stars & Stripes flying and, to his surprise, "old Milroy some 60 feet on the pole in a basket viewing, but our forces all hid." This did not surprise Buckeye sergeant James Dalzell of the 116th Ohio, who observed, "The sharpshooters could see him [Milroy] sitting there, eye-glass in hand, all day long. He was a remarkably plain and attractive target. . . . His clothing was riddled. His cap twice pierced. The flag-staff a foot through shot off over his head. The box he sat in was bored full of holes. The flag was shot down above him twice and again." According to the Union sergeant, Milroy would go down, pick up the banner, wave it defiantly at the enemy in a shower of lead, and then replace it as best he could on its pole.[54]

By midday, steady sunshine had burned off the last remaining clouds and the temperature was hot and the humidity high. Many of the men in Allegheny Johnson's unengaged brigades, without the excitement of battle to occupy their attention, were quite uncomfortable. Confederate Second Corps artillery staff officer Lt. Samuel H.

53 "The Loss of Winchester: A Narrative of the Investment and Abandonment of the Place," *New York Times*, June 28, 1863.

54 Firebaugh diary entry for June 14, 1863, SHC; Dalzell, "A Lucky Blunder," 96.

Pendleton had spent a miserable night in the fields off of the Front Royal Pike without bedclothes or overcoat. Now, with little to do, he listened to the distant sporadic firing. About the same time, chafing for more action after his morning adventures, Harry Gilmor, after rubbing neat's-foot oil on his horse's injured leg, rode to see General Ewell on the heights beyond the Millwood Pike southeast of town. The commander dispatched Gilmor on a scouting mission out the Berryville Road.[55]

Several hundred yards east of the Front Royal Pike south of Winchester, Brig. Gen. John M. Jones, a brigade commander in Johnson's division, advanced sharpshooters from the 25th Virginia to a low ridge in front of a large farmhouse. About noon, a middle-aged woman and her beautiful teenage niece Annie walked out to the firing line. A mile to the west, a long Rebel line of skirmishers of the 1st and 3rd North Carolina was moving down the same ridge. However, she noticed a body of Union cavalry riding straight at the skirmishers across the shallow valley. "Oh, dear, dear," the girl wailed, "all our poor men will be killed." Someone told her to look at the crest to the west, where the main line of Steuart's 1st and 3rd North Carolina regiments had just emerged from the woods in a mile-long line and began advancing behind the skirmish line. The skirmishers paused, fired once, and then fell back to Tar Heels' main line. The cavalry, undaunted, kept coming until the North Carolinians fired a volley. The horsemen then retired with a few saddles emptied. Annie, thrilled with the outcome of the brief encounter, joyously shouted her encouragement and clapped her hands repeatedly.[56]

Also about noon, General Milroy began reinforcing his forward lines with companies of infantry from the Main and Star forts. He sent the rest of the men of the 18th Connecticut from the Star Fort to their camp site of the previous night (in the earthworks at the eastern foot of Apple Pie Ridge below the Main Fort). Company F advanced to a line of rifle pits on the Smithfield estate northeast of town and knelt down, where the Nutmeg infantry began exchanging fire with skirmishers from the Stonewall Brigade. According to Pvt. James M. Smith, the firing there became "pretty brisk." Rumors reached him that General Hooker was approaching in the rear of the Rebels with reinforcements, "but I don't believe it," Smith admitted.[57]

The artillery on both sides grew quiet in the late forenoon as targets moved out of sight or effective range. The fitful skirmishing continued, more intense at times than others, but the Confederates were not making a determined attempt to rush the forts.

---

55 Entry for June 14, 1863, Samuel H. Pendleton Diary, 1861-1864, Accession #9878, Albert and Shirley Small Special Collections Library, UVA; Gilmor, *Four Years in the Saddle*, 86.

56 King, *My Experience in the Confederate Army*, 12.

57 James M. Smith diary entry for June 14, 1863.

Some of the officers remained convinced the Rebels would leave and head to Martinsburg or Harpers Ferry. Inside the forts, Union soldiers debated Ewell's intentions. "Everyone was in suspense all day," wrote a member of the 116th Ohio. "That dread silence meant something, all deeply felt, but what was the strategy progressing none seemed able to discover." About noon, Milroy began positioning fresh troops as reserves. He shifted Lt. Col. William McKellip and Companies C, E, G, H, and K of the 6th Maryland out of the Star Fort to the extreme left of the Main Fort. He also ordered Colonel Schall's 87th Pennsylvania, its men exhausted from the fighting thus far, to retire to the Main Fort.[58]

After the weary men of the 87th had retired and arrived at the rifle pits, "then a flag of truce came from the other side, the bearers asking General Milroy to surrender," recalled Corporal Denues. "That officer replied that he would fight until the freezing over of a future place of punishment and when that place froze over he would slide away on the ice." When the men heard of his brash reply, they gave Milroy a great cheer. The general wanted to abide by the common rules of battle, and, if attacked, he intended to burn the town. Supposedly, Ewell replied that if any house was burned, he would hoist the black flag and give no quarter. Some Southern papers later claimed Ewell threatened to hang any captured Yankees in retaliation if Milroy burned Winchester. Northern papers quickly picked up the story.[59]

About 1:00 p.m. General Elliott ordered Companies I, K, and part of B of Lt. Col. Moses Granger's 122nd Ohio to deploy in southern Winchester. There, they became involved in some of the day's sharpest skirmishing when they advanced rapidly upon a rifle pit and stone wall manned by what they estimated to be a battalion of Rebel infantry. The Buckeyes fired three volleys and, according to Lt. James Hartley, a Rebel left the ranks to run into a nearby house. There, a woman, perhaps the soldier's wife, met him at the door, threw her arms around him, and watched in horror as a nearby soldier shot the fleeing soldier down. "I would not care if every Rebel was served the same way if they will not lay down their arms and behave themselves," Hartley noted with some satisfaction. "Some of our fellows were shot at on Sunday from the windows and the Scamps took every advantage of us that they could," he added. When the 123rd Ohio of Ely's brigade arrived to relieve them, the Buckeyes of the

58 *Philadelphia Press*, June 26, 1863; *Baltimore Sun*, April 19, 1904; *Charleston* (SC) *Mercury*, June 22, 1863, citing unnamed Richmond newspapers.

59 *Philadelphia Inquirer*, July 4, 1897. Sgt. James Dalzell of the 116th Ohio claimed Milroy rejected Ewell's surrender demand from his flagpole perch, crying out, "Go to hell! Tell Gen. Ewell to come and take me." James M. Dalzell, "Milroy Swore at Rebs from Box on Pole," *Winchester Evening Star*, February 1, 1922; *Semi-Weekly Wisconsin (Milwaukee)*, June 26, 1863, citing Richmond papers of June 18. See also the *Raleigh Register*, June 20, 1863, quoting a gentleman who had left Winchester on the morning of June 16.

122nd retired to the works around the Main Fort. Colonel William H. Ball, the 122nd's commander, would later praise Granger, five officers, and the men for displaying a high degree of courage and coolness in the sharp foray.[60]

While Milroy continued to move his troops about in the early afternoon, in Washington his silence about the specific nature of his opponents became intolerable. Frustrated by a lack of solid intelligence about Rebel whereabouts, President Lincoln wired General Hooker at 1:14 p.m., "Do you consider it possible that 15,000 of Ewell's men can now be at Winchester?" He also instructed Middle Department commander Maj. Gen. Robert C. Schenck to order Milroy to remove his troops to safety northward to Harpers Ferry: "He will be gobbled up if he remains, if he is not already past salvation." Lincoln from afar and many of the Union troops in and around Winchester were thinking the same thing. To reinforce the gravity of the situation, the general-in-chief of the U. S. Army, Henry Halleck, early that afternoon wired Schenck in Baltimore, "If you have not executed my orders to concentrate your forces at Harpers Ferry, you will do so immediately. Troops, stores, &c., at New Creek, Grafton, [West Virginia] &c., should be carried west the moment danger approaches. Unless there is a more prompt obedience of orders," Halleck concluded in a direct and ominous threat, "there must be a change of commanders. See to this immediately."

It was too late. General Schenck could not extricate Milroy before the Rebel noose tightened around Winchester. "I was doing all I could," he later declared in defense of himself, "and suppose that General Halleck, as is often the case with all ours, was a little excited by the news he had heard." Halleck had made a recent leadership change, assigning the more experienced Brig. Gen. Daniel Tyler to command the garrison at Martinsburg, replacing Col. Benjamin F. Smith. That also was too little, too late.[61]

Concerned about the "overwhelming masses of the enemy about me," Milroy had kept his forces well in hand and in immediate connection with the forts. As early as Saturday evening after learning of the presence of part of Lee's army in force below Winchester, Milroy had made up his mind to act on the defensive, economizing his forces and waiting until the enemy had massed for a final attack. If relief did not arrive, he thought he could force his way through the weakest portion of the Rebel lines and escape. Confederate movements on Saturday only served to reinforce his mistaken thoughts, and he continued to believe the real attack would come from the direction

60 Hartley, *Civil War Letters*, 42; Moses M. Granger, "The 122nd Ohio at Winchester," *National Tribune*, August 12, 1909.

61 *OR* 27, pt. 1, 38; pt. 2, 16; *OR* 51, 1055.

of the Romney Road to the rest. Milroy's conclusion would prove to be a fateful decision.[62]

Meanwhile at Winchester, while Washington awaited news from Milroy, the 5th Maryland soldiers deployed in the black cemetery on Camp Hill maintained their fight with the Confederate 2nd Maryland Battalion. According to Dr. Charles Goldsborough, who maintained his field hospital on the reverse slope, the Rebels were slowly pressing ahead. Sergeant Charles Troeger, a young German, periodically crept from the shelter of a tombstone to the board fence enclosing the graveyard so he could get a better and closer shot at the Rebels, most of whom were still behind the distant stone wall. His comrades had cautioned him several times about the grave risk he was taking, but Troeger ignored the sound advice. He was crawling forward once more when a Minié ball struck him in the lower throat just above his breastbone and killed him. During a lull in the skirmishing, Dr. Goldsborough sent some men to retrieve Troeger's corpse. He pressed a nearby black man to carry Troeger to the edge of town, where he placed the sergeant beneath a tree. In the early afternoon, the Federals twice left their stone wall to attack the Maryland Confederates. Major William Goldsborough's Rebels repulsed both efforts, but Lt. Joseph E. Quinn of Company E, 2nd Maryland was captured, explained one eyewitness, "due to his own indiscretion."[63]

Sometime about 2:00 p.m., Capt. Charles B. Morgan and his detachment of the 12th Pennsylvania Cavalry (which had been sent west out the Pughtown road at 7:20 a.m. to determine whether Ewell had moved west) returned from its reconnaissance without meeting or detecting any traces of the enemy. Morgan's report relieved Milroy's apprehensions of an immediate attack from that direction, "and induced me to turn my attention to the approaches in the other directions," he later wrote. Milroy's staff officer, Capt. Frederick Palmer, provided insight into Milroy's state of mind at this time. "It became the generally settled belief that [the Confederates] had passed up the Valley to Harpers Ferry, leaving us to be attended to on their return, which idea was confirmed by the heavy firing heard in that direction," wrote Palmer. "When ever a body of the enemy did appear, our guns were turned upon them instantly, but not a single artillery response could be obtained, and we could not account for their mysterious silence, save by the theory that they had taken their guns with them, and

---

62 OR 27, pt. 2, 46.

63 *Gettysburg Star & Sentinel*, April 2, 1902; Goldsborough, *The Maryland Line*, 95. It is believed that Heyward Shepherd is buried in this cemetery, which is known today as Orrick Cemetery. Shepherd, a free black, was the first man to die during John Brown's 1859 raid on Harpers Ferry when two of the raiders shot him. See Noyalas, http://www.shenandoahatwar.org/The-History/The-People/Heyward-Shepherd, accessed December 8, 2013.

had left only sufficient force to engage us at skirmishing at long range." If Morgan had been instructed to reconnoiter in another direction, he could not have missed finding large bodies of Confederate troops. Deceived by Morgan's news, Milroy took no additional major steps to fend off the coming disaster.[64]

Meanwhile, while Milroy continued to underestimate the danger his men faced at Winchester, the adventure-loving Confederate Maj. Harry Gilmor completed his voluntary scouting mission out the Berryville Pike and headed back to General Ewell via the Valley Mill Road. During his return, he encountered a "Jessie Scout" in a narrow lane leading to Griffith's woolen factory along Abram's Creek. Earlier in the war Maj. Gen. John C. Fremont authorized the formation of a group of Union spies dressed in Confederate uniforms. To distinguish each other, the spies, soon known as "Jessie Scouts," wore white handkerchiefs around their neck, with the long end dangling over a shoulder. Gilmor had wisely taken the precaution of donning a similar handkerchief. The Union spy drew his pistol and slowly rode forward toward the stranger riding a dappled gray. After a brief exchange of small talk, Gilmor captured the spy and appropriated a pair of handcuffs, which the Union man intended to use on a Rebel he thought was hiding in the factory. When the Jessie Scout tried to break away, Gilmor thrust his saber into his chest. He knelt beside the victim and gave him brandy, but within five minutes the man was dead. Gilmor swapped horses, tying injured Old Bill to a pine tree. Before he had ridden too far, however, three or four Union vedettes hidden in a clump of trees fired on him, killing Gilmor's new mount. The Southern major pulled off the valuable saddle as fast as he could and raced back to his own horse and galloped away. When Old Bill came up lame, Gilmor had no choice but to leave him in the custody of the miller's son at Swartz's Mill, where he mounted a mustang. When he found that mount unsatisfactory, Gilmor swapped it for yet another mount, his fourth, and rode off to Ewell's headquarters.[65]

Back in Winchester, meanwhile, about 3:00 p.m., the 87th Pennsylvania relieved the 67th Pennsylvania on the forward line southeast of Winchester. The 87th's Company A was moving down Main Street when a stray Rebel cavalryman, who

---

64 OR 27, pt. 2, 46, 70 and 55. Morgan's failure to detect the presence of so many Confederates stumped Milroy. "I am still at a loss to know how Captain Morgan could have made the tour which he reported without seeing or encountering the enemy, for within two hours after he made his report the enemy opened upon me." Ibid.

65 Gilmor, *Four Years in the Saddle*, 87-88; Gillespie 1873 map; Garland R. Quarles, *Some Old Homes in Frederick County, Virginia* (Stephens City, VA: Commercial Press, 1999), 116-18. Factory co-owner Aaron H. Griffith, a Quaker, was a staunch Union man who had married into the prominent Hollingsworth family (his wife was Mary P. Hollingsworth). His and his two brothers' prosperous business was known as the Friendly Grove Woolen Factory. Their father was a pioneer in the region's textile industry. The factory closed in 1904.

apparently had lingered in the town after Goldsborough's Marylanders withdrew, appeared suddenly and fired at Pvt. Henry C. Ginter. The ball pierced his belt plate and lodged in his cartridge box without piercing his skin. He then rode off. Refreshed by their brief early afternoon rest at the Main Fort, the Keystoners renewed the skirmishing. For some reason, Company H remained at the rifle pits and did not join the rest of the regiment.[66]

About 3:30 p.m., some of Johnson's Rebels advanced to the eastern and southeastern edges of town along the Berryville and Front Royal roads, but well-directed fire drove them back on their supports in some confusion. The supporting troops took the hint and fell back into the sheltering woods. Milroy saw this from his perch and thought the Rebels were being routed. He ordered the 87th Pennsylvania and 18th Connecticut to press the matter and, at the same time, instructed General Elliott to advance south across Bower's Hill to retake Milltown southwest of Winchester. As soon as Colonel Ely's skirmishers approached the woods, however, they discovered much of Johnson's division drawn up in force. A heavy volley chased them back faster than they had come.[67]

By about 4:00 p.m., many of the pro-Union citizens had seen enough and began evacuating the forts and headed out on the Martinsburg Pike in the hope of getting well out of Winchester before darkness fell. Milroy ordered his supply train, almost 660 wagons, to also retire. Several sutlers, many of German-Jewish descent, had pitched their tents near the John McVicar house north of Winchester on the Martinsburg turnpike. Twenty-year-old Kate McVicar believed one of the sutlers was "the most frightened man we saw during the war." Frightened by the relentless skirmishing and mounting casualties, he had spent most of the day in their cellar, even though none of the family members deemed the danger great enough to retreat there themselves.[68]

About the same time, Milroy sent Colonel Ely out of the Main Fort with a relief party to clear the Rebels from the vicinity of Cemetery Hill south of Winchester. This force included infantry, a squadron of cavalry, and Lt. Jonathan B. Hanson with two detachments of the 1st Massachusetts Heavy Artillery dragging their pair of 24-pounder howitzers. From the ramparts of the Main Fort, the Wheeling Battery's Pvt. George McClelland watched the Bay State gunners "plant their artillery and then cut a lot of boughs and cover the guns completely." According to McClelland, some of the 13th Pennsylvania Cavalry charged the 2nd Maryland Battalion. The troopers rode

---

66 Prowell, *History of the 87th Pennsylvania*, 85.

67 OR 27, pt. 2, 79; *Philadelphia Press*, June 26, 1863.

68 McVicar Collection, Handley Library.

as close as they dared before wheeling about and retreating to the Union lines. Lieutenant Colonel Herbert's Rebel Marylanders jumped over the stone wall and followed them as the horsemen retreated behind Hanson's hidden guns. Timed perfectly, the cannoneers unmasked their brace of howitzers and fired three or four rounds of canister "with murderous effect" into the Marylanders' ranks. The Rebels wavered and broke. The guns soon stopped firing to avoid hitting the Pennsylvania troopers, who galloped back out front amongst the confused Rebels, several of whom they captured.[69]

During the afternoon, Lt. Col. Hazel J. Williams and Companies A and F of the 5th Virginia, part of Walker's Stonewall Brigade, regained possession of the Baker house. Skirmishers fired from the loopholes in the walls, forcing the nearby 18th Connecticut to huddle in their rifle pits. "We had to lie low or zip would come a bullet, and at times many of them," recalled Pvt. Charles Lynch. When they spotted Ely's Union reinforcements approaching with the pair of artillery pieces, Williams' Virginians sent word back to division commander General Johnson, who ordered Capt. Lycurgus Grills' skirmishers from Company E to fall back 200 yards to the woods. Ely ordered one of the 1st Massachusetts Heavy Artillery's 24-pounder howitzers—whose crew included the battery's commissary, Isaiah McDonald—to open fire on the brick Baker house. A few shells crashed through the walls and scattered the sharpshooters. "No more trouble came from that point," deadpanned Private Lynch.[70]

Major Williams had quickly abandoned the house to dissuade the Yankees from shelling it any further. However, his decision exposed the center of the skirmish line to flanking fire. Williams fell with a severe thigh wound. Major James W. Newton rushed the reserves into action, restoring the line and temporarily halting the Federals, who together with the howitzers retired to the Main Fort. Milroy's expedition resulted in

---

69 *Wheeling Sunday Register*, April 26, 1891. One of the 13th Pennsylvania Cavalry's enlisted men, 19-year-old Donegal-born Michael Dougherty, was kept busy that day carrying dispatches from one point of the field to another, often under hostile fire. His fellow Irishman, Major Kerwin, later presented him with a gold medal in recognition of his bravery. Years later, Dougherty received the Medal of Honor for heroism in an October 1863 firefight along the Rappahannock River. After being captured there and spending months in the Andersonville prison camp, he survived the catastrophic sinking of the troopship *Sultana* while making his way home to Bristol, Pennsylvania. For more on Dougherty, see James T. Navary, ed., *The Prison Diary of Michael Dougherty: Union Survivor of Two Years Confinement in Confederate Prisons* (Createspace, 2009), and Robert P. Broadwater, *Civil War Medal of Honor Recipients: A Complete Record* (Jefferson, NC: McFarland, 2007).

70 *OR* 27, pt. 2, 45-46; 72, 500, 516, 521; Alfred Seelye Roe, *History of the First Regiment of Heavy Artillery Massachusetts Volunteers, Formerly the Fourteenth Regiment of Infantry* (Worcester, MA: The Regimental Association, 1917), 65; Lynch diary entry for June 14, 1863.

the death of a Confederate captain, the wounding of a major and several enlisted men, and the seizure of 11 prisoners.[71]

The 110th Ohio's Lt. Henry Rush left the West Fort about noon to walk back to his regiment's campsite near Winchester to get medicine for a sick comrade. From that point he watched the brief shelling of the Baker place and apparently other homes as well. "Off yonder in the city suburbs, and in costly mansions beyond, would drop exploding bombs and drive out rebels like rats from burning barns," penned the preacher. "Here and there," he concluded in poetic prose, "went up smoke and flame that told how relentless was war when mansions of luxury, adornments of art, or even human life, defied its imperious tread."[72]

Late in the afternoon, Ely pushed forward parts of the 18th Connecticut and 6th Maryland, along with elements of the 110th Ohio, from the earthworks west of Winchester. Their advance shoved some of Johnson's advanced Confederates down through a ravine and over a nearby hill. Buckeye Lt. Charles Gross and three other soldiers were well in advance of the main line of battle. When they looked back, they discovered the primary line falling back. At the same time, Gross discovered seven Rebels lying by a stone wall and exclaimed, "Let's get those fellows!" As the blue-clad quartet double-quicked toward the prone Southerners, one of the enemy jumped up and started to run away. He ignored the Buckeyes' collective order to "Halt!" and kept running, dodging several bullets until he jumped another stone fence and huddled tightly behind it. The other six Confederates, having lost any appetite they may have had in trying to duplicate the feat, surrendered. Two of the Union soldiers escorted the captives to the rear while Gross and the fourth man chased the fellow who had escaped. When the duo approached within a few yards, the Rebel rose from behind the wall still clutching his musket, but promptly dropped it when Gross ordered him to surrender. The dejected Johnny climbed over the wall and walked out to meet his captors.[73]

Gross instructed his comrade to take the reluctant prisoner to the rear, adding, "I will get his gun for a relic." Gross claimed the trophy and was just starting back when several Rebels on another nearby hill leveled their rifle-muskets and opened fire. Gross had about 400 yards of open ground to traverse before he could reach shelter.

71 OR 27, pt. 2, 72, 500, 516, 521. General Walker later presumed the skirmishers had wasted their ammunition, but Newton quoted the captain in the 18th Connecticut posted in Mount Hebron Cemetery who said he lost 15 men killed or wounded in the action. His men could not even expose themselves without endangering their lives. The 5th Virginia lost 3 killed, 16 wounded, and 10 missing during the day.

72 Rush, *Life and Writings*, 231.

73 Gross, "Sketch of Army and Prison Life."

After running about halfway, with the Rebels in full pursuit, he turned, took aim, and fired. Without waiting to see the results, he resumed his flight for life with rounds of lead buzzing past his head. Utterly exhausted, Gross reached the summit of Cemetery Hill and dropped to the ground, unable to run another step. He was hoping the Confederates would conclude he had been hit and give up the chase, but hi strategy failed miserably. The Rebels kept firing, and a hail of leaden missiles plowed into the dirt on either side of him. The tired Gross jumped up started walking back to Winchester, but the whistling of the Minié balls gave him what he described as "new inspiration," and he picked up the pace until he reached the cover of a board fence, which he used to shield himself as he entered a nearby cottage. To his surprise, two or three other weary Union men were lying on the floor in an equally exhausted condition.[74]

Afternoon Action at the Glen Burnie Stone Wall

About 2:00 p.m., as Captain Morgan returned from his unsuccessful cavalry reconnaissance and brisk skirmishing continued south and east of Winchester, action renewed to the west-southwest of Bower's Hill. The Wheeling Battery's Capt. John Carlin sent Lt. Ephraim Chalfant's section out of the Main Fort west-southwest to one of the narrow ridges across the Romney Road. The pair of guns was ordered out to cover the withdrawal of Colonel Klunk's 12th West Virginia, whose men had been on the skirmish line for much of the day. The exhausted Mountaineers pulled back, leaving Lt. James R. Durham and two companies of skirmishers along their well-defended stone wall to contest Gordon's Georgians. Klunk's men had spent long miserable hours hunkered down in an untenable situation, because showing their heads above it invited a quick death or horrendous injury. A line of Confederates near another stone wall about 150 yards distant maintained a constant musketry, killing three Mountaineers, one at a time, who dared to rise to return fire.[75]

About 4:00 p.m., General Elliott advanced the bulk of the 12th West Virginia, with the 122nd and 123rd Ohio on its left. Klunk moved his regiment up to the familiar stone wall, halted his main line, and ordered Lieutenant Durham to advance against the protected Rebels. The order must have struck Durham as madness, for the young lieutenant turned to his men, and shouted "Good-bye!" and "Come on!" before jumping over the wall. He and his skirmishers advanced about 30 yards, the bullets

---

74 bid.

75 OR 27, pt. 2, 80-81; W. F. Beyer and O. F. Keydel, eds., *Deeds of Valor: How America's Civil War Heroes Won the Congressional Medal of Honor* (Detroit: Perrien-Keydel, 1901), 210-11.

Lt. James R. Durham, 12th West Virginia Infantry, received a Medal of Honor
for his heroic actions at Second Winchester. W. F. Beyer and O. F. Keydel, eds.,
Deeds of Valor: How America's Civil War Heroes Won the Congressional Medal of Honor

flying thick and fast on all sides, when Durham felt a sharp pain in his right hand. Six
or seven of his men fell, and two men who had advanced too far simply surrendered
rather than risk being shot while retreating. Ignoring his hand wound, Durham
remained out front and in command. Instead of advancing against his obviously weak
thrust, the Georgians surprised everyone by retiring behind several other stone walls.
A relieved Durham ordered his men to withdraw, taking their wounded with them.
Two or three more men fell injured before they reached the regimental line. There,
Durham discovered that his right hand and forearm had been shattered. Despite the
intense pain, he walked into Winchester on his own and reported to the hospital.
Durham would later receive a Medal of Honor for "extraordinary heroism."[76]

Klunk, with his regiment still sheltered behind the stone wall, looked around for
support, but the 122nd and 123rd Ohio, who were supposed to advance on his left,
were now retiring. Without the Buckeyes to protect his flank, Klunk worried about his

76 Ibid.

advanced position, so he recalled Durham's remaining skirmishers. Gordon's men, meanwhile, had returned to the parallel stone wall 150 yards to his front so advancing was no longer an option because of their heavier firepower. With the Buckeyes still withdrawing north toward the Main Fort, Klunk decided to follow suit, though he had no orders to do so. His men left the sheltering wall as best and quickly as they could, a few soldiers falling in the process. Once out of the sight of the Georgians, Klunk reformed his men and marched toward the two guns of the Wheeling Battery posted on one of the narrow ridges across the Romney Road.[77]

The withdrawal of the West Virginia infantry may not have been as orderly as Klunk later reported. Lt. Ephraim Chalfant's section had scarcely taken position on the low ridge when the gunners heard yelling off to their left. In that direction they saw members of the 12th West Virginia "racing down toward us like a flock of frightened sheep," Pvt. George McClelland claimed. "I never hated anything so badly in my life. It was our own Marshall and Ohio county boys." An officer tried to rally them, recalled the private, but "he could as easily have rallied a streak of forked lightning." The West Virginians rushed past the startled cannoneers to the rear, where they sought cover behind walls, trees, and fences. When the Rebels did not follow them, the Mountaineers regained their composure, formed into line, and advanced to the protective rifle pits, where they stacked arms and lay down to rest. McClelland blamed the trouble on a mistake by Klunk. The colonel successfully rallied the men, but instead of ordering them to march to the rear as intended, he began his command by stating, "Retreat, retreat." The regiment immediately obeyed, taking off in disorder before he could complete his instructions.[78]

About 4:00 p.m. and concurrent with his orders to Ely and howitzers to advance, Milroy sent Carlin's other two sections of guns out the Romney Road to rendezvous with Chalfant's pair of pieces. However, they did not go into battery. Because all was then quiet in that area, they went into park to await further developments. Milroy intended for them to support the 122nd and 123rd Ohio in a renewed assault on Gordon's line.[79] The day-long skirmishing reinforced Milroy's belief that the primary threat came from Johnson to the east and southeast and Gordon to the south in the vicinity of Bower's Hill. The Union commander was simply unable to realize that the Confederate noose was tightening around Winchester. Captain Morgan's morning and midday scouting mission would sadly prove inaccurate in reporting the area west of Winchester to be clear of Rebels. Jubal Early was on the march.

---

77 *OR* 27, pt. 2, 81.

78 *Wheeling Sunday Register*, April 26, 1891.

79 Ibid.

Chapter 7

Sunday, June 14, afternoon and evening

"The pine mountain fairly blazed with cannon."

— *Pvt. Lorenzo Barnhart, 116th Ohio*[1]

Jubal Early's Flanking Movement

While General Milroy remained naively confident that he could hold Winchester, General Early finished preparations for his flanking maneuver west of town to strike at the West Fort. While the various skirmishes were being waged southeast and east of town, Early shifted the rest of Brig. Gen. John Gordon's Georgia brigade to the extreme southern part of Bower's Hill, and supported them with Colonel Herbert's Marylanders and Captain Griffin's Baltimore Light Artillery. Early also dispatched Captain Hupp's Salem Virginia Artillery to bolster Griffin and repositioned the two Maryland cavalry companies on the flanks. Once satisfied these arrangements were sufficient to hold the Yankees in place, Early ordered his other three infantry brigades under Harry Hays, William Smith, and Isaac Avery, together with Lt. Col. Hilary P. Jones' artillery battalion and Capt. Willis J. Dance's twelve reserve guns, to prepare to march.[2]

Early utilized local resident James Carr Baker, who he deemed as "a very intelligent and patriotic citizen" with a son in the Confederate army, to guide the long column into position for the planned attack. Captain Thomas K. Cartmell, a local military scout with family ties to the Baker clan, also volunteered to act as a guide. For

---

1 Barnhart, *Reminiscences*.

2 OR 27, pt. 2, 440; Early, *Autobiographical Sketch*, 244.

Cartmell it was all personal. The former provost marshal of Winchester under Stonewall Jackson regarded Milroy as "the lowest type of that class of commanders whose mode of warfare was to persecute women and children. . . . The brutalities of this ruffian and braggart, so well remembered to this day, were a disgrace to the soldiery of America; and his name is never mentioned except to point to his infamy and ultimate overthrow." As far as Cartmell was concerned, Jubal Early was the right man for the work of overthrowing Milroy.[3]

At 11:00 a.m., Early sent some of Gordon's Georgians to relieve the 7th Louisiana's skirmishers and ordered General Hays to withdraw his men from the front lines. After reforming his brigade about 11:30 a.m., Hays followed Baker and Cartmell south on an "old road" that kept the column out of view of the 12th West Virginia and other prying Union eyes. Behind Hays trailed "Extra Billy" Smith's Virginia brigade and Colonel Avery's four regiments of Tar Heels. The 54th North Carolina brought up the end of the column escorting Jones' artillery battalion. The day had become quite hot, so Hays ordered a short break once his men reached the Cedar Creek Grade not far from the J. N. Bell homestead. When the advance resumed, the column trudged and rolled west for a couple of miles with the heights closer to town screening them from Federal view, and passed over Sandy Ridge.[4]

Baker and Cartmell guided the dusty column off the road northward across the Cloverdale farm, across the open fields near Stribling's Run and through several patches of light woods that allowed the passage of Hilary Jones' artillery limbers and caissons. The advance guard did not spot any Federal pickets although they did encounter a pair of "very ordinary looking men" whose presence raised concerns. Always suspicious, Early ordered them placed under guard. The guides and the head of the column arrived soon thereafter at the Romney Road, with North Mountain and Petticoat Gap off to their left. Early paused here at an 18th-century stone farmhouse "Walnut Grove" in rural Stonewall Township. He was now about three miles west of Winchester.

There, Early consulted with the home's owner, ardent Southern sympathizer Dr. John S. Lupton, who reported the Yankees had posted pickets about half a mile down

---

3   Early, *Autobiographical Sketch*, 244; Thomas K. Cartmell, *Shenandoah Valley Pioneers and Their Families: A History of Frederick County, Virginia* (Winchester, VA: The Eddy Press, 1909), 385-86. Cartmell was married to Annie (Baker) Cartmell. A private in the 11th Virginia Cavalry after his stint as Provost Marshal, he served as a special scout in the Secret Service.

4   Henry H. Dedrick to Mary E. A. Dedrick, June 14, 1863, Winchester, Virginia, Henry H. Dedrick Papers, Manuscript #0332, VMI; *The Spirit of the Age* (Raleigh, NC), August 10, 1863. Dedrick served in the 52nd Virginia in Extra Billy Smith's brigade. The "old road" may have been the narrow farm lane on the Cook property, which led southward to the Cedar Creek Grade.

The Cedar Creek Grade southwest of Winchester in 1945 near the spot where Jubal Early's column turned off on their flank march.

Handley Regional Library

the road. To discourage any probing eyes from that direction, Early dropped off Col. Kenneth M. Murchison's 54th North Carolina from Avery's brigade to watch his rear. The remainder of the division followed Baker north along a narrow, tree-lined country lane leading to the western side of the low ridge Early planned to use to launch his assault against Union-held Flint Ridge. The two suspicious men picked up earlier were left behind at Lupton's house, where Murchison's provost guard kept a watchful eye on them.[5]

The lengthy Confederate column followed the relatively flat dirt lane northward. It was getting hot in the early afternoon sunshine and there were no convenient sources of fresh drinking water along the soldiers' path. Thankfully they did not find any Yankees blocking their way. After a short distance the Rebel vanguard spotted a teenaged girl riding on horseback carrying a large bundle of clothes tied up with a sheet. Her younger brother was walking behind her. The sight of a moving column of troops frightened her because she thought they were Yankees. When she discovered they were Confederates, the girl enthusiastically pulled off her bonnet, waved it over her head as she hurrahed the troops, and burst into tears of joy. She informed Early and his staff officers that Yankees had been shelling the woods dangerously close to her father's house, and their parents had sent her and her brother away for their own

---

5   Beck and Grunder, *Second Battle of Winchester*, 41; Early, *Autobiographical Sketch*, 244; Cartmell, *Shenandoah Valley Pioneers*, 386. Dr. Lupton is believed to have planted the first commercial apple orchard in the Shenandoah Valley in the 1850s, and within twenty years was one of the most successful apple growers in Virginia, despite early skepticism from neighboring farmers. Confederates used his sprawling farm, which eventually encompassed 4,000 acres, at various times as a campsite, including the Rockbridge Artillery in late January 1862. During Milroy's occupation of Winchester, Lupton supposedly hid dried corn in his attic while awaiting the Confederate army's possible return. Squirrels darting in and out of the building, however, revealed the corn's presence to Union officers. Part of the old country lane used by Jubal Early to get into position is today's Echo Lane.

safety. Convinced the girl was telling the truth, Early permitted the children to continue their journey.[6]

The Rebel vanguard arrived behind the low ridge in front of Little North Mountain, not far from the Pughtown Road, between 3:30 and 4:00 p.m. Halting his column near the Parish farm well out of the enemy's line of sight, Early and his aides ascended the slope and carefully observed the distant enemy position to ascertain if they could launch an assault from that position. To their satisfaction, the ridge was a perfect place to form troops without being seen, and the route eastward was passable. It also offered a good artillery platform to soften the enemy defenses prior to committing the infantry. According to a staff officer, the Union guards were "marching to and fro at ease and looking southward where skirmish lines were exchanging the sharpshooter's leaden salutations."[7]

With battle looming, civilian guide Baker thought it wise to return to his house and excused himself. Early thanked him for his help and asked his other volunteer, Thomas Cartmell, to rush back to General Gordon and the other troops along south Bower's Hill near the Valley Pike and direct them not to enter Winchester until any fire from Early's direction ceased. Cartmell apparently agreed, but disobeyed because he wanted to stick around long enough to see the artillery open fire to see where the shells landed.[8]

"Old Jube," meanwhile, examined his new position more carefully. It was perfectly suited for his offensive purposes. Union-held West Fort was about three-fourths of a mile to his front, and so within easy range of his guns. A heavy stand of pine trees crowned the ridge, and in several places had been partially clear-cut. To Early's amusement, several notices tacked to the trunks announced, "General Milroy orders all of the timber east of this point to be cleared off." The work had not been finished, and the remaining trees offered ready cover for his deployment and shade from the afternoon heat.[9]

---

6   Early, *Autobiographical Sketch*, 245.

7   Unknown Confederate staff officer, hand-written note, June 14, 1863, Box 25, John Warwick Daniel Papers, Special Collections, UVA.

8   Cartmell, *Shenandoah Valley Pioneers*, 386.

9   Ibid., 246; OR 27, pt. 2, 153. Captain W. Alonzo Powell, Milroy's chief engineer, had dispatched work crews cutting trees up to Saturday morning when Milroy recalled them to man the defenses. Powell later testified that the West Fort would not have fallen had the tree line been clear cut back 1,500 yards from the earthworks, as originally intended. There was simply not enough time to finish the labor-intensive job before the Confederates arrived. He also planned to construct two traverses and add another flanking entrenchment to one of the lunettes.

View from Early's lines across toward Flint Ridge and the site of
Battery #6 and the West Fort. *Scott Mingus*

The lay of the land would allow Early to ease a brigade of infantry well forward
unnoticed to within a short distance of the enemy fortifications. A large cornfield on
Mrs. Brierly's farm on the northern slope of the ridge near the Pughtown Road offered
enough concealment to move artillery to the edge of the woods. Guns placed there
would face southeasterly toward the West Fort and easterly toward Battery #6 and the
distant Star Fort. South of the cornfield, beyond the thick pine woods, were a mature
untended orchard and the remains of an abandoned farmhouse known locally as
"Folk's old house" directly opposite the West Fort. The eastern hillside there had been
cleared, offering an excellent viewshed for Jones' guns.

Harry Hays sent word to bring up the infantry. His Louisiana Tigers had already
marched nearly ten miles on a hot day and were exhausted, so Early hustled them into
the trees behind the planned jump-off point. The grateful soldiers packed into the
welcome shade, stacked arms, and caught some much-needed rest. Avery's North
Carolinians and Extra Billy Smith's Virginians moved up to support the assault, but
responsibility for the main attack would fall to the Louisianans.[10]

The Federals garrisoning the West Fort and Battery #6 on Flint Ridge remained
ignorant of the impending threat. Milroy had ordered most of these troops into the
unfinished works just that morning, assigning Col. J. Warren Keifer to the command,

10 Smith's brigade formed into battle line in Mrs. Brierly's cornfield before resting in the
nearby woods, while Avery split his troops, sending the 57th North Carolina farther north.
They eventually crossed the Pughtown Road and occupied the unfinished works to the north of
West Fort and the Pughtown Road.

independent of the previous brigade organizational structure. Keifer had 323 men from his own 110th Ohio, led this day by Lt. Col. William N. Foster, inside the West Fort and nearby rifle pits. They were supporting four Ordnance Rifles of Lt. Wallace F. Randolph's Battery L, 5th U. S. Artillery which were unlimbered inside the low earthen fort. Off to their right on a small knoll was the predominantly German Company C of the 116th Ohio, which along with two more of Randolph's guns manned Battery #6. Company C's northern flank dangled somewhat in the air, but no one suspected trouble. "The boys were laying on the parapets in the sun," Pvt. Lorenzo Barnhart later wrote. "We came to the conclusion the confederates had all went to church to get religion, but they were only fixing to kill all of us."[11]

Unseen by Keifer's men, Generals Early and Hays, together with some of their staff officers, crept forward through the pine trees to ascertain the best lines of approach. To their surprise, no Federal pickets or lookouts had been posted to watch the western approaches. A few soldiers lounged outside the walls under the shade of a large tree, and others leisurely watched Bower's Hill to the south, where John Gordon had thrown forward skirmishers and his Georgians were slowly advancing toward Winchester.[12]

"We have taken possession of a hill on the enemy's extreme right," the Louisiana Guard Artillery's W. B. Bailey noted in his diary that afternoon. "Col. Jones is placing artillery in position." Hilary Jones began deploying his twenty guns in two separate positions from which they could be hand-pushed forward once Early gave the order to fire. This was a rather common artillery technique known as "creeping," which guarded against potential mistakes by allowing the officers to safely reconnoiter the position the guns would occupy as well as their intended targets. Captain Willis Dance, who commanded Lt. Alexander A. Cochran's section of the Charlottesville Artillery and two guns from the Louisiana Guard, as well as eight from his own 1st Virginia Artillery Battalion, unlimbered the dozen pieces on an elevation near Folk's old house in the untended apple orchard. The cannoneers could see the rear of Colonel Klunk's line of West Virginians in the distance and the supporting infantry, artillery, and cavalry facing south contesting Gordon.[13]

Captain James Carrington used the cover of Mrs. Brierly's extensive cornfield to move his eight guns behind a high stone wall at the edge of the woods. Dance and

11 Wildes, *Record of the One Hundred and Sixteenth Regiment Ohio Infantry*, 57; Keifer, *Slavery and Four Years of War*, 10; Barnhart, *Reminiscences*; OR 27, pt. 2, 58.

12 Early, *Autobiographical Sketch*, 246-47. As Gordon advanced, several pro-Confederate civilians shouted, "Go to it gray coats; kill the nasty rascals!"

13 Bailey diary entry for June 14, 1863; Early, *Autobiographical Sketch*, 246-47; OR 27, pt. 2, 494-95. This elevation is 994 feet above sea level at its crest.

Carrington were about 250-300 yards apart, which would enable them to catch the West Fort in a plunging cross-fire. However, Carrington's position was vulnerable to partial enfilade from Randolph's two Union rifles in Battery #6. Carrington's men removed enough rocks from the wall to form embrasures for the gun tubes, taking care to avoid detection as they loaded their first rounds. Runners brought extra ammunition from the caissons, and the officers selected potential targets and estimated ranges.[14]

Jones kept a few cannon in reserve behind the center of the ridge to relieve Carrington or Dance, if needed. These guns included four outdated smoothbore howitzers of the 2nd and 3rd Richmond Howitzers (their modern rifles were in Dance's gun line). "That was most mortifying to me," William White complained, "for I dislike seeing one 'section' of the company always being 'ordered in,' whilst the other does nothing but 'bring up the rear.'" White was considering a transfer to another battery, one with rifles, because he was tired of the frequent taunts directed at the howitzers that, as some joked, constituted "Granny Pendleton's Reserve."[15]

While the gun line was being formed, Early positioned Lt. Col. James H. Skinner's 57th North Carolina to protect Carrington's batteries from an enemy attack from the Pughtown Road. Colonel Avery's other three regiments (the 54th North Carolina was still protecting the Romney Road near Dr. Lupton's house) were arrayed in battle line a quarter-mile directly behind Hays, followed by Smith's Virginians in a third line. Early ordered Hays to rouse his men from their rest in the woods and move them down the slope to the eastern edge, arranging their lines so they could advance quickly once ordered to do so. The Tigers slipped silently forward through the heavy pine thickets.[16]

Across the intervening distance, Colonel Keifer did not anticipate any trouble because his own front to the west had been completely quiet. About 3:00 p.m., the Union colonel rode over to the Main Fort to meet with General Milroy. Once there, the Buckeye lawyer-turned-soldier unsaddled his horse and requested it be fed and watered. In the Main Fort he found the commander in high spirits. Milroy did not

---

14 Stiles, *Four Years under Marse Robert* (New York/Washington: Neale Publishing Co., 1904), 192; Wise, *The Long Arm of Lee*, 2: 602-603. Carrington's guns were on a low rise about 960 feet above sea level; the West Fort and Battery #6 were both located on Flint Ridge at 900 feet above sea level.

15 White, "A Diary of the War," 186. The 53-year-old white-bearded Brig. Gen. William N. Pendleton nominally commanded Lee's reserve artillery, but after a questionable performance at Shepherdstown the previous September his duties now were largely administrative, including coordinating the ordnance and ammunition logistics.

16 Early, *Autobiographical Sketch*, 247.

expect a serious fight, he explained, and the enemy was only "trying to scare him out of the Valley." He referred to the simple skirmishing, and thus the relative quiet of the day, as evidence of his opinion, and that his cavalry patrols had failed to see any signs of enemy activity in Keifer's front. After meeting for an hour or so, Milroy left to visit the 122nd and 123rd Ohio to prepare them to attack Bower's Hill. Keifer, meanwhile, visited with other officers and waited for his horse to be delivered to him so he could ride back to the West Fort.[17]

Unbeknownst to the colonel, Harry Hays was forming his brigade of veteran infantry into lines of battle to assault the West Fort. "It was necessary to storm this place, and, as usual, whenever anything daring or dangerous is to be done, the Louisiana Brigade was ordered up," concluded the 5th Louisiana's Capt. Samuel H. Chisolm. Hays called his officers together and briefly explained his expectations. "I have seldom seen men look so serious," Chisolm added, "but we knew that General Hays would lead the charge, and we were willing to follow." Once the conference over, the captain ordered the boys to throw off their blankets and other unnecessary items, and "in a moment all hands knew that the ironclad brigade had to make good again its name."[18]

Hays planned to attack in a double line, with the 7th and 9th Louisiana up front and the 8th and 5th following. The 6th would advance off to the right, providing flank cover in case the Yankees in the Romney Road area counterattacked. Hays sent his trusted adjutant, Capt. William J. Seymour, to report to General Early that his preparations were complete and his brigade was ready to advance. Early's reply instructed Hays to wait until the artillery barrage dismounted some of the enemy guns before commencing his attack.[19]

The battle-ready Louisianans and their fiery leader burned with impatience, as well as some anxiety, as the minutes ticked past. The front line infantry surveyed the steep hill to the east and found it covered with recently felled timber, with two lines of breastworks crowning its summit. It looked formidable, but not impregnable to a frontal assault. "Many times before [we] enjoyed the honor of being selected for similar work," observed Pvt. Bartlett Napier. On two occasions Hays prepared to move his men out, but on both occasions Early sent couriers to stop him. Early was extra cautious, and even perhaps a little skeptical, that Milroy could have possibly left

---

17 Keifer, *Slavery and Four Years of War*, 11.

18 Chisolm, "Forward the Louisiana Brigade," 449. Chisolm places this at 5:00 p.m., but the time was almost certainly an hour before, based upon many other accounts.

19 *OR* 27, pt. 2, 477; Col. William Monaghan, "Movements of General Ewell," in *Richmond Enquirer*, June 23, 1863; Seymour account, GNMP.

his entire right flank completely exposed without placing a single picket or lookout west of Flint Ridge. When Hays inquired a third time, Early denied the request yet again.[20]

During the lull before Early's artillery opened fire, General Smith, a former Virginia governor, five-term U. S. congressman, and early Confederate congressman, delivered a characteristically lengthy speech to his men. Seeking a return to the Old Dominion's governorship, Smith never missed an opportunity to talk. For 30 minutes while his Virginians waited behind the ridge, "Extra Billy" "gave us some interesting reminiscences of his career, and what impressed me most deeply was his talk of his domestic life," recalled Maj. John W. Daniel. Smith spoke about his wife and family, and the principles and rules of conduct that had guided him in life. "I will not repeat his language, for it was not used for such quotation," continued Daniel, "but the wisdom of his utterance, and its elevated affectionate tone—the picture he drew of home as it should be, and of domestic peace, happiness and duty; these are things that must linger in the heart of all who heard him. A beautiful and impressive picture indeed it was, all the brighter for its dark background." Smith's infantrymen were well behind the Louisiana men in front, but word had passed through the ranks that the coming attack would be difficult, prompting one Virginian to fret, "thay was so well fixt I thought we would not get them out."[21]

Several soldiers of the 13th Virginia, part of Smith's brigade, hailed from Winchester and boasted to Jubal Early they would "do the work up clean if he would let us go and see our girls." The general better known for cursing and vitriol laughed in reply and said he would think about it. Early was not a particularly popular officer in the Army of Northern Virginia, and he cared little about cultivating the favor of his men or his peers. "I saw much of Jubal Early," the 13th's J. W. Baker recalled later in life. "To me he appeared as one who had fallen from a great height. His sneering cynicism and wickedness were beyond belief."[22]

---

20 Napier Bartlett, *A Soldier's Story of the War* (New Orleans: Clark and Hofeline, 1884), 181.

21 Bell, *Memoirs of Governor William Smith*, 117-18; Robert H. Depriest to his wife, June 15, 1863, Robert H. Depriest Letters, Virginia State Library. Smith had been governor during the Mexican War.

22 S. D. Buck, *With the Old Confeds. Actual Experiences of a Captain in the Line* (Baltimore: H.E. Houck and Co., 1925), 87-88; J. W. Baker, "War Reminiscences," in *Clinch Valley (Virginia) News*, April 22, 1921.

Early's Attack
on the West Fort
5:30–7 p.m., June 14, 1863

contour interval: 25 feet
US, CS artillery
sections (2 guns)

miles

0   0.75

Hal Jespersen

The Cannonade

It was about 5:00 p.m. when General Early satisfied himself all was ready, the enemy had not spotted his flanking movement, and it was time to attack. A signal gun opened fire. A solid iron round sailed over the forts and whistled into Winchester proper. "The surprise was complete, the distance not great, and the effect overwhelming," concluded one of Early's artillerists. Within moments, the "whole posse of guns opened and kept firing as fast as possible," wrote Rebel Lt. J. Warren Jackson. "We have opened with 20 guns on the enemy's fortifications," Louisiana Guard artilleryman W. B. Bailey scribbled, "and he is taken completely by surprise." Griffin's two Rebel batteries on southern Bower's Hill also opened fire. "As fearful a fire ensued from all points upon us as can be imagined," recalled a Union soldier. "Such hissing, seething, breaking and bursting of shells was scarcely ever heard. This continued until long after dark." The barrage impressed a soldier in Colonel Klunk's 12th West Virginia. "The rebels thro the day had not fired a cannon, but now opened upon us with not less than 30 pieces," he wrote. "The firing continued with unabated fury for about one hour."[23]

Randolph's and Alexander's stunned Union artillerists abandoned their dinners and stopped feeding their horses as they scrambled to the man their guns. Inside the irregular confines of the Star Fort, the 1st New York Cavalry's Lt. William Beach was enjoying a perfect June day when the Confederate iron rain shattered the Sabbath calm. Some of the hissing shells arced overhead and landed in the parked supply train. The teamsters, their reverie also at an end, worked at a feverish pace to move their wagons to safer locations outside Winchester. Out on the Romney Road, Carlin's Wheeling battery remained in park. A cavalryman had dropped a carbine out that way earlier in the day, and Cpl. Thomas J. Moffat picked it up. He was looking at the firearm when six or eight pieces of artillery open off their right. "What's that?" Carlin cried. "What's that?" The battery commander shaded his eyes and looked in the direction of the unexpected artillery thunder. Whatever it was, it was something serious and the artillery firing didn't peter out, but instead picked up. Carlin yelled out orders and his battery countermarched, galloping as hard as the horses could run in the direction of the Main Fort.[24]

---

23 OR 27, pt. 2, 77; Jackson, "Going Back in the Union at Last," 12; Stiles, *Four Years Under Marse Robert*, 193; Wise, *The Long Arm of Lee*, 603; Bailey diary entry for June 14, 1863; "The Loss of Winchester: A Narrative of the Investment and Abandonment of the Place"; "H.C.H.", "With the 12th Virginia."

24 *Baltimore Sun*, June 19, 1863; Beach, *The First New York (Lincoln) Cavalry*, 236. The 9th Louisiana's Tom Reed mentioned hearing a pistol as the signal just before Jones opened. Some

General Milroy was still with the 122nd Ohio near the Main Fort after ordering another charge on Bower's Hill. He was by this time directing his various troops personally, without regard to brigade integrity and largely ignoring protocol by sending orders through his brigade commanders Elliott, Ely, and McReynolds. The Buckeye regiment's field officers had protested the order, arguing their force was too weak because the Confederates had at least two full regiments and artillery to oppose the effort. Milroy responded by ordering the 123rd Ohio to support the 122nd regiment, which was at that time prone just outside of musket range. The 123rd Ohio arrived just as the men of the 122nd were preparing to rise and launch their assault, "which would have sealed our fate," believed Sgt. David H. Danhauer. Just then, Early's cannonade began.[25]

The outburst caught Milroy completely unaware, though to his credit he recovered quickly and sent out a flurry of orders. "The fight was upon [Milroy], and he had to face it," was the candid observation made by one Confederate officer. Milroy tried to consolidate his defensive front by ordering the 12th Pennsylvania Cavalry back almost a mile from its exposed position along the Pughtown Road to the defenses south of the Main Fort. Milroy ordered Colonel Ely to withdraw his forces from southeast and east of Winchester back through the town to the Main Fort. His men almost immediately became heavily intermingled with Elliott's infantry which was withdrawing under the intense skirmish fire of Gordon's Georgians advancing on the 122nd and 123rd Ohio. Captain William F. Martins' heavy artillery opened from the West Fort in reply to Jones's Rebel tubes. The thunder, low and heavy, reverberated for miles in every direction.[26]

The townspeople reacted with surprise and wonder when Alexander's guns in the Star Fort also opened in response to Jones' barrage. They, like the blue-clad defenders, had grown accustomed to the "sullen, stubborn cannonade, which had kept up unceasingly throughout the day," according to a lady. The sudden burst of fresh artillery fire northwest of town triggered new rumors of oncoming Federal reinforcements. Women who had left their houses and gone into the streets hoping to welcome back their beloved sons and brothers expressed terrible disappointment at the prospect. Many of these Confederate sympathizers stood in anxious groups, alternating between hope on the one hand and fear on the other. "We eagerly

---

Confederate accounts place Jones' opening shots at 6:00 p.m. but Cartmell and others state it was indeed 5:00 p.m.; *Wheeling Sunday Register*, April 26, 1891.

25 *Zanesville* (OH) *Courier*, July 22, 1863.

26 David Powell, "Shenandoah Valley: Milroy's Defense of Winchester in June, 1863," *National Tribune*, May 16, 1889; OR 27, pt. 2, 69.

devoured every exaggerated story that crazy and excited imaginations could suggest," she added.[27]

The 5th Maryland's Dr. Charles Goldsborough was still with Sgt. Charles Troeger's body under the shade tree behind Camp Hill when General Early was getting ready to open fire. The division's medical director, Dr. Daniel Meeker, arrived from Winchester. Goldsborough asked him what he thought about the situation. "I do not think they intend to attack the fortifications; they are too strong for them," the director responded. In his opinion, the Rebels intended to raid the B&O Railroad and possibly take Martinsburg, about "which we can do nothing to defend ourselves." Just then, the first loud artillery explosions erupted, startling the medical men and the nearby infantry on Camp Hill. Meeker set his spurs and dashed back into town bound for the Star Fort.[28]

Ohio's Colonel Keifer, who was still inside the Main Fort waiting for his horse, heard the stunning roar of artillery "in broad daylight from a quarter where no enemy was known to be." Worst of all, at least for Keifer, it was coming from his front. The colonel halted a passing wagonmaster and appropriated his horse, which he rode on a wild five-minute gallop to the eastern base of the ridge just below the West Fort. Once there, the Buckeye officer jumped off and raced uphill through a storm of exploding shell into the stronghold's open backside. The rush of shells, reported another Buckeye, was "as if hell itself had burst its bolts and bars and was bringing fire and tempests on the world." Every eye turned westward.[29]

Meanwhile, to the north of the Main Fort, Lieutenant Colonel McKellip's five-company battalion of the 6th Maryland braved a storm of iron from what he counted as 30 guns belching a flight of shells and solid shot across his route to the Star Fort. The Marylanders crossed a deep ravine and began marching up to the hill, raising a cloud of dust that attracted the attention of the distant Confederate gunners. McKellip's pride swelled when he looked back on his trailing 300 men and "found them facing a storm with the same degree of coolness that would be manifested in ordinary drill. No excitement, the line well dressed, and the step as measured and perfect as could have been desired on a dress parade." McKellip and his men reached the fort and took up positions in the rifle pits. Also hustling to the bastion was a portion of the 18th Connecticut, a move that drew "a hot fire" from the enemy. The orderly sergeant of Company H was wounded in his breast, but everyone else slipped through the metal storm and made it safely to the rifle pits on the south side of the

---

27 "Leaves from a Diary Kept by a Lady."

28 *Gettysburg Star & Sentinel*, April 2, 1902; *National Tribune*, December 18, 1884.

29 Keifer, *Slavery and Four Years of War*, 11-12; *Philadelphia Press*, June 26, 1863.

fort, where they tried to make themselves small as shells burst over and around them.[30]

Hilary Jones' veteran artillerists hurled rounds at the West Fort at a rapid rate, catching the Union stronghold in a plunging crossfire from two major positions that also happened to be 60 and 90 feet higher. The incoming rounds "tumbled [the boys] off the parapets like turtles drop off a log into the water," admitted the 110th Ohio's Private Barnhart. The distant pine mountain "fairly blazed with cannon." Some Unionists suffering under the fire thought that as many as 60 guns had opened upon them instead of the 20 pieces Jones had in action between his two positions Our fire, boasted Harry Hays, was "so well directed . . . that in a few minutes the enemy were forced to seek shelter behind their works, "and scarcely a head was discovered above the ramparts."[31]

"Our artillery opened a rapid and well directed fire upon the redoubt," recorded Hays' staff officer Seymour. "Some of the shells explode over the work while others strike the parapet, tearing great holes in it and sending dirt high up in the air." Seymour continued: "So taken by surprise were the Yankees that they made no response for several minutes, when, recovering themselves, they replied with considerable spirit." One of the Confederate artillerists agreed: "We got possession of a hill which commanded their main works and in an hour or so drove them into their main fort." Early in the fight the Rebels largely ignored the Star Fort, at least according to Baltimore artillerist Fred Wild, who claimed the enemy concentrated fire on the West Fort and Battery #6, "whilst we were peppering them good." Captain Alexander and his Baltimore battery officers personally sighted their Union guns using the standard Pendulum-Hausse device, firing at Carrington's position at ranges of 1,500 to 1,700 yards. Alexander claimed he drove some of the Confederate batteries off the ridge three times, dismounting two guns in the process.[32]

In Front Royal some 20 miles to the southeast, Lucy Buck and her family wondered what the fighting in the direction of Winchester meant. She had never heard "such a succession of rapid and heavy firing in my life—we all went out to listen and felt very anxious to ascertain the cause of it." Marcus, Lucy's father, listened to the fighting as he wrote in his diary: "From 4 to 7 P.M. the roar of artillery from both sides

---

30 *Baltimore Sun*, April 19, 1904; James M. Smith diary entry for June 14, 1863.

31 Barnhart, *Reminiscences*; OR 27, pt. 2, 477.

32 Seymour account, GNMP; Wild, *Capt. F. W. Alexander's Baltimore Battery*, 60-61; J. Peter Williams to his wife, June 16, 1863. Confederate accounts state that Carrington and Dance several times repositioned their guns to improve their firing positions; Alexander interpreted this shifting as being the result of his guns driving the Rebels from the ridge.

was deafening and incessant. Horrid cruel war, how I wish I could arrest it and give my people peace and independence."[33]

Thomas Cartmell, the civilian guide who had disobeyed General Early until he had a chance to observe the artillery fire, finally pulled himself away from the smoke-shrouded ridge after the third volley from Jones' 20 pieces. The guide hastened south and then back east along the route they had earlier taken in an effort to locate General Gordon as ordered. Exactly what happened to him remains unclear, but he failed to rendezvous with the Georgian that evening. Partisan cavalryman Harry Gilmor, meanwhile, viewing the spectacle from General Ewell's hilltop headquarters along the Berryville Road, marveled at the "magnificent spectacle," as the forts "belched forth fire . . . the firing was terrific." "Never heard such cannonading in all my life," exclaimed young Kate Sperry at her home on South Loudoun Street. Sperry was specifically worried that "our town will yet be blown to atoms." Union officers standing near Cornelia Peake McDonald's home along the Romney Road initially believed the "blaze of fire from those western hills" marked the belated arrival from a rumored Federal relief column from Cumberland, Maryland. Shouts of "Mulligan has come!" echoed through the streets. When General Milroy and his staff galloped past not ten feet away, Kate Sperry caught sight of what she described as his "pale, agitated face" and felt sorry for the Union commander. He bowed low, the plume of his hat almost touching his horse's mane as he headed for his lofty observation post in the Main Fort. Hundreds of his retreating soldiers hustled through the town in an effort to reach the forts.[34]

Among them was Chaplain Joseph Brown of the 6th Maryland, who had been busy ministering to the wounded in one of the downtown hospitals. As Rebel shells began to fall nearby and "a general fight commenced," he hustled to rejoin his comrades in McKellip's battalion who had redeployed outside the Star Fort. "I was shelled out of the hospital," the Methodist preacher from Cherry Hill, Maryland, later penned, "and took my stance with the reg[iment] behind the rifle pits at the Star Fort until nearly dusk."[35]

Well to the west of the Star Fort, in the old orchard on the higher southern part of the Confederate-held ridge, artillery Capt. Willis Dance lost the use of one of his rifled cannon. The 1st Rockbridge Artillery had recently replaced its two 10-pounder Parrott

---

33 Lucy Buck, *Sad Earth, Sweet Heaven: The Diary of Lucy Rebecca Buck*, ed. William P. Buck (Birmingham, AL: Cornerstone, 1973), 197; Marcus Blakemore Buck diary entry for June 14, 1863.

34 Cartmell, *Shenandoah Valley Pioneers*, 386; Gilmor, *Four Years in the Saddle*, 89; McDonald, *A Woman's Civil War*, 155–56.

35 Brown diary entry for June 14, 1863.

Rifles with 18-pounder, four-inch Blakely guns imported from England. This was the first opportunity these Rebel gunners had to use them in action. Unfortunately, one of the Blakely pieces, according to an observer, "choked" when a defective shell lodged halfway down the barrel and could not be rammed home or removed, rendering the gun useless for the rest of the fight.[36]

The incoming Rebel crossfire presented significant problems for Battery L's Lieutenant Randolph in the West Fort and Battery #6. If he focused on his closest target (Carrington's eight guns), then Dance's artillerists to the south had the opportunity to sight their dozen guns "with the greatest deliberation," almost assuring a hit even at a range of three-quarters of a mile. When Randolph turned his heavily outnumbered guns to fire at Dance, Carrington moved forward to pound the Federals from a closer position. Distributing his fire evenly between the two Rebel positions seemed to have little to no effect. Jubal Early watched the opening round of the fight with growing satisfaction. The Yankee attempt at counter-battery, he observed was made in a "very wild manner." Hilary Jones believed his well-directed rounds so disrupted the enemy they "[shot] wildly over our heads."[37]

During one of Carrington's forward movements, the Charlottesville Artillery's Sgt. John Hunter narrowly escaped injury when a 20-pounder Parrott shell from the Main Fort passed completely through Madge, his diminutive chestnut mare. The round just missed Hunter's legs, showering him with the horse's blood and gore, before exploding a few yards away. Hunter calmly stepped off Madge, who was already dead, as she gently sank to the ground. He glanced at the bloody horror and exclaimed, "Well, poor little Madge!"[38]

Artillery Maj. Robert Stiles also told of another casualty, a crewman in Capt. Asher Garber's Staunton Artillery. The man was trotting abreast of the rear gun as the battery was passing single file through a pair of old stone gateposts flanking a country lane Garber was using to move to a new firing position. The washer hook of the gun carriage, according to Stiles, caught the unsuspecting artilleryman and disemboweled him, "dragging the poor wretch along by his intestines, which were literally pulled

---

36 White, "A Diary of the War," 187. Although White says it was a defective shell, it is conceivable the crew rammed the wrong type of shell down the barrel, a relatively common occurrence in batteries with mixed guns and ammunition—especially during the high stress of live combat.

37 Wise, *The Long Arm of Lee*, 603; Early, *Autobiographical Sketch*, 247; OR 27, pt. 2, 494. James C. Zimmerman of the 57th North Carolina wrote his wife on June 19 that "a shell would go over us at almost every second," but luckily no one in the rear ranks was injured by the misaimed overshots.

38 Stiles, *Four Years under Marse Robert*, 195-96.

from his body in a long, gory ribbon." However, Garber did not report any fatalities in his command, so Stiles' memory of the event may have been faulty.[39]

It only took Jones about 15 minutes to wreck Battery L's caissons and limbers and kill or wound about four dozen horses, according to later counts. Inside the scant protection of the West Fort and the nearby Battery #6, Randolph was down to two operational 3-inch rifles with his other guns dismounted or with their wooden wheels crushed. His men spiked three of the disabled guns and ran their caissons down the eastern slope for protection. Carrington's skillful repositioning of his guns thwarted repeated Federal attempts to knock them out. New York cavalryman William Beach watched as the Star Fort's Maryland artillerists occasionally responded to some Rebel shot that revealed the location of an enemy gun.[40]

Jones soon had company in his attempts to silence the Federal guns. The Confederate Baltimore Light Artillery on Bower's Hill just left of the Valley Pike threw its first shell into the center of the Main Fort. Captain Wiley Griffin's Marylanders opened a furious cannonade, momentarily throwing Ely's and Elliott's retreating infantry regiments into the "greatest confusion."[41] The accuracy impressed a correspondent for the *Richmond Whig*. "Just here we must say that it never was our fortune to see a battery so skillfully handled as the Baltimore Battery; from first to last it maintained its position, receiving the fire of the siege guns undismayed, and sending back from its magnificent guns shell after shell. All honor to this glorious battery," continued the writer. "We do not write this to praise a friend, because we do not know one member of this company, but having witnessed their heroism in receiving the enemy's fire, and the skill with which they sent their death-dealing missiles, we feel that it is due them."[42]

"About five o'clock we were heavily shelled by the rebs," artilleryman William H. Moffett of Alexander's Baltimore Battery wrote. In response, Lieutenant Leary's section limbered and wildly galloped northward from Winchester through a gauntlet of enemy artillery rounds. From the elevated position of the Star Fort, Fred Wild watched as the limbers and caissons thundered directly toward him. To his surprise, none of the cannoneers were killed or wounded under the heavy iron rain and everyone made it safely inside the fort. To the south, Milroy and his staff rode into

39 Ibid, 196-97.

40 *Baltimore Sun*, June 19, 1863.; *Richmond Examiner*, July 4, 1863; J. Warren Keifer, *Official Reports of J. Warren Keifer, Major General of Volunteers* (Springfield, OH: Daily Republic Steam Job Office, 1866), 6; OR 27, pt. 2, 146; Beach, The First New York (Lincoln) Cavalry, 236.

41 Hands, "Civil War Notebook," 91.

42 Reprinted in the *Raleigh Weekly State Journal*, July 2, 1863.

Fort Milroy. "We must and should hold the Main Fort from any attack," the army commander informed everyone within hearing distance.[43]

Lieutenant Colonel William Nelson's reserve Rebel artillery battalion unlimbered on Bower's Hill and on the low ridges recently vacated by Colonel Klunk's 12th West Virginia. Nelson's orders were to "give the fellows in the big fort a pounding," recalled cannoneer A. S. Hardie. The command consisted of Kirkpatrick's Amherst and Massie's Fluvanna Artillery, both Virginia outfits, and Milledge's Battery from Georgia. The guns dropped trail and added their iron and thunder to the deafening bombardment.[44]

Cornelia Peake McDonald's house was once again under the path of artillery rounds. "It seemed as if shells and cannon balls poured from every direction at once," observed Cornelia, who watched the hasty retreat as Carlin's limbered guns and caissons of the Wheeling Battery galloped through her yard on their way up to the Main Fort. Many horses exhibited bloody wounds, and the cannoneers, some of whom were also injured, were "pale with fright." Behind the guns came "hurrying groups of stragglers, and officers without swords, and some bareheaded." These men were likely from the 12th West Virginia, which had been supporting Carlin and were also hastening to the Main Fort. Several refugees crowded onto Cornelia's porch to catch their breath while others ran through the streets in panic. "Ambulances were backed up to let out their loads of wounded and horses reared frantic with pain from their bleeding wounds," she observed. "Some were streaming with blood, and looking wild, and their poor eyes stretched wide with pain and fright." Comrades carried Pvt. J. N. Waddell, who had been badly injured near Tidball's Spring when the Mountaineers had retired with some haste from the Glen Burnie stone wall.[45]

Word spread throughout Winchester that the Confederates had moved artillery into the Union rear, cutting off the Union lines of retreat and leaving them with no option but surrender. "Of course, we believed it," a pro-Confederate lady wrote. "How could we help it? But it was in fear and trembling lest we might again be disappointed." When a Union regiment (possibly the 5th or 6th Maryland on the way to the Star Fort) marched past her house, she stopped a passing soldier and asked how the fight was going. "We are driven in," was his dejected reply. They had fought on

43 Hands, "Civil War Notebook," 90-91; W. H. Moffett to Dear Father, June 16, 1863, Maryland Heights, MHS; Wild, *Capt. F. W. Alexander's Baltimore Battery*, 59, 61; *Zanesville* (OH) *Courier*, July 22, 1863.

44 A. S. Hardy, "Terrific Fighting at Winchester," in *Confederate Veteran*, vol. 9, March 1901, 114; *Wheeling Sunday Register*, April 26, 1891.

45 McDonald diary, entry for June 14, 1863; Waddell, "Milroy at Winchester: A Veteran of the 12th Va. Gives His Experiences."

and off throughout the day with nothing to eat and could stand it no longer. "I never saw anything to equal the spirit of these rebels," added the nameless Union infantryman. "They rush forward like devils, perfectly regardless of danger." The woman recalled feeling "a little bit sorry" for the passing troops because they looked so tired and hungry.[46]

Several blocks away, the full import of the bombardment did not escape pro-Confederate "devil diarist" Mary Greenhow Lee. Knowing that "human beings are being hurled into eternity, perhaps unprepared, whether friends or enemies," terrified her. The distressing affair only added "to the horror when we know so many of our friends must be suffering from wounds [and] we cannot get to them, to give them comfort."[47]

At the 110th Ohio's old campsite north of Winchester, Confederate overshots dropped through the roof of the regimental hospital despite its identifying yellow flag waving overhead. Doctors hustled their patients into the cellar. In spite of the danger, the hospital steward dispensed quinine and anesthetic to Lt. Henry Rush, who had requisitioned it for his sick friend in the West Fort. As the young lieutenant emerged into the bright sunshine, a live shell rolled hissing through the campground. The regiment's playful dog "ran after the missile," bemoaned Rush, "clasped it with his jaws and was instantly blown to pieces by its explosion."[48]

While making his way back to the West Fort, Rush passed in front of the Main Fort, where he observed an open shed supported by four corner posts. Beneath the canopy sat Mrs. Cotterell, the wife of Company E's wagonmaster, cradling her baby. She had been in Winchester visiting her husband for only a few days. "Are you not afraid to remain here?" Rush inquired. "I find no other shade," she responded, "and I s'pose I'm as safe here as anywhere." The baby smiled up at the uneasy officer, who with regret went on his way.[49]

As the bombardment intensified, Rush paused to scan the Rebel gunnery positions with his field-glasses. He concluded at least 32 Confederate guns were firing from various locations. Continuing on his way, he passed several squads of Rebel prisoners, most but lightly guarded. One of the captives caught his attention and bragged, "Hit'll be you'uns turn to be taken next. We'uns'll soon have you 'uns, without you 'uns is party peert gittin' out o' this." Rush finally reached the West Fort

---

46 Anonymous, "Leaves from a Diary of a Lady."

47 Mary Greenhow Lee diary, entry for June 14, 1863.

48 Rush, *Life and Writings*, 231-32.

49 Ibid. According to Rush, the mother and child were captured on June 15 and taken to Richmond, where the baby became ill and died.

where, to his relief, "no essential changes had taken place except that two of the guns at our extreme left had been dismounted and the horses killed."[50]

About half an hour after Jones opened fire, Carlin's Union battery halted in the rear of the Main Fort and awaited orders. Someone counted 24 guns playing on that one fort, but Pvt. George McClelland "thought 2,400 was nearer the number." The drivers dismounted while they waited. Just as McClelland, the swing driver, slipped from the saddle, a shell passed over the fort and struck the hard-packed ground near an infantryman standing between the battery and the fort. The soldier spun around three or four times like a top and fell hard to the ground—but was otherwise unharmed. The shell failed to explode, but rebounded right across McClelland's recently vacated saddle.[51]

Orders arrived for the battery to head south to the small redoubt where Carlin's command had camped for the past two or three months. There was a hollow between the Main Fort and small redoubt, though both were on the same ridge. Just as the battery was descending the steep hillside, a shell burst in front of McClelland's caisson and wounded the two lead horses. Lead driver Dick French and McClelland dismounted to unhook them. Normally, the lead driver replaced the swing driver, but French, seeing a chance to avoid further danger, declined to do so. McClelland climbed back into his saddle, but was so frightened he later admitted he hardly knew his own name. He pulled too high on the harness and the horses stayed put. "Go on, go on!' the drivers behind him shouted. McClelland whipped his off-horse, but all it did in response was kick. He next struck its shoulders, which convinced the horse to rear and snort. In desperation, he spurred his saddle-horse, which "tried to dance a horn pipe" on its rear feet. Crying like a baby, the teenaged artillerist yelled for Dick French, as did several other frustrated drivers. Grumbling the entire way, French arrived and took his rightful place.[52]

McClelland tumbled to the bottom of the hollow and crossed the stream with some difficulty. When he tried to negotiate the opposite slope, he had to stop to rest numerous times. He finally got up the courage and the strength to reach the redoubt, where he dropped into the surrounding ditch and found three or four other equally terrified men already cowering there. McClelland wormed his way along the ditch to the entrance and, in between incoming shells, darted inside and huddled under the parapets. Corporal George Smith ordered the teenager to take a bucket and go back down to the stream to fetch water to cool a gun. McClelland refused, citing his bad

50 Rush, *Life and Writings*, 233.

51 *Wheeling Sunday Register*, April 26, 1891.

52 Ibid.

nerves. Another soldier came by with a full pail, letting him off the hook. McClelland and Sgt. Scott Riley did carry ammunition from the caisson. Every time a shell passed overhead, the teenager threw himself to the ground or hugged the walls, eliciting intense laughter from other more experienced men. A shell fragment struck Riley in his back, cutting short his laughter. Fortunately for him the chunk was at the end of its course and only knocked the wind of out him. Nearby, the caisson's frightened horses trembled in their harnesses. When one was hit, its mate would look at its injured companion with wild-eyed wonder, and would scarcely move to allow his stricken companion to fall.[53]

The Attack on the West Fort and Battery #6

The cannonade lasted almost 45 minutes, the roar of artillery echoing through the pine woods where the Louisiana Tigers anxiously awaited the order to advance. Hays could tell the Confederate long-arm was having success suppressing Union guns on Flint Ridge, and believed he had a good chance of carrying the Union position. Hays, according to his official report, ordered his men to advance "at about 6 or 6.30 o'clock." "At a given signal the well-known voice of Harry sang forth," recalled the 5th Louisiana's Capt. Samuel Chisolm. The Tigers, yelling wildly, surged down the heavily wooded slope. The 9th Louisiana's line was already disorganized by the time it reached the bottom of the hill. The men had to halt and reform before moving forward again. This, in turn, forced the trailing 5th Louisiana regiment to halt. After clearing the canopy of trees at the base and emerging into the late afternoon sunlight, the brigade advanced through 300 yards of corn and wheat fields. Soldiers jumped over wooden fences and pressed forward through the trampled fields. About the halfway point, Hays shouted, "Hoist those colors in the Ninth!"[54]

"Suddenly in the afternoon a dark mass of infantry was seen creeping out of the woods," wrote a member of the 116th Ohio, recalling the first moment he spotted the real threat to Union-held Flint Ridge. Skirmishers from Keifer's 110th Ohio opened fire with Henry repeating rifles as soon as the Confederate infantry stepped into range. "Extra Billy" Smith's reserves on the ridge behind the Tigers watched in fascination. "After a heavy fire of half an hour, I saw coming out of the wood a half mile to my right, our old division moving in a line of battle by brigade front and marching as if on parade," was how the 13th Virginia's Pvt. Sam Buck described the proud moment.

---

53 *Wheeling Sunday Register*, April 26, 1891.

54 Merl E. Reed, ed., "The Gettysburg Campaign: A Louisiana Lieutenant's Eye-witness Account," in *Pennsylvania History*, vol. 30, no. 2, April 1963; Chisolm, "Forward the Louisiana Brigade," 449; Thomas Reed, *A Private in Gray*, 37.

"Steel and shot tore through their ranks," continued the former Tiger, "but still they pressed on and on until within a short distance of the fort."[55]

From a distance, one of Edward "Allegheny" Johnson's staff officers surveyed the dramatic scene. "It was a picturesque battle," he penned. "Early's Artillery opened vigorously on the north of the forts. We could see the flash of his guns, sixteen discharges per minute, while the Stars and Stripes waved defiantly amid the bursting shells in the rolling smoke, the sun sinking red and angry behind the western clouds, the advance and retreat of the skirmishers with the sharp crack of the rifle, while cavalry and artillery gallop into position and infantry file in column."[56]

General Ewell, his staff, and Maryland cavalryman Harry Gilmor strained to observe the long-awaited assault through the drifting smoke that now obscured the area. It appeared as though Jubal Early had the advantage, as the number of Yankees streaming away clearly suggested. An occasional rifle volley and Rebel Yell from the Tigers broke through the smoky cacophony as the Louisiana troops moved closer to the forward Union rifle pits. Gilmor noted, "There broke on our expectant ears heavy volleys of musketry and the terrible, long, shrill cry of the two [lines] of the Louisiana Tigers."[57]

The 6th Louisiana, early on dubbed the "Irish Brigade," approached a small stone house on a farm leased by Samuel Yonley. Alma and her younger sister Lizzie, Yonley's two daughters, watched as Confederates streamed by "with banners flying and our own and the enemy's shells screaming over." Early's flanking movement had also caught them by total surprise. "The storming of those breastworks was the grandest sight my eyes ever beheld," gushed Lizzie.[58]

When Hays' first line reached the western base of the ridge, Jones' artillery ceased firing to avoid hitting them. Colonel Keifer and his Buckeye officers ordered their men to fix bayonets, reload, and watch the fields to their front. Within a few moments,

---

55 Dalzell, "A Lucky Blunder," 97; S. D. Buck, *With the Old Confeds*, 87-88. This was one of the first documented cases of the Henry rifle being used in combat. See Joseph G. Bilby, *A Revolution in Arms: A History of the First Repeating Rifles* (Yardley, Pa.: Westholme Publishing, 2006), 108. This was the earliest recorded use of the Henry by an organized unit in the Eastern Theater and perhaps in the war.

56 McKim, *A Soldier's Recollections*, 146.

57 Gilmor, *Four Years in the Saddle*, 89-90.

58 Jones, *Lee's Tigers*, 159–60; OR 27, pt. 2, 63; John J. Rivera, "Two Heroines of the Shenandoah Valley," *Confederate Veteran*, no. 8, November 1900, 495. Elizabeth A. "Lizzie" Yonley later became known as the "Maid of Winchester" for her humanitarian efforts. According to the 1860 census of Hampshire County, Virginia, where they lived at the time, Lizzie was just 16 and Alma 18 at the time of the battle. The family was forced to relocate to Winchester when their large farmhouse was destroyed by Union troops.

Union Private Barnhart and the others watched as Confederate infantry "come out of the brush, out of a ravine." The astonished Keifer counted at least five regiments in deep column of attack, and later claimed the advance regiment carried the U. S. colors, perhaps mistaking an early-war Confederate banner for the Stars & Stripes. Because of the cover, the Rebels approached his lines without much trouble.[59]

On the western declivity about 100 yards from the works, however, the Louisianans encountered a long line of *abatis* that slowed their ascent. "We came to a kind of stockade," the 9th's Pvt. Tom Reed observed. "This was made of trees fallen or dragged, with the tops of them outward, forming the breastworks, and the small ends of the limbs were cut sharp. Now, we had to pass through this mass of stuff before getting to the rifle pits, but this did not stop us." The 110th Ohio's Lt. Henry Rush deemed the obstacle a "labyrinth of trunks and interlocked limbs. . . . On and on they come, loading and firing, climbing and clambering forward through that tumble of timber as if it were sweet to die for Jefferson Davis."[60]

Keifer's nearly 500 defenders rose from behind their works. "We would get to shoot only one shot," Private Barnhart recalled, "then use our bayonets and club with our guns." The Rebels heavily outnumbered the inexperienced Ohioans but, for a brief instant, the Buckeyes held their own. "They came in desperate order," continued Barnhart. "We gave them a volley low down in their legs. They dropped out of ranks. We made large gaps in their lines, but they did not stop, for they closed the gaps shoulder to shoulder. . . . They had been in such scraps before." The Union fire, thought Lieutenant Rush, "was fast, furious, and well-aimed . . . but there seemed to be thousands pressing forward from the rear."[61]

Colonel Keifer later claimed his infantry fire, coupled with Randolph's shells, had a "fearful effect, mowing down his advance Regiment almost to a man. My sharpshooters shot down the officers on horseback, but only for a few moments could we check the enemy's advancing column. . . . Many Confederate officers and men were seen to fall, and the head of the column wavered." Keifer almost certainly believed what he wrote, reality was something altogether different, for his men inflicted far fewer casualties than he recalled. Several men in the 6th Louisiana advancing up as the ridge on Hays' right fell. A Minié ball slammed into Capt. George Ring's left ankle, disabling him for eight months. In the center, when the 9th

---

59 OR 27, pt. 2, 477; Keifer, *Official Reports*, 6.

60 Clement A. Evans, ed., *Confederate Military History: A Library of Confederate States History* (Atlanta: Confederate Publishing Co., 1899), 19:255; Reed, *A Private in Gray*, 37; Rush, *Life and Writings*, 233-34.

61 Barnhart, *Reminiscences*.

Louisiana's Cpl. James G. Barnett slumped to the ground, his comrades carried the 32-year-old farmer from Livingston Parish to the rear. A surgeon amputated his leg. Captain John J. Rivera suffered a gunshot in his side during the ascent. As Tom Reed stepped near the *abatis*, he watched as a Rebel raised the regiment's flag, which had been knocked to the ground. A shell fragment struck the bearer, James Stewart, on the head and killed him.[62]

After his men finally cleared the *abatis*, Harry Hays ordered them to charge. In response, the Tigers, "yelling like fiends," quickly surged forward. The Yankees only had time to fire off a few weak rounds that failed to halt the Rebels' momentum. The long ditch in front of the earthworks proved to be only a momentary obstacle. "The dead pile up till the living stand on them and fire into us over the crest of our own works," recalled Ohio Lieutenant Rush. According to Capt. Samuel Chisholm, the 5th Louisiana held its fire until within 20 steps of the breastworks. "They gave us a volley," Private Barnhart wrote, "then came onto us with bayonets and a yell like Indians." A few terrified Buckeyes turned and raced for the rear as the wave of howling Louisianans closed on them.[63]

Randolph's two remaining operational 3-inch rifles blasted four or five rounds of canister, but they "did not appear to have a particle of effect," the lieutenant rued, likely with some surprise. The Rebels simply closed ranks and kept coming. With some difficulty, the Tigers scrambled across the ditches and up the steep dirt embankments. Lieutenant John Orr, the Canadian-born adjutant of the 6th Louisiana, was among the first of the Irish regiment to reach the West Fort. As the 23-year-old officer crested the wall, he spotted a three-man Union color guard carrying off their banner. The officer leaped toward them and slashed wildly with his sword, grabbing at the flagpole. One of the defenders stabbed him in the side with a bayonet thrust and raced off with their colors. Orr would survive his painful wound, but was done fighting. Off to his left, Maj. J. Moore Wilson was the first of the 9th Louisiana to mount the works, with Pvt. Tom Reed close behind him. Wilson shouted, "Come on boys!" Reed yelled back, "I am here!" as he also scrambled atop the wall.[64]

---

62 Keifer, *Slavery and Four Years of War*, 11; Andrew B. Booth, *Records of Louisiana Confederate Soldiers and Louisiana Confederate Commands*, 3 vols. (Spartanburg, SC: Reprint Co., 1984). On July 26, the one-legged Barnett was captured at the Jordan Springs hospital. He was paroled in early August and never fought again. He returned to Livingston Parish, and lived a long life before dying there in October 1918.

63 Rush, *Life and Writings*, 234; Chisolm, "Forward the Louisiana Brigade," 449; Barnhart, *Reminiscences*.

64 OR 27, pt. 2, 74, 478; Janet B. Hewitt, Noah Andre Trudeau, and Bryce A. Suderow, eds., *Supplement to the Official Records of the Union and Confederate Armies*, pt. 2, Record of Events, vol. 24,

Well to the rear, the one-legged Richard Ewell struggled to contain his growing excitement. "The enemy stood firm for a while," Major Gilmor noted, "and Old Ewell was jumping about on his crutches, with the utmost difficulty in keeping the perpendicular. At last the Federals began to give way, and pretty soon, the Louisianans, with their battle-flag, appeared on the crests charging the redoubts." Through his field glasses, Ewell thought he spotted Jubal Early's familiar form. His eyes welled with tears of exuberance as he shouted, "Hurrah for the Louisiana boys! There's Early; I hope the old fellow won't be hurt!" Just then, a spent bullet struck the corps commander in the chest and almost knocked him to the ground. Shocked staff officers rushed to his side, as did medical director Dr. Hunter Maguire. A quick examination revealed an ugly black bruise, but no serious damage. Maguire ordered the general to lie down and rest, and took away his crutches to make sure he did so, chiding, "had better let those sticks alone for now." The irrepressible Ewell, however, was "soon on his feet again, or rather, on the only one he had left," joked Gilmor.[65]

Milroy, observing from his flagpole lookout, would claim at least 10,000 men attacked Keifer's position, and that his officers counted 17 Rebel colors. "The rebel General Ewell is reported with his glass to have spied General Milroy in the lookout," a New York newsman wrote, "and to have exclaimed, 'There's that d—d old Milroy, who would stop and fight, if the d—l himself was after him.'"[66]

The 5th Louisiana's Captain Chisolm grabbed a pistol from a Yankee officer and "pitched into them right and left." The combat inside the fort was brief, violent, and at times, hand-to-hand. Private Michael Gleason of the 6th Louisiana died from a Yankee gunshot shortly after leaping into the fort from the parapet. The 110th Ohio's

---

serial 36 (Wilmington, NC: Broadfoot Publishing, 1994), 80, Reed, *A Private in Gray*, 37.Orr survived his wound and returned to duty. He was captured later in the war and spent months in the Johnson's Island prison camp near Sandusky, Ohio. After the war, he moved to Austin, Texas.

65 Gilmor, *Four Years in the Saddle*, 90. Confederate spy Belle Boyd and a wounded Rebel officer watched the combat from a hill near the Martinsburg Road. Several civilians, for the most part mounted on emaciated horses and those mules not yet confiscated by Milroy's soldiers, joined them. The spectators scattered when Union artillery lobbed a shell in their direction. Belle Boyd, *Belle Boyd, In Camp and Prison*, 2 vols. (London: Saunders, Otley, and Co., 1865), 1:250-51. The 19-year-old Boyd, a celebrity for her assistance in helping Stonewall Jackson capture Front Royal in the 1862 Valley Campaign, was returning to her parents' home in Martinsburg following an extended tour of the South. She was within four miles of Winchester when she first heard the artillery. Anxious to see the outcome, she rode onto the heights, joined by the unidentified crippled officer, and sat for some time "absorbed in the struggle that was going on beneath us." Mounted on a white horse on the hilltop and accompanied by other riders, she made a conspicuous target for Union artillerists three-quarters of a mile away.

66 OR 27, pt. 2, 46, 63; "The Defence and Evacuation of Winchester," 486.

Lorenzo Barnhart exaggerated the Rebels' strength: "We used our gun stocks to [club] them [in] the front and to the rear. We clubbed them a while but to no use. Oh, we hurt some of them, but what could 80 soldiers do to 70 or 80 thousand." In the bloody close-quarter confusion, it must have seemed as if the earth had torn open and spilled endless numbers of Rebels from the ground. "They overcrowded us, but we made it hot for them for a moment. [We] were clubbing with the butts of guns, and thrusting the bayonet at and through each other," added the Buckeye. "For a moment it looked like H—l."[67]

Tigers swarmed through the redan and its flanking entrenchments, seizing Lt. Paris Horney and sending him to the rear. A Louisianan used his musket to club Sgt. Mathias McAnally in the head. The 6th Louisiana's Maj. William H. Manning demanded that Cpl. John R. Rhoades surrender, but the defiant Buckeye ran his bayonet through the luckless Louisiana officer's abdomen and into his spine. As Rhoades struggled to withdraw it, another Southerner swung a musket at him. Rhoades managed to partially deflect the blow, but suffered a severe gash in his scalp. Dazed and bleeding, he fell down and announced his surrender. A Tiger would have none of it, and thrust the muzzle of his rifle against Rhoades' head. A Rebel lieutenant, however, knocked the gun downward and heatedly reprimanded the private for trying to shoot a helpless prisoner.[68]

Harry Hays, only a few minutes after beginning his triumphant assault, watched as his Louisianans' bright red battle flags fluttered above the fortifications. Dozens of terrified Buckeyes streamed out the open reverse side and down the uneven slope toward the Main Fort, throwing away accoutrements and abandoning their supplies, guns, and even battery wagons. The rest, however, soldiered on. After having three horses shot from under him, Battery L's Lt. Wallace Randolph fell with a severe wound. Lieutenant Edmund Spooner assumed command. From the now silent Confederate artillery line, Robert Stiles, volunteering in the Charlottesville Artillery, believed, "The surprise was complete, the distance not great, and the effect overwhelming."[69]

---

67 Chisolm, "Forward the Louisiana Brigade," 449; Barnhart, *Reminiscences*.

68 John R. Rhoades Papers, Rutherford B. Hayes Presidential Center, Fremont, Ohio; Pope, *The Weary Boys*, 41; *Richmond Enquirer*, June 23, 1863; Rush, *Life and Writings*, 235-36. Though believed mortally wounded, Major Manning survived and later led the 6th Louisiana in the 1864 Overland Campaign. In 1864 Paris Horney died in a prison in Columbia, South Carolina. Mathias McAnally, the Rev. Henry Rush's choir director before the war, was exchanged, but died in a Union hospital in Louisville, Ky.

69 Lt. James C. Bush, *"The Fifth Regiment of Artillery," The Army of the United States: Historical Sketches of Staff and Line with Portraits of Generals-in-Chief*, ed. Theo. F. Rodenbough (New York:

Meanwhile, the 7th and 8th Louisiana regiments veered northeast toward Battery #6. "Over the crest of the near hill upon our right, column after column of Confederates are coming at a double quick," the 110th Ohio's Lieutenant Rush observed. "Glancing in that direction a few moments, I vividly remember that nearly as quickly as one can count three, that many times their advance colors went down. As bearer after bearer fell, another would spring to his place, lift up and start forward with the fallen flag."[70]

Keifer realized his position was hopeless. Rebels had pierced the center of his line and now outnumbered his men inside the West Fort. "The trenches and breastworks were of such character as to afford no obstructions to the entrance of the enemy," he complained. Stubborn fighting continued, but Keifer did not order a retreat until Hays attacked his exposed flanks.[71] When that time came, the retreat quickly became a rout. "The Yankees did not know that we were on them until they saw us standing over them," the 9th Louisiana's Tom Reed explained. "Then you ought to have seen those fellows run, and as they ran down the hill we poured it into them, but they soon scampered away and we were in possession of the breastworks." Very few of the Unionists, chided Captain Chisholm, "dared to cross bayonets with us, the balance outrunning quarterhorses. All those who stood their ground were soon rolling in their own blood and many who ran were shot in the back." An 18th Connecticut soldier in the rifle pits surrounding Carlin's battery, observing the distant debacle in the West Fort, later claimed the Confederates clubbed the brains out of men after they surrendered.[72]

"We did not surrender, we just quit and every man for himself," admitted Ohio Private Barnhart. "I seen my chance to get in a ravine close by and follow it. I did and then had to cross a level piece of ground to get our last resort and Fort. While crossing

Maynard, Merrill, and Co., 1896), 383; OR 27, pt. 2, 74; Stiles, *Four Years under Marse Robert*, 192. Stiles, a Yale-educated Kentucky native who was raised in New York City and Connecticut, moved to Richmond before the war to practice law. He joined the Richmond Howitzers and later served on a volunteer basis in the Gettysburg campaign with the Charlottesville Artillery. Lieutenant Randolph would be left behind in Winchester to recuperate; Rebels would capture him when Winchester fell. In 1910, the then General Randolph, in ill health, committed suicide. Randolph and Spooner had been promoted to lieutenant on May 16, 1861, and assigned to the 5th U. S. Artillery. Later in 1863, Spooner was assigned permanent command of Battery H, 5th U. S. following the death of Lt. Howard M. Burnham at Chickamauga.

70 Rush, *Life and Writings*, 234.

71 Keifer, *Official Reports*, 6; Keifer, *Slavery and Four Years of War*, 11.

72 Reed, *A Private in Gray*, 37; Chisolm, "Forward the Louisiana Brigade," 449. See also Larry B. Maier, *Gateway to Gettysburg: The Second Battle of Winchester* (Shippensburg, PA: Burd Street Press, 2002), 122.

this, I was in plain view of them. They seen me get away. They sent the shot after me, but I would not halt. I went ahead towards the [Main] Fort with their bullets plowing the ground around my feet. I looked to be hit any moment, but I ran the Gauntlet all safe. My clothes were pierced with bullets, but my skin was not cut. I did not want to serve my time in a confederate prison." Barnhart eventually reached the Main Fort and flung himself down on the ground just outside its earthen walls. "We dared to slacken our retreat."[73]

Keifer's retreating men were thankful the Rebels' aim was often wild. Some managed to keep their sense of humor despite the terrifying ordeal. As Henry Rush clamored up the slope to the Main Fort's entrenchments, he "did not pause to inspect the quality of the soil or pick up geological specimens." He looked down toward Winchester and then to the fields to his left, where hundreds of men were falling back and ascending the long slope to safety. Keifer managed to save all except 40 or 50 men left as casualties or prisoners. The Regular artillerymen were among the last to leave the fortifications. "Not till the enemy had planted their colors upon the works did my men leave their guns," boasted Lieutenant Spooner. He and 18 cannoneers escaped to the Main Fort while the Tigers bayoneted those men still trying to work the two remaining pieces. Spooner later praised Keifer's infantry for their support in the face of overwhelming odds, declaring, "Men never fought better than those men did."[74]

With the West Fort now firmly in Rebel hands, Hays turned his full attention to Battery #6. The Yankees there had begun scrambling out when they saw their comrades abandoning the West Fort. While artillerists in Battery #6 labored to carry off their two pieces, Hays spotted an opportunity to capture the guns. The aggressive brigadier faced the 7th Louisiana to the left and ordered the regiment to open fire. Their volley dropped several limber horses, halting the section's retreat.[75]

A soldier of the 116th Ohio took in the spectacle of the fight raging in front of him and left a wonderful account:

> I went on the hill in a fair view, and for a few minutes watched the artillery fight. The enemy was using his 24 guns to the best advantage. Our forts were replying vigorously. The roar of the cannons was terrific; it was one eternal thunder, the explosion of the shells making a sort of echo. The guns kept a continual pouring forth of fire and smoke, a dense vapor filled the air, piled together like huge mountains and the mild rays of the setting sun

73 Barnhart, *Reminiscences.*

74 Rush, *Life and Writings*, 236; Bush, "The Fifth Regiment of Artillery," 383; *OR* 27, pt. 2, 74, 112, 146.

75 *OR* 27, pt. 2, 478.

reflected beautifully on these smoky clouds. Nothing could be more grand and sublime than this sight, and indeed it would have been delightful to have beheld it, had it not been for its terrible effect. [The men of Company C of the 116th Ohio fighting in the outer defenses of Battery #6] were completely enveloped in smoke. They nobly stood their ground until charged on by five times their number. I joined the boys in the ravine below and told them we had better move our wagons, as quickly as possible, for the enemy would soon have possession of the outer fort, and then would turn the guns upon us.

The Buckeye of the 116th regiment was right. A few minutes later, the Confederates seized the fort at bayonet point. "The rebel flag-bearer shook his flag defiantly as he ascended the rampart, and yelling like a demon."[76]

The remaining Yankees streamed to the rear as fast as possible. Many could not escape. Captain Frederick H. Arckenoe of Company C, 116th Ohio was calmly firing his pistol when a Tiger put a Minié ball through his forehead. The lifeless Prussian immigrant pitched to the ground, not far from the body of Sgt. Oswald Heck, who was shot through the mouth. "The Captain was a gallant officer and we regret his loss," lamented one of his men. Two of Arckenoe's privates fell wounded, and the Louisianans captured about one-third of his entire company, including 2nd Lt. Levi Lupton and 27 enlisted men. Lieutenant James P. Mann and the remaining survivors reassembled in the Star Fort north of Battery #6.[77]

The victorious Tigers paused to plunder the bountiful supplies found inside the abandoned West Fort. "We drove the Yankees pell-mell from their breastworks," Lt. J. Warren Jackson boasted, but the 8th Louisiana captured "but few of them as they were rather too nimble for us." Perhaps of even more importance to the young officer was the discovery of "plenty of Coffee ready made & warm, soup & light bread. We evidently took [them] by surprise as they were just preparing their supper." The 116th Ohio had drawn new Model 1861 Springfield rifle muskets on April 3. Many of these weapons (as well as a handful of Henry repeaters) and a large supply of ammunition were now in the Tigers' hands. The victory had come with surprising ease, with the casualties much lower than anyone anticipated. Both astounded Capt. William Seymour and Hays' other staff officers.[78]

76 "Letter from the 116th O.V.I."

77 Wildes, *Record of the One Hundred and Sixteenth Regiment*, 57; "Letter from the 116th O.V.I." Levi Lupton died in a prison camp in Charleston, SC. Arckenoe, educated at some of Germany's finest military schools, traveled to the U. S. after the failed Revolution of 1848. He enlisted in the 116th Ohio Volunteer Infantry in September 1862. Company C consisted of many Germans, who deeply mourned his loss.

78 Jackson, "Going Back in the Union at Last," 55; Seymour account, GNMP.

While the Rebels ate abandoned food and stuffed what was left into their haversacks, the dismounted lieutenant colonel of the 9th Louisiana, William Raine Peck, labored up and over the earthworks and collapsed against the wall. Weighing more than 300 pounds and standing six-and-a-half feet tall, Peck was one of the largest men in the Army of Northern Virginia. His size prevented him from keeping up with his charging regiment. The wealthy cotton planter struggled through the *abatis* and the ditch-covered slope, and once inside the fort, used the wall to support his weight while he wheezed and gasped for breath. "Big Peck," as he was called, drew a mix of cheers and laughter when he exclaimed, "Bully! Bully! By God! Bully! For the old Ninth, by God!"[79]

Harry Hays congratulated his men on their victory while wishing his triumph had been more decisive, ruing the difficulty his men had encountered getting over the ditches and embankments once they had reached the works. These obstacles, coupled with the enemy's "precipitate flight," had significantly reduced the number of Yankees killed, wounded, or captured. Still, the capture of the six-gun battery, with all its caissons and trappings except for the horses gunned down by the 7th Louisiana, was quite a trophy.[80]

While Hays' men were fighting in the fort, the 27th Virginia's Ordnance Sgt. Watkins Kearns rode up Bower's Hill, where he could clearly hear the infantry engagement raging off to the north. Eventually word came that a brigade from Early's division had captured a battery of nine [six] guns, and cheers went up along the line. The sergeant's revelry, however, proved short-lived as orders arrived to move the ammunition wagons into a new position behind Allegheny Johnson's Second Brigade. He reluctantly spurred his horse back to the southeast to the wagon park off the Front Royal Pike.[81]

Ecstatic about the stunning victory, division commander Jubal Early rode up to congratulate Harry Hays and study the remaining Union positions. With the intervening deep and rugged ravines between the West Fort and the two forts still under Milroy's control, Early judged that an assault against Fort Milroy and the Star Fort would be very difficult and likely bloody. However, the aggressive Early also wanted to finish off the Yankees with one final concerted push. The division leader consolidated Hays' front and brought up a pair of Colonel Avery's North Carolina regiments and "Extra Billy" Smith's Virginia brigade. "Milroy was in retreat down the valley," Maj. J. W. Daniel recalled, "and amidst the smoke and screaming shells I saw

79 Reed, *A Private in Gray*, 37.

80 *OR* 27, pt. 2, 478.

81 Kearns diary entry for June 14, 1863, VHS.

again Smith's brigade coming up, the General, as usual, in front, full of the eagerness of battle."[82]

Smith's Virginians, despite the continued Federal fire raining on the abandoned West Fort area, were anxious to share in the spoils the Louisianans were enjoying. "The ridge had been heavily timbered," recalled one of "Extra Billy's" boys, Pvt. James William Baker of the 13th Virginia. "When we looked up at the fort we saw that General Milroy had cut all the trees, thrown them in rows down the ridge—trimmed them up, so they were splinter-jagged everywhere, and had done all this just to keep us out of rations. He ought to have known we had to eat. Could not put it off too long. So when they told us we had better go up through the impediments and get that fort we did so at once. Rough climbing, but we were as gaunt as hounds, as active as cats; so in twenty minutes we had the fort and plenty to eat in reach. So Mr. Milroy got no good that time out of all his toil and labor."[83]

The Virginians sheltered on the reverse slope of Flint Ridge behind Avery's prone line. "Gen. Smith was standing on the right of a long line of infantry, lying flat on their faces under a terrible fire," artillery Maj. Robert Stiles related, "and erect, with his folded arms, securing his horse's bridle rein, and, save the artillery men following their guns, just then changing position at a gallop, he was the only human being I saw erect upon that field. As the cannoneers dashed by with faces blanched, lips pressed against the teeth, and eye-balls straining out of their sockets," he continued, "I saw Gen. Smith bow politely, and heard him greet each one as he passed, in a rich, smooth, full, clear voice; 'How do you do, Sir! how are you today, Sir!' and I noted, too, the effect upon the men; for each lifted and threw back his head proudly as if he felt—Gen. Smith must have noticed me, especially; I certainly meant to do my full duty in this fight, at least." The white-haired sexagenarian Smith received a minor flesh wound when a spent shell fragment struck him, but he stayed with his men. He had survived a severe wound to his shoulder and two other wounds at Sharpsburg, so this fresh injury proved little more than a minor annoyance.[84]

The Federals Counterattack and a Second Cannonade

Before long, Jubal Early and his officers in the captured works noticed distant Federals massing in three columns near the Main Fort, apparently intent on

---

82 Early, *Autobiographical Sketch*, 248; John W. Daniel Papers, Manuscripts Division, Special Collections Department, UVA.

83 J. W. Baker, "War Reminiscences," *Clinch Valley (Virginia) News*, April 22, 1921.

84 *Richmond Sentinel*, July 11, 1863; Bell, *Memoirs of Governor William Smith*, 54.

recapturing Flint Ridge while simultaneously pushing through Gordon's line on Bower's Hill. Hays' five reformed regiments awaited orders while two of the captured guns opened fire on the closest advancing Yankees, with infantrymen from the 5th and 6th Louisiana operating the pieces. According to Hays, these impromptu artillerists managed to fire a few well-directed rounds. Meanwhile, the Union line moving on Gordon's position "retired precipitately," Early noted, "and the enemy's whole force seemed to be in great commotion."[85]

The advancing Yankees included most of the remainder of the 116th Ohio, which left its rifle pits to the right and rear of the Star Fort. Milroy had ordered the Buckeyes to reinforce their comrades on Flint Ridge, but Keifer's line had since collapsed and Rebel battle flags now waved over the works. Colonel James Washburn, however, dutifully obeyed orders and led his regiment down from the Star Fort. Some of his men questioned the "senseless order," among them Sgt.-Major James Dalzell. "What name the fool bore who gave that order I never could find out," grumbled the Caldwell resident, "and don't want to know now." At the double-quick, they started over the ravine-filled, shallow valley toward the ridge. They soon had company when the 5th Maryland left its trenches in front of the Main Fort to support the attack.[86]

When Milroy realized the Rebels were overrunning the West Fort, he had also ordered Colonel Schall and the 87th Pennsylvania to advance from the rifle pits near the Main Fort to support Lieutenant Wallace's Battery L, 5th U. S. Artillery inside the besieged bastion. He had earlier ordered the Keystoners to the Star Fort, but they changed direction and headed for Flint Ridge. At least one of Schall's line officers did not go forward. Captain Vincent C. S. Eckert, a prewar shoe salesman and newspaper editor from Hanover, claimed he was too ill to lead Company G in the charge. Other lame excuses followed, and Eckert failed to tender any instructions to his bewildered subordinates.[87]

The 87th, with Company G now under new, braver leadership, advanced well to the left of the 116th Ohio, with the 67th Pennsylvania remaining stationary in supporting distance in the rifle pits surrounding the Main Fort. When the 87th's

---

85 *OR* 27, pt. 2, 44.

86 *Athens* (OH) *Messenger,* July 9, 1863; Dalzell, "A Lucky Blunder," 98. The 116th's Company A, badly mauled at Bunker Hill, apparently did not participate. According to Sgt. George A. Way, "We stood for full four hours under a fire of thirty rebel cannon but did not loose [sic] a man." *The Spirit of Democracy (Woodsfield, Ohio),* July 1, 1863.

87 Prowell, *History of the 87th Pennsylvania,* 72, 75; Brandt database, YCHT. Earlier in the war the *Hanover Spectator* deemed Eckert a "prodigious ass." In September 1863 he was dishonorably discharged for disobeying a direct order. His reputation was ruined by his battlefield failure, and he never returned to Hanover. He spent the rest of his life in Baltimore and Harrisburg.

skirmishers reached the top of the ridge between the Main Fort and West Fort, they discovered the enemy ready "to wipe us of existence," Cpl. Charles Z. Denues recounted. They halted and hugged the ground while the main line ascended the slope. However, when the line arrived, the West Fort hilltop was "solid full of Confederates," according to Cpl. John Keses, a 40-year-old Prussian immigrant and former maker of whips. Keses counted seven lines of battle in reserve behind the fort, so "we acted on the maxim that 'discretion is the better part of valor.'" Under fire, the regiment retreated toward the Main Fort (Fort Milroy), saved only by the terrain that sheltered them from Rebel artillery fire. "Had there not been a steep decline," Keses later wrote, "there would not have been many of these boys to tell the story." After sundown, the Pennsylvanians took position in the rifle pits on the eastern side of the fort facing the Pughtown Road and the more distant Martinsburg Pike.[88]

Off the 87th's right flank, meanwhile, the 116th Ohio had advanced half a mile across broken terrain toward Flint Ridge. Realizing the fortifications were lost, Milroy sent an aide galloping to the Buckeyes to order them to retire to his position without delay. The foot-soldiers "obeyed with a hearty good will I assure you," Cpl. George K. Campbell wrote, echoing Corporal Keses in the 87th Pennsylvania, "for had we continued per [the] first order there would not have been one [left] to tell the tale." The supporting 5th Maryland also fell back.[89]

The 13th Pennsylvania Cavalry's Col. James A. Galligher had been injured in a nasty fall from his horse. He was recuperating in the William and Mary Fahnestock house immediately east of Battery #6 when the fighting broke out. Doctor Charles Goldsborough had just reached the house to attend to Galligher when hundreds of Federals, including his own 5th Maryland, scrambled eastward across the ravines. The doctor and the colonel joined the exodus and made it safely to the fortifications. When the masking Union infantry had retired far enough, two guns in the Star Fort opened against Flint Ridge. Captain Alexander brought two more guns to bear. However, there was not enough available space on the western side of the fort to bring his third section into play.[90]

Despite the enemy artillery bursts, Jubal Early's Rebel provost began policing recently captured Flint Ridge. Armed guards escorted sullen Union prisoners to designated holding areas in the rear. Quartermasters scoured the fortifications and

88 *Philadelphia Inquirer*, July 4, 1879; John C. Keses account, USAHEC; Prowell, *History of the 87th Pennsylvania*, 75. The north-south section of the old Pughtown Road is now Fairmont Avenue.

89 *Athens* (OH) *Messenger*, July 9, 1863; *Philadelphia Press*, June 26, 1863.

90 Wise, *The Long Arm of Lee*, 604; *National Tribune*, December 18, 1884; *Baltimore Sun*, April 19, 1904. This house still stands just off of modern VA Route 522.

collected weapons, accoutrements, supplies, and other abandoned equipment. The Tigers and Smith's Virginians ate well, feasting on confiscated beef and other Yankee foodstuffs. The 7th Louisiana's Lt. Charlie Pierce found a fine sword, which he proudly carried for the rest of what would soon be called the Gettysburg campaign.[91]

Curiosity got the better of the 9th Louisiana's Pvt. Thomas Reed, who descended the eastern slope and found some Union caissons with good draft horses still hitched to them. Reed plundered through the caissons and found some clean underwear, two dry blankets, and some stationery. Satisfied with his haul, the private ascended the ridge and returned to his company. He was telling his comrades about the horses when Lieutenant Colonel Peck interrupted, offering Reed $100 if he would go back and get him one of those horses. Reed slipped back into the valley, where he worked and tugged to loosen one of the animals from its harness. When an enemy artillery round burst nearby and its hot iron fragments whizzed uncomfortably close to the Alabama native, Reed scrambled for safety. The idea of getting a hundred bucks from "Big Peck," however, convinced him to go after the horse once more. When another shell burst near him, however, Reed concluded he was its target and raced back up the hillside to find shelter. When he explained to "Big Peck" the dangers of his adventure, the huge officer ruefully responded, "Well, you had better let the horses alone."[92]

As the sun set, a brief lull in the cannonade ensued. "Just then the gorgeous western sky would have shamed the rich coloring of the old Venetian schools, and put to blush the more modern and masterly imitations of sunset glory," the 110th Ohio's Lt. Henry Rush poetically painted. "The stillness was as tranquil and undisturbed as if this had been the prelude of millennial peace. Standing by the side of Gen. [Col.] Keifer, I called his attention to the glory of this evening sky. Before any reply was possible," he continued, "all the vast semi-circle of rebel batteries burst into sublime and deafening chorus."[93]

By this time, Dance's Rebel batteries together with Carrington's eight guns had limbered and moved with some difficulty across the uneven valley toward the West Fort. The cannoneers strained to hold on as the limbers and caissons bounced along the rough terrain. "I was watching one of the enemy's batteries trying to cross a ravine

---

91 James Gannon, *Irish Rebels, Confederate Tigers: A History of the 6th Louisiana Volunteers, 1861–1865* (Campbell, CA: Savas Publishing Co., 1998), 179. Lt. M. McNamara, "Lieutenant Charlie Pierce's Daring Attempts to Escape from Johnson's Island," *SHSP*, vol. 8, 1880, 61. When much of his brigade surrendered at Rappahannock Station in November 1863, Pierce reluctantly broke the prized sword over his knee. He handed the hilt to his captor. He tried unsuccessfully to escape from Johnson's Island and was not paroled until the war's end.

92 Reed, *A Private in Gray*, 38.

93 Rush, *Life and Writings*, 237.

on the opposite hill," wrote the 1st New York Cavalry's James Stevenson from inside the Star Fort, "when Captain Alexander [the Baltimore Battery] trained a gun on the point of crossing, which was very rugged, and just as the caisson attempted to cross he fired, filling the air with the debris of the demolished machine, while our troops rent the air with shouts of triumph." The distant Confederate caisson, together with whoever was riding on it, "blew up with a terrific crash, and looked just like pictures one sees in books," Fred Wild recounted. "And then the shouting and the hurrahing all along our line, and the cheering encouraged our boys to renewed vigor. Our little Lieutenant Peter Leary, Jr., whom the boys did not think much of, up to that time, stripped off his coat, and took a hand in loading and firing a cannon in his shirt sleeves, cheering and hurrahing at every successful shot, and there were many such, and our battery proved itself a good one."[94]

One of Alexander's well-aimed shots knocked another enemy gun on its side. Another caisson emerged from under the trees and was making a turn when a shell burst directly overhead, stampeding the horses down the slope and into a ravine. Fred Wild wanted to get a better view of the distant action, so he and a comrade mounted the parapet. Moments later, "whiz! whiz! whiz! whistling bullets came dreadfully close. We did not have to be told to get down from there, but did so at once, as the bullets were emphatic enough," recalled Wild. "I had done one of the most foolish things of which a soldier could be guilty; I did not know that sharpshooters were stationed in favorable positions in every battle to pick off officers, and fools like myself; 'Fools will venture, where wise men fear to tread.' And up to this day I think that, that was the nearest to death's door that I had ever been."[95]

A couple of Carrington's Rebel pieces careened around the West Fort earthworks, where sometime after 7:00 p.m. his artillerists unlimbered on the open and relatively flat rear and in the fields south of Flint Ridge. New York cavalryman William Beach watched as the enemy limbers entered the abandoned works, wheeling and unlimbering in "gallant style."[96] Captain Alexander's four serviceable guns in the Star Fort greeted the Rebel field pieces as they deployed near the West Fort with a steady barrage of case shot and percussion shells. Nearby Union troops cheered when a round burst in the enemy ranks. "We fired as accurately as we could," Lt. H. Eugene Alexander, the battery commander's brother, related. "We had to work our guns on

---

94 Stevenson, *Boots and Saddles*, 189. Baltimore artilleryman E. N. Moffett confirmed the explosion of the caisson in a letter to his father on June 16 from Maryland Heights (Moffett Papers, MHS); Wild, *Capt. F. W. Alexander's Baltimore Battery*, 60.

95 Ibid., 60-61.

96 *Charleston* (SC) *Mercury*, June 22, 1863; Beach, *The First New York (Lincoln) Cavalry*, 238.

Artillery pieces and limbers in the Star Fort; although uncertain, some accounts suggest these are the captured guns of Capt. F. W. Alexander's Baltimore Battery after Second Winchester. *Handley Regional Library*

our knees, the shell killing our horses and wounding our men," recalled a Union artillerist. "But we gave them as good as we sent, the big fort helping us all the time."[97]

Captain Dance's Rebel artillerists, having by this time also unlimbered on Flint Ridge near the West Fort, resumed fire. They tossed a few shells at the distant fleeing Yankees, increasing their panic and confusion. Dance next turned his attention to the Main Fort and began bombarding it, while keeping some of his guns in position in case of any renewed Yankee attempt to retake the abandoned fortifications. Dance lost an injured horse and a man with a slight flesh wound to his right arm. The wounded man later rejoiced in the almost bloodless victory, sincerely thanking God for it.[98]

Robert Stiles, acting as the Number 6 crewman on one of Carrington's guns, passed ammunition from the limbers to the loader. As enemy shells burst overhead, the Presbyterian preacher's son instinctively slammed down the lid of the ammunition chest to prevent hot fragments from prematurely detonating the lethal ordnance. He and other Confederate artillerists were at a loss to explain why the initial Federal counter-battery fire was so uncommonly accurate until someone noticed a practice target marker standing in between two of their guns. The Union artillerists had

97 "Letter from an Officer in the Wheeling Battery," *New York Herald*, June 22, 1863.

98 *Baltimore Sun*, April 19, 1904; Wise, *The Long Arm of Lee*, 604; Beach, *The First New York (Lincoln) Cavalry*, 238.

practiced for just such an occasion, and so had determined in advance how to cut their fuses. The Rebel crews moved the guns several dozen yards downhill, and thereafter Milroy's rounds passed harmlessly overhead.[99]

However, just before dark, an exploding shell severely injured Capt. Charles Thompson of the Louisiana Guard Artillery, one of Jones' battery commanders, when one of the iron fragments tore off his left arm near the shoulder joint. Somehow the critically wounded officer managed to remain calm. Thompson turned his horse toward his unsuspecting men in an effort to hide the magnitude of his horrendous injury. "Keep it up boys! I'll be back in a moment," he called out before slowly heading down the western slope toward the rear. Before Thompson reached his limbers, however, he fell dead from his saddle from the shock of the injury and heavy loss of blood.[100]

Lieutenant Beach was inside the Star Fort and witnessed the incident. "[A] gallant officer on a spirited horse" rode out in front of the captured works, he recalled. "A shell from one of Alexander's guns seemed to strike directly beneath the horse, bursting and raising a cloud of smoke and dust that enveloped the horse and the rider. Loud and long were the cheers that again broke from the Union men." One of Captain Thompson's cannoneers, Sgt. Albert M. Riddle, put the blame for his commander's death squarely on the medical team: "Left our Capt. yesterday. He had his hand shot off & died from want of surgical attendance." The unfortunate Captain Thompson was the only man struck by the Union counter-battery fire, although the bombardment also wounded three artillery horses, one of them severely.[101]

During the prolonged exchange, one of Alexander's cannoneers in the Star Fort had his leg ripped off by a jagged piece of hot iron and expired the next day. The Unionists also lost valuable horse flesh. "A beautiful black wheel horse had a piece torn out of his throat as wide as your hand and bleeding terribly," Wild recalled in describing the horrific wound. "Every time he exhaled, a spurt of blood came out with the air. He appeared to know that he was going to die; I put my hand over the wound expecting to ease him but this turned the blood into his lungs and he had to cough up the clotted blood; the sweat was pouring from his shiny black body. He was trembling as if cold," continued Wild, "his moments were few, and as our fort was too small to

99 Stiles, *Four Years under Marse Robert*, 192-94.

100 Ibid., 192-94, 197. In other accounts, Thompson bled to death from a wounded left wrist before he could be treated.

101 Beach, *The First New York (Lincoln) Cavalry*, 238; Albert Mortimer Riddle Diary, entry for June 15, 1863, George J. Mitchell Department of Special Collections & Archives, Bowdoin College, Brunswick, Maine.

be encumbered with dead horses, the wounded ones were led out into the open where the leaden hail soon finished them."[102]

At one point during the iron exchange, a shell fragment from a ball Wild estimated at four inches in diameter tumbled along the ground, "at times standing still like a spinning top." He was going to give it a kick, but an instinct told him not to do so. "This innocent looking thing touched against a cannon wheel, glanced off and broke a horse's leg," he wrote. "What might it have done to mine, if I had kicked it?" The Rebels were firing "an allotment of railroad iron . . . in chunks of various lengths, which made a terrible roaring noise. This was a wise economy of the enemy (every shot we fired cost ten dollars) and where no accurate shooting was required and terrifying noise was a factor, the railroad iron answered every purpose and cost much less."[103]

George W. Morehead of Colonel Klunk's 12th West Virginia had a clear view of the impact of the accurate and concentrated Confederate artillery fire. "They silenced the Baltimore Light Artillery," Morehead scribbled in his diary, "charged battery 4 and captured it and forced our men to fall back to the main fortification. They then tried to take the Star Fort by storm but met with a severe repulse." According to Sergeant Riddle of the Louisiana Guard Artillery, his piece of Thompson's battery alone fired 142 rounds of shell, while the other gun in his section burned through 105 rounds. The spirited duel, concluded Riddle, "was a terrific battle at the heights of Winchester."[104]

The rifled sections of the Richmond Howitzers were also heavily engaged, while their antiquated shorter-ranged smoothbore howitzers necessarily remained idle behind the main gun line. With his pieces in park, William White had a chance to move up and watch the artillery duel from a relatively safe spot. The strongly built star-shaped fort quickly drew his attention. In White's opinion, it would cost heavily to carry it with an infantry assault. However, he scratched in his journal, "we can make it too hot for them to remain in it, and they will be compelled to surrender or cut their way out."[105]

---

102 Wild, *Capt. F. W. Alexander's Baltimore Battery*, 59, 61.

103 Ibid., 63. The claim of firing railroad iron may be dubious; other account do not mention it.

104 George W. Morehead diary, entry for June 17, 1863, West Virginia State Archives, Charleston; Riddle diary entry for June 15, 1863.

105 White, "A Diary of the War," 187. The two howitzer sections only suffered one slight casualty, Lt. Lorraine Jones of the 2nd Richmond Howitzers. White noted that his company did not fire a single shot, "but, like the little boy in the rock-battle, we *holler'd* and I suppose that will count."

"Toward dark the cannonading commenced again & now [is] quite fierce," penned the 27th Virginia's ordnance sergeant, Watkins Kearns. He and the rest of the rear echelon troops were mere onlookers by this stage of the battle. "From where our train is we can see the shells bursting high in the air," he described. "Countless shells flew in every direction, with long fiery tails like comets," marveled Private McClelland of Carlin's Wheeling Battery. He regained his composure and watched the arcing shells with fascination. Bursts of flames erupted at intervals along the Main Fort.[106]

When Captain Martins' heavy siege guns in the Main Fort fired, the 87th Pennsylvania's George Blotcher described how they had the advantage "because our guns were higher up and we could fire over the town of Winchester and miles beyond where the enemy could hardly reach us to do any harm." One of Martins' cannoneers, Pvt. James F. Hodgdon, suffered significant injuries when a charge prematurely exploded. His comrades carried him into Winchester to a field hospital for care.[107]

Inside the town, meanwhile, terrified citizens, hospital patients, and Union wives and sweethearts huddled as the artillery duel continued long after the musketry stopped. Periodically, a round would detonate directly overhead, raining its red-hot shell fragments onto the rooftops and into the streets. One of Confederate Dr. Abram S. Miller's friends, a woman remembered only as Betsey, was leaving her house when one shell burst just outside the front gate and several more exploded above the house. To another resident, it felt as though "every shell from our artillery bore us a message from home. But in our rejoicing the sad certainty would obtrude itself, that some *must* fall before the murderous fire that was showered upon them, and each waiting, anxious heart could only pray to Almighty God that their loved ones might be spared."[108]

The sun was just setting when the Confederates spotted Milroy's wagons moving off past the Star Fort northwest toward Pughtown. General Ewell correctly concluded the wagons might try to escape in the dark, possibly by way of the Martinsburg Road, and directed division commander Edward Johnson to assemble a force to prepare to cut off the potential escape routes. It was also likely the Yankees might try to remove their light artillery, so Ewell ordered Harry Gilmor to take command of all the cavalry he could find and circle the town to try to cut them off. Gilmor took Hanse McNeil's company of partisan rangers and part of the 1st Maryland Cavalry and set off, though it would be all for naught. As night fell, he and four men became separated from the

---

106 *Wheeling Sunday Register*, April 26, 1891; Kearns diary entry for June 14, 1863, VHS.

107 Blotcher diary, June 14, 1863, YCHT; *OR* 27, pt. 2, 73.

108 A. S. Miller to Dear Julia, June 16, 1863, Handley Library; "Leaves from a Diary Kept by a Lady."

main party in the woods and pine thickets near the Berryville Road when they took a different route and became lost. After searching for two hours, Gilmor became "so completely puzzled that I was very near entering Winchester, where the enemy still held possession. Having despaired of joining the company, five of us turned into a barn and slept till morning."[109]

When Gilmor was setting out on his useless journey, Edward "Allegheny" Johnson was pushing his Virginia skirmishers from the Stonewall Brigade closer to Winchester. From her home north of Winchester, Kate McVicar watched opposing infantry off to the east fire at one another on the Wall and Burgess properties. "Puffs of white smoke and the sharp crack of rifles came from there," she later recalled. Several shells fired at the forts exploded near her house, convincing her family to seek shelter in their cellar. The firing claimed the lives of the 18th Connecticut's Stephen H. Oakley and George W. Pickett, both of whom died on Company G's skirmish line. Oakley and Pickett were among the last known Union battlefield fatalities incurred that night.[110]

The dramatic and noisy artillery duel continued into the enveloping darkness of that humid Virginia evening. The flashes, thought Confederate staff officer Randolph McKim, produced what he called a "lurid, weird effect." Inside the Main Fort, the beleaguered Federals not manning the guns or busy with other important tasks huddled wherever they could find some form of protection. According to an observer from Georgia, his comrades were dropping three shells every minute inside the embattled fort. "I think it was the most beautiful sight I ever witnessed," exclaimed the Stonewall Brigade's Ted Barclay. Lieutenant Colonel Herbert's civilian guide, young Robbie Barton, agreed with the sentiment when he described the cannonade as a "splendid display."[111]

At one point Federal chain-shot, which flew attached to no ideology, tore off a portion of the roof from staunch Unionist William Fahnestock house. "This was the time the firing was heaviest," Cornelia Peake McDonald penned, "and the terror so great." Atop Cemetery Hill east of Winchester, Emma Riely and a companion could see the soldiers huddled inside the forts by the light of the explosions. The duo was standing in the darkness observing the pyrotechnics when a Union regiment suddenly trotted past them, double-quicking its way to the fort. "Run home, girls," one of the

---

109 Gilmor, *Four Years in the Saddle*, 90-91.

110 McVicar Collection, Handley Library; Walker, *History of the Eighteenth Connecticut*, 113.

111 McKim, *A Soldier's Recollections*, 147; *Augusta* (GA) *Chronicle and Sentinel*, June 28, 1863; Ted Barclay to Hannah Barclay Moore, June 19, 1863, near Sharpsburg, Maryland, Washington and Lee University; Colt, *Defend the Valley*, 257. Robbie Barton deemed Milroy an "arch villain."

soldiers cried out, "get ready, the Rebs are coming!" Emma and her friend scurried home.[112]

By 9:00 p.m. Carlin's and Martins' guns were down to nothing but grape and canister, their shells and solid shot having been expended. Although no one died or was seriously injured inside the Main Fort, several Rebel shells had fallen into its interior but failed to explode. The concussions from Martins' thunderous guns, however, caused permanent hearing loss for some of the soldiers. Private William Strater of the 87th Pennsylvania, who with his comrades was providing close support for the 24-pounders, lost all the hearing in his right ear and suffered some impairment in his left. During the excitement, a sutler wagon tipped over, dumping its contents on the ground. James A. Fellers, another member of the 87th Pennsylvania, crept out in the darkness and bayoneted a large wheel of cheese. Struggling with the weight, he carried the delicious prize back into his lines to share with his lucky friends.[113]

Chaplain Joseph Brown of the 6th Maryland had being helping man the rifle pits near the Star Fort until Lt. Erastus S. Norval ordered him to leave. Once out, he followed "a regular stampede with the wagons and cavalry" out the Martinsburg Road until order was finally restored. Shot and shell rained around them until about 8:30 p.m., when the Union firing temporarily ceased after one last blast from a gun in the Main Fort. Heeding a friend's advice not to return to the Star Fort until morning, the chaplain Brown lay down near some wounded men on the porch of a house and fell fast asleep.[114]

The Final Confederate Push on the Main Fort

A little after 9:00 p.m., the Rebel guns fell silent. Moments later, according to many Union accounts but few Confederate ones, long waves of gray infantry began slowly descending the eastern slope of Flint Ridge, tramping east toward both the Main and Star forts. After Hays' Tigers stepped off, "Extra Billy" Smith's men rose to dress ranks. "Hays sent for us to support him," John Lewis Poe, a 24-year-old private in the 49th Virginia, wrote. "[Avery's] North Carolina soldiers had to lay down and let

---

112 McDonald, *A Woman's Civil War*, 160; *Athens* (OH) *Messenger*, July 9, 1863; Macon, *Reminiscences of the Civil War*, 79-80. This regiment may have been part of the 18th Connecticut trying to return to the Main Fort. Several companies were still east of town skirmishing with the Stonewall Brigade when darkness fell.

113 *Athens* (OH) *Messenger*, July 9, 1863; Brandt database, YCHT; Prowell, *History of the 87th Pennsylvania*, 90. Fellers would lose a leg at the 1864 Third Battle of Winchester (also known as the battle of Opequon).

114 Brown diary entry for June 14, 1863.

us walk over them. Some of our boys said, 'Lay down there, tar heels, and let these Virginians get over you.' You ought to have heard them curse and rare [roar]. I did not say a word."[115]

As the prospect of annihilation loomed, many of Milroy's men steeled themselves for a possible fight to the death. "Just as the sun set in the gold and glory of a ripe summer Sunday," the 116th Ohio's Sergeant-Major Dalzell observed, "the long lines of gray were seen to be moving into mass preparing for a final charge." He was glad Milroy still had 5,000 effective men and all the artillery except that captured on Flint Ridge. "Our rifle-pits were filled with determined, picked men," Dalzell added, admitting, "I was not in them. The rest of us hugged the fort." He believed the men, their equipment, the wagons, and everything they had would soon be in Rebels hands, "and theirs too, tall the dark-eyed maidens who had so charmed us with their divine wrath."[116]

"The sun went down and every moment we expected to meet the charge, and defend ourselves to the last," recalled the 87th Pennsylvania's Lt. Col. James Stahle. Corporal John C. Keses echoed the resolution: "Every man of us stood with fixed bayonet, gun at half-cock, and resolute face." Milroy gave his orders in a low voice: "Not a shot until the rebs reach the rifle-pits. Then give them hell, and receive them with the bayonet." For a while, silence reigned along the Union front on that young moonless and clear night. "You could have heard a pin drop in our great fort" observed Sergeant Dalzell. "On the west of the fort appeared the indistinct and faint line of an army moving like a grim shadow upon us," he added. When the advancing Rebels reached the outward rifle pits, a volley forced them back. Keses claimed that "almost at the close of the day, the Rebels made three unsuccessful charges on our works. We were surrounded by an unbroken line of battle which, like a wave, was coming upon us." When Milroy cried "Fire!" the Unionists with small arms and holding lanyards "poured death into the enemy." Not truly understanding the situation, Keses believed, "We had gained a victory that day and had kept almost two Corps from walking over us as they had boasted."[117]

As Ewell pressed the assault, Milroy ordered Carlin's Wheeling Battery to return to the Main Fort from their redoubt on the northern part of Bower's Hill. "I tell you

115 "John Lewis Poe's Account, The War of 1861 to 1865," dictated January 29, 1926, to his daughter-in-law Eva Poe; courtesy of descendant Daryl Poe; OR 27, 2, 489. Some accounts suggest General Smith started the taunt and that his men picked it up. The regimental historian of the 87th Pennsylvania, George R. Prowell, believed the artillery duel stopped about 8:00 p.m., but most other accounts place it about an hour later.

116 Dalzell, "A Lucky Blunder," 99.

117 Ibid., Stahle Papers and John C. Keses account, USAHEC.

we jerked our guns and carriages out of that little old redoubt in a hurry," Private McClelland admitted. Their infantry support, including some of the 18th Connecticut, moved down to the front of the abandoned redoubt. Just as the battery reached the northeastern corner of the Main Fort, the men heard yelling from the redoubt. Those who turned to look spotted two sheets of flame about 25 yards apart as the Mountaineer infantry and the oncoming Rebels fired into one another. "I suppose finding the battery was not there, they did not make a determined effort," McClelland concluded. The Confederates soon fell back. Carlin brought his limbers and caissons into the Main Fort and placed the rifles in position on the walls. Two more Southern thrusts were turned back, according to Federal accounts.[118]

The 87th Pennsylvania's Cpl. Charles Z. Denues, fighting from the rifle pits in front of the Main Fort, recalled how the Rebels came at them without pausing to fix bayonets. "As they came up we mowed them down, and they retreated in disorder," claimed Denues, "leaving their dead and wounded on the field." The 116th Ohio's Sergeant-Major Dalzell estimated some 900 bodies lay waiting burial in the morning. Another soldier in the 116th Ohio offered a more realistic assessment when he recorded that the Confederates finally retired, "but with what loss we are unable to tell."[119]

Most Confederate accounts suggest far fewer casualties than Union reminiscences suggest. "We charged the breastworks one half of a mile long and I didn't see but one man killed," John Lewis Poe recalled. "[W]e took it so quick they did not have time to kill many of us. This was the fastest double quicking we ever did. We drove them back to the town, and they began to shell us. One shell burst just in front of our company and Jemmy Brown, the next man to me, was wounded." Brown was one of only three men in Smith's sizable brigade wounded during the entire battle.[120]

"It was a hot place," confirmed the 18th Connecticut's Pvt. Charles Lynch. "The roaring of the big guns, explosion of shells, rattling of musketry, was something fearful. The charging of both sides was hot work. We drove the enemy back and they also forced our lines back. Darkness put an end to the carnage and I had passed through the battle unharmed. . . . The casualties were great as I could not help seeing. It gave me an opportunity to see what a horrible thing war really was." Part of the 18th Connecticut remained on the Smithfield skirmish line while the rest moved from the

---

118 *Wheeling Sunday Register*, April 26, 1891; Walker, *History of the Eighteenth Connecticut*, 112.

119 *Philadelphia Inquirer*, July 4, 1897; Dalzell, "A Lucky Blunder, 100; *Athens* (OH) *Messenger*, July 8, 1863.

120 *Athens* (OH) *Messenger*, July 9, 1863; Poe, "John Lewis Poe's Account."

rifle pits into the Main Fort. Stephen Oatley of Company G was killed during this movement.[121]

"God mercifully directed the shells," the 6th Maryland's Lieutenant Colonel McKellip remarked, "for we lost but four or five men by all that furious cannonade." After repulsing Early's assault on the Main Fort, Milroy fully expected an attack on the Star Fort. He pulled his Marylanders out of the rifle pits back into the Star Fort, where they supported the Baltimore Battery. "I don't think ten thousand men could have taken us, from the calmness and firmness which the Sixth Maryland evinced," Lt. H. E. Alexander opined. The 67th Pennsylvania remained in the rifle-pits outside the fort.[122]

About 9:30 p.m., Col. Andrew McReynolds, the commander of Milroy's Third Brigade which was mostly congregated around the Star Fort, told Captain F. W. Alexander of the Baltimore Battery to expect an attack on the Star Fort within the next half hour. The crews loaded the guns with canister and prepared for the impending assault. Alexander ordered Fred Wild to take charge of the magazine and stow the ammunition. As the various rounds were handed to him, he stacked each in a manner that would allow him to easily find and hand it out in the dark, if need be. Any light under that circumstance would have been extremely hazardous. "Confederates were going to charge on our fort," explained Wild, "and as they were coming up, we fired grape and canister into them as fast as the guns could be loaded, and with the thousands of muskets blazing away and the shells flying through the air, were followed by a streak of fire like a sky-rocket, and the flash of the shells from the heavy guns as they burst over the enemy, made a display of pyrotechnics that was awfully, terribly grand!" Following the final repulse of Early's infantry, sporadic artillery fire continued until about 10:00 p.m., when at last the guns of all varieties fell silent.[123]

The firing had stopped, but the battlefield was anything but quiet, as Lieutenant Rush recalled:

No more firing, all was now silent—no, not silent, for the saddest of sounds came out of the darkness. Calls from our wounded could be heard from the ground over which but a few hours before we had made our retreat. The various names of officers or comrades could be heard in plaintive appeals from the wounded for help from us who could neither answer nor give aid. But saddest of all were the groans heard through all the long,

---

121 Lynch, *Civil War Diary*, 20; James M. Smith diary entry for June 14, 1863. The 18th Connecticut had been organized in August 1862 but had spent most of its service time in various posts around Baltimore, including Fort McHenry.

122 *Baltimore Sun*, April 19, 1904; Wild, *Capt. F. W. Alexander's Baltimore Battery*, 61.

123 Ibid., OR 27, pt. 2, 87.

sleepless, terrible night-hours from our own hospital. They were mingled with the grating sound of surgeons' saws . . . Beneath bloody tables lay hands and feet and arms and limbs, transcending all treasures of gold—glad but gory offerings upon our country's altar.[124]

Captain Alexander's Baltimore Battery offers a stunning example of the often overlooked intensity of the fighting at Second Winchester. By the time the fighting ended on June 15, his Maryland command had only 168 rounds left out of the 1,187 on hand the previous day. According to his returns, his sextet of guns had fired 70 percussion shells and 95 rounds of case shot while skirmishing south of Winchester on the 13th and 14th, and then 10 rounds of canister, 359 percussions shells, and 456 rounds of case shot while manning the Star Fort (where only four guns could be brought to bear on the Rebels). Adding in the defense of Berryville and the brief skirmish at Locke's Ford, Alexander's battery had fired 1,019 rounds.[125]

Alexander's younger brother Eugene reported disabling two Rebel guns and a limber on Flint Ridge, in addition to Carrington's caisson blown up during his eastward movement from the Little North Mountain extension. Union artillery losses in the battery were surprising light. Two of the Baltimore artillerymen had been wounded, one by enemy metal and another when the turbulence from a passing artillery round flung him off the parapet. Five battery horses were down, and Alexander had no more than 20 rounds left per gun, with no reserve ammunition. Eugene praised the cannoneers: "Though it was the first time they had been under fire, not a man flinched, but they fought without excitement, and as coolly and regularly as if on drill, jesting and talking as it were mere pastime." A nearby Pennsylvania cavalryman thought the guns were "well managed."[126]

To the west, Jubal Early established a strong skirmish line under the command of Lt. Richard J. Hancock of the 9th Louisiana, leaving Hays on Flint Ridge with Smith's Virginians behind them. He moved the 57th North Carolina of Colonel Avery's brigade across the Pughtown Road into a small unfinished set of fortifications known in some accounts as Battery #7, kept the 54th North Carolina on picket duty on the Romney Road, and placed Avery's remaining two regiments in the rear to prevent any Yankee surprise. While the men congratulated one another on the successful attack and the rich bounty of captured supplies, Hilary Jones' artillery quartermaster distributed a cache of Union artillery swords amongst the battalion's sergeants. "It was

124 Rush, *Life and Writings*, 238-39.

125 1863 Monthly Returns, Baltimore Battery of Light Artillery Records, MHS.

126 Wild, *Capt. F. W. Alexander's Baltimore Battery*, 61; *Harrisburg Patriot and Union*, July 4, 1863. Carlin's West Virginia battery had 35 rounds per gun left, having fired an average of 265 rounds per gun.

The Yonley sisters comforted the wounded in their father's rented house near the West Fort. *Confederate Veteran*

the best managed affair Hayes ever had anything to do with," was the rather odd way the 8th Louisiana's Lt. J. Warren Jackson described the day's fighting. According to Hays, his brigade lost two officers and 10 men killed, and eight officers and 59 men wounded out of some 1,200 men he carried into battle. The two days of sharp fighting had cost the Tigers a total of 14 dead, 78 wounded, and three missing. The 6th Louisiana, which bore the brunt of the fire in the assault against the West Fort, lost 43 men killed and wounded, with 14 more coming from the 9th.[127]

Medical stewards and litter bearers hauled Hays' wounded to temporary field hospitals, including the damaged Fahnestock house (immediately east of Battery #6), where injured Louisianans mingled with wounded Yankees under the care of Mary Fahnestock. The surgeon of the 6th Louisiana, 24-year-old Kentucky-raised Dr. Charles H. Todd, treated many of his regiment's wounded at Samuel and Maria Yonley's small stone farmhouse southwest of the West Fort. The Yonley's two oldest girls, Alma and Lizzie, actively and generously ministered to their unexpected guests. Years later, Capt. John J. Rivera recalled their unselfish kindness. "[Yonley's] devoted daughters, notwithstanding the bursting shells and the parental admonition to remain in a place of comparative safety, went about the stricken soldiers and ministered to

---

127 Richard J. Hancock, "Billy Singleton Got the Flag," in *Confederate Veteran*, vol. 15, July 1907, 308; *Richmond Daily Dispatch*, June 25, 1863; Jackson, "Going Back in the Union at Last," 55; Stuart Sifakis, *Compendium of the Confederate Armies: Louisiana* (New York: Facts on File, 1992), 78–80. Keifer claimed the Confederates lost 100 men killed and 400 wounded. He based this on secondhand information from Winchester citizens and Confederate prisoners taken in the weeks after the battle (see *OR* 27, pt. 2, 64). He lost 55 of his own men.

their needs in every practical way," wrote Rivera. "That entire night, they were zealous in their attentions, and for several weeks they kindly nursed several [men], the severity of whose wounds did not permit removal." Alma had held the captain's hand while the surgeon painfully probed his side for a bullet. Rivera would never forget "the cool serenity of her courage as he looked into her blue eyes beaming with sympathy and encouragement, while she unflinchingly aided the surgeon in his search. She was as tender and kind to the wounded in her care as she was brave under fire."[128]

Meanwhile, two men of the Rockbridge Artillery found a little mule equipped with a saddle and bridle and presumed it was U. S. property. Since they were afraid of mules, even small ones, they turned it over to their comrade Pvt. Edward Moore, who spent a pleasant hour riding around the area. Moore planned to keep the mule for the rest of the campaign, but a member of the Richmond Howitzers claimed it in the morning as his own and took it away.[129]

While Private Moore surveyed the landscape from the back of a mule, Winchester residents emerged from their houses. "The stars were our only sentinels that night," a pro-Confederate lady penned, "and we walked abroad through the streets to enjoy the freedom of which we had been deprived so long." During Milroy's "military despotism," no one had been allowed outside their homes after dark. Sentinels had orders to shoot at any lights seen burning after 9:00 p.m. Now, with that hour having come and gone, Ewell's campfires burned brightly from every hill south, east, and west of town, "watchful guardians of the security," she rejoiced. A death-like calm prevailed throughout the night. Few residents went to bed early.[130]

While the pro-Southern residents quietly celebrated, Milroy reorganized and repositioned his forces. He resumed the brigade integrity which he had abandoned for much of the day. Brigadier General Washington Elliott's First Brigade now occupied the Main Fort and its flanking entrenchments, while Col. William Ely's Second Brigade manned the town and the intervening space between it and the Main Fort. Colonel Andrew McReynolds' Third Brigade continued to hold the Star Fort. Scouts

---

128 Rivera, "The Heroines of the Shenandoah Valley," 496. After the war, both sisters married and moved to Little Rock, Arkansas. Alma V. Chapman died in 1891. Captain Rivera was a New-York born former New Orleans newspaper printer. He moved to New York City, worked in the newspaper business, and outlived all the other field officers of the 6th Louisiana. In 1900, he, John Orr, and another surviving Tiger presented Lizzie Heironimus with a commemorative medal to thank her for her gracious care for the wounded at Second Winchester. The 6th Louisiana's Dr. Charles H. Todd (1838-1916) was a relative of Mary Todd Lincoln. His father, War of 1812 veteran 71-year-old Charles S. Todd, had offered to enlist in the Union army at the start of the war, but was denied because of age.

129 Moore, *The Story of a Cannoneer*, 187.

130 "Leaves from a Diary Kept by a Lady."

Private Richard Bassford of the Baltimore Light Artillery helped work the guns in the Star Fort on June 14. He was captured the following day at Carter's Woods.
Jonathan A. Noyalas

who filtered out from the Star Fort to reconnoiter returned with ominous news for McReynolds: the Rebels were moving their heaviest guns through a hollow to the high ground north of the Pughtown Road, where they could command his position and shell them easily once the sun rose.[131]

By now many of the embattled Union soldiers were questioning the wisdom of Milroy's decision to stay and fight at Winchester. The 87th Pennsylvania's George Blotcher counted himself among the doubters. "It looked now like the whole rebel army were down on us," he feared. "Why ever such an event happened is strange to me and others, having so many scouting parties and scouts from time to time up the valley and letting such a large force sweeping down on us, without giving Gen. Milroy due warning. It would have been folly for Gen. Milroy to remain here," added the German immigrant, "should he have known the result beforehand."[132]

Many of the German sutlers who serviced the division for a profit were in agreement. Late in the evening, some of them took their account books and other private papers to John McVicar's house near the Martinsburg Road, where they begged the family to take care of them because the Rebels were surrounding the town. The McVicars agreed, and eventually returned the documents to their owners after the war.[133]

"We had no time to eat the whole day of the fight," remembered the 87th Pennsylvania's Cpl. John Keses, "and during the night no fire was allowed to be made,

131 *Baltimore Sun*, April 19, 1904.

132 *Gettysburg Compiler*, June 29, 1863; Blotcher diary, June 14, 1863, YCHT. According to researcher Dennis Brandt, Blotcher tossed his diary onto a bonfire as Milroy's men destroyed extra baggage in preparation to leave Winchester on June 15. He began a new diary in 1864 and after the war tried to reproduce the earlier entries from memory and surviving letters.

133 Kate McVicar Collection, Handley Library.

even for coffee, lest we draw the enemy's fire upon our fortification. In our trenches we could hear them massing artillery into position to shell us by daylight. It was a bad place to sleep; nevertheless many men had a nap for an hour or so." Edmund Snyder served in the 123rd Ohio. Unlike the men of the 87th Pennsylvania, the Buckeyes "lay in the rifle pits that night with strict orders that no man should sleep, for a night attack was expected."[134]

"Through some bad generalship at this period we only had about one hour's ammunition for the artillery, and it was evident that we either would have to surrender in the morning or retreat that night," wrote a soldier of the 12th West Virginia with the benefit of hindsight. "The men were greatly disappointed when they found they had to retreat. No one imagined anything else but that there was ammunition enough in the magazine to blow up the Southern Confederacy. But there was not enough there to destroy the magazine."[135]

"At dark the battle ceased and an ominous silence reigned," recalled the 1st New York Cavalry's Captain Stevenson, "while the heads and hearts of our boys were busied with thoughts of the morrow." After dark he rested in a tent just outside of the Star Fort, "musing on the events of the two previous days, and sending up a silent prayer to the Father of all mercies to protect us in the struggle, which I knew to be inevitable on the coming day." When a loud gurgling noise at the tent flap startled Stevenson, he discovered there a grotesquely injured artillery horse "whose throat had been severed by a piece of shell, trying to get his head inside the tent; while the blood flowed from his nostrils, and he seemed by his loud moans to ask for assistance. Finally he staggered and fell, and in a short time was dead." The gruesome scene shook the New Yorker. "The darkness of the night; the close proximity of the enemy; the dead and wounded lying so close by, in an improvised hospital, moaning with pain, had given rise to serious thoughts," he mused, "and this strange apparition at the tent door filled me with a dread of impending evil, and I was compelled to jump to my feet and walk about to dispel my unhappy thoughts."[136]

While Stevenson paced and others slept or kept watch in the darkness, General Ewell finalized his plans for the morrow. As the Union defenders suspected, he intended to renew the bombardment in the morning in conjunction with a general assault on the two remaining Federal forts. Even before it was fully dark Jubal Early had sent an aide, Lt. William G. Callaway, to order General Gordon to advance his

134 Keses manuscript, YCHT; Edmund P. Snyder, *Autobiography of a Soldier of the Civil War* (Privately published, 1915), 8.

135 "H.C.H.," "With the 12th Virginia."

136 Stevenson, *Boots and Saddles*, 190.

Georgians from Bower's Hill northward in the morning and seize the Main Fort. The brigadier was uncharacteristically nervous. "My command was lying almost in the shadow of a frowning fortress in front, in which General Milroy, of the Union army, was strongly intrenched with forces which we had been fighting during the afternoon," he wrote in a letter to his wife Fanny. "In the dim twilight, with the glimmer of his bayonets and brass howitzers still discernible, I received an order to storm the fortress at daylight the next morning. To say that I was astounded at the order would feebly express the sensation which its reading produced; for on either side of the fort was an open country, miles in width, through which Confederate troops could easily pass around to the rear of the fort, cutting off General Milroy from the base of his supplies, and thus forcing him to retire and meet us in the open field. There was nothing for me to do, however, but to obey the order."[137]

Early's and Johnson's troops, the latter still occupying the now quiet ground south and east of Winchester after Union Colonel Ely had withdrawn most of his troops earlier in the evening, settled into their respective campsites, with many sleeping anxiously on their arms while Early's pioneers worked to reverse the Flint Ridge fortifications to provide better cover for Jones' artillery. Contrary to Gordon's premonition, however, many men fully expected a major victory in the morning, one that would finally rid the Valley of the hated Milroy. "The position of the Yankees was utterly hopeless now," a member of Dance's 1st Virginia Battalion thought, "for in the morning we would have torn them to pieces with our artillery." With his Artillery Reserve now fully deployed in addition to the two divisional battalions, Ewell now had dozens of cannon aimed at the pair of Yankee fortifications. Ordnance officers worked well into the night preparing stockpiles of ammunition for the expected renewal of the artillery duel. About 10:00 p.m. the Rockbridge Artillery and other reserve batteries unlimbered on Flint Ridge to renew the bombardment in the morning.[138]

William White and some cannoneers from the 3rd Richmond Howitzers and the Powhatan Artillery spent a thankless night taking their limbers to Flint Ridge and hauling Randolph's captured Union guns to the rear in the darkness. The Powhatan artillerymen moved to replace their inferior howitzers with a pair of captured Union 3-inch rifles. However, to White's dismay, his company was detailed to haul one of Randolph's guns to another battery, and they were unable to retain it to replace what White considered to be an "abominable" howitzer. He seethed at the injustice,

137 Goldsborough, *The Maryland Line*, 96; John B. Gordon, *Reminiscences of the Civil War* (New York: Charles Scribner's Sons, 1904), 68.

138 *Charleston* (SC) *Mercury*, June 22, 1863, citing unnamed Richmond newspapers; Diary of Robert Sherrard Bell, Old Courthouse Civil War Museum, Winchester, Virginia.

commenting in his diary, "We returned to our former camp in no pleasant mood, just as day was breaking." The disgruntled gunners threw themselves on the ground to catch a few moments of sleep, for the day ahead promised plenty of hard work.[139]

One of the Stonewall Brigade's veterans, John Garibaldi of the 27th Virginia, believed General Johnson had made the correct call in not aggressively moving toward the artillery-studded forts that evening. The Yankees were "too well fortified to charge on their fortifications but we could have taken them with a heavy loss, so the commander of our corps General Ewell left a gap open thinking that they will try to get out during the night and thus make its escape, and he fell on the right plan."[140]

In Winchester, young Gettie Miller hoped "our men will catch old Milroy. . . . They say they have him surrounded. I expect our men will come here tomorrow. It will be splendid to see the rebels again. We have not seen them for six months. It seems such a long time."[141]

139 White, "A Diary of the War," 188, 190.

140 John Garibaldi to his wife, Sarah, June 16, 1863, Camp Stephenson, Winchester, Virginia, Letter #13, Manuscript #284, Garibaldi Papers, VMI.

141 Gettie Miller diary entry for June 15, 1863.

Chapter 8

Sunday, June 14

"They were getting away as fast as their legs could carry them."

— *Capt. James I. Harris, 30th North Carolina*[1]

Fighting at Martinsburg

While
Generals Early and Johnson attacked and maneuvered against the overmatched Milroy at Winchester, Maj. Gen. Robert Rodes started his Confederate division at daybreak on "a very fatiguing march of 19 miles" from Summit Point and Berryville. His goal was the seizure of Martinsburg, where more than 1,200 Federals under Col. Benjamin F. Smith guarded the Valley Pike and the sprawling Baltimore & Ohio Railroad complex.

Martinsburg was a prosperous town of 3,300 people and the seat of Berkeley County, which would soon be part of the new state of West Virginia. Established in 1773, Martinsburg was situated on a broad elevation in the Lower Shenandoah Valley about 12 miles south of Williamsport and some 20 miles north of Winchester. Several roads radiated from the town, including the north-south Valley Pike, the Charles Town (Charlestown) Road, and well-used routes to Shepherdstown to the east, Hedgesville to the northwest, and Boyd's Gap in the North Mountain range to the west. Early settlers included Germans, Quakers, and Scots-Irish, whose descendants maintained mills, farms, and light industry, or worked for the railroad or associated enterprises. Several stately mansions dotted Martinsburg, the most prominent of which was "Boydville." The Georgian-style plastered stone manor was the home of Confederate Lt. Col. Charles J. Faulkner, a Minister to France during the Buchanan administration and Stonewall Jackson's assistant adjutant general. His two-story

---

1   Taylor, "Ramseur's Brigade in the Gettysburg Campaign," 28.

house just south of town was a popular hub of antebellum society and the center of a sprawling farm and estate.[2]

Martinsburg's strategic location and the presence of several important railroad shops and warehouses there made it an inviting target for both armies once war erupted in April 1861. Three months later in July, when some of Maj. Gen. Robert Patterson's Union soldiers attempted to raise the Stars and Stripes over the home of Benjamin and Mary Boyd, a verbal altercation broke out and their daughter, Maria Isabelle, pulled out a pistol and killed Pvt. Frederick Martin of the 7th Pennsylvania. Although she was acquitted of the charges, Maria Boyd—or "Belle" as she is better known to history—turned her talents to espionage and became a relatively effective spy for the Confederate high command. Because he was soldiering in the 2nd Virginia (part of what would become the famous Stonewall Brigade), Benjamin Boyd was not home when his daughter shot Martin. Most of Martinsburg's residents leaned strongly to the Union, but a significant number of others, such as the Boyds, fervently supported the Confederacy.[3]

Martinsburg changed hands many times during the Civil War. Union troops occupied the city beginning in October 1862. The troops that made up the Union garrison holding the town during the second weekend of June 1863 consisted of Col. Benjamin F. Smith's Third Brigade, 1st Division, Eighth Corps. The 31-year-old Smith was a West Point graduate and a career soldier with considerable experience in the western territories and distant states before the war, including fighting Comanches in Texas, putting down disturbances in Kansas, and serving in the Mormon Expedition. Now, in June of the war's third year, he commanded the 500 men of his own 126th Ohio, 600 men of Col. Edward C. James' 106th New York (off-site at Camp Hopkins in an oak grove on North Mountain along the B & O northwest of Martinsburg), Capt. William F. Firey's Company B of the 1st Potomac Home Brigade Cavalry, and Capt. Thomas A. Maulsby's six-gun West Virginia battery. The colorful Captain Firey, educated in medicine at the University of Pennsylvania, had made a considerable fortune in California's gold rush of 1849. He returned to his hometown of Clear Spring, Maryland, in 1853 and opened a medical office. In 1861, Firey recruited a company of cavalry that saw considerable action in western Virginia and

---

2 Leon, *Diary of a Tar Heel Confederate Soldier*, 31; Files of the Berkeley County Historical Society, Martinsburg, West Virginia. Boydville, erected in 1812, is at 601 S. Queen Street. At the time of the war, several smaller outbuildings, including Faulkner's law office and the caretaker's home, surrounded the manor house. Faulkner's son, a European-educated VMI cadet who served in the 1864 battle of New Market would be a two-term U.S. Senator at the turn of the century.

3 The Belle Boyd house is at 126 E. Race Street.

Alfred Waud sketches of Martinsburg. *Library of Congress*

Maryland over the next two years. Few of Smith's infantry, however, had "seen the elephant."[4]

Rumors of a major Confederate incursion had been circulating for some time before the head of the Confederate army made its appearance. "An impression seemed to prevail among the citizens that the rebels were going to clear out the valley," Capt. Jonathan S. McCready of the 126th Ohio observed. "I do not know that the soldiers paid much attention to it. The prevailing opinion seemed to be that we could whip them if they came—that is, the soldiers thought so, or a good many of them, but not so the citizens." Milroy sent a ciphered message via courier to Colonel Smith that if he [Milroy] could not safely evacuate, he could sustain himself and hold his position five days. Without the prospect of Milroy's division joining him, and with no other reinforcements on the way, Smith later complained that he had "no force to support him."[5]

All day on Saturday, June 13, news of the Rebel approach caused considerable commotion in Martinsburg. The ominous boom of artillery from the direction of Winchester cast a pall over the pro-Union residents. Many of the women despaired at

4   *Franklin and Marshall University Obituary Record: A Record of Deceased Alumni…* (Lancaster, PA: Franklin and Marshall College Alumni Association, 1897), 1:38-39.

5   Ibid.; *Cadiz* (OH) *Republican,* June 29, 1863; OR 27, pt. 2, 174.

the idea of being captured if the town fell. Most merchants packed up to leave, and many offered their wares at significantly lower prices than normal. As evening approached so did a rain storm. The darkness and hard shower combined to further dampen moods and turned the dirt side roads into sticky ribbons of mud.[6]

That Saturday night, Colonel Smith took the precaution of ordering his men to strike their tents and load their supplies and baggage into wagons. He marched his own regiment, the 126th Ohio, a short distance out of town shortly before dark, but when word arrived the Confederates were not expected until morning, Smith's force returned to camp. The eight companies of Colonel James' 106th New York arrived shortly after 7:30 p.m. after receiving Smith's telegraphed orders to march the nine miles south from the trackside Camp Hopkins. James left behind 11 sick men, the hospital tents, and medical stores in the care of Dartmouth-educated assistant surgeon Dr. Frederick H. Petit. The healthy riflemen and their supports camped on the sprawling 300-acre John W. Stewart estate "Aspen Hall" on a hill just north of town near the railroad, while the Buckeye pickets maintained a south-facing watch along the Valley Pike.[7]

The 106th New York regimental band found comfortable quarters in a nearby barn. Many of the other soldiers slept outside on rubberized blankets as protection from the damp rain-soaked ground. Mrs. Mary Stewart remained busy cooking and providing a meal for some of the more fortunate soldiers. None of the New Yorkers quite knew what to expect. "We don't know the minute we will be attacked," exclaimed a private named Henry Gaddis. "There has been talk we will be going to Harpers Ferry on the cars." Their night, for a multitude of reasons, proved a restless one.[8]

In addition to his own demi-brigade, Colonel Smith had a handful of men from the 13th Pennsylvania Cavalry and gained the use of Lt. Frank Martindale's Company H of the 1st New York Cavalry, which arrived from Bunker Hill on Saturday night after holding off Albert Jenkins' Rebel troopers long enough to allow Colonel McReynolds' 42 wagons to escape. Those wagons and their cavalry escort moved

---

6 James R. Droegemeyer, "The Battle of Martinsburg, June 14, 1863," The *Berkeley Journal*, no. 27, 2001, 53.

7 McCready letter to the *Cadiz* (OH) *Republican*, cited in Susan G. Hall, *Appalachian Ohio and the Civil War, 1862-1863* (Jefferson, NC: McFarland, 2008), 225-26; *OR* 27, pt. 2, 37-40; West Virginia Civil War Trails wayside marker for Camp Hopkins, located near 570 Allensville Road north of Hedgesville, West Virginia. Three days later the Rebels captured the camp, pilfered most of its contents, and marched away, leaving Dr. Petit and the very sick men behind in the hospital tent.

8 Droegemeyer, "The Battle of Martinsburg," 57-58.

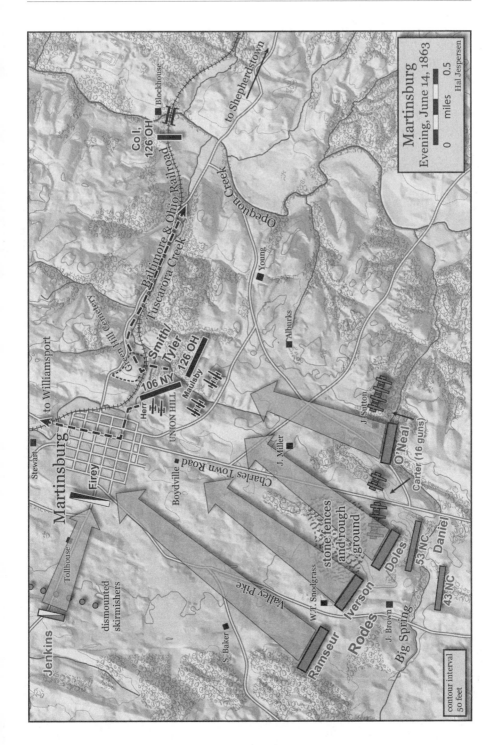

Martinsburg
Evening, June 14, 1863

Hal Jespersen

0   0.5
miles

contour interval
50 feet

farther northward that night. The rest of the wagon train moved about three miles along the road to Williamsport and rested there.[9]

The Sabbath, June 14, opened under a cloudy sky. The Union soldiers rose early, prepared breakfast, and awaited orders to advance. Mary Stewart fed some of the grateful New Yorkers congregated around her Aspen Hall manor house. Their repast ended abruptly about 8:00 a.m. when the head of Jenkins' cavalry drove in Smith's vedettes along the turnpike south of Martinsburg. About the same time, 64-year-old Brig. Gen. Daniel Tyler and two staff officers, Capt. Max Woodhull and Lt. Edmund L. Tyler (one of the general's sons), arrived on a special early train from Harpers Ferry. Tyler, an 1819 graduate of West Point and former railroad executive, had departed Baltimore at midnight with instructions from Maj. Gen. Robert Schenck to use the troops at Martinsburg to support and cover the supposed retreat of Milroy's command from Winchester northward to Harpers Ferry. Special Orders No. 159 left the exact details to Tyler's discretion, but suggested Bunker Hill as a suitable position to make a stand if he found the Rebels in force between his newly assigned command and Milroy. Schenck cautioned Tyler to "keep constantly in communication meanwhile with General Milroy." After arriving at Harpers Ferry at 5:00 a.m., Tyler consulted with Brig. Gen. Benjamin F. Kelley, whose scouts reported Rebel cavalry in the Valley—but no infantry. With that false assurance, Tyler's train continued on to Martinsburg.[10]

When Colonel Smith told Tyler his vedettes reported the enemy was advancing in force on the Winchester Pike, the old general deferred what to do next to Smith, who was well into his preparations to meet the threat. That decision would generate some controversy as to who was responsible for the defense of Martinsburg. Tyler, the ranking officer, would later offer the rather bizarre claim that Smith's small command, to which he was a "perfect stranger," was not commensurate with his rank as a brigadier general, and that he had left Harpers Ferry expecting a much larger force. While still inside the train station at Martinsburg, Tyler had the telegraph operator tap out a message to inform General Schenck the Rebels were only three miles away.[11]

Tyler moved to an office in the Market House, where he established headquarters and performed a series of largely administrative duties. Concurrently, Colonel Smith, meanwhile, began deploying his men to resist the oncoming Rebel cavalry. He

---

9 Beach, *The First New York Cavalry*, 235; Grant, "Letter from Lieut. W. J. Grant." The next morning, they learned that Jenkins had taken Martinsburg and had then crossed the Potomac River at Williamsport before. They went to Chambersburg, Pennsylvania, and then on to Carlisle and Harrisburg, pursued the entire way by Jenkins' horse soldiers.

10 *OR* 27, pt. 2, 33, 57 and 198.

11 Ibid., 198.

Brig. Gen. Daniel Tyler, commander of the Union garrison at Martinsburg. *Library of Congress*

certainly did not consider Tyler to be in overall command, because "he showed me no orders and gave me no explanation why he was there." Smith supposed Tyler's role was merely as an inspector general sent by Schenck, the same role Tyler had performed a few days earlier when he accompanied Lt. Col. Donn Piatt to visit Martinsburg, Camp Hopkins, and Winchester.[12]

"Got orders to fall in as the rebels was approaching," an Ohioan mentioned in his diary. "We form a line of battle at 9 oclock A.M. and march out to Winchester Road." Colonel Smith stayed behind in Martinsburg to give some last minute instructions to his quartermasters and commissary officers. The 126th Ohio formed in the fields a mile south of town, sheltering behind a wall of limestone rocks on the northern end of a low narrow hill overlooking the turnpike. Captain Maulsby's relatively new 3-inch Ordnance Rifles unlimbered on high ground covering the roads from both Winchester and Charles Town, the most likely avenues of Confederate approach. Shortly after 10:00 a.m. the New Yorkers joined them. Seven companies crossed the road to their right and took position on an open hill. Colonel James threw Companies B and G a half-mile out as skirmishers, and Lt. Col. William H. Harlan did the same with the Buckeyes. Company K of the 106th remained east of the macadamized turnpike to support the guns, while scouts rode out on each flank to watch for any threatening movements.[13]

At Colonel Smith's request, General Tyler rode out to view the scene. The threatening situation took an ominous turn mid-morning when Capt. William H.

12 *Court of Inquiry Relative to the Evacuation of Martinsburg by the Command of Brig. Gen. Daniel Tyler*, NARA, Archives I, Record Group 153, Records of the Advocate General Office, Court-Martial Files, 17.

13 Anonymous diary entry for June 14, 1863, "Diary of a Civil War Soldier in Company F 126th Ohio Volunteer Infantry"; *The Union Army: A History of the Military Affairs in the Loyal States, 1861-65* (Madison, WI: Federal Publishing Co., 1908), 6:587; OR 27, pt. 2, 16, 37, 40 and 198; Steve French, "The Battle of Martinsburg," *Gettysburg Magazine*, no. 34, January 2006, 11-12.

Boyd and Company C of the 1st New York Cavalry trotted in with a message from Milroy: Ewell's Second Corps of between 15,000-18,000 Confederates was at Winchester. Tyler dispatched Captain Woodhull to ride to the telegraph office to relay the information to headquarters in Baltimore. A courier arrived with the disconcerting news that Bunker Hill was now in Confederate hands. It would have been useless for Tyler or Smith to try a diversion to aid Milroy's retreat, for it looked as though the Winchester commander had no intent to execute one. Tyler assumed a strong force of Rebels had attacked General Milroy, and took the initiative to order Smith's baggage train to move toward Williamsport and make its way to Pennsylvania.[14]

Trouble arrived soon thereafter. "In looking down the valley we could plainly see a dense cloud of dust arising, indicating a great force moving to stir up such a cloud," observed the 106th's surgeon Dr. Calvin Skinner. Within a few minutes the New Yorkers could see a large enemy force approaching from the south, and "could distinctly hear the rebel yell." Corporal Frank B. Williams served in the 50th New York Engineers assigned to the Union garrison at Harpers Ferry. He later reported that he had been helping with a pontoon bridge across the Potomac River at Williamsport earlier that morning. Williams arrived at Martinsburg just in time to learn the enemy was nearby. The corporal decided to stick around to observe what was going to transpire.[15]

The Confederates approaching within sight of Martinsburg belonged to General Jenkins, who deployed his brigade's skirmishers in a wide arc near Big Spring. The rolling farmland was dotted with stone walls and stands of trees, and cut by a series of ravines. Shortly after 11:00 a.m., "skirmishing began sharply and was kept up all day," the 126th Ohio's Captain McCready wrote. The ordained minister had maintained his religious duties while his regiment occupied Martinsburg, including officiating at the weddings of two of his soldiers to local pro-Union women. Now, his inexperienced men faced the dismounted veteran Rebel skirmishers, many of whom carried Enfield rifles as they sheltered in the distant fields and behind fence lines. The crackle of the fitful musketry carried into downtown Martinsburg, where many residents huddled in their cellars for protection.[16]

When a sizeable portion of Jenkins' mounted Virginians moved into range, Maulsby's guns opened fire. "Our artillery was too much for them," recalled Corporal

14 OR 27, pt. 2, 17, 38 and 198.

15 Dr. Calvin Skinner, "A Surgeon's Story," *The Franklin Gazette*, Malone, NY, August 17, 1894; Frank B. Williams, "Our Army Correspondence. From the 50th (Engineer) Regiment," *Rochester Democrat and American*, June 29, 1863.

16 Hall, *Appalachian Ohio and the Civil War*, 180, 225-26; French, "Battle of Martinsburg," 11; Droegemeyer, "The Battle of Martinsburg," 60.

Williams. "They wheeled and scampered back to the woods from whence they came." The noisy demonstration scared the horse of Captain Moorman B. White, which carried the 14th Virginia Cavalry officer straight into Federal lines. The new prisoner confirmed the Federals were battling Jenkins' cavalry brigade, and went on to brag that by nightfall they would be facing 30 guns and up to 30,000 men—a claim General Tyler brushed aside as impossible.[17]

Teamsters with the wagon train three miles north of Martinsburg listened to the roar of Maulsby's guns off to the south and understood what it signified. The men hastily hitched their draft horses and mules, and within minutes the lengthy procession of wheeled vehicles was tracing the Valley Pike northward as fast as possible. The heavily laden supply wagons occasionally careened nearly out of control on the turns as drivers frantically whipped their teams. The teamsters crossed the Potomac at Light's Ford at Williamsport and continued on all the way to Hagerstown, Maryland.[18]

In an effort to avoid being flanked, just before noon Colonel Smith moved his Buckeyes and the artillery back toward Union Hill, a narrow rise just south of Green Hill Cemetery. This new location on the high ground was better situated to protect the vital roads running to Williamsport and Shepherdstown. With bugles blaring, the Ohioans withdrew while Smith kept James's New Yorkers south of town to fend off any probing Confederate patrols. General Tyler, meanwhile, having returned to the downtown Market House, sent word on to Smith about noon that a retreat would in fact be necessary, but that he should hold on until the baggage train had reached safety, at which time the entire force would march to Williamsport and beyond to Harpers Ferry.[19]

Four of Captain Maulsby's rifles on Union Hill faced south. About 300 paces away in what proved to be a rather confined space for the guns and limbers, Smith positioned Lt. John S. S. Herr's section above a steep limestone cliff overlooking the Charles Town Road. These guns faced west to counter the Rebel cavalry. Smith formed his own 126th Ohio behind some stone walls to protect the guns and redeployed his skirmishers in a wide arc in the fields south and southeast of town. Firey's cavalry and the Pennsylvanians protected the western approaches to

17 Williams, "Our Army Correspondence"; French, "Battle of Martinsburg," 11; Robert Driver, *14th Virginia Cavalry* (Lynchburg, VA: H.E. Howard, 1988), 20.

18 Grant, "Letter from Lieut. W. J. Grant."

19 Ibid. According to Martinsburg historian James R. Droegemeyer, Union Hill supposedly gained the name because of local Union sympathizers who lived there. Period maps designate it as Shower's Hill. See French, "Battle of Martinsburg," 13.

Downtown Martinsburg, as it appeared in 1864, by artist James E. Taylor.
Western Reserve Historical Society

Martinsburg, with a company of the 1st New York Cavalry watching the Valley Pike to Williamsport.[20]

Meanwhile, feverish efforts to raise Winchester continued in the various telegraph offices across the area. "Harpers Ferry reports slight current from Winchester battery, which proves the wire is not broken. It is probably on the ground," concluded Martinsburg's telegrapher George W. Baldwin. "Cannot work to Winchester at present." Whether the wires had been cut or were just "on the ground," concerns about Milroy's position increased.[21]

Around midday General Jenkins sent Capt. William A. Harris, one of General Rodes' staff officers, together with a small escort forward under a flag of truce to demand that the Federals surrender. If the commander refused, explained Jenkins' message, he was "respectfully requested to notify the inhabitants of the place to remove forthwith to a place of safety. Small-arms only will be used for one hour upon the town after your reception of this note. After that, I shall feel at liberty to shell the town, if I see proper. Should you refuse to give the necessary notification to the inhabitants, I shall be compelled to hold your command responsible." Jenkins did not

---

20 French, "Battle of Martinsburg," 12; *OR* 27, pt. 2, 18.

21 *OR* 27, pt. 2, 174.

have any artillery with his column, and was betting the Federals did not know that small detail.[22]

Colonel Smith drafted a terse reply and sent it to General Tyler for his endorsement. "Martinsburg will not be surrendered. You may commence shelling as soon as you choose. I will, however, inform the women and children of your threat." Once Smith notified the inhabitants of the looming danger, large numbers of civilians crowded the roads north of town in their effort to escape. "They at once commenced a grand hegira over the fields towards Maryland," observed veteran *New York Herald* journalist F. G. Chapman. "We still waited for the expected bombardment, occasionally shelling the enemy at long range wherever they appeared."[23]

When the two o'clock hour passed without so much as a single Rebel shell, Colonel Smith, satisfied a major attack was not imminent, pulled the 106th New York back toward Union Hill near the Buckeyes. At nightfall, he informed Colonel James, they would all retreat to Williamsport on the Valley Pike and then head to Harpers Ferry. James' skirmishers reformed in the fields to the south linking with the Buckeye's skirmish line. Jenkins responded by lengthening his lines to cut off the roads south and west of Martinsburg.

General Tyler had counted on using the railroad to evacuate his and General Milroy's troops to Harpers Ferry, but when he returned to the depot he discovered every car and engine had already been sent away, and there were no locomotives or rolling stock within range to help him. At 3:00 p.m., Tyler wired General Schenck and President Lincoln that Milroy was in a "tight place" at Winchester, and "if he gets out, it will be by good luck and hard fighting. Not a straggler from his army is yet in; it is neck or nothing." Tyler added, "We are besieged here; have had a little skirmish. I imagine our rebel friends are waiting for grub and artillery." The message exasperated the already frustrated Lincoln, who replied, "If you are besieged, how do you dispatch me? Why did you not leave before being besieged?"[24]

Captain Henry C. Yontz and Company I of the 126th Ohio were on detached duty guarding a blockhouse where the railroad crossed Opequon Creek a couple of

---

22 Ibid., 17, 38, 198 and 548. After the war, Captain Harris was a congressman and U. S. Senator from Kansas. He was Rodes' Chief of Ordnance during the Gettysburg campaign. Some accounts place Jenkins' flag of truce at noon or 1:00 p.m.; others state as late as 2:00 or 3:00 p.m.

23 F. G. Chapman to editor, June 19, 1863, Maryland Heights, Maryland, as printed in the *New York Herald*, June 27, 1863.

24 *Daily Milwaukee News*, June 21, 1863, citing a Baltimore-based correspondent who mentioned the B&O rolling stock and locomotives, except what was needed for military purposes, had been sent to that city; OR 27, pt. 2, 18 and 174; pt. 3, 109.

miles east of town. "At three o'clock an order was received to retreat by the Williamsport Road, which could not be executed," Pvt. John H. Gilson recalled, "as the enemy in large force occupied all the roads except the Shepherdstown road, on which our troops were now posted." Some of Jenkins' forward pickets intercepted the isolated Buckeyes as they attempted to rejoin their regiment, capturing the entire company except for two officers and thirteen men.[25]

It was likely about this time or soon thereafter that General Tyler, unable to locate Colonel Smith, ordered Lieutenant Colonel Harlan to fire upon his own skirmish line in the mistaken belief the men were Rebels. Harlan refused, and explained he had placed them in position himself and knew they were his men. Tyler relented, averting a potential tragedy.[26]

The skirmishing resumed about 3:00 p.m. according to *New York Herald* correspondent Chapman. "Sometimes it would die away, then it would revive, and so rapidly would it become that you would suppose the battle was fairly begun," recalled Ohio Captain McCready. "These skirmishes, however, which precede a battle, are rather harmless affairs. It was thought that two or three rebels were killed, during the day, but they kept at long range."[27]

Albert Jenkins gradually fed more troops into the combat, massing his dismounted cavalry south and west of the town. Some of his men did not like his aggressive posture, especially with Rodes' infantry and artillery still not up. "It was a dreadful thought to contemplate a pitched battle," explained the 17th Virginia Cavalry's Lt. Addison Smith. "Now it seemed strange to us why we should fight this battle when in our rear lay enough infantry to have swallowed them up easily. But Gen. Jenkins was eager for a chance to distinguish himself and his command, and was determined to storm the place."[28]

About 5:00 p.m., Jenkins attempted to turn Captain Firey's right flank and occupy the town. However, Maulsby's guns in general, and Lieutenant Herr's two westward-facing Ordnance Rifles in particular, checked his efforts. Concerned about the potential for high casualties, Jenkins decided to await the arrival of General Rodes, though his men did sever the telegraph lines in the area. An hour later Colonel Smith, also anticipating the arrival of Rebel infantry, detached the left wing of his Ohio

---

25 Ibid., 39; John H. Gilson, *Concise History of the One Hundred and Twenty-sixth Regiment, Ohio Volunteer Infantry* (Salem, OH: Walton, 1883), 10; Droegemeyer, "The Battle of Martinsburg," 75.

26 *OR* 27, pt. 2, 199.

27 Hall, *Appalachian Ohio and the Civil War*, 226.

28 Kesterson, *Campaigning with the 17th Virginia Cavalry*, 26.

regiment under Lt. Col. Frederick E. Embick and placed it behind Maulsby's four southern-facing rifles a short distance in front of the main force. When Jenkins renewed his long-distance skirmishing, Smith sent orders for his skirmishers and pickets to fall back just before sunset.[29]

Rodes' Division Joins the Fighting

Robert Rodes marched his infantry division out of Bunker Hill after a noontime lunch break. When the column passed through the village of Smithfield, the residents' friendly reception pleased Pvt. Samuel Pickens of the 5th Alabama, part of Col. Edward O'Neal's brigade. "A lady was standing before her door with a bucket of nice warm light bread & buttered & pitcher buttermilk; as I passed by she gave me [a] slice & poured milk in my cup. I enjoyed it very much & only wished for more." The passing troops cheered the local ladies busy waving handkerchiefs in welcome. A martial band added to the festivities. Pickens stopped at several houses to purchase milk and butter, but Jenkins' horsemen had already made off with much of the excess food. The 30th North Carolina's Lt. William Ardrey appreciated the cups of cool water, "all kinds of eatables," and bouquets of flowers that greeted he and his comrades in Ramseur' passing brigade. However, the column did not tarry, but marched onward toward Martinsburg. "The troops marched hard the latter part of the day & we had very little rest," Pickens later complained.[30]

Ramseur's road-weary infantry tramped within sight of Martinsburg just before sunset. Before any infantry deployed, General Rodes sent the rest of Jenkins' cavalry to the left and rear of Martinsburg. As far as the frustrated Rodes was concerned, Jenkins had not been showing enough aggressiveness. He intended to dismount the horse soldiers and send them forward as skirmishers to gain possession of the town and cut off the enemy's avenues of retreat toward Hedgesville and Williamsport, and instructed Jenkins to report what force, if any, he had discovered in and to the left of Martinsburg.[31]

To his artillery commander, Rodes sent orders to "take the best position for his artillery to enable him to silence the opposing battery, which was annoying us." Carter turned off the hard-packed gravel turnpike to the right and began unlimbering his sixteen guns on the heights between the pike and the Charles Town Road. The cannoneers of the Jeff Davis Artillery brought their pieces to bear on Union Hill. "The

29 *OR 27*, pt. 2, 18, 40.

30 Hubbs, *Voices from Company D*, 178; Ardrey diary entry for June 14, 1863.

31 *OR 27*, pt. 2, 548.

first shot from Reese's battery passed over Captain Maulsby's four nearest pieces and plunged into the farthest [Herr's] section, killing and wounding several horses and demoralizing the infantry support," recorded Confederate gunner John Purifoy.[32]

"The first volley burst above our heads," Pvt. Henry Gaddis of the supporting 106th New York admitted. "The next volley struck about a rod in front of us in the face of the hill. There was an artilleryman killed and one or two horses killed. I had never seen shells look so fiery before." These first Rebel rounds threw Herr's infantry supports, the right battalion of the 106th New York, into some confusion. The men fell back some distance, but their officers rallied them and they resumed their position a few minutes later. Meanwhile, in Tyler's opinion, Maulsby's initial counter-battery fire was "at one time so effectually as almost to silence the rebel guns." Rebel cannoneer Purifoy observed, "Captain Maulsby fired six rounds, from each of his four pieces." Captain Charles W. Fry's Orange (Virginia) Artillery lost one man killed and one wounded. However, before long Carter's other two batteries, the King William (Virginia) Artillery and the Morris (Virginia) Artillery, took position and unlimbered.[33]

Shortly before Reese opened, Colonel Smith received notification that all of his wagons had crossed the Potomac at Williamsport. With that news, he issued orders for his men to prepare to fall back to the ferry on the turnpike. However, ten minutes later the enemy artillery opened from three different points just as he ordered his pickets and skirmishers to fall back slowly and cautiously. The fire was so concentrated "it cannot be wondered at that the men were thrown into temporary confusion." He passed word for his outnumbered Buckeye regiment to retire and for Maulsby to prepare to limber his guns. "The air was howling with the sound of flying shot and the explosion of shells," recalled reporter F. G. Chapman.[34]

As Carter's field pieces barked, Rodes' infantry deployed. According to Louis Leon, the 53rd North Carolina "felt like driving the devil out of his own stronghold, as we had to march in quicktime a distance of twenty-five miles; therefore we certainly were not in the very best humor." They were about to take out that ill-humor on Smith's Federals. "[D]ispositions for the attack were made," recorded the 30th North Carolina's Capt. James Harris. "From all the information we could gain the lowest estimate we could place on the enemy's strength was 5,000. As had been the case at Berryville, our plan was to attack at two or three different points at once. Our brigade, when within one mile of the town, moved off to the left of the turnpike while [Brig.

---

32 Ibid.; Purifoy, "With Jackson in the Valley," 384.

33 Droegemeyer, "The Battle of Martinsburg," 70; Purifoy, "With Jackson in the Valley," 384; *OR* 27, pt. 2, 549.

34 *OR* 27, pt. 2, 38; *New York Herald*, June 27, 1863.

Gen. Alfred] Iverson moved to the right and occupied the heights fronting those on which the town was built." Rodes placed O'Neal's Alabamans and Maj. Eugene Blackford's sharpshooters on the right to support the artillery with the brigades of Brig. Gen. George Doles and Iverson to their left. Ramseur pushed forward toward Jenkins and the town on the left while the 43rd and 53rd North Carolina of Brig. Gen. Junius Daniel's brigade remained in reserve. The rest of Daniel's regiments were well in the rear protecting the supply wagons.[35]

As the road-weary infantrymen settled into position, Lieutenant Colonel Carter concentrated on the distant Yankee guns on the hillside. An unknown artillery officer enjoyed a bird's eye view of the concentrated cannonade. "In the brief space of twenty minutes," he wrote, "before our infantry could get into position—we had the enemy flying in great haste from the 'ragged rebels.'" A shell landed in the street in front of the Conrad house and another burst in the garden, tearing off a raspberry bush and damaging another remembered Confederate Lt. Launcelot M. Blackford. The family sheltered in their cellar during the cannonade.[36]

The cannonade was intense, but brief and relatively bloodless. Several inexperienced Federals exaggerated or misunderstood its duration, and also wildly exaggerated the size of Rodes' command. Private David Close, a teenager serving with the 126th Ohio, claimed "the enemy threw about 200 shells at us which came screaming over our heads some bursting and scattering the pieces all around others would strike the ground and scatter the earth in every direction." Close believed "30,000 rebels attacked 1,500 of us, and of course we could not hold out long against so many of the enemy." One of the New Yorkers, Henry Gaddis, claimed the Rebels were "thick as hair on a dog," and estimated their strength at "nine or ten thousand." He added, "Our battery kept throwing a few pills to the rebs. They were so far from us our muskets were of no use." Leaving his skirmishers in place to cover the retreat, Colonel Smith directed his Ohio regiment down a ravine on the northern slope of Union Hill. The men splashed across Tuscarora Creek to John Street, turned east, crossed the railroad tracks using Mead's Bridge, and disappeared around the eastern side of Green Hill on what was then called the Shepherdstown Road. They would

---

35 Taylor, "Ramseur's Brigade in the Gettysburg Campaign," 28; *OR* 27, pt. 2, 18, 57; *Charlotte Observer*, Nov. 16, 1892; Leon, *Diary of a Tar Heel*, 31.

36 *Macon* (Ga.) *Telegraph*, July 1, 1863, citing extracts from an unsigned letter to the *Petersburg* (Va.) *Express*; L. M. Blackford to Dear Father, June 28, 1863, Blackford Family Letters, Albert and Shirley Small Special Collections Library, UVA. Blackford was the brother of Maj. Eugene Blackford, who commanded Col. Edward O'Neal's sharpshooter battalion. Another sibling named William served on Jeb Stuart's staff. Sixty-three-year-old David H. Conrad was an attorney in Martinsburg.

cross the Potomac at Boteler's Ford and follow the canal to Maryland Heights near Harpers Ferry.[37]

The shelling also provided all of the incentive that Cpl. Frank Williams needed to make haste to return to Williamsport. "Not wishing to become acquainted with the rebels and to prevent familiarity," Williams mounted his horse and headed away from the sound of the guns. "I shall never forget the touching scene which I witnessed leaving Martinsburg," he wrote. "The women and children were congregated outside of the town." Williams sympathized with them—they could see the Confederate artillery hammering their homes and farms, "with hundreds of these Southern gentlemen rushing in to plunder and destroy." Williams put spurs to his horse and headed off to Williamsport, the sound of the guns growing fainter as he rode.[38]

"The surprise came so suddenly upon us that the surroundings did look fearfully," the 106th's Dr. Skinner related, "as if our last moment had come; yet the whole thing did look so ludicrous that one could hardly help laughing while shaking with fear. Here the pickets were rushing in as fast as their feet could carry them; the infantry hastening to the nearest ravine or ditch, cowering down as close as possibly to mother earth. The artillerymen deserted their guns, or all but one." Skinner went on to admit that he "exercised his pedal extremities just as effectively as the men that surrounded him." Colonel James rode up and down the wavering line shouting in a stentorian voice, "Steady, men! Steady, men!" as shells rained down, one bursting near his horse's hooves without causing any injury. At each explosion, he bowed his head until it nearly touched the mane of his mount. Nearby battery horses became nearly unmanageable under the barrage. One overshot landed in the Green Hill Cemetery, scattering chunks of monuments in every direction.[39]

Meanwhile, General Tyler had been too busy "stimulating" Maulsby's battery and assisting Colonel James in the rallying of the New Yorkers to notice the 126th Ohio's hasty departure. "It had now become apparent that the enemy was in force on our front with at least a brigade of infantry and a superior force of artillery and cavalry, and were threatening our right," reported Tyler, "and that the moment for retreat had

---

37 David Close to My dear Aunt and Uncle, New York City, August 24, 1863, Donald Close collection, 126th Ohio Volunteer Infantry homepage, http://frontierfamilies.net/family/DCletters.htm#mberg, accessed October 12, 2013. David Close was captured at the Wilderness in May 1864 and sent to Andersonville Prison in Georgia where he died in October at the age of 20. OR 27, pt. 2, 456; French, "Battle of Martinsburg," 20-21. The road east of Green Hill no longer exists

38 Williams, "Our Army Correspondence."

39 *Franklin Gazette*, August 17, 1894. See also the Edward Christopher James Papers, Box 14, Beinecke Rare Book and Manuscript Library, Yale University, New Haven, Connecticut.

come." "All were ordered to retreat," Henry Gaddis corroborated, "James in quick time, succeeded in getting all the soldiers to a man together, save those who had already fled, and, immediately moved down the hill by a right flank march." Reporter F. G. Chapman described the chaotic scene: "The One Hundred and Sixth New York was immediately drawn up, and marched steadily down the hill out of range, with colors flying and every man in his place. Although the shot flew in every direction above, beside and around them, not a man was injured who stood in the ranks. One had his knapsack knocked from his back, and many met with hairbreadth escapes. The quartermaster's horse was shot from under him. This is the first time this regiment has been under fire."[40]

To his dismay, Tyler soon learned Colonel Smith had left without notice, taking his Buckeyes with him. Tyler ordered the 106th New York to follow suit, and had Captain Maulsby throw a few shots at the enemy and limber and follow. With Smith out of sight, however, Colonel James was uncertain which direction to go. Tyler told him to head toward the Williamsport (Valley) Pike, assuming Smith had taken that particular route. The regiment had advanced but 200 yards before the aged general directed Colonel James to move his regiment to the Shepherdstown Road, with the cavalry eventually trotting along behind it. With one of his guns upset in a ravine, Lieutenant Herr limbered the other rifle and, with his two caissons, moved off behind James. To Tyler's shock, "by some mistake not yet explained," Maulsby's other two sections descended the ravine, entered Martinsburg, and made their way to the Williamsport Pike and galloped off and disappeared. Tyler and Captain Woodhull went looking for them, but they had gone too far for him to recall them to take the Shepherdstown Road.[41]

Surprisingly, the prolonged skirmishing and cannonade thus far had killed and wounded only a handful of Federals. In the haste of the retreat, one of the 106th New York's loaded ammunition wagons overturned while fording Tuscarora Creek and had to be abandoned, as had two ambulances whose drivers had unhitched the teams to lead them off to safety. Colonel James left behind about 20 sick or lame men who simply could not keep up with the column. James also lost Lt. William A. Merry of Company A, who had been busy calling in the outposts at the time of the withdrawal. Cut off by the advancing Confederates, the unfortunate lieutenant had no choice but to surrender.[42]

---

40 OR 27, pt. 2, 18; Droegemeyer, "The Battle of Martinsburg," 72; *New York Herald*, June 27, 1863.

41 OR 27, pt. 2, 18-19.

42 Ibid, 40.

Dr. Skinner ran back to the grove where he had left his ambulances, only to find the wagons were no longer there. As far as the good doctor was concerned, he was responsible for their disappearance. Dr. Skinner ran down a wooded ravine and crept along it in an effort to reach the regiment, dodging behind several large oak trees as shells exploded around him. One round burst above his head, which he described as "making a report similar to a rotten pumpkin dropped on the frozen ground." Farther down the ravine he spotted band director John Esputa also thus far successfully dodging the flying iron by running around trees. "Doctor, wasn't that an old cuss?" the musician cried. "Come, hurry up, or we shall be captured!" Together, the medical man and musician hastened on and managed to join the Buckeye regiment as it passed muddy Tuscarora Creek. Skinner mounted Lieutenant Herr's remaining gun and rode across the stream. When he looked back on the wooded hillside a half-mile distant, Skinner spotted the abandoned ambulances. He asked Adjutant Henry W. Clark if he could borrow his fleet Kentucky horse to ride down to his vehicle to retrieve his surgical case. "Doctor, you may have the horse, but will it pay?" asked Clark. Skinner made the perilous trek, grabbed his instruments, and eventually returned to the regiment.[43]

With some of Captain Maulsby's guns silenced and darkness fast setting in, General Rodes remained determined to do everything in his power to keep the remaining Federals from making good their escape. Rodes ordered Stephen Ramseur's brigade, the closest infantry command to Martinsburg, to "advance with speed upon the enemy's position," followed in turn by his other brigades. To the surprise of everyone who witnessed it, a very beautiful young lady rode up to Ramseur and offered to show him the routes around the town. She was still trotting beside him when Union artillery began firing at the gray line of men. Moving on the left of Rodes' line, Ramseur's brigade, with Alfred Iverson's men aligned on his right, poured through the Faulkner "Boydville" estate and nearby fields as they rushed toward the town and Union Hill. The Yankees "had their infantry and cavalry drawn up on a high hill in front of the city behind stone fences," according to the 2nd North Carolina's Capt. John Gorman. "With a cheer we attacked the hill, and after a few random shots the enemy broke and fled through town, and those that succeeded in escaping never stopped till they had placed the Potomac between us and them." "There was such confusion & terror & running to & fro by the Yankees & citizens that I never before witnessed," recalled Maj. Charles Blacknell of the 23rd North Carolina, part of Iverson's command. "Before we got half way the black rows of Yankees were plainly seen on the heights beyond the town," observed Tar Heel Captain Harris. "It was their backs however which we saw, for they were getting away as fast as their legs could carry them."[44]

Meanwhile, the 17th Virginia Cavalry, largely dismounted with Jenkins leading the charge on horseback, advanced beyond the turnpike under an intense infantry and artillery fire. Despite some enemy reports to the contrary, they lost few troopers doing so. The Virginians obliqued across the road and chased off the forward Union skirmish line from a series of stone walls on the Faulkner property (Boydville). "Our skirmishers were charged upon by the rebs," Private Gaddis of the 106th New York reported, "and when they drove our boys past the woods where our battery could see them the battery opened up on them and piled them on the road at a fearful rate."[45]

The advancing Virginians raised a howl, held their fire, and continued toward the town. One of the Union rounds knocked General Jenkins' horse out from under him. He "seemed perfectly wild in his fighting humor," recalled Lt. Addison Smith. His men, having charged almost a mile on foot, were exhausted by the time they reached the outskirts of Martinsburg.[46]

As the Union infantry withdrew, Jenkins sent Captain Crawford's 57-man mounted Company F charging "through town like a streak of lightning and on after the flying wretches," according to the 30th North Carolina's Capt. James Harris, whose men were hustling up in support. However, effective work by Martindale's company of the 1st New York Cavalry, as well as Captain Firey's Marylanders and the troopers of the 13th Pennsylvania, slowed Crawford and bought precious time for the retreating Federal infantry. "The rebel cavalry came down the road on full charge, yelling like wildcats," reported *New York Herald* correspondent F. G. Chapman. "Our retiring pickets were driven before them, but they were gallantly met by our cavalry, and, with the aid of a few well directed shells, repulsed with considerable loss."[47]

According to the 17th Virginia Cavalry's Sgt. Isaac H. Brisco, his screaming company charged down a street through a "sheet of flame on both sides." He survived a one-on-one melee with a pistol-carrying Union trooper by using his saber to slash the Yankee's head. "We charged through the town and rode over them scattering them in all directions," wrote Pvt. James H. Hodam. "About a thousand prisoners,

---

44 OR 27, pt. 2, 548; Eugene Blackford Memoirs, USAHEC, 221; John C. Gorman to Friend Holden, June 22, 1863, NCSA and GNMP; Taylor, "Ramseur's Brigade in the Gettysburg Campaign," 28.

45 Droegemeyer, "The Battle of Martinsburg," 68-69.

46 Kesterson, *Campaigning with the 17th Virginia Cavalry*, 27.

47 Taylor, "Ramseur's Brigade in the Gettysburg Campaign," 28; *New York Herald*, June 27, 1863.

nine pieces of artillery and an immense amount of war material fell into our hands here. The artillery was captured by our regiment and in the fight our Chaplain Samuel Shepperd, revolver in hand, rode down and captured a New York colonel and fine roan horse. The 'Rev Sam' was a fighting Parson who never shirked duty on the field, or in the camp, but he loved a fine horse extremely well."[48]

The stubborn Federals withdrew toward the Potomac River with Jenkins' men in hot pursuit. Reporter F. G. Chapman later interviewed some of the Federal soldiers. "It is said by stragglers who remained near the scene that shortly after our forces left the rebels charged our position with their usual amount of yelling, but, much to their chagrin, found that the birds had flown."[49]

Ramseur's men arrived in town shortly after the evacuation of the Union cavalry. Unlike those of rabidly pro-Confederate Berryville, most of Martinsburg residents leaned toward the Union cause. As the first Rebels descended the hill into the town about 8:00 p.m., Susan Nourse Riddle, the daughter of one of Martinsburg's leading merchants, was one of the few who rejoiced at seeing the gray uniforms. "Oh! The joy at seeing it once more," she penned in her diary. "Another & another & soon the town is full. Such a happy comfortable night we have not spent for six long nights. May we not forget to 'Bless the Lord' this happy Sabbath night."[50]

Other Southern sympathizers followed to enthusiastically welcome the arrival of Ewell's soldiers, telling them they had "been long expecting us and they want us to stay with them now for they are tired of the domineering disposition of the yankey troops." Some Rebels who recorded their experiences, however, described their reception as decidedly unfriendly. "This place Martinsburg is one of the hottest Union holes I ever saw," reported a soldier of the 6th Alabama of O'Neal's brigade. "The men of course hold their peace but the women, bless their soles some of them look sour & crop eyed at us. Pout their pretty lips & turn up their little noses at us as we approach them if indeed we presume to be so impertinent as to do so (& who could like it)."[51]

---

48 Hodam, *The Journal of James H. Hodam*, 60. Hodam greatly exaggerated the number of prisoners (most accounts suggest 200) and guns (five). No "New York colonel" was captured, although a second lieutenant named William Merry left behind with the rear guard was taken prisoner.

49 Kesterson, *Campaigning with the 17th Virginia Cavalry*, 27; *New York Herald*, June 27, 1863.

50 Susan Nourse Riddle diary entry for June 14, 1863, in Droegemeyer, "The Battle of Martinsburg," 29.

51 Thomas S. Taylor to his sister, June 16, 1863, Civil War Letters of Thomas S. Taylor, http://www.usgennet.org/usa/al/state1/military/6th/letters/taylor6.htm, accessed September 24, 2013.

A "huge column of smoke now was high in the air," noted the 30th North Carolina's Captain Harris, "& I thought that the rascals had fired the town. It proved to be the long platform at the station on which was piled long rows of corn & hay. Our reception was all that we could have desired. The ladies seemed wild with joy. They showered bouquets on us and running out in the street met us, shaking hands, howd'ye, howd'ye, howd'ye." In a bit of good-natured competition between the North Carolina brigades, added Harris, "It was said that Iverson's brigade had about fifteen minutes the start of ours, but so rapid was our movement that we got into town [a] full fifteen minutes before he did. We stopped in the street a few minutes and then moved rapidly forward again on the road toward Williamsport. We did not go more than a mile however before we were ordered back."[52]

With Ramseur's pursuit halted, General Tyler and his beleaguered Federal infantry made good their escape during the dark night by retreating out the Shepherdstown Road. "We forded a brook about knee deep," recalled the 106th New York's Henry Gaddis. However, much of the artillery was not as fortunate as the foot soldiers. Lieutenant Herr's remaining gun and two caissons fell in behind the 106th and made good their escape. Captain Maulsby, however, had never received contrary orders from Smith or Tyler and, seeing neither, followed his original instructions and headed for Williamsport. One caisson from Lt. James C. Means' section broke down on North Queen Street at the B&O crossing and had to be abandoned. The remaining four guns and three caissons continued rolling north out of town pursued by elements of the 17th Virginia Cavalry and the 34th Battalion, Virginia Cavalry. The Rebels caught up with the fleeing Yankees about one mile north of Martinsburg. "The left wheel of the first carriage came off," Means reported. "Of course, the others had to stop. We could not get past as the road was narrow and filled with soldiers. The men who were trying to replace the wheel were captured, and here my section was captured."[53]

The other section of guns under Lt. George W. Graham surrendered in the roadway to a large group of Rebel cavalry. During these events a bullet struck Captain Maulsby and shattered his right knee joint. The wound disabled him for life. However, the captain, his officers, and most of his men and horses, as well as some nearby infantrymen, managed to escape to Williamsport. The 17th Virginia Cavalry's Lt. Addison Smith discovered the new rifle musket, knapsack, and blankets of a

---

52 OR 27, pt. 2, 39; Taylor, "Ramseur's Brigade in the Gettysburg Campaign," 28. Harris noted, "By 9 o'clock p.m. we were lying on the ground just on the edge of town, that would rival Seven Pines for roughness."

53 Droegemeyer, "The Battle of Martinsburg," 74.

Pennsylvania soldier named Joab Smith and took special delight in finding a picture of Smith's sweetheart and her personal letters to him.[54]

Meanwhile, after quick-timing a couple of miles east on the Shepherdstown Road, the 106th New York caught up with the rear of the slower moving 126th Ohio. Luckily, Lt. Jesse F. Wyckoff of the 1st New York Cavalry knew the countryside. Because of his coolness and knowledge, he "did more than any other man in the column to assure the safety of the command," Tyler later reported. The reunited force reached the Potomac River about 1:00 a.m. The general rode ahead through the darkness with a small escort to examine the ford. A volley rang out from the Maryland riverbank, but the shooters turned out to be Union pickets who mistook Tyler's group for Rebels. Fortunately, no one was hurt.[55]

The men waded across swollen Boteler's (also known as Packhorse) Ford with water up to their armpits from the recent rains. Once across, Dr. Skinner found his missing horse in the hands of his orderly, "who pretended to be watching anxiously for me; but my saddle had flown into Maryland." The Union column followed the Chesapeake & Ohio Canal towpath ten miles down to Harpers Ferry. It was a "sorry and tedious night," recorded the exhausted and frustrated surgeon. "Worse than all, the road leading to Harpers Ferry was very sandy and soft, and the wet and heavy brogans so chafed their feet that most of the men were laid up for several days, unable to walk." Once there, those who were still ambulatory slowly climbed the 1,000-foot Maryland Heights and reported the next morning at 10:00 a.m. The 126th Ohio's Captain McCready, a pious man, rejoiced that their deliverance was nothing short of a "signal mercy from Divine Providence. . . . All reflecting men in the Regiment . . . so regard it." It is unlikely many of the sick and infirm men left behind, or Pat Haverfield and Samuel Ferguson, who had abandoned vast sutler stores, felt the same way. "The forced march to Maryland Heights from Martinsburg was long and fatiguing," was how Colonel Smith later rationalized the effort, "but we congratulate ourselves that we held in check a whole day a vastly superior force of the enemy, leaving him an

---

54 *Court of Inquiry*, 8-10; OR 27, pt. 2, 199-200; Kesterson, *Campaigns of the 17th Virginia Cavalry*, 267. No soldier by the name of Joab Smith is listed, however, in the Pennsylvania Civil War Soldiers Card Files or in Samuel Bates' *History of the Pennsylvania Volunteers*. A Jacob Smith is listed in Company I of the 126th OVI which was at Martinsburg. A piece of special legislation to grant Maulsby a veterans pension indicated that his wound "is in the right leg near the knee, entirely destroying the knee joint, his knee is flexed at an angle of 45 degrees, and he is compelled to use a crutch at all times, and it becomes more difficult and painful for him to move around as his age increases." See Report No. 1480, 59th Congress, 1st Session. *Thomas A. Maulsby Report to Accompany S. 4775* (U. S. Senate Committee on Pensions, Washington, DC: U.S. Government Printing Office, 1906), 1.

55 OR 27, pt. 2, 19, 39.

empty town, as far as supplies were concerned, when he expected to find a depot stores with everything he desired."[56]

Almost immediately, a controversy arose as to the wisdom of the decision to try to defend Martinsburg with so few men, and inexperienced ones at that. *New York Herald* newsman F. G. Chapman interviewed members of the 106th New York on Maryland Heights. "Had not a retreat been previously ordered," he penned, "it is probable that a longer resistance could have been made; but with so few to resist so many, the result could hardly have been else than disastrous. As it is, we have reason to congratulate ourselves upon an escape which now seems a miracle."[57]

"There seems to be some blundering in not reinforcing the place," observed Cpl. Frank B. Williams of the 50th New York Engineers. "The Rebels outnumbered ours considerably. This was seen when they charged upon us and took the town." Still, he continued, "All the rolling stock of the Baltimore & Ohio Railroad was sent away; the Rebels did not get much."[58]

Some of the sick men Dr. Skinner had to leave behind managed to escape into Maryland. Most of the others, including George Gates, Jesse Irish, and William T. Hubbard, were too weak to leave and fell into enemy hands. So did the three medical officers of the 126th Ohio who stayed with their charges. In his diary that night, Private Hubbard overestimated the enemy strength: "Rebs take possession of the place. Force about 40,000 strong . . . self captured as prisoner 6 o'clock PM. Received good treatment from the Rebs." He later amended the enemy force as between 15,000 and 18,000 men. Despite their losses and retreat, morale and martial pride remained high among the Union soldiers who had retreated. This fact prompted Maj. Gen. William H. French, who relieved Tyler on June 26, to write, "The troops under Colonel Smith, from Martinsburg, 1,500 men, were under excellent discipline, and perfectly reliable."[59]

"The enemy destroyed many of the stores at Martinsburg," reported Confederate General Ewell, "but 6,000 bushels of grain and a few quartermaster's and commissary stores fell into our hands. The results of this expedition were 5 pieces of artillery, 200 prisoners, and quartermaster's and subsistence stores in some quantity." Confederate

56 Ibid., 39; *Franklin Gazette*, August 17, 1894; Hall, *Appalachian Ohio and the Civil War*, 228, 231. McCready was killed at the Wilderness in May 1864.

57 *New York Herald*, June 27, 1863.

58 Williams, "Our Army Correspondence."

59 William T. Hubbard Diary, entry for June 14, 1863, Franklin County Historical and Museum Society, Malone, New York; *OR* 27, pt. 1, 488. Hubbard had enrolled as a wagoner and now was a private in Company C.

losses totaled seven men killed and an unstated number of wounded. Robert Rodes confirmed the seizure of 40 rounds of rifled artillery ammunition and a rather minor amount of small arms and ammunition, and was more than pleased to capture the two "excellent" ambulances. He placed one of George Doles' Georgia regiments in town as a provost guard and set the appropriate officers to work gathering prisoners, "who were concealed in the houses of many of the Union families of the town." He also placed armed guards around the Federal military hospitals, including a brick Lutheran church. Meanwhile, Jenkins' cavalry began destroying the railroad tracks on either side of town, and several of his poorly armed men appropriated Union muskets and pistols.[60]

Despite the windfall of bounty, complained Alabama artillerist John Purifoy, "This was another of the numerous cases when the attack was made too late in the day to reap all the advantages that were available, as the infantry escaped because of the darkness. Before leaving Martinsburg," he continued, "the four captured rifle guns, with horses and equipment complete, were turned over to Reese's company, the Jeff Davis Artillery. The old guns of the company, two Rome, Ga., rifles, one bronze Napoleon, and a twelve-pounder howitzer, and the greatly worn equipment, which had been in constant use for about two years, were turned in to the Confederate Ordnance Department."[61]

Deep into the night, detachments from Rodes' division continued mopping up the battlefield and town. "I was engaged until 2 o'clock in collecting the guns and horses," wrote an artillery officer, a task he found extremely fatiguing. "Martinsburg," he added, "is strong for the old Union, and several Yankees were found concealed in the houses, even after the owners had sworn that none were there. All that part of Virginia, I fear, with but very few exceptions, is unsound to the core."[62]

As a soldier from the 126th Ohio quickly discovered, the life of a prisoner was anything but pleasant. "In guard hous to day Rebils wont let no one speak to us wont let us poot hed out of windows," wrote the unidentified Buckeye in his diary. "They fired on us for looking out Started with us to day at 4 oclock for Winchester We arrived there at 12 oclock at night all most ded got nothing to eate." The ordeal of the prisoners had only just begun.[63]

---

60 Ibid., pt. 2, 442 and 549; *The Union Army*, 6:587. Harris noted that Jenkins' cavalry returned with spoils, including five cannon and "some of the finest artillery horses I ever saw."

61 Purifoy, "With Jackson in the Valley," 384.

62 *Macon* (Ga.) *Telegraph*, July 1, 1863, citing the *Petersburg* (Va.) *Express*.

63 Anonymous, diary entry for June 16, 1863, Winchester, Virginia, "Diary of a Civil War Soldier in Company F, 126th Ohio Volunteer Infantry."

Milroy Plans to Evacuate Winchester

Ewell's Confederates had forced the Federals out of Berryville, Bunker Hill, and now Martinsburg, but the beleaguered General Milroy stubbornly clung to his remaining forts at Winchester. Three sergeants from the 1st New York Cavalry rode in from Martinsburg after slipping past the Rebels ringing much of the important Valley town. They carried with them a message from General Schenck who directed Milroy to fall back to Harpers Ferry. At 9:00 p.m., Milroy convened a council of war with his three brigade commanders. His inspector general and chief of staff, Maj. J. Lowry McGee, later claimed the general took him aside before the meeting and in an impressive manner told him, "I have been persuaded to call a council of war. It may decide to surrender, but I will never surrender to any d——d Rebels. If the council decides to surrender, I want you to get your three companies of West Virginians together, and at their head we will go to Harpers Ferry or to hell."[64]

Milroy's troops had only one day's rations left, and his artillery ammunition was nearly spent. Recent information suggested the enemy on the following morning could bring as many as 100 guns to bear upon his embattled and much smaller command. "Our position at Winchester," Milroy later explained, "although affording facilities for defense which would enable an inferior to maintain itself against a superior number for a limited time, could not be successfully defended by the limited means at my command against such an army as surrounded me." Milroy expressed his concern that retreat was impossible and they might be forced to surrender in the morning. His subordinates listened intently, but at least initially, remained silent. "My opinion was not called for," recalled Col. J. Warren Keifer, "but I volunteered to say that I could start that night, avoiding roads and the enemy, and escape with my command by mountain roads over Apple Pie Ridge and safely reach Maryland." In Keifer's opinion, his confident comments "led General Milroy to order a retreat northward on the Martinsburg Pike with a hope that the Confederate line of investment could be there broken so as to let the infantry and cavalry through. The artillery, trains, camp equipage and supplies were to be abandoned."[65]

According to Milroy, "The propositions concluded upon in that council were, that in consequence of the entire exhaustion of our artillery ammunition, it was impossible to hold the post against the overwhelming forces of the enemy, and that a further prolongation of the defense could only result in sacrificing the lives of our

---

64 Theodore F. Lang, *Loyal West Virginia from 1861 to 1865* (Baltimore: Deutsch Publishing Co., 1895), 199.

65 Beach, *First New York (Lincoln) Cavalry*, 242; *OR* 27, pt. 2, 47; Keifer, "The Story of a Flag," 419.

soldiers without any practical benefit to the country." Milroy continued: "We owed it to the honor of the Federal arms to make an effort to force our way through the lines of the beleaguering foe; that the artillery and wagons should be abandoned, and the division, brigade, and regimental quartermasters instructed to bring away all public horses, and that the brigades, in the order of their numbers, should march from the forts at 1 o'clock in the morning, carrying with them their arms and the usual supply of ammunition." Colonel Keifer later recorded, "My request to be allowed to escape with my command led General Milroy to assign me to lead and command the advance of his army on its retreat towards Martinsburg."[66]

Keifer had quartered in the comfortable Sherrard house for months. Once he learned of the plan to evacuate the forts, he rode into Winchester to visit the Rielys, with whom he had become friends. The family had taken in one of the three Sherrard sisters, Lizzie, who had contracted typhoid fever. Inside the Kent Street house, Emma Riely was sitting up with Lizzie when the colonel arrived. "The town was as still as death," Emma later recalled. "We could hear horses' hoofs on the cobble stones a long way off, but when they stopped in front of the house our hearts went pit-a-pat, not knowing whether friend or foe." When Keifer knocked on the door, Emma, her aunt, and her sisters discussed who could be calling at such an unearthly hour. Keifer identified himself, mentioning that he and a friend wanted to speak with them as they might not get another chance. The Riely women hastily dressed and went downstairs, where the colonel told them the Rebels would be there in the morning. He presented two bottles of fine brandy, one for Lizzie and the other to be given with his compliments to Major Goldsborough and Captain Emack of the Maryland Line. Back on May 30 at Middletown, Keifer had negotiated a flag of truce with the Confederate officers and they had spent several pleasant hours together. "He said he would feel very anxious to hear about Miss Lizzie and hoped she would soon recover," Emma recounted, "and bade us good-bye."[67]

"It was a moonless, intensely dark night that came down upon Winchester," recalled the 1st New York Cavalry's Lt. William Beach. "Those not on guard or picket took what rest they could. The artillery and infantry were in the fort. The cavalry were on the slopes of the hills. If any slept it was by their horses, keeping hold of the reins. No one felt like predicting what the next day would bring forth. All knew that they were surrounded by superior numbers," the lieutenant continued, "but hoped that there might be found some opening by which they could break through the lines

---

66 Prowell, *History of the 87th Pennsylvania*, 72; OR 27, pt. 2, 47; Keifer, "The Story of a Flag," 419.

67 Macon, *Reminiscences of the Civil War*, 81; Pope, *The Weary Boys*, 37.

drawn around them." Grim reminders of their possible fate abounded as the plaintive cries of the wounded broke the stillness.[68]

Meanwhile, the 122nd Ohio's Sgt. David Danhauer sat on an empty ammunition box "contemplating in all of its disagreeable forms our surrender in the morning." He overheard General Elliott summon the commanding officers of his regiments to appear before him. Elliott informed them of the decision to cut their way through to Harpers Ferry. The news relieved Danhauer, although he knew it would be a hazardous undertaking. He believed it could have been done much easier 24 hours earlier, and saved the artillery and trains to boot. He was not certain whether they could now be saved.[69]

General Ewell suspected that Milroy might try to abandon his forts. Accordingly, late that evening he dispatched cavalryman Maj. Harry Gilmor to order Maj. William Goldsborough and his three companies of 2nd Maryland skirmishers to "press on into Winchester at the break of day, and if possible ascertain at intervals during the night what the enemy was doing." Scouts returned with news the Yankees were indeed evacuating the forts, and the report went up the command chain to Ewell.[70]

Ewell reacted quickly to the news by ordering Ed Johnson's division to cut off Milroy. General Johnson reported that he was to move by the right flank with three brigades and a portion of his artillery to a point on the Martinsburg Pike two-and-a-half miles north of Winchester. The plan had the double purpose, he supposed, of intercepting the Union retreat and attacking them in their fortifications from the North. He sent word to George Steuart's and Jesse Nicholls' brigades and to artillery battalion commander Lt. Col. Snowden Andrews to ready their men to march to the Berryville Road. He also sent word to General James Walker, whose line was nearest the enemy, to follow after advancing his skirmishers to the town to conceal the movement and ascertain the position of the enemy. Ewell planned to leave John M. Jones' brigade and the remainder of Andrews' battalion under Maj. Joseph W. Latimer in reserve to prevent any escape attempt on the Berryville Road. With his plan in hand Johnson set off, hopeful he might bag Milroy's entire force.[71]

68 Beach, *The First New York (Lincoln) Cavalry*, 242.

69 *Zanesville* (OH) *Courier*, July 22, 1863.

70 Goldsborough, *The Maryland Line*, 95-96.

71 *OR* 27, pt. 2, 500-501.

Chapter 9

Monday, June 15, morning

"Then it seemed as though the earth swallowed up a great portion of our host."

— *Cpl. John C. Keses, 87th Pennsylvania*[1]

Williamsport, Maryland, and Chambersburg, Pennsylvania

"Fatigued,

but hopeful, and encouraged by the results of our glorious battle of yesterday, at Martinsburg, Virginia," the 14th Virginia Cavalry's Lt. Hermann Schuricht wrote, "we were called by the sound of the bugle to mount horses." It was 2:00 a.m. on June 15, a pitch dark moonless night about three hours before sunrise.

After a brief side trip to reconnoiter Dam No. 5, Albert Jenkins' cavalry brigade splashed across Light's Ford on the Potomac River opposite Williamsport, Maryland. Scouts slipped into the sleeping village about 3:00 a.m. and severed telegraph wires; the bulk of the brigade arrived by nine that morning. The German-born Lieutenant Schuricht rejoiced when the inhabitants extended a kind welcome. Tables with plenty of milk, bread, and meat were set up in the street, and the Virginians enjoyed a delicious, if hasty, breakfast.[2] "The river was low and we had no difficulty in crossing,"

---

1 John C. Keses manuscript, MSS 31121, YCHT.

2 U. S. Naval Observatory; "Jenkins' Brigade in the Gettysburg Campaign: Extracts from the Diary of Lieutenant Hermann Schuricht, of the Fourteenth Virginia Cavalry," *Richmond Dispatch*, April 5, 1896. Dam No. 5 was about seven miles upriver (west) from Williamsport. Stonewall Jackson had tried unsuccessfully to destroy it in December 1861 to hamper the transport of Allegheny Mountain coal on the C&O Canal to Washington. Schuricht translated his diary from German to English and submitted portions to the newspaper "to give some additional evidence assisting to establish the historical truth."

recalled the 17th's Lt. Addison Smith. "On the bank of the river was the small town called Williamsport. We were soon in it. Found the citizens well disposed toward us, and they set long tables along the road well loaded with good eatables, that the hungry soldiers might help themselves, which thing nearly all did, taking a piece as they passed along." Another Virginian, however, suggested the locals exhibited only a "smothered expression of sympathy" for the passing troopers.[3]

"We were very anxious to cross the Potomac as we regarded Maryland as part of the enemies country," recorded Pvt. James H. Hodam of the 17th Virginia Cavalry, "but in this we were somewhat mistaken, as we soon found many very loyal people to the South in many sections of the state." Hodam and the rest of the regiment splashed across the Potomac. "The first object I saw on the other side was a large siege gun stuck in a sandbar where the Federals had left it."[4]

Once his men had eaten and rested, General Jenkins pushed forward into Maryland. Ahead of their vanguard, Union Col. Andrew McReynolds' fleeing baggage train careened toward Pennsylvania with Capt. William H. Boyd and his Company C of the 1st New York Cavalry screening its rear. A reporter later described the train as "an immense one, counting of upwards of five hundred wagons (four horses to a wagon) and is about three miles in length. . . . Both horses and drivers bear evidence of the hardships endured on the retreat. Very many of the wagons were driven by contrabands," he continued, "who rode the wheel-horse, while their families all sit perched upon the top of the load. Here, on one wagon, were old white-haired crones, and on another would be little negro children, who had fallen asleep from sheer exhaustion, while the sun beat full on their upturned faces. Over all was thrown a yellow mantle of dust. Eyelashes, eyebrows, flesh, and wool were powdered so thickly as to give the caravan a most motley and grotesque appearance."[5]

Throngs of pro-Union refugees from the Shenandoah Valley and Maryland also raced northward in an effort to avoid meeting Jenkins' Rebels. Hundreds of Keystoners joined the exodus. "On this day we witnessed the greatest excitement which had occurred up to that time during all the history of the war," observed

---

3 Addison A. Smith, *"A Story of the Life and Trials of a Confederate Soldier and the Great Loop He Made in Three Years,"* manuscript in Jackson County Public Library, Ripley, West Virginia; "W. K. to Messrs. Editors, June 19, 1863," *Richmond Enquirer*, June 30, 1863.

4 Hodam, *Journal of James H. Hodam*, 61.

5 Stevenson, "The First Cavalry," 639; "General Milroy's Wagon Train," *Adams Sentinel (Gettysburg, Pa.)*, June 23, 1863. The wagon train would eventually reach safety in Philadelphia's Fairmount Park. Boyd's men turned back at Harrisburg and contested Jenkins' advance, losing Cpl. William H. Rihl in a sharp skirmish on June 22 near Greencastle, Pennsylvania. Rihl was the first Union soldier killed on Pennsylvania soil.

Chambersburg merchant Jacob Hoke. "Early that morning, farmers from the southern portions of Franklin County fled before the Confederate invaders and headed down the road to Harrisburg, carrying with them their stock and valuables. The road was crowded with wagons, horses and cattle. Following this initial group of refugees came large numbers of colored persons, men, women, and children, bearing with them huge bundles of clothing, bedding, and articles of house-keeping."[6]

Fear increased when more than 40 fleeing military supply wagons galloped through Chambersburg at 10:00 a.m., their drivers confirming civilian reports of Confederates approaching Pennsylvania. Never before had the townspeople witnessed "such wild excitement and consternation." A few of McReynolds' careening wagons lost their wheels and crashed. Exhausted horses fell dead in the streets. Angry teamsters swore at balky animals at the top of their lungs while lashing them with whips. As the "grand stampede" continued, every man and horse was "animated with the singular desire of salvation from Rebel clutches." Order returned only when the provost lieutenant, Charles W. Palmer, brandished a cocked revolver and forced the teamsters to halt. The "extraordinary spectacle" frightened the already nervous residents.[7]

"This morning pretty early Gen. Milroy's wagon train (so we were told) came," wrote Canadian-born Rachel Cormany, a Chambersburg resident and the wife of a Union cavalry sergeant serving in the Army of the Potomac. "Contrabands on ahead coming as fast as they could on all & any kind of horses, their eyes fairly protruding with fear—teams coming at the same rate—come with the covers half off—some lost—men without hats or coats—some lost their coats as they were flying, one darky woman astride of a horse going what she could. There really was a real panic," she added. "All reported that the rebels were just on their heels." Jenkins' oncoming brigade was the first of Robert E. Lee's commands to enter Pennsylvania. His outriders reached Chambersburg just after nightfall.[8]

Milroy Evacuates Winchester

Meanwhile, in Winchester (about 65 miles south of Jenkins' advancing troopers), General Milroy contemplated how to save the command he had kept in place far too long against the advice of his superiors. He hoped to slip his division away in the same

---

6   Jacob Hoke, *The Great Invasion* (Dayton, OH: W. J. Shuey, 1887), 97-98.

7   *Chambersburg Valley Spirit,* July 8, 1863; *Chambersburg Repository,* June 16, 1863.

8   James C. Mohr, ed., *The Cormany Diaries: A Northern Family in the Civil War* (Pittsburgh: University of Pittsburgh Press, 1982), 328-29.

inky darkness that had enveloped Jenkins' brigade at Williamsport. Milroy ordered his men to destroy as much equipment as possible and then steal away north toward Martinsburg via the Valley Pike. Staff officer Capt. Zebulon Baird carried the message to each regiment stationed around the Main Fort. There, he found many of the soldiers asleep in their tents or in the rifle pits. Company officers quietly roused their men and instructed them to conduct the evacuation as silently and as quickly as possible, for Rebel sentinels were posted no more than 200 yards away. Milroy called in his pickets, but had to abandon some who could not make their way safely back to the lines.[9]

"We slept in the trenches until 12 o'clock, when we were aroused," a private in the 123rd Ohio later informed his father in a letter home. "Co. B was called [to] one side and told by Major [Horace] Kellogg that we were to skedaddle, and that Co. B was to go to the wagon yard, mount the horses, and make the best of our way through. We all succeeded in getting horses, except about ten or fifteen men."[10]

Inside the Star Fort, Colonel McReynolds delivered the same orders to Capt. F. W. Alexander, who immediately voiced his displeasure. As chief of artillery, he asked to visit Milroy to seek permission to take his battery out with him. McReynolds consented and Alexander rode south to the Main Fort. He was unable to locate Milroy, but caught up with his adjutant general, Maj. John A. Cravens. Speaking for Milroy, Cravens insisted the order was peremptory and was to be strictly obeyed. Nothing on wheels or anything that could make noise would be permitted with the men. The goal, repeated the major, was perfect silence and secrecy. Besides, he added, all of the other guns had already been spiked. The disappointed Alexander remounted his horse for the return trip to the Star Fort to carry out the instructions.[11]

The Wheeling Battery's Capt. John Carlin also questioned the decision to abandon his guns. According to his estimates, his men had fired 265 rounds of ammunition per gun during the previous two days of fighting. He still had 35 rounds left for each one, or more than enough to cover the retreat. At 2:00 a.m. he received Milroy's orders via General Elliott to spike his pieces, destroy the remaining ammunition, cut up the harnesses, and carry away only the saddles and bridles. Carlin reluctantly complied with the order, but later complained he could have taken his guns and equipment out and rendered good service doing so. Crews hastily sawed the carriages into pieces and spiked the guns in the positions where they had fired their last

9   Prowell, *History of the 87th Pennsylvania*, 74.

10 *Norwalk (Ohio) Reflector*, June 30, 1863.

11 *OR* 27, pt. 2, 47, 87.

shots. Nearby infantrymen stuffed 40 rounds into their cartridge boxes and additional rounds into their pockets, fixed bayonets, and prepared to march.[12]

Captain Carlin mounted as many cannoneers as he could on spare horses with the drivers riding their team animals. "Everything was in confusion," admitted 17-year-old Pvt. George McClelland. Lieutenant Chalfant's section had lost two caisson horses, so McClelland worried he would have to walk. Luckily, Martin Beamer allowed the youth to ride behind him. The retreat, for the most part, was conducted in an orderly fashion. "Not a man faltered," proudly remembered an officer of the Wheeling battery. "We stood to our guns and held our position as long as our ammunition lasted, then put for the big fort, having first spiked our guns and cut up the harnesses." The West Virginians were leaving the fort at the same time Captain Martins' Massachusetts Heavy Artillery company was marching down the same hillside. The unarmed McClelland noticed the Bay Staters' composed appearance and their muskets. "It was the only time that I ever wanted a musket," added the officer, "or envied a man whom I saw carrying one."[13]

In the rifle-pits in front of the Main Fort, Lt. Henry Rush and his comrades in the 110th Ohio heard the muffled sounds of wheels moving behind them, the low murmuring of men, the quiet treading of their brogans, and the occasional neighing of a horse—but weren't sure of the meaning. Someone passed along the line and in a low voice commanded, "Attention. Immediately in line, without knapsacks or blanket— nothing but arm and ammunition . . . March." They filed out of the entrenchments and followed Col. J. Warren Keifer down the long slope to a ravine that led to the Martinsburg Pike. According to Lt. Charles Gross, the Buckeyes "folded their tents like the Arabs and as quietly stole away."[14]

At 2:00 a.m., "whispered orders were passed down the line" for the 123rd Ohio to fall in. "Every man was given eighty rounds of cartridges and we stole silently out in the darkness," Pvt. Edmund P. Snyder recounted. Company B was detailed to ride away on horses, while Company D, the provost guard, would bring up the rear to deter any stragglers. Shortly after 2:00 a.m. most of Elliott's weary command was underway after dumping excess ammunition into the cisterns. Soldiers used rifles butts to break open boxes of hardtack so the passing soldiers cold jam their haversacks full of the tasteless crackers. The 12th Pennsylvania Cavalry led the way, followed by the 110th,

---

12 *History and Roster of Maryland Volunteers, War of 1861-6*, 1:817; Dalzell, "A Lucky Blunder," 100; D. M. Bliss, "With Milroy at Winchester. A Vivid Pen Picture of Stirring Days Long Ago," in *National Tribune*, June 10, 1915.

13 "War Sketches, Being Anecdotes and Experiences of West Virginia Warriors," *Wheeling Sunday Register*, May 3, 1891; "Letter from an Officer in the Wheeling Battery."

14 Rush, *Life and Writings*, 240; Gross, "Sketch of Army and Prison Life."

123rd, and 122nd Ohio, with Colonel Keifer in temporary command of all three Buckeye regiments. They tramped more than a mile through a sheltering ravine to a dirt path leading to the Martinsburg Pike, aiming to avoid detection by prying townspeople who might sound the alarm.[15]

Tension grew within the ranks of Elliott's evacuees as it did with the thousands of troops waiting their turn to leave Winchester. No one was certain the escape would be successful, or if at any point hordes of howling Confederates would suddenly appear out of the darkness and attack them. Those still in the forts and entrenchments listened, mostly expecting that enemy gunfire would greet the long procession as it snaked its way northward to the turnpike. Concerns grew by the minute in the still night that Rebel pickets would pick up the sound of the moving column and launch an attack on the vulnerable formation. With no artillery protection and with the regiments strung out along the road, it would be nearly impossible to organize an effective defense.

In a hospital north of Winchester, Sgt. Edward Muhliman of the 116th Ohio made up his mind to leave with the retreating troops. He felt well enough to at least make the attempt, despite have been prostrated with illness for several days. Young Muhliman, who left his studies at Baldwin College to enlist the previous autumn, was not alone. As word of the evacuation spread, scores of other patients decided to try their luck with the column rather than risk certain capture by remaining behind. Among them was the 18th Connecticut's Lt. Col. Monroe Nichols, who left his sickbed to take command of his regiment.[16]

Colonel William Ely's brigade, second in line, also began preparing to leave. "We were roused up [in the] night to make preparations to leave," the 87th Pennsylvania's Cpl. Jacob M. Herr noted in his diary. "Our ammunition having run out as I feared; we spiked all the guns and marched out of the fort at two Oclock. We had to leave everything behind but what we had on our backs. The rebs get a great many things but what they need most they won't get. We leave about two days rations and all our wagons all our camp equipeige and knapsacks. But our horses and ourselves mostly all got out, and our cannon will not do them any good."[17]

---

15 Snyder, *Autobiography of a Soldier of the Civil War*, 8; E. H. Forster [Forester], "From the 123rd," *Tiffin (Ohio) Weekly Tribune*, June 26, 1863. The latter account claims the 123rd Ohio was the advance regiment of infantry, but other primary accounts suggest it was the 110th Ohio that led the way immediately behind the cavalry; OR 27, pt. 2, 47, 58; Hewitt, *History of the 12th West Virginia*, 44.

16 Civil War Archive of Edward Muhliman, 116th Ohio, Co. E, privately owned; Walker, *History of the Eighteenth Connecticut*, 113.

17 Herr diary entry for June 15, 1863.

"Every man who wished mounted a horse, but outside of horses we left everything we could not destroy," recalled the 87th's Cpl. John C. Keses. "Our double column of infantry, cavalry, and men mounted on battery and train horses and some few loyal citizens seeking a place of safety within our lines—I remember seeing a few young fellows with their sweethearts—and our band was moving along regularly." The 116th Ohio lost its way in the darkness and confusion, and eventually fell in behind Ely's column.[18]

It was not until after 3:00 a.m. that McReynolds' brigade, the last of the three brigades to leave, slipped out of the Star Fort along with Captain Alexander's mounted cannoneers trailing the 13th Pennsylvania Cavalry. The soldiers assigned to defend the Star Fort had endured a rough night. "Expecting them to charge on us and our regiment was put inside the fort. The 67th Pa. staid in the rifle pits below as our Batterys had run out of ammunition," recounted Pvt. George Washington Hamilton of the 6th Maryland. "We found there was no chance to hold out any longer so they made ready to start from there if possible. The guns were spiked and the artillery rode the horses. We started about three o'clock on the morning of the 15th on the pike toward Martinsburg." The prospect of a one-sided firefight weighed heavily on their minds. According to George's brother, Cpl. Hiram N. Hamilton, the 6th was very low on ammunition, with only about five rounds left per man.[19]

To McReynolds' rear, the 1st New York Cavalry descended the hill into the ravine. "It was a weird procession passing in silence, without a spoken word, through the midnight darkness," explained Lt. William Beach. The "silence" Beach described was comprised of the shuffle of thousands of feet, the clanking of bayonets against tin canteens, the muted curses from the throats of stumbling men, and the occasional braying of balky mules. Flankers lined both sides of the miles-long column to watch for Rebels. "It was a very delicate undertaking to steal away with about six or seven thousand men, including three regiments of cavalry, and the artillery and team horses with their jingling harness, without being discovered," observed cavalryman James Stevenson. "Orders were given in a whisper, and the hearts of the officers and men beat rapidly with varying emotions." Huge crowds of pro-Union civilians, black residents of Winchester looking for protection, and the relatives and immediate family

---

18 John C. Keses Papers, CWTI Collection, USAHEC.

19 Hamilton diary, entry for June 15, 1863; Hiram Hamilton to his niece Anna, June 25, 1863, Maryland Heights, Maryland, private collection. The Hamilton brothers, from Cecil County, unfortunately each died five days apart in mid-August 1863 of disease contracted while in the service.

members of the soldiers and other non- combatants joined in the "weird procession."[20]

The column soon met the abandoned supply train parked in the middle of the turnpike and filed around it on either side. Wheeling cannoneers McClelland and Beamer broke from the mob and rummaged through the wagons looking for their knapsacks, but "we might as well have tried to find a needle in a haystack," McClelland complained. He found a sword and kept it for his protection as they resumed their journey. Ahead of them in the column, the 87th Pennsylvania's Pvt. George H. Dittenhaffer suffered a painful groin injury when his horse jumped a fence and threw him against the saddle pommel. Somehow he managed to stay with the column. His wife Elizabeth, a laundress, had borrowed a swift horse and rode along with the escaping teamsters.[21]

The road was so crowded and the jam of horses and mules so great that Baltimore Battery's Fred Wild was compelled to take his feet out of the stirrups periodically and kneel or squat on the saddle for fear his legs might be broken in the crush of beasts and wagons. He and a lifelong friend became separated from the battery, but resolved to stay together no matter what tribulations they faced. Horses threw shoes on the hard macadam surface or came up lame. Wounded and sick men or those with worn or ill-fitting brogans began to fall out of the march route. Others, exhausted from a lack of sleep and poor or inadequate food, dropped down by the roadside to rest. Knapsacks, unwanted accouterments, and personal items of every description littered the pike. The latter sections of the column began to look more like a disorganized mob than a military procession.[22]

Milroy's escape did not pass unnoticed. A work detail from the 31st Georgia had been digging redoubts all night on the northern crest of Bower's Hill. Tired from their exertion with picks and shovels, Pvt. Gordon Bradwell and his comrades threw themselves on the clover to snatch a few moments of sleep. A low rumbling noise startled them awake. The sound, which they likened to the sudden movement of many trains, came from the north side of the distant fort. Someone suggested the enemy had rushed out and was escaping. "This proved true in part," Bradwell wrote, "for they

20 Beach, *The First New York (Lincoln) Cavalry*, 241; *Baltimore Sun*, April 19, 1904; Stevenson, *Boots and Saddles*, 191-92.

21 *Wheeling Sunday Register*, May 3, 1891; Brandt database, YCHT; Prowell, *History of the 87th Pennsylvania*, 89.

22 Ibid., Wild, *Capt. F. W. Alexander's Baltimore Battery*, 64.

had massed all their forces on that side and rushed down the hill upon our drowsy soldiers so unexpectedly that they made no resistance."[23]

Most of the other Confederates and the residents around Winchester did not realize Milroy was evacuating. Brigadier General John B. Gordon, plagued throughout the long night with premonitions he would die that morning attacking the Main Fort, slept little. As he planned the assault deep into the night, he could not stop thinking about the dreadful slaughter that surely awaited his men. The night was mostly behind him when he sat down by his bivouac fire with pencil and paper in hand. He composed what he thought would be his last letter to his wife, Fanny. When he finished, Gordon summoned his quartermaster and handed him the letter with instructions to deliver it to her if he died. With that sad chore completed, he mounted his horse and, in the darkness briefly addressed his assembled troops, encouraging them to go with him into the fort. Long before dawn his brigade advanced and quietly ascended the long slope climbing toward the waiting rifle pits and fort. He expected a storm of shell and ball to erupt into their faces, but only silence met them as they swept into the empty fort.[24]

"About half past one Monday morning," wrote one of Gordon's relieved Georgians known only as Will to an Augusta newspaper, "we were roused up to march. The Yankees were leaving and we had to follow them. Captain Milledge was the first man in the fort, and had the honor of hauling down the stars and stripes." However, the 9th Louisiana's Lt. Richard J. Hancock argued that one of his forward skirmishers, Billy Singleton, outraced a Georgian into the vacated fort and hauled down its immense flag. "All covered up" with the colors, Singleton triumphantly returned to the skirmish line 200 yards away. With the Yankees gone, the Confederates started collecting the spoils. "Mrs. Milroy and the Misses Milroy, who had been in the fort, lost all their wardrobe," gloated Will, "and the way the soldiers were pulling on the silk dresses was quite laughable."[25]

The 31st Georgia's Pvt. Gordon Bradwell told a much different story. His work party received orders to cease efforts on the redoubt and return to their commands. According to Bradwell, he entered the silent fort and General Gordon galloped in on a large black U. S. army horse that his men began calling "Old Milroy," supposing it to belong to the enemy general. Gordon supposedly rode up to the flag pole in the center of the fort, dismounted, and personally hauled down the colors. He placed one end of them on his saddle. Remounting, Gordon spurred his horse and sailed out of the sally

23 Bradwell, "Capture of Winchester," 331.

24 Gordon, *Reminiscences*, 68-69.

25 *Augusta (Ga.) Chronicle and Sentinel*, June 28, 1863.

port ahead of his men while the 'Star Spangled Banner' floated more than thirty feet behind him. Colonel Clement A. Evans, commander of the 31st Georgia, noticed that the Stars and Stripes no longer fluttered over the ramparts of the fort. He promptly ordered his regiment to fall in to prepare to march to pursue the Yankees because he realized that the hauling down of the flag meant Milroy's troops had fled.[26]

Meanwhile on Flint Ridge, Company D of the 13th Virginia Infantry lounged nearby as Gens. Jubal Early, Harry Hays, and "Extra Billy" Smith conferred: "While I was resting on the grass at the [West] fort three generals rode up," wrote Pvt. J. W. Baker, who continued:

> I always liked to hear what they had to say. They were the boys that got you in trouble. One said, 'we shall have to leave a regiment here to guard the captured stores.' Another said, 'We will leave the 49th.' The ranking general said, 'We will leave the 13th Virginia; half her men are behind wounded, and she has done far more than her part of the fighting.' A few more minutes after, these called for 20 volunteers to go down to the fort on the pike near the town. I was the first man that reached them. But this is no time for chroma[ne] nor blue ribbons. I volunteered because it was the safest thing in sight. No danger of walking over the blue grass for a mile in the dark, but how would you like to walk the same field in day light swept by grape and canister? Always go when it is the best thing. Some times you have to volunteer when it is the very worst thing. We went down to the fort. Listened, could hear nothing. Climbed in, found all kinds of supplies, with one bottle of whiskey. The enemy had left everything that could rattle and sneaked off in the dark. Just below the fort 400 wagons were parked. I climbed onto these and every citizen that came along I gave him a suit of clothes, a ham or meat, sugar and coffee, anything and as much as he would take. These Shenandoah Valley people never got tired of being good to us, and I was doing my best to pay them back.[27]

South of Winchester, meanwhile, Lt. Col. James Herbert and Maj. William W. Goldsborough got the men of the 2nd Maryland Battalion up early and prepared them to assault the Main Fort. As they marched under the cover of woods and ravines to get into position for the planned assault, they received the gratifying news that "although the cage was ours, the birds had flown."[28]

---

26 Bradwell, "Capture of Winchester," 331; Stephens, *Intrepid Warrior*, 190. Gordon in his reminiscences did not mention personally hauling down the flag, which may be hearsay on the part of Private Bradwell. It is likely a Georgia soldier recovered the prize, which was eventually sent up through the command chain and presented to General Ewell.

27 J. W. Baker, "War Reminiscences," in *Clinch Valley* (Va.) *News*, April 22, 1921.

28 McCullough diary entry for June 15, 1863.

Maj. Gen. Edward "Allegheny" Johnson, the commander of one of Ewell's divisions.
Library of Congress

Several members of "Extra Billy" Smith's brigade also rejoiced in the unexpected turn of events. "Day broke this morning to show us the fort vacated by the enemy," wrote a happy Capt. Henry W. Wingfield of the 58th Virginia. "This was a relief to us, as we were ordered to charge it at day." Part of the concern coursing through the Virginian's ranks was a lack of faith in their aged leader who, while personally brave, had not demonstrated brigade-level command abilities since his appointment earlier in the year. "Extra Billy received a large majority of the votes cast," Wingfield confirmed in his diary on May 28 in a reference to his commander's current gubernatorial aspirations. "I am disposed to think that his heavy army vote was the result of his unpopularity as Brigadier and were cast with the hope of freeing themselves from him in the army." Luckily for Smith's men, they did not have to find out how the controversial political general with no military training—the oldest general in the Army of Northern Virginia—would fare in an attack against a fort full of Yankee guns.[29]

Another interested distant onlooker was Ordnance Sgt. Watkins Kearns of the 27th Virginia. "Cannonading again at Winchester & musketry," he hastily penned in his diary. "Does not last long however. The Yankees have left & our flag now waves over the fort." "I had the pleasure of seeing the Stars and Stripes hauled down," proudly reported another Confederate soldier, "& the Confederate banner waving from the flagpole."[30]

As noted earlier, General Johnson left John M. Jones' brigade and Latimer's artillery battery to cut off any escape routes and to deal with any residual Yankees at Winchester. These forces deployed astride the Berryville Road. Youthful Lt. John M.

29 W. W. Scott, ed., "Two Confederate Items," in *Bulletin of the Virginia State Library* (Richmond: David Bottom, Superintendent of Public Printing, 1927), 26-27.

30 Kearns diary entry for June 15, 1863; J. Peter Williams to his wife, June 16, 1863.

Steptoe, an 1857 VMI graduate, had also spent a nervous night worrying about the "most formidable works that this army has ever encountered." Jones ordered the charge, but luckily for Steptoe and his comrades, "as fortune would have it, when light came the hill was discovered to be deserted and the enemy gone." Confederate troops began rounding up the many Union pickets left behind when Milroy retreated. The sullen captives included a detachment of 60 men of the 110th Ohio under Lt. Thomas Weakley. "After a most gallant resistance, they surrendered," their commander, Colonel Keifer, later said. He had received a false report they had evacuated with the wagon train, so he had marched off without them.[31]

Johnson's March to Stephenson's Depot

While Milroy evacuated Winchester, Confederate Maj. Gen. Edward "Allegheny" Johnson marched the bulk of his division eastward to intercept the fleeing Yankees. Brigadier General George Steuart's brigade led the way on the Berryville Road, with 1st Lt. David C. Grayson's Company K (the "Page Volunteers") of the 10th Virginia in the van behind Johnson and his escort. They marched about 100 yards ahead of the rest of the regiment and the trailing 1st and 3rd North Carolina regiments. Some of Lt. Col. R. Snowden Andrews' artillery battalion rumbled behind them. Nicholls' Second Louisiana Brigade, under the temporary command of Col. Jesse M. Williams, followed, with the rest of the guns bringing up the rear.[32]

Somehow, a misunderstanding left the entire Stonewall Brigade behind. After dark on Sunday night, Johnson sent staff officer Lt. Oscar Hinrichs to instruct General Walker to go forward, sending Maj. James Newton's 5th Virginia skirmishers through the town, if practical. As Walker prepared for the move, the divisional medical director, Dr. Robert T. Coleman, arrived and mentioned the rest of the division was marching on the Berryville Road and the Stonewall Brigade should follow it. An alarmed Walker dispatched one of his aides, Lt. Robert W. Hunter, to find Johnson and ascertain his expectations. As Hunter rode off into the night, Walker ordered Major Newton to send the left wing of the skirmishers into Winchester to discover whether the Yankees still held the town. The skirmishers quietly entered the streets, detected no Federal presence whatsoever, and returned to Walker with the report the enemy had retired to their fortifications. Lieutenant Hunter located General Johnson and returned to Walker's headquarters about 11:00 p.m. with orders that the

---

31 John M. Steptoe to My Dear Hannie, June 25, 1863, near Winchester, Virginia, 1862-1865 Correspondence of the Steptoe Family of Bedford County, Virginia, Albert and Shirley Small Special Collections Library, UVA; Pope, *The Weary Boys*, 42; *OR* 27, pt. 2, 64.

32 T. H. Lauck, "The Little Corporal's Story," in *Confederate Veteran*, vol. 29, Feb. 1921, 180.

brigade was indeed to follow the rest of the division. It took time to call in the skirmishers and get the men ready, but the Stonewall Brigade finally marched away about 1:00 a.m.[33]

Well ahead of them, Johnson's column took a circuitous route toward Jordan's White Sulphur Springs, a popular resort hotel that more recently doubled as military field hospital along Lick Run four miles from Winchester. "The night was a starlit one and the roads were mostly hidden in the shade of big, overhanging trees," wrote Cpl. Theodore H. "Sonnie" Lauck of the 10th Virginia. "The 'boys' were on edge from the start, for they intuitively felt that something peculiar and important was ahead of them." Lieutenant Grayson's lead company, including Lauck, tramped over Devil's Backbone ridge, across Lick Run, and reached the hotel. Johnson drew in his mount outside the resort's front gate. Johnson, Grayson, and a guard detail under Corporal Lauck approached one of the largest buildings. The general knocked on a side door and, without waiting for a response, turned the doorknob and entered the dark hallway. Roused out of his sleep, proprietor Edwin C. Jordan, Sr. emerged holding a flickering candle. Johnson put his finger to his lips and spoke with Jordan in low tones. As they prepared to leave, Mrs. Jordan woke, lit a lamp in the upstairs bedroom, sat on the windowsill, and asked Lauck's detail about what was transpiring. "I dunno, mum," came the reply, just as Johnson had instructed them to reply. "Why, you are the strangest men I ever met!" she shot back.[34]

Grayson's company returned to the road and resumed its march. The men had not gone 100 yards before they heard the woman emit a "most horrifying scream" and exclaim, "Oh, what are you going to do with my husband?" Her agonizing cry alarmed Lauck, but he quickly surmised she was a Union sympathizer and that General Johnson, somehow knowing this fact, had arranged a fictitious arrest so she would not know her husband's true intent. After walking a few hundred yards farther, they heard a peacock screaming "in such an outrageous manner that Company K would have lost its shoes if they had not been tied on, and more than one man came back to earth again cussin' mad, swearing that that blankety peacock would wake every Yankee picket in five miles of us."[35]

---

33 OR 27, pt. 2, 516, 525.

34 Lauck, "The Little Corporal's Story," 180. Johnson likely used Woods Mill Road (today's Virginia Route 660) to reach Jordan Springs Road. The historic Jordan Springs, at 1160 Jordan Springs Road (Virginia Route 664), remains a popular wedding and special occasion venue.

35 Ibid. In his memoirs, J. W. F. Hatton of Dement's battery gave a much different account of what appears to be the same incident. Jordan, a strong Confederate sympathizer, agreed to lead the column but used the ruse to placate his wife. Both Union and Confederate forces used the

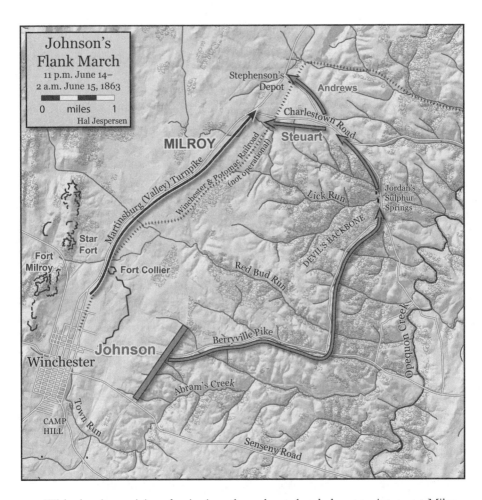

Johnson's
Flank March
11 p.m. June 14–
2 a.m. June 15, 1863

0   miles   1
Hal Jespersen

With that inauspicious beginning, the column headed out to intercept Milroy. After moving some distance on the Berryville Road, Jordan, the proprietor of the hotel, informed Johnson that he would need to cross fields and traverse some rough terrain in order to carry out Ewell's plan. Jordan suggested the Union enemy would certainly retreat along the Martinsburg Pike. Just south of Stephenson's Depot, about five miles from Winchester, a deep railroad cut masked by woods paralleled the turnpike about 200 yards away. Jordan explained to the general that this terrain feature would afford excellent shelter for troops in case of an engagement. Believing the enemy would discover his movement and probably escape if he used Ewell's

buildings as hospitals at various times during the war, enjoying the comforts of the therapeutic sulfur springs.

instructed route, Johnson decided to follow Jordan's advice. About 2:00 a.m., the resort owner guided the lengthy column northward on the Charles Town Road (present-day Route 761). The route forked southeast of the burned-out Stephenson's Depot, with the left-hand lane passing over the Winchester & Potomac's railroad cut on a small wooden bridge before intersecting the northeasterly-running turnpike. The right-hand route (present-day Route 664) passed the depot before meeting up with the pike.[36]

First Contact

Sometime about 3:30 a.m., Lieutenant Grayson halted Company K of the 12th Virginia of Steuart's brigade at the bridge, which was about a half-mile south of the ruins of the railroad station and a quarter-mile from the turnpike. The Virginians sat down to rest by the roadside near the intersection with the Milburn Road, a dirt farm lane which ran south along the tracks. Nearby was a wooden building with a scale used by local farmers to weigh their hay for market. Stars twinkled above and the warm night was deathly quiet. Grayson asked Corporal Lauck to take position on the bridge. Lauck slid his gun onto the floor, put his hands to his ears, and turned in the direction of Winchester. Before long he heard the sound of neighing horses and the confused murmur of a moving column of men. The Yankees, he quietly informed Grayson, were deserting Winchester. Grayson listened for a few moments and agreed. Just then, Johnson and his staff rode onto the bridge. "General, the Yankees are evacuating Winchester," Grayson announced. "Hush! Let me listen!" Johnson responded. He and his staff guided their horses across the span toward the pike, from which point they discerned the Union movement. Meanwhile, Corporal Lauck dutifully shouldered his gun and stood guard. About five minutes later the brigade's adjutant, Capt. George Williamson, rode onto the span from behind Lauck. All was quiet momentarily, but soon Lauck and Williamson could hear advancing horsemen coming from their front. Lauck called "Halt!" Presuming the riders were General Johnson and his staff returning, he responded with a standard rifle salute. Just then, a gunshot pierced the silence and a bullet fanned Williamson's left ear. Without orders, Lauck turned quickly to his right, dropped to his right knee, and fired at a dark blur in the middle of the road. Williamson was drawing his pistol from its holster when someone yelled, "Skirmishers out!"[37]

36 OR 27, pt. 2, 501.

37 Lauck, "The Little Corporal's Story," 180.

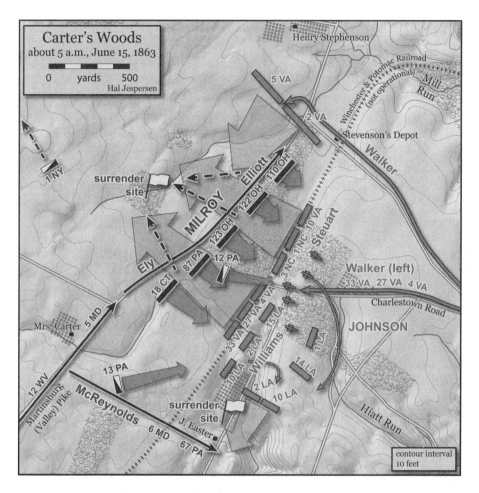

The shadowy horsemen who had shot at the Confederates were the advance scouts of Lt. Col. Joseph Moss's 12th Pennsylvania Cavalry. They had ridden four miles on the turnpike from Winchester and were now probing eastward in the darkness. A few of the riders in the front rank fired at the poorly silhouetted Rebels before wheeling their horses and heading back to Moss's main body. According to Johnson's staff officer Lt. Randolph McKim, "I happened to be in the front and was thus the first to discern in the dim dusk of early morning the approach of a column of the enemy's cavalry." He snapped off a quick pistol shot in their direction. He, General Johnson, and the rest of the party returned to the bridge as the Federals returned in more force. Grayson's company fanned out and peppered the oncoming Yankees. "The attack of the enemy was prompt and furious," a Federal trooper commented, "and though our men were nearly exhausted, they returned the fire sharply and defiantly, but owing to the extreme darkness, the firing on both sides was

Postwar view of Mrs. Carter's house along the Martinsburg Road.

Ben Ritter via Jerry Holsworth

not very effective at first." Lieutenant Colonel Moss sent a courier back to the turnpike to inform General Elliott that he had encountered the Rebels.[38]

Moss rushed Companies G and F of the 12th Pennsylvania forward to reinforce his vanguard. "There was opened one of the bloodiest battles on record," Keystone Pvt. John H. Black proffered with exaggerated flair. The two Keystone companies launched a mounted charge that sent the 10th Virginia's pickets scrambling back into some woods owned by a widow named Mrs. Susan Pitman Carter. Saber-wielding Federal cavalrymen recklessly chased them back into the timber line, where telegraph wires stretched between the trees in the inky blackness sent some of the horses and riders tumbling. "There was confusion and mix up," Pvt. Malden Valentine explained. "My horse went down by bullet or wire." When the stunned trooper recovered from the fall, he found himself staring at the business end of a Rebel's rifle. Valentine wisely surrendered, carrying a carpetbag full of the company's records as his captor escorted him to the rear. The encounter confirmed Johnson's supposition that Milroy had indeed evacuated the forts and was retreating to Harpers Ferry. The Federal cavalrymen were likely screening this movement. Johnson sent a courier galloping

38 OR 27, pt. 2, 48; McKim, *A Soldier's Recollections*, 148.

back down the Charles Town Road with orders to bring up Steuart's brigade to engage the Yankees.[39]

The rest of the 10th Virginia was in the lead, with the 1st and 3rd North Carolina trailing them. As they arrived on the scene, Allegheny Johnson directed General Steuart to deploy his three regiments to the right of the Old Charles Town Road on elevated wooded ground and in a nearby open field. Johnson also sent word for the rest of his division to come up. As Steuart's men were arriving, a bullet whizzed over the column, followed a few seconds later by another and then a third. If there was any doubt the Yankees were near, the lead fusillade confirmed that danger indeed lurked just ahead. "Just as the head of the column was crossing the bridge, it was fired into, causing momentary confusion," Steuart later confirmed in his report.

Notwithstanding the difficulty of crossing fences and unknown terrain in the dark, Steuart directed the 10th Virginia toward the railroad cut to the right of the bridge, with the 1st North Carolina in tow. Stone-and-rider fencing lined both sides of the cut for several yards north and south of the bridge. Tar Heel Lt. Col. William M. Parsley changed front on his first company, initially facing the direction of the gunfire before his men clamored over the fencing and dropped into the protective cut. Ahead of Parsley was a open field about 200 yards wide stretching to the northern portion of Carter's Woods (the Charles Town Road bisected her timber). General Johnson, who was watching the deployment, moved the 1st and 3rd North Carolina to the left (west) of the cut beyond the woods, keeping the 10th Virginia in place along the tracks. Fronted by a heavy line of skirmishers, Steuart's position appeared to be a very strong one. "I found Colonel [E. T. H.] Warren there in the very loveliest place he'd ever found on a battle field," was how the 10th Virginia's Corporal Lauck explained it, with "four feet of perfectly trustworthy yellow clay embankment towering above his head."[40]

Once in position, the 1st and 3rd North Carolina began shooting at the shadowy enemy troopers, while the forward skirmishers of the 10th Virginia maintained their fire. Their Minié balls struck both flanks of Lieutenant Colonel Moss's two 12th

---

39 John H. Black, David J. Coles, and Stephen D. Engle, *A Yankee Horseman in the Shenandoah Valley: The Civil War Letters of John H. Black, Twelfth Pennsylvania Cavalry* (Knoxville: University of Tennessee Press, 2012), 46, (as Black penned in a letter to his fiancée on June 16 from Centerville, Pennsylvania); McKim, *A Soldier's Recollections*, 148. For more on the cavalry's action that morning, see Maier, *Leather & Steel: the 12th Pennsylvania Cavalry in the Civil War.* It is likely the wires were not strung by the Rebels as some Yankees later claimed, but were already in place for other purposes.

40 Lauck, "The Little Corporal's Story," 180; James I. Metts, "Jordan Springs Battle," in *Confederate Veteran*, vol. 29, Feb. 1921, 104-105; OR 27, pt. 2, 507. The stone walls had two "riders," newly installed wooden fence rails set on X-shaped cross beams on top of the rocks.

Pennsylvania companies, which fought back with "great spirit and determination." Seeing his men and officers milling about in confusion and some falling, Moss ordered his right battalion to charge to its relief. When a bullet brought down Moss's horse hard upon him, Maj. Darius Titus assumed command of the regiment. The troopers maintained a defensive position for about 15 to 20 minutes, holding the vital turnpike open as General Elliott hastened the leading infantry composed of three Ohio regiments forward. Elliott sent his assistant adjutant-general, Capt. J. Elliott Jacobs, dashing back down the pike to inform General Milroy of the developing and potentially very dangerous situation. At that time Milroy and his staff were approaching the intersection of the Martinsburg Pike and the road to Summit Point. His main column was still strung out all the way back to Winchester, and it would be some time before Ely's brigade came up. Unknown to Milroy, McReynolds' brigade was just then departing Winchester.[41]

Elliott halted his advance north of the widow Susan Pitman Carter's farmhouse and began deploying his men. A "tall, beautiful girl . . . a rich, ripe brunette, commanding and statuesque," stood on the veranda watching the long column, recalled the 116th Ohio's Sgt. James Dalzell. Mrs. Carter's 22-year-old adopted daughter, Susan Mary Pitman, he continued, was one of the "stateliest, queenliest, sauciest girls in all that old valley. Not a man in our army but had heard her tongue abusing the hated Yankees, and not one of all our forces whom she had not captivated with her dark beauty . . . and never more bewitching than when she poured torrents of abuse upon us as we passed by her door . . . her sweet little curses were music to us." Pitman, he believed, was an inspiration to both armies.[42]

Elliott's brigade did not have an easy march. The sounds of small arms fire reverberated through the dark countryside, increasing the anxiety and fear of the blue-clad soldiers who soon realized the Confederates had intercepted the retreating column. The 123rd Ohio filed off the turnpike to the left while Col. J. Warren Keifer's understrength 110th Ohio, down the 60 men left behind at Winchester, continued northward. The 122nd Ohio halted.[43]

---

41 OR 27, pt. 2, 70.

42 Dalzell, "A Lucky Blunder," 103. After John Carter died in 1842, Susan Carter adopted Susan Mary Pitman, the daughter of her brother Joseph. Mrs. Carter owned a 173-acre farm where much of the fighting would occur. "Her farm produced wheat, corn, Irish potatoes, and hay. In 1850, she owned 8 horses, 8 head of cattle, 2 oxen, 2 sheep that provided 125 pounds of wool, and 33 hogs. She also owned at least 7 slaves." ("Interrupted by War" state wayside marker at Rutherford's Farm, Virginia Historical Society).

43 OR 27, pt. 2, 47, 58-59.

Confusion reigned for several minutes. "I was ordered to form on the One hundred and tenth Ohio Volunteer Infantry," the 122nd Ohio's Col. William Ball mentioned. "When completing the formation, I was ordered to form in rear of the One hundred and twenty-third Ohio Volunteer Infantry. Just as that formation was being made, I was ordered to follow the One hundred and tenth Ohio Volunteer Infantry, which had been moved off the field some time before and was out of sight." According to Elliott, Milroy's aide, Capt. Zebulon Baird, galloped up and took personal command of Col. William Tecumseh Wilson's 123rd Ohio. He led that regiment off in the darkness, leaving Elliott temporarily unaware of its whereabouts; the reason remains uncertain. Milroy later stressed, "I did not give the order for the One hundred and twenty-third Ohio to be detached from General Elliott on the battle-field Monday, June 15, and Captain Baird informs me that he received no such order from me; that he gave no such order to Colonel Wilson or any other officer of that regiment."[44]

For his part, Baird later reported,

> I immediately rode forward toward the front, and met Major Cravens of General Milroy's staff. He directed me to ride forward, and order the two regiments [110th and 122nd Ohio] which had filed to the left some distance back to the Martinsburg Road, and place them in line of battle there, fronting the woods in which the enemy appeared to be. I immediately proceeded to execute this order. When I arrived at the front of the column, I was about delivering the order to Colonel Keifer . . . , when I saw General Elliott, whom I supposed was with General Milroy. I apologized to General Elliott for beginning to give this order to his colonels when he was present. General Elliott then explained to me that he had filed those regiments to the left with reference to forming his line of battle.[45]

Meanwhile on the Charles Town Road, Capt. William F. Dement's 1st Maryland (CSA) Artillery was marching in close support of Steuart's infantry columns. Under Allegheny Johnson's orders, sometime after 3:00 a.m. battalion commander Lt. Col. Snowden Andrews sent Lt. Charles S. Contee and the lead gun, which had temporarily parked some 200 yards from the burned railroad depot, to assist General Steuart. Johnson directed the lone piece to a low ridge along Milburn Road in the left rear of the bridge. Andrews, riding in the lead, came thundering up the road to the bridge yelling, "In battery, action, front!" However, a heavy stake-and-rider fence lined the road. The cannoneers simply did not have the time to dismantle it to allow Contee's

---

44 Ibid., 59, 68.

45 *OR* 27, pt. 2, 136.

Lt. Col. Richard Snowden Andrews, who commanded the artillery battalion assigned to Johnson's division.

U.S. Army Heritage and Education Center

gun and limber to pass through it, so as many men as could be quickly gathered leaned hard against it and finally knocked it over. With the obstacle gone, the drivers of the No. 1 gun swung to the left off the road and moved into position, unlimbering the Napoleon on the ridge as ordered.[46]

When the second cannon arrived, Contee ordered Sgt. John G. Harris and his artillerymen to push the No. 1 gun down onto the bridge while Sgt. John E. Glasscocke positioned the No. 2 gun behind them on higher ground in support. Crews loaded both pieces with canister. Lieutenant Colonel Andrews instructed Contee to hold the bridge as long as there was a man left. Bullets peppered the position and a few exposed cannoneers were hit. "We received a volley of minnie balls," confirmed a soldier in Glasscocke's No. 2 gun crew several days after the fighting, "but it was so dark we could not see the enemy, who continued to fire upon us."[47]

According to the 3rd North Carolina's John B. Casteen, some of the Tar Heels discerned a shadowy group of riders moving along a nearby hill, likely in an attempt to flank the Confederate position. Some of the soldiers thought it was General Milroy and his escort trying to escape in the lingering darkness, but it was actually additional elements of the 12th Pennsylvania Cavalry that Moss had brought forward from the turnpike. Someone remarked to Allegheny Johnson, "General, the cavalry is flanking us." Johnson, who was sitting on his horse about 50 yards behind the main battle line, exclaimed in a low steady voice, "Let them come! Let them come! That is what I want them to do. Turn that battery on them." Johnson also instructed the nearby

---

46 J. W. Owens, "Heroic Defense of Bridge at Stephenson's Depot, Va.," *Confederate Veteran*, vol. 29, no. 2, February 1921, 41; Tunstall Smith, ed., *Richard Snowden Andrews: Lieutenant-Colonel Commanding the First Maryland Artillery… A Memoir* (Baltimore: The Sun Job Printing Office, 1930), 48.

47 OR 27, pt. 2, 501, 541; McKim, *A Soldier's Recollections*, 149; "The Battle of Winchester: The Maryland Battery," *Richmond Enquirer*, June 22, 1863.

infantrymen, "Be quiet men, be quiet. I want them to think there is only a handful of you."[48]

All remained quiet as the enemy horsemen drew closer. General Johnson rode over to the bridge, brandishing his trademark walking cane when he arrived. "Why in the hell don't you open that battery?" he is said to have yelled at Contee, not realizing his own skirmishers masked the guns. The Virginia and North Carolina infantrymen in Steuart's main line along the railroad embankment also had to withhold their fire. "As ammunition and everything else was scarce in the Confederacy," Lt. James I. Metts of the 3rd North Carolina explained, "I sat on the bank watching the Yanks in the woods and told the boys to hold their fire until they came out in the field, then give it to them heavy."[49]

When four more of his cannon teams arrived, Andrews deployed Capt. Charles Raine's pair of 3-inch rifles and Lt. William Lambie's two Napoleons on the low ridge along Milburn Road off to Contee's left (south). Andrews soon rejudged the situation and shifted Lambie's pieces 200 yards to the right of the Charles Town Road to protect against a flank attack. When Johnson received word the Yankees were attempting to turn his left flank, he sent two companies of the 3rd North Carolina, including Lieutenant Metts and Company G, back into the open field south of the bridge. The flankers proved to be nothing more than some of Moss's cavalry, who retired when confronted. The Tar Heel skirmishers finally fell back just before dawn, entering the railroad cut and passing under the bridge to rejoin their regiment. Andrews' guns now enjoyed a wide and clear field of fire to do their work. Although visibility was still limited, the battalion commander ordered, "Load and fire at will! Commence firing!"[50]

Lieutenant Lambie's first two shots did more harm than good. The 10th Virginia's Corporal Lauck had climbed halfway up the 10-foot-high western embankment to fire from behind the stone-and-rider fence. A stone wall ran perpendicular from his position to the Martinsburg Pike. When one of the artillery

48 "Memories of the Confederacy," *Wilmington* (NC) *Morning Star*, May 7, 1917. Casteen's twin brother Jacob had also served in the same regiment, but had died in June 1862 in a Richmond hospital of typhoid fever. John would survive Second Winchester, the maelstrom of Culp's Hill at Gettysburg, sharp fighting at Payne's Farm during the Mine Run Campaign, and the hell of the Wilderness, only to be captured at Spotsylvania during the dawn attack against the Mule Shoe. He would spend the rest of the war in prisons at Point Lookout in Maryland and then in Elmira, New York.

49 Metts, "The Jordan Springs Battle."

50 *OR* 27, pt. 2, 507, 541; *SHSP*, March 1877, 3:138; Metts, "The Jordan Springs Battle," 104. Metts mistakenly believed the enemy riders were Milroy and his staff. The gun position has been deemed "Battery Heights," though no formal name seems to exist.

rounds fired from behind him, something struck him on the top of his head. The puzzled corporal dropped down into the cut and discovered a 16-inch chunk of freshly torn wood. Private Utz of Company L replaced him along the wall, but he too quickly dropped back into the cut, bleeding from both thighs after another cannon blast. Lauck scrambled up the eastern embankment, climbed on top of its damaged stone wall, and thundered, "Cease firing over there! You are wounding your own men!" In the dim light he could just make out a cannoneer stop mid-swab with his ramrod near in the barrel of one of the pieces. The 10th Virginia had no more trouble from guns firing too low in the darkness. "The cannoneers had neither light nor knowledge to go by, so they must be excused," Lauck explained, "but somebody blundered."[51]

Despite the darkness and uncertainty of the exact enemy position, Lambie and Contee opened "the most deadly and terrific fire I ever witnessed," recorded Major Titus of the 12th Pennsylvania Cavalry. His dismounted Keystoners retired in good order several yards until shells began dropping among them. Much to General Elliott's surprise, the troopers quickly mounted their horses and rode completely off the battlefield without his orders.[52]

The sound of the unexpected cannonade reverberated throughout the area. "We expected to be attacked in the rear by Confederate cavalry. We never for one moment expected any trouble in front," admitted Maj. Alonzo Adams of the 1st New York Cavalry, the commander of Milroy's rear guard. Startled townspeople in Winchester woke up and wondered about the source of this new night-time firing well off to the northeast. At the Taylor Hotel, the 18th Connecticut's James Sawyer noted that the uninjured fat Ohio drummer boy had risen very early and stepped outside. Within a few moments the lad burst into the room and yelled with excitement, "Boys, come out and hear the firing!" When Sawyer reached the street, the booming of cannon indicated that a battle of no small magnitude was in progress. Just north of Winchester, the exhausted Chaplain Joseph T. Brown of the 6th Maryland was sleeping on the front porch of a house when the noisy events shook him awake. To his surprise and dismay, he learned "the entire division had moved off toward Harpers Ferry." He could not see the fighting, but could hear it "very distinctively."[53]

---

51 Lauck, "The Little Corporal's Story."

52 *OR* 27, pt. 2, 70; *SHSP*, March 1877, 3:138; Metts, "The Jordan Springs Battle," 104.

53 Sawyer, "Abandoned at Winchester," 11; Brown diary entry for June 15, 1863.

Col. William H. Ball, commander of the
122d Ohio Volunteer Infantry.
U.S. Army Heritage and Education Center

The Initial Fighting at
Stephenson's Depot

As the Confederate artillery continued
to roar, Milroy tried to make sense of the
tactical situation as best as he could in the
pre-dawn darkness. The two lead regiments
of Elliott's brigade had halted on the
turnpike shortly after Moss's cavalry went
forward to probe the enemy position. Now,
Milroy sent Colonel Keifer and the 110th
Ohio forward to relieve Moss's cavalry and
feel the enemy's position. "Some straggling
shots notified us that the enemy were on the pike near us," Keifer recounted. "I halted
and faced the men in line of battle toward the pike, and, though still dark, a personal
investigation revealed the fact that the Confederates were in confusion, and the
commands they were giving also indicated that they were greatly excited." He found
General Elliott some distance in the rear and obtained his commander's consent to
charge the Rebels. His command "charged rapidly across the road without firing,"
Keifer later stated. Despite the darkness, "it fortunately struck the enemy's flank."[54]

Upon being notified of the unfolding situation, Milroy ordered Col. William H.
Ball's 122nd Ohio to advance on Keifer's right in case of an opportunity to turn the
Rebels' left flank. By then, Keifer was already moving forward and was out of sight in
Carter's Woods. "The regiments being so separated," Ball recalled. "I did not engage
the enemy as soon as the One hundred and tenth. I formed on the right of the One
hundred and tenth Ohio Volunteer Infantry, and the two regiments advanced within
the skirt of the woods and engaged the enemy, who occupied the woods with infantry
and artillery." Keifer assumed overall command of the joint attack.[55]

During their eastward advance across the uneven ground, Keifer's Buckeyes
entered a depression and believed they had passed Johnson's left flank. Intense Rebel

54 Keifer, *Slavery and Four Years of War*, vol. 2, 14.

55 *OR* 27, pt. 2, 68.

fire soon changed that optimistic opinion. Keifer pointed toward the woods from which the muzzle blasts came and gave the command to charge. "Forward we went in with a double quick," reported Pvt. Alonzo Barnhart. The ranks cheered as the line briefly surged ahead before stumbling through the underbrush and trees and becoming somewhat disordered. Colonel Keifer halted to dress his lines and fire off an initial volley. "When we got close enough we gave them a volley of minnie balls for their breakfast," Barnhart added. He believed the hail of bullets had surprised the Rebels. "They were dumbfounded for a while. They did not know what it meant from the outside of their lines."[56]

Johnson quickly reacted by repositioning the 3rd North Carolina to repel the attack. When he learned that the van of Nicholls' Louisiana brigade under Colonel Williams was coming up, he directed the Tar Heels to return to their original position. Johnson personally led Lt. Col. Ross E. Burke's 2nd Louisiana and Maj. Thomas Powell's 10th Louisiana left onto the Milburn Road, where the regiments changed face, advanced, and engaged the oncoming 122nd in a sharp firefight. Only the flashes from the muzzles indicated their relative positions. Johnson sent Lt. Col. David Zable and the 14th Louisiana north of the Charles Town Road. Zable left half of the regiment to support the gun line and moved the rest to support Steuart's line in the railroad cut.[57]

The steady pressure from the two Union regiments soon forced Steuart's skirmishers back out of the woods. "After a sharp action," the 122nd Ohio's Colonel Ball recalled, "the line was advanced at least 100 yards and to within 20 paces of the enemy's artillery, where a terrible fire was maintained for fifteen or twenty minutes by both parties. The artillery was driven back over 100 yards, and for a time silenced by the fire of our rifles." In the canopy of smoke and limited visibility, General Milroy believed the Buckeyes were driving the enemy with their "incessant, heavy, and murderous fire of musketry." He later praised Colonel Keifer, who "especially distinguished himself by the display of the qualities of a brave soldier and a judicious and skillful officer." The Rebels quickly retired to the shelter of the railroad cut and Contee's guns soon blazed away at the distant enemy muzzle flashes. Keifer had his work cut out for him.[58]

Milroy apparently at some point rode into the woods to make his own assessment of the situation. Charles McCabe, the baritone-voiced chaplain of the 122nd Ohio,

---

56 OR 27, pt. 2, 62, 507; Barnhart, *Reminiscences*; Lauck, "The Little Corporal's Story."

57 OR 27, pt. 2, 501, 512-515; W. G. Lloyd, "Second Louisiana at Gettysburg," in *Confederate Veteran*, vol. 6, Feb. 1898, 417.

58 OR 27, pt. 2, 48, 68.

Detail from the Snowden Andrews' monument at Stephenson's Depot showing
Contee's stout defense of the Charles Town Road bridge. *Scott Mingus*

watched the "Grey Eagle" dash from place to place with his staff in tow. McCabe
"wondered as he galloped forward toward the rebel line of earthworks if he knew that
a reward of ten thousand dollars had been offered to any man who would take him,
dead or alive."[59]

With Carter's Woods clear, the Ohioans traded heavy musketry with Colonel
Warren's 10th Virginia and Zable's Louisianans. The right companies of the 10th
Virginia defended a low portion of the railroad embankment and had to fire from their
knees to get any protection. Most of them fired as many as 60 rounds during the
engagement, while the left companies, under much less pressure and in better cover,
fired about half that number. When Warren sent word to Steuart that the enemy was
pressing him hard and his supply of cartridges was nearly gone, the brigadier moved
the 1st North Carolina northward in support. He also dispatched part of the 3rd

59 *The Rome* (NY) *Daily Sentinel,* April 12, 1899.

North Carolina. Under intense fire, Keifer fell back into the shelter of the oak trees. The failed effort was compounded when General Elliott's aide-de-camp, Lt. William L. Shaw of the 110th Ohio, had his horse shot from under him. "By order of Colonel Keifer," Ball recounted, "the two regiments then retreated beyond the range of the enemy's infantry" and reformed.[60]

A sizable number of dead and wounded Yankees littered the field in front of the 10th Virginia. Corporal T. H. Lauck ran along the cut to take up a new firing position below the bridge when he ran into an unarmed Yankee who apparently had stumbled over the embankment. Blood streamed from beneath the man's slouch hat, and he was either crazy from his head wound or scared out of his wits. Lauck grabbed his shoulder and asked, "Have you any cartridges?" The Yankee did nothing but mumble nonsense in return and tried to pull away. Lauck held him with one hand and used his other to peer into his cartridge box. When it realized it was nearly full, he pulled the box and sling off the dazed Buckeye and sent him on his way to the rear as a prisoner.[61]

Contee's No. 2 gun south of the bridge continued belching fire under "a shower of Minnie balls such as I never heard before," a Confederate artillerist related. With a cheer, the 110th and 122nd Ohio regiments bravely pushed forward again, firing at will. Their Minié balls mostly passed harmlessly over the heads of the Confederates concealed behind the railroad cut, which had sturdy stone walls flanking the bridge on either side. "I could see the Yanks dodging behind the trees," recalled the 3rd North Carolina's Lieutenant Metts, "and they did not advance much nearer than the edge of the woods, which was about one hundred yards from us into the field, for our boys poured the shot and shell into them heavy." Only a handful of Tar Heels were down. Private George Rose of Company D lay dead in the railroad cut and Lieutenant Craig and others had been wounded. General Steuart and his mounted staff officers, including young Lt. Randolph McKim, remained exposed, as were Contee's valiant gunners on the bridge. Keifer's attack soon stalled under the withering fire. His two regiments maintained their relative positions for almost an hour.[62]

Snowden Andrews' gun line continued harassing the two distant Ohio regiments. Half an hour after the cannonade started, Lt. J. Harris Stonestreet galloped onto the field with the guns of Captain Dement's left section. The two smoothbore guns were unlimbered to the right of the road on high ground behind Steuart's infantry to support Lambie's Napoleons. Atop the bridge, Lieutenant Contee kept up the morale of his cannoneers in the face of a hail of whistling Minié balls. By this time, the No. 2

---

60 Ibid.; *OR* 27, pt. 2, 68.

61 Lauck, "The Little Corporal's Story."

62 *Richmond Enquirer*, June 22, 1863; McKim, *A Soldier's Recollections*, 159.

gun had exhausted its ammunition and was out of the fight. "Give it to them boys, give it to them!" Contee bellowed repeatedly. A few days before the battle, a young private named William T. Wooten had been arrested for showing disrespect to an officer. He was released until the impending fight was over, but by this time he had heard enough of Contee's loud exhortations. "Charlie Contee, if you don't shut your mouth I will pick you up and throw you off the bridge," Willie yelled.[63]

The Fighting Escalates

Meanwhile, additional Union regiments—the 87th Pennsylvania, 18th Connecticut, 5th Maryland, 12th West Virginia, and 116th Ohio—began arriving on the turnpike south of the bridge near Carter's Woods. Milroy planned to outflank the Confederate line and lead his men to safety. It was not to be. Just then, Col. Jesse Williams' hidden Louisianans suddenly fired a volley from the railroad cut. Two more came in quick succession. The effect of the ambush was telling. "This was a murderous trap which was not seen in the gray dawn of that fatal morning, and it was first discovered by the flash of rebel rifles," recorded the 18th Connecticut's chaplain, the Rev. William Walker.[64]

"The cavalry were to the right of us, marching in fours or parallel to the infantry lines," the 18th's Charles Lynch recalled. "They broke and ran through our lines, causing much confusion." The "cavalry" was a column of fours of more than 800 government horses and mules, largely ridden by non-combatants, civilians, convalescents, and clerks. Milroy's assistant quartermaster, Capt. Mark L. DeMotte, commanded them. A soldier in the 116th Ohio recorded the stampede. "The teams, being unhitched from the wagons, were marching at the right of the column between our men and the enemy and consequently received the first three volleys of the enemy's fire, which frightened them so badly that some of them became unmanageable, threw their riders and broke the ranks of the column, which for a moment caused some confusion. The men, however, were soon rallied and fearlessly and in good order went into the battle."[65]

Captain DeMotte, an Indiana native and antebellum prosecuting attorney, attempted to move the rest of the riders left (west) of the road toward some timber. His shaken command was halfway to safety when the distant Rebel artillerymen

---

63 *OR* 27, pt. 2, 541; *Richmond Enquirer*, June 22, 1863; August James Albert, "Account of Service in the Civil War," MHS; *Washington Post*, December 5, 1920.

64 Walker, *History of the Eighteenth Regiment*, 114-15; *National Tribune*, December 18, 1884.

65 "Letter from the 116th O.V.I."; Lynch, *Civil War Diary*, 21.

spotted it and opened fire. The rounds unnerved the horses. Their riders, having ordinary wagon bridles and lacking saddles, quickly lost control of their mounts. The terrified animals knocked several soldiers of the 12th West Virginia against the fences lining the turnpike, injuring some soldiers and smashing several rifles. DeMotte tried to rally the refugees in a wheatfield a quarter-mile from the road, to no avail.[66]

It was "a terrible time," one of the riders, the 18th Connecticut's Pvt. David Emerson, remembered. "For five minutes the bullets flew around me as thick as hail-stones, but as soon as I could get my mule out of the way, I made him jump over a rail fence into an orchard, and when the mule jumped, as much as twenty bullets struck the rails." The orchard proved to be just out of the Rebels' musketry range, so Emerson relaxed a bit before Rebel artillery began to play upon the position. He and the other riders moved into another field until the Confederate gunners spotted them once more and opened fire. Some of Captain DeMotte's motley command soon started off for Cumberland, Maryland, leaving the battlefield behind them.[67]

Meanwhile, Lt. Col. Monroe Nichols and his officers managed to reform the shaken 18th Connecticut. General Milroy, with his two leading Ohio regiments still embattled, decided to up the ante. He rode over to the 87th Pennsylvania and ordered Col. John Schall to advance, hoping to seize the rightmost Rebel cannon (Glasscocke's No. 2 gun of Contee's section). Milroy needed to drive off this gun and its supporting infantry, the 3rd North Carolina. Schall accordingly threw out Capt. John Fahs and Company A as skirmishers and pushed eastward toward Mrs. Carter's woods.

Unfortunately for the Yankees, it was still too dark to discern friend from foe with any certainty. The 18th Connecticut, having just reformed after the confusion from the stampede, mistook Schall's movement for the enemy and began firing. Four Pennsylvania riflemen—Privates Sylvester Golding, John C. Hoffman, Lazarus J. Klinedinst, and Peter Free—closed within long range of Glasscocke's cannoneers and opened fire. However, lead from the 3rd North Carolina and the 18th Connecticut's friendly fire soon pinned them down and mortally wounded Free. When Milroy realized what was happening, he quickly rode over to the 18th Connecticut and excitedly ordered the men to cease fire. In some cases, he had to resort to knocking their rifles upward with his sword to get their attention. The respite allowed Colonel

---

66 OR 27, pt. 2, 116; "H.C.H.", "With the 12th Virginia"; DeMotte eventually lost 150 of the riders as prisoners.

67 David Emerson to *Dear Transcript, New Creek, West Virginia, June 17, 1863,* cited in *Dear Transcript: Letters home from the boys and regiments of Windham County written to the editor of their hometown newspaper, 'The Windham County Transcript.'* (Danielson, CT: Killingly Historical & Genealogical Society, 2009), 293.

Schall and his field officers to reform their stunned Keystoners. Once all was in order, the 87th Pennsylvania advanced toward the Rebel-held timber, but met a withering fire from Raine's distant batteries, as well as Sergeant Glasscocke's solitary gun. Most of the Pennsylvanians soon fell back in the darkness 150 yards to a brush-choked ravine housing Hiatt Run. In their isolated position close to the Rebel line, Golding, Hoffman, and Klinedinst did not realize the regiment had withdrawn. Caught in a cross-fire, they dared not rise. Lying beside the dying Free, they managed to keep firing on the Rebel gunners.[68]

While this transpired, the 18th Connecticut's Lieutenant Colonel Nichols spotted the 5th Maryland marching away. Ignoring how sick he was, Nichols galloped after the Marylanders and induced the regiment's officers to return and fight. They finally formed a line of battle to the left of the Nutmegs. General Milroy, with the situation growing more critical by the minute, tried another assault to drive Williams' and Steuart's troops away and clear the turnpike. He sent the 18th Connecticut and the 5th Maryland forward, with the 87th Pennsylvania soon advancing from the sheltering Hiatt Run ravine to join in this second assault. Colonel Ely, having arrived on the scene, led the regiments forward through the dark woods into a field of "high and tangled" clover that worked to slow the Union advance. Charles Lynch and his comrades in the 18th Connecticut's color company (Company C) tramped ahead with no little anxiety because in the distance they could see that Raine's Rebel battery was "well posted and supported." It proved to be ugly business. According to the 18th Connecticut's Chaplain Walker, "The Union forces could see nothing else as they charged into the woods, and up the cross road, hence the rebels had every advantage, and were not slow to improve it."[69]

A bullet struck Colonel Schall's sorrel during the 87th Pennsylvania's approach to Carter's Woods. The officer calmly dismounted the mortally wounded beast and continued leading his men forward. "Come on, boys!" Lt. William H. Lanius shouted, waving his sword and urging Company I forward. "We'll give them hell!" The Pennsylvanians managed to slash their way 40 yards into the timber before stalling under a heavy fire. Private William Emenheiser escaped serious injury when a minié ball glanced off his U. S. belt plate and another passed through his blanket roll, slashing his back between his shoulder blades. As Emenheiser discovered after the battle, his unrolled blanket displayed fourteen holes. When the Rebel gunners focused their pieces on the main battle line of the 87th Pennsylvania, the prostrated Golding,

---

68 Prowell, *History of the Eighty-seventh Regiment*, 76-85. The 21-year-old Peter Free, a farmer from York County, died on July 4, 1863.

69 Ibid.; OR 27, pt. 2, 48; Walker, *History of the Eighteenth Regiment*, 114-15; *National Tribune*, December 18, 1884.

Hoffman, and Klinedinst took advantage of the respite to implement a bold plan. The trio sprang to their feet and reportedly seized a nearby Rebel caisson, which they rolled back toward the woods. Fear of an explosion, however, overcame the men and they abandoned the trophy. Colonel Schall skillfully withdrew his regiment into the field, where he ordered the men to lay down. His skirmishers maintained a brisk fire for about 30 minutes while Colonel Ely withdrew the 18th Connecticut and 5th Maryland. They had failed to make any significant headway against Williams' Louisianans or Steuart's 3rd North Carolina along the railroad.[70]

General Milroy spent much of the fighting at Carter's Woods riding with two staff members and some orderlies—and fuming. Believing that Ely might capture the Rebel guns with proper support, Milroy made four calls for the 1st New York Cavalry and 12th Pennsylvania Cavalry to return to the field and charge. According to Arch Rowand of Milroy's escort, Company K of the 1st West Virginia Cavalry, the general "seemed crazy for awhile" after being told the cavalry would not return. "He cursed and swore like a madman while grape and canister and shell were flying all around for awhile. He seemed perfectly indifferent whether he lived or not."[71]

An officer in the 1st New York Cavalry later explained what had happened earlier to that regiment:

> It was too dark yet to see exactly what the situation was. The artillery firing was severe. Even in the perils of that cannonading one could not help admiring the brilliant bursts of spiteful red fire, as the shells in quick succession exploded in the darkness overhead. It was magnificent as well as terrific. There was no use in staying there. For the moment the only thing seemed to be to make a grand crash through the blazing line in front. The order rang out, 'Draw sabres! Forward! Trot!' The men gathered their reins, grasped firm hold of their sabres, fixed themselves firmly in their saddles, clenched their teeth, and spurred their horses into a gallop.

The New Yorkers pounded northward on the fence-lined turnpike toward the fight at Carter's Woods. However, they found the Rebels too well posted. "It would have been a grand charge, like that of the Light Brigade at Balaklava," Beach believed,

---

70 Prowell, *History of the 87th Pennsylvania*, 76, 83. During one of the 87th's attacks, Cpl. Johnston Skelly was mortally wounded. Some accounts suggest he was the fiancée of Virginia "Ginny" Wade, the only civilian to be killed in the battle of Gettysburg.

71 Archibald H. Rowand to Dear Mother, June 21, 1863, Winchester, Virginia, Harry Rowand Collection, excerpts published in the *Pittsburgh Post-Gazette*, May 3, 1998, and posted on-line at http://www.jessiescouts.com/JS_Letters_1863_June_21.html, accessed March 22, 2013. After the war Rowand received a Medal of Honor for his 1864 work as a "Jessie Scout" (a spy group which dressed in Confederate uniforms to deceive the enemy).

"but at a fearful sacrifice of life, with nothing to gain but the name. The men would have made the charge, and Major Adams would have led them in it." Just then "someone with some sense," either a staff officer or one of the regiment's junior officers, appeared at the head of the galloping column and ordered the horsemen off to the left of the road. They moved rapidly across a farm field as the Rebels fired on their right flank. The riders soon rode out of range of the musketry and out of the fight.[72]

Milroy's Final Charges in the Center

Milroy desperately needed to clear Lieutenant Contee's pesky cannon from the bullet-torn bridge, as well as the Rebel gun line on the ridge. When help arrived in the form of Captain Baird and the 123rd Ohio, Milroy decided to try to turn both of Johnson's flanks simultaneously. He would send Colonel McReynolds' brigade past the far left of the Rebel line. He had earlier sent an orderly riding south to hurry along the New Yorker, who was riding with his adjutant, Lt. James Stevenson, well ahead of his slow-moving column. McReynolds and Stevenson trotted forward to meet Milroy, who they found sitting on their horses alongside the turnpike. Milroy reportedly asked McReynolds where his command was. Receiving an unenthusiastic answer that it was "all right," Milroy tersely responded, "You ought to be with your command." He urged McReynolds to hurry his troops forward. The two officers had parted ways, riding in opposite directions.[73]

Now, with McReynolds' brigade on the scene (likely between 4:00 and 4:30 a.m.), Milroy rode north to complete his preparations for the assault. In the center, the 123rd would angle toward the 3rd North Carolina in the railroad cut and Contee's two guns, while the 87th Pennsylvania, 18th Connecticut, and 5th Maryland again went for Glasscocke's gun, Raine's battery, and Williams' Louisianans. The 12th West Virginia and 116th Ohio would remain in support, awaiting orders, and look for an opportunity to break through. Meanwhile, Colonel Keifer would take the 110th and 122nd Ohio farther north to attack the right of Johnson's line. Colonel Wilson formed his 123rd Ohio regiment into line of battle left of Ely's reformed regiments, fixed bayonets, and sent out skirmishers across the road. Colonel Ely briefly drilled all of the troops in this sector under enemy fire before telling Milroy he was ready for orders. The line soon pressed forward.

72 Andrew McReynolds, "The Evacuation of Winchester," *Baltimore American*, June 21, 1863, reprinted in the *New York Evening Express*, June 22, 1863; Beach, *The First New York (Lincoln) Cavalry*, 243.

73 OR 27, pt. 2, 48; Stevenson, *Boots and Saddles*, 192-93.

The 123rd Ohio soon encountered the same problem as the 12th Pennsylvania Cavalry had earlier in the night. "The rebels had used the telegraph wires and other means to obstruct the approaches to their battery," 19-year-old Pvt. Edwin H. Forester noted. Another Buckeye recounted, "Just across the road in their front was an orchard, between the trees of which wire had been tied, doubtless for the purpose of catching our cavalry. At another place they had felled trees to prevent our escape." Nevertheless, the infantrymen pressed on. Yet another Ohioan recalled, "In the storm of grape and canister Col. Wilson, Lieut. Col. Hunter and Maj. Horace Kellogg rode their horses as coolly as though it were simply a hailstorm, which, undoubtedly, contributed greatly in keeping the regiment so firmly to its work." "My little band went in with a yell amidst a shower of grape, canister and musketry such as I never witnessed before, and never wish to see again," reported Colonel Wilson. "We got within fifty yards of their guns, which were unmanned several times by our boys, but the odds were too terrible to engage them hand to hand, and all we could do was retain our position, hoping for support." Shocked by a shell fragment that carried away his haversack and nicked him, the 123rd Ohio's Capt. Charles H. Riggs sat down by a stump, stunned and out of the fight. Caught in what Wilson deemed a "heavy and murderous fire of musketry," this wave also failed to dislodge the Rebels.[74]

Milroy kept desperately trying to dislodge the Rebels to open the pathway to Martinsburg. His troops were stubborn in their determination to succeed. "Again and still again they were rallied and charged, but in vain," 19-year-old Private Forester of the 123rd Ohio recollected as the newly arrived Buckeyes kept trying to push through the Rebels. "The rebels opened with grape and canister, shot down the flag, and inflicted heavy loss upon the regiment on the second charge." Forester suffered painful wounds in his hands and a wrist, but remained on his feet. Another Buckeye, Pvt. W. H. Bruder, described the engagement as a "fierce but short-lived whirlwind of rebel wrath." This ill-fated attack proved to be the bloodiest yet, even though the Confederates could not depress the barrels of their cannon sufficiently to fire upon the Union regiments when they drew near the railroad cut. The Southern musketry, however, was intense and unrelenting. The 123rd's Maj. Horace Kellogg suffered a severe wound to his foot and soon retired from the field.[75]

---

74 Granger, "The 122nd Ohio at Winchester." *Norwalk* (OH) *Reflector*, June 30, 1863; *Sandusky* (OH) *Register*, December 22, 1863; Keyes, *Military History of the 123rd Ohio*, 47-49; OR 27, pt. 2, 48; Forester, "From the 123rd." The unfortunate Riggs died of disease while a prisoner of war September 15, 1864, at Charleston, South Carolina. For more, see the *Tiffin* (OH) *Weekly Tribune*, October 20, 1864.

75 Forester, "From the 123rd"; Bruder Journal, USAHEC. Kellogg managed to avoid capture and escaped. He later was promoted to lieutenant colonel.

Private Edmund P. Snyder of the 123rd Ohio was experiencing his first combat. "At the last charge a bullet struck my gun below the first band, shattered the stock and beat the ramrod out at right angles so that I couldn't draw it out," he recalled. "I dropped the gun and picked up another, plenty of them were scattered about the field." The coolness of the officers and men around him impressed Snyder. "A lieutenant at my left stood right out in the open, firing a little pepper-box of a revolver, and the Colonel, just at my right, rode his horse right up to the front. A shell cut a limb from a tree—the battle was in a strip of woods—that fell across the horse's neck. He coolly threw the limb off, all the time shouting words of encouragement to the boys and giving them an example far more effective than words." A German immigrant named Jake Dorn, a veteran of eight years' service in the Prussian army, was a member of Snyder's company. According to Snyder, Private Dorn was the best drilled and most disciplined solder he had ever met. "He knew that we were ordered to take that battery," wrote Snyder, "and when the battle was over his body, with a bullet through the center of his forehead, was found nearer to the guns than any other."[76]

Several of Wilson's riflemen concentrated on disabling the gun crew. "The only thing the men could do was to load and fire and shoot down the gunners," was how the 123rd Ohio's W. H. Bruder explained the desperate situation. Cannoneers successively fell until only Lieutenant Contee and Pvt. Benjamin Welsh Owens remained uninjured, but "they continued undauntedly serving their piece in its perilous position," boasted staff officer Randolph McKim. "Every discharge the recoil carried the gun almost over the side of the bridge, but before it could roll over, these brave men were at the wheel rolling it back into its place." An admiring Pvt. J. W. F. Hatton agreed. "Every man save one at the gun near the bridge was picked off severely wounded," he wrote. "This one man remained at the gun, trying to fire it himself, till reinforcements reached him. His name was Owens." Hatton deemed him a "brave man."[77]

When Lieutenant Contee finally fell with a painful leg injury, Private Owens, Lt. John A. Morgan of the 1st North Carolina, and Pvt. James A. Matthews of the 10th Virginia moved in to work the gun, despite Matthews' company commander hollering at him that he was "too brave" and to get off the bridge. McKim and General Johnson

76 Snyder, *Autobiography of a Soldier of the Civil War*, 9.

77 Bruder Journal, USAHEC.; McKim, *A Soldier's Recollections*, 150-51; Hatton memoirs. In 1917 Owens, a native of Anne Arundel County, Maryland, received a medal for his actions at the bridge. In 1999, admirers erected an 8-foot statue on a pedestal in his memory at Mount Calvary Southern Episcopal Church in Lothian, Maryland. *Fredericksburg Free-Lance Star*, June 10 and 19, 1999. Johnson, a division commander, had no business carrying ammunition for an artillery piece, a detail that should have been assigned to a common soldier.

dismounted and carried ammunition forward from the caisson before McKim helped man the endangered artillery piece. The 123rd Ohio again pulled back, suffering more dead and wounded in the failed effort. Among the Union victims was W. H. Bruder, who had been carrying off a wounded comrade when a Rebel Minié ball struck and killed him. An awestruck Pvt. S. Thomas McCullough of the 2nd Maryland Battalion watched the Federal attacks. "Again belched forth the boys of war, and again and again," he explained, "many lie and shattered forces of the foe reeled back in confusion and disarray."[78]

After fighting continuously for more than an hour and a half, Steuart's infantrymen were running out of ammunition. "The situation was exceedingly critical," admitted General Johnson. Lieutenant McKim agreed: "The centre now engrossed our attention, for the enemy were making desperate efforts to break through at the bridge. The situation was serious, for the ammunition of the Third Brigade was all but exhausted—one round only left. That little wooden bridge witnessed one of the most superb displays of dauntless intrepidity that was seen during the whole war. The men serving the piece planted there were fearfully exposed."[79]

"The whistling of their bullets was tremendous," related Pvt. August James Albert, Jr., who was out of action with a shattered left arm. "What made me realize even more their number," he added, "was the rattle those made that struck the wooden uncovered bridge on which we were standing, making a sound very much like a watchman's alarm rattle." Not wanting to be shot in the back, the wounded Albert walked backward off the bridge with his face to the enemy and blood streaming down his sleeve. When dizziness overtook him, he sat down by the side of the road until comrades came to his aid and bound his arm to slow his blood loss. Later, one of Albert's friends named William Brown surveyed the dead and injured Union soldiers heaped in front of the bridge and related his story to him. Brown counted more than 50 of "their poor fellows lying just in front of our gun, most of them torn to pieces by our short range shot," recalled Albert, who added, "May God forgive us." One of the wounded Confederates was Willie Wooten, the impudent private who had threatened

78 McKim, *A Soldier's Recollections*, 150-51; Lauck, "The Little Corporal's Story"; *OR* 27, pt. 2, 502, 541; *Richmond Enquirer*, June 22, 1863; Bruder Journal, USAHEC. Bruder survived his injury; McCullough diary entry for June 15, 1863.

79 *OR* 27, pt. 2, 441-42, 501; Tunstall Smith, ed., *Richard Snowden Andrews: Lieutenant Colonel Commanding the First Maryland Artillery* (Baltimore: The Sun Job Printing Office, 1910), 48; McKim, *A Soldier's Recollections*, 150-51.

to toss Lieutenant Contee off the bridge. Wooten was down with a dangerous wound thought mortal by those around him.[80]

Private McCullough of the 2nd Maryland Battalion left a vivid account of the fighting. Andrews' artillerymen, he observed,

> had to stand alone the terrible onslaught made upon them, and nobly so they did it—on came the enemy swarming on their front, like the locusts of Egypt, but no sooner had they come within point blank range of their guns, then the curling smoke and the trembling air, told of the top rate energy of the men who stood by them—again and again hurling forth the death dealing missiles—cheer on cheer rent the air—the earth trembled and the sound of the conflict rolled far away into the distance—when suddenly the bull boys of war hushed their growling, everyone was still and the smoke wreaths of the battle drifted away and lo: a spectacle such wounds to bleed the hearts of rivals, met the astonished gaze—the broken and many lie ranks of the foe, reeling, discomfited and defeated, beyond range of the guns, that had already, in so short a space of time, piled the intervening space, with thousands of their wounded and slain.[81]

"Our canister is exhausted," wrote cannoneer Pvt. James W. Owens, who was out of commission with a wound, "and our case shots are cut to explode at a quarter of a second, and swathes are mowed in their ranks like grain before a reaper." Owens, despite his painful wound, finally retired to the rear, dashing from tree to tree to avoid being shot in the back. However, the brace of guns had taken quite a toll just when the exhausted, frantic Federals thought they could break through.[82]

Some of the attackers began to question the wisdom of continuing the fight. A frustrated Pvt. Edmund Snyder of the 123rd Ohio typified the growing sentiment: "Milroy ordered us to capture that battery when we could easily have passed it on the flank and continued on the retreat or compelled the enemy to come out and fight in the open. He evidently knew nothing at all about the situation. Three times we charged their position," he added, "and every time were repulsed with frightful loss." The regiment's assistant surgeon, Dr. William B. Hyatt, was among the wounded.[83]

---

80 Albert account, MHS; *Richmond Enquirer*, June 22, 1863. Dr. Hunter Maguire gave Albert a one in ten chance of living if he did not amputate the arm; the injured private quickly acquiesced. Artilleryman William T. Wooten was not as fortunate; he expired from his severe shoulder injury.

81 McCullough diary entry for June 15, 1863. McCullough badly exaggerated the number of Union dead and wounded, which was more likely in the dozens, not thousands.

82 Owens, "Heroic Defense of Bridge."

83 Snyder, *Autobiography of a Soldier of the Civil War*, 8.

To the south of the embattled 123rd Ohio, the rest of Ely's attacking regiments were also in trouble as they attacked the railroad cut. "A long line of fire streamed from thousands or rifles, interrupted now and then by the blaze of the battery," recalled a member of the 18th Connecticut. "Trees were peeled in all directions." The fatalities in this failed third charge included the New England regiment's youthful, Yale- educated Capt. Edward L. Porter. Two other Nutmeg captains suffered severe wounds but survived their ordeals.[84]

"The battle raged here for nearly 3 hours which we could not withstand any longer," admitted the 87th Pennsylvania's George Blotcher. "Having no field pieces … it would have been folly for us to stand there to be butchered up without any mercy." "After making three successive charges on them we were compelled to fall back," Cpl. Jacob M. Herr confirmed. "We were fighting at a disadvantage, and had a smaller force then [sic] they had. They were in the woods and had two batteries while we had to fight them in the open field and had no cannon." However, he added, General Milroy "was on the battlefield all the time, encouraging the troops."[85]

After pulling back toward the turnpike, Colonels Wilson and Ely sheltered their weary men behind a rise of ground. Lieutenant Colonel Monroe also rallied his 18th Connecticut and reformed them for another go at the strongly positioned Rebels. By then, desperation was starting to set in for Milroy's beleaguered division. The 18th Connecticut, this time unsupported, made a final frantic attempt to break Johnson's defensive line, also to no avail. "That was a hot fight in that early June morning," penned Charles Lynch. "The cannon and musketry firing was a great and awful sight to us young fellows, who were getting our first lessons in a real battle, a hard one and against great odds." Off in the distance, Pvt. David Emerson, one of the riders in Captain DeMotte's motley command, followed the unfolding action. "Our men were fighting like bulldogs," he said, but he expected that "they are all cut to pieces."[86]

Although the round was almost certainly not intended for him, during the final charge General Milroy barely escaped death when a shell grazed his leg and fractured a thigh bone in his black horse. Arch Rowand of the 1st West Virginia Cavalry and two other troopers were riding behind the general when the shell did its damage. The

---

84 Croffut and Morris, *The Military and Civil History of Connecticut*, 353; *New London* (CT) *Day*, April 30, 1892. Captain Porter was the third generation of his family to graduate from Yale. His father was the post surgeon at Fort Trumbull in New London.

85 Blotcher diary entry for June 15, 1863, YCHT; Herr diary entry for June 15, 1863.

86 Lynch diary entry for June 15, 1863. David Emerson to *Dear Transcript, New Creek, West Virginia, June 17, 1863, cited in Dear Transcript: Letters home from the boys and regiments of Windham County written to the editor of their hometown newspaper, 'The Windham County Transcript.'* (Danielson, CT: Killingly Historical & Genealogical Society, 2009), 293.

round also knocked down the horse of the man riding on Rowand's left. At the same time, another Rebel shell severed the leg of Pat Farley, who was just to the right. Rowand dismounted and handed his own horse to Milroy, who mounted the animal. He asked Rowand to lead the injured horse off the field, find his servant, and return with his white horse. Rowand complied and a few minutes later returned with the requested horse. As Milroy was in the act of dismounting from Rowand's horse, he gave it a profanity-laced compliment before riding off northward on the white one to look after the 110th and 122nd Ohio.[87]

McReynolds' Flanking Movement

In Winchester, now that it was light outside, several residents climbed once more onto their roofs to get a better understanding of what was transpiring. One lady had a clear view of Milroy's forts—and not a single Yankee was anywhere to be seen. It was obvious they had fled during the night, and the roar of battle could be heard well to the north of town. "Still the cannonading continued, and at intervals furious volleys of musketry," she recounted. "It immediately occurred to me that they were trying to cut their way through."[88]

General Milroy was desperately trying to turn both of Johnson's flanks simultaneously. While Colonel Keifer's Buckeyes moved northward, two of Col. Andrew McReynolds' regiments, the 6th Maryland and 67th Pennsylvania, arrived on the Martinsburg Pike and filed off to the right well south of Carter's Woods. Colonel John W. Horn and Lt. Col. William A. McKellip urged their Marylanders to keep close and step off promptly. The men used the cover of a stone wall along a dirt road to approach the left flank of Nicholls' Louisiana command near Milburn Cemetery. This movement, however, did not go totally unnoticed, and word quickly reached General Johnson. A career soldier in his third decade of service, the 47-year-old Virginian had fought in the Mexican War, Seminole Wars, and the Mormon Uprising in the Utah Territory. He was unflappable, determined, and not afraid of combat.[89]

"I can see him [Johnson] now, as I write," recalled Lieutenant McKim, "riding up and down, vehemently giving orders, and waving the big cane which he carried instead of a sword, because of the lameness which resulted from his wound at the battle of Alleghany [sic; where he received the nickname "Allegheny" Johnson]. His bravery and regardlessness of danger was an inspiration to the men, who responded with

---

87 Archibald H. Rowand to Dear Mother, June 21, 1863.

88 "Leaves from a Diary Kept by a Lady."

89 *OR* 27, pt. 2, 150-52. The dirt road is now McCann's Road.

alacrity to his example." Johnson sent a flurry of staff officers about the battlefield with orders as the situation unfolded. McKim narrowly escaped injury when he rode south to position the Louisianans' left flank. He rode along the western slope of the low ridge along Milburn Road, with Captain Raine's two guns higher on the elevation. However, he drifted too far up the hillside just as a cannon discharged its round at McReynolds' flanking column. A solid shot whizzed past his head, and the airwaves it created almost knocked him from his horse.[90]

About that time, Col. Jesse Williams arrived on the field with the 1st and 15th Louisiana regiments, which had been held in reserve to support Andrews' artillery line. As he rode to the front, Williams observed McReynolds' movement and ordered the 2nd and 10th Louisiana to change front perpendicular to the Martinsburg Road and attack the flanking force. To defend against this threat, the Marylanders and the 67th Pennsylvania formed into a line of battle off the dirt lane, but "the men had closed up too much," according to Lt. Colonel McKellip of the 6th, "and there was a little confusion; that is, it was necessary to take ground to the left." Once they were in proper order, they quick-timed to the Winchester & Potomac Railroad. Raine's section of Rebel rifles opened on them there at a range of about 600 yards. (Lt. Col. Andrews had previously repositioned these guns 200 yards to the left-rear and at a right angle from their previous position on the Milburn Road ridge.) The Federals made it to the shelter of the railroad as shells exploded above and around them.[91]

McReynolds ordered Maj. Michael Kerwin's 13th Pennsylvania Cavalry to charge Williams' left flank in an effort to drive off the guns. The Irish Dragoons had already had a scare when Captain DeMotte's motley command had earlier skedaddled near them. "The large and unofficered body, of course, ran at the first fire," the 13th's Sgt. George W. Nailer recalled, "creating some apprehension of panic, which was, however, by no means shared by the really military force." Undaunted, the regiment galloped toward the Rebel guns. "Some of the best fighting of the war was done at this time," Nailer claimed. "I never in my life, and others who have been in service for two years say the same, that was the hottest fighting ever done in western Va. The rebels shot rail road iron, from 12 to 20 inches long. I saw horses cut in two by one of the pieces. A whole set of 4's close in my rear was ground to powder."[92]

---

90 McKim, *A Soldier's Recollections*, 149-50. Johnson was also sometimes called "Old Clubby" due to the heavy walking stick that he used as a result of his combat wound. The battle was known as either The Battle of Camp Allegheny or Battle of Allegheny Mountain.

91 *OR* 27, pt. 2, 150-152, 512.

92 "From George Nailer to his parents, July 7, 1863, George W. Nailer Papers, Manuscript, Archives and Rare Book Library, Emory University, Atlanta; "Maryland Heights," *Philadelphia Inquirer*, November 6, 1863. Set of 4's refers to a team of four horses.

The energetic Johnson quickly moved Lambie's artillery section and one of Stonestreet's guns south of the bridge to support Captain Raine's battery. They hurled several rounds at the oncoming Union cavalry, forcing them back in some confusion. Several horses panicked and the situation deteriorated. "An officer dashed in among us and gave orders for every man to get away as best he could," one Keystoner recalled. "This order ended all discipline, and away we went, every one looking out only for himself . . . and as we left the field of battle farther and farther behind us, the noise became less and less until it died out altogether. We thus continued to madly dash on, but to where we knew not. We had only one object in view, and that to escape from our enemy."[93]

"The noise was terrific, and the danger great," McReynolds' adjutant, Capt. James Stevenson, recalled, "and we, at the head of the column, did not know that we had been deserted by the Thirteenth until we had got through the fire. On looking back over the field we saw the teams and artillery horses charging wildly to the rear, and our infantry running in all directions, with the charging enemy close behind them; and we knew then that the day was lost." "Away we started in all directions," wrote another trooper. "Every man was running for himself. Among the crowd of running men were infantrymen, artillerymen, sutlers, cavalrymen, servants and citizens who had followed us for no known reason. We must have presented a very fine appearance as we scattered down the valley."[94]

"The Thirteenth Pennsylvania cavalry, under Major Kerwin, fought desperately, but were forced to fall back under the murderous fire; every regiment began to take care of itself, and it attempted, and a portion of it succeeded, in forcing a passage by the east toward Harper's Ferry," observed a Union artillerist. Most of the cavalrymen headed for Berryville, but they captured a Confederate courier who told them the town was in Rebel hands, so they headed instead for Charles Town and eventually Harper's Ferry.[95]

Colonel McReynolds, who later claimed his troops "fought like devils," pulled back the 6th Maryland and 67th Pennsylvania and rode off to find the missing 1st New York Cavalry. The Empire State horsemen had been at the extreme rear of Milroy's column, but McReynolds was unable to locate them. He did not know they had ridden farther northward. He soon galloped off to the right to rejoin his two infantry

---

93 Ibid., 541; *Philadelphia Inquirer*, June 13, 1897. The 13th Pennsylvania Cavalry finally arrived on Bolivar Heights near Harpers Ferry about 4:00 p.m. where ladies presented the famished troopers with bread, cake, pie, and coffee.

94 Stevenson, *Boots and Saddles*, 194.

95 "The Loss of Winchester: A Narrative of the Investment and Abandonment of the Place"; McIlhinny, "Milroy at Winchester."

regiments, but now he could not locate them either. Accompanied only by two orderlies, the Irishman found himself virtually alone on the confused battlefield. Realizing his plight, he put spurs to his horse and fled the field. He splashed across Opequon Creek and headed for Harpers Ferry via the Charlestown Road. The brigade commander's battle was over.[96]

Meanwhile, Confederate Colonel Williams moved his Pelican Brigade by their left flank parallel to the Yankees until they discovered about 1,000 of the enemy. The Louisianans opened fire "with great success," in his opinion. The ever-present General Johnson arrived on the scene and personally took charge of the 2nd and 10th Louisiana. He kept the 1st and 15th Louisiana in reserve until needed. Williams later moved the latter two regiments to different positions as circumstances necessitated, but they were not actively engaged.[97]

When it became apparent the fighting to the north was not going well, McReynolds' two regiments tried to chop their way through the Rebel left. "We passed through the tunnel or arch, and down by a ravine, that protected us from the enemy's battery," the 6th Maryland's Lt. Colonel McKellip remembered. When the 67th Pennsylvania reached the John Easter house a great many soldiers broke ranks to get water and rest in the shady fenced-in yard and outbuildings. McKellip, in the van of the trailing 6th Maryland, stood in front of the gate and gave orders that none of his men could enter the premises. "From that point . . . the Sixty-seventh Pennsylvania ceased to be an organized regiment," he later reported.[98]

The 2nd Louisiana and the left wing of the 14th Louisiana, commanded by Capt. J. W. T. Leech, suddenly attacked the disorganized 67th. A brief but severe firefight ensued. The exhausted Pennsylvanians, having gotten little sleep since Friday night, could not put up much of a fight. Seventeen men, including Capt. Lynford Troch, died; 38 were wounded; and almost 400 surrendered. Col. John F. Staunton and 117 men scattered and escaped into nearby woods. The captives included 15-year-old William Keller, perhaps the youngest sergeant on the field. The 67th's battle flag became the 2nd Louisiana's prize. The regiment's popular major, Harry White, had

---

96 *OR* 27, pt. 2, 110.

97 Ibid., 512-14. "After marching all night," Captain E. D. Willett of the 1st Louisiana reported, "the regiment was formed into line of battle to the left of the Charlestown road, as a support to the Second, Tenth, Fourteenth, and Fifteenth Louisiana Regiments, but was soon after wheeled to the left, and advanced about 200 yards, to repel and attack upon the flank. Observing the enemy to be moving to our left, the regiment was moved by the left flank in a parallel line with them, and at a distance of 150 or 200 yards. We were then marched back to our original position, which was on the right of the Fourteenth Louisiana Regiment."

98 *OR* 27, pt. 2, 150-52. The tunnel was actually a railroad overpass.

Maj. Harry White of the 67th Pennsylvania Volunteer Infantry, who was also at the time a state legislator. *Library of Congress*

dismounted to fight on foot with his men and now was a prisoner. He was also a leading Republican in the Pennsylvania State Senate. Without his pivotal vote, the other 32 members deadlocked evenly between Republicans and Democrats and could not pass partisan legislation.[99]

Spotting the oncoming Rebels, Colonel Horn filed the 6th Maryland some 200 yards to the right into an open field. He formed into battle line and moved up the crest of the hill, where he encountered more Louisianans and Raine's rifled guns, a formidable line "too strong for us to cope with." Horn, McKellip, and Maj. Joseph W. Hill considered the situation to be hopeless because they were alone after the 67th Pennsylvania disintegrated. They withdrew to a heavily wooded ridge by the right flank in fairly good order. With all the chaos on the rest of the battlefield, they marched away, with every company maintaining its organization. Part of Company I, 1st Massachusetts Heavy Artillery joined them as they left the area. The gunless battery "had officers with it; they behaved well, and marched through in good order."[100]

The men of the 6th Maryland finally spotted an opportunity to make good their escape. "It was best to try to get around if we could so we started through the woods and by keeping through deep ravines and by making a circuitous route managed to elude them although they tried hard to cut off the retreat. There was a large force of

99   Ibid., 515; Edgar, *My Reminiscences of the Civil War*, 129; Scott, *History of Jefferson County, Pennsylvania*, 167; W. G. Lloyd, "Second Louisiana at Gettysburg," in *Confederate Veteran*, vol. 6, February 1898, 417. Adding the soldiers sick in the hospitals or captured elsewhere, the 67th lost more than 700 men in total. The enlisted men received paroles in October, well before Keller turned 16 on Christmas Day. When he enlisted he had told the recruiting officer he was 20. He finished the war as a 2nd Lieutenant, and received praise for valor at Sailor's Creek in 1865. The charismatic Harry White tried several times to escape from Libby Prison, earning him solitary confinement. After the war he was a two-term U. S. Congressman and an unsuccessful candidate for governor in 1872.

100 OR 27, pt. 2, 150-52.

cavalry followed us and pick up a good many of our stragglers," recounted George W. Hamilton in his diary. The unwell Hamilton, who was suffering the debilitating effects from heat exhaustion, fell out about 18 miles from Harpers Ferry. Along with three other men from his company, he headed toward Maryland Heights overlooking Harpers Ferry. The trio eventually made it to safety, their long and trying ordeal finally at an end.[101]

Debacle at Carter's Woods

By this time the embattled Yankees were in serious trouble, for a signal gun from Winchester warned Milroy that additional Confederates were now marching against his rear.

Unbeknownst to Milroy, Brig. Gen. John Gordon's brigade of Georgians had marched through town and was now heading north on the Martinsburg Pike toward the sound of the growing battle. When Milroy learned this, he realized his only hope of extracting the remnant of his division was to move farther north away from this new approaching threat. Colonel Keifer's 110th and 122nd Ohio regiments were, according to Milroy, "still maintaining their fire on the left with unabating energy. I then gave instructions that my forces unengaged and trains should retreat under cover of the contest, taking the Martinsburg road for a short distance, and then turning to the right." A long column of the 5th Maryland and 12th West Virginia, along with Milroy's mounted cannoneers, assorted rear echelon troops, several pro-Union residents, and some of the soldiers' wives and sweethearts, began moving past Carter's Woods.[102]

Anticipating Milroy's movement northward, "Allegheny" Johnson sent staff officers racing over to have General Steuart refuse his line at a sharp angle to the rear. Lambie's and Stonestreet's guns continued raining shells into the woods north of the Charles Town Road as Colonel Keifer slid the 110th and 122nd Ohio northward. Broken tree limbs tumbled down on the weary Buckeyes. Keifer had done a masterful job on that morning maintaining discipline despite mounting casualties. With their ammunition exhausted, his men retreated out of the woods into an open field, passing the helpless wounded. "These were upturned faces whose pleading, pitiful, despairing

---

101 Hamilton diary entry for June 16, 1863.

102 OR 27, pt. 2, 48; "The Evacuation of Winchester: A Defence of General Milroy," *Baltimore American and Commercial Advertiser*, July 6, 1863. The writer (known only as "B.") was a member of the 5th Maryland.

expression is in memory and heart today," remembered Lt. Henry Rush many years later.[103]

Milroy had yet to grasp the true gravity of his situation. Shortly after dawn, General Johnson pushed the late-arriving Stonewall Brigade forward to cut the Yankees' escape route on the Martinsburg Pike. Despite being weary and footsore, the Virginians hustled forward to the beat of heavy volleys of musketry. The three rear regiments (4th, 27th, and 33rd Virginia) swung south through the fields and then turned west toward the turnpike, while the 2nd and 5th Virginia continued to Steuart's position and formed in a clover field to the right of the Charles Town Road. Capt. Henry Kyd Douglas, Stonewall Jackson's former staff officer who was now attached to Johnson's staff, located General Walker and informed him that his entire command was needed on the right to cut off the Union retreat. Accordingly, Walker directed staff officer Lt. Charles S. Arnall to recall the 4th, 27th, and 33rd Virginia from the left and move them to support the 2nd and 5th Virginia on the right. Walker personally led the latter two regiments through the field to the right of the woods held by Steuart's brigade. They crossed the railroad and reached the Martinsburg Pike without encountering the enemy. That would soon change.[104]

"A strong and almost impregnable cordon of boys in grey" began surrounding Colonel Ely's regiments was how the 87th Pennsylvania's Lt. Col. James Stahle described the rapidly deteriorating situation. A large body of Walker's Rebels pushed past the regiment's left flank. Desperation and fear set in as the Pennsylvanians realized that fresh Confederate reinforcements had arrived. Realizing his position was compromised, Colonel Schall quickly ordered a retreat. He was frustrated that Milroy was nowhere to be found since he rode off to check on the 110th and 122nd Ohio. "I received no further orders," Schall later complained, "and could give no further instruction to my officers, as to our course." The move was executed with some uncertainty as Williams' Louisianans poured on musketry. Captain Wells A. Farrah, one of the most popular men in the Keystone regiment, was shot dead. His fall added to the confusion that was already coursing through the ranks. The Confederates firmly pressed the issue and the Union regiment lost cohesion and began breaking apart. Privates William H. Newman and John C. Hoffman dropped into the brush-choked ravine, where the thirsty soldiers drank the warm water flowing in Hiatt Run. Within seconds a line of Rebels topped a nearby hillside and shouted, "Surrender you blankety blank little Yanks." The duo darted through the ravine and across a field with

---

103 Rush, *Life and Writings*, 243-45.

104 *OR* 27, pt. 2, 517, 524. Arnall, the adjutant of the 5th Virginia, served as acting assistant adjutant general of the brigade.

Firing line of the 5th Maryland and 18th Connecticut at Carter's Woods.
William C. Walker, *History of the Eighteenth Regiment Conn. Volunteers*

the zip of Minié balls ringing in their ears. When the 87th's Pvt. Valentine "Tiny" Grove spotted a large number of overcoats lying on the field, he threw a dozen coats over his back and began to retreat all by himself. A Rebel promptly caught him by the arm and demanded, "Yank, I want you and your coats." Grove obeyed and surrendered.[105]

"Our little band was moving along regularly until we struck the picket line," claimed the 87th Pennsylvania's Cpl. John Keses. "Then it seemed almost as though the earth swallowed up a great portion of our host." The Rebels handily drove off the desperate attackers, shooting down men and horses by the score. The concussion from a bursting artillery shell flung Cpl. John T. Allison over a nearby fence. When he finally regained his senses, Allison found himself a prisoner of war. According to a Hanover, Pennsylvania, newspaper, its hometown Company G had "fought until it was considered madness to contend any longer." Once that moment arrived, many of the men began heading for the rear.[106]

---

105 Prowell, *History of the 87th Pennsylvania*, 85-86, 88. The 37-year-old Farrah was a prosperous and well known merchant from Wellsville in northwestern York County.

106 Keses manuscript, YCHT; Brandt database, YCHT; *Hanover* (PA) *Spectator*, June 26, 1863. The Spectator was one of the few female owned and operated newspapers in the county during the mid-19th century.

A large group of Pennsylvanians was approaching the Charles Town Road, where the wounded Contee's two guns were still blazing, when, recalled Stahle, "at last we knew we are entirely surrounded. There was nothing to do but surrender, or cut our way through at any cost, and the price will be: Death in all its shapes, bleeding wounds, desolate homes, widows and orphans." He reported that "the command came quick and sharp, 'by companies into line,' and 'forward.' Going but a short distance [Milroy] came thundering down the road, his grey hair streaming in the wind, his white horse flecked with sweat and foam, his hat waving in his hand as he shouted, 'The Eighty-seventh will charge that battery!'"[107]

This final attempt to break out was short, intense, and ultimately unsuccessful. Part of the 87th, supported by equally desperate elements of the 18th Connecticut and 5th Maryland, came within 60 yards of Contee's No. 2 gun, under Sergeant Glasscocke. A few Federals then surged toward it. "The Yankees made a final charge and got nearer than before, and we thought we were about to be captured," one of the anxious cannoneers recalled. They had exhausted their ammunition and were trying to withdraw when the Yankees came at them. However, because two or three dead horses were entangled in the harness, the crew was unable to withdraw the gun to safety. The 18th Connecticut's Cpl. William C. Tracy claimed to have bayoneted two of the artillerists. Tracy was turning to retreat when his cartridge box was blown completely off, but he managed to escape injury. Some of the surviving No. 2 cannoneers, hearing there was still ammunition left in the No. 1 caisson, raced over, grabbed the rounds, and hustled back to their bronze Napoleon. Their quick thinking and equally quick action helped drive the Yankee mass backward. "Their infantry fought desperately to cut their way out," reported a member of the Chesapeake Artillery. "They charged our batteries over and over again, but were driven back with terrible slaughter."[108]

The artillerists manning Contee's No. 2 artillery piece later expressed frustration with the the lack of support they received, especially from those who allegedly huddled in the railroad cut while the Federals attacked them. "So terrific was their fire," Pvt. J. W. F. Hatton complained, "that our infantry in the railroad cut received paralysis and refused to run up to shoot lest their bodies would be exposed to instant death."[109]

107 Stahle Papers, USAHEC.

108 *Richmond Enquirer*, June 22, 1863; *Zanesville* (OH) *Courier*, July 22, 1863; "Military Items," in *Hartford* (CT) *Courant*, July 17, 1863; J. Peter Williams to his wife, June 16, 1863.

109 John William Ford Hatton Papers, LOC.

Pvt. James C. Maguire was one of the bandsmen of the 87th Pennsylvania captured at Carter's Woods. The New York native survived captivity, returned home to his wife and five children, and resume his career as a tailor.
Chester Urban/Chris Buckingham

One officer in the 87th Pennsylvania claimed that General Milroy, unable to extricate his beleaguered command, lost his presence of mind that morning. The officer would later claim that Milroy uttered, "I know not what in God's name to do! Men, save yourselves!" before dashing off, trailed by most of his staff. The 5th Maryland's Dr. Charles Goldsborough described Milroy galloping "from the field with others off to the left, with the most pained expression on his face I ever saw. . . . I thought at the time his show was a poor one." Dement's Confederate battery fired some long-range shrapnel rounds at the general's party, but none of the iron rounds struck a target. "Everything was in confusion by this time," recorded George Blotcher of the 87th Pennsylvania. "By this time the fields were all dotted by scattered troops in all direction and the enemy close behind." The regiment's bandsmen threw away their heaviest instruments to lighten their load in their effort to get away.[110]

"We held the enemy in check until the General, his staff, and escort, left the field, guided by scouts through fields, on to Harpers Ferry," reported Charles Lynch of the 18th Connecticut. As the horses galloped away, whatever discipline remained with the weary infantrymen collapsed. "It was every man for himself, and the devil take the hindmost," admitted the 18th's Color Sgt. George F. Torrey. Unwilling to allow the flag to be captured, Torrey cut the silken flag from its staff, wrapped it around his chest, and covered it by donning his coat. Torrey slipped away in the confusion.[111]

An unidentified officer of the Wheeling battery who had escaped from the Star Fort mounted on one of the battery's horses also heard General Milroy yell to the men

---

110 *Harrisburg Patriot and Union*, July 4, 1863; OR 27, pt. 2, 442; Blotcher diary, YCHT; Keses manuscript, YCHT.

111 Lynch, *The Civil War Diary*, 21-22; *History of Battle-Flag Day*, September 17, 1879 (Hartford, CT: Lockwood & Merritt, 1879), 119; Walker, *History of the Eighteenth Regiment*, 440.

to look out for themselves. The officer and the survivors of the battery put spurs to their horses and made a flanking move to make good their escape. Most of the artillerists successfully escaped largely because they were mounted, and survived to fight another day. That was more than could be said of many of their comrades in the infantry.[112]

The Stonewall Brigade continued encircling Milroy's beleaguered command. The 2nd and 5th Virginia wheeled to the left straddling the Martinsburg Pike to block that escape route. The smoke and fog was so dense in the early light of day that the men on both sides could only see a few steps in front of them. Through the haze the Virginians spotted a faint column moving in the fields east of the pike and opened fire. However, some thought that perhaps they were firing on friends and the effort ceased. General Walker rode forward to ascertain their identity, turned his horse quickly back toward his own lines, and ordered his men to open fire once more. The Virginians also advanced, maintaining as heavy a fire as possible as they closed the distance with the Yankees.[113]

As Maj. James Newton led the 5th Virginia forward in tandem with Col. J. Q. A. Nadenboush's 2nd Virginia, many of the remaining Federals retreated into some woods west of the pike. Within a few minutes, a white flag was spotted waving amidst the trees. General Walker ordered his two regiments to cease firing, but to continue advancing toward the Yankees. Private Samuel Gray, the youngest member of Company E of the 87th Pennsylvania, concealed himself in a gully about one-half mile west of Carter's Woods. As the Virginians approached, he fired a shot and raced off amidst a shower of bullets. After running a long distance to the north, Gray eluded a squad of Confederate cavalry by darting behind a tree. His freedom would prove fleeting.[114]

The Union officer waving the white flag proved to be Colonel Ely. After the 18th Connecticut's final assault failed and they streamed back through Carter's Woods, Maj. Henry Peale had directed the regiment to move to the right and get away. The men retreated northwest into the meadows and pastures across the Martinsburg Pike. "For some reason, best known to himself," related Charles Lynch, "the Colonel [Ely] ordered a halt and surrendered to the enemy." While Peale, Lynch, and some 300 men kept going, Ely discovered he was nearly surrounded and decided to order what was left of the 18th Connecticut and 87th Pennsylvania, as well as some of the 5th

---

112 Letter from an Officer in the Wheeling Battery."

113 OR 27, pt. 2, 517.

114 OR 27, pt. 2, 524; *Wheeling Sunday Register*, May 3, 1891; Prowell, *History of the 87th Pennsylvania*, 88.

Maryland, to surrender. Most of the men stacked their arms as Ely waved the white canvas side of a rubberized blanket to notify the Rebels of his intentions.[115] "I at this time almost envied our boys who were killed (for there were many of them)," grumbled the disgusted James Smith of the 18th Connecticut.[116]

After halting near the tree line, the Virginians stood and watched as hundreds of Yankees slowly emerged from under the canopy. The 2nd and 5th Virginia "took too yankey ridgements and the bregde general," was how a Virginia private named Robert H. Depriest put it. "The officers road up to ours and gave up thare swords and horses." The men of the Stonewall Brigade loudly cheered their victory, but Walker moved quickly to silence them. As the men fell silent, he rode over next to the crestfallen Colonel Ely and remarked, "You gave us a lot of trouble yesterday and today." When Walker asked how Ely had broken his sword, the captured officer explained it had happened in the fighting. "You deserve to keep it," came Walker's generous reply. Ely had his soldiers stack their arms. Although many soldiers questioned the wisdom of Ely's decision to surrender, 18-year-old Pvt. Charles Porter, fighting in his first battle, waxed realistic. "We were thoroughly wearied by three days' incessant watching and fighting, and badly cut up by three successive charges," he explained, "and were twenty-five miles from supports, and entirely surrounded." Ely risked "great and useless slaughter" by resisting further.[117]

Across the fields to the south of Ely's surrender site, a large gaggle of Union prisoners taken earlier in the fighting stood at Mrs. Carter's house under a cordon of guards. West Virginia artilleryman Pvt. George McClelland, his appropriated sword now in Rebel hands, watched as the distant Union soldiers march forward with their arms at carry and their colors flying proudly overhead until they stopped in the field and began stacking arms and throwing off accoutrements. Confederates separated the captured officers from the roughly 300 captured enlisted men. Major Newton of the 5th Virginia took charge of the enlisted, and some soldiers from his regiment marched them down the pike to Stephenson's Depot. On their way, they encountered Sam Gray, the 87th Pennsylvania youth who had raced off after firing a final shot at the enemy. "Don't run any farther," a playful Virginian called out. "We 'uns have Martinsburg now." An unidentified colonel rode up, studied the young man for a few

---

115 Lynch diary entry for June 15, 1863; Walker, *History of the Eighteenth Regiment*, 118. In February 1864 Ely, with 108 other officers, escaped from Libby Prison in Richmond, but he was recaptured four days later after walking 42 miles. In May he returned to the 18th Connecticut after being exchanged.

116 James M. Smith diary, entry for June 15, 1863.

117 Depriest to Dear wife, June 15, 1863, Library of Virginia; Porter, "Daring and Suffering," 7.

moments, and teased, "That's the Yank I want to send home for a pet." After guarding Gray and the other prisoners at the depot for a short time, the 5th escorted them back to Susan Carter's house and turned them over to the 10th Virginia's Colonel Warren.[118]

At the Carter house, the new Yankee captives came under Miss Sue Pitman's relentless, sharp-witted tongue. "There she stood as the battle rages, firm and passionless as a statue," recalled the infatuated Sgt.-Major James Dalzell of the 116th Ohio who knew how to wield a poetic pen. "She stood unmoved, her arms folded, like a beautiful but pitiless goddess gazing down at the battle." Dalzell marveled that the beautiful "Spirit of the Battle" had somehow avoided being shot because her house was in the very center of the carnage and the contest had raged all around her for some time. Bullet and shell holes pockmarked the Carter house, but there she stood, bravely holding court on the veranda and rejoicing at the obvious Confederate triumph over Milroy's hated despots.[119]

Meanwhile, 280 men under the 87th Pennsylvania's Lt. Col. James Stahle escaped the fiasco by heading northwest across the pike through several fields and eventually reached Hancock, Maryland. Stahle's commanding officer, Col. John Schall, mounted a black stallion that belonged to Colonel Ely and led a separate contingent of 180 men toward Harpers Ferry. During the exhausting night march from Winchester, Pvt. James Fellers had shared part of the cheese wheel he had bayoneted from the overturned sutler wagon. He lost another chunk when the regiment engaged Johnson's Confederates around Carter's Woods. Now, on a march to escape, he divvied up the remainder, gladly accepting donations in return from his appreciative comrades.[120]

Corporal John Keses had a close call. His leather shoes, hard and cracked from wading creeks, hurt his feet so much that he fell behind. Firing to the rear was still brisk, so he pressed on. After passing through some woods, he and other footsore men hid in an adjoining clover field. Rebels approached the edge of the field and fired a few rounds before marching away. The Pennsylvanians waited until the coast was clear and then headed for the distant mountains. Corporal William M. Gill and several others finally discarded their brogans because their swollen and ulcerated feet could no longer take the agony. Their escape was not without some additional peril. "The

118 Ibid.

119 Dalzell, "A Lucky Blunder," 104.

120 Prowell, *History of the 87th Pennsylvania*, 81, 90; Schriver diary entry for June 15, 1863, YCHT.

Rebel Cavalry tried to gobble us up," penned George Schriver, "but we turned on them and emptied a few saddles and they left."[121]

One unfortunate Keystoner who did not make it out was George Dittenhaffer. Still nursing his groin injury, the unlucky 35-year-old private hobbled along until Confederates overtook him. Unbeknownst to the private, his laundress wife Elizabeth had made good her escape on her fleet horse, but Albert Jenkins' Confederate cavalry would eventually ride her down and capture her and scores of other refugees. Corporal Adam Morningstar was injured while leaping a ditch. A fleeing horse barreled into Pvt. John McConnell and knocked his head against a tree. Most of the regimental band fell into Rebel hands. Civilian sutler John M. Warner of Gettysburg, Pennsylvania, together with his wagonload of valuable merchandise, also fell into enemy hands.[122]

Chaos Reigns

Meanwhile, the 123rd Ohio's Colonel Wilson, realizing that Confederates blocked his route of retreat, looked behind his regiment and spotted Ely's white flag waving in the distance. Wilson briefly considered making a dash on horseback to cut his way out with some of men, but realized "the lives of many of my boys would no doubt have been sacrificed in the attempt. The sacrifice would have been too great for the results that might have been attained." Wilson reluctantly surrendered his remaining men. "A few minutes later," Capt. J. W. Chamberlain wrote, "we found ourselves with a new commander, in the person of Brigadier-General Walker, commanding the 'Old Stonewall Brigade.'" Walker's Rebels escorted their prisoners to the rear.[123]

Captain David S. Caldwell, a 42-year-old minister from Wyandot County, was one of Wilson's men now in Southern hands. "I was not without company in this unenviable position, for there were about one hundred and eight or ten officers besides myself, and some four thousand enlisted men captured at the same time," he later wrote. "The officers ranked from Colonel down to Second Lieutenant. Of the number of officers before mentioned, there were twenty-one belonging to my own

121 Keses manuscript and Schriver diary, both at YCHT.

122 Prowell, *History of the 87th Pennsylvania*, 89; Brandt database, YCHT.

123 *Norwalk* (OH) *Reflector*, December 22, 1863; William T. Wilson diary entry for June 15, 1863; Chamberlain, "Scenes in Libby Prison," 343.

regiment, including our Colonel, Lieutenant Colonel, seven Captains, and twelve Lieutenants."[124]

The fate of the 123rd Ohio's Company B was a happier one. The outfit had been detached to the wagon yard to secure the horses prior to the evacuation of Winchester. About daybreak and after riding four miles, the men heard scattered gunfire. "Then came the sound of hurried commands to the infantry forming in line of battle; then the crash of musketry," related Pvt. Henry Clapp. "Soon word came back to us that our troops were surrendering and that we should escape if possible." The company was opposite an orchard with a low stone wall between it and the pike when the glum news arrived. The Buckeye company's cavalry escort went over the wall and galloped through the orchard, with the mounted infantrymen behind them. The gunfire excited Clapp's horse, which charged over the wall and under the trees, almost knocking off its rider. The party reached a side road leading to the mountains, where Clapp and his comrades followed the cavalry at a "wild gallop."

Inexperienced at the art of riding a steed at full speed, Clapp still had his heavily laden knapsack on his back and his rifle musket slung over his shoulder. "There did not seem to be a concert of action between these articles and my horse. When he was going down they would be going up, and vice-versa, and I between them was getting the worst of it. I realized that it was necessary to throw some of my ballast overboard. My knapsack," he continued, "contained my scanty change of clothing and some useful little articles brought from home. I disliked to part with it, but it would not do to drop my musket. I had enlisted to save the Union, and I could never do it without a gun." Off went the knapsack. Clapp and most of Company B made it to the B&O Railroad station near Hancock, Maryland. Once there, they turned the horses over to the local cavalry commander and piled into boxcars for the welcome ride to safety. Another young Buckeye, Pvt. Ed Forester, and some comrades escaped by dodging into the woods. They lived on berries and water for three days before reaching Pennsylvania.[125]

While Ely and Wilson were surrendering, the 5th Maryland and some members of the 12th West Virginia formed as best they could and desperately attempted to cut their way through Walker's 4th, 27th, and 33rd Virginia. "The [1]4th La. and [3]3rd Va. brigades met the first assault," recalled the 4th Virginia's Pvt. Ted Barclay. "The enemy greatly outnumbering them drove them back a short distance, when Gen Johnson galloping along the line and told them the Stonewall [Brigade] was coming to

124 D. S. Caldwell, *Incidents of War and Southern Prison Life* (Dayton, OH: United Brethren Printing Establishment, 1864), 3-4.

125 *Norwalk* (OH) *Reflector*, December 22, 1863.

their support and they soon rallied and in turn drove the enemy; our brigade fired very few shots." According to the 5th Maryland's surgeon, Dr. Charles Goldsborough, the final charge was "a bloody one—the men fighting with desperation, although our line was fast melting away." Portions of the two regiments managed to break out and head for safety, but the rest threw down their rifled-muskets and threw up their hands. The 33rd Virginia seized the Marylanders' flag. At some point in the swirling fighting, the 12th West Virginia's Simon B. Siglin and his kinsman William Siglin were both killed. There would be plenty of mourning in Monroe County when that sad news reached home.[126]

The rest of Colonel Klunk's mountaineers and Col. James Washburn's 116th Ohio had formed a battle line just west of the turnpike and north of the bridge. They were near the section of Carter's Woods long occupied by Colonel Keifer's Ohioans. They remained under fire for several minutes before being ordered to the left of the Rebel line, beginning a series of frustrating and useless countermarches under fire. Before they tramped very far, they received orders to "make the best of our way to Bunker Hill," recalled Lt. Col. Thomas Wildes. After marching about half a mile, they men received orders to return to the fight, which by this time had shifted west of the pike. They turned onto a farm lane that ran at right angles to the road and marched for some distance before heading into the fields toward the rear of the 2nd and 5th Virginia. Before reaching the Rebels in the woods, Washburn received orders from Maj. J. Lowry McGee of Milroy's staff to fall back to the lane and make his retreat the best way possible. By then the firing had all but ceased, and "to attack the enemy at that time and place would effect no good," explained Washburn. After reaching the dirt lane, he encountered one of Milroy's scouts who was well acquainted with the country and offered to guide them over the West Virginia mountains to the Potomac River.[127]

The 116th Ohio moved off to the left into some woods, "skirmishing with an unseen foe," Lt. Colonel Wildes later recounted. The Buckeyes finally reached an open field, where they halted and reformed. There, they found Klunk's 12th West Virginia, some of Keifer's 110th Ohio, fragments of other regiments, a battalion of the 1st New York Cavalry, and about one-half of Moss's 12th Pennsylvania Cavalry. They settled on a course of retreat and Colonel Washburn took command of the infantry

---

126 Ted Barclay to Hannah Barclay Moore, June 19, 1863, near Sharpsburg, Maryland, Washington and Lee University; Walker, *History of the Eighteenth Regiment*, 115, 440; John B. Sheets diary entry for June 13, 1863, transcribed by Dale Harter, *The Harrisonburg-Rockingham Historical Society Newsletter*, vol. 31, no. 1, Winter 2009.

127 *OR* 27, pt. 2, 66; "Letter from the 116th O. V. I.," Thomas F. Wildes, Bloody Run, Pennsylvania, June 23, 1863, in *Athens* (OH) *Messenger*, July 2, 1863.

and Maj. Alonzo Adams the cavalry. Washburn marched away with his new impromptu command with the cavalrymen guarding their rear. "Knowing precisely the direction to take, and the point to make," Wildes added, "we were enabled in the confusion following the engagement, aided by the mist of early dawn, to get well on our way before we were discovered by the rebels." These remnants of Milroy's command headed for Berkeley Springs, West Virginia, hoping to march from there to Hancock, Maryland.[128]

One of the men in Washburn's column was the 12th West Virginia's 30-year-old Lt. James Durham, the heroic officer who had led a charge over the stone wall near the Glen Burnie estate the previous afternoon (for which he would later receive a Medal of Honor). Despite his shattered right arm, Durham accompanied the Mountaineers in their withdrawal. Still bleeding profusely, he somehow rode 45 miles on a saddle-less horse to escape capture. It would be six months before he could rejoin the regiment in the field.[129]

After their frantic gallop northward on the turnpike and subsequent movement into the fields west of the turnpike, the 1st New York Cavalry began slowly trotting away from the debacle. Major Adams halted the regiment, "as if he wanted to see all that was to be seen," Lieutenant Beach scorned. Someone urged the unpopular commander to go on instead of waiting longer where nothing could be done. "I am in no hurry to get out of here," Adams is said to have responded. His arch-rival Major Quinn exploded, thundering "I noticed you *were* in a hurry to get out of where you were a few minutes ago." Many of his supporters exclaimed, "Hurrah for Major Quinn!" or "Bully for Tim Quinn!" Some shouted, "Quinn take command and lead us out, and let the other major stay if he wants to!" Lieutenant Beach and scores of men had no confidence in Adams' strategy. "Reckless bravado was not always the courage that won," he later mused.[130]

"The whole brigade was a disorganized mob," declared James Suydam of the 1st New York Cavalry. "And it is evident that every man was for himself." Suydam and a handful of other Union horse soldiers from the 12th and 13th Pennsylvania Cavalry regiments made their escape by jumping their horses over a fence and then dashing through the woods. One of the troopers rode a white horse, and the Confederates mistook him for Milroy who was also known to ride a white horse. Consequently, "they threw shells at our party for 4 miles and the Rebel cavalry tried to flank us, but

---

128 Wildes, *Record of the One Hundred and Sixteenth Regiment Ohio Infantry*, 59-60.

129 Beyer and Keydel, *Deeds of Valor*, 211. Durham survived the war with the rank of captain. He died in 1904 and is buried in Arlington National Cemetery.

130 Ibid., 244.

we escaped and were obliged to pass through Charles Town, the place where John Brown was executed, but the rebs to our good luck were not there and we then came to Harper's Ferry." The rest of the survivors of the 1st New York Cavalry "led the vanguard of what remained of Milroy's Army, fighting our way through a tremendous force placed between us and Martinsburg for the purpose of surrounding us. Here it was that our regiment charged upon a rebel battery, taking it but being without infantry support could not hold it." The New Yorkers did not stop until they reached Hancock, Maryland, on the Potomac River.[131]

Colonel Keifer Breaks Out

To the north of Ely's and Wilson's surrender sites, the remaining men in the 110th and 122nd Ohio regiments remained full of fight. The man who led them, the capable Colonel Keifer, was a frustrated man that morning. Despite his best efforts, he knew next to nothing about how the fight was progressing at other points along the line. When the firing died down and nothing was left to be heard except occasional shots from the direction of Winchester, he concluded the object of the attack was accomplished so far as possible and the non-combatants had sufficient time to escape. "It was now day—dawn, and we could not hope to further surprise the enemy or long operate on his flank," he explained. "About 5 A.M., therefore, I ordered the whole line withdrawn from the woods, and resumed the march northward along the Martinsburg road. I was soon joined by Generals Milroy and Elliott and by members of their staffs, but with few men. Milroy had personally led a charge with the 87th Pennsylvania and had a horse shot under him, but there was no concert of action in the conduct of the battle."[132]

Milroy knew time was rapidly running out. He pointed northward and told Kiefer, "Every man fight your way through to Harper's Ferry. Do not go on the pike, it is patrolled by the enemy, and you will be captured." The quick-minded Keifer rode closer to Milroy. As he did so, a bullet cut through the leg of his pants and just missed his ankle. "General," asked the unfazed officer, "shall I oblique my regiment to the left and charge those fellows yonder in the woods?" It was a bold risk, for Keifer was offering to charge the Rebels despite his exhausted ammunition in order to give them the impression that reinforcements were arriving from Harpers Ferry. Milroy thought a moment and replied, "Yes, if you think you can, do it."[133]

---

131 Black, *A Lincoln Cavalryman*, 128, 130; "Veritas," letter of July 24, 1863.

132 Keifer, *Slavery and Four Years of War*, 1:167.

133 Rush, *Life and Writings*, 243-45.

Monument to Lt. Col. R. Snowden Andrews near Stephenson's Depot. *Scott Mingus*

Keifer moved his regiment into oblique line a few hundred feet to the left and ordered the advance. The Confederates took the bait. Apparently concerned it was a trap, they yielded their ground rather stand or countercharge. Keifer's bold tactic opened gaps in the Rebel lines and some of the Buckeyes surged through, albeit disordered and split apart. "The retreat was now in full progress," admitted Pvt. Lorenzo Barnhart, "the two columns by different routes—and it was impossible to unite them." He and several other soldiers made their escape, leaping across a wide brook.[134]

As a result of Keifer's quick-thinking, the 110th Ohio would exit the fighting with one of the lowest percentages of men captured that fateful morning. "It was Keifer's strategy that saved Milroy's army—that hewed the gap and swung the gate of its escape," believed Lieutenant Rush. "Milroy was a brave, daring, dashing General, but he had not the coolness and instant calculation for a critical and unforeseen situation."[135]

Meanwhile, Colonel Ball's 122nd Ohio was facing its own predicament. "What some of the other regiments were doing all this time, I know not," Sgt. David Danhauer wondered. "I fear they were not doing their duty." As the left of the 2nd Virginia approached from the turnpike, according to Lt. James J. Hartley, they "got us to cease firing by hallooing to us to cease firing for God Sake that we were firing on our own men. And a part of them were dressed in our clothes so that we could hardly tell whether they were our men or not." At some point in the swirling fighting, the 122nd's Capt. Charles J. Gibeaut was killed in action.[136]

George Steuart's 1st and 3rd North Carolina and 10th Virginia climbed out of the railroad cut and headed toward the beleaguered Ohioans. "I don't remember in what order the colonel got us out of the cut," the 10th Virginia's Cpl. "Sonnie" Lauck said,

---

134 Ibid.; Barnhart, *Reminiscences*, OR 27, pt. 2, 49.

135 Rush, *Life and Writings*, 245.

136 Hartley, *Civil War Letters*, 40-42; *Official Army Register*, Part 5, 218.

"but I know that we passed a dead horse badly mangled lying at the corner of the woods directly in front of the howitzer with an officer's saddle on it, showing that there was at least one brave man in front of us who had doubtless tried to get his men to charge across that deadly open space, but in the three charges they made against us failed to get them to leave the shelter of the big trees."[137]

"Our brigade [Steuart's] was quickly formed in line of battle," the 1st North Carolina's Cpl. William H. Proffit wrote to his father a few days later, "stretching across the road on which the Yankees were retreating. The Yanks then saw that their only hope to escape depended upon breaking our line & forcing their way through, and I tell you they went to work in good earnest. They raised a most hideous yell and came at us like they expected to accomplish all their designs. Our boys lay low and kept their cool until the Yankees came within about 30-40 steps when a most deadly volley was poured into them which caused them to change direction quickly."[138]

The 122nd Ohio's Lieutenant Hartley deemed the precarious position a "hornet's nest" as Steuart moved to cut them off. "We then found we had been surrounded on every side and had to cut our way out, which we did with as hard fighting I expect as ever was done by a set of men." Company A's Sergeant Danhauer narrowly missed serious injury when a bullet zipped through his pants leg. Standing next to him, Pvt. Samuel Maxwell suffered a gunshot wound to his arm. Instead of surrendering, Col. William Ball and a large portion of the regiment decided to fight their way to safety. "The Rebs had it fixed and fixed well to take all of us if we had not fought like Bulldogs," Hartley added. After extricating themselves, he and Company E took off as the Rebels "sent a shower of bullets after us which appeared to fly almost as thick as hail in any hail storm that I ever had seen." He and 46 of his company safely made it to Harpers Ferry.[139]

The Fighting Ends

The battlefield around Carter's Woods and the Martinsburg Pike-Charles Town Road intersection had degenerated into mass confusion in the morning mists and wafting gun smoke. The Union lines had broken at nearly every point. To complete the rout, the capable Lt. Col. Snowden Andrews decided to charge through the

---

137 Lauck, "The Little Corporal's Story."

138 William H. Proffit to Dear Father, Camp near Sharpsburg, Maryland, June 22, 1863, Proffit Family Letters, Wilson Library, UNC-Chapel Hill. Corporal Proffit would not survive the year, dying in October in a hospital in Gordonsville, Virginia.

139 Hartley, *Civil War Letters*, 40-42; *Zanesville* (OH) *Courier*, July 22, 1863.

enemy's shattered lines with Stonestreet's section of guns and open fire into their rear. However, a shot from a Union sharpshooter struck him in the arm. Although the wound was severe (and his third of the war), the round missed striking any bone. After he staunched the bleeding, Andrews rode back to the bridge only to find Lieutenant Contee lying on its deck surrounded by dead and wounded gunners. Though in considerable pain from a broken bone in one leg and a nasty flesh wound in the other, Contee raised himself and said with no little satisfaction, "Colonel, I have a sergeant and two men, and the enemy is retreating." By this time, 14 men and 18 horses had been shot and Contee had precious little case shot left. Andrews' had ordered him to hold the bridge until the last man—and so he had. According to Pvt. James W. Owens, an admiring Robert E. Lee later exclaimed that the "heroic self-sacrifice of those men was a second Thermopylae." Like the ancient Greeks, Contee's cannoneers had bravely withstood overwhelming odds to buy time for the rest of the army.[140]

Late in the fighting the 27th Virginia spotted a large contingent of Yankees attempting to escape toward Jordan Springs. However, before he could attack them Lt. Col. Daniel M. Shriver received orders to move back past the turnpike to help in the fighting there. "The Yankees are running as fast as they can," noted Lt. Alfred M. Edgar. "We too are running as fast as we can and yelling our best." There, they captured scores of Federals as well as the 5th Maryland's regimental colors and a company flag. General Johnson, however, had spotted the group trying to flee toward the springs. He ordered one of Raine's guns to intercept them. Seeing the limbered cannon approaching, several hundred enemy soldiers surrendered to seven nearby Confederate infantrymen. The 27th's John Garibaldi later gushed, "This was the cheapest victory ever was achieved without the loss of so many lives."[141]

One of the last Confederates to die at Carter's Woods was Capt. John S. R. Miller. A former soldier in the antebellum U. S. Army in Utah and Nebraska, Miller at the outset of the war joined the 1st North Carolina as its adjutant. Severely wounded in

140 OR 27, pt. 2, 542; Smith, *Richard Snowden Andrews*, 96; Owens, "Heroic Defense of Bridge," *Richmond Enquirer*, June 22, 1863. Unfortunately for Andrews and the Confederacy, his third wound ended his battlefield service. The unlucky officer was first struck during the Seven Days' Battles. He recovered and was in command of artillery at Cedar Mountain when he was almost disemboweled by an artillery fragment. The intrepid officer had the presence of mind to hold his intestines in place when he fell from his horse, but spent hours on the battlefield before help found him. He defied all odds by recovering, but the wound outside Winchester that June ended his career in the field and sent him to Germany as an envoy. Andrews survived the war and lived for another four decades before dying in Baltimore in 1903. An impressive monument along the Martinsburg Road (present-day Route 11) commemorates his heroism and that of Contee's cannoneers.

141 OR 27, pt. 2, 527, 541; Wise, *The Long Arm of Lee*, 607; John Garibaldi to his wife, Sarah, June 16, 1863, VMI.

the foot at Mechanicsville in late June 1862, the young Tar Heel recovered and assumed command of Company H. Late in the fighting on June 15, a small party of Union soldiers was trying to gain the regiment's rear. "He met them," a comrade recalled, "and in the last volley of enfilading fire before surrendering a fatal ball pierced his temple and killed him instantly; thus has fallen another brave son of North Carolina."[142]

Allegheny Johnson himself got caught up in the excitement. He reportedly captured 30 demoralized Yankees by using nothing more than his opera glass. Johnson and Milroy had tangled numerous times during the early days of the war with Johnson besting the Grey Eagle more than once on the field of battle. However, Milroy had launched a successful sneak attack upon Johnson's Camp Allegheny using spies during the winter of 1861-1862, infuriating the Confederate general. Further, some of Milroy's troops had inflicted the severe wound to his ankle at McDowell, so Johnson had nursed a particular hatred for the Grey Eagle. "General Johnson had a special aversion to Milroy," noted a Winchester newspaperman, "and wanted to capture him."[143]

Johnson's eyes flashed as he contemplated the prospect of seizing the opportunity to deliver a *coup de grace* to his long-time adversary. Alas, his effort to do so would not come to fruition. "General Johnson, in his eagerness, pursued with his staff and bodyguard until he was far in advance of any organized troops and simply commanding skirmishers," recounted staff officer Maj. Henry Kyd Douglas. "In rushing across the Opequon Creek he rode into a deep hole, and both horse and rider were soon foundering in the depths. With assistance he reached the shore safely and one of the pursued Federals jumped into the creek, rescued the General's hat and brought it to him and surrendered. This called a halt to our part of the pursuit, and we returned to the troops." Once again, and to his great disappointment, Johnson's despised foe had slipped from his closing grasp.[144]

At least one Confederate regiment attempted an impromptu pursuit. "So the infantry gathered up the wagon horses and mules and mounted them," related the 33rd Virginia's John Casler, "bareback and in every way, as best they could. They were the hardest looking cavalry regiment I ever saw, with their knapsacks and blankets around their shoulders; with their long rifles and no saddles, and blind bridles, and

142 *North Carolina Standard* (Raleigh), July 22, 1863. See also William H. Proffit to Miss R. L. Proffit, Shepherdstown, West Virginia, June 18, 1863, UNC-Chapel Hill. Miller, of Caldwell County, was one of the few fatalities in the 1st North Carolina that day.

143 Gregg S. Clemmer, *Old Alleghany: The Life and Wars of General Ed Johnson* (Staunton, VA: The Hearthside Publishing Co., 2004), 449-450.

144 Douglas, *I Rode with Stonewall*, 242; Noyalas, *"My Will is Absolute Law"*, 112.

mounted on mules and horses promiscuously. Away they went down the pike, as hard as they could go, yelling and firing, as if it were big fun for an infantry man to be mounted in any shape. They were after the wagon train ahead of the infantry, and made a fine capture." Casler opined that, "General Ewell was a good officer, and our corps preferred him to any other after we had lost General Jackson. He did well in routing Milroy from Winchester, but Jackson (in my opinion) would have marched all night the night we went into camp, and by daylight would have had his line of battle around Winchester, and captured the whole command. Our corps was rather anxious to capture Milroy, as he had tyrannized over the citizens of Winchester, insulting ladies (so it was reported), and rendering himself obnoxious in different ways—more so than any Federal General had done during the war; and if he had been captured by some of our men he would have fared badly." Captain James H. Wood of the 37th Virginia, however, believed, "If there was a lack of wise leadership on the part of the enemy it was in not retiring in time."[145]

According to General Walker, the Stonewall Brigade seized 713 non-commissioned officers and privates, 83 commissioned officers, and six stands of colors. His prisoners included Colonels Ely and Wilson, Lieutenant Colonels Monroe Nichols of the 18th Connecticut and Robert S. Northcott of the 12th West Virginia, and two or three other field officers. Another captive was English-born Lt. Thomas Morley of the 12th Pennsylvania Cavalry, who had served as a young officer in the 17th Lancers in 1854 during the famed "Charge of the Light Brigade" during the Crimean War. "We succeeded in capturing five regiments without firing a shot," proudly claimed one of Walker's men. "In fact we took more prisoners than we had men in our brigade." However, John O. Casler of the 33rd Virginia bemoaned the fact that he and his fellow soldiers had not arrived sooner. "We were in their rear, and if we had been one hour sooner," he argued, "we would have had our line formed across the road and captured the whole 'outfit.'"[146]

After hearing news of the overwhelming victory, a jubilant Lt. Gen. Richard Ewell sent a courier galloping off to find General Rodes at Berryville and order him to intercept the fleeing Milroy, "but he [Rodes] was not in position to intercept him,

---

145 Casler, *Four Years in the Stonewall Brigade*, 167; James H. Wood, *The War: "Stonewall" Jackson: His Campaigns and Battles, the Regiment as I Saw Them* (Cumberland, MD: Eddy Press, 1910), 137.

146 James Falkner, "A 17th Lancer in the American Civil War: Thomas Morley," The Victorian Military Society website, http://www.victorianmilitarysociety.org.uk/index.php/research/2012-09-09-11-20-22/archive/49-a-17th-lancer-in-the-american-civil-war-thomas-morley, accessed February 24, 2013; John P. Welsh to Becky, June 15, 1863, Welsh Family Papers, State Library of Virginia, Richmond; John O. Casler, *Four Years in the Stonewall Brigade* (Girard, KS.: Appeal Publishing Co., 1906), 166. Walker's mixed bag of prisoners came from the 18th Connecticut, 123rd Ohio, 5th Maryland, and 87th Pennsylvania.

Jenkins' cavalry being already (10 a.m. 15th) on the Potomac, near Williamsport." Many Confederate infantrymen, still milling about the area near Carter's Woods and Stephenson's Depot, expected to pursue the fleeing Yankees, but no orders came. "I sespect we will go on. We are wating for the wagons to come up to cook I recon," later penned the 2nd Virginia's R. H. Depriest in a letter home to his wife.[147]

Milroy fled the field before the battle ended, drawing scorn from many of his previously loyal men when the story spread among the prisoners. "It was mortifying, indeed," wrote one of the 18th Connecticut, "to be compelled to surrender to the rebels, who were dirty, ragged, and insulting in their taunts and jeers. They asked our boys how they liked to fight under Milroy. How they liked the situation; and taunted them with being Milroy's thieves. Inquired if we had not better staid at home, and said they were on their way to Philadelphia, Baltimore, and Washington."[148]

"The only thing I regret is that old Milroy made his escape," grumbled a Virginia artillerist. "He got out yesterday morning with the cavalry." Despite the failure to nab Milroy, the Confederate victory was nearly complete. They had every reason to gloat.[149]

147 OR 27, pt. 2, 442; Depriest to Dear Wife, June 15, 1863, Library of Virginia.

148 Walker, *History of the Eighteenth Regiment*, 119.

149 J. Peter Williams to his wife, June 16, 1863.

Chapter 10

Monday, June 15, afternoon and evening

"What had become of Lieutenant or Captain or Colonel So and So?"

— *Pvt. I. G. Bradwell, 31st Georgia*[1]

After the Stephenson's Depot fight

It took less than two hours to rout the overconfident Yankees, and now the important turnpike to the Keystone State was wide open. General Ed Johnson, normally an unflappable professional described by gunner W. Owens as "apparently a man without emotion," was beside himself with unbridled joy. Johnson rode to a house on the Charles Town Road behind his lines to visit Snowden Andrews' wounded artillerists who had been taken there. Tears glistened in his eyes and his voice choked with emotion when he exclaimed, "Men of the 1st Maryland, you have been fighting like men of your own State and have captured a stand of Maryland colors. They rightfully belong to you, and you shall have them."[2]

Johnson had not needed the reinforcements that marched to the sound of the guns from Winchester, including Col. I. E. Avery's 54th North Carolina from Jubal Early's division. Still guarding the Romney Road east of Dr. Lupton's house, the rattle of musketry in the direction of the Martinsburg Road woke the Tar Heels in the pre-dawn darkness. "Then the truth was clear that Milroy was attempting to escape," a

---

1 Bradwell, "The Capture of Winchester," 332.

2 Owens, "Heroic Defence of Bridge." Andrews went to the Milburn Road house of John Easter, whose brother in Baltimore knew Andrews. The colonel stayed there until July 4 or 5, when he was well enough to rejoin his battery near Hagerstown during Lee's retreat from Gettysburg. See Smith, *Richard Snowden Andrews*, 48-49). The old 1st Maryland had been reconstituted as the 2nd Maryland.

soldier wrote. "Every man was up in a moment, with musket in hand, eager to go to the assistance of the Stonewall Brigade. Soon orders came; we marched in double quick about five miles, but were too late to fire a gun. The Yankees had shown the white feather and were marching back towards Winchester under guard." The North Carolinians went into camp and rested for the rest of the day.[3]

Ahead of the Tar Heels, Brig. Gen John Gordon's Georgia brigade approached the battlefield. After taking possession of the garrison flag at the Main Fort in the pre-dawn hours, Gordon had sent an officer to communicate with General Early before moving "as rapidly as possible in the direction of the firing, distinctly heard, on the Martinsburg pike. My brigade reached the point where a portion of Johnson's division engaged the retreating enemy only in time to assist in collecting horses and prisoners." The baritone Rev. Charles C. McCabe, who had serenaded General Milroy the night before the battle, and the 122nd Ohio's surgeon, Dr. William M. Houston, were among the prisoners brought to General Gordon. McCabe had retreated from Winchester with the 122nd Ohio's commissary, who asked him what he had done with his tent. "I folded it up," McCabe had answered just as firing started at Carter's Woods. McCabe and Dr. Houston had panicked initially, each running in different directions in their confusion. Colonel Ball and their regiment had eventually cut their way through to safety, but the preacher and physician "held a council of war" behind a tree. "Chaplain," Houston stated, "I want you to stay with me and help with the wounded soldiers." They decided to stay behind. Soon, a Rebel provost-marshal encountered them and escorted them to General Gordon.[4]

When the charismatic Georgian learned why these two men had lingered when they could have slipped away with their unit, he sympathetically told an orderly, "Let them have fifty soldiers and all the ambulances they want to help get their wounded off the field." McCabe and Houston enlisted several other captives to help with the task. When they were finished, they presented themselves to General Early, who had taken overall command in Winchester. McCabe announced, "General Early, we are a company of surgeons and chaplains who have stayed behind to look after the wounded; we have finished our work and would like very much to be sent through [the Confederate line] to our regiment." Early smiled, turned to McCabe, and remarked, "You are a preacher, are you?" When McCabe answered in the affirmative, the volatile Early answered, "Well, you preachers have done more to bring on this war than anybody, and I'm going to send you to Richmond." The Southern capital was 150

---

3   The *Spirit of the Age*, August 10, 1863.

4   OR 27, pt. 2, 491; Maryniak, Benedict R., *The Spirit Divided: Memoirs of Civil War Chaplains* (Macon, Georgia: Mercer University Press, 2007), 188-89.

miles away, protested the reverend, while Harpers Ferry was only 30 miles away. Early responded by saying, "They tell me you have been shouting, 'On to Richmond'" for a long time, and to Richmond you shall go." To their dismay, McCabe and Houston were headed for Libby Prison instead of Harpers Ferry.[5]

Meanwhile, General Gordon's soldiers continued policing the battlefield. A long line of captured wagon and artillery trains clogged the turnpike. While the Georgians paused to allow them to pass, Pvt. Gordon Bradwell noticed hundreds of U. S. army horses and mules grazing on a field of clover. The 1st North Carolina Infantry rode up mounted on captured horses and its members boasted they would henceforth serve as cavalry. The news prompted some jealousy within the ranks of the Georgians, but the Tar Heels eventually had to turn over their mounts to the quartermaster and return to the ranks of "Jackson's foot cavalry." Before they did, however, they "rode all day & overtook several straggling Yankees which we carried back with us," reported Cpl. William H. Proffit. "Our boys enjoyed the sport very much."[6]

Near Private Bradwell and the clover field stood a grove of trees. "All the bright colors of the rainbow, all the finery displayed in the most fashionable shops of a city seemed assembled there in that strip of woods," wrote the private. "What could it mean? In a few minutes they started toward us, two and two, led by a gray-clad soldier. When they reached us, we found they were the wives and sweethearts of our enemies, who, in their haste to follow the army, had put on their most costly attire and mounted the army wagons and horses in an effort to escape. As they passed us all were in tears and excited our sympathy by their hasty inquiries as to what had become of Lieutenant or Captain or Colonel So and So." Guards escorted the frightened women and children into Winchester, where the pro-secessionist women rejoiced at their sudden change in fortune. "Some of them were dressed elegantly," recalled Kate McVicar, "and how they did bewail the loss of their baggage and being captured by the Rebels."[7]

Confederate soldiers eventually identified General Milroy's personal baggage wagon among the hundreds of abandoned military and sutler wagons. Stories circulated that the wagons contained a box of silverware bearing the Logan name

---

5 Ibid. Reverend McCabe was released later in 1863, but his health was broken. He resigned his chaplaincy on January 8, 1864, and returned to Ohio. The fiery Methodist eventually recovered and resumed his prolific ministry and public service until his death in 1906. The 41-year-old Dr. Houston was held in Libby Prison for five months before returning to his role as the 122nd Ohio's surgeon. He became the surgeon-in-chief of the 2nd Brigade, 3rd Division, 6th Corps in January 1864. Houston mustered out on June 26, 1865. He died in 1900.

6 OR 27, pt. 2, 491; Bradwell, "The Capture of Winchester," 331-32; William H. Proffit to Dear Father, Camp near Sharpsburg, Maryland, June 22, 1863, UNC-Chapel Hill.

7 Bradwell, "The Capture of Winchester," 331-32; McVicar Collection.

taken from the mansion the Grey Eagle had appropriated for his own use. Old John M. Mayson, well known to Winchester's senior citizens, watched as Rebels discovered many other items seized from the Logan house for use in the Union headquarters. Rumors spread that Milroy had been captured or that he had escaped during the night disguised in civilian or women's clothing. Later and less sensational reports confirmed his escape from the battlefield with his cavalry escort. Another tale circulated that the Yankee attack had killed or maimed old William "Extra Billy" Smith. This, too, was soon refuted. Very much alive and unharmed, the 65-year-old general once again won the governorship. "We defeated the enemy badly at Winchester on Saturday," announced some Northern newspapers still unaware of the disaster at Carter's Woods. "They made five attacks, were driven back with heavy loss, and at the last onslaught were effectively routed after a severe battle." A correspondent in Baltimore was smart enough to add the caveat, "Such, at least, is the information now at hand."[8]

Near Stevenson's Depot, Col. Jesse Williams' Second Louisiana Brigade secured enough captured horses branded "U. S." to mount nearly the entire brigade. The Louisianans triumphantly rode back toward Winchester making sure to pass Harry Hays' First Louisiana Brigade's camp north of town. They arrived just as Hays' Tigers were sitting down to the special treat of fresh coffee brewed from captured Yankee stores. Some of Hays' men celebrated their own prize that morning when Col. William Monaghan and a 30-man patrol of the 6th Louisiana seized 250 Yankees and their colors, a matter of intense pride for the Southern Irishmen.[9]

Other patrols roamed the region searching for hidden Yankees. About 20 members of Captain Alexander's Baltimore Battery and other Federal soldiers had taken refuge in a barn off the Martinsburg Pike. In an effort to keep their weapons out of Rebel hands, Pvt. Fred Wild stashed his short sword under the barn. He and his comrades also removed the chambers from their revolvers, broke off the barrels, and threw the pieces every direction. Before long, a lone Confederate officer approached with a black servant carrying a string of captured pistols slung over his shoulder. When the Rebel learned the Yankees revolvers had been broken apart, he forced one of the cannoneers to collect the pieces at gunpoint. He departed as a "fierce looking" cavalryman took his place. The rider dismounted when he saw Wild and extended his hand in surprise and pleasure. The two had been schoolmates in Baltimore before the war. Wild did not have such luck when more Confederate horsemen arrived. One swapped his broken down nag for the youth's beautiful gray. Wild tenderly kissed his

8   McVicar Collection; *Raleigh Register*, June 20, 1863; "Letter from Baltimore," correspondence of the *Philadelphia Inquirer*, reprinted in the *Daily Milwaukee News*, June 21, 1863.

9   M. H. Ackerd, "Early's Brigade at Winchester," in *Confederate Veteran*, vol. 29, February 1921, 264; *Richmond Enquirer*, June 23, 1863.

trusted horse goodbye before the Rebel led it away. Another cavalryman snatched Wild's gaudy red-tasseled, black-plume felt hat from his head and replaced it with a "dilapidated, torn and ragged old straw hat." Yet another Rebel took that hat and left Wild with a gray VMI cadet cap several sizes too small. Once that final humiliation was complete, Wild and his comrades were marched back into Winchester.[10]

A young lieutenant from the Rebel 2nd Maryland Battalion rode up to an unidentified soldier of the 110th Ohio and exclaimed, "You are riding a d——n fine horse. You are my prisoner—come with me." The pair headed back down the turnpike to Winchester, with the Baltimore officer allowing the Buckeye to remain mounted. After entering town, the pair visited one of the Rebel's friends and left their horses there. When the Rebel asked the Yankee if he wanted to eat, the Buckeye replied yes and mentioned his lady-friend Susan's home. To his astonishment, the Rebel told him to go there himself because he wanted to visit others. "The citizens along the street were a little suspicious to see me by myself," the Ohioan recounted, "and the Rebel soldiers, as I passed them, stared at me, as much to say, 'who are you, old fellow, that you are allowed to run around here with impunity?'" When he arrived at Susan's residence, she prepared a late breakfast for him while her family expressed sorrow at his situation and hoped he would get through it safely. After a time, his captor arrived but remained only long enough to admonish his prisoner to remain put until he returned. The Buckeye did as instructed until evening, when he walked down to the Winchester courthouse. After conversing there with fellow officers, he was taken to the Main Fort. Luckily for him, Susan and his other friends had supplied him with goods and food he somehow managed to smuggle into his temporary prison.[11]

The Rev. George H. Hammer, the popular Presbyterian chaplain of the 12th Pennsylvania Cavalry, claimed some of the Rebels mistreated two fellow chaplains at Carter's Woods. "I have seen men angry with passion," he wrote to a Philadelphia paper, "but I have never beheld such maddened fiendishness of feeling as that poured out upon us, and the more especially as General Milroy eluded their grasp and was beyond their power. Could they have captured him they would have torn him limb from limb," Hammer added. "He was hated with a perfect hatred, which I imagine arose from the manner in which he compelled all Rebels, whether soldiers or civilians, to keep time to Uncle Sam's music." To Chaplain Hammer, this unbridled hatred contributed to an ugly incident. "Under the sanctity of the flag of truce, two of our chaplains (not then captured), visited the field of slaughter to gather up the wounded,

10 Wild, *Capt. F. W. Alexander's Battery*, 68. According to weapons expert Phil Spaugy, Wild's "short sword" was likely a Model 1840 Light Artillery sabre issued to horse artillery units such as Alexander's, and not the Model 1832 short sword issued to the foot or garrison artillery units.

11 "Adventures of a Union Prisoner," *Xenia* (Ohio) *Sentinel*, September 1, 1863.

hear their last whisper, and bury the dead. They had hardly entered the field before they were insulted, and from one of them (Chaplain [Edward C.] Ambler of the 67th Pennsylvania), a valuable watch was taken . . . and himself threatened with violence."[12]

The stunning victories bolstered the Rebels' already high confidence. "We caught Gen. Robert Huston Milroy and his troops at Winchester," gloated Pvt. W. P. Snakenberg of Williams' 14th Louisiana, "and before he knew much we were nearly all around him. We fought hard and quick and got everything he had." Ironically, that same day a Republican newspaper in Harrisburg predicted, "The Rebels want plunder. The cut-throats who first rallied under the flag of secession were won to that infamous cause by inducements held out of invading the North, where plunder would pay for all the hardships of battle, and the revenge thus afforded satisfy the bitterest hatred which modern Democracy has ever created for freedom."[13]

Sergeant A. M. Riddle of the Louisiana Guard Artillery mourned the loss of his commander, Capt. Charles Thompson, but was pleased with the outcome: "Enemy whipped & driven back," he told his diary. Riddle went on to note that he saw more Yankee prisoners than at any previous time in the war since the surrender of the garrison at Harpers Ferry, and he rejoiced that his battery had picked up 115 usable rounds of Union artillery ammunition. The question about the enemy commander's whereabouts, however, lingered: "Heard Milroy was taken but doubt it."[14]

"[Milroy] got off himself, but it was a tight squeeze," recounted Capt. John Welsh of the Stonewall Brigade's 27th Virginia. "Our Brigade had no fighting to do, we made a charge on one lot of them but they did not stand for us to give them a fire." The veteran was astonished by the overwhelming outcome: "We . . . succeeded in capturing five regiments without firing a shot, in fact we took more prisoners than we had men in our Brigade." Rumors spread that the hated Union commander was a prisoner. "Old Milroy clothed himself in citizen's clothes, and attempted to escape, but was taken," was the mistaken belief of a Virginia artilleryman. Another Confederate regretted Milroy's escape, "as he was greatly wanted by us for his many crimes and outrages against helpless citizens of the Valley."[15]

---

12 George Hammer, "Union Prisoners in Richmond," *Philadelphia Inquirer*, November 6, 1863.

13 "The Civil War Memoirs of W. P. Snakenberg, Company K, 14th Louisiana Infantry Regiment," in *Amite* (LA) *News Digest*, October 3, 1984; *Charlotte Observer*, November 16, 1892; *Harrisburg Evening Telegraph*, June 15, 1863.

14 Riddle diary entry for June 15, 1863. Riddle estimated the number of captives at 8-9,000.

15 William G. Bean, "A House Divided: The Civil War Letters of A Virginia Family," in *Virginia Magazine of History and Biography*, vol. 59, no. 4, October 1951, 417; *Charleston* (SC) *Mercury*, June 22, 1863, citing unnamed Richmond newspapers; Isaac G. Bradwell, "The Burning of Wrightsville, Pa.," in *Confederate Veteran*, no. 27 (1919), 300.

An officer of the 10th Virginia in Steuart's brigade realized soon after the fighting that the 1st and 3rd North Carolina regiments, as well as his own, had been dangerously exposed early in the contest at the railroad cut. "If the Federals had deployed even one regiment in the field on the south of the country road and charged with confidence," Cpl. T. H. "Sonnie" Lauck argued, "they would have swiped us out of the cut and into our graves or Northern prisons, taking us, cannon and all, back with them."[16]

Assessing Milroy's losses

The fighting at Winchester and Stephenson's Depot was devastating for the Union cause in general and for Milroy in particular. Published accounts varied in the exact totals. One of the first reports came from an anonymous "gentleman from the Valley," who informed the Richmond newspapers that Ewell had taken 6,000-7,000 prisoners, 2,800 horses, 400 to 500 wagons, and $1.5 to $2 million in government stores. Those figures soon were widely repeated in other Southern papers, but the number of captives seems too high.[17]

The *Philadelphia Press* and *New York Herald* gave the final tally as 95 killed, 348 wounded, and 3,358 prisoners. In addition, continued the correspondent, the Rebels seized four 20-pounder Parrott Rifles and a pair of 24-pounder howitzers abandoned in the Main Fort, 17 3-inch rifles left behind by the light artillery batteries, 300 loaded supply wagons, and 200,000 rounds of small arms ammunition. Milroy also lost enough provisions to feed 10,000 men for two months, a six-month supply of clothing, almost all of his men's personal possessions, private baggage, books and papers, a dozen large sutler stores, huge quantities of medical supplies, and other materiel. All that was left of Milroy's command was 3,900 men scattered across the northern reaches of the Shenandoah Valley. "Not a thing was saved except that which was worn or carried upon the persons of the troops," lamented a northern newspaper correspondent.[18]

Milroy's aide-de-camp, Capt. Frederick A. Palmer of the 18th Connecticut, later tabulated the loss as 7 officers and 88 enlisted men killed; 12 officers and 336 enlisted men wounded; and 144 officers and 3,856 enlisted men captured or missing for a total of 4,443 men lost from all causes in the Second Division, Eighth Corps. He listed the

---

16 Lauck, "The Little Corporal's Story."

17 *Charleston* (SC) *Mercury*, June 22, 1863, citing unnamed Richmond newspapers.

18 Philadelphia Press, June 26, 1863; New York Herald, June 22, 1863; *Hartford* (CT) *Courant*, June 24, 1863; *Charlotte Western Democrat*, July 7, 1863.

67th Pennsylvania as having the most men captured, with 714. Behind them were the 18th Connecticut at 513 prisoners and the 123rd Ohio at 445.[19]

In recent years, modern authors and researchers have also weighed in. J. David Petruzzi and Steve Stanley, in their landmark *The Gettysburg Campaign in Numbers and Losses*, state that Milroy lost 96 killed, 349 wounded, and 3,999 captured or missing. Author David J. Eicher repeats the early newspaper accounts of 95 killed, 348 wounded, and about 3,358 captured.[20]

General Ewell reported taking 4,000 prisoners. One difficulty in assessing how many Union soldiers were captured stems from the large number of infirmed men being treated in the Winchester hospitals who also fell into Ewell's hands. The National Park Service's David W. Lowe states, "Union casualty figures for Second Winchester vary widely because about two thousand Union soldiers not belonging to Milroy's command were in field hospitals in the city and were often added to the number of captured and missing." Captain Palmer's post-battle table combines those soldiers in Milroy's division who were taken prisoner in the town and hospitals, as well as on the battlefield. However, Ewell also likely captured untold scores of soldiers from other commands who had been taken to Winchester earlier in the war, or had remained there under medical treatment when their regiments had departed. Ewell's talented cartographer, Jedediah Hotchkiss, counted about 2,000 prisoners taken in Winchester, not including those taken at Stephenson's Depot/Carter's Woods or those seized elsewhere during the pursuit of the fleeing Yankees. Allegheny Johnson took about 3,500 captives there, according to his estimates.[21]

Confederate losses were remarkably light given the complexity of the operation. General Ewell reported only 309 casualties. Eicher believes Ewell only lost 47 men killed, 219 wounded, and 3 missing, 40 less than Ewell's 1863 tally. Petruzzi's more recent study suggests 49 killed, 1 mortally wounded, 238 wounded, and 12 missing, for a total of 300. Discrepancies aside, it was an overwhelming Confederate victory, one that shocked the North and energized the South. Second Winchester, wrote Rebel artilleryman Maj. Robert Stiles after the war, "was one of the most perfect pieces of work the Army of Northern Virginia ever did." Flushed with a dazzling debut as a corps commander, Ewell directed the chaplains to hold religious services in their

---

19 OR 27, pt. 2, 53.

20 J. David Petruzzi and Steven A. Stanley, *The Gettysburg Campaign in Numbers and Losses* (El Dorado Hills, CA: Savas Beatie, 2012), 16-17; David J. Eicher, *The Longest Night: A Military History of the Civil War* (New York: Simon & Schuster, 2001), 494.

21 OR 27, pt. 2, 453; David W. Lowe, *Study of Civil War Sites in the Shenandoah Valley of Virginia* (Washington, DC: U.S. Department of the Interior, National Park Service, Interagency Resources Division, 1992), 73.

respective regiments "in acknowledgement of Divine Favor at such times as may be most convenient."[22]

Winchester

As dawn was breaking, and while the fighting still raged around Carter's Woods, Maj. William Goldsborough and three companies of the 2nd Maryland Battalion moved cautiously through Winchester's quiet streets. Not a single enemy was seen. The Yankees had retreated, "leaving their fortifications and everything—wagons, knapsacks, guns, stores, etc.—in the greatest confusion," one of Company C's officers later wrote. The Marylanders could hear artillery fire from the direction of the Martinsburg Pike, but remained wary that the Yankees still lurked in the forts.[23]

"There's a Confed!" came a joyous shout from a nearby window. A pro-secessionist woman on her rooftop had turned her attention from watching some Yankee deserters seeking refuge in some old stables to the streets. "Bless your heart, you dear Reb!" she screamed with delight. The soldier looked around until he spotted the woman, and yelled in a thick Irish brogue, "Where are the Yankees?" The Winchester resident motioned toward the stable before running downstairs to recover a hidden Confederate flag and rush outside, "anxious to be the first to welcome our returning braves." Citizens began filling the streets. Only Goldsborough's companies had thus far entered the city, but "as each soldier appeared he was seized and shaken by the hand and a dozen questions put to him."[24]

Once past the adulation, Goldsborough led his men north out of town. The sun was not yet up. When they drew near the Star Fort the major called a halt. Pretending he had not heard the order, Lt. George Thomas continued on and discovered a large body of almost 200 enemy cavalry. The officer boldly ordered them to surrender, and the stunned Yankees complied and dismounted. Thomas secured the horses for his own command and singlehandedly marched the sullen prisoners back into town to turn them in to the provost. The sight was so comical that Major Goldsborough administered only a mild reprimand to the gallant young officer for disobeying his order. Sergeant Thomas Barron of Company C hauled down the Star Fort's flag. After mopping up, most of Goldsborough's Marylanders filed back into Winchester. "We were soon on duty guarding the prisoners," William H. Lyons reported. He and his

---

22 Ibid.; Eicher, *The Longest Night*, 494; Petruzzi and Stanley, *Numbers and Losses*, 17; Stiles, *Four Years Under Marse Robert*, 192.

23 Goldsborough, *The Maryland Line*, 95-96; *Richmond Whig*, June 23, 1863.

24 "Leaves from a Diary Kept by a Lady."

comrades began appropriating abandoned Union stores. "I was in a sutler's shoproom soon after we arrived," boasted Lyons. "We got plenty of things we needed."[25]

Major General Jubal Early arrived in Winchester a short time later at the head of several regiments, with John M. Jones' Virginia brigade detached from Johnson's division trailing his command. A "shout of the wildest joy" came from the jubilant, and almost disbelieving, pro-secessionist crowd that had gathered outdoors. The scene was one of "wildest excitement," according to one woman. Flags and sunbonnets (the secret secessionist sign during Milroy's occupation) waved in every direction. Confederate flags long hidden now dangled from windows. "Our men were passing in one direction and the Yankee prisoners were being brought in in squads from the opposite point," she added. One of the prisoners supposedly exclaimed, "Gracious heavens! This is a sight worth witnessing. I couldn't believe it when I've read accounts of these receptions. I don't wonder [why] you fellows fight so."[26]

The patients housed in the Taylor Hotel first learned of their fate when the fat Ohio drummer boy ventured out half an hour after Snowden Andrews' artillery ceased firing. He rushed back upstairs to his room where the 18th Connecticut's James Sawyer noticed the lad arrived with dilated eyes and a white face. "Boys," the musician uttered, "there was a rebel down in the yard, and he raised his gun to shoot me!" The uninjured Ohio lieutenant sharing the room with his wounded brother calmly remarked that the army must have retreated, and in doing so abandoned the patients as prisoners. Stepping outside, Sawyer and the others noted a long line of Confederates standing in the street with their backs to the hotel. They right-faced and marched away, but the situation was clear. The Rebels now controlled Winchester.[27]

Some patients later claimed the Confederates robbed them. George R. Maguire of the 13th Pennsylvania Cavalry was confined to bed with typhoid fever. An unnamed Rebel major "not only took my arms," Maguire complained, "but robbed me of $212 in money, my watch, and all the clothing I was possessed of, except one suit. I was removed from the house at which I was to the hospital. Here we were treated with great indignity, simply because we belonged to Milroy's army." It would only get worse for Maguire. "We were allowed no liberty whatever. Every privilege was curtailed, and we were immured in a small hospital crowded with the dead and dying, and not allowed to show ourselves outside under penalty of being shot."[28]

---

25 Ibid.; Lyons diary entry for June 15, 1863. The "cavalry" was a mixed bag of riders.

26 "Leaves from a Diary Kept by a Southern Lady."

27 Sawyer, "Abandoned at Winchester," 11.

28 "Statement of the Agent of the Thirteenth Pennsylvania Cavalry, Mr. George R. Maguire," *Philadelphia Inquirer*, August 18, 1863. Maguire would experience several weeks of captivity in

Main Street in downtown Winchester. *U.S. Army Heritage and Education Center*

The detainees in the hospitals included more than a dozen doctors and several chaplains. They and scores of patients, both Union and Confederate, lined the broad porches of the Taylor Hotel to stare at the incoming gray infantry. One of the recuperating invalids happy to see Goldsborough and his Maryland Rebels was Capt. William Rasin, the trooper severely wounded in the melee after the June 12 Newtown ambush. One of Early's bands broke out their instruments and played *Dixie* in front of the hotel. When they reached the chorus of the next song, "The Bonnie Blue Flag," a group of ladies began singing. By degrees, the entire crowd lining the street joined in, followed by the soldiers, until the words echoed throughout much of the town. "It was a day worth living for," was how one resident put it, "and I felt almost repaid for having remained within their lines during eight long, weary months."[29]

Hundreds of jubilant Rebels strolled around town receiving the heartfelt thanks of most of its visible residents. Artillerist Henry R. Berkeley marveled at the unbridled joy: "The citizens seemed perfectly wild with joy, many old ladies and gentlemen rushing out on their porches in their night clothes, and waving flags, handkerchiefs and various other garments, while children and young girls shouted and hurrahed until

the Winchester hospital before finally being removed to Staunton, some 96 miles up the Valley. Having no rail transportation to Richmond at the time, he and the other prisoners camped outside on a hill for four days. Luckily, he and four other officers escaped and made their way to Union General Averell's lines in Hampshire County, West Virginia.

29 "Leaves from a Diary Kept by a Lady."

their strength failed them." The 25th Virginia's Pvt. John R. King, part of Jones' brigade, spotted "a large old lady on a porch bouncing from one end to the other, clapping her hands and shouting: 'Thank the Lord, Milroy is gone.'" The anti-Yankee Mary Greenhow Lee also rejoiced: "[F]or the first time in six months, the air is not polluted by their immediate presence." The Union evacuation and defeat allowed the Logan family to reclaim possession of the handsome mansion that had served as Milroy's headquarters and family residence for the past several months. The Logan home, reported a newspaper in Raleigh, North Carolina, looked "as well as ever."[30]

"At last our men, our dear men, have come," exclaimed a diarist. "Their advent has almost crazed me with delight, to think we are again free. I can't realize it at all. We had heard so many false rumors that we had nearly given up in despair." Another joyous pro-secessionist woman, Maggie Miller, wrote that "a feeling of gratitude and thankfulness to our Divine Protector, for our deliverance from a bondage so galling, pervades our whole being. I believe our prayer for piece will soon be answered," she concluded. "Piece! and independence! and war too without any earthly power!" Some of the most telling prose came from one of the youngest diarists, Gettie Miller. "We heard that General Elliott was killed. I would rather it had been old Milroy, but I do not want any of them killed," she explained, seeing the war through child's eyes. "I want them to go back to their homes and stay there and never poke their noses in the south. We ought to have a high wall between us so they could not come over."[31]

Not surprisingly, pro-Union citizens held a diametrically opposing viewpoint. "The Rebels took possession of our town at 5 o'clock this morning," penned Julia Chase. "And we are now in Dixie. Oh what a sad, sad day this has been to us." Several residents became embroiled in arguments with Confederate soldiers. "[I] had about as much fun in the way of an argument with a Union lady as I could have wished," observed Capt. James Harris of the 30th North Carolina.[32]

Greenbury S. Robinson, a black civilian cook and servant for Company A of the 87th Pennsylvania, took advantage of the chaos and confusion during the raucous celebration. The 21-year-old peacetime barber was captured at Carter's Woods, but escaped by removing his military coat and disappearing into a crowd of blacks lining

30 Henry R. Berkeley and William H. Runge, ed., *Four Years in the Confederate Artillery: The Diary of Private Henry Robinson Berkeley* (Chapel Hill: The University of North Carolina Press, 1961), 47; King, "My Experience in the Confederate Army and in Northern Prisons"; Mary Lee diary entry for June 14, 1863; "From Winchester," *The Daily Progress*, July 17, 1863.

31 "Leaves from a Diary Kept by a Lady"; Margaret Miller to Caspar Coiner Henkel, June 29, 1863, Winchester, Virginia, Henkel Family Letters 1787-1907, U. S. National Library of Medicine, Bethesda, Maryland; Gettie Miller diary entry for June 15, 1863.

32 Taylor, "Ramseur's Brigade in the Gettysburg Campaign," 29.

Winchester's streets. Rebels detained 37-year-old Walburga S. Shultz, a Prussian-born laundress and nurse whom the 87th affectionately called "the mother of the regiment." Her husband John was a private in Company E. She had a U. S. flag and $300 in cash concealed under her dress as Rebels led her and her daughter away. Another civilian prisoner was Gettysburg, Pennsylvania's John M. Warner, whose brother George served in Company H of the 87th Pennsylvania. Lame since a childhood fall and so unable to shoulder a musket himself, John had still tried to do his part by accompanying his brother's regiment to Winchester as a sutler.[33]

A pro-Union Winchester maiden saved another flag. Right before abandoning the Main Fort, the 110th Ohio's Colonel Keifer ordered his men to raise the post's colors to indicate its occupancy. Rebels later boxed the trophy for shipment to Richmond, but Quaker-born Annie Jackson broke into the crate and took it. She hid it for the rest of the war, though sometimes broke it out to wear under her outer skirt.[34]

Milroy's vast stores in the warehouses and abandoned forts attracted considerable interest from the awestruck Southern soldiers. "Such an abundance of plunder they had never seen before," the 13th Virginia's Alexander Hunter recounted, "and each man in the regiment was arrayed in style. There were creature comforts and almost forgotten delicacies too numerous to mention which went far to swelling the full tide of that earthly content which rolled in upon each mans soul and reflected itself in each lineament of his face." Second Corps artillery staff officer Lt. Samuel H. Pendleton was tasked with inventorying the cache of supplies seized inside the Main Fort. While doing so, he happily appropriated "a nice pair [of] all cloth pants and writing materials sufficient for a 12 mos. siege." Corporal James P. Williams of the Chesapeake Artillery recalled how "all of our men equipped themselves with gum-blankets, overcoats, canteens, knapsacks, in fact everything they want, & are now ready for anything." He also found some Yankee photographs, which he mailed to his sister.[35]

Hundreds of army horses had changed hands. "My men captured a horse of magnificent appearance and handsomely caparisoned," wrote General Gordon. "He was solid black in color and dangerously treacherous in disposition. He was brought to me by his captors with the statement that he was General Milroy's horse, and he was at

33 Brandt database, YCHT; Prowell, *History of the 87th Pennsylvania*, 89; Brandt, *From Home Guards to Heroes*, 323. Robinson later became the servant for the 39th U. S. Colored Troops.

34 Keifer, "The Story of a Flag," 420-21. Keifer and his wife Eliza had previously socialized with Annie Jackson. She sent the flag to him in January 1922. Keifer later presented it to the Ohio Historical Society for preservation.

35 Alexander Hunter, "Thirteenth Virginia Infantry Humor," in *Confederate Veteran*, vol. 16, no. 7, July 1908, 339; Pendleton diary entry for June 15, 1863, UVA; James P. Williams to Dear sister, June 16, 1863, Winchester, VA, Library of Virginia.

once christened 'Milroy' by my men. I have no idea that he belonged to the general," continued Gordon, "for that officer was too true a soldier to have ridden such a beast in battle—certainly not after one test of his cowardice." Staff officer Henry Kyd Douglas also ended up with a new mount he promptly named "Dick Turpin." Despite it being "the most willful, but the toughest, beast I ever owned or rode, he proved invaluable. He was given me because he was so violent no one would have him."[36]

While many celebrated and others inventoried, General Johnson set about reforming his division for a possible move north in pursuit of the Yankees and ordered up his supply trains. "Ordered to move our wagons out on the Martinsburg turnpike," the Stonewall Brigade's Watkins Kearns scribbled in his diary. "Moved through Winchester which is filled with prisoners." The long and rumbling procession of wagons slowly headed north. The path of Milroy's retreat was easy to recognize because discarded debris was scattered along the roadside. The Rebel ordnance train halted at Carter's Woods. "Mrs. Carters house [has] been taken for a hospital," Kearns recalled. "See Miss Sue Pitman. In god spirit. The house & grounds seem to have suffered very much from the soldiers. A cannon ball passed through the roof."[37]

When Gordon's brigade approached Mrs. Carter's house, the Georgians frequently broke ranks to collect souvenirs and articles of possible use for the continued push northward. "Along the roadside were strewed muskets, knapsacks, sutlers' wagons, and everything you could think of," wrote a soldier from Augusta known only as Will to the editor of the *Augusta Chronicle and Sentinel*. "I got a splendid sabre and belts, a saddle, and lots of small things, and plenty of paper and envelopes on which I am now writing. I am very sorry to inform you that old Milroy and about 1000 men made their escape. However," he continued, "we done well—capturing great supplies and have driven them out of this part of Virginia."[38]

Some in Ewell's command believed the victory could have been much greater. "It was believed Milroy's command 'would be scooped up,' as Genl. Early curtly said," bemoaned military scout Thomas Cartmell. "Someone east of town was to blame. Rodes passing through Berryville on time, drove all before him in such shape, he

---

36 Gordon, *Reminiscences*, 102; Douglas, *I Rode with Stonewall*, 242. The captured horse proved unworthy at Gettysburg where Gordon complained, "His fear of Minié balls was absolutely uncontrollable. He came near disgracing me in the first and only fight in which I attempted to ride him. Indeed, if it had chanced to be my first appearance under fire with my men, they would probably have followed my example as they saw me flying to the rear on this elephantine brute." Union accounts suggest Milroy rode a borrowed white horse at the time of his escape, his own mount having been killed.

37 Kearns diary entry for June 15, 1863, VHS.

38 *Augusta* (GA) *Chronicle and Sentinel*, June 28, 1863.

Ewell's stepson, Maj. G. Campbell Brown.
Tennessee State Archives

mistook his orders and never stopped until he reached Martinsburg, capturing guns, stores, and a few prisoners. Had he halted at some point under cover of timber near old Hackwood, until the Stonewall [Brigade] appeared," Cartmell continued, "there would doubtless have been a complete surrender."[39]

In 1886, Ewell's stepson Campbell Brown explained the failure to aggressively pursue the enemy. "We never estimated Milroy's strength at more than 6,000 of all arms—and were unaware any considerable body of infantry succeeded in passing Johnson's blockade of the road," Brown wrote Union Gen. Henry J. Hunt, the commander of General Meade's artillery at Gettysburg. "We knew that his cavalry & all who could get horses had made their way out. It was singular that we never suspected the retreat of anything like a body of troops toward Hancock, at the time nor afterwards. Our underestimate of Milroy's force aided the darkness in covering the escape of these, as we thought all the organized infantry force had surrendered, and consequently made no systematic search for them."[40]

A few miles to the north, when General Rodes learned of Johnson's smashing triumph, he left the 6th and 26th Alabama of Colonel O'Neal's brigade to secure Martinsburg and led the balance of his division toward Williamsport late that morning. "My Regt. & the 26th Ala. which constitute a part of our Brigade was left at this place 2 days ago as a provost guard & Our company at present has very good quarters," reported Thomas S. Taylor of the 6th Alabama. "It is guarding the Commissary Ordnance & quartermaster stores, captured by our forces at this place & we are in a large building possibly a market house. We can sleep very comfortably at night on the brick floor. We were all very proud of our position because all of us were very tired &

---

39 Cartmell, *Shenandoah Valley Pioneers*, 386. The "Hackwood" estate east of Winchester played a significant role in the Third Battle of Winchester in 1864.

40 Campbell Brown to Henry Hunt, July 17, 1886, Gettysburg Discussion Group, *http://www.gdg.org/Research/Hunt/hajuly17_1886.html*, accessed January 15, 2014.

our feet were blistered all over from excessive marching." Although the Alabamians were comfortable, "we everywhere get the cold shoulder of those of the Union sentiments." Taylor and his comrades had no idea what lay ahead for them. "Our Regiment may stay at this place a week, 2 weeks, or even a month & it may be ordered somewhere else in less than 2 hours," he observed. "A soldier's life is one continued disappointment & suspense. We never know what the future has in store for us & we are often disappointed in our expectation."[41]

The 106th New York's Pvt. William Hubbard and several other ill Union prisoners were convalescing at the home of Mrs. Ann Woolf when the Rebels arrived. Hubbard penned in his diary that the Rebels destroyed a railroad bridge, but for him the important news was that at six o'clock in the evening, he received a parole. He would not have to march south to a prison camp, unlike his healthier comrades.[42]

While the captive New Yorkers and Ohioans pondered their fate and chatted with their Alabama guards, the rest of General Rodes' Confederates marched north toward the Potomac River. Rodes described the move as "the most trying march we had yet had, most trying because of the intense heat, the character of the road, and the increased number of barefooted men in the command." This was the first day his troops began to exhibit unmistakable signs of exhaustion, with "absolutely worn-out" stragglers falling out along the route. "A halt at Williamsport was absolutely necessary from the condition of the feet of the unshod men. Very many of these gallant fellows were still marching in ranks, with feet bruised, bleeding and swollen." Only the best of soldiers, he added, "could have made such a march under such circumstances." The stalwarts who endured the march arrived opposite Williamsport late that afternoon and camped along the river. The divisions under Early and Johnson, meanwhile, remained near Winchester to police the prisoners and collect the spoils. Early camped near the John H. Rutherford farm about three miles north of town while Johnson rested his men on the Stephenson's Depot battlefield.[43]

"From Winchester to Stephenson the road was strewn with plunder," recorded Lt. Henry H. Harris, an engineer assigned to Ed Johnson's staff and battling a bad case of the mumps. "Sent out burial parties who reported one Negro, two Confederates, and forty-three Yankees." Guards marched thousands of prisoners from Carter's

---

41 Taylor to his sister, June 16, 1863. Both regiments would fight at Gettysburg.

42 Hubbard diary entry for June 15, 1863. The following day, Hubbard simply wrote, "Union soldiers start for Richmond as prisoners."

43 *OR* 27, pt. 2, 550. Rutherford bought the farm from the heirs of John Carter in the 1840s. He and his wife lived with Carter's sister-in-law, the widow Susan Pitman Carter, on her adjoining farm until he built his own house in 1857. He managed Carter's farm in addition to his own. The Rutherford house was torn down ca. 1963. A Civil War Trails marker marks the site.

Woods to the captured forts. Ironically, Milroy's stout bastions upon which he had so confidently staked his army's survival became prison pens for the men who built them. "We were nearly starved while prisoners, and were very roughly treated," complained Lt. Elmer E. Husted of the 123rd Ohio's quartermaster staff. "The rebels took from me everything except one shirt, pants, stockings and tobacco box. I lost $150, a part of which did not belong to me." "Went to the Fort, and here we are, pinned all hands in a small Fort without any shelter from the hot sun, and laying in the dirt, half of us without blankets of any kind, and water very poor," lamented a solider of the 18th Connecticut, "but we do the best we can and let things take their course."[44]

"A couple of tents were then put up for the accommodation of the commissioned officers," a captain in the 123rd Ohio later related, "but which failed to prevent the wind from annoying us very much by blowing sand from all directions. Weary and worn out, and having eaten nothing during the day, we were compelled to lie down at night without even a 'hard tack' to refresh us." A captive from Col. B. F. Smith's 126th Ohio captured by Rodes' men at Martinsburg on the 14th complained, "Woak up this morning & found my self very sore & hungry. there is [prisoners] leaving for Richmond to day. there had beene a bout 2000 men left. we have drawn some hard tacks & spoilt meat and God knows when we will get any more." The plight of the Federal prisoners of war inevitably became much worse before it got better.[45]

Among the sullen captives was Chaplain Joseph T. Brown of the 6th Maryland. Rebels escorted him to the Main Fort, where by that evening he was joined by "many others, 2,000 or more by evening." He noted they only got "one meal to day bread & watter no rations. Men are like wolves. Slept in a tent put up for the officers."[46]

One of the women who had suffered under Milroy's tyranny returned to Winchester "to see Milroy surrender," she gloated in her diary, "but when we arrived there were found the town indeed occupied by our troops but the brave Milroy had skipped out like a wolf in sheep's clothing." She went by the Main Fort "to see the wreck of fancied greatness. It was crowded with prisoners and it was good to see those who had trampled us down in their brutal pride and might, guarded by our brave men.

---

44 W. Harrison Daniel, ed., "H. H. Harris Civil War Diary, 1863-1865," in *The Virginia Baptist Register*, 1996, no. 25, 1769; *Norwalk* (OH) *Reflector*, July 21, 1863; James M. Smith diary entry for June 15, 1863. Lieutenant Husted was released rather quickly and sent in early July from Belle Isle in Richmond to Camp Parole in Annapolis, Maryland. He received his pay and then headed on to Camp Chase in Columbus, Ohio, as the shattered regiment began reorganizing.

45 Keyes, *The Military History of the 123rd Ohio*, 119; Anonymous, "Diary of a Civil War Soldier in Company F, 126th Ohio Volunteer Infantry." The unknown soldier and hundreds of other Winchester victims held in Richmond were paroled by the end of June and transported by ship from City Point, Virginia, to Annapolis.

46 Brown diary entry for June 15, 1863.

I could not help triumphing when I saw those who had ridden over our fair lands on their splendid horses as if it had been their birthright, tramping on foot through the dust and hot sun, guarded by our men on horseback."[47]

Among the captives taken to Winchester was Cpl. Philip M. Shive, a bandsman of the 87th Pennsylvania. As he entered the fort, one of the guards called out "Hello, Philip! What are you doing here?" Shive recognized the soldier who accosted him as an old friend, formerly from his hometown of York but now in Confederate service. Also in captivity was Sgt. William Cutter, an Ohioan who had served as Milroy's postmaster since their days together in western Virginia earlier in the war. He was confined with the civilians and women because the Rebels suspected him of being an officer in disguise "because he was so well dressed and exhibited elegant manners."[48]

The multitude of prisoners included Capt. F. A. Patterson of the 3rd West Virginia Cavalry. Patterson joined the regiment on June 12 after being on recruiting duty. His upcoming 21 months of captivity shattered his health, and he later filed a claim for back pay, only to find that he was the victim of a bureaucratic foul-up. Although mustered into the army with a commission dating from November 1862, someone forgot to enter his name on the official regimental rolls when he arrived in Winchester. The invalided widower with no children would not receive his pay until 1866 after Congress passed a bill directing the secretary of war to release the funds.[49]

Another prisoner being held in the iron-fenced courthouse yard was the 110th Ohio's Lt. Charles Gross. Several Rebels were bringing in baggage captured from the 18th Connecticut including new dress coats, caps, knapsacks, stationery, and other items. Gross wanted one of the coats because he was only wearing an old blouse without rank insignia he had donned on Saturday morning when he started out to take command of the picket line. He had only grabbed a day's rations because he fully expected to be relieved on Sunday. However, in the hurry and confusion of the actions early on the Sabbath, no one came to relieve him. Gross asked a Rebel guard for permission to exchange coats because his blouse was very thin. The Rebel hesitated, worried he explained that the officers would see him do so. Gross pleaded his case, and the guard finally relented: "Exchange quickly." The Buckeye officer gladly did so. Gross was walking toward the courthouse elated with his trade when he realized his discarded old blouse contained all of his money. He had pinned two $10 bills between

---

47 Harrison diary entry for June 17, 1863.

48 Prowell, *History of the 87th Pennsylvania*, 89; Lt. Col. Robert Northcott letter in *Report on the Treatment of Prisoners of War, by the Rebel Authorities, during the War of the Rebellion; To which Are Appended the Testimony Taken by the Committee, and Official Documents and Statistics, etc., Report No. 45, 40th Congress, 3rd Session, House of Representatives* (Washington, DC: GPO, 1869), 1105.

49 U. S. House of Representatives, 51st Congress, Report #1349, NARA..

the lining and the outer part. He hastened back to the pile of goods in search of the old coat, but was unable to locate it. When the sympathetic guard explained that several other men had picked up clothing since he had left, Gross studied the other prisoners in the off-chance he might spot his nondescript unmarked blouse, to avail.

Guards escorted Gross and his comrades to the Main Fort, where several thousand others were being held. Unable to forget the loss of his cash, the Buckeye major continued studying the clothing of his fellow captives. When he saw one who looked familiar, he asked him to please take off his coat for a minute to let him see it, reassuring the man that he would hand it back to him. The curious soldier unbuttoned the blouse and handed it to Gross, who realized there was no telltale pin attached to the lining. He was about to return it when he reached into the lining where, to his delight, he pulled out the two $10.00 bills. Gross handed the dumbfounded man the blouse and walked away "as happy as a man could be under the circumstances."[50]

Meanwhile, the 5th Maryland's surgeon, Dr. Charles Goldsborough, encountered his older Rebel brother, Maj. William Goldsborough of the 2nd Maryland, who had been appointed provost marshal in recognition of his recent gallantry. The major gave his doctor-brother a parole and a pass. Dr. Goldsborough ventured out to the battlefield and collected wounded Connecticut boys, bringing them to the regiment's hospital in the cramped Methodist church. One of the first things he did was extract a bullet from a lieutenant he saw fall at Carter's Woods from a gunshot to his body.[51]

Hundreds of other wounded men, Union and Confederate, found their way or were taken to the downtown hotels. John S. Apperson, a hospital steward in the Second Corps Medical Department, found several missing soldiers at the Taylor Hotel who had been taken prisoner in the June 12 cavalry skirmish near Newtown. Dr. Harvey Black established a temporary field hospital in the York House, and Apperson helped transfer captured medical supplies to that site. "A large amount is sent to Dr. Black," Apperson penned in his diary, "including [anything] that a Yankee notion vendor could have—shoes, boots, trunks—medicines, confectionaries. Any quantity of medical & blank books, paper and ink. The captured Yankee mail was brought in and we oppened [*sic*] some of it—a very tedious job."[52]

---

50 Gross, "Sketch of Army and Prison Life." Gross likely removed his rank insignia to avoid standing out as an officer to enemy sharpshooters. The practice became commonplace by 1864 in both the Eastern and Western Theaters.

51 Walker, *History of the Eighteenth Regiment*, 441. Assistant surgeon, Dr. H. Lindsley Pierce, was also taken prisoner in the church. He died "of disease and bad treatment" at Libby Prison on November 5, 1863. A victim of pneumonia and diarrhea, Pierce left a young widow Katie and a baby son Norval born that May. Widow's Pension Claims, Harvey L. Pierce, NARA.

52 Apperson, *Repairing the March of Mars*, 463.

Several Confederates passed the captured Federal letters around, finding special amusement in notes from loved ones back home. A Richmond newspaper, tired of the routine mocking in Northern papers about the stereotypical poor education received by most Southerners, fired back: "Among the letters captured at Winchester was one from a Yankee girl at Somerville, Ohio, to her sweetheart in the army. The following is an extract: 'You ort to See Sum Rebs Letters that Tom Bort hum With him. Whar they bin Ritin to thar galls and if I cud get holt of sum of them Secesh hussies how i woud tar ther her for Em i am a gud union gal as ever you ort to See how them Rebel husseys Spel you Kin hardly Reed it they Spel the Durdndest Wurds you did ever Seen I sous Rite nomor but Remain your Expected Wif til Deth.'"[53]

Major John G. Campbell of Hays' First Louisiana Brigade sent a few Yankee documents to the *Richmond Enquirer* for publication. "I am afraid if that worthy successor of the immortal Jackson, Gen. Ewell, continues the campaign in the manner he has begun," added Campbell, "it will tend to increase the ranks of the Copperheads more than these precious publications have diminished them." One of the captured papers was a beautifully printed commission of William F. Wallace as a first lieutenant in the 5th U. S. Artillery. Campbell also enclosed several other documents, including copies of one of Union Maj. Gen. Benjamin Butler's speeches and court-martial proceedings. That same day's mail brought an envelope from Capt. Jacob J. Hill, the assistant quartermaster of the 31st Virginia, full of several recent dispatches between Milroy and Schenck the *Enquirer* gleefully reprinted.[54]

According to a newspaper in Staunton, Virginia, the haul of enemy military intelligence included a February 15th report from Michael Graham, the former head of Maj. Gen. Nathaniel Banks' secret service when he commanded at Winchester, to Major General Halleck. Banks relayed his wife Catherine's observations she had made while traveling as a spy from Mount Jackson up the Valley to Staunton and then on to Richmond before finally arriving in Washington. Mrs. Banks traveled part of the way with two women she believed to be Rebel spies. Union Brig. Gen. Benjamin F. Kelly had endorsed Graham's report, "Respectfully referred to Brig. Gen'l Milroy for his information."[55]

The 3rd Richmond Howitzers' William White noticed what he described as the "strange women" who flocked to see the prisoners at the Main Fort or who strolled the streets—"mothers, but not wearing the marriage ring; camp followers of Milroy

53 "Ohio spelling," *Richmond Daily Dispatch*, June 30, 1863.

54 "Yankee Documents and Milroy's Departure," *Richmond Enquirer*, June 22, 1863. Campbell signed his letter as a captain but was promoted to major dating from June 3, 1863.

55 *Staunton Spectator*, July 7, 1863.

and his now dissipated army." He also chastised the pro-Union portion of the local populace who were "of the lower class," some of whom were being held captive inside the Main Fort.[56]

Some of the celebrating Southern soldiers milling about the streets of Winchester imbibed freely in alcohol. The assistant surgeon of the 3rd North Carolina, Thomas F. Wood, was on foot leading his sore-backed horse and so did not accompany Steuart's brigade during Johnson's movement to Stephenson's Depot. Dr. Wood was walking through Winchester when he encountered an officer he only indentified as "Col. B." riding a good saddle horse he had captured. "The Col. was under the influence of liquor," Wood gloated, "and was in search of whiskey and gave me the horse for a canteen of whiskey." Wood did not get to keep his new mount for long because a quartermaster found out about the swap and took charge of the horse. "I was therefore obliged to pursue my journey on foot," grumbled the young surgeon from Wilmington.[57]

That first night, the prisoners tried to bolster their flagging spirits despite the miserable conditions. "Some one started to sing 'Columbia the Gem of the Ocean' followed by 'My Country Tis of Thee,' and so on, all the patriotic airs we could think of, then 'My Old Kentucky Home,' 'Annie Laura,' and other sentimental songs," recalled Pvt. Fred Wild, one of Captain Alexander's artillerists in the Baltimore Battery. "'Tramp, Tramp, Tramp' had not been composed, or we would have made the welkin ring with it, it would have been so appropriate. One cannot express the feeling which these songs awakened, and how they cheered the down hearted, unless he had experienced such surroundings." Although the singing helped bolster their sagging morale, the circumstances remained less than ideal. At least one sullen captive battled nagging doubts about his own performance in the battle. The 18th Connecticut's Capt. Henry C. Davis would pen a letter from Libby Prison to two friends in Washington in which he stated that he hoped he had "acted an honorable part" in the fighting.[58]

Several Confederates later reflected on the fighting and what General Ewell's next steps would be. "It was a very noisy battle, but not very many were killed," recalled James E. Hall of Company H, 31st Virginia. "History will detail the plans of the attack, and therefore it is useless for me. The 31st Regt. lost only some two or three

---

56 White, "A Diary of the War," 191.

57 Donald B. Koonce, ed., *Doctor to the Front: The Recollections of Confederate Surgeon Thomas Fanning Wood, 1861-1865* (Knoxville: U. of Tennessee Press, 2000), 96. The only colonel in Steuart's brigade whose surname began with B was Lt. Col. Henry Brown, 1st North Carolina.

58 Wild, *Memoirs and History of Capt. F. W. Alexander's Baltimore Battery*, 80; Henry Clinton Davis to John Eastman and James Stevens, Libby Prison, Collection of the Connecticut State Library.

men. I got out safely," he added, "as I hope to do again in the one that is now pending. I expect we are going into Maryland."[59]

"I am well and in the land of the living, dear Wife," the 3rd North Carolina's Pvt. John Futch recounted in a letter home written on captured Union stationery. "We have had another Battel at Winchester and to praise the help of God our army is again crowned with victory." Reassuring her that he had not been involved in the fighting that had cost his company four men, Futch went on to mention the capture of "any quantities of commissary stores such as flour bacon Molass[es] coffee sugar rice" and fresh beef. "We will fair well as long as the Yankee comissary lasts," he added. Still, a march into Maryland and perhaps beyond loomed, with the grim prospects of more fights and additional danger. "You musant be oneasy about me and tak the best Cear of your Self and I Will the Same," he penned the next day. "I hope the lord Will spear me to Com and Se you all again."[60]

Other Confederates reflected on the merits of their new leader. "That's the way to gain a victory — annihilate the enemy at a blow," gushed the 5th Louisiana's Capt. Samuel Chisolm in a post-battle letter to his brother. "The genius shown by Ewell surpasses even the immortal Jackson. He is fast becoming the hero of the whole army, as Jackson was only nine months ago." "We had not much hard fighting to get the town of Winchester," explained Sgt. Daniel Sheetz of the 2nd Virginia. "We got all that the enemy had and the greater part of them."[61]

A North Carolina newspaper gloated, "A Yankee Colonel who escaped from Winchester when that place was captured by Gen. Ewell, wrote to his father in Philadelphia as follows: 'I cannot give particulars of the battles, which beat all within my knowledge. Suffice it to say that Gen. Milroy's account, which I have seen, is a mere white-washing affair, not giving any true facts. Gen. Milroy did not bring away a gun, team, ambulance, or a third of his command.' The Yankee General Milroy reported to his master, Abe Lincoln, that he saved most of his army and trains, but one of his Colonels lets the truth out, and shows that Milroy lied."[62]

---

59 James Edmond Hall and Ruth Dayton Woods, ed., *The Diary of a Confederate Soldier* (Lewisburg, WV: n. p., 1961), 81. Hall's hope came true. He survived Gettysburg and the war.

60 John Futch to Martha Ramsey Futch, June 18 and 19, 1863, North Carolina Digital Collections, North Carolina Department of Cultural Resources. Private Futch, lonely and grieving over his brother Charley's death at Gettysburg, was reported absent without leave from August 11-31, 1863. He was court-martialed and shot for desertion in early September.

61 Chisolm, "Forward the Louisiana Brigade," Dennis E. Frye, *2nd Virginia Infantry*, (Lynchburg, Va.: H. E. Howard, 1984), 52-53.

62 *Charleston* (SC) *Mercury*, June 22, 1863, citing unnamed Richmond newspapers; *Hartford* (CT) *Courant*, June 24, 1863; *Charlotte Western Democrat*, July 7, 1863.

When he learned of the stunning victory, Robert E. Lee sent a message to Jefferson Davis: "God has again crowned the valor of our troops with success—Early's division stormed the enemy's entrenchments at Winchester, capturing their artillery, &c." Many of the men in Ewell's Second Corps echoed the sentiment. "Rejoice in the glorious victory which, to use our good old chieftains expression, God has given us," the 33rd Virginia's Capt. George Rust Bedinger expressed in a letter to his brother. He was perhaps more thankful for the "innumerable stores and plunder of every description to an immense account."[63]

That evening, a jubilant General Ewell ordered the Confederate flag raised over Fort Milroy, which he renamed "Fort Jackson" in honor of the late Stonewall. One of his senior staff members, Maj. Alexander S. "Sandie" Pendleton, had asked the girls of the town to make a set of colors for Fort Jackson from two captured U. S. flags. To repay them for their labor, the youthful officer distributed several pairs of ladies' shoes seized from a sutler's inventory. He kept a few pairs to send to his sisters in Lexington, where their father William Nelson Pendleton had been the rector of Grace Church before becoming Lee's chief of artillery.[64]

The makeshift, hand-sewn standard was raised with a 13-gun salute to fly defiantly over the heads of hundreds of sullen Union prisoners held in the re-christened bastion. Several of Winchester's pro-Confederate women gave Ewell three loud cheers. The new corps leader thanked them and asked that they call for a speech by General Early. Repeated cries of "Speech from General Early!" rang out from the throng of women, but Old Jube disliked the attention and unexpected invitation. "Ladies," he calmly remarked with a tip of his hat, "I could never find the courage to address one of you—of course I can't speak to a hundred."[65]

After the brief ceremony, Ewell, Early, and some staff members headed for ardent secessionist Mary Lee's comfortable home and drank tea in her yard. Mrs. Lee and the other women in the household regaled the generals with stories of the fighting around town as seen from their viewpoint. Mary found Ewell quite charming, though he was "rather abrupt in his manners but is enthusiastic & quick." She invited Ewell to establish his headquarters in her house.[66]

63 "Victory at Winchester," *Raleigh Register,* June 20, 1863; G. R. Bedinger to Dear Diddy, June 16, 1863, Camp near Winchester, Virginia, Bedinger-Dandridge Family Papers, Duke University, Durham, North Carolina.

64 Alexander S. Pendleton to his fiancée Kate Corbin, June 18, 1863, 3 miles north of Winchester, Virginia, William Nelson Pendleton Papers, SHC, UNC-Chapel Hill.

65 Hotchkiss diary entry for June 15, 1863; Nye, *Here Come the Rebels!,* 123.

66 Mary Greenhow Lee account, Handley Library.

Ewell also issued a congratulatory order to the men of the Second Corps that echoed the piety of the lamented Stonewall Jackson:

> The Lieutenant General commanding asks the men and officers of the Corps to unite in returning thanks to our Heavenly Father for the signal success which has crowned the valor of this command. In acknowledgment of divine Favor, Chaplains will hold religious services in their respective regiments at such times as might be convenient. With wonderfully small loss—less than 300 killed, wounded and missing—we have carried strong works defended by an abundance of superior artillery, capturing over 3,000 prisoners and large quantities of military stores. . . . Such a result should strengthen the reliance in the righteousness of our cause which has inspired. . . our troops.[67]

Many of Ewell's men were as jubilant about their one-legged commander, who had emerged victorious in his first battle in the late Stonewall's role. "I admire General Ewell . . . he values the lives of his men," wrote one to a hometown paper. "While Jackson was loved and all willing to follow where he led, he did not regard the life of man but rushed ahead carrying by storm everything before him." Opinions on Ewell's caution and adversity to risking his men would change after Gettysburg, but for now he received high and well-earned praise. "I think we have a very good successor to Gen Jackson," opined the Stonewall Brigade's Ted Barclay. Many of his comrades concurred. The prospects for the summer campaign had brightened considerably.[68]

Richmond

The news of General Ewell's nearly bloodless capture of Winchester and a large portion of Milroy's command was received enthusiastically in Richmond. John Beauchamp Jones, working as a clerk in the War Department, kept a detailed diary filled with insight into how the Confederate high command functioned. According to Jones, Richmond "has been gladdened" by Lee's message to President Davis about the smashing victory. Subsequent reports indicated its magnitude. "If we caught Milroy," added the clerk, "the impression prevails that he was hung immediately, in accordance with the President's order some time since, as a just punishment for the outrages inflicted by him on our helpless old men, women, and children." With such an auspicious beginning to the second invasion of the North, the civilians of

---

67 General Order No. 44, June 15, 1863, Jubal A. Early Papers, Microfilm Reel C596, VHS.

68 "At Sharpsburg Again," in *Macon* (GA) *Telegraph*, July 2, 1863; Ted Barclay to Hannah Barclay Moore, June 19, 1863, near Sharpsburg, Maryland, Washington and Lee University.

Richmond were understandably optimistic. How the future would unfold remained to be seen.[69]

The news Winchester was no longer "under the power of the Abolitionists" increased speculation as to Lee's ultimate intentions. "But few people know what our Generals intend to do before they undertake any important movement," editorialized the *Rockingham Register.* "General Lee is first-rate at keeping secrets, and so are the few to whom he is obliged to entrust his designs. Hence, the movement upon the enemy at Winchester was almost a profound secret, until it burst upon him 'like a clap of thunder from a cloudless sky.'" After praising Ewell and recapping the battle, the paper added, "What our troops in the Valley intend to do next, we cannot say; but this we will 'guess:' they do not intend to stand still or to sit down in inglorious ease and permit the summer to end without striking a blow for their country that will be far more important than the recovery of Winchester, however important that may seem to be and really is, to our people."[70]

---

69 John B. Jones, *A Rebel War Clerk's Diary at the Confederate States Capitol,* 2 vols. (Philadelphia: J. B. Lippincott, 1866), 1:350.

70 *Rockingham* (VA) *Register,* June 19, 1863.

Chapter 11

June 16 through June 30

"Verily when it comes to this, a Soldier's life is tough."

— *Pvt. James M. Smith, 18th Connecticut*[1]

Early on the morning of June 16, guards escorted most of the captive Union officers from the overcrowded forts through downtown Winchester before confining them in the iron-fenced courthouse yard. General Early detailed his local guide, Capt. Thomas K. Cartmell, to record the names of the officers, their regiments, and other pertinent information. As the day wore on, the prisoners complained of extreme hunger. When told the Confederates were in the same predicament until rations could be issued, several Union soldiers revealed that they knew the location of a large lot of sutler's supplies. A guard detail accompanied two prisoners into a storeroom across from the Taylor Hotel and came out with barrels of crackers, canned food, cheese, and other edibles that they distributed to the hungry Yankees.[2]

"I think it was not until after we were in the Court-house, that any rations were issued to us," recalled Capt. David S. Caldwell of the 123rd Ohio. "You may well imagine that by that time, we had the most intense relish for what ever might be set before us in the shape of food, as we received but very little during the fight on Saturday and Sunday, previous to our capture on Monday morning." "Today we are in the fort as prisoners of war," 19-year-old Pvt. Phillip A. Huffman of the 123rd Ohio wrote in his diary that Tuesday. "And a miserable place it is too. We had to live on raw meat and water until this evening we got some bread. They took the officers off to

---

1 James M. Smith diary, entry for June 16, 1863.

2 Cartmell, *Shenandoah Valley Pioneers*, 386.

Richmond." The next day he added, "Today we was in the fort and it seemed like a year to me."[3]

According to James M. Smith of the 18th Connecticut, some of the men were reduced to eating raw potatoes to stave off hunger. "Verily when it comes to this, a Soldier's life is tough," he admitted. Several sympathetic pro-Union Quaker ladies of Winchester gave a basket of provisions to 26-year-old Capt. John W. Chamberlin to be distributed among the regiment's officers. Confederate quartermasters finally arrived late that evening with bread and meat.[4]

Early and his provost had to deal with another set of prisoners, for at least 47 wives and children of Union soldiers had fallen into Confederate hands. He authorized the 87th Pennsylvania's Chaplain David C. Eberhart, a former medical student who doubled as the regiment's dentist, to look after the comfort and welfare of 15 laundresses being held in the Main Fort. Eberhart's other duties included assisting the wounded in the Taylor Hotel. He and baritone Chaplain Charles McCabe of the 122nd Ohio also took charge of 17 officers' wives, including Jennie Maish, the young Winchester resident who married the 87th's Capt. Lewis Maish the previous winter. Jennie had attracted Confederate attention through her determined efforts to supply food to the soldiers of the 87th who had been captured in her house.[5]

In addition to the regular battlefield haul of prisoners and military items, the newfound spoils of war included the seizure of some of the Winchester region's free blacks suspected of being escaped slaves. On Tuesday, June 16, William R. Gilmer of the 37th Virginia wrote his sister Martha that they had taken 4,000 prisoners "besides several negroes." Sergeant Isaac V. Reynolds of Jenkins' 16th Virginia Cavalry's letter to his wife mentioned the "boys capturing negroes & horses." "Many darkies were captured," wrote a Winchester grandmother named Ann C. R. Jones, "amongst them the Braxton family except the head of it, vile old William. I do hope for his own sake, as well as ours, he will yet be caught." According to the 52nd Virginia's Pvt. Henry H. Dedrick, "They brought a yankee past and his wife was with him and she was a black one at that. Dr. [John] Lewis asked him if that was his wife. He said yessir and the[y] had took a good many negroes and we got a good many of them back."[6]

---

3 Caldwell, *Incidents of War*, 4; Edna J. Carmean, ed., *Uncle Phil and the Rebbles* (Annville, PA: Lebanon Valley College Press, 1989), 51.

4 James M. Smith diary entry for June 16, 1863; Keyes, *The Military History of the 123rd Ohio*, 119-20.

5 Prowell, *History of the 87th Pennsylvania*, 81.

6 William Reeves Gilmer to Dear sister, June 16, 1863, Winchester, Virginia, Gilmer Family Letters, UVA; I. V. Reynolds to Dear Wife, Harrisonburg, Virginia, August 9, 1863, copies in Duke University, Southern University, and the Illinois Historical Society, transcribed by

Some members of the 33rd Virginia Infantry of Walker's Stonewall Brigade took the opportunity to visit friends and relatives. "I think we shall move to the Potomac today as we are order[ed] to march at eleven," youthful Capt. George R. Bedinger wrote to his brother. "I shall endeavor to get home for an hour. I suppose you will come charging down bag and baggage before soon." The popular former University of Virginia student added with some satisfaction, "I have seen the girls in Winchester." For so many of Ewell's men, their last memory of Winchester was the warm farewell they received as they marched away to an unknown fate in the summer campaign.[7]

The ultimate destination of the army remained a mystery, but rumors circulated that the objective was a bit farther north: Pennsylvania. "I will tell you now that I survived another storm and that it pleased God to let me come out unhurt from the battle field," wrote the thankful 27th Virginia's Sgt. John Garibaldi on June 16 to his sister. "We have now here in the valley about forty thousand men, the corps of Lieutenant General Ewell," he continued, "and what is the object for taking us here I am not able to tell you. I know that it wasn't necessary to take opposite of forty thousand men here to whip and take seven or eight thousand yankees. We feel very much tired out from marching around Fredericksburg to this place," added the Italian-born Garibaldi, "and we are now under marching orders again. We cooked three days rations, and filled up our haversacks with it and we are to be ready to march by eleven o'clock."[8]

Some Confederates turned their minds to the recently fallen and much lamented Stonewall. "If the spirits disembodied can see what goes on in this world," Maj. Sandie Pendleton penned to his fiancée Kate Corbin on June 17, "I am sure that General Jackson has felt unfeigned pleasure since yesterday. Twas a sight worth seeing the joy of the good people of Winchester as our men passed yesterday at daylight. Old men and maidens vied with each other in demonstrations almost frantic. The suspense they had been kept in, knowing the terrible strength of the fortifications erected by the enemy and defended by numerous artillery, made them all the more violent in their manifestations of delight in being free." He wished that Kate could have seen the

---

Gregory Lepore, http://russellvets.org/letters/reynolds2.html, accessed December 30, 2013; Colt, *Defend the Valley*, 259; Henry H. Dedrick to Mary E. A. Dedrick, June 1863, Winchester, Virginia, Henry H. Hedrick Papers, VMI. Dr. John Lewis was the surgeon of the 52nd Virginia.

7 Stephens, *Intrepid Warrior*, 203; George Bedinger to Diddy, June 16, 1863, Camp near Winchester, Bedinger-Dandridge Papers, Duke University. Captain Bedinger would never return to Winchester or see his brother again; he died on July 3 at Gettysburg. He was only 22.

8 John Garibaldi to his wife, Sarah, June 16, 1863, Camp Stephenson, Winchester, Virginia, VMI. Garibaldi was born in Genoa, Italy, on April 30, 1831, and came to the U. S. in 1851.

"wondrous amount" of stores captured from the Federals and particularly the sutlers. "There was candy in profusion and ladies' wearing apparel of various sorts."[9]

On June 17 the artillerists of the 3rd Richmond Howitzers (also known as Company D, 1st Virginia Artillery) rejoiced in finally replacing their two obsolete short-range light howitzers with captured Federals 3-inch Ordnance Rifles. They were amazed to learn that one of the captured guns had belonged to Company D, 1st West Virginia Artillery (Carlin's battery). "We are Virginians," wrote William White, "and they are God knows what!—mostly born in Hesse-Cassel or Hess-Darmstadt— Hessians any way . . . but times have changed, and the 'Blue Mountain boys' hire them now!" The Germans, continued White, "are a liberty-loving people and fight well when they are in a good cause, but frequently they get on the wrong side of the fence, and then they get mostly soundly drubbed. The funny part is money will put them on either side."[10]

Ewell, meanwhile, prepared to push his Second Corps northward. Part of Early's division, including John Gordon's and Harry Hays' brigades, departed Winchester on the afternoon of June 16 and marched north toward Martinsburg, passing the site of the Carter's Woods/Stephenson's Depot fight. The rest of Early's men and those of Johnson's division remained in and around Winchester. Johnson's division moved out the next day. In Martinsburg, the convalescing and recently paroled Pvt. William Hubbard of the 106th New York watched as Johnson's veterans tramped through the town. "Another force of Rebels 6,000 came in this morning," he recalled, though he had no idea where they were bound, neither did the Rebels tramping in the ranks. "We are not stopping here," declared Ewell's able chief of staff Sandie Pendleton, who was also privy to the plans of the Confederate high command. "Jenkins, with his cavalry brigade, is already at Chambersburg [Pennsylvania]—Rodes's division moving to Hagerstown and Johnson's crossing at Shepherdstown. We are going to Harrisburg."[11]

The youthful staffer was correct. On June 18, Jubal Early moved out of Winchester with the rest of his brigade and Lt. Col. Hilary Jones' artillery battalion, leaving "Extra Billy" Smith's 13th and 58th Virginia and Colonel Avery's 54th North Carolina behind to guard the prisoners and process the captured stores. "I was given a detachment of men and sent to patrol Winchester, and there remained until the army returned," the 13th's Pvt. J. W. Baker recounted. "No people acquitted themselves

9 Alexander S. Pendleton to his fiancée Kate Corbin, June 18, 1863, 3 miles north of Winchester, Virginia, William Nelson Pendleton Papers, SHC, UNC-Chapel Hill.

10 White, "A Diary of the War," 191.

11 Hubbard diary entry for June 17, 1863; Lee, *William Nelson Pendleton*, 278.

better than did the women of this town. The wounded were everywhere, and night and day they cooked, made beds, dressed wounds, removed parasites, no service too menial for them to perform. How noble a woman can be when she stoops to serve."[12]

That same hot Thursday, the 106th New York's William Hubbard was depressed that "no news or information can be had of the 106th Regt. or 126 Ohio Regt." He watched from Mrs. Ann Woolf's house as Early's division and Jones' artillery passed through Martinsburg. "Rebs shure of success," he penned in his diary. "I seen a number of Negroes armed in the Rebel ranks going this evening." The Rebels, continued the New Yorker, had used the Odd Fellows Hall to house their sick men who had suffered "quite a number of Deaths." Hubbard praised the loyal women of Martinsburg for demonstrating their very strong Union sentiment both in talk and acts. They were continuously bringing in provisions, tobacco, cigars, and other things for the comfort of the men. They kept up their kindness despite the presence of "Secesh" soldiers and Southern sympathizers, waiting with great interest for the Yankees to make their appearance.[13]

With Milroy's division of the Eighth Corps shattered and no longer combat worthy, "there is much less obstruction to the contemplated invasion of Pennsylvania," penned a Baltimore-based correspondent. "A feeling is gaining ground here, even with the Union men, that unless the people of the North more fully realize the solemn importance of their position, and cease to divide amongst themselves on mere partisan or political questions, there will be no regrets at seeing the rebels penetrate even as far as New York, teaching disloyal men a practical lesson that they may better understand the value of their country, and learn that republican liberty is not to be trifled with." He continued exhorting his *Philadelphia Inquirer* readers: "Now is the hour for unity, and the indignant ignoring of all partisan issues."[14]

News of the stunning outcome of the Winchester fighting spread quickly throughout the Confederacy. "God be thanked for the glorious news," penned a

---

12 J. W. Baker, "War Reminiscences," in *Clinch Valley* (VA) *News*, April 22, 1921. The 54th NC had a new commander, Col. Kenneth M. Murchison. He had recently been promoted to replace Col. J. C. S. McDowell, who was mortally wounded during the Chancellorsville campaign.

13 Hubbard diary entries for June 18-21, 1863. Early's division included the Louisiana Tigers which had a mulatto man named Charles Lutz in the ranks as well as several men of Caribbean origin. Gordon's brigade included several Native Americans from Georgia. Perhaps it was these darker-skinned soldiers which Hubbard saw and mistook as "Negroes." No accounts have surfaced of any sizeable number of African-Americans in the division. For more on Lutz and the ethnic make-up of the First Louisiana Brigade, see Mingus, *The Louisiana Tigers in the Gettysburg Campaign*.

14 *Daily Milwaukee News*, June 21, 1863.

North Carolinian Catherine Ann Devereux Edmondston. "Great news, which stirs every fibre of our hearts & bodies with thankfulness. God has indeed blessed us."[15]

Ewell's Confederates remained optimistic as they tramped onward. "One week ago the boasting Genl Milroy with his defiant host was occupying the hills about your illfated town confident of resisting the advance of any number of depised rebels that might dare approach," declared Dr. Caspar C. Henkel of the 37th Virginia on June 21. In a letter to his cousin Maggie, the surgeon reiterated that the "noble, self-sacrificing, good people of Winchester were in awful suspense between hope & fear" under Milroy's reign. Ewell's "sturdy, brave Confederates [overcame] the fierce resistance of the guilty enemy," capturing most of them except "their miserable leader." Henkel claimed Milroy reached Harpers Ferry with 800 horsemen "in very good order & reported to the war department that all had arrived safely at that point with very little loss. Oh! what heaven forsaken unblushing liars!"[16]

Reaction in Washington, D.C.

When word of Milroy's crushing defeat filtered into the War Department in Washington, President Abraham Lincoln met with his general-in-chief, Henry Halleck, and Secretary of the Navy Gideon Welles to discuss the loss. Someone needed to be blamed for the debacle, concluded Halleck, and Milroy and Schenck were the logical candidates. Welles, never shy with his opinions, lambasted Halleck and placed the blame for Milroy's disaster squarely on the general-in-chief. "I cannot learn from the War Department how early Milroy was warned from here that the Rebels were approaching him and that it would be necessary for him to fall back. Halleck scolds and swears about him as a stupid, worthless fellow. This seems his way to escape censure himself and cover his stupidity in higher position. . . . Halleck sits, and smokes, and swears, and scratches his arm . . . but exhibits little military capacity or intelligence; is obfuscated, muddy, uncertain, stupid as to what is doing or to be done." Milroy, concluded Welles, would become "the scapegoat, and blamed for the stupid blunders, neglects, and mistakes of those who should have warned and advised him." The naval secretary believed, and correctly so, that Halleck should bear some of the

---

15 Catherine Ann Devereux Edmondston, Beth G. Crabtree and James W. Patton, eds., *Journal of a Secesh Lady: The Diary of Catherine Ann Devereux Edmondston 1860-1866* (Raleigh: North Carolina Division of Archives and History, 1979), https://civilianwartime.wordpress.com/2013/06/20/god-be-thanked-for-the-glorious-news-which-reached-us-last-night-cw150/, accessed May 20, 2015.

16 Caspar C. Henkel to cousin, June 21, 1863, near Sharpsburg, Maryland, Henkel Family Correspondence, Modern Manuscripts Collection, History of Medicine Division, National Library of Medicine, National Institutes of Health, Bethesda, Maryland.

blame for failing to act soon enough to make sure Milroy's command could be safely withdrawn from Winchester. In fact, it was already clear the political powers intended to make an example of Milroy.[17]

Given the magnitude of the disaster at Winchester, the War Department decided to do what it could to clamp down on the information being disseminated about it. One of the first attempts was by Federal officials to muzzle the newspapers. Reporter F. G. Chapman informed his superiors at the *New York Herald*, "I could not telegraph you for the reason that the War Department has prohibited correspondents from sending over the wires any war news of whatever character." The effort, however, proved unsuccessful.[18]

Destination Harpers Ferry and Western Maryland

As noted earlier, the confusion at Carter's Woods brought about by the darkness, conflicting orders, and determined Confederate action broke apart and scattered Milroy's force. A large portion of the beaten division headed off toward Harpers Ferry, while another sizable group trickled northwest toward the West Virginia mountain range. Among the first Eighth Corps soldiers to reach safety were Pvt. David Emerson and the detachment of the 18th Connecticut in charge of the quartermaster's horses and mules. They had left the fields near Carter's Woods during Milroy's second charge. Emerson rode his mule bareback and for the last 52 miles led a second mule with a halter. Emerson and his little band reached Cumberland, Maryland, on June 16. He left both mules there, wearily climbed on top of a railcar filled with hay, tied his handkerchief around his eyes, and fell sound asleep within a few minutes. Someone shook him awake when the train pulled into New Creek, West Virginia. "I never was so used up in my life," he wrote his hometown newspaper, "but I feel better now." He felt even better when he learned the Rebels had seized Cumberland and cut the rail line just hours after his train had rolled out.[19]

Milroy's routed soldiers were making their escape when Confederate Capt. John H. "Hanse" McNeill's partisan rangers arrived on the scene after returning from their scouting expedition with Harry Gilmor. "We captured over one hundred fifty prisoners," bragged one of McNeill's rangers, "between eighty and ninety horses, many of them having splendid harness, and a large number of saddles, revolvers,

---

17 Gideon Welles, *Diary of Gideon Welles: Secretary of the Navy Under Lincoln and Johnson*, 2 vols. (Boston: Houghton-Mifflin, 1909), 1:328, 331.

18 *New York Herald*, June 22, 1863.

19 *Dear Transcript*, 293.

carbines, etc." The swirling mass of rangers only added to the confusion and chaos that befell the survivors of Milroy's division. Most of the survivors managed to slip away and McNeill's men moved on to other pursuits.[20]

Milroy and General Elliott joined 18 officers and 305 enlisted men of Colonel Keifer's 110th Ohio and an equal number of the 122nd Ohio during the hasty flight toward Harpers Ferry. Keifer's Buckeyes were lucky to get out of the final bloody chaos that was Carter's Woods. "The cavalry became panic-stricken and, commingling with the mules and horses on which teamsters and others were mounted, all in great disorder took wildly to the hills and mountains to the northwest, followed by infantry in somewhat better order," recalled Keifer years later. "The mules brayed, the horses neighed, the teamsters and riders indulged in much vigorous profanity. . . . Citizens on Apple Pie Ridge who witnessed the wild scene describe it as a veritable bedlam." Keifer had collected as many men as possible and struck out in the direction of Harpers Ferry. A wounded captain named E. A. Shepherd was helped off the field, but soon collapsed from weakness and exhaustion. Keifer had no choice but to leave the unfortunate officer behind to his fate.[21]

By the time Old Grey Eagle caught up with Keifer and the rest of the men he was thoroughly exhausted. He later told Mary that he had not slept at all during the preceding two nights and after escaping the Confederate trap fell asleep in the saddle. He remained on his mount only because loyal aides propped him up in the saddle to keep him from toppling off. Milroy and Elliott arrived at Harpers Ferry about two o'clock that afternoon. Other survivors, singly and in groups, trickled in throughout the course of the day. All of them remained at Harpers Ferry for nearly two weeks before eventually leaving to join the Army of the Potomac after the battle of Gettysburg.[22]

Throughout June 16 and 17, Capt. Frank Bond's company of the 1st Maryland Cavalry (Confederate) actively pursued and harassed the disordered enemy. At one point Lt. James A. V. Pue and a squad of six soldiers boldly charged into the midst of almost 100 demoralized Yankee refugees. Most raised their hands in surrender.

20 *Rockingham Register*, July 31, 1863; Scharf, *History of Western Maryland*, 268; C. Armour Newcomer, *Cole's Cavalry, or Three Years in the Saddle in the Shenandoah Valley* (Baltimore: Cushing & Co., 1895), 50. Some of the last Union soldiers to reach Harpers Ferry belonged to Capt. George Vernon's company of Cole's Cavalry, which had spent the day covering Milroy's retreat by patrolling the roads from Charles Town and beyond to the Potomac River.

21 Keifer, *Slavery and Four Years of War*, 1:167; OR 27, pt. 1, 8.

22 Milroy to Mary Milroy, June 16, 1863, Milroy Papers; OR 27, pt. 2, 22; Prowell, *History of the Eighty-seventh Regiment*, 87. Eventually, these troops were incorporated into Maj. Gen. William H. French's division of the 8th Corps which was transferred to the Army of the Potomac's Third Corps on July 10, 1863.

However, a few resisted and desultory firing broke out. The heavily outnumbered Pue withdrew and allowed the Federals to continue their determined quest for safety. After this experience, Captain Bond masked his strength by opening fire from ambush when he encountered similar parties. Only after the Yankees stacked arms would Bond reveal his small numbers—much to the disgust of his new prisoners. With these tactics he eventually rounded up an eclectic collection of more than 500 prisoners of all arms.[23]

The 12th and 13th Pennsylvania Cavalry, escorting some of Milroy's escaping infantrymen, encountered heavy musket and artillery fire outside Bunker Hill that only served to further demoralize the horsemen. When the small force of infantry was unable to cut its way out, Major Michael Kerwin's 13th Pennsylvania tried to break free and also failed. Kerwin knew the foot soldiers could not keep up with his troopers and decided to abandon them to their fate in an effort to save his own command, which made for Harpers Ferry. "We arrived there after noon, more dead than alive, crossed over the Potomac, and went up on Maryland Heights," recalled Sgt. S. T. Linn of Company F. "We tied our horses to trees, and dropped down on the ground and went to sleep—a hungry sleep at that, not having had time to cook anything the last three days, not even coffee." Before long, some officers of one of the New York heavy artillery units assigned to the garrison at Harpers Ferry visited the refugees. The Empire State men fed the hungry cavalrymen and their horses, and even cooked meat for the new arrivals. "We were utterly worn out with loss of sleep and our rough trip from Winchester," admitted Linn.[24]

An officer of the 13th Pennsylvania Cavalry described his regiment's losses and the route he and his comrades followed to reach safety at Harpers Ferry. Noting they were fortunate to cut their way out, the Pennsylvanian mentioned that his "colonel, however, is missing, two majors, half the officers, and half the regiment. With a portion [of the 13th Pennsylvania] I rode by a circuitous course to avoid the swarming bands which had passed to our front to intercept us, and, running the gauntlet of shells, finally forded the Potomac at Shepherdstown, and arrived here this morning. We must have ridden 70 miles after the battle, without a halt," he concluded, "save for such few minutes as was necessary to reconnoiter."[25]

Milroy's crushing defeat at Winchester alarmed the garrison at the confluence of the three rivers. "At present appearances, there is every prospect of Harpers Ferry being again under rebel domination," wrote a member of the 50th New York

---

23 Bond, "Company A, First Maryland Cavalry."

24 Linn, "The Cavalry at Winchester."

25 *Philadelphia Inquirer,* June 23, 1863.

Engineers on June 16. The Union soldiers expected Ewell's army to pay them a visit next, so they took steps to transfer horses and other animals across the Potomac River into Maryland. "Harpers Ferry is considered safe and impregnable," a Baltimore-based correspondent for the *Philadelphia Inquirer* penned, perhaps forgetting that Stonewall Jackson had captured it less than a year earlier. Others apparently did not think the place all that stable, for as he noted, "Large reinforcements have been sent up towards that place from Washington, sufficient, it is hoped, with the forces already along the lines to repel the invaders." This time and to the surprise of many in the Union ranks, the Confederates bypassed Harpers Ferry and headed straight into Maryland.[26]

In Baltimore, meanwhile, General Schenck was forced to contend with the disaster that had befallen Milroy's command. After retreating from Martinsburg, General Tyler assumed command of the forces at Harpers Ferry. "Colonel McReynolds is on his way to you," Schenck wrote Tyler. "General Milroy has been ordered to turn over his command to you. You will organize and bring it into the best condition you can as soon as possible and report your force, or whole probable force, at the earliest moment you can. General Halleck says, if you are besieged you will soon be relieved." Schenck also ordered Milroy to move from Harpers Ferry by way of Harrisburg to Bloody Run (now Everett), where he was to assume command of the troops gathering there.[27]

While the rest of the survivors of Elliott's brigade headed toward Hancock, Maryland, the rest of the 122nd Ohio Infantry made a grueling 34-mile march to Harpers Ferry by the most direct route its members could find. The Buckeye contingent safely arrived at Bolivar Heights just outside the town about six o'clock that evening, having made remarkably good time after the heavy fighting at Carter's Woods. The next day the Ohioans moved on to and up Maryland Heights, where they remained until July 1, their harrowing ordeal finally at an end. On June 19, the *Philadelphia Inquirer* reported that 74 of the 123 men of Alexander's Baltimore Battery had also reached welcoming safety at Harpers Ferry, and that "whatever loss they

---

26 Williams, "Our Army Correspondence"; *Daily Milwaukee News*, June 21, 1863.

27 *OR* 27, pt. 3, 127. Bloody Run, now called Everett, is in Bedford County in south-central Pennsylvania. Some accounts suggest it was originally named for a nearby creek that was the site of a battle between white settlers and Indians. Other sources claim the name stemmed from an earlier incident in 1768 during the French & Indian War (Seven Years' War) when troops under English general John Forbes slaughtered beef cattle near the creek. The town was renamed in 1873 for famed orator Edward Everett, the keynote speaker at the dedication of the Gettysburg National Cemetery. See *History of Bedford, Somerset, and Fulton Counties, Pennsylvania* (Chicago, 1884), 313.

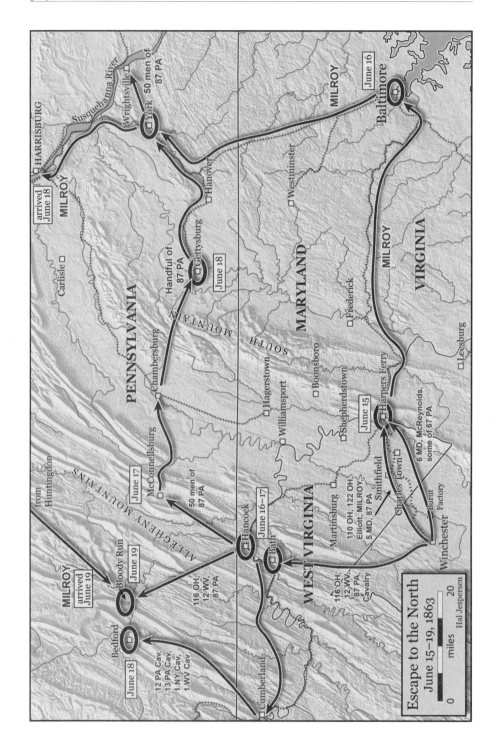

Escape to the North
June 15–19, 1863

Hal Jespersen

0   miles   20

sustained was in the retreat, and as they were all mounted, it is believed that but few were captured."[28]

Several hundred soldiers of the 18th Connecticut reached Harpers Ferry "after a long and tedious march," wrote Charles Lynch in his diary. "Tired and discouraged we dropped to the ground for rest and sleep. Our regiment was badly broken up. Many killed, wounded, and prisoners. The trials of the past few days were something fearful to endure. It was wonderful that we came out as well as we did. Short of rations, sleeping on the ground." After a couple of days' rest these men marched through the town there and up rugged Maryland Heights, where they remained for about two weeks.[29]

The pending arrival of Milroy's remnants muddled the Union command situation there. "Don't give General Milroy any command at Harpers Ferry," Halleck instructed Schenck on June 15, the day Johnson ripped apart much of the Eighth Corps at Stephenson's Depot outside Winchester. "We have had enough of that sort of military genius." That same day, however, Milroy sent a telegram announcing his arrival at Harpers Ferry with the remnants of his command. "Spiked all my guns on Sunday evening, and left with the whole of my command at 1 o'clock on Monday morning, bringing all the horses of my artillery and wagons, but was interrupted by an overwhelming rebel force, with artillery, four miles this side of Winchester, on the Martinsburgh road, and after a desperate fight of two hours, I got through," he wrote. "We were pursued by a large cavalry force, who picked up a number of my weary boys." The moniker "weary boys" stuck to the veterans of Milroy's division, for whom the name became a badge of honor.[30]

Pursuant to Halleck's direct orders, Schenck directed Milroy to turn over command to General Tyler and report in person to his headquarters in Baltimore. The next day, in an effort to lessen the impact of his relief, Schenck suggested to the defeated officer that a force of the enemy "set loose to come upon you in such overwhelming force & rapidly as the Rebels did, I think you made the best resistance you possibly could. . . . You can help me in person here or have a short leave of absence, if you prefer it, in order to rest after the hard & bloody work you have fought through, or you may stop awhile if you think it best to aid in reorganizing & getting

28 "History of the Marches, Skirmishes, & Battles of Co. F, 122 Ohio Vols. from May 1, 1863 until May 1, 1865," Papers of Co. F, 122nd O.V.I., Ohio Historical Society, Columbus; *Philadelphia Inquirer*, June 19, 1863.

29 Lynch, *Civil War Diary*, 22-23.

30 OR 27, pt. 2, 171, 176; "The Battle at Winchester: Official Dispatch from Gen. Milroy. His Outer Fortifications Carried by Storm. He Spikes His Guns and Cuts His Way out. Our Loss About 2,000 in Killed, Wounded and Prisoners," *New York Times*, June 17, 1863.

back into shape & good condition as quick as possible for methodical work & resistance if attacked again, your own brigade & men you understand." Schenck signed the letter, "With much respect & regard, your friend."[31]

As ordered, Milroy reported to the department commander, received new orders, and boarded a train to return to Harpers Ferry. When the train arrived in Frederick, Maryland (21 miles from Harpers Ferry) Milroy learned Confederates had cut the telegraph wires ahead and were now between the two towns. Milroy had no choice but to turn the train around and return to Baltimore early on the morning of June 18. Once there, the Grey Eagle boarded a Northern Central Railway train to Harrisburg, Pennsylvania, hoping to reach the remnants of his command by that indirect route.[32]

Milroy's arrival in the Keystone State's capital elicited a stream of editorial sarcasm from unsympathetic Northern newspapers. A *New York World* reporter was particularly biting in his commentary. After accepting the early news that Milroy had "contended with superhuman gallantry against [a] vastly superior force," the newsman now admitted that "truth and daylight always dawn at last. While Milroy was galloping up and down Harrisburg streets to keep his spirits up, he was suddenly astonished by the apparition of a great number of his own lost soldiers. We do not doubt his first impulse was to order them under arrest," mocked the newsman, "for a soldier who has been reported as lost by [a] general, is clearly guilty of insubordination in coming to life again. But curiosity seems to have got the better of discipline in the mind of Milroy, and he at once set about finding out what had become of his army." The Grey Eagle reported losing 2,000 men, but 3,100 refugees had recently returned to their regiments. The math simply did not add up if Milroy was telling the truth about his losses. "He must content himself now with the station of chief recruiting officer of the nation. His qualifications for this post are indisputable," continued the *New York World* editorial. "By placing Milroy in supreme command therefore, we shall evidently avoid the necessity of conscription. The more battles he loses, the more forces we shall have in field."[33]

The 6th Maryland marched into Harpers Ferry on June 18 with their flags flying, their arms at ease, and singing "Hail Columbia" with the regiment's commander, Col.

---

31 *OR* 27, pt. 3, 127; Robert C. Schenck to Robert H. Milroy, June 16, 1863, Baltimore, Robert Cumming Schenck Papers, Miami University Archives, Oxford, Ohio.

32 "Our Baltimore Letter," *Philadelphia Inquirer*, June 19, 1863. Researcher Steve French believes these cavalrymen may have been a small patrol diaptched by Harry Gilmor. That officer had ordered Capt. T. Sturgis Davis to scout to Frederick, Maryland, with 10 men and the next day he moved on Frederick with the 1st Md.Cavalry Battalion. See Gilmor, *Four Years in the Saddle*, 92-94.

33 "The Rout at Winchester," *New York World*, reprinted in the *Portland* (ME) *Weekly Advertiser*.

John W. Horn, riding at its head. Although they had been surrounded and forced to surrender at Stephenson's Depot, the Confederates failed to disarm the men or place guards over them. "Colonel Horn knowing the county well, and seeing an opportunity to escape by a side road, formed his men in line, and in the darkness of the evening moved quickly off." Horn adeptly guided his men on a circuitous route to the ferry by using farm roads and thus bypassing the towns of Berryville, Smithfield, and Charles Town, "rejoicing with neither an enemy in front or pursuers in their rear." They intentionally misled the local citizens by claiming to be the advance guard of the Army of Potomac seeking the road to Berryville instead of admitting that they had escaped from the Confederate trap at Winchester. "We are here, in our own state again, what there is left of us," penned a relieved Cpl. Hiram Hamilton of the 6th Maryland. "We numbered near 800 men when we marched to Winchester, 290 some is all that is left."[34]

"What a sad sorry wreck we all were when we marched up to our old camping ground of the past winter," admitted the 6th's frustrated Lt. Col. William McKellip. "Many were shoeless, some were in their stocking feet, and altogether we presented a condition pitiable in the extreme." "It seemed like as if they had risen from the dead," a reporter for the *Baltimore American* recorded, "and their return caused great astonishment. The gallant fellows were in a sad condition after so severe a march and fight, but were full of spirit and gratification that they had escaped the clutches of the enemy."[35]

Finally safe at Harpers Ferry, Pvt. Thomas Crowl of the 87th Pennsylvania took a few minutes to write to his sister Mary. While on "the road to Martinsburg 4 miles the Rebs attacked us, and there we fought them hard for 1 hour and a ½. But with all they cut us all to peaces. We had 800 men in our Regt when we went in to them and now we have but 132 in all. We have only 10 men in our company."[36]

The soldiers of the river garrison watched as Milroy's broken regiments filed onto Maryland Heights. Private Archibald T. Kirkwood of the 7th Maryland Infantry informed a friend that "the 5th Md has got 4 left all we have seen the 87th Pen has got about 100 left [Capt. Murray] Crosses Company had got 19 in it not a commissioned officer in that company they are either killed or taken prisoners James Thompson is

34 "War News," *The Cecil* (MD) *Whig*, June 20, 1863; *Richmond Daily Dispatch*, June 22, 1863, citing the *Baltimore American*; "Newspaper Reports; Winchester and Harpers Ferry"; Hiram Hamilton to his niece Anna, June 25, 1863, Maryland Heights, Maryland. Hiram and his brother George both died of typhoid fever later that summer, only five days apart.

35 McKellip, "Gen. Milroy's Retreat."; *New York Times*, June 19, 1863.

36 Thomas O. Crowl to Dear Sister, June 16, 1863, Harpers Ferry, West Virginia, Crowell letters, USAHEC.

Capt. William H. Boyd, the intrepid commander of Company C of the 1st New York (Lincoln) Cavalry, who shepherded Milroy's wagon train to Harrisburg safely.
U.S. Army Heritage and Education Center

one of the missing there was a big loss on both sides but from all accounts the rebs paid dear for their trip." Kirkwood added, "We have been in line of battle ever since [the morning of June 16] and not allowed to leave any distance from the line." The 7th's Maryland's Pvt. Daniel Mowen watched from atop Maryland Heights as Milroy's wagons made their way toward safety. "We could see the wagon train wending its way across the valley. All kinds of rumors were afloat, and we were living under constant expectation of something turning up."[37]

Captain Boyd and the wagon train

The passage of the wagon train and the ordeal of the men took a severe toll. "After a terrible march from Berryville via Bunker Hill, Martinsburgh and Williamsport, we arrived here yesterday morning with all our trains safely," reported Lt. James Touchstone, the regimental quartermaster of the 6th Maryland. "We lost all of our camp equipage and was without tents until December following, being exposed during that time to all kinds of weather without shelter of any kind," wrote Lt. Colonel Joseph Hill, "and it was the exposure aforesaid and the mental strain caused by his anxiety for the safety of his Wagon Train which led to a protracted illness, necessitating his [Lt. Touchstone's] resignation and subsequently caused his death from consumption."[38]

---

37 Archibald T. Kirkwood to his father, June 18, 1863, Kirkwood Papers, MHS; Daniel H. Mowen manuscript, *The Globe* newspaper files, Middletown Valley Historical Society, Middletown, Maryland.

38 "Newspaper Reports; Winchester and Harpers Ferry"; Affidavit of Joseph C. Hill, James Touchstone pension file, RG 94, NARA. Touchstone's brief dispatch was quoted in the June 19, 1863, *New York Times*. Touchstone resigned his commission and died in 1872 from tuberculosis contracted in the field.

Under the superb leadership of the intrepid Capt. William H. Boyd and his Company C of the 1st New York Cavalry, the wagon train covered about 120 miles before reaching the safety of the Union fortifications protecting Harrisburg. "During the entire afternoon Market Street was occupied with army wagons from Milroy's division, which rumbled across the old bridge, and from thence past the railroad depot and out to a camp ground on the other side of the canal," reported a newspaper correspondent. "These wagons were mostly drawn by four horses, though there were some mule teams among them. Dust was the prevailing feature of the vehicles, from the ears of the horses to the hat rims of the teamsters. Some of the wagons were filled with hay and some with tents, while from many peeped the black faces, grinning mouths and white teeth of contrabands, large and small, of both sexes." It took several hours for the entire wagon train to pass completely, "giving the spectators a far better idea of the dust, turmoil and fatigue of war than they could get in any other way."[39]

Once Boyd delivered his charges to the Union authorities in Harrisburg, he and his troopers headed south again to resist Ewell's invasion of their native Pennsylvania. "Then he began a system of partisan warfare, dashing upon the enemy in front and on both flanks, causing them to think there was a large force in their front, and preventing them from doing much mischief that they otherwise might have done, and helped to save the State capitol from the invaders," recounted Capt. James H. Stevenson of the 1st New York Cavalry. "From the 15th of June, when they left Winchester, to the 15th of July, this company was never out of sight of the enemy, and seldom a day passed without their having a fight. They captured many prisoners, and a vast amount of property, beside saving untold thousands to the people of the Cumberland Valley."[40]

Not everyone saw Boyd's service as heroic. Sergeant George W. Nailer of the 13th Pennsylvania Cavalry was a schoolteacher in Carlisle before the war. He knew that part of the Keystone State very well. "The First New York Cavalry have been trying to gain the praise by publishing great feats in the N. Y. Herald, but they do not say where they were on Sunday, and where they skedaddled to on Monday morning," he groused in a letter to his parents. "I know for certainty that they were driven as far as Carlisle, if not further." Nailer did not realize that Boyd's company had been given such an important task to complete or that he had dogged the advance of Jenkins'

39 "Newspaper Reports; Winchester and Harpers Ferry."

40 Stevenson, "The First Cavalry," 639; Despite being credited to the 1st New York Cavalry, Boyd's company was recruited in Philadelphia and Company K was from Grand Rapids, Michigan. One of Boyd's troopers, Cpl. William H. Rihl of Philadelphia, was the first Union soldier killed north of the Mason-Dixon Line during the Gettysburg campaign when one of Jenkins' troopers killed him on June 22 on the Fleming farm along the Valley Turnpike just north of Greencastle. A handsome monument marks Rihl's final resting place.

cavalry. All he knew was that Boyd and his men had ridden all the way to Harrisburg—and that bothered him a great deal.[41]

The March of the Hodgepodge Brigade

In large groups, small parties, and individuals, the survivors of Milroy's ruined division had made their escape from the Stephenson's Depot battlefield. Realizing the enemy was in Martinsburg in force, Milroy had ordered his closest troops to march west and head for the Baltimore & Ohio Railroad at some point near Hancock. "We then quickly moved to the left, westward, through a piece of woods, skirmishing with an unseen foe as we went, until we reached an open field beyond, where we halted and reformed," recounted Lt. Col. Thomas F. Wildes of the 116th Ohio Infantry. The Buckeye officer discovered that the little disorganized force consisted of elements of the 12th West Virginia and the 6th Maryland, plus fragments of several regiments, a battalion of the 1st New York Cavalry, and about half of the 12th Pennsylvania Cavalry.[42]

The ranking officers, Col. James Washburn of the 116th Ohio and Maj. Alonzo Adams of the 1st New York Cavalry, conferred and settled on a course of retreat with the infantry in advance and the cavalry covering the rear of the column. "Knowing precisely the direction to take, and the point to make, we were enabled in the confusion following the engagement, aided by the mist of early dawn, to get well on our way before we were discovered by the rebels. When they did discover us, they followed with a considerable force, determined to cut us off from a gap in the mountains, which we were aiming, with all speed, to reach." The New York horse soldiers "did splendid service now in protecting the rear of our column, and preventing the enemy's cavalry from obstructing our march." The detachment of the 12th Pennsylvania dashed ahead to seize and hold the mountain pass. "By dint of hard marching, and considerable maneuvering and skirmishing, we reached the gap, and

---

41 Nailer to his parents, July 7, 1863. To reward his magnificent performance during the Gettysburg campaign, Boyd, who had just been promoted to major in the 1st New York Cavalry, was promoted again to colonel in August 1863 and assigned command of the newly mustered 21st Pennsylvania Cavalry. Boyd was badly wounded leading his troops in the May 1864 battle of the Wilderness and as a consequence had to be discharged because of disability. But the intrepid Canadian turned Philadelphian who recruited the Civil War's first company of volunteer cavalry left his indelible mark on the Second Battle of Winchester and the rest of the campaign that followed. For a detailed biographical sketch of Col. William H. Boyd, see Eric J. Wittenberg, "Col. William H. Boyd, Part 2," http://civilwarcavalry.com/?p=3849, accessed May 20, 2015.

42 Wildes, *Record of the 116th Regiment*, 59-60.

entering the narrow mountain pass, we were safe against further successful pursuit by almost any amount of force."[43]

These men marched northward along the Frederick-Morgan Turnpike to Bath, where they rested a few hours. Many of the men took the opportunity to bathe and relax in the sulfurous waters of Berkeley Springs. "As we were starting [to march] again," recalled Wildes, "we learned that a force of rebel cavalry was trying to get possession of certain mountain roads ahead of us a short distance, in order to cut us off from the ford of the Potomac at St. John's Run." He continued: "Hastily throwing a few companies forward, to command these roads, we moved out quickly, and crossed the ford without molestation, but we were scarcely across before the enemy appeared on the opposite bank of the river. From here we sent our horses and mules to Cumberland." The bedraggled refugees of Carter's Woods continued on to Hancock.[44]

This motley force, dubbed the participants as the "Hodgepodge Brigade," consisted of about 80 troopers of the 13th Pennsylvania Cavalry, about 275 troopers of the 12th Pennsylvania Cavalry, eight officers and 350 enlisted men of the 1st New York Cavalry, Captain Carlin and about 50 men of the Wheeling Battery, 650 men and officers of the 12th West Virginia, 500 men and officers of the 116th Ohio, 80 officers and men of the 123rd Ohio (with 35 prisoners of war in tow), 30 officers and men of an engineering detachment, a small contingent of the 87th Pennsylvania, and about 200 teamsters and another 100 or so stragglers—indeed a ragtag hodgepodge command that fit well with its temporary name. Colonel Washburn remained in command of the infantry portion of the motley force while Major Adams continued to lead the mounted detachment.[45]

A trooper of the 13th Pennsylvania Cavalry shared his saga. He "only left the field when it had been cleared of all but a few drivers of artillery, and then joined the forces to the left. We passed through Bath at dark, crossed the Potomac River into Hancock, reaching it at about 9 P.M.," he wrote. "Next morning, Col. James A. Galligher, of the Thirteenth Pennsylvania Cavalry, took command of all the forces in the place appointing First Lieut. John W. Berks, of the same regiment, Adjutant General, and Major Timothy Quinn, of the First New York Cavalry, Provost-Marshal. The Major appointed Capt. [Joseph K.] Stearns and Lieut. [Erwin C.] Watkins, of his regiment, as his Assistants, and order was immediately established. Capt. Alexander and Lieut.

43 Ibid.

44 Ibid. Bath was also known as Berkeley Springs Post Office.

45 Ibid., "The Loss of Winchester."

McKee, of Gen. Elliott's Staff, were on hand as Quartermasters and for commissary supplies, and every man was well taken care of."[46]

"After the retreat was ordered we all took to the mountains every man for himself," the 87th Pennsylvania's Cpl. Jacob M. Herr recorded in his diary. "But after traveling in the mountains awhile there was about two thousand of us got together. We were then commanded by Col. Galacher. The casualties of our company are a few as I know J. Hoffman, D. Wickey, D. McClellan wounded. The Col. [John Schall] had his horse shot from under him, but he escaped. We are tired and hungry for we had no sleep for three nights and on our feet all the time, and nothing to eat but some onions that we got along the road, we ate without salt or bread. We are encamped tonight 10 miles from the Potomac."[47]

Another small group of survivors from the 87th Pennsylvania independently arrived in Hancock, where its members encountered Lt. Col. James A. Stahle and Maj. Noah Ruhl. Ruhl informed them that since the location of Colonel Schall and the rest of the regiment was unknown, they were free to head home if they desired. Ten men including William E. Culp and David G. Myers reached Gettysburg on June 19, where rumors spread that the Rebels had killed or captured all of the officers of Company H. Several other Pennsylvanians eventually returned to York County, where they helped defend the mile-and-a-quarter-long multi-purpose covered bridge over the broad Susquehanna River. One of these soldiers informed the *York Gazette* that members of the 87th "singly and in squads are roaming through the country seeking their way home." Corporal Henry Bowman and Jacob Moon had been convalescents in the hospital in Winchester. When the retreat started, they secured two horses and escaped to New Creek, West Virginia. They would not arrive in Bloody Run until the evening of June 21.[48]

Some of the 87th's refugees were not as fortunate. Lieutenant Henry Morningstar of Company G had managed to escape the Confederates swarming around Carter's Woods and, despite his ruptured groin, walked with great difficulty to the eastern slope of the West Virginia mountains. The small squad of men included Privates Daniel Stine and Alfred Wilt. Supposing they were safe, the small group sat down to rest. Confederate partisan Hans McNeill and his rangers, however, rounded them up

---

46 "The Loss of Winchester; A Narrative of the Investment and Abandonment of the Place," *New York Times*, June 28, 1863.

47 Herr diary entry for June 15, 1863.

48 Sarah Broadhead and Salome Myers Stewart accounts, GNMP; *York* (PA) *Gazette*, June 23, 1863; Herr diary entry for June 22, 1863. For much more on the defense of the world's longest covered bridge see Mingus, *Flames Beyond Gettysburg*.

and escorted captives to Martinsburg. The next day they were being held prisoner in Winchester.[49]

The Hodgepodge Brigade bivouacked on North Mountain that night before resuming the march about midnight on the 16th. The refugees arrived at Hancock about noon. "The men, of course, by the time were much exhausted from two or three days; fighting, little sleep since the fight began three days before, little to eat for the last day or two, and hard marching," recounted a soldier of the 12th West Virginia. "It is believed that the men generally, got something to eat here." Unfortunately, their respite would not last long.[50]

Three hundred Confederate cavalrymen from Brig. Gen. John D. Imboden's Northwestern Brigade advanced on Hancock and burned the canal boats on the C & O Canal, but a detachment of Union cavalrymen under command of Colonel Galligher of the 13th Pennsylvania Cavalry drove them off. Another 700 of Imboden's grayclad horse soldiers made a flank move toward St. John's Run intending to destroy a large culvert over the canal near Hancock. Galligher's troopers drove them back after an hour's skirmishing, saving the culvert, with two troopers of the 1st New York Cavalry slightly wounded during the fight. Brigadier General Benjamin F. Kelley, who commanded the Department of West Virginia and had jurisdiction there, ordered Galligher to escort the infantry to Cumberland, Maryland. Kelley moved his headquarters to New Creek, West Virginia. As the ranking officer on the scene, Galligher assumed command of the Hodgepodge Brigade.[51]

As darkness fell on the night of Tuesday, June 17, and in compliance with Kelley's order, the Hodgepodge Brigade marched to Little Orleans Station on the B & O Railroad. This nondescript whistle stop was along the Potomac River near the mouth of Fifteen-mile Creek. Colonel Washburn had received a report that a special train would be waiting for them there to take them to Cumberland. The men marched the 20-plus miles during the night and morning and arrived near the station about noon, but, "greatly to the disappointment of the men, who were nearly worn out, we found no train waiting for us," reported Washburn. They waited several hours for the train to arrive but it never appeared. Instead, they received the unwelcome news that Imboden's cavalrymen occupied Cumberland.[52]

"Ascertaining there that the enemy were in possession of the place, we left the main road at Flint Stone, and reaching Chaneysville, sixteen miles from here, at dusk,

49 Prowell, *History of the 87th Pennsylvania*, 86-87.

50 Hewitt, *History of the Twelfth West Virginia*, 48.

51 "The Rebels at Hancock," *Philadelphia Inquirer*, June 19, 1863.

52 OR 27, pt. 2, 66.

we halted over night, and left next day for here, arriving at 3 o'clock P.M.," reported a Pennsylvania horse soldier. "All the troops above enumerated have not-reached here, but will during the day. Four miles this side of Chaneysville we saw pleasant faces for the first time, and at Rainsburgh the doors of the houses were thrown open, and the inhabitants, led off by Mr. Samuel Williams, spread their hands and their boards for our comfort. It was encouraging to come from a country of vinegar visages and hard tack, to a clime of milk and honey and happy people." By June 19, they had reached Bedford, Pennsylvania. "Here we are, however," concluded the correspondent. "Our next point is not yet learned. Col. Galligher is in communication with Gen. Schenck. We find the North alarmed, and justly so, indeed." The same soldier noted, "Ten millions of dollars will be spent to drive back the invaders after the gray scamps will have destroyed as much more. If Winchester was worth having at all, why not properly reinforce it. It is the key to Western Virginia, Western and Central Pennsylvania, situated as it is up the Shenandoah Valley. Further on north we have Martinsburgh, Hagerstown. Williamsport, Shippensburgh, Carlisle, Harrisburgh; in fact, that place."[53]

The withdrawal of the survivors of Carter's Woods from Hancock drew severe criticism. According to the *Philadelphia Inquirer*, the roughly 1,600 survivors who made it to Hancock "were so disorganized and demoralized by the absence of their officers that they fled, like startled sheep, at the mere report of an advance of the enemy." Indeed, Milroy's "weary boys" were demoralized, disorganized, and susceptible to rumors. As the 116th Ohio's Sgt. George A. Way lamented, "[we] now for over five days have passed through what no one but a soldier could endure, hunger, thirst, lack of sleep and numerous other privations only known to that army which has retreated in an enemy's country without supplies."[54]

The 18th Connecticut's Lt. Horatio Blanchard described his escape from the maelstrom at Carter's Woods. "We cut our way through the skirmishers, and then their cavalry dashed after us. We ran through a cleared lot, over a hill, and doubled and came back and laid down in the grass," he recalled. "The cavalry passed on. We could see them all around us, and expected every moment to be taken, but, thank God! they did not see us. We lay in the grass till all had left, and then started [for Martinsburg]." Lieutenant Blanchard had lost everything but his sword and revolver in the fighting. As he and his comrades approached Martinsburg, they learned the Confederates held

---

53 "The Loss of Winchester: A Narrative of the Investment and Abandonment of the Place," *New York Times*, June 28, 1863.

54 "Our Winchester Campaigns," *Philadelphia Inquirer*, June 19, 1863; *The Spirit of Democracy (Woodsfield, Ohio)*, July 1, 1863.

Early 20th century postcard of downtown Bloody Run, now Everett, Pennsylvania. *Scott Mingus*

the town and instead headed for Bloomery Gap, where they arrived on Tuesday night.[55]

The regimental historian of the 18th Connecticut described his unit's subsequent ordeal as "almost five days of almost unprecedented marching." For three nights, he explained, "the column marched constantly and longest rest at one time was thirty minutes. Generally a stop of five minutes was made each hour. The route pursued was circuitous, to avoid the rebels, and it was thereby made all the more tedious and embarrassing. The days were very hot, and F. G. Bixby, then orderly of Company D, says that many of the men fell out on account of heatstroke." He continued: "One day the men were short of water, and it was so hot that their tongues swelled terribly." The men safely made their way to Bloody Run, arriving there on the morning of June 23. Another detachment of the 18th made its way to Harpers Ferry, where it joined Tyler's command.[56]

Many other survivors dribbled into camp at Bloody Run. "The boys had very hard times on that retreat, marched both day and night, without anything to eat," said a soldier of the 116th Ohio. "Some of them gave out on the way, hid in the mountains, and finally joined the Regiment again at Bloody Run, Pennsylvania." Once they

---

55 Walker, *History of the Eighteenth Regiment*, 146-47.

56 Walker, *History of the Eighteenth Regiment*, 60-61.

arrived there, they still had no tents, no pots and pans, no replacement clothing, and little else but what they had carried on their backs, all of which left the Buckeye to conclude, "we are now in very desperate circumstances." No one who had reached Bloody Run had any idea how many of their comrades had been killed or wounded, or what had happened to the missing men of their regiment. By noon on June 19 the bulk of the Hodgepodge Brigade had arrived. The long journey of the "Weary Boys" was finally over.[57]

Rushing there to greet them was a correspondent from the *Philadelphia Inquirer*, who had jumped a train to do so. The reporter arrived at daylight on the 18th in Huntingdon, a rail stop more than 40 miles to the northeast where, to his great surprise, he found the vanguard of six or eight stragglers who had escaped the Winchester fight. "It was evident from the confused story they told that they had left at or about the time Milroy's advance guard had been attacked," he wrote, surmising they had not seen the main part of the fight. He telegraphed the news to his editor from Hopewell, the southern terminus of the Pennsylvania Railroad in 1863. Once he had done so, he boarded an old stage coach and started the rough journey over the mountains on what would be an intensely hot day. The ride to Bloody Run was an eye-opening affair, during which the newsman encountered more than 50 stragglers from various regiments of Milroy's shattered command. "Some were traveling in groups, some on foot, alone, others were mounted on steeds, perfect specimens of the Rosinante breed, and others had hired hacks and wagons to convey them forward." Despite the driver's tight schedule to deliver the mail in a timely manner, the reporter convinced him several times to stop so he could converse with the refugees and hear their "perilous and hair-breadth escapes."[58]

When the stagecoach reached Bloody Run, its passengers discovered other stragglers including about 80 cavalrymen who had just crossed the Juniata River above the town and were now heading toward them. "The people of Bloody Run had learned that some two hundred and fifty cavalry had succeeded in concentrating themselves here, and had assumed some definite shape and organization. This was cheering, indeed," explained the Philadelphia reporter. "I and my fellow passengers began to congratulate ourselves with the belief that many who were supposed to be prisoners had escaped, and that General Milroy's estimate of two thousand killed, wounded, and missing, would be greatly reduced." In fact, despite the stream of refugees that number was too low. Eight miles from Bloody Run the party encountered many more stragglers slowly making their way toward Bedford in an effort to join their regiments.

---

57 "Letter from the 116th O.V.I."

58 "Our Bedford Letter," *Philadelphia Inquirer*, June 18, 1863.

When he arrived at his hotel the reporter met Major Adams of the 1st New York Cavalry, who told him he had 250 men with him, "worn and jaded by long marches, but who were together and fit for service." He also met Lieutenant Colonel Moss of the 12th Pennsylvania Cavalry and learned he was also from Philadelphia, specifically the 24th Ward. Moss had another 400 men with him and expected another 100 by tomorrow noon. A few officers of the 13th Pennsylvania Cavalry, including Colonel Galligher, had joined in with the other two regiments while en route to Hancock since their own regiment was no where to be found. "The people of this town have shown a great deal of attention and hospitality to the retreating soldiers," the newsman added. "They have opened their houses to them, and not even the commonest private suffers. They deem the arrival of this force most opportune for the protection of their property."[59]

"We are now in glorious Old Pennsylvania," wrote the thankful 116th Ohio's Sergeant Way, "where the citizens (God bless them) sympathize with us in all our afflictions, not by words but by actions, they supply us with load after load of eatables, and throw open their houses as we pass, with the exclamation: 'Come in and partake of what we have got!' Yes, we are now safe, and a happier set of boys, than we of the 116th Ohio, considering circumstances, were never heard of." He figured the regiment had lost some 300 men, but all praise was due to Colonel Washburn for saving the remnants. Sergeant Way speculated they would be sent to some military base to recruit and refit, because "we have lost every thing, company books, clothing and all."[60]

The infantrymen of the 12th West Virginia had their own ordeal reaching Bloody Run. They first marched as far as Little Orleans Station before halting for the night on June 16. "It was getting dark when we picked our resting ground. We were sleeping in a cemetery and I pillowed my head on a little mound which I took for the grave of a small child," explained Lt. David Powell. "In the night I awoke and found that my head was not pillowed on the mound of the dead but upon an ant hill whose inhabitants were terribly alive. They had rebelled and feasted upon my neck, face, and hands until I was almost flayed." Adding insult to his negligent injury, Powell "felt I would burn up" in the next day's relentless heat. The Mountaineers struggled on toward Bloody Run and finally arrived there on the 19th. Captain W. B. Curtis of Company D sent a message to a Wheeling newspaper delineating his casualties and expressing his deep thanks to the Pennsylvania citizens for their kindness and hospitality in furnishing them food and shelter. "Long may they live to enjoy the

59 Ibid.

60 *The Spirit of Democracy (Woodsfield, Ohio)*, July 1, 1863.

blessings of the government they are willing to sacrifice so much to defend and protect," he added.[61]

"I have had nothing to eat since Sunday noon," complained wagon master Henry M. Durfey of the 18th Connecticut Infantry on June 18. "One of the men just brought in a loaf of bread for five of us. No sleep till last night since Friday night; slept and fed in a wheat field last night." The next morning, June 19, a cavalryman galloped up, reined in his mount, and informed Durfey that Confederate cavalry was within just four miles of his position, alarming news that prompted Durfey to get his wagon train moving toward Pennsylvania. They left Hancock and rumbled on another seven miles, but were driven back by Rebel cavalry. The next day, Durfey started for Cumberland, but when his wagons reached Flintstone, 30 miles from Cumberland, Durfey learned Imboden's cavalry already held the town, so they abandoned the wagons and took to the woods. They spent the night there before heading for Bedford, Pennsylvania, 26 miles away. "We have received nothing to eat for forty-eight hours, except what we begged as we jogged along," recalled Durfey. When the teamsters arrived at Rainsburg, they found some friendly locals who fed them and 28 refugees of the 18th Connecticut. Their journey ended the next morning, June 22, at Bloody Run.[62]

The widely scattered survivors of the Carter's Woods debacle sought safety wherever they could find it, carrying with them alarming reports of the magnitude of the Federal disaster. After initially making it to safety at Harpers Ferry, several exhausted members of the 5th Maryland stumbled into Frederick, Maryland, about 50 miles north of the Winchester battlefields. "They appeared much worn out, and did not know much about the casualties that occurred, except that only about twenty of the regiment had made their escape, the remainder being killed, wounded or captured," was how one correspondent described it.[63]

Reports circulated that Milroy's men were committing outrages against the civilian populace on their journey northward, but nothing could be proven. There were a few accounts of soldiers disguising themselves as civilians to make their escape. According to 15-year-old John Cabell Early, who was traveling north to join his division commander uncle Jubal, "When we got into Maryland we found the natives very hostile and vindictive toward the South, and we were warned to be very careful, as there were a great many Union soldiers in citizen's clothes, and there had been

---

61 "David Powell Reminiscences," David Powell Papers, USAHEC; *Wheeling Daily Intelligencer*, June 25, 1863.

62 Walker, *History of the Eighteenth Regiment*, 59-60.

63 "Important from the Potomac," *Baltimore Sun*, June 19, 1863.

considerable bush-whacking and might be more, as the Southern Army had gotten far away."[64]

Nevertheless, the indomitable spirit of the men of the Hodgepodge Brigade impressed Colonel Washburn. "I cannot speak too highly of the good order and discipline displayed by both officers and men during the whole affair," he reported. "Especially would I commend the cheerfulness and patience with which the men endured the march of five days, averaging nearly 30 miles per day, and with scarcely one ration of food during the whole march." Washburn had every reason to be proud of these men; after three days of combat at Winchester they successfully completed a long and arduous march under adverse circumstances and yet remained a viable combat command.[65]

The Plight of the Union Prisoners of War

While their comrades who had escaped capture headed to Harpers Ferry, Bloody Run, or other places of safety, the Eighth Corps prisoners at Winchester faced a long journey to Richmond. There was no direct route to get to the Southern capital, so they would have to travel more than 200 miles, nearly half of it on foot. As the first 1,600 prisoners prepared to march on June 16, the 58th Virginia's Col. Francis H. Board of "Extra Billy" Smith's brigade addressed his men who, along with Avery's 54th North Carolina, had been assigned to escort the prisoners up the Shenandoah Valley to Staunton. There, they would be loaded onto rail cars of the Virginia Central Railroad for the 135-mile trip to Richmond. "Men, these Yankees have fallen into our hands by the fortune of war," Board declared. "I want them treated like gentlemen. If I hear of any insults or abuse, it will be punished." A soldier of the 18th Connecticut remembered the Confederates treated them kindly, and he and his comrades "always had the feeling of comrades towards them rather than of enemies."[66]

For some men the trip quickly turned into a grueling ordeal. Still pleased with the recovery of his two $10 bills from the lining of his old discarded blouse, the 110th Ohio's Lt. Charles Gross started the long trek he knew so well south to Staunton. Before long, however, a sharp nail worked its way up through the heel of his boot and a painful blister formed on the bottom of his foot. It "was not a very comfortable

---

64 John Cabell Early, "A Southern Boy's Experience at Gettysburg," in *Journal of the Military Service Institution*, vol. 43 (January-February 1911), 418-19.

65 *OR* 27, pt. 2, 67.

66 J. H. Sawyer, "Memory of Carter's Farm: Humane Treatment of 1,500 Yankee Prisoners on Weary March from Winchester to Staunton, Va.," The *Bolivar* (OH) *Breeze*, June 25, 1914.

thing to march on," he related, "but we were not allowed to mind a little thing like that."[67]

On the night of June 17, the soldiers of the 54th North Carolina bathed and several men donned fresh Union pants, shirts, and boots. The Tar Heels cooked rations and caught as much sleep as they could. The next morning, they took charge of 1,984 prisoners and marched them 96 miles south along the Valley Turnpike to Staunton. Private Phil Huffman of the 123rd Ohio kept a diary throughout his service in the Civil War. His entries captured the ordeal of the march:[68]

Thurs. June 18: We started for Richmond today. We came about ten miles and it commenced raining which made it rather disagreeable.

Fri. June 19: This morning we started at daylight and it was an awful hot day. It is about 60 miles to Staunton yet.

Sat. June 20: Today we marched 20 miles towards Staunton to a town called Newmarket. We are now about 40 miles from Staunton.

Sun. June 21: Today we are marching as prisoners of war. We came about 15 miles.

Mon. June 22: We were marching today and are now within 13 miles of Staunton. We are now in the heart of Rebeldom. The roads are completely lined with people to see the Yankeys.

Tues. June 23: We came ten miles today and are in camp in the woods.

Wed. June 24: We started from Staunton for Richmond today at twelve oclock and will have to ride all night one hundred and thirty-six miles.

Because they had little in the way of food or water, the march was a grueling ordeal.[69]

Private Charles Kelly of Jenkins' 16th Virginia Cavalry was posted in rural Shenandoah County. His regiment moved up into Pennsylvania after their fighting at Berryville and Martinsburg, but he remained behind at the regimental base camp to

---

67 Gross, "Sketch of Army and Prison Life."

68 *The Spirit of the Age*, August 10, 1863.

69 Cremeans, *Uncle Phil and the Rebbles*, 51. Huffman was a prisoner at Belle Isle and Libby Prison until he was paroled on July 14. Fortunately, his stay in the horrific confines of these death traps was mercifully short.

care for about 60 horses unfit for duty. For several days he watched the seemingly endless procession of prisoners from Milroy's division tramp past on their way into captivity. They were a motley group, with some half-naked and others barefooted or bareheaded. Some of the prisoners told him that if they got home they would never come out to fight again. According to Kelly, the accompanying Confederates were not in much better condition: "Our men that were guarding them looked like they was dead on their feet."[70]

Many of the ill and infirmed struggled to keep up with the passing column. Private George "Tony" Miller of the 87th Pennsylvania had been hospitalized multiple times that because of typhoid fever. Now, as a prisoner of war, the young father from Glen Rock stumbled along using a cane for support. The prisoners from Milroy's cavalry and artillery had it especially rough. These men were used to riding, not long marches on foot, and their heavy boots were designed for horseback riding, not long walks. The result was weary and footsore men. As one soldier put it, "the boys begin to act like old men, limping along, pretty foot-sore, but in good spirits." By contrast, the long march did not seem to bother many of their comrades in the infantry, who were accustomed to such treks.[71]

"The many trampling feet stirred up the white lime dust, which overhung the column in a choking cloud," recalled a soldier of the 18th Connecticut. "The pangs of thirst began to torment. The steady monotonous tramp was held hour after hour. Past pleasant farmhouses, through shady groves, where the cool shadows were so inviting; over clear brooks, where there would be a short, struggling halt for water; forward, the Blue and the Gray pressed on together." On June 18 another member of the 18th Connecticut noted the passage of an important anniversary. "10 Months ago today we were mustered into the U. States Service," he scribbled into his diary. "Quite a contrast between now and then. Then we were just taking up arms and today we are marching without arms as prisoners of war to Richmond, and such is a Soldier's fate."[72]

---

70 Charles Kelly to his wife Martha, June 30, 1863, and Charles Kelly to dear brother, June 27, 1863, both written in Shenandoah County, Virginia, in Gregory Lepore's Russell County Civil War Website, http://russellvets.org/letters/ckelly.html, accessed May 20, 2015.

71 Dennis W. Brandt files, 87th Pennsylvania Pension Records, YCHT; Wild, *Memoirs and History of Capt. F. W. Alexander's Baltimore Battery*, 76; James M. Smith diary entry for June 21, 1863.

72 J. H. Sawyer, "Captured at Winchester. A Day's March Down the Valley After the Disaster to Milroy's Forces," *National Tribune*, October 23, 1913; James M. Smith diary entry for June 18, 1863.

"The citizens are generally strong 'secesh,'" a member of the 54th North Carolina recalled, "and are as kind to the rebel soldiers as they can be, giving them milk, butter, cheese, vegetables, &c. at every town; and also the farmers along the road would sell us chickens at the old price of 10 to 15 cents." The Confederates, however, made few if any arrangements to make sure their prisoners were properly fed.[73]

Some of the captives received a pint of flour for each man, who then had to figure out how to make and bake his own dough cakes. The Rebels "seemed to have a high opinion of the Yankees as rustlers," recalled a soldier of the 123rd Ohio. "They seemed to think we'd get along if we got the raw material." So they did. "We formed messes of five or six comrades, put our flour together on a poncho, mixed it up into a stiff paste, heated flat stones, greased them over with bacon, spread the paste on a la slapjack and the job was soon done. This made a highly concentrated article of diet. A little heavy and hard to digest, but our continuous outdoor life and fatiguing marches fitted us for the work, and our greatest trouble was to get enough of it."[74]

Things were no better for the officers. Their horses were now Confederate property, so they were on foot like their men. Such was the case of the 123rd Ohio's Col. William T. Wilson, who on the night of June 19 noted in his diary, "Rained hard in evening just in time to wet us thoroughly before we got into the building," where they spent the fitful night. "Slept but little," he added.[75]

Captain David S. Caldwell, also of the 123rd Ohio, was bitter about the treatment he and his comrades received. "During our march to Staunton, we were necessitated, by our unfortunate condition as prisoners of war, to submit to the most contemptible treatment, and outrageous insults, that an enraged and diabolical enemy could heap upon us," he wrote. "This detestable treatment was not confined, neither was it most rampant among the soldier guards; but the citizens outrivaled even the soldiers in the exhibition hate and virulence. They seemed to take intense delight in hurling their anathemas upon us with unmitigated fury, such as 'd———d Yankees,' 'Milroy's thieves and robbers,' 'black abolitionists,' 'every one of you, ought to be hung,' &c. &c."[76]

---

73 *The Spirit of the Age*, August 10, 1863.

74 Snyder, *Autobiography of a Soldier of the Civil War*, 10.

75 William T. Wilson diary, entry for June 19, 1863.

76 Caldwell, *Incidents of War*, 4. Caldwell, it turned out, had the last laugh. On February 10, 1864, Caldwell was one of the 109 Union officers who escaped from Libby Prison via a tunnel that they had dug in just 17 days of hard labor. 48 were recaptured, 2 drowned in the James River, and the rest, including Captain Caldwell, made it back to the Union lines. Caldwell rejoined his regiment, and was present for the Army of Northern Virginia's surrender at Appomattox Court House on April 9, 1865. Caldwell's book documents his travails in prison, the escape, and his

A member of the 18th Connecticut noted that as the column passed through Strasburg, "the secesh hatred was more viciously displayed here than in any previous place. The men, however, were getting accustomed to their treatment and did not mind it much. Instead, they often responded with some Union song appropriate to the occasion, or dealt out a little Yankee wit."[77]

Private Harry Fink soldiered faithfully in the 87th Pennsylvania despite being bowlegged and in his early 50s, which made marching quite a chore for the fifer. About halfway to Staunton, one of the most unusual events of any prisoner march of the war occurred when an unidentified Confederate officer in the guard detail inquired, "Where are your musicians?" Fink stepped forward along with Pvt. Lewis Renaut. "Take the front line," ordered the officer. Fink and Renaut, with two drummers tagging along behind, moved to the head of the long column. To the surprise of the astonished Yankees, the Southern guards distributed fifes and drums to the men. "What shall we play?' asked Fink. "Anything," replied the 58th Virginia's Col. Francis H. Board, who was sitting nearby on his horse. The musicians led off with *Yankee Doodle*, which triggered polite applause from their captors. They followed with *When Johnny Comes Marching Home* and then *The Girl I Left Behind*. "Very good," Board announced. "Give us another tune." Fink, who was making eye contact with the mounted colonel, held his fife up to his mouth with one hand and struck up *The Star-Spangled Banner*. Some of the prisoners joined in the chorus while others cheered. To their amazement, the guards applauded and Board laughed, enjoying the fun. After the impromptu concert, the Rebels collected the instruments and the column resumed its wearisome march to Staunton.[78]

The footsore prisoners were entering the town when a guard asked Fink to play once more. The resourceful Pennsylvania native plucked a leaf from a tree, placed it between the palms of his hands, and blew *Yankee Doodle*. That creative trick amused the guards, prisoners, and even some of the civilians lining the sidewalks. "I thought the Yanks were wild men, but they are just like the rest of us," recorded an old man who had just set eyes on a Union soldier for the first time.[79]

---

return to duty. See "Escape of One Hundred and Nine Commissioned Yankee Officers from the Libby Prison—A Scientific Tunnel—Their Underground Route to Liberty," *Richmond Examiner*, February 11, 1864. After the end of the war, Caldwell devoted the rest of his life to preaching the gospel. For more about the audacious escape of the Union prisoners of war from Libby Prison, see Joseph Wheelan, *Libby Prison Breakout: The Daring Escape from the Notorious Civil War Prison* (New York: Public Affairs, 2010).

77 Walker, *History of the Eighteenth Regiment*, 123.

78 Prowell, *History of the 87th Pennsylvania*, 227-28.

79 Ibid.

An Ohio captain was part of a party of 108 officers being marched south under the command of Capt. Henry W. Wingfield of the 58th Virginia. After being stripped of their accoutrements, they were given blankets before starting the trek. The captives did not eat during their first day on the road and did not receive flour and meat until the afternoon of the second day. The enlisted men overtook the officers that day, but "we were not allowed to communicate with them," complained an officer in the 123rd Ohio. To make matters worse, it began to rain heavily. "At night we were obligated to take up our quarters in an old log stable," the officer added, "which was more thoroughly infested by fleas than was particularly pleasant or convenient to us. Wet as we were, we laid down and attempted to gain a few hours repose, but alas, no chance for that desired boon. All night long the inhabitants of the stable could be heard visiting their maledictions on the fleas."[80]

Marching about five miles behind the officers was a mixed group of 1,500 enlisted men from a variety of Milroy's broken and demoralized regiments. The motley assemblage included the 110th Ohio infantryman whose captor, the lieutenant of the 2nd Maryland Battalion, had allowed him to visit his lady friend Susan all day June 15 after surrendering near Carter's Woods. The Buckeye now found himself in a much different predicament, trudging the long macadamized turnpike to Staunton with 173 other unfortunates from his regiment. "Now you may imagine, that was anything but pleasant to a young man who had never walked ten miles in his life," he would write is distant sister, "but I determined to go through or die in the attempt." He bought his food along the way, paying a dollar a dozen for biscuits and 50 cents each for pies. The second night out the Rebs put them up in the hospitals at New Market, where the defiant Buckeye was able to purchase two pounds of crackers for "the small sum of two dollars."[81]

Dr. Charles T. Sempers, the 6th Maryland's regimental surgeon, remained behind to care for the wounded when the rest of his regiment retreated from Stephenson's Depot. On June 20, he and about 400 other prisoners, including surgeons and regimental chaplains, also began their trek to Richmond. "Surgeons and chaplains were allowed to go about at will," he noted in his diary. "General commanding Reb forces assured us we were not regarded as prisoners." He noted that the officers were sheltered in nearby houses, but that the enlisted men were left to their own devices in the open fields.[82]

80 Keyes, *The Military History of the 123rd Ohio*, 120.

81 *Xenia (Ohio) Sentinel*, September 1, 1863.

82 Charles T. Sempers diary entries for June 20-25, 1863, Cecil County Historical Society, Elkton, Maryland.

The inclusion of the noncombatant chaplains in the column of prisoners irked Rev. George H. Hammer of the 12th Pennsylvania Cavalry. He and the rest of the chaplains had been ordered to report to the Union Hotel and await further orders. "Bear in mind we were not considered as prisoners," he wrote. "This they utterly disclaimed; but were only said to be detained by the necessity of the case, until certain movements had been made, when we would be sent through the lines to Harpers Ferry." The distinction, he quickly learned, was one without a real difference. "Contrary to promises and express declarations (for let me tell you, the Rebels are the greatest liars unpunished—they take to lying as easily and as naturally as a duck takes to the water), we with others, some having preceded us, were marching on foot to Staunton."[83]

Complaining that every contact with the hard packed turnpike "seemed to burn the foot to a blister," Chaplain Hammer struggled to keep up with the column. "Half-clad, many shoeless and hatless and unfed, the cavalcade was a sorrowful one. The sufferings of the trip I cannot express. Nothing to eat but what we begged or bought off citizens who hated us intensely, shut their doors in our faces, and from appearances would have been far better pleased with a visit from even his Satanic majesty himself. Indeed, unless the guard had interfered in our behalf, we should have fared very badly. There were indeed some noble Union exceptions, but they were the exceptions, and not the rule."[84]

The Union prisoners trudged on through driving thunderstorms and under a hot sun to cover the 96 miles from Winchester to Staunton in four-and-a-half days. On Monday, June 22, a Staunton resident watched as the first 1,600 Yankees arrived in town about 10:00 a.m. "The prisoners were much better clothed than the Confederates who guarded them," observed Joseph A. Waddell, one of the town's prominent civilians. Another 1,900 tramped into town the following day, just as the first trainloads began departing for Richmond. On the 24th Waddell continued, "The guard of the prisoners—a North Carolina regiment—although generally dirty, and some of them ragged, looked stouter and more hardy than the Yankees. Several of our poor fellows were barefooted." The following day, Waddell watched as a number of female Northern camp followers passed by him on their way to the depot. He reported that precisely 4,321 prisoners, including 45 women and children, had arrived during the week.[85]

83 *Philadelphia Inquirer*, November 6, 1863.

84 Ibid.

85 Joseph A. Waddell, *Annals of Augusta County, Virginia, from 1726 to 1871* (Staunton, VA: C. Russell Caldwell, 1902), 482.

By then the exhausted, dust-covered prisoners were a sorry-looking lot. "Many were sore, sick, and weary," observed one of Capt. Alexander's Baltimore artillerists. Once the column arrived in Staunton, the prisoners were counted off into groups of 80 and loaded onto freight cars of the Virginia Central Railroad. "The one I happened to get into had been used as a cattle car and had not been swept clean, as there was plenty of evidence as to what it had been used for before we were huddled into it," observed the same artillerist. "There was no room to lie down, one could sit on the floor with his knees to his chin and if he wished to stretch his legs, he had to poke them over the tops of others, perhaps with his feet in some one's face, naturally there was very little sleep, but a great deal of growling that night." He noted that one facetious comrade piped up, "Cheer up boys, the worst is yet to come," a lament that soon became the byword of all of the prisoners aboard that cramped freight car.[86]

James Smith of the 18th Connecticut also left a vivid description of the horrible trip to Richmond. "We were soon piled into some old freight cars, 50 in a car, and we started, and it was the roughest riding I ever saw. We had no seats and had to sit on the car bottom and go the best way we could," recalled. "We had no rations, and as a natural consequence we were pretty hungry. The first place we came to was Fisherville, distant as near I could learn, 134 miles from Richmond. Passed through a very mountainous country, and it seemed as though the old car would go over, it swayed so bad." The train passed through two mountain tunnels as it wound its way out of the high country. "The darkness of night put an end to sight-seeing, and we disposed ourselves as well as circumstances would permit for the night. There seemed to be an 'aching void' in my stomach that nothing but food would fill, but that was out of the question." A trooper of the 12th Pennsylvania Cavalry also unfortunate enough to find himself on the train long recalled that "long, weary night ride" to Richmond. It took nearly a full 24 hours to complete the miserable trip. One-half of the 54th North Carolina was detailed to guard the prisoners while the other half lounged at Staunton until June 28 before heading north to cover the Potomac River crossings.[87]

After having suffered the taunts of the Virginia civilians, the unlucky prisoners suffered more indignities upon reaching the Southern capital. "We were marched through one side of the city to our destination," the Reverend Hammer recounted for a Philadelphia paper, "the chaplains and surgeons glad at their arrival, having been fed with the idea that they would be passed through at once to the United States. The following will show how near we came to the truth of our hopes, and how exceedingly

86 Wild, *Memoirs and History of Capt. F. W. Alexander's Baltimore Battery*, 82-83.

87 James M. Smith diary entry for June 22, 1863; Malden Valentine, "Saved Philadelphia. Milroy's Stubborn Resistance Gave Time for the Army of the Potomac to Get Up," *National Tribune*, November 19, 1908; *The Spirit of the Age*, August 10, 1863.

green we had been to be so easily gulled." Frustrated with by the betrayal, he added, "Upon our nearing the prison, the first thing that attracted our attention was a sign reaching out from the corner of the building on which were ominous and not very classic words, 'Libby & Son, ship chandlers and grocers.' The second sight, all the window openings in the part of the building facing us, filled with human heads, rising one above another, which we soon recognized as belonging to Union prisoners, and our fellow sufferers who had preceded us." Above the din of the guards and jeers of a crowd of boys on the street, Hammer heard the sarcastic cries of "fresh fish, fresh fish!" Another cry of warning followed: "Look out for your money!"[88]

He soon learned what the catcalls meant. After registering inside the office, Hammer and the other newly arrived officers were marched into a large hall, where they endured individual examinations by the prison inspector. Hammer decried this mistreatment by the Rebels. "I have said before they would lie; I must now add they will steal. Everything of value was taken from us—canteens, haversacks, gum blankets, in some cases our woolen blankets, our money and valuables, private papers and pocket diaries, lists of dead and wounded, and even last messages from brave martyrs to their friends," he continued, "nothing being retained but the few things that seemed to be a part of ourselves and necessary to conceal our nakedness." The chaplains were not only ones to suffer this indignity. "The Surgeons, whose private property is always respected in war, were likewise stripped of their effects. Their green sashes as badges of their profession were taken from them; their pocket cases of instruments abstracted, the pocket medicines confiscated, so that upon our induction into the mysteries of Libby we had fewer things to care for, fewer still to lose."[89]

The enlisted men also faced hardships. "We were the objects of great curiosity to the people of Richmond as we were marched through the streets from the train to Castle Thunder, an old tobacco warehouse, where we were kept a day and night," recalled Edmund Snyder of the 123rd Ohio. "They jeered us, made disparaging remarks about our personal appearance, and all the time we were not allowed to reply." So began their stint as prisoners of war in Richmond. Most of the enlisted men ended up at Belle Isle, also in Richmond, while the officers usually ended up in the notorious Libby Prison.[90]

Typical of their experiences was an account by 20-year-old Pvt. Albert Miller of the 67th Pennsylvania, who found himself incarcerated at Belle Isle:

---

88 *Philadelphia Inquirer*, November 6, 1863.

89 Ibid.

90 Snyder, *Autobiography of a Solder of the Civil War*, 10. Like his comrade Huffman, Snyder was paroled thirty days later.

There was six of us boys bunched together and we got a piece of canvas and four poles, we put them up for shade, they marched us every day. I don't know for (why) unless to punish us in the hot sun and had us stand in line for an hour or two taken us out one side taken us in on the other side. We had to take our shade along if not some that didn't have would get it. On our way around was a small stream of water with a narrow foot bridge across it, only cross it by single file that would have take a long time to pass over. They gave enough of bread and black-bean soup boiled in the muddy James river water to create a very strong appetite for no more.[91]

Everyone rued their circumstances and most blamed General Milroy for their predicament. For one chaplain, Milroy's meddling in Winchester's civilian affairs almost brought tragedy. A captured soldier from Piqua, Ohio, escaped from Richmond and made his way back home, where he reported some grim news. Back in early June, the 110th Ohio's Chaplain James Harvey learned the Rebels were approaching Winchester. The popular prewar pastor of a church in Delaware, Ohio, sent his wife north beyond danger. Milroy dispatched a contraband mulatto girl named Sarah Jenkins to travel with her. Sarah was owned by W. J. Shumate of Augusta County. After the fighting at Winchester, Chaplain Harvey stayed behind to minister to the wounded and was captured. Reports of the missing slave girl and Harvey's involvement were forwarded to Richmond authorities and, according to the escaped prisoner, Harvey was to be hung for his part in "running off the slaves." Once safely back in Ohio, Mrs. Harvey emphatically denied her husband's involvement and stressed the entire affair was done strictly on Milroy's orders. Ironically, she had not seen the mulatto since an unsympathetic conductor kicked Sarah off a train on the way north—despite having a paid ticket. Fellow pastors soon took up the cause by writing a series of letters on Harvey's behalf. Governor David Tod of Ohio became involved, and in the end the chaplain was not executed. His health, however, was broken. Harvey accepted a medical discharge after his exchange in October.[92]

General Ewell had also sent another set of prisoners southward, this group being the unfortunate wives and children of Milroy's division who had not escaped Winchester. Because of General Rodes' movement into Maryland, Jubal Early did not think it wise to transport noncombatants through the lines to Harpers Ferry or other nearby Union outposts for fear they might reveal details of Confederate strength or movements. Instead, his provost officers marshaled wagons and ambulances to carry

---

91 "Civil War Experience Dictated by Albert Miller, between 1930 and 1937," Ellen Mowrer Miller Papers, Iowa Women's Archives at the University of Iowa Library Archives, University of Iowa Libraries, Iowa City.

92 *Staunton Spectator*, July 10, 1864; *Daily Ohio State Journal*, July 14, 1864.

these women and children on the long ride south to the railhead at Staunton. When they arrived in the Confederacy's capital city, the women had to wait while government officials completed the arrangements for their transfer. The civilians were kept under guard and in some cases under restraint. On July 2, the women and children arrived at Fort Monroe at Hampton Roads, Virginia, for their eventual transport via sea to Annapolis, Maryland. The ordeal proved overwhelming for some of the women as well as those who loved them. "My wife and child were captured at Winchester, Va., and confined in Castle Thunder," complained Lt. James Kane of the 13th Pennsylvania Cavalry. "They were robbed of their trunks, clothing, and money—everything except what they wore on their persons. My wife will never be well."[93]

Milroy's failure to make adequate arrangements for the safety of the wives of his officers put them in harm's way and heaped unneeded stress upon his men. "Many of the poor bearers of shoulder straps are going around with exceedingly long faces, moaning not like Rachael for children, but for their other selves, whom the exigencies of the occasion prevented them from taking away," reported the *New York Herald.* "Quite a number of officers had had their wives with them." These already demoralized officers now bore the added burden of worrying about the safety and well-being of their loved ones who were left to the tender mercies of the Confederates and whose whereabouts were unknown.[94]

General Milroy Goes to Bloody Run

While his sullen prisoners headed to Staunton and eventual confinement in Richmond, a chagrined Milroy planned to rejoin his remaining men. On June 18, General Schenck informed Maj. Gen. Darius N. Couch, the commander of the Department of the Susquehanna headquartered in Harrisburg, "General Milroy and staff have just left here by the Northern Central Railroad, for Harrisburg to proceed at once to find the wandering 3,000 from Winchester who went north from Hancock yesterday." Schenck asked Couch to meet Milroy at the train station and lend whatever

---

93 "Wives and Children of Yankee Soldiers Captured at Winchester," in *Confederate Veteran,* vol. 30, Nov. 1922, 422; James Kane to E. D. Townsend, Asst, Adjt. Gen., May 7, 1864, U. S. Army Hospital, Annapolis, Maryland, House Report 1980, Serial Set vol. 2603; United States House of Representatives, April 27, 1888 (NARA).Unfounded rumors quickly spread that the Confederates had incarcerated the women and children in the infamous Castle Thunder Prison in Richmond.

94 "The Battle of Winchester: Authentic Details of the Contest," *New York Herald,* June 22, 1863.

assistance he could to Milroy's efforts to locate his command. "They may be made serviceable for the present for operations in Pennsylvania, offensive or defensive."[95]

Milroy spent a day in Harrisburg consulting with Pennsylvania Gov. Andrew G. Curtin and General Couch. The regimental band of the 23rd New Jersey Militia serenaded Milroy at his Harrisburg hotel a scant few days after his stunning defeat at Carter's Woods. Still, the mood at the Jones House was festive and upbeat. According to a reporter, "The General was called on for a speech, and responded to the call in a very able manner. General Couch also made a few remarks, which were approved by the men giving three hearty cheers for the General, the Union, General Milroy, and several other distinguished Generals."[96]

That day Couch reported that 1,700 of Milroy's men were in Bedford, "most of them, I fear, without arms. The rebels could not have been in much force near Hancock, or these men would have been captured. General Milroy leaves this evening to join his men. I may hold him in that section until he reorganizes. Their presence will be valuable." Milroy was understandably anxious to find his command, so he set out for McConnellsburg in an effort to do so.[97]

By June 19, Milroy had established his headquarters at Bloody Run. His adjutant, Lt. John O. Cravens, and his chief of staff, Maj. J. Lowry McGee, were present there with him. "I found 2500 of my weary worn out boys," at Bloody Run reported Milroy in a letter to his wife Mary. "They all thought I had been killed, and when they saw me they shouted and yelled and were almost crazy with joy as they crowded around to shake hands with me. Nearly all the infantry had their feet badly blistered. In some cases their boots and shoes which they had not had off for over a week were filled with blood and matter." Shouts of joy and serenades aside, the defeat weighed heavily on the general. "There is so much disappointment and anguish in my defeat and retreat from Winchester that it is painful for me to think of it and relate the facts to you."[98]

That same day Milroy ordered Colonel Galligher to report to him, along with all forces under his command then in Bedford, including the 12th Pennsylvania Cavalry, 1st New York Cavalry, and a portion of the 13th Pennsylvania Cavalry. These units joined the 116th Ohio and the 12th West Virginia at Bloody Run, which meant Milroy could now muster a rather substantial armed force of some 2,500 men. Schenck

---

95 *OR* 27, pt. 3, 201.

96 *Harrisburg Evening Telegraph*, June 23, 1863. The Jones House stood at Second and Market Streets on Market Square in downtown Harrisburg. Abraham Lincoln had stopped there briefly on Feb. 22, 1861, en route to his inauguration in Washington.

97 *OR* 27, pt. 3, 202-3.

98 Milroy to Mary Milroy, June 21, 1863, Milroy Papers.

ordered Milroy to march his command to Chambersburg and then on to Harrisburg, where it would join Couch's command in the defenses of the capital of Pennsylvania. Milroy thought the order premature and said as much. He wanted time to reorganize his shattered command and reunite it around Harpers Ferry. "I want to go back to Winchester for many reasons," he informed Schenck. "I have learned a wealth of experience in the Valley & would like to have a chance to make use of it."[99]

For the local citizenry, the arrival of a significant force of Union soldiers came not a moment too soon. "The whole population of this quiet, retired village has turned out to receive them," reported one correspondent. "Cheering is going on from the inhabitants, and the troops are cheering back again." "Handkerchiefs wave, fair women and ardent young girls shed tears of joy. The juveniles kindle bonfires upon the streets, and the century-old town of Bedford feels as if there was new blood poured into her veins, and hot young sensations leaping through her heart and brain. Sensations in Chestnut Street scarcely parallel it. They are all completely armed, and know how to shoot. Rebel raids toward this point are rapidly becoming dangerous."[100]

"Upon hearing of our coming," wrote Lt. Colonel Thomas F. Wildes of the 116th Ohio on June 18, the people of that place prepared a glorious feast for us. Long tables were placed in the middle of the principal street, which were loaded with warm and cold meats, potatoes, bread, pickles, splendid hot coffee, and great bowls and pails of milk. We were nearly starved, and no meal we ever ate was so heartily relished. The good people of Bloody Run," he added, "will be remembered as long as there is a member of the 116th living."[101]

Another observer left a colorful description of the refugees streaming north from Winchester:

Union soldiers, ragged, dusty, often hatless and coatless, with and without muskets or accoutrements of any kind; lank, long-haired rebels from the ridges around Bath and Berkley Springs; negroes of every shade or color from the tottering old ex-slave with back bearing more stripes than the nation's emblem, to the chubby tot, bow-legged and scant of clothing; buxom maidens in black and tan, with the conventional turban, under which stuck out like sprigs of a dog-collar, a row of short, tightly-twisted curly plaits, all able to

---

99 "Movements of Gen. Milroy," *New York Times*, June 20, 1863; *OR* 27, pt. 3, 220; Milroy to Schenck, June 22, 1863, Schenck Papers.

100 "Reports from Bedford," *New York Times*, June 24, 1863. On June 30, Confederate cavalry under the command of Brig. Gen. John D. Imboden clashed with Capt. Abram Jones' company of the 1st New York Cavalry at McConnellsburg, just 25 miles away from Bloody Run.

101 Wildes, *Record of the One Hundred and Sixteenth Regiment*, 61.

bearing burdens of bundles big as feather beds, tied up in ragged shawls and more ragged sheets; dogs of every imaginable breed, color, size and condition; wagons, carts and sleds, even, piled high with household effects of away back, fashion and finish, all rushing pell-mell, helter-skelter, to the great unknown North, for safety and freedom.[102]

"We reached Bloody Run on the 19th," recorded the historian of the 116th Ohio. "Milroy was as good as his word, and met us on the next day after our arrival. It was a sad meeting. The 'Old Grey Eagle' looked gloomy and broken hearted but we drew up in line to receive him, and as he approached, presented arms, and cheered him loud and long. Stacking arms, officers and men gathered about to shake his hand and learn the fate of his little army. Many a heart was saddened at the news that our old associates of the 123rd were prisoners." Milroy inspected the bedraggled soldiers and correctly determined they were not combat effective. He left them to await further orders and rest. For the time being, their role in the Gettysburg campaign was over. That night, Couch informed Milroy that 8,000 mounted Confederates were in Hagerstown and he should prepare to meet them, if necessary.[103]

The next day, on June 20, Milroy informed Couch of his arrival at Bloody Run and that his 2,500 troops there were "all badly supplied with ammunition, and no rations." There was a great deal of confusion over who had jurisdiction over Milroy's survivors. Were they still subject to Schenck's orders even though they had left the Middle District? Or, did they report to General Couch because they now were within the Department of the Susquehanna? As it turned out, both department commanders claimed authority. That same day, Couch instructed Milroy to disregard any orders coming from anyone but him, and to shift his base of operations to Chambersburg. Not long after receiving that cable Milroy received a message from a frustrated Schenck who demanded, "You have not reported to me since you left Harrisburg. You will at once inform me where you are, with what force, how engaged, and the condition of the troops you have found."[104]

At 1:50 p.m. on June 20, Schenck received instructions from Halleck to place Milroy under arrest. "I relieved [Milroy] of command . . . and ordered him to report here," replied Schenck. "I then sent him back to Harpers Ferry to assist in collecting and reorganizing those of his troops who were saved under General Tyler. . . . In the meantime I heard of a large body of his men . . . had gone up to Pennsylvania. I ordered him to proceed by Harrisburg to Bedford, to find and take charge of them."

102 "M. E. K.", "Border Land in War Time," *Toledo Blade*, October 4, 1894.

103 Wildes, *Record of the One Hundred Sixteenth Regiment*, 59-61; OR 27, pt. 3, 222.

104 Ibid., 235-56.

Still unclear as to whom Milroy was to report, Secretary of War Stanton instructed Couch to arrest Milroy. Ewell's infantry was about to enter Pennsylvania, however, and Couch declared that Milroy "cannot be relieved at this moment." Halleck, however, insisted Milroy be relieved of command and placed under arrest.[105]

Colonel Andrew T. McReynolds, meanwhile, took time to reflect on the dismal retreat from Winchester and the fortunes of the outcome. "Gen. Elliott was the hero," he exclaimed. "Gen. Milroy is a brave gallant soldier, and has my deepest sympathy." Over time, the New York colonel would grow more disillusioned with Milroy's performance at Winchester and add his voice to the growing chorus of anti-Milroy sentiment.

While McReynolds and other refugees from Milroy's division rendered strong opinions of their leaders, other soldiers in letters and diary entries mostly recounted the battle, the trek northward, or their present circumstances. "Still at Bloody Run," wrote the 87th Pennsylvania's Jacob Herr on June 21. A kind-hearted farmer had given them quarters in his barn. "This place appears like home, well, we can almost call it home for it is in Penna. The citizens are very kind to us. They give us everything we ask for, but there are some Copperheads through here. We have good living here, almost too much so. All we have [we] got from the neighboring farmers." He added the next night, "All our duty as yet is picket, eat, and sleep which comes very nice to us." Contemplating the martial origins of the colonial name Bloody Run, he added. "To see the battlefield on which our forefathers bled and died, awakens a new thought in a soldier of the present rebellion. Just think how our fathers fought for this government, now why should not we sacrifice everything to sustain it."[106]

Many relatives and loved ones back home, meanwhile, remained anxious about the uncertain fates of their family members. Julie Hawkins, from Lebanon, Connecticut, shared rumors about local men of the 18th Connecticut Infantry in a letter to a friend. One missing soldier they both knew was William Perry. "I rather think he will get war enough before he gets home," she penned, "if he ever does get home perhaps he never will." Mrs. Joseph Tilden, she continued, had not yet heard from her husband, and some were speculating the private and father of two had been killed in the recent fighting, "but it is all guess work. She is feeling very bad, [and] I hope he is living." Private Tilden had little stomach for war, but decided enlisting was better than being drafted and assigned wherever the government decided he was

---

105 Ibid., 237 and 263.

106 Andrew McReynolds, "The Evacuation of Winchester," *Baltimore American*, June 21, 1863, reprinted in the *New York Evening Express*, June 22, 1863; Herr diary entries for June 21-22, 1863.

needed. "I think I would have run the risk of that if I had been in his shoes," added Julie added.[107]

Ohioan James R. Morris located the 116th Ohio in Bloody Run and received a full accounting of the outfit's missing and the wounded left behind in the hospital in Winchester. He submitted the list to his hometown newspaper in Woodsfield, Ohio. Morris reassured readers he had many letters from soldiers, most containing money for their relatives and friends back home. "In my humble judgment," he added, "from what the men and officers say, there was a great blunder committed at Winchester. Who is responsible is not for me to say."[108]

Many other participants in the recent fighting in the Lower Valley disagreed as to who was responsible for the disastrous result, or even whether the appropriate level of praise was being doled out to the proper commands. Infighting and finger-pointing ruled the day. "Of the cavalry, here or elsewhere, I have nothing to say," concluded the 116th Ohio's Sgt.-Major James M. Dalzell. "That some of them, especially the 1st New York, did their duty, I will not deny, but that they deserve the fulsome praise that has been so copiously lavished upon them, I most emphatically deny." He was not alone in leveling criticism at Milroy's cavalry.[109]

Several Northern newspapers jumped into the issue. Some blamed Generals Halleck and Schenck, or an ever popular target, the horse soldiers. "The questions which spring to every lip are these," suggested the editor of the *Washington National Intelligencer.* "What were Gen. Milroy's cavalry about that they did not give timely warning of the rebel movement? How was it that the forces in Berryville were so utterly surprised as to be almost defenceless? Why was Winchester, when it was so strongly fortified, so well mounted with artillery, so strongly garrisoned, so feebly defended? Why was it not held as obstinately as Foster held Washington, North Carolina?" The *New York Times* agreed: "The facts then are, by Gen. Milroy's showing, that 15,000 rebels whipped him out of his fortifications, he having 10,000 men to defend them with. Such a result is inexplicable. He should have been able with such a force to hold his works against 30,000 assailants, and but for his own admission, we could not credit his failure."[110]

---

107 Julie A. Hawkins to Ever remembered Susie, Lebanon, Connecticut, July 5, 1863, Alan Crane collection. Joseph Tilden survived his wound, which turned out to be rather slight, and later mustered out with his regiment on June 27, 1865, at Harpers Ferry.

108 James R. Morris to Ed. Spirit, Huntingdon, Pennsylvania, June 23, 1863, printed in *The Spirit of Democracy (Woodsfield, Ohio),* July 1, 1863.

109 *Philadelphia Press,* June 26, 1863.

110 "Our Winchester Campaigns," in *Washington* (DC) *National Intelligencer,* June 20, 1863; "The Battle of Winchester: Milroy's Retreat," *New York Times,* June 19, 1863.

On June 21, six days after the Stephenson's Depot fiasco, a West Virginia newspaper reported that Milroy's troops "are expecting marching orders immediately. It is feared that Ewell is in Williamsport, but the opinion here is that he is not at that point, unless Lee is about to cross below."[111] Milroy's men, meanwhile, continued trickling into the camp set up at Bloody Run. Another 400 reached that place on June 22, and some 2,000 Pennsylvania militia and emergency troops joined the swelling force there. The latter troops appalled Milroy, a Regular martinet who frowned upon the nonprofessionals. "They are mostly a wild undisciplined mob, and a greater curse and terror to the people of the country then the rebels," he complained to Schenck. "They . . . plunder and steal as they go and come and go and do about as they please."[112]

In the wake of the defeat and confusion that followed, some of the men simply went home. Late on June 24, more than 30 cannoneers led by Captain Carlin and Lieutenants Chalfant and Richards of Battery D, 1st West Virginia Artillery, surprised their loved ones when they rode their battery horses into Wheeling. They left Bedford early on Wednesday morning and were now dusty and travel-worn. "[T]king everything into consideration, they were in good spirits," wrote a local newsman. The men planned to remain in town until they could procure new guns, at which time they would reenter the service. The artillerists all agreed the affair at Winchester was the "huskiest muss they ever were in," continued the reporter. The battery's third section under Charles Theaker was not with them because it had escaped in a different direction to Harpers Ferry. Captain Carlin claimed to have fired 1,600 rounds, and told the interviewer that his boys "almost cried" when ordered to evacuate and spike their guns. According to the captain, he heard reports that some stragglers made it as far as Washington, Pennsylvania, before reporting to Bloody Run. Carlin remained optimistic about those still unaccounted for: "the friends of the missing battery boys feel no alarm about their safety. He feels confident that all will yet turn up, and report themselves at this point."[113]

Meanwhile, also on June 24, Schenck told Milroy to have all his troops ready to march to either Harrisburg or Baltimore, as needed. The order was the last thing Milroy wanted to hear because it all but guaranteed he would not soon earn an opportunity to redeem himself. As far as he was concerned, what happened at Winchester was not his fault, and he expected to command troops in the field again. I am still detained at this place on account of the Rebel forces," the Union general wrote

---

111 *Wheeling Daily Intelligencer*, June 23, 1863.

112 *Cleveland Morning Leader*, June 23, 1863; Milroy to Schenck, June 22, 1863, Schenck papers.

113 *Wheeling Intelligencer*, June 25, 1863.

to his wife Mary the following day. "They are now within 20 miles of this place, stealing horses and cattle, and robbing the country and my force is so crippled and destitute of everything that I cannot advance to meet them, and I look for them to come and attack me. My sore-footed boys will give them a bloody reception."[114]

Whether because the Bureau of Military Intelligence had fewer than 20 operatives because the War Department simply overlooked it, no one in a position to do anything about it thought to send anyone to Harpers Ferry or Bloody Run to interview Milroy's officers and men about the identity and strength of the Confederates who had driven them from the Valley. In addition, neither Milroy nor anyone else in southern Pennsylvania (or in Washington) knew where the major elements of Lee's army were or their ultimate intentions. Milroy only knew Rebel cavalry was operating in the vicinity, so he prepared his men as best he could to counter them if case they moved farther north and threatened his position in the Bedford-Bloody Run region.[115]

Schenck and Couch, meanwhile, continued squabbling about who should have command of Milroy's troops at Bloody Run. Couch steadfastly insisted he needed them to counter the obvious Confederate threat, while Schenck pulled out all the stops to have the troops join him at Baltimore. Of the 110 officers and 2,236 enlisted men at Bloody Run, explained Schenck, "one-fifth of them are without arms, many without shoes. They need to return, if only for reorganization." That afternoon, however, Couch instructed Milroy to seize and hold the mountain passes between Bedford and Bloody Run "at every hazard. That section of country must be covered and held."[116]

While Couch and Schenck carped, criticism of Milroy continued to mount. "In my opinion Milroy's men will fight better under a *soldier*," wrote Maj. Gen. Joseph Hooker, the commander of the Army of the Potomac, to his chief of staff Maj. Gen. Daniel Butterfield. Hooker was himself embroiled in controversy with the War Department concerning who had authority over the troops at Harpers Ferry (including Milroy's remnants assembled there). Just days later he would be relieved of command, with Maj. Gen. George G. Meade appointed in his place.[117]

On June 26, the order relieving Milroy of command finally reached him. General Couch replaced him with 31-year-old Col. Lewis B. Pierce of the 12th Pennsylvania

114 *OR* 27, pt. 2, 297; Milroy to Mary Milroy, June 25, 1863, Milroy Papers.

115 Edwin C. Fishel, *The Secret War for the Union: The Untold Story of Military Intelligence in the Civil War* (Kent, OH: Kent State University, 1996), 460.

116 *OR* 27, part 3, 325-6.

117 *Report of the Joint Committee on the Conduct of the War, at the Second Session, Thirty-eighth Congress* (Washington: Government Printing Office, 1865), 287-88.

Cavalry, who had been serving as Milroy's inspector general. The Pennsylvania colonel was instructed to assume command of the entire force assembled at Bloody Run. Pierce, who was loyal to Milroy and did not want the command, reluctantly agreed. "In obedience to [orders] I assume the command of the forces now here," he wrote in a broadside issued to his troops. "I am aware that you in having your General taken from you, have met with an irreparable loss. That loss no one feels or regrets more than myself." The separation between Milroy and his troops, declared Pierce, "will not be final." He went on to exhort the soldiers to do their best to defend the local population, and to "amply avenge the death of our fallen brothers in arms, and wipe out even the memory of our recent reverses."[118]

The news of his relief devastated Milroy, who seems not to have anticipated it despite the shellacking he had taken at Winchester. "I am ordered to leave you, and report to General Schenck at Baltimore," he told his troops before departing. "With anguish, I bid you farewell. If we do not meet again, I shall watch your course and your actions with the deepest solicitude. I always expect to point with pride to you as brave soldiers, whom I have had the honor to command. Our cause is clouded with adversity now, but will be ultimately successful. Hope on, fight on, and may God protect you until we see our cause triumph, and peace restored." With that, the Grey Eagle took leave of the wreckage of his division.[119]

On June 27, General Halleck ordered Milroy to be arrested and held in Baltimore for a court of inquiry. Milroy immediately obeyed and reported to Schenck's headquarters. "I have no idea why I was ordered here until my arrival, when Schenck

---

118 Special Orders No. 16, June 26, 1863, Milroy Papers. Pierce was born in LeRaysville, Bradford County, Pennsylvania, on September 2, 1831. He was a merchant and farmer before the war, and was elected to serve as Auditor of Public Accounts of Bradford County from 1858-1861. He was commissioned lieutenant colonel of the 12th Pennsylvania Cavalry on November 7, 1861 and was promoted to colonel on April 21, 1862. Pierce was deeply unpopular with the men. He was dismissed from the service on August 7, 1864 for "utter worthlessness and inefficiency as an officer," but was reinstated on October 15, 1864, after a military commission found that his dismissal was "founded on insufficient evidence." However, he was mustered out on December 15, 1864 "for incompetency, upon the recommendation of the Commanding General, Middle Military Division." Roger D. Hunt, *Colonels in Blue: Union Army Colonels of the Civil War. The Mid-Atlantic States: Pennsylvania, New Jersey, Maryland, Delaware, and the District of Columbia* (Mechanicsburg, PA: Stackpole Books, 2007), 133-34.

119 Prowell, *History of the 87th Pennsylvania*, 82. Only the mounted elements of the Hodgepodge Brigade saw further action in the Gettysburg campaign; the rest of Milroy's Weary Boys had no further involvement. For a good discussion of the role played by the refugees of Winchester for the rest of the campaign, see Steve Hollingshead and Jeffrey Whetstone, *From Winchester to Bloody Run: Border Raids and Skirmishes in Western Pennsylvania During the Gettysburg Campaign* (Everett, PA: privately published, 2004).

informed me that he had received a peremptory order on the 20th from tyrannical prejudiced brute Halleck to place me in arrest," he complained to his wife. "General Schenck and Major General Couch (in whose department I was) both remonstrated stating that the most vital interest of the public service required that I should remain with my men and defend that portion of Pennsylvania from the Reb forces there, advancing on it," he continued, "but no consideration of public good induce the vindictive old brute to forgo the chance to crush and disgrace me."[120]

The news did not sit well with some of his loyal followers. "The arrest of Gen. Milroy, under the circumstances, was a cruel injustice to a heroic and patriotic officer, "for which there was neither provocation nor excuse," declared his chief of staff, Maj. J. Lowrey McGee of the 3rd West Virginia Cavalry. The general agreed that Milroy "was not prepared to meet Lee's army," and that "prudence dictated that he should fall back," but he also argued, "in view of the recent peremptory order to hold the position until further orders his brigade commanders agreed with him that he had no discretion in the premises, and it was clearly up to him to encounter any force that might confront him." Consequently, he continued, his commander had done nothing wrong or worthy of being relieved of command let alone arrested.[121]

Once in Baltimore, Milroy fired off a missive to President Abraham Lincoln protesting his relief. John Palmer Usher of Indiana, Lincoln's secretary of the interior, hand-carried the letter to the president. Lincoln told Usher that he was Milroy's friend, but he could not intervene in the matter. "Old Abe seems to be a mere tool for Halleck," declared the disgusted Milroy. "Usher promised he would not cease till he got me released." He begged Usher to intervene with Halleck on his behalf. The Grey Eagle firmly believed the West Pointer harbored severe prejudices against officers who had not graduated from the academy, and against Milroy in particular. "Halleck hates me without cause," he told Usher, "with the blind unreasoning hatred of an Indian & I can ask or expect nothing but injustice from him."[122]

Lincoln responded to Milroy in a calm, straightforward manner: "You have lost a division and, prima facie, the fault is upon you. And while that remains unchanged for me to put you in command again, is justly to subject me to a charge of having put you there on purpose to have you lose another." The chief executive also pointed out the obvious when he noted, "You hate West Point generally, and General Halleck

120 Special Order No. 172, Schenck to Milroy, June 27, 1863, NARA; Milroy to Mary Milroy, June 30, 1863, Milroy Papers.

121 McGee, "Milroy at Winchester."

122 Milroy to Mary Milroy, June 30, 1863, Milroy Papers; Milroy to John Usher, June 28, 1863, in Roy P. Basler, ed., *The Collected Works of Abraham Lincoln*, 8 vols. (New Brunswick, NJ: Rutgers University Press, 1953), 6:309.

particularly; but I do know that it was not his fault that you were at Winchester on the 13th, 14th, and the morning of the 15th—the days of your disaster."[123]

Milroy's continued pleas to command once more in the field fell on deaf ears. "I have never in my life been so entirely wretched and miserable," he admitted to Mary on June 30. "Life has never had many attractions for me and were it not for you and the children would not long endure in its agony." To his everlasting regret and anger, the only part Milroy would play in the Gettysburg campaign was as the Union commander who presided over a stunning defeat. For the former commander of the Second Division of the Eighth Corps, life had taken on the trappings of a Greek tragedy.

The Second Battle of Winchester quickly faded into the background, overshadowed by the bloody conflagration just two weeks later in Pennsylvania. Compared to the butcher's bill at Gettysburg, the human cost at Winchester was minimal. But for the men of Milroy's command and for the Grey Eagle himself, the lesser of the engagements forever remained a life-changing affair.[124]

123 Ibid., 6:308.

124 Milroy to Mary Milroy, June 30, 1863, Milroy Papers.

Chapter 12

The Aftermath

"I would court demand and defy the most rigid scrutiny into my conduct."

— *Maj. Gen. Robert H. Milroy, commanding Second Division, Union Eighth Corps[1]*

The Old Grey Eagle Pines for Action

Robert Milroy's frustration increased with each passing day he spent marking time. While the armies waged the largest battle of the war at Gettysburg during July's first few days, the relieved general pleaded with General Halleck to be released from arrest so he could take the field. "I love my country dearer than life or wife or children and since the beginning of the war have devoted every faculty of my soul and body to the salvation of the Union," he declared. He went on to tell the general-in-chief his version of the story of Second Winchester. After pointing out that he had never shirked his duty, Milroy begged, "Place me in the 'fore front' of the battle, even in Hell itself rather than this position of disgraceful inactivity during the present crisis of my country. After the crisis is passed I would court demand and defy the most rigid scrutiny into my conduct." Halleck remained unmoved.[2]

Once he was relieved from command and placed under arrest, Milroy prepared his after-action report for Second Winchester and sent it to his superior, General Schenck. The disgraced general also implored President Lincoln to examine the document: "Look at my report. My destiny is in your hands. I ask nothing but justice. Having been denied the privilege of participating in the glorious battle of Gettysburg and that which will complete the destruction of Lee's army, adequate justice cannot

---

1 Milroy to Halleck, July 2, 1863, Abraham Lincoln Papers, LOC.

2 Ibid.

Col. Lewis B. Pierce of the 12th Pennsylvania Cavalry, Milroy's acting inspector general, and his successor in command of the division. *Ronn Palm*

now be done me." His pleas fell on deaf ears. Desperate to redeem his tarnished reputation and chafing at being sidelined, Milroy continued agitating for a court of inquiry to clear his name.[3]

By July 14, the survivors of Lee's Army of Northern Virginia were finally back in Virginia after a tense four-day standoff with the Army of the Potomac along the banks of the Potomac at Williamsport, Maryland. Lincoln was extremely frustrated by General Meade's failure to trap and destroy the wounded Rebel army. On July 16, while still in a melancholy mood, Lincoln and his personal secretary John Hay spent a few minutes discussing Milroy's pleas for justice. "Had a little talk with the President about Milroy," Hay scrawled in his diary. "Says Halleck thinks Schenck is somewhat to blame for the Winchester business. President says, however, you may doubt or disagree from Halleck he is very apt to be right in the end."[4]

Milroy's Soldiers React to Second Winchester and Their Commander's Fall from Grace

While Milroy anxiously sought redemption, opinions varied widely within the ranks of the Eighth Corps as to his personal performance at Second Winchester. Many of his loyal men longed for his return. Their new commander at Bloody Run, Col. Lewis B. Pierce, did not inspire confidence among his new charges. "Gen. Milroy has been relieved, and Col. Pierce of the 12th Pa. Cavalry is now commanding us," the 12th West Virginia's Sgt. Milton Campbell informed his sister. "We will never be in any danger whilst he is in command, for upon the least intimation of the approach of the 'Rebs' he moves on toward Pittsburg on the double quick. We heard that

3 Milroy to Lincoln, July 13, 1863, Milroy Papers; reprinted in the *Raleigh Weekly State Journal*, July 2, 1863.

4 Michael Burlingame and John R. Turner Ettlinger, eds., *Inside Lincoln's White House: The Complete Civil War Diary of John Hay* (Carbondale: Southern Illinois University Press, 1997), 63.

[Confederate General] Imboden with six thousand rebs was marching on Bloody Run," he continued, "and I assure he got us away from there in a hurry." Despite Milroy's obvious leadership shortcomings, some of his men believed him to be a stout fighter, unlike Pierce. "The men are all down on him and want our old Milroy back with us," wrote the sergeant. "He never runs until he sees something to run from. This old fool will march us to death to get away from nothing. If he continues this much longer, most of the men here will leave and go home."[5]

A Union soldier left an especially cogent analysis of the fall of Winchester, written just three days after the end of the battle. His letter was originally published in the *Philadelphia Ledger*, which suggests he was a member of the 13th Pennsylvania Cavalry (a Philadelphia-raised unit). The soldier noted he had been stationed at Winchester since February 5, 1863, and that he had scouted up and down the length of the Shenandoah:

> I knew long since that 7,000 men could never hold it—in our interviews with the rebel officers, on flag of truce occasions, they always said that as soon as the grass grew they were coming, and, sure enough, did come, and with at least 30,000, and what then were we?—nothing to them," he declared. "The only wonder is that we were not surrounded and captured in a body. What has been the result? Why, a Union retreat—everything lost, guns, wagons and the equipage of every camp, officers' baggage and all. Gen. Milroy is safe, and so am I, but where are hundreds of others who went into Winchester at the call of the country? Echo does not answer where—it says this time, dead.[6]

However much the unnamed soldier despised Milroy, many of the general's former soldiers strongly advocated for him to be restored to command. Major Alonzo Adams of the 1st New York Cavalry penned his after-action report from Bloody Run. After declaring that his men remained firm in their belief in their cause, Adams wrote, "Nor is our confidence in the skill and dauntless courage of our late commander at all shaken on account of the temporary disaster at Winchester, which might have occurred to any other commander under heaven with greatly superior numbers against him, directed by a wily foe, who had more than once succeeded in deceiving and evading the highest and most skillful commanders in our army." Adams finished strongly: "We who have best known Maj. Gen. R. H. Milroy, and have learned by association to respect his private virtues as a man and his skill and great devotion to his

---

5   Milton Campbell to Dear sister, July 1, 1863, in Fluharty, *Civil War Letters of Lt. Milton B. Campbell*, 49.

6   "The Loss of Winchester: A Narrative of the Investment and Abandonment of the Place."

country as a soldier, will love and appreciate him not the less because he is a terror to and maligned and traduced by rebels and rebel sympathizers."[7]

Lieutenant James Hartley of the 122nd Ohio also reflected on the recent debacle at Winchester during his sojourn at Harpers Ferry. "If I was going to fight the Rebels there again," he offered, "I would rather be on the outside and undertake to take the place from them than to be on the inside and try to defend it. It will take more men to defend the place than it will to take it. It can be surrounded," Hartley continued, "as we were at anytime and all communications cut off." The 110th Ohio's Colonel Keifer offered a simple conclusion when he observed that Second Winchester was "a most sanguinary battle."[8]

"Thus fell the gate which opened to the rebels the Cumberland Valley," a Union officer who thought little of Milroy complained to a Harrisburg newspaper in early July. "Had the place been commanded by a competent and watchful General, it would doubtless have been held until reinforcements by railroad from Harpers Ferry and Baltimore could have reached the point, and thus averted all the calamities following Ewell's devastating raid. Further comment is useless." Edmund P. Snyder of the 123rd Ohio remained bitter about how the disaster had unfolded. Milroy, he wrote many years later, "was a fighter, just a fighter, with no judgment or discretion and wholly unfit to command a larger force than a regiment." Writing from Libby Prison, the 116th Ohio's Dr. Josiah L. Brown offered a terse statement that summed up the sad affair: "Milroy got whipped."[9]

Others questioned Milroy's culpability for the disaster that befell his command. A member of the 116th Ohio explained the problem with the Winchester defenses: "It is also true, that he had built quite extensive fortifications sufficient probably for 40,000 men, but not having a force sufficient to man these works, the outer works must necessarily fall into the hands of the enemy, and then instead of aiding us in the defense, did materially aid the enemy in driving us from our position. Why we were not reinforced I do not know." The Buckeye soldier's point was well-taken and added further confirmation that Winchester had required a large force to hold it.[10]

On July 10, the troops from Harpers Ferry, including Milroy's refugees from Carter's Woods, reinforced the Army of the Potomac's Third Corps, which had been

---

7   OR 27, pt. 2, 86.

8   Hartley, *Civil War Letters*, 42; Keifer, "The Story of a Flag," 419.

9   Snyder, *Autobiography of a Soldier of the Civil War*, 8; Dr. Josiah L. Brown to his wife Mary, June 22, 1863, Libby Prison, Richmond, Josiah L. Brown Papers, Archives & Special Collections, Ohio University, Athens.

10   "Letter from the 116th O.V.I."

wrecked eight days earlier at Gettysburg. Unhappy with his change of venue, a soldier of the 122nd Ohio penned a letter home on July 21 to complain about his circumstances. "We are all sick of the Army of the Potomac, and we are all in hopes that we will get back in our old corps and under our old General Milroy," he wrote. "I did think after our battle at Winchester that Milroy made a poor thing of it. But since matters have come to light I know there is no general in the service who could have done any better or as well. He is the man for me any how." As late as August, the men of his division still expected Milroy would return to command them. Old Grey Eagle, however, would never command troops in the Eastern Theater again.[11]

The officers of the 122nd Ohio wrote directly to Milroy on July 21, telling him they were "going to work energetically—and apply or petition the proper authorities that be and see if we can once more have you restored to us." The Buckeyes declared their fealty to their old commander. "We want no other commander than Genl. Milroy and so far as your old Division is concerned," they added, "this feeling I do know to be unanimous." Other officers of his former command wrote to Lincoln to plead for the return of their hero. "We feel that we would rather fight under the leadership of this veteran soldier than that of any other commander," they declared, "and no other man living can inspire the officers and men of this Division with the same amount of courage, zeal and enthusiasm in the work of crushing out this infamous rebellion."[12]

The proxy war, meanwhile, continued apace. An anonymous Ohio soldier in a Western Theater regiment penned a letter that found its way into a newspaper. "The unaccountable defeat of Milroy, and his disorderly retreat in which he lost more than half of his command, is still shrouded in deep mystery in the West. We think it smacks of cowardice," he declared. "I do not believe the fault lies with the soldiers, those soldiers, were as brave as any other soldiers, anywhere." The unidentified scribe finished by accusing Milroy of being a coward: "Some gain fame and lose it because it was not well gained, and I fear that little Gen. Milroy had was of this character."[13]

The accusation offended a soldier of the 116th Ohio, who promptly sprang to Milroy's defense. "No one who knows Milroy will ever call him a coward. And no one will make this charge a second time in the hearing of any of the men of his old Division," exclaimed the angry Buckeye. "Was it cowardly to save 4,000 men at the very last moment they could be saved? Was it cowardly to check the advance of Lee's

---

11 Black, "Civil War Letters," 179; Black, *A Lincoln Cavalryman*, 134.

12 122nd Ohio to Milroy, July 21, 1863, Milroy Papers; Officers in Milroy Division to Lincoln, July 23, 1863, Lincoln Papers.

13 Newspaper clipping in letter from the 116th Regiment, August 23, 1863, in Paulus, *Papers of General Milroy*, 4:159.

army for three days, and thus give the Potomac army . . . time? Was it cowardly of him because he did not remain . . . to be shelled by a hundred guns of the enemy, and have his command all killed or, captured?" The indignant soldier concluded, "General Milroy will come from under this cloud pure and undefiled, notwithstanding . . . the jealousy of West Point Generals. Mark this."[14]

A West Virginian sounded a similar note. "Some may think that Gen. Milroy was surprised, that he did not suppose that he was engaging a vastly superior force, or that he retreated from a strong position, and from a force not much greater than his own," he wrote. "If you had formed any such opinion you are laboring under a grand mistake. Our scouts reported the rebel force in the valley at 50,000, while prisoners which we took on Friday reported the same thing. For several nights a strong picket force had been sent out." It seems not to have dawned on the writer that if indeed his statements were true, they served only to reinforce the notion that Milroy made a critical error in not promptly evacuating Winchester.[15]

Confederate Reactions

S. Thomas McCullough served in the 2nd Maryland Battalion, part of Edward "Allegheny" Johnson's division of Ewell's Corps. McCullough was among the first to put pen to paper and sum up the results of the Second Battle of Winchester just hours after the June 15 Stephenson's Depot battle:

> The capture of Winchester was a most brilliant affair, placing in our possession some 6,000 prisoners, 33 guns, three or four hundred loaded wagons, besides immense quantities of ordnance, commissary and sutler's stores, a large number of horses, all of their camp equipments—in consequence, fared quite sumptuously during the remainder of the day [on June 15]. Plenty of canned fruit, pure coffee, sugar, etc., which we had almost come to look upon as thoughts of a diseased imagination and not realities of memory—we also got a supply of articles a little more useful, and substantial, such as hats, pants, shirts, etc."

McCullough overestimated the number of prisoners and the guns captured, but it was plain for even the men in the ranks to see that General Ewell had secured a rather easy and complete victory at Winchester.[16]

14 Ibid., 4:161-62.

15 "H.C.H.", "From the 12th Virginia."

16 McCullough diary, entry for June 15, 1863.

Major Henry Kyd Douglas, who served on Allegheny Johnson's staff, left an insightful comparison of the generalship of the adversaries at Winchester. "The movement of Ewell was quick, skillful and effective—in fact, Jacksonian," he praised, while "the defense of Milroy was devoid of all military intelligence and actually discreditable. In the two days, the Federal troops were driven out of the Valley, without a battle."[17]

Dr. Abram S. Miller, the regimental surgeon of the 25th Virginia, very much liked what he saw of Old Bald Head's performance during the opening act of the Gettysburg Campaign. "Gen. Ewell had all the eatables captured at Winchester divided amongst the men such as candies segars &c. which gave great satisfaction," he wrote to his wife on June 19. "They are all very much pleased with it. They did not get much apiece but they like the principle, and I think that he will make himself equally as popular as Gen. Jackson was at the same time he will make them do their duties, I think he is the right man to fill Jackson's place. He is a splendid fighter, and was very popular with his old division. He managed the affairs about Winchester very well."[18]

Milroy's withdrawal, however, remained a source of great disappointment to the Confederates. "It is a matter of regret that Milroy escaped," expressed Capt. John C. Gorman of the 2nd North Carolina. "His acts had been so oppressive and outrageous, that if caught, he would probably have met his just fate as a felon and outlaw."[19] Lieutenant Alfred M. Edgar of the 27th Virginia wrote prophetically, "It looks like a farce to call [Second Winchester] a battle. It is certainly a bloodless victory, but we have had some very bloody ones, so this is a desirable change, if it is somewhat tame. We may have more bloody ones in the future, and I greatly fear bloody failures also. 'The end is not yet.'"[20]

Reactions in the Northern press

The press on both sides of the Mason-Dixon line, meanwhile, excoriated the beleaguered general. Most of the Northern newspapers lambasted Milroy for the debacle. A sarcastic Ohio editor writing for the *Dayton Daily Empire* entertained his readers with a three-line poem dedicated to the "doughty hero": "He fled full moon, In the month of June, And bade the rest keep fighting." The editor concluded with a

---

17 Douglas, *I Rode with Stonewall*, 242-43.

18 Miller to his wife, June 19, 183, Miller Collection.

19 John C. Gorman to Friend Holden, June 22, 1863, NCSA and GNMP. See also the *Statesville* (NC) *Landmark*, April 12, 1932.

20 Edgar, *My Reminiscences of the Civil War*, 129.

scornful, "So much for Milroy."[21] One Pennsylvania paper called it "the most disgraceful defeat of the war. By the bad management, the want of cool courage and capacity, in Milroy, he lost everything." Mocking Milroy for fleeing the battlefield, the editor declared, "Such an officer is a disgrace to our army. He should be cashiered and dismissed the service without an hour's delay."[22]

The *New York Tribune* also minced few words:

> We rejoice to hear that Judge Advocate General [Joseph] Holt is preparing the documents for a court-martial in the case of Gen. Milroy, charged with evacuating Winchester with cowardly precipitation, leaving millions' worth of arms, munitions, &c., to the Rebels, and sacrificing the bulk of his command to save his own neck. We do not know nor judge that he did other than his whole duty in the premises. We trust that he will have a fair, impartial trial, and be honorably acquitted if the facts will warrant; *but* if he be proved guilty, we trust he will be inexorably shot. That will be a light penalty for the offenses of which he stands accused. We shall gladly see him vindicated; but, if he *is* guilty, we pray the Court and President to have mercy on the country.[23]

The *New York World* was perhaps the most vitriolic of the Northern publications, lambasting Milroy's "feeble defense of Winchester," and likening it to the previous Union disasters at Harpers Ferry and Holly Springs. "Milroy's record is a very bad one," announced the editor, who believed the Lincoln administration had made a terrible mistake assigning him to command such an important position. "Like most feeble men, he has been violent and tyrannical," added the writer. "He is an Abolitionist of the most violent type, and our readers will remember a letter he wrote not long since, threatening to set his soldiers upon the track of Democrats, to hunt them down after the war was over." The editorial finished with a warning: "Generals of the Butler and Milroy stamp are terrible fellows on paper, or when they have women and children to deal with; but fighting men is not in their way. There is everything to fear at Harpers Ferry if Milroy is left in command of it."[24]

---

21 *Dayton Daily Empire*, October 31, 1863.

22 "The Battle of Winchester," *Columbia Democrat and Bloomsburg General Advertiser*, July 4, 1863.

23 "Milroy," *New York Daily Tribune*, July 6, 1863.

24 Reprinted in *The Spirit of Democracy (Woodsfield, Ohio)*, July 1, 1863. Holly Springs is a reference to a successful mounted raid by Confederate Maj. Gen. Earl Van Dorn upon U. S. Grant's supply depot at Holly Springs, Mississippi, in December 1862.

Reactions in the Southern and International Press

Lawson, the *Richmond Whig* reporter who was in Winchester during the battle, soon after the fighting labeled Milroy a "vulgar brutish, thieving devil" who had committed multiple outrages upon the "oppressed and downtrodden people" of Winchester.[25] At least one Southern newsman offered Milroy some backhanded praise for his efforts at Second Winchester. "Milroy has been charged with many ugly things, one of which was knowing more about browbeating non-combatants than handling soldiers," he editorialized, "but it will always be remembered by friend and foe alike that he did not leave Winchester that day without a fight." Milroy, he continued, "did not show his heels until obliged to. He had five to one opposed to him, and yet he did not give way until pushed with the bayonet." With that praise finished, the writer picked up the common theme that Milroy ran off and abandoned his men: "When he did go it was a helter skelter to avoid a force already on his flank, and Milroy and staff were the first at the Potomac, leaving over 3,000 prisoners and nearly all his artillery in the hands of the Confederates."[26]

Even the respected overseas *The Times* of London jumped into the debate. Adding some international flair to the matter, the venerable English newspaper blasted Milroy in its July 6 edition. "General Milroy," it observed, was "one of the political adventurers of the school of Butler, Schenck, and [Brig. Gen. Milo] Hascall, who have left the desk for the camp, for their advancement and the shame of their country, is the same redoubtable warrior who threatened the 'Copperheads' and peace party, and who otherwise rendered himself notorious by armed hostilities against newspaper offices that were unable to resist." The correspondent who filed the piece was of the firm belief that Milroy received his command for political, and not military, reasons "at a moment when the President was out of temper with the slow and cautious movements of all the officers who had received a military education at West Point." As bad as this was, the Englishman was just warming up.

It was Milroy's duty to be prepared at Winchester, but as soon as Ewell's divisions appeared "he became alarmed, and lost his self-control and presence of mind. Instead of holding out or offering the best resistance possible, until General Hooker should send or come to the rescue, he made up what little of his mind was left to the sad conclusion that he was outnumbered and outgeneraled, and that nothing was to be done but to retreat as rapidly as he could." The newsman mocked Milroy for "most

---

25 *Richmond Whig*, as quoted in the *Raleigh* (NC) *Weekly State Journal*, July 2, 1863.

26 "Sixteen Years After: Why Lee Invaded the North," *The Cuthbert* (GA) *Appeal*, April 28, 1882.

gallantly" announcing to the world that he had desperately cut his way out through a vastly superior force, adding:

> It turns out, however—for private letters from officers and soldiers will come to legit, facts, however carefully suppressed, will be made known, and truth will vindicate itself, whoever may be hurt in the process—that General Milroy reached Harpers Ferry with only 1,700 men out of 7,000; that he left all his artillery, ammunition, baggage and stores, estimated to be worth to the Confederates nearly $5,000,000; and, moreover, that he ran a great deal faster than any of his army.

The English reporter was far from finished with his biting sarcasm. He scorned the notion that many of Milroy's men were "wondering at the remarkable agility of their commander in getting away so easily, perhaps sparked by his fear of being captured and possibly being hung." General Lee, continued the paper, "in reporting the capture of Winchester, announces, 'that God has once more crowned the valour of our troops with victory.' The New York World takes exception to the phrase, and thinks it ought to have stated that 'God has once more crowned the folly of General Milroy with confusion;' while the Herald, less sarcastic and more appropriately in earnest, declares that Milroy, whose incompetency was well known to the War Department, should be immediately arrested, tried by court-martial, and shot, as an example for the future." Edwin Stanton was not immune to the vitriolic pen, which added that the war secretary "should be removed from the War-office to make room for an abler administrator."[27]

The Formal Inquiry into the Debacles at Second Winchester and Martinsburg

Throughout the summer, Robert Milroy continued requesting a court of inquiry to clear his name. In a letter written from his comfortable room at Coleman's Eutaw House in Baltimore on July 22, Milroy complained to Schenck's chief of staff, Lt. Col. Donn Piatt, that the "blame still wrongfully attaches to me." Politicians from Indiana and elsewhere also poured on the pressure to have Milroy restored to command of his division. These entreaties continued falling upon deaf ears. Neither Lincoln nor Halleck was about to restore Milroy to command. However, the steady pressure did finally prod President Lincoln into appointing a court of inquiry. The hearings would convene in Washington on August 7 to determine whether Milroy was culpable for

---

27 The Times (London, England), July 6, 1863.

the devastating defeat. Lincoln's order stipulated that the court was to evaluate several matters, including: "whether the orders of the General-in-Chief in regard to the evacuation of Winchester were complied with; and, if not, why by whom were they disobeyed. . . . [W]hether the retreat of the command was properly conducted, and the public property suitably cared for, and, if not, what officer or officers were in fault. . . . [and] whether the retreat from Martinsburg was properly conducted, and the public property suitably cared for; and, if not, what officer or officers were at fault." Major General Ethan Allen Hitchcock, a grandson of Revolutionary War general Ethan Allen, together with Brig. Gens. William F. Barry and John J. Abercrombie—all West Point alumni, a prospect that must have horrified Milroy—were assigned to serve as the members of the court. Captain Robert N. Scott was selected to serve as the judge advocate presiding.[28]

The proceedings were scheduled to begin at the War Department headquarters on August 7, 1863, but the lack of a suitable room postponed its opening until August 8. Milroy arrived until 12:30 p.m. After the special order convening the court was read aloud, he was asked whether he had any objections to any of the members assigned to the court. Milroy replied no, and asked for permission to employ counsel and the granting of a brief continuance to give his attorney a reasonable opportunity to prepare. The court granted both requests and adjourned until Monday, August 10, which was extended one additional day at Milroy's request.[29]

On August 11, when General Hitchcock did not appear, he was relieved from duty on the court and Brig. Gen. Gustavus De Russy was assigned to take his place. When it was discovered De Russy was not available, the proceedings were delayed another three days. Finally, on August 14, it appeared that things were finally ready to proceed. Milroy applied to Secretary of War Edwin M. Stanton to modify the order of reference in the case to appoint at least one major general to the court, and to defer the proceedings until the application could be acted upon. The court granted Milroy's request to postpone the proceedings, but determined the next day that Milroy had no right to object. Eight days after its originally scheduled opening, the proceedings finally commenced.[30]

The court of inquiry entertained nearly three weeks of testimony. Milroy was the first witness sworn. "I supposed," he explained in candid fashion, "that with my

---

28 R. H. Milroy to Donn Piatt, July 22, 1863, Baltimore, NARA; *OR* 27, pt. 2, 88-89.

29 The entire transcript of the court of inquiry appears in the *Official Records*, volume 27, pt. 2, 88-201, which also includes the findings of the Judge Advocate General as to both the Winchester and Martinsburg portions of the proceedings.

30 *OR* 27, pt. 2, 90-91 and 183-84.

fortifications, I was able to stand some two or three times my own force." That simple statement explained his conduct of the Battle of Second Winchester. Milroy also defended his actions by correctly pointing out that Winchester "is the key to the Baltimore & Ohio Railroad. Let this point be abandoned, and our forces withdrawn to Harpers Ferry, and no force that it would be practicable for our Government to place at Harpers Ferry, and at points along the Baltimore & Ohio Railroad west of that place, would or could secure it against raids from the enemy. That railroad," he concluded, "has not been nor never can be kept from destruction while this place is occupied by the rebels."

Milroy also claimed he had no choice but to hold Winchester because the "Union men and women of this and adjoining counties have been so often disappointed and abandoned to the demons of treason, that they have become very timid and doubtful, but our six months' occupation here has begun to give them confidence in, and many of them have come out and taken a decided stand for, the Union." He also claimed, incorrectly, that "the leading influential secessionists of this place, in private counsel among themselves, have determined, upon the first serious reverse to their cause in Virginia, to come out boldly and take the stump for reconstruction."

Milroy went on to make this rather astonishing claim: "I never received orders to withdraw from there." In fact, he continued, "if I left there without fighting, I would have disobeyed General Schenck's positive orders. If I had withdrawn without demonstrating the fact that I could not stay there, it would have been disobedience to my orders." Milroy also audaciously claimed his actions were responsible for the Union victory at Gettysburg. "I checked the advance of Lee's army three days. That was certainly doing something for the country. If they had been allowed to go on, they would have had three days longer for pillage and robbery in Pennsylvania, and probably ten times as much property as I lost would have been destroyed in that time."[31]

Colonel Andrew McReynolds, the commander of Milroy's Third Brigade, had little to say on behalf of his former commander once he took his seat in the witness chair. When asked who should be held responsible for the debacle, McReynolds stated without hesitation, "I suppose the commanding officer is held responsible." When asked why Milroy's command was in Winchester, the colonel replied, "It was generally understood to be a 'running command.' It was viewed generally as a position to be run from, if attacked by a heavy force with artillery; one not to be held obstinately. I have heard General Milroy speak of his dissatisfaction in not being allowed to make advances when he thought it advisable and that he was to run ... at the approach ... of

31 bid., 93, 97, and 178.

the enemy." McReynolds also told the court that he believed it was a mistake to call his brigade back to Winchester from Berryville, even though it represented a significant portion of Milroy's command. "I should have gone to Harpers Ferry," he declared.[32]

After demanding to be released from having to testify, and then requesting a court of inquiry of his own to evaluate his performance during the campaign, General Schenck appeared before the court. His testimony, perhaps to the surprise of some, supported his former subordinate. "One of the principal duties assigned to me was the protection of the Baltimore & Ohio Railroad," declared Schenck. "I did not believe that any number of pickets stationed immediately on and scattered along the road itself, would insure its protection, and especially against cavalry raids, which we had most and constantly to apprehend. . . . I thought . . . Winchester should be occupied [because the town] was one of the keys to the approaches north." Schenck concluded by firmly denying Milroy had disobeyed any order of his relating to the evacuation of Winchester. He also claimed that, given proper time and good intelligence, he would have concentrated his forces at Winchester, "where I believe I could have held up Lee's army in front or outside of the fortifications until Hooker could come up."[33]

---

32 Ibid., 112-15.

33 Ibid., 167-68. Schenck also sent his chief of staff, Lt. Col. Donn Piatt, to the White House to present his protest. Piatt left a detailed account of his visit with Lincoln, as follows: General Schenck was summoned to appear, and, instead of appearing, drew up a protest, that he directed me not only to take to the President, but read to him, fearing that it would be pigeon-holed for consideration when consideration would be too late. It was late in the afternoon, and riding to the White House, I was told the President could be found at the War Department. I met him coming out, and delivered my message. "Let me see the protest," said the President, as we walked toward the Executive Mansion. "General Schenck ordered me, Mr. President, to read it to you." "Well, I can read," he responded, sharply, and as he was General Schenck's superior officer, I handed him the paper. He read as he strode along. Arriving at the entrance to the White House, we found the carriage awaiting to carry him to the Soldiers' Home, where he was then spending the summer, and the guard detailed to escort him drawn up in front. The President sat down upon the steps of the porch, and continued his study of the protest. I have him photographed on my mind, as he sat there, and a strange picture he presented. His long, slender legs were drawn up until his knees were level with his chin, while his long arms held the paper, which he studied regardless of the crowd before him. He read on to the end; then looking up said: "Piatt, don't you think that you and Schenck are squealing, like pigs, before you're hurt?" "No, Mr. President." "Why, I am the Court of Appeal," he continued, "and do you think I am going to have an injustice done Schenck?" "Before the appeal can be heard, a soldier's reputation will be blasted by a packed court," I responded. "Come, now," he exclaimed, an ugly look shaking his face, "you and I are lawyers, and know the meaning of the word 'packed.' I don't want to hear it from your lips again. What's the matter with the court?" "It is illegally organized by General Halleck." "Halleck's act is mine." "I beg your pardon, Mr. President, the Rules and Regulations direct that in cases of this sort you shall select the court; you cannot delegate that to a subordinate any more than you can the pardoning power;'" and opening the book, I pointed to the article. "That is a point," he said, slowly rising.

A number of other officers testified on other matters, and General Tyler discussed his handling of affairs at Martinsburg. The court examined a small mountain of the evidence, including many telegrams and other dispatches sent and received by the various officers involved. On September 17, Judge Advocate General Joseph Holt released his report of the findings of the court.[34]

After summarizing the testimony and addressing the questions assigned to him, the court concluded as follows:

1. That the General-in-Chief, prior to the attack upon Winchester, had repeatedly instructed General Schenck to maintain only a small force at that place, and to use it only as an outpost, concentrating his forces principally upon Harpers Ferry, and that General Schenck had disregarded these instructions, viewing them as suggestions merely.

2. That it was owing to General Schenck that at the time of the attack and evacuation there were at Winchester any more troops, munitions, &c., than would have been sufficient for a mere outpost.

3. That up to the time of the evacuation, General Milroy was under orders from his commanding officer, General Schenck, not to retreat at once, but to hold his post until further orders, with further orders had not been received up to the time of the evacuation, though telegraphed for by General Milroy.

4. That in giving this order, General Schenck was doubtless somewhat influenced by the representations which General Milroy himself had, in the most confident and extravagant terms, repeatedly made as to his ability to hold the post against a large force of the enemy.

5. That, further, the order of General Schenck was issued without reference to or knowledge of the fact that the army of Lee was then approaching Winchester, but in contemplation merely of an attack by the usual Valley force of the enemy or by Stuart's cavalry.

"Do you know, Colonel, that I have been so busy with this war I have never read the Regulations. Give me that book, and I'll study them to-night." "I beg your pardon, Mr. President," I said, giving him the book, "but in the meantime my general will be put under arrest for disobedience, and the mischief will be done." "That's so," he replied. "Here, give me a pencil," and tearing off a corner of the paper General Schenck had sent him, he wrote: "All proceedings before the court convened to try General Milroy are suspended until further orders. A. LINCOLN." The next morning I clanked into the court-room with my triangular order, and had the grim satisfaction of seeing the owls in epaulettes file out, never to be called together again. Piatt, *Memories of the Men Who Saved the Union*, 40-2.

34 The text of Holt's report on General Milroy's conduct at Winchester is in Appendix B, and his report on General Tyler's conduct at Martinsburg is in Appendix C.

6. That the time of giving this order, General Schenck had from his superior officers no intelligence whatever of the approach of Lee; that he received no such intelligence until it was too late for him to prevent the disaster at Winchester, and that, on the contrary, all the intelligence received by him, both from his superior and inferiors in rank, was of a nature to quiet any apprehension that he might have left as to the probability of an advance by Lee or any portion of his army upon Winchester.

7. That the evacuation of Winchester by General Milroy was as well ordered as could have been expected under all the circumstances, and that the loss of most of the public property, which was abandoned, was inevitable.

8. That during the retreat the troops of General Milroy were not kept well in hand, but were very much dispersed, but that this was in great part owing to their being obliged to force their way through a body of troops superior in numbers, and in some part also (in the opinion of the majority of the witnesses) to a want of active co-operation on the part of Colonel McReynolds, commanding Third Brigade, in the engagement with the enemy, and in the efforts used for securing a safe retreat.[35]

There was plenty of blame to go around, some of which tarred Generals Halleck and Schenck, as well as Colonel McReynolds, but the crux of the findings was clear: the court of inquiry vindicated Milroy, who was relieved from arrest two days later.

However pleased Milroy was by this result, however, he did not think the findings would be a complete until the president endorsed them. "There has not yet been any announcement, official or otherwise of any decision upon the evidence for the Court of Inquiry in which I was concerned," he wrote the president a day after the ruling. "In the multiplicity of your duties this matter may have escaped your notice. The treatment I have received from my Government by being suspended from command at the most important crisis of the country and placed in arrest and the continuance of that arrest for three months have occasioned me so much misery." This was the first of many letters Milroy would pen to badger the chief executive into taking action.[36]

Lincoln, of course, had been following the proceedings and was aware of the findings. By October 27 he had had enough of Milroy's hectoring, and replied:

> In June last a division was substantially lost at and near Winchester, Va. At the time, it was under General Milroy as immediate commander in the field, General Schenck as department commander at Baltimore, and General Halleck as General-in-Chief at Washington. General Milroy, as immediate commander, was put in arrest, and

35 Ibid., 196-7.

36 Assistant Adjutant General James A. Hardie to Maj. Gen. Henry W. Halleck, September 19, 1863, NARA; Milroy to Lincoln, September 20, 1863, Lincoln Papers.

subsequently a court of inquiry examined chiefly with reference to disobedience of orders, and reported the evidence.

The foregoing is a synoptical statement of the evidence, together with the Judge-Advocate-General's conclusions. The disaster, when it came, was a surprise to all. It was very well known to Generals Schenck and Milroy for some time before that General Halleck thought the division was in great danger of a surprise at Winchester; that it was of no service commensurate with the risk it incurred, and that it ought to be withdrawn; but, although he more than once advised its withdrawal, he never positively ordered it. General Schenck, on the contrary, believed the service of the force at Winchester was worth the hazard, and so did not positively order its withdrawal until it was so late that the enemy cut the wire and prevented the order reaching General Milroy. General Milroy seems to have concurred with General Schenck in the opinion that the force should be kept at Winchester at least until the approach of danger, but he disobeyed no order upon the subject. Some question can be made whether some of General Halleck's dispatches to General Schenck should not have been constructed to be orders to withdraw the force, and obeyed accordingly; but no such question can be made against General Milroy. In fact, the last order he received was to be prepared to withdraw, but not to actually withdraw until further order, which further order never reached him.

Serious blame is not necessarily due to any serious disaster, and I cannot say that in this case any of the officers are deserving of serious blame. No court-martial is deemed necessary or proper in the case.

A. Lincoln."[37]

Milroy's name was officially cleared.

Most of Milroy's men rejoiced at the news and hoped it would open the door for their beloved Grey Eagle to be restored to them. "The Judge Advocate General of the U. S. Army has rendered his decision in the case of our Gen. Milroy," declared Sgt. Milton Campbell of the 12th West Virginia, "and had decided that the disaster at Winchester was not attributable to any fault of Gen. Milroy, but lays the whole affair on Gen. Schenck and Col. McReynolds of the 1st N. Y. Cavalry. I knew Gen. Milroy would come out all right. If our generals were all Milroys," he added, "there would have been no rebellion to day."[38]

Judge Advocate General Holt also issued findings with respect to Brig. Gen. Daniel Tyler's conduct of matters at Martinsburg:

37 OR 27, pt. 2, 197. The introduction of paragraphs is for reading purposes only.

38 Milton Campbell to Dear sister, October 25, 1863, in Fluharty, *Civil War Letters of Lt. Milton B. Campbell*, 78.

Upon the whole testimony it is believed that the following conclusions are properly arrived at:

1. That Colonel Smith handled his command skillfully during the day (June 14), but that he withdrew from the field too abruptly, and without giving the desirable attention, or communicating with certainty, to a part of his command the final orders for the retreat.

2. That General Tyler was at fault in keeping the two sections of Maulsby's battery on the field (as is found by the court), after the infantry supports had retired, and in finally neglecting, after assuming command over the battery, to direct Captain Maulsby as to his line of retreat.

3. That Maulsby's four guns were lost principally because of this action and neglect on the part of General Tyler and partly because of the neglect of Colonel Smith to convey a positive order to Maulsby as to the direction of the retreat.

4. That General Tyler would have more strictly complied with the instructions of his commanding officers if he had assumed command of the brigade upon his arrival at Martinsburg, in accordance with General Schenck's order of June 13, taken in connection with the communication from the latter of the 14th, that if General Tyler had so assumed command, it is probable that the errors which were committed at the time of the attack by the enemy in force, in consequence of there being practically two commanding officers in the field, might have been avoided.[39]

Unlike Milroy, Daniel Tyler was found culpable for the losses sustained by his command at Martinsburg and relieved of command at Harpers Ferry on July 2. The authorities shunted the officer off to Wilmington, Delaware, where Tyler commanded the Department of Delaware until January 19, 1864, when he was relieved. Tyler resigned his commission on April 6, 1864. He was older than the retirement age of 65, and the taint of his failure at Martinsburg stained his military service.[40]

---

39 *OR* 27, pt. 2, 200-01.

40 Warner, *Generals in Blue*, 514. After the war, Tyler settled in Alabama, founded an iron manufacturing company, and became president of the Mobile & Montgomery RR, pursuits he had engaged in successfully before the war. He also bought large tracts of land in Guadalupe, Texas. He died wealthy on November 30, 1882.

Epilogue

The March into Undeserved Obscurity

"I humbly hope that I may be relieved from the further useless waste of time."[1]

— Maj. Gen. Robert H. Milroy, U.S.

Major

General R. H. Milroy may have been absolved of responsibility for the disaster at Winchester, but that did not mean the Union high command was in any hurry to put him back in charge of troops in the field, his aggressive letter-writing barrage notwithstanding.

"I would be glad to see Gen. Milroy, were it not that I know he wishes to ask for what I have not to give," was how President Lincoln saw the situation on October 19, 1863. Nearly a month later on November 16, the desperate general wrote to Secretary of War Stanton. "I have the honor to state that my leave of absence expired yesterday," he began. "I respectfully report for duty. I hope that I will be pardoned for stating that having been exiled from duty for near five months, I feel painfully impressed with the utter loss of this valuable time to the county, to the service and to myself, and I humbly hope that I may be relieved from the further useless waste of time."[2]

---

1 R. H. Milroy to Edwin M. Stanton, November 16, 1863, NARA.

2 Handwritten note by Lincoln, October 19, 1863, found at http://www.shapell.org/ manuscript.aspx?abraham-lincoln-avoids-general-milroy. Milroy wrote on the back of Lincoln's note, "I had asked Old Abe for his decision on the evidence in my case before the Court of Inquiry, referred to him for his decision. I had been after him several times about it &

Later that month Milroy received a sympathetic note from one of his former subordinates. The 116th Ohio's Lt. Col. Thomas F. Wildes expressed strong criticism of General-in-Chief Henry Halleck and cast the ultimate blame for the bloody defeat at Winchester squarely on Halleck and Col. Andrew McReynolds; the latter officer was, by this time, leading an anti-Milroy cabal. "But will not the coming session of Congress make an effort to rid the country and the army of this terrible Ogre?" Wildes continued. "Must his spleen and his personal animosities, together with his blind partiality for West Pointism ruin the nation and blast the reputation of all who do not bend the suppliant knee to 'His Bigness'"?[3]

To Milroy's great lament, he ended 1863 still on marking time on the sidelines. "What a miserable world," he complained to his wife Mary in February 1864.[4] Unable to get anywhere with Lincoln, Stanton, or Halleck, Milroy tried a new tactic by directed his letter-writing campaign at the new general-in-chief, Lt. Gen. Ulysses S. Grant. Milroy begged Grant to put him in command of a division of cavalry. Grant, who knew next to nothing about Milroy, asked General Meade what he thought of the idea. "I should not judge him qualified to command a division of cavalry," responded the head of the Army of the Potomac. That ended that discussion.[5]

Finally, on May 6, 1864, orders arrived instructing Milroy to report to Maj. Gen. George H. Thomas, the commander of the Army of the Cumberland, at Nashville, Tennessee. When he arrived in Nashville, Milroy learned that Thomas had moved into Georgia. Milroy detrained at Maj. Gen. William T. Sherman's headquarters and met with Sherman to implore for a field command. When Sherman declined, Milroy moved on to Thomas's headquarters and made the same plea. To his chagrin, Thomas also declined. Instead, he wanted the Grey Eagle to help organize new regiments reporting for duty in hostile territory, not unlike the environment he had faced at Winchester.

Milroy assumed command of Sub-District No. 1, where he was responsible for defending about 150 miles of the tracks of the Nashville and Chattanooga Railroad. While he did not get the front-line field command he so desperately wanted, he did get a consolation prize: His troops included his old regiment, the 9th Indiana. Chasing guerrillas and dealing with disloyal civilians, however, was not to Milroy's liking. He

---

the other side is his ans[wer], Oct. 19"; R. H. Milroy to Edwin M. Stanton, November 16, 1863, NARA.

3   Thomas F. Wildes to R. H. Milroy, Nov. 25, 1863, Martinsburg, WV, Milroy Papers.

4   Milroy to Mary Milroy, February 28, 1864, Milroy Papers.

5   George G. Meade to Ulysses S. Grant, April 8, 1864, in John Y. Simon, ed., *The Papers of Ulysses S. Grant*, 18 vols. (Carbondale: Southern Illinois University Press, 1979-1991), 10:279.

never gave up trying to persuade Thomas or Sherman to return him to a more active command. When those attempts failed, he petitioned President Lincoln once again, to no avail. "I see no prospect of being sent to the front or getting more honorable service," he told Mary in August. "I am very sick of this lifeless monotonous service."[6] Instead, Milroy continued with the same unfulfilling duties that had occupied so much of his time at Winchester.

General John B. Hood's invasion of Tennessee in November 1864 changed things. On December 4, troops under Milroy's command defeated an effort by Maj. Gen. William B. Bate's infantry division to destroy Blockhouse No. 7 protecting the railroad crossing near Overall's Creek west of Union-held Murfreesboro. After this skirmish, Bate's soldiers linked up with Maj. Gen. Nathan Bedford Forrest's cavalry and moved against Murfreesboro itself. On December 7, Maj. Gen. Lovell Rousseau, Milroy's commander, sent Milroy out into the field with seven regiments of infantry and a cavalry detachment—about 3,000 men—to find and stop the Confederates. Never one to shy from a fight, Milroy found them and attacked. After shifting his men onto Forrest's flank, Milroy struck a second time and Bates' Rebels fled the field. The disgraced Grey Eagle had defeated the vaunted Nathan Bedford Forrest in a stand-up fight. "The rout was complete, infantry and cavalry running in every direction," wrote Rousseau with some exaggeration. "The fight was well-conducted by Major-General Milroy and the troops behaved most gallantly."[7]

Except for this bright moment of success against Forrest and Bate, however, Milroy soon found himself back in the tedium of his regular duty battling occasional guerrillas and partisans. Hood's army was soundly defeated outside Nashville on December 15-16, and the Confederates left Tennessee. Convinced the "West Point aristocracy" remained aligned against him, Milroy complained to Mary that his popularity with the troops in the ranks caused the academy graduates to consider him "as a trespasser upon their special rights," with "the baleful eyes of the infamous Halleck were fixed on me. What little reputation I have acquired is so small, so insignificant, in comparison to what it would have been, had I been fairly dealt by and justly treated, that I regard it as nothing—almost with contempt. I feel entirely hopeless."[8]

Nothing changed as the final months of war ground on in early 1865. Milroy continued dealing with bushwhackers and guerrillas, all the while unsuccessfully

---

6 Milroy to Mary Milroy, August 8, 1864, in Paulus, *Papers of General Milroy*, 1:372; Noyalas, *My Will is Absolute Law*, 140-47.

7 *OR* 45, pt. 1, 614.

8 Milroy to Mary Milroy, January 1, 1865, in Paulus, *Papers of General Milroy*, 1:489-90.

lobbying his superiors. Not even the surrender of the most of the Confederate forces in April 1865 stopped his efforts. On July 11, 1865, General Thomas sent Milroy the following order: "In accordance with instructions received from the Lieut. Gen. Comdg. Armies of the United States, Maj. Gen. R. H. Milroy U. S. Vols. will proceed to his residence at Rensselaer, Ind." The Grey Eagle's military career had reached an undignified and unfulfilling end.[9]

Deprived of an opportunity to fully redeem himself, Milroy spent the rest of his days fighting on a different type of battlefield by defending his actions at Winchester. In mid-November 1867, he made an ill-advised trip to Winchester to give a speech in support of Ulysses S. Grant's campaign to obtain the Republican nomination for president in 1868. "Milroy, the great military chieftain," mocked one Southern writer, "thought he would become Milroy the great orator and statesman." The Grey Eagle's talk broke down in a cacophony of catcalls and interruptions from the crowd. "I am more accustomed to fight than to speak," he exclaimed at one point, to which one wag cried out, "Where's Ewell?" Another also drew laughs with, "Hurry up, General Early is coming!" Milroy continued with his prepared remarks. "Congress in its wisdom has proposed certain measures as conditions precedent to your restoration to the glorious Union," he began, which triggered a flurry of acerbic responses, including "What measures has Congress taken about John Arnold's cow?" "Yes, where's John Arnold's cow?" came a chorus of voices. Others sarcastically asked about Mrs. Logan's missing piano and spoons, as well as other items many residents suspected Milroy had appropriated for his own use.[10]

To his credit Milroy somehow managed to regain his composure and struggle on, but the biting sarcasm wore on his nerves: "Spoons!" "General Ewell's coming, who made you fly in your shirt-tail!" "You never did anything but steal and rob, and burn houses when you were in the Army!" Milroy periodically raised both hands as if to ward off the verbal blows in an attempt to continue, but no words came out of his mouth. Sensing that the old general was now firmly on the defensive, the hostile audience unleashed a broadside of barbed comments that brought down the house. Finally, an Irishman on the far edge of the crowd cried out in a clear, distinctive voice above the uproar, "Faith, Gineral, we've had enough of yer speech, now bring out Mrs. Logan's piano and play us a tune!" One more Milroy was outnumbered and nearly surrounded in Winchester. He gave up the effort and again retreated from Winchester in frustration.[11]

---

9   Thomas to Milroy, Special Orders 18, July 11, 1865, in Paulus, *Papers of General Milroy*, 3:164.

10   D.H. Hill, *The Land We Love*, Vol. 5, No. 3, 277-78.

11   Ibid.; *Central Missourian (California, Missouri)*, Nov. 23, 1867.

Milroy, who was nothing if not stubborn, insisted on continuing his pro-Grant speaking tour. He appeared in Front Royal the following Wednesday. "At that place," a hostile editor railed, "his presence excited the same disgust exhibited in Winchester." A gentleman approached Milroy and said, "General, allow me to present you with a spoon." Taken aback, Milroy responded, "What do you mean, sir? Do you mean to insult me?" The citizen confirmed Milroy's understanding by retorting that he thought he would give him one spoon in an effort to prevent him from stealing the rest. "Things were getting too hot for the General," the editor mocked. "He 'fell back' like he did from Winchester."[12] A few weeks later the writer added, "The visit of Milroy to Winchester, and of [Maj. Gen. Benjamin "Beast"] Butler to Richmond, were two of the most *ultra* exhibitions of 'brass'—vulgarly called 'cheek'—that have ever occurred in this or any other country."[13]

In 1868, the *Winchester Journal*, a Unionist newspaper, strongly defended Milroy's harsh treatment of the Confederate sympathizers who resided there and took the residents of the city to task for heckling him the year before:

> The loyalists of the Valley have but one opinion of Gen. Milroy. No other officer executed his duties to such universal satisfaction, or is held in such universal respect. He recognized that the war existed, that the rebels in arms were an enemy, that it was his duty, so far as possible, to protect loyalty wherever found. Gen. Milroy, by reason of his great executive ability, gave better protection to Union men and women than any other man who commanded in Winchester. This is the secret of rebels' dislike of him. This was the reason for the shameful treatment they gave him on the occasion of his speech to a Republican meeting in this place, a year ago.[14]

The *Delphi Times*, an Indiana newspaper took immediate issue with this assessment:

> All know that, as a General, Milroy was a miserable failure. The sacrifice of millions of dollars worth of Government property in his disastrous retreat from Winchester was only equaled during the war by [Dixon S.] Miles' surrender of Maryland Heights. That he is personally brave, perhaps it would be wrong to deny. It is not characteristic of his family to be cowardly. But while a man may possess what is called 'bull-dog' courage, he may be guilty of cowardly and tyrannical actions. A man at the head of an army who would

12 "General Milroy at Front Royal," *Alexandria Gazette*, November 1, 1867.

13 *Alexandria Gazette*, January 16, 1868.

14 "General Milroy and His Conduct at Winchester," *The Delphi Times*, September 18, 1868, citing the *Winchester Journal*.

oppress an unprotected woman—and bear in mind the *Winchester Journal* does not deny the charge of its contemporary that General Milroy sent Mrs. Logan from her home among strangers, is certainly so far as that deed is concerned, not acting the part of a brave man. The General attempts to excuse himself for doing what he did in her case by saying she was a spy."[15]

There was simply no way to escape it: The consequences of Robert H. Milroy's actions at Second Winchester colored the rest of his life.

While defending his wartime actions Milroy also had to make a living, and he set about doing so by founding a mining company in Indiana. He would spend the rest of his life trying to clear his name, even to the point of begging President Grant to publish all the documents associated with his court of inquiry in the hope that doing so would clear his name for posterity's sake. Instead, Grant appointed Milroy marshal for the Wyoming Territory and then Superintendent for Indian Affairs for the Washington Territory. Milroy held this post until it was abolished in 1875. He retired from public life and spent the rest of his days reading and studying because he was too poor to do much else.

In 1890, a bill was introduced in Congress to increase the Grey Eagle's military pension to $75.00 per month. "He retired from the military service of the Government poor in purse, and has been compelled to struggle ever since with that poverty," declared the legislative report. "He is now seventy-four years of age, is worn out, he is in poverty and want, he is unable to perform any labor or do anything towards his subsistence, his whole dependence is upon the efforts of his old wife, who is herself over sixty-two years of age, in keeping boarders, where they now live, at Olympia, in the State of Washington." The report emphasized Milroy's faithful military service and the advancing age of both he and his wife Mary as a justification for passing the pension bill. "General Milroy was in twenty-one principal and considerable battles of the war, besides he was present in many skirmishes. He risked his life, he ruined his health in the military service of his country, he served faithfully and well, and, in the opinion of your committee, ought not be left to die neglected and in utter poverty, but ought to have granted to him by the Government what will support him and his wife during his remaining years, which necessarily must be short."[16]

15 Ibid.

16 "Mary J. Milroy: Report to Accompany S. 3348," Report No. 1891, House of Representatives, 51st Congress, 1st Session, May 5, 1890 (Washington, DC: U.S. Government Printing Office, 1890). Congress eventually passed the special piece of legislation, and Milroy's wife Mary spent the rest of her life on the pension rolls.

The handsome monument to Robert H. Milroy in Milroy Park, in the general's hometown of Rensselaer, Indiana. *Judy Kanne*

Robert Huston Milroy died "in utter poverty" on March 29, 1890, while Congress was considering the bill to increase his pension. Bad luck plagued the aging general all the way to the grave.[17]

The people of Rensselaer raised the money to erect a handsome monument to their hometown hero's memory that was dedicated in Milroy Park on July 4, 1910. Several family members, including his children, attended the ceremony. Judge E. P. Hammond, who served under Milroy's command in the 9th Indiana and went on to a distinguished career as a jurist, gave the oration. "It is a great personal gratification to preside at the dedication of the monument to this distinguished soldier, and especially on the anniversary of the birth of the Republic," declared Hammond. "While the nation at large is celebrating the day, we might well, rejoice in this event which more particularly concerns our own community and state. The monument is to the valor not only of General Milroy, but to those who were his comrades in arms. It is a memorial to the honor of all."

After noting the work done to raise the necessary funds to pay for the monument, Judge Hammond continued:

> General Milroy has been dead twenty years. He may not have been great, in the ordinary sense of the term as applied to ancient and modern warriors. However, if the term great be limited to pure patriotism and bravery, then no general ever lived who was more entitled to the name than Milroy. He had no conception of fear. Of him, Major Benham of the regular army remarked in action, 'There goes Milroy. The rebels may kill, but cannot scare him.'"

If courage was a mark of greatness, there is no doubt of Milroy's worthiness. However, there was much more to the measure of military greatness, and Judge

---

17 Noyalas, *My Will is Absolute Law*, 165-75.

The historical marker in Milroy Park. *Judy Kanne*

Hammond recognized that Milroy fell far short of that standard. Nevertheless, the monument to the Grey Eagle stood as a handsome recognition of his service to the preservation of the Union.[18]

Many of his former soldiers remained loyal to their old commander for the rest of their lives. "Ever since that time I have waited for justice to be done our beloved General Milroy," wrote D. M. Bliss, a veteran of the Wheeling Battery, in 1915. "I am now within a few days of 70 years old. I still hope the recognition may yet come, as I sit my desk and recall the battle and look back to the time when I sat on the ramparts of the fort, the cold chills run up and down my back. Then I rejoice in the fact that I helped save the Union."[19]

The savagery of Second Winchester paled in comparison to the bloodletting that occurred on much of the same ground in September 1864; Third Winchester further shoved the events of June 13-15, 1863, into deeper obscurity. It is unclear whether

18 Louis H. Hamilton and William Darroch, eds., *A Standard History of Jasper and Newton Counties Indiana. An Authentic Narrative of the Past, with an Extended Survey of Modern Developments in the Progress of Town and County*, 2 vols. (Chicago: The Lewis Publishing Co., 1918), 1:120.

19 Bliss, "With Milroy at Winchester."

Grey Eagle realized that the larger and later battle cast his own debacle there deeper in shadow. If so, perhaps he was silently grateful.

Analysis

The first battle fought at Winchester on May 25, 1862, seems not to have imparted any wisdom to the Union high command. In that engagement, some 16,000 Confederates under Stonewall Jackson (primarily the same soldiers who fought and won Second Winchester) attacked and defeated Maj. Gen. Nathaniel Banks' 6,500 men on some of the same ground that would be fought over one year later. The forces in both battles were of similar size and makeup. Instead of learning from Banks' error that Winchester was all but indefensible in the face of a superior enemy, Milroy believed that strong static defenses—similar to a Maginot Line mentality the French would adopt after the First World War—would be adequate. He was wrong, and his command met a fate similar to the one Banks' troops suffered, only with twice the losses. To the great misfortune of the loyal men who followed him into battle, Milroy (and some of his superiors) failed to learn the very visible lesson of First Winchester.

There is no question that Richard Ewell's first battle after his return to duty was executed brilliantly. "Ewell's triumph was complete," concluded Col. Wilbur Sturtevant Nye in *Here Come the Rebels!*, his excellent study of the Confederate invasion of Pennsylvania. "It is not too much to say that his victory at Winchester represented the zenith of his military career. In a single rapid offensive he had eliminated all opposition in the Valley, and had cleared the path for the passage of his own and the other two corps into the North. The Union garrison at Harpers Ferry remained," continued Nye, "but had been so intimidated that it was strictly on the defensive. It did not even have to be contained or watched."[20]

Ewell's subordinates also performed very well at Second Winchester. Jubal Early designed and executed an excellent plan to carry the West Fort on June 14, and his plan drove Milroy's forces from Winchester. Edward "Allegheny" Johnson's troops performed well at Carter's Woods, delivering the decisive attack that led directly to the capture of about one-half of Milroy's division. Robert Rodes masterfully executed the movement on Martinsburg, where his division seized that important town for the Confederacy. Albert G. Jenkins' largely unproven cavalry command demonstrated that Lee's faith in them was well-placed; leading the Confederate advance into Pennsylvania was their first stint of "regular" service with the Army of Northern Virginia.

---

20 Nye, *Here Come the Rebels!*, 123.

Winchester National Cemetery. *Scott Mingus*

The only critical observation that can be leveled at the Confederate conduct of the movement on Winchester and its aftermath is that so much of General Milroy's command escaped to fight another day. To be fair, no one on the Confederate side could have anticipated the timing of the Union withdrawal or such a devastating rout, and the Southerners were simply not prepared or properly equipped to pursue two different enemy groups heading in two different directions. Perhaps better planning and crisper execution of the pursuit of Milroy's shattered command might have bagged the entire force, but under the circumstances, and with no ability of hindsight, it is not clear Ewell could have done anything more to bring Milroy's refugees to bay beyond what he did that June.

Some of the Union veterans picked up on Milroy's boasts and claimed their ill-fated stand at Winchester delayed Ewell's advance into Pennsylvania enough to allow sufficient time for Union forces to concentrate to meet the Confederate threat in the Keystone State. "Where the battle would have been if Lee's army had reached Pennsylvania two or three days sooner may be difficult to tell," declared Sgt. John M. Griffith of the 87th Pennsylvania, who had fallen wounded in the Bunker Hill fighting on June 13, "but evidently they would have found less resistance, and might have gone on to Harrisburg." Another veteran also engaged in a bit of excuse-making when he declared, "Winchester and Gettysburg are twain, and are connected by time and events. Had there been no Winchester, Harrisburg would have suffered the fate of [being burned like] Chambersburg [in 1864]." These assertions—a defense mechanism of sorts—seek to rationalize the decision to hold the city, and thus justify the controversial decision to remain in Winchester and the Union debacle that followed from it.[21]

An unidentified Confederate officer argued along similar lines in his own effort to explain the unexplainable: Lee's defeat at Gettysburg. The soldier went so far as to call the fighting at Second Winchester "Lee's fatal mistake." He continued: "What had such a handful of men as that under Milroy to do with one of the most daring moves that had been attempted during the war? Lee had started for Pennsylvania with nearly the whole Federal army in his rear. In the midst of his march he turned aside from his main line and spent four days in battling with a man who knew nothing but how to fight. In the fight with Milroy," he added, "Lee lost four whole days of marching. . . . It was this delay and the losses he sustained at Winchester that located the battle at Gettysburg and gave Gen. Meade the victory. Lee lost the victory of his northern campaign through the obstinate and fool-hardy fighting of Milroy at Winchester." The unnamed Southern officer concluded with this stunning declaration: "Milroy's defeat was Gen. Lee's overthrow, and must end in the hopeless submission of the South. I curse the day that Lee turned aside to fight Milroy." The claim serves as a means to explain Lee's defeat in Pennsylvania, though it is true that if Ewell had not been delayed in the northern reaches of the Valley, the campaign would have evolved in a different manner. Whether the delay made it possible for the Union forces to fight and win Gettysburg, however, is impossible to know.[22]

The crushing defeat at Winchester had another unforeseen consequence. In the days immediately following Gettysburg, the Union high command scrambled to reinforce the battered Army of the Potomac. The fighting cost the army more than 20,000 casualties and shattered the First Corps and Third Corps, in particular; General Meade needed reinforcements. On July 10, Maj. Gen. William H. French, who assumed command of the troops at Harpers Ferry after the General Tyler was relieved, was ordered to report to Meade's army with his roughly 10,000 troops for assignment to the Third Corps. The survivors of Milroy's division made up a significant portion of French's command. The addition of 10,000 men was welcome, but that number could have been as high as 14,000 men—or an entire small corps— had Milroy's command not been shattered at Second Winchester. The loss of so many men, in turn, impacted the battle readiness of the Third Corps.

*   *   *

---

21 Griffith, "Milroy at Winchester"; Eschelberger, "All Stand Up for Milroy."

22 Powell, "Shenandoah Valley."

By mid-autumn of 1863, many of the surviving prisoners returned to the ranks. The paroled and exchanged members of the 87th Pennsylvania returned "in good spirits" to their regiment just before the Mine Run campaign. To their dismay, rumors circulated for many months that the men would be required to pay for their lost equipment, tents, weapons, and supplies. Lieutenant Col. James Stahle refuted this falsehood in a letter to a Gettysburg newspaper in April 1864.[23]

Earlier that summer of 1864, Early's former division, now under John Gordon, tangled with some of Milroy's old forces again, this time at the battle of Monocacy near Frederick, Maryland. There, the 87th Pennsylvania acquitted itself particularly well, gaining a measure of revenge against the men who captured their stores, knapsacks, ambulances, and wagons at Second Winchester. However, other veterans of Second Winchester fared less well. The 67th Pennsylvania's Col. John F. Staunton, by then commanding a brigade in the Sixth Corps, never got his 900 men into action. For some reason he triggered delays, and then a total stoppage, of the train on which he and his men were riding; they arrived at Monocacy after the battle ended. A court martial found Staunton guilty of disobeying orders and "shameful neglect," and he was cashiered from the army in August 1864. A little more than a year had passed since he had allowed the 67th Pennsylvania to fall into disarray in the face of the enemy at the Easter farm at Carter's Woods.[24]

* * *

The civilians of Winchester thought Milroy's departure freed them from the heavy-handedness of Union occupation. They were wrong. Yankee troops returned and reoccupied Winchester almost immediately after the retreat of Lee's army following its defeat at Gettysburg. The Union soldiers remained there for most of the rest of the war, seizing it for the final time in September when the third, largest, and last battle of Winchester was fought—this time with Jubal Early in command of the remnants of Stonewall Jackson's old Army of the Valley.[25]

---

23 *Adams Sentinel*, April 19, 1864. Obviously, a detailed discussion of the retreat of Lee's Army of Northern Virginia and its pursuit by the Army of the Potomac in the days after the battle of Gettysburg strays far beyond the scope of this study. For a detailed treatment, see Eric J. Wittenberg, J. David Petruzzi, and Michael F. Nugent, *One Continuous Fight: The Retreat from Gettysburg and the Pursuit of Lee's Army of Northern Virginia, July 4-14, 1863* (El Dorado Hills, CA: Savas Beatie, 2008).

24 Files of the Monocacy National Battlefield, National Park Service.

25 A detailed discussion of the Third Battle of Winchester strays far beyond the scope of this study. For the best discussion of Third Winchester, see Scott C. Patchan, *The Last Battle of*

*   *   *

After the fighting, the families of the men who were killed came from near and far to claim the corpses of their loved ones from the battlefield and take them home for burial. Many of the rest who did not make that journey are now in the Winchester National Cemetery. Almost surely a handful of remains lay scattered about the old battlefield. In late October 1892, the remains of two Federal soldiers were brought to Winchester for interment in the National Cemetery. One originated from the Fisher's Hill battlefield, which was fought during the 1864 Shenandoah Valley Campaign. The other was likely one of Milroy's own men. John Kenney discovered human bones and five brass buttons quarrying rock near Stephenson's Depot. The remains were just fifteen inches below the surface in the open field where Milroy was attacked. The bones were turned over to the cemetery on October 21 and buried as unknown.[26]

Today, much of the battlefield has been developed and is unrecognizable as a killing ground. The remains of the Star Fort have been preserved as a small park in the middle of a recent subdivision of densely packed tract homes. The hill where Jubal Early placed his artillery for the assault on the West Fort houses a large farm equipment dealership, and a busy Virginia state highway bisects that portion of the battlefield. Much of the Stephenson's Depot area, which was pristine only a decade ago, is now filled with a massive housing development. Only bits and pieces of the battlefield, such as the Star Fort and most of the Kernstown section of the battlefield, remain unsullied by the unrelenting march of progress. It is difficult for the mind's eye to envision the savage fighting that raged at Carter's Woods, as just one example, in the midst of such massive development.

*   *   *

As those old veterans gradually died off, memories of the Second Battle of Winchester and the important role it played in the development of the Gettysburg Campaign faded. So, too, did attempts to rehabilitate Milroy's reputation. By that time, if not before, Second Winchester had come to be seen as an insignificant prelude to Gettysburg, a gross oversight that does not do justice to the veterans of either side. Second Winchester was more of an afterthought in the public's mind rather than the Greek tragedy it surely was.

Winchester: Phil Sheridan, Jubal Early, and the Shenandoah Valley Campaign, August 7 - September 19, 1864 (El Dorado Hills, CA: Savas-Beatie, 2013).

26 *Alexandria* (VA) *Gazette*, October 22, 1892.

Appendix A

Driving Tour of the
Second Battle of Winchester

This

first tour is courtesy of the Shenandoah Valley Battlefields Foundation and Prof. Jonathan A. Noyalas, and is used with their gracious permission.

* * *

Begin the driving tour at the Opequon Presbyterian Church in Kernstown (217 Opequon Church Lane, Winchester, Virginia). Visitors are encouraged to visit the Kernstown Battlefield Association property which borders the church to the north to explore this phase of the engagement more closely. The KBA property currently is open May-October on Saturdays and Sundays. For more information, visit www.kernstownbattle.org

Stop 1: Opequon Presbyterian Church

Standing near the signs which discuss the two battles of Kernstown, look to the north. You are viewing the historic Pritchard Farm. The prominent rise of high ground behind the red-brick Pritchard House is known as Pritchard's Hill. After the skirmish near Newtown and Middletown on June 12, 1863, Union Maj. Gen. Robert H. Milroy set up a defensive line to protect the southern approaches to Winchester. On the morning of June 13, Confederate Lt. Gen. Richard S. Ewell divided his force and sent Maj. Gen. Edward "Allegheny" Johnson's division to strike Winchester via the Front Royal Road while Maj. Gen. Jubal Early's division marched toward Winchester on the Valley Pike. To protect the Valley Pike, Milroy turned to Brig. Gen. Washington Elliott. In an effort to slow Early's advance, Elliott posted infantry and two guns from Battery D, 1st West Virginia Artillery commanded by Lt. Charles C. Theaker atop Pritchard's Hill. As Early's column

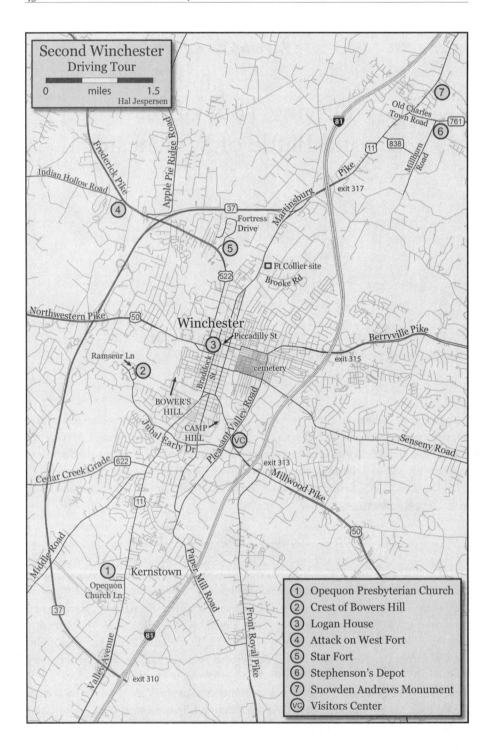

Second Winchester
Driving Tour

0   miles   1.5
Hal Jespersen

① Opequon Presbyterian Church
② Crest of Bowers Hill
③ Logan House
④ Attack on West Fort
⑤ Star Fort
⑥ Stephenson's Depot
⑦ Snowden Andrews Monument
ⓥ Visitors Center

approached Kernstown, Theaker's guns opened on the Confederates. General Early moved Brig. Gen. Harry Hays' First Louisiana Brigade (the famed "Louisiana Tigers") to flank the guns. Heavily outnumbered, the West Virginia section and Elliott's supporting infantry withdrew from this hill north to Winchester.

Directions to Stop 2: Follow Opequon Church Lane back to Rt. 11. Turn left on Rt. 11 and get in the left lane when it becomes two lanes. Follow Rt. 11 north for 2.1 miles and then turn left onto Jubal Early Drive and then get into the left lane. Follow Jubal Early Drive for 0.9 miles and then turn right onto Ramseur Lane. In less than 0.1 mile pull over to the right when you see the water tower on your right side; it marks the crest of Bower's Hill.

Stop 2: Crest of Bower's Hill

By the late afternoon of the 13th, Elliott's command reformed on the north side of Abram's Creek (to your south, or left) while Early's men pursued. In an effort to slow the Confederate advance, the remaining guns of Capt. John Carlin's Battery D, 1st West Virginia Artillery took position on the crest of Bower's Hill. When the Confederates closed to within 800 yards of the base of Bower's Hill, Carlin's gunners opened fire. When the fire commenced a Union soldier recorded its impact on Early's men: "The word 'fire' was given and crushing and crushing went grape and canister through the masses of men. The cry of 'Oh, Lord, Oh, Lord' came loud and plaintive, full one-fourth of a mile away."

Sensing that the Confederates were stunned, Elliott launched an attack with the 123rd Ohio and two companies of the 12th West Virginia in the fields which once stood to your south. At the same time the 12th Pennsylvania Cavalry launched an attack against the Confederates closer to the Valley Pike. As night descended over the battlefield Union troops held their position atop Bower's Hill.

Directions to stop 3: Follow Ramseur Lane for 0.1 mile and turn left onto Mahone Drive. Follow Mahone to the stop sign and turn left onto Meadow Branch Avenue. When Meadow Branch Avenue becomes two lanes at 0.4 miles stay in the left lane. Follow Meadow Branch Avenue for 1.0 mile and then turn left onto Valley Avenue (note at 0.6 miles it will become Braddock Street). At 1.5 miles pull over on the the right at a metered parking spot for your next stop, the large tan and white columned building to your left (just before the intersection with Piccadilly Street).

Stop 3: Logan House

This stately structure served as General Milroy's headquarters during his nearly six-month occupation of Winchester. In April 1863 Milroy expelled the Logan family from their home and exiled them from Winchester on the charge that they mistreated a Union scout. After the fighting subsided on the 13th, General Milroy held a council of war and ordered his regiments into the three fortifications his division had spent nearly half a year constructing—West Fort, Star Fort, and Fort Milroy. When the sun rose on June 14, Confederate Lt. Gen. Richard S. Ewell looked to Bower's Hill and saw that Elliott's men had vacated the position during the night. He promptly sent Brig. Gen. John B. Gordon's brigade, the Maryland Line, and two artillery batteries to secure the heights. Ewell next put in motion his plan to drive Milroy from his fortifications north and west of town.

Directions to Stop 4: From the parking space proceed to the intersection of Braddock and Piccadilly streets. Turn left on Piccadilly Street. Note that a 0.1 mile Piccadilly bends to the right and becomes Fairmont Avenue. When the road becomes two lanes after 1.1 miles get into the left lane. You are now on Rt. 522 North. After 1.7 miles turn left at the traffic light onto Indian Hollow Road and proceed into the parking area for the Virginia Farm Market. Proceed on foot to the interpretive marker beside the picnic shelter and orient yourself looking south. West Fort, your next stop, will be marked by the tree line to your front.

Stop 4: Attack on the West Fort

On the morning of the 14th, General Ewell determined that if he was going to break Milroy's command he first needed to capture the smallest of Milroy's fortifications—the West Fort, marked by the tree line to your front. Only a few remnants of West Fort remain today. To accomplish his mission, Ewell turned to Early's division to execute a flank march. With the aid of local guides, Early marched his command from Bower's Hill to the west and then north to strike the West Fort. Early's division completed the flank march of nearly ten miles in the early afternoon and prepared to assault the West Fort. About 5:00 p.m. (some accounts suggest 6:00 p.m.) Early placed two battalions of artillery on the ridges north and west of the West Fort (the area to your right) and ordered them to open fire. After an artillery barrage of forty-five minutes the fire slackened and Hays' Louisiana brigade spearheaded the attack. As they charged through the orchard they encountered fire from the Union defenders—the 110th Ohio, one company of the 116th Ohio, and six cannon. When Hays' brigade neared the base of the West Fort, the Union soldiers, some of whom were armed with Henry repeating rifles, unleashed a furious fire. Once Hays' soldiers regained they composure, they stormed the ramparts and captured the West Fort. Now Ewell turned his gaze to Milroy's two remaining fortifications.

Directions to Stop 5: From the Virginia Farm Market parking area return to Rt. 522. Turn right onto Rt. 522 South and get into the left lane. At 1.4 miles turn left into the crossover and cross Rt. 522

Hay's Louisiana Tigers swept from right to left in this view as they
headed toward the West Fort. *Scott Mingus*

*onto Fortress Drive—paying attention to oncoming traffic. Proceed a short distance on Fortress Drive until
you see the Star Fort site sign on your right. Pull onto the grassy area near the sign, and then follow the path
and directional signs into Star Fort's interior.*

Stop 5: Star Fort

Initially constructed as a series of gun emplacements in 1861 and dubbed "Fort
Alabama," it was not until Milroy occupied Winchester in 1863 that these emplacements
were expanded into the formidable Star Fort. During the Second Battle of Winchester
troops from Col. Andrew McReynolds' brigade defended Star Fort along with artillery
from Capt. Frederick W. Alexander's Baltimore Light Artillery. After the Confederates
captured the West Fort the guns from the Star Fort lobbed shells into it forcing the
Confederates on three occasions to pull back to the reverse slope of the West Fort for
cover. As darkness descended over the battlefield, the firing stopped. At approximately
9:00 p.m. Milroy held a council of war and determined to withdraw. By 3:00 a.m. on June
15, Milroy's command had abandoned Winchester.

*Directions to Stop 6: Turn left back onto Fortress Drive and drive back to the intersection with Rt.
522. Turn right onto Rt. 522 North and get into the right lane. After 0.6 miles take the ramp onto Rt. 37
North. Follow Rt. 37/11 North for 3.8 miles and then turn right onto Rt. 761. Follow Rt. 761 for 0.3
miles and then turn right onto the Old Milburn Road (a gravel road) and pull off at the interpretive
markers on your right.*

Stop 6: Stephenson's Depot

General Ewell sensed that Milroy might withdraw during the night so he ordered Maj.
Gen. Edward Johnson's division north to Stephenson's Depot to cut off any potential
Union retreat route. Johnson established his line here facing to the west with its center
anchored near the bridge. In the early morning hours of June 15, Johnson's division fired
into Milroy's column which hoped to escape via the Martinsburg Pike. Milroy's brigade

commanders attempted to organize, but the destructive fire from Johnson's division, coupled with panicked sutlers, teamsters, and African Americans who feared a return to slavery, made the efforts futile.

Ewell inflicted heavy losses on Milroy's command at Second Winchester. The Federals suffered a total of 4,443 casualties, 95 of whom were killed, 318 wounded, and the rest captured. Ewell suffered minimal losses—47 killed and 219 wounded. After the defeat at Winchester, Union General-in-Chief Henry Halleck ordered Milroy's arrest. Although a court of inquiry later exonerated Milroy for his defeat, the pain of that loss burdened him the remaining years of his life.

Directions to Stop 7: Continue on Milburn Road for 0.4 miles and then turn right onto Rt. 838 (McCann's Road). Follow this road for 0.5 miles and then turn right into Rt. 11 North. Follow Rt. 11 North for 1.0 mile to the Emmanuel Methodist Church parking lot and then proceed to the large stone and bronze monument on your last stop.

Stop 7: Snowden Andrews Monument

This monument, erected to the memory of Lt. Col. Richard Snowden Andrews, was dedicated on December 4, 1920. Andrews commanded an artillery battalion in Ewell's corps and it was two of his guns, commanded by Lt. C. S. Contee, which anchored the center of Johnson's line at the bridge located near your previous stop. Andrews was wounded during the action on the morning of the 15th while directing his artillery fire. Andrews' family commissioned the monument.

This concludes your driving tour. For more information about Civil War sites in the area, please visit the Winchester-Frederick County Visitors Center and Civil War Orientation Center. It is located at 1400 S. Pleasant Valley Road, Winchester, phone 877-871-1326. Open daily 9:00 a.m. to 5:00 p.m. at the time of this publication. For more information, see their website at www.visitwinchesterva.com. They can provide lodging and restaurant information, as well as Civil War brochures and directions.

Other nearby sites of interest

- *Old Town Winchester*—The hub of Winchester's restaurant and specialty shopping district. Along this walking mall is the historic Frederick County Court House, now an interesting Civil War museum. Note the Confederate statue in front. Union prisoners of war crowded into this fenced-in lawn in the days following the Second Battle of Winchester. Also note the newly restored Taylor Hotel which in the first half of 1863 was a significant Union hospital.

- *Stonewall Jackson's Headquarters*—451 N. Braddock Street, phone 540-667-3242. This historic house, constructed in the Gothic Revival style, served as General

Jackson's headquarters throughout the winter of 1861-62. Owner Lt. Col. Lewis T. Moore of the 4th Virginia invited Jackson to use the house. The Winchester-Frederick Historical Society now administers the property which is a National Historic Landmark.

- *Museum of the Shenandoah Valley and Glen Burnie*—901 Amherst St./Rt. 50, Winchester, phone 540-662-1473. A superb collection of relics and artifacts with appropriate interpretation. Some of the sharpest skirmishing of the Second Battle of Winchester occurred on this property and adjoining land on June 14, 1863 when the 12th West Virginia and its supports engaged elements of Brig. Gen. John B. Gordon's Georgia Brigade. Remains of an old stone wall at the southern edge of the property near the John Kerr Elementary School mark the Mountaineers' line.

Extended Driving Tour
The Outlying Skirmishes and Rodes' Advance on Martinsburg

Begin at the Winchester-Frederick County Visitors Center and Civil War Orientation Center (1400 S. Pleasant Valley Road, Winchester). You may also choose to begin from Old Town Winchester (the Loudon Street walking mall), in which case you should drive to E. Boscawen Street and proceed east to the first tour stop. Alternatively, E. Piccadilly and E. Cork Streets will also take you east to East Lane where you can turn left from Piccadilly or right from Cork to get to the tour stop.

Directions to Stop 1: From the Visitors Center parking lot, turn right and drive northeast on S. Pleasant Valley Road. In this general area was the advanced skirmish line of Steuart's brigade of Allegheny Johnson's division which contested Union troops on Camp Hill. The 18th Connecticut's campsite was off to the left near what is now the Shawnee Springs Preserve. Turn left onto E. Cork Street and follow the black iron fencing around Mount Hebron Cemetery. Turn right on S. East Lane and continue half a block to the cemetery's entrance at 305 E. Boscawen Street. The 18th Connecticut and other Union troops, including the 67th and 87th Pennsylvania and 5th Maryland at times, occupied parts of Cemetery Hill on June 13 and 14, 1863, as they skirmished with Walker's Stonewall Brigade.

Stop 1: Stonewall Cemetery

This historic site contains the graves of 2,575 Confederate soldiers who died on the region's battlefields and at the military hospitals. They include Capt. Charles Thompson, one of Jubal Early's artillery battery commanders at Second Winchester. A shell fragment mangled his left arm during the artillery duel after the Louisiana Tigers seized the West Fort. The well-regarded commander of the Louisiana Guard Artillery bled to death on

"Winchester, Va., Sept. 1885, across the town to Milroy's fort, from Camp Russell."
U.S. Army Hertage and Education Center

Flint Ridge. Burials are by arranged by state with the Virginia section naturally being the largest. During the June 1863 fighting this cemetery was between the opposing Union lines in Mount Hebron Cemetery and Confederates skirmishers farther to the east.

Directions to Stop 2: You may walk north to the Winchester National Cemetery. Woodstock Lane marks the northern boundary of Mount Hebron Cemetery and the southern boundary of the National Cemetery. To drive, head back to East Lane. Turn right on N. East Lane and drive to Rt. 7 / National Avenue. Make a right turn and drive 0.3 miles. Find a parking spot anywhere along the street and walk to the National Cemetery at 401 National Avenue, Winchester, (540) 825-0027.

The Stonewall Cemetery at Winchester. *Scott Mingus*

Stop 2: Winchester National Cemetery

This graveyard marks the final resting place for Union soldiers who fought and died at the battles of Winchester, New Market, Front Royal, Snickers Gap, Harper's Ferry, Martinsburg, and Romney. Monuments recall several Union regiments including the 18th Connecticut and 123rd Ohio which both fought at the Second Battle of Winchester. Note also the Pennsylvania state memorial—the 12th and 13th Pennsylvania Cavalry were part of Milroy's division of the Eighth Corps, as were the 67th and 87th Pennsylvania infantry regiments. The interments include dozens of soldiers killed or mortally wounded at Second Winchester as well as earlier victims of disease who perished in the temporary hospitals downtown.

Directions to Stop 3: To continue to Berryville proceed straight on Virginia Rt. 7 / National Avenue to the intersection with N. Pleasant Valley Road. Reset or mark your odometer reading. Drive 8.3 miles east. As you cross Baker Lane, to your left at 806 Berryville Avenue once sat Josiah L. Baker's sturdy brick house which played a prominent role in the June 14, 1863, skirmishing as well as in the Third Battle of Winchester in September 1864. The house was demolished in 1969. As you approach I-81, much of "Allegheny" Johnson's Confederate division occupied the heights to the right of the road stretching southward past Senseny Road. Continue on Rt. 7, entering the "Berryville Canyon" paralleling Ash Hollow Run. Cross over Opequon Creek and continue toward Berryville.

Turn right onto Business Rt. 7 East/ W. Main Street. During the 1863 skirmish at Berryville, Brig. Gen. Albert Jenkins' Confederate cavalry moved to this road to cut off Union Col. Andrew McReynolds' brigade's access to the Winchester Pike. As you approach the town you will pass through land which saw action during the September 3-4, 1864, battle of Berryville during the 1864 Valley Campaign (Brig. Gen. Joseph Kershaw's division was astride the road facing elements of the Union Eighth Corps). At the second traffic light in town, turn left onto Church Street. Drive one block to the old Clarke County Court House (on your right) and park.

Stop 3: Downtown Berryville

Proceed to the court house grounds. Note the statue of the Confederate soldier, hat in hand, mourning his fallen comrades. At the time of publication, there is a small museum at the court house. You may wish to stroll around downtown Berryville; a walking tour with 20 stops is available. Brochures outlining this tour are available at the Berryville Planning and Zoning office at 15 E. Main St. or at the Berryville Main Street office at 5 S. Church Street.

The historic town traces its origins to an old country tavern at the intersection of the Winchester Turnpike (Business Rt. 7) and the Charles Town Road (U. S. Rt. 340). Colonel Andrew McReynolds had his men construct earthworks and rifle pits to cover the main approaches to town; no traces remain today. Midday on Saturday, June 13, 1863, Confederate Maj. Gen. Robert E. Rodes' division advanced from the south on the Charles Town Road (S. Buckmarsh Street). McReynolds had evacuated Berryville prior to Rodes'

The Pennsylvania Monument in the National Cemetery. The 67th and 87th PA Infantry
and 12th and 13th PA Cavalry fought at Second Winchester. *Scott Mingus*

arrival, leaving a rear guard of artillery, cavalry, and infantry to delay the Confederates. These troops delayed Rodes and then managed to extricate themselves to the north to Summit Point, W. V.

Directions to Stop 4: Return to your car and drive to the end of the road and carefully turn around (dead end). Return to Main Street and turn right. At the traffic light turn right and head north on U. S. Rt. 340 (Lord Fairfax Highway). Drive two miles, passing Rt. 7, to Summit Point Road (Rt. 611) and make a left turn. Drive 2.9 miles, crossing into West Virginia. Summit Point Road will become Leetown Road/Kearneysville-Virginia Line Road. Continue 2.5 miles. The road will become Hawthorne Street in Summit Point. Rodes' division camped outside of town on the night of June 14 after pursuing McReynolds' fleeing column. Turn left onto Summit Point Road and drive west for 3.0 miles. Immediately past the Virginia state line (where the road becomes State Line Road) when the road ends, turn right at the stop sign onto Swimley Road. Follow this about 1.9 miles to the Opequon Creek bridge and pull over in a safe spot.

Stop 4: The Skirmish at Locke's Ford

In the late afternoon of June 13, 1863, Colonel McReynolds' rear guard under Lt. Col. William McKellip of the 6th Maryland Infantry was crossing Opequon Creek at Locke's Ford (just north of where the bridge is today). Jenkins' vanguard, the 36th Battalion, Virginia Cavalry, attacked the 1st New York Cavalry in the fields and woods near the sharp road bend east of the creek. McKellip's troops, pursued by several of the Virginians, fell back across the creek. Union artillery fire from a gun of Alexander's Baltimore Battery and a volley from the Marylanders halted the Confederates, and a counterattack by the New Yorkers ended the fighting. McReynolds' main column and read guard would safely reach the Star Fort at night.

Directions to Stop 5: Return to your car and carefully pull back onto Swimley Road/Brucetown Road. Continue west 3.3 miles through the hamlet of Brucetown to Clear Brook where you will make a right turn onto U. S. Rt. 11, the historic Valley Turnpike/Martinsburg Road. Drive 5.5 miles north back into West Virginia to Bunker Hill. Park anywhere you can in the village near the intersection with Rt. 26. The parking lot of the Methodist Church is a convenient spot if open.

Stop 5: Bunker Hill

Four companies of Union troops (about 200 infantrymen from the 87th Pennsylvania and 116th Ohio) under Maj. William T. Morris garrisoned Bunker Hill in mid-June 1863. Upon the approach of Jenkins' cavalry on the late afternoon of June 13, 1863, Morris formed a line stretching from today's Rt. 11 northeasterly to the Smithfield Road (today's Rt. 26). The Rebel cavalry attacked, driving the Union soldiers back into the village where the remnants took refuge in two fortified brick churches. Those men unable to take shelter were captured, shot, or cut down with sabres. Jenkins, lacking any artillery, was unable to seize the churches, and called off the attack at dark. In a driving rainstorm in the middle of the night, Major Morris withdrew his men to safety.

Bunker Hill Presbyterian Church is at the intersection of Rt. 11 and Runnymeade Road/Rt. 26 on the west side of the Valley Pike. The original structure was built in 1853. The street address is 9802 Winchester Pike. Henry and Sarah Bowers' stone tavern sat diagonally across the pike in 1863. The one-story brick Methodist Episcopal Church is along Runnymeade Road just west of the Presbyterian Church. Constructed in the early 1840s, it served as a hospital and stable at various times during the war. By 1863 part of the flooring and most of the pews had been taken as firewood. In 1912 the congregation moved to a new location two blocks to the south. Now known as the "Boyd Building" for an early parishioner, Gen. Elisha Boyd, who donated the land, the Civil War-era church remains in use as a community recreation center.

Farther west on Runnymeade Road is the long driveway which leads southward to the historic Edgewood Manor, a privately owned home which General Boyd built in 1839 for his son John. Confederate Brig. Gen. J. Johnston Pettigrew died here after being wounded

The Clarke County Courthouse and Confederate Soldier Monument in Berryville. *Scott Mingus*

Modern bridge just upstream of the wartime Locke's Ford. *Scott Mingus*

at Falling Waters during Lee's retreat from Gettysburg. Generals Lee, Jackson, and A. P. Hill met here in September 1862 during the retreat from the battle of Sharpsburg.

You may also wish to turn east on Rt. 26 and drive less than a mile to the Mill Creek Historic District, an interesting early industrial-commercial center along Mill Creek. Several old historic buildings pre-date the Civil War. This was a thriving complex of sturdy houses, water-powered grist mills, and supporting buildings during the time Major Morris's men occupied Bunker Hill.

Directions to Stop 6: From the center of Bunker Hill drive 9.7 miles north on U. S. Rt. 11 toward Martinsburg. This is the route Jenkins' cavalry, and later Rodes' division, used on Sunday, June 14, 1863, to approach the Union defenses at Martinsburg. As you pass Paynes Ford Road south of Martinsburg, this is the approximate place where Rodes formed into battleline near Big Spring and began advancing. Earlier, Union Col. B. F. Smith's men had occupied nearby hills while skirmishing with Jenkins' cavalrymen. The terrain has been significantly altered in recent years by extensive quarrying. Once in downtown Martinsburg, turn right on W. King Street/Rt. 11 and find a convenient place to park.

Stop 6: Martinsburg

On June 14, 1863, Union Col. Benjamin F. Smith commanded 1,300 troops garrisoning Martinsburg. As Jenkins' Confederate cavalry approached during the morning, Smith sent most of his forces south to some hills just north of Big Spring. There they skirmished throughout much of the day with Jenkins' cavalrymen. Union Brig. Gen. Daniel Tyler arrived from Washington, but deferred tactical command to Smith. In midday General Jenkins demanded the surrender of the town, but Smith and Tyler refused. Smith formed a new line on Union Hill east of town and immediately south of Tuscarora Creek (south of today's E. John Street). To reach John Street from your parking space, proceed to S. Queen Street and turn right. In one block turn left onto E. John Street and drive to its end. The creek will be off to your right, as will Union Hill. Six guns crowded onto the rise, four facing south and two facing west, with the 106th New York and 126th Ohio providing infantry support.

When General Rodes arrived with his Confederate division, he deployed his artillery south of Martinsburg in fields just north of what is now Paynes Ford Road (Rt. 19) and bombarded the distant Federals while Jenkins' cavalry moved west of the town. Colonel Smith led his 126th Ohio Infantry from the field (without General Tyler's knowledge) using what is today Rt. 36 toward Shepherdstown, West Virginia. Tyler soon also retreated with the 106th New York and the remaining troops, abandoning the sick and wounded in the town's hospitals. In the confusion, Smith's artillery, under Capt. Thomas A. Maulsby, tried to take the road to Williamsport, only to be cut off. The Confederates captured five of the six guns, as well as about 150 men.

Historic Martinsburg dates from the 18th century. The town was home to several important families during the Civil War years, including famed spy Belle Boyd. Her parents' house is now a museum located at 126 E. Race Street. "Aspen Hall" is at 405 Boyd

Top: Modern view of the Bunker Hill
Presbyterian Church. *Scott Mingus*
Left: Modern view of the building that was
formerly the Bunker Hill Methodist Church.
Scott Mingus

Avenue (off W. Race Street three blocks north of the intersection of King and Queen streets). This elegant Georgian-style house on a hill above Tuscarora Creek was the centerpiece of the Stewart farm where the 106th New York camped the night before the battle of Martinsburg. The home was also periodically used as a Union hospital; extensive bloodstains still remain on the original floor boards. Parts of the sprawling B & O railroad complex along Tuscarora Creek have been preserved as the Martinsburg Roundhouse Center at 229 E. Martin Street. To visit it, return to Rt. 11/N. Queen St. and head south. In two blocks, turn left on E. Burke Street. After crossing the RR tracks, turn left on N. Center Street.

Just south of downtown at 601 S. Queen Street is "Boydville," once the centerpiece of the 300-acre estate of Gen. Elisha Boyd. About 13 acres remain, including the privately owned manor house which during the Civil War was home to the Hon. Charles J. Faulkner, a Confederate staff officer who had been a U. S. congressman in the early 1850 and then the Minister to France during the Buchanan administration. Confederate troops skirmished with Colonel Smith's Federals on this plantation during the June 14, 1863, fighting at Martinsburg.

This concludes the Extended Driving Tour. You may wish to return to Winchester and explore other Civil War sites in the area, including the Cedar Creek battlefield south of town on Rt. 11.

Orders of Battle:
Second Winchester and Martinsburg[1]

!

Second Winchester

Federal

Middle Department, Eighth Army Corps

SECOND DIVISION
Maj. Gen. Robert Huston Milroy, Commanding
[About 8,700][2] (103k, 3mw, 349w, 4,210m = 4,657)[3] 53.5%

First Brigade: Brig. Gen. Washington Lafayette Elliott
[2,989] (24k, 121w, 1,214m = 1,359) 45.5%

110th Ohio Volunteer Infantry, Col. Joseph Warren Keifer
[569] (4k, 51w, 210m = 265) 46.6%
116th Ohio Volunteer Infantry, Col. James Washburn
[619][4] (8k, 29w, 141m = 178) 74.2%
122nd Ohio Volunteer Infantry, Col. William Henry Ball
[810] (8k, 25w, 380m = 413) 51.0%
12th Pennsylvania Cavalry, Col. Lewis Burton Pierce
[620] (4k, 12w, 156m = 172) 27.7%
13th Pennsylvania Cavalry ("Irish Dragoons"), Col. James A. Galligher
[655] (0k, 1w, 247m = 248) 37.9%

---

1 Adapted/updated from OOBs in J. David Petruzzi and Steven Stanley, *The Gettysburg Campaign in Numbers and Losses* (Savas Beatie, 2013), and John H. Eicher, http://www.gdg.org/research/OOB/EicherOOB.htm, and information from regimental morning reports and other primary sources. Numbers for some regiments remain uncertain.

2 The estimate includes noncombatants, men sick in the hospitals, and those on detached duty. Some soldiers may have been double counted on the duty rosters and on the sick lists.

3 *OR* 27, pt. 1, 193 lists Milroy's casualties as seven officers and 88 men killed, 12 officers and 336 men wounded, and 144 officers and 3,856 men captured, for a total of 4,443 casualties.

4 According to the 116th OVI's signed morning report book (captured June 16 by the 2nd North Carolina of Ramseur's brigade and preserved in the North Carolina State Archives), on June 13 the regiment had 30 officers and 589 enlisted men present for duty.

1st (West) Virginia Light Artillery, Battery D, Capt. John Carlin
Six 3-inch ordnance rifles
[95] (0k, 3w, 80m = 83) 87.4%

Second Brigade: Col. William Grosvenor Ely (c)
[3,305] (52k, 173w, 1,752m = 1,977) 59.8%

18th Connecticut Infantry, Lt. Col. Monroe Nichols (c), Maj. Henry Peale
[820] (18k, 46w, 534m = 598) 72.9%
5th Maryland Infantry, Maj. Salome Marsh
[645 est.] (0k, 5w, 315m = 320) 49.6% est.
123rd Ohio Volunteer Infantry, Col. William Tecumseh Wilson (c), Lt. Col. Henry B. Hunter
(w/c), Maj. Horace Kellogg (w), Capt. Frederick K. Shawhan
[720 est.] (21k, 62w, 466m = 549) 76.3% est.
87th Pennsylvania Infantry, Col. John William Schall
[750 est.] (11k, 21w, 293m = 325) 43.3%[5]
12th (West) Virginia Infantry, Col. John B. Klunk
[440 est.] (6k, 36w, 191m = 233) 53.0%
1st (West) Virginia Cavalry, Company K, Capt. Thomas Weston Rowand
[65] (0k, 1w, 11m = 12) 18.5%
3rd (West) Virginia Cavalry, Companies D and E, Capt. James R. Utt
[125] (0k, 1w, 71m = 72) 57.6%
5th United States Artillery, Battery L, Lt. Wallace Fitz Randolph (w),
Lt. Edmund Dana Spooner
Six 3-inch ordnance rifles
[90] (3k, 1w, 77m = 81) 90.0%

Third Brigade: Col. Andrew Thomas McReynolds
[1,925] (20k, 3mw, 52w, 993m = 1,068) 55.5%

6th Maryland Infantry, Col. John Watt Horn
[580] (1k, 6w, 167m = 174) 26.5%
67th Pennsylvania Infantry, Lt. Col. Horace Blois Burnham
[830] (17k, 38w, 736m = 791) 5.3%
1st New York (Lincoln) Cavalry, Maj. Alonzo Whitney Adams
Maj. Timothy Quinn (temporarily)
(Adams was placed under arrest on June 13 then restored to command later that day) [420] (2k,
3mw, 3w, 56m = 64) 15.2%
Baltimore Battery, Maryland Light Artillery, Capt. Frederick William Alexander
Six 3-inch ordnance rifles
[123] (0k, 5w, 34m = 39) 31.7%
1st (14th) Regiment Massachusetts Volunteer Heavy Artillery, Company I,
Capt. William F. Martins (c), Lt. Jonathan B. Hanson
Four 20-pounder Parrott rifles, two 24-pounder howitzers
[105] (0k, 3w, 45m = 48) 45.7%

---

5 Brandt, *From Home Guards to Heroes*, 246.

Not at Winchester, but helped cover Milroy's Retreat

Cole's Battalion, 1st Potomac Home Brigade Cavalry, Maj. Henry Alexander Cole
[Strength not known] (Losses not reported)
Company A, Capt. George Washington Frederick Vernon
[40] (Losses not reported)
Company B, Capt. William Firey
(Detached at Martinsburg)
Company C, Capt. Albert M. Hunter
(Losses not reported)
Company D, Capt. Pierce K. Keirl (resigned June 18, 1863)
(Losses not reported)

INDEPENDENT
Capt. George Denton "Dent" Summers
Company F, 2nd Potomac Home Brigade Cavalry
[About 40] (Losses not reported)

CONFEDERATE

Army of Northern Virginia

ELEMENTS OF EWELL'S SECOND CORPS
Lt. Gen. Richard Stoddert Ewell, commanding
[14,008*] (52k, 244w, 13m = 309) 2.2%
*Strength & losses do not include Rodes' division at Berryville and Martinsburg

EARLY'S DIVISION[6]
Maj. Gen. Jubal Anderson Early
[6,350] (30k, 143w, 3m = 176) 2.8%

Hays' First Louisiana Brigade ("Louisiana Tigers"): Brig. Gen. Harry T. Hays
[1,272] (14k, 78w, 3m = 95) 7.5%

5th Louisiana Infantry, Maj. Alexander Hart
[206] (1k, 6w = 7) 3.3%
6th Louisiana Infantry, Col. William Monaghan
[255] (7k, 36w = 43) 16.9%
7th Louisiana Infantry, Col. Davidson Bradfute Penn
[255] (1k, 22w, 1m = 24) 9.4
8th Louisiana Infantry, Col. Trevanion Dudley Lewis
[296] (2k, 3w, 2m =7) 2.4%
9th Louisiana Infantry, Col. Leroy Augustus Stafford
[260] (3k, 11w = 14) 5.4%

---

6 Early's Second Winchester casualty field report, Gettysburg Campaign, NARA.

Hoke's Brigade: Col. Isaac Erwin Avery
[1,750] (1k, 3w = 4) 0.2%

1st North Carolina Battalion, Maj. Rufus Watson Wharton
[77] (1w = 1) 0.0%
6th North Carolina Infantry, Maj. Samuel McDowell Tate
[515] (No losses reported) 0.0%
21st North Carolina Infantry, Col. William Whedbee Kirkland
[445] (No losses reported) 0.0%
54th North Carolina Infantry, Col. Kenneth McKenzie Murchison
[408] (No losses reported) 0.0%
57th North Carolina Infantry, Col. Archibald Campbell Godwin
[305] (1k, 2w = 3) 1.0%

Smith's Brigade: Brig. Gen. William "Extra Billy" Smith
[1,180] (0k, 3w = 3) 0.3%

13th Virginia Infantry, Col. James Barbour Terrill
[102] (No losses reported) 0.0%
31st Virginia Infantry, Col. John Stringer Hoffman
[270] (0k, 1w = 1) 0.4%
49th Virginia Infantry, Lt. Col. Jonathan Catlett Gibson
[281] (0k, 1w = 1) 0.4%
52nd Virginia Infantry, Lt. Col. James Henry Skinner
[255] (0k, 1w = 1) 0.4%
58th Virginia Infantry, Col. Francis Howard Board
[272] (No losses reported) 0.0%

Gordon's Brigade: Brig. Gen. John Brown Gordon
[1,850] (15k, 59w = 74) 4.0%

13th Georgia Infantry, Col. James Milton Smith
[322] (3k, 10w = 13) 4.0%
26th Georgia Infantry, Col. Edmund Nathan Atkinson
[320] (0k, 12w = 12) 3.8%
31st Georgia Infantry, Col. Clement Anselm Evans
[260] (0k, 8w = 8) 3.1%
38th Georgia Infantry, Capt. William L. McLeod
[350] (6k, 13w = 19) 5.4%
60th Georgia Infantry, Capt. Walter Burrus Jones
[305] (6k, 16w = 22) 7.2%
61st Georgia Infantry, Col. John Hill Lamar
[293] (No losses reported) 0.0%

Artillery Battalion: Lt. Col. Hilary Pollard Jones
[298] (1k, 2w, 1mw = 4) 1.3%

Carrington's Battery, Charlottesville (Virginia) Artillery,
Capt. James McDowell Carrington

Four 12-pounder Napoleons
[75] (1k, 1w = 2) 2.7%
Tanner's Battery, Richmond (Virginia) "Courtney" Artillery,
Capt. William A. Tanner
Four 3-inch ordnance rifles
[95] (No losses reported) 0.0%
Garber's Battery, Staunton (Virginia) Artillery, Capt. Asher Waterman Garber
Four 12-pounder Napoleons
[64] (0k, 1w = 1) 1.6%
Thompson's Battery, Louisiana Guard Artillery,
Capt. Charles Thompson (mw), Lt. Charles A. Green
Two 3-inch ordnance rifles, two 10-pounder Parrott rifles
[64] (0k, 1mw = 1) 1.6%

JOHNSON'S DIVISION
Maj. Gen. Edward "Allegheny" Johnson
[6,473] (22k, 101w, 10m = 133) 2.1%

Steuart's Brigade: Brig. Gen. George Hume Steuart
[2,178] (14k, 54w = 68) 3.1%

1st North Carolina Infantry, Lt. Col. Hamilton Allen Brown
[396] (5k, 14w = 19) 4.8%
3rd North Carolina Infantry, Maj. William Murdock Parsley
[585] (9k, 34w = 43) 7.4%
10th Virginia Infantry, Col. Edward Tiffin Harrison Warren
[282] (0k, 6w = 6) 2.1%
23rd Virginia Infantry, Lt. Col. Simeon Taylor Walton
[251] (not engaged)
37th Virginia Infantry, Maj. Henry Clinton Wood
[264] (not engaged)

Nichols' Second Louisiana "Pelican" Brigade: Col. Jesse Milton Williams
[1,038] (2k, 13w = 15) 1.4%

1st Louisiana Infantry, Capt. Edward D. Willett
[172] (0k, 1w =1) 0.6%
2nd Louisiana Infantry, Lt. Col. Ross Edwin Burke
[236] (2k, 9w =11) 4.7%
10th Louisiana Infantry, Maj. Thomas N. Powell
[226] (0k, 3w = 3) 1.3%
14th Louisiana Infantry, Lt. Col. David Zable
[218] (No losses reported) 0.0%
15th Louisiana Infantry, Maj. Andrew Brady
[186] (not engaged)

Walker's "Stonewall Brigade": Brig. Gen. James Alexander Walker
[1,346] (3k, 19w, 10m = 32) 2.4%
2nd Virginia Infantry, Col. John Quincy Adams Nadenbousch

[335] (0k, 2w = 2) 0.6%
4th Virginia Infantry, Maj. William Terry
[257] (No losses reported) 0.0%
5th Virginia Infantry, Lt. Col. Hazael Joseph Williams (w),
Maj. James William Newton
[370] (3k, 16w, 10m = 29) 7.8%
27th Virginia Infantry, Lt. Col. Daniel McElheran Shriver
[148] (No losses reported) 0.0%
33rd Virginia Infantry, Capt. Jacob Burner Golladay
[236] (0k, 1w = 1) 0.4%

Jones' Brigade: Brig. Gen. John Marshall Jones
[1,446] (0k, 1w =1) 0.07%

21st Virginia Infantry, Capt. William Perkins Moseley
[183] (No losses reported) 0.0%
25th Virginia Infantry, Col. John Carlton Higginbotham
[280] (No losses reported) 0.0%
42nd Virginia Infantry, Lt. Col. Robert Woodson Withers
[252] (No losses reported) 0.0%
44th Virginia Infantry, Maj. Norvell Cobb
[227] (No losses reported) 0.0%
48th Virginia Infantry, Lt. Col. Robert Henry Dungan
[252] (0k, 1w = 1) 0.4%
50th Virginia Infantry, Lt. Col. Logan Henry Neil Salyer
[252] (No losses reported) 0.0%

Artillery Battalion: Lt. Col. Richard Snowden Andrews (w),
Maj. Joseph White Latimer
[380] (3k, 14w = 17) 4.5%

Dement's Battery, 1st Maryland Battery, Capt. William Fendley Dement
Four 12-pounder Napoleons
[105] (2k, 13w = 15) 14.3%
Brown's Battery, 4th Maryland "Chesapeake" Artillery,
Capt. William Dawson Brown
Four 10-pounder Parrott rifles
[81] (Not engaged)
Carpenter's Battery, Alleghany (Virginia) Rough Artillery,
Lt. William Thomas Lambie
Two 12-pounder Napoleons, two 3-inch ordnance rifles
[99] (1k, 1w = 2) 2.0%
Raine's Battery, Lynchburg (Virginia) "Lee" Battery, Capt. Charles James Raine
One 3-inch ordnance rifle, one 10-pounder Parrott, two 20-pounder Parrotts
[95] (No losses reported) 0.0%

Artillery Reserve: Capt. Archibald Graham
[85] (No losses reported) 0.0%

1stVirginia Battalion
1st Rockbridge (Virginia) Artillery
Two Blakely rifles, two 20-pounder Parrott rifles
(Captured two 20-pounder Parrotts at Winchester and disposed of the Blakely guns)
[85] (No losses reported) 0.0%

UNATTACHED, "MARYLAND LINE"
Lt. Col. James Rawlings Herbert

2nd Maryland Battalion, Lt. Col. James Rawlings Herbert,
Maj. William Worthington Goldsborough
[400] (Lost "17 men wounded, some mortally"[7]) 4.3%
(Assigned to Steuart's brigade after the Second Battle of Winchester)
2nd Baltimore Light Artillery, Capt. Wiley Hunter Griffin
Four 10-pounder Parrott rifles
[106] (No losses reported) 0.0%
Company A, 1st Maryland Cavalry, Capt. Frank A. Bond
[~50] (No losses reported) 0.0%
Company B, 1st Maryland Cavalry, Capt. George Malcolm Emack
[~50] (No losses reported) 0.0%

CAVALRY DIVISION

Jenkins' Brigade, Brig. Gen. Albert Gallatin Jenkins
[1,072] (1k, 1w, 2m = 4+) 0.4%+

14th Virginia Cavalry (7 Companies), Col. James Addison Cochran
[268] (1k, 2m = 3) 1.1%
16th Virginia Cavalry, Col. Milton Jameson Ferguson, Maj. James Henry Nounnan
[265] (Unknown losses)
17th Virginia Cavalry, Col. William Henderson French
[242] (0k, 1w = 1) 0.4%
34th Battalion, Virginia Cavalry, Lt. Col. Vincent Addison Witcher
[172] (Unknown losses)
36th Battalion, Virginia Cavalry, Maj. James W. Sweeney (w),
Capt. Cornelius Timothy Smith
[125] (Unknown losses)

Artillery (not present)
Jackson's Battery, Charlottesville (Virginia) Horse Artillery,
Capt. Thomas Edwin Jackson
Two 12-pounder howitzers, two 3-inch ordnance rifles
[113] (No losses)

7   William H. Lyons diary entry, June 14, 1863, Maryland Historical Association.

Order of Battle at Martinsburg
(adapted from *OR* 27, pt. 1, 193)

Federal

Middle Department, Eighth Army Corps

FIRST DIVISION

Third Brigade: Col. Benjamin Franklin Smith, nominal commander,
Brig. Gen. Daniel Tyler, assigned to command on June 14, 1863
[About 1,300] (4k, 9w, 149m = 159) About 12%

106th New York Infantry, Col. Edward Christopher James
[About 600]
126th Ohio Volunteer Infantry, Col. Benjamin Franklin Smith
[About 500]
Company B, 1st Maryland Potomac Home Brigade Cavalry,
Capt. William Firey
[About 40] (Losses not reported)
1st (West) Virginia Light Artillery, Battery F, Capt. Thomas A. Maulsby
Six 3-inch ordnance rifles
[About 100] (Losses not reported)

UNATTACHED

Company H, 1st New York (Lincoln) Cavalry, Lt. Franklin Gray Martindale
[About 30] (Losses not reported)
Elements of the 13th Pennsylvania Cavalry
[About 30] (Losses not reported)

Confederate

RODES' DIVISION
Maj. Gen. Robert Emmett Rodes
[About 8,000] (Losses not reported; Union estimated Rodes at 7 killed)
(Strengths are based on the battle of Gettysburg, from Petruzzi and Stanley)

Daniel's Brigade: Brig. Gen. Junius Daniel
[2,157] (Losses not reported)

32nd North Carolina Infantry, Col. Edmund Crey Brabble
[465] (Losses not reported)
43rd North Carolina Infantry, Col. Thomas Stephens Kenan
[583] (Losses not reported)

45th North Carolina Infantry, Lt. Col. Samuel Hill Boyd
[460] (Losses not reported)
53rd North Carolina Infantry, Col. William Allison Owens
[409] (Losses not reported)
2nd North Carolina Battalion, Lt. Col. Hezekiah L. Andrews
[240] (Losses not reported)

Doles' Brigade: Brig. Gen. George Doles
[1,329] (Losses not reported)

4th Georgia Infantry, Lt. Col. David Read Evans Winn
[341] (Losses not reported)
12th Georgia Infantry, Col. Edward S. Willis
[327] (Losses not reported)
21st Georgia Infantry, Col. John Thomas Mercer
[287] (Losses not reported)
44th Georgia Infantry, Col. Samuel Prophet Lumpkin
[364] (Losses not reported)

Iverson's Brigade: Brig. Gen. Alfred Iverson Jr.
[1,380] (Losses not reported)

5th North Carolina Infantry, Capt. Speight Brock West
[473] (Losses not reported)
12th North Carolina Infantry, Lt. Col. William Smith Davis
[219] (Losses not reported)
20th North Carolina Infantry, Lt. Col. Nelson Slough
[372] (Losses not reported)
23rd North Carolina Infantry, Col. Daniel Harvey Christie
[316] (Losses not reported)

O'Neal's Brigade: Col. Edward Asbury O'Neal
[1,685] (Losses not reported)

3rd Alabama Infantry, Col. Cullen Andrews Battle
[350] (Losses not reported)
5th Alabama Infantry, Col. Josephus Marion Hall
[317] (Losses not reported)
6th Alabama Infantry, Col. James Newell Lightfoot
[382] (Losses not reported)
12th Alabama Infantry, Col. Samuel Bonneau Pickens
[317] (Losses not reported)
26th Alabama Infantry, Lt. Col. John Chapman Goodgame
[319] (Losses not reported)

Rameur's Brigade: Brig. Gen. Stephen Dodson Ramseur
[1,023] (Losses not reported)

2nd North Carolina Infantry, Maj. Daniel Washington Hurtt
[243] (Losses not reported)

4th North Carolina Infantry, Col. Bryan Grimes
[196] (Losses not reported)
14th North Carolina Infantry, Col. Risden Tyler Bennett
[308] (Losses not reported)
30th North Carolina Infantry, Col. Francis Marion Parker
[276] (Losses not reported)

Artillery Battalion: Lt. Col. Thomas H. Carter
[378] (1k, 1w = 2) 0.5%

Reese's Battery, Jefferson Davis (Alabama) Artillery, Capt. William J. Reese
Four 3-inch ordnance rifles
[79] (No losses reported) 0.0%
Carter's Battery, King William (Virginia) Artillery, Capt. William P. Carter
Two Napoleons, two 10-pounder Parrott rifles
[103] (No losses reported) 0.0%
Page's Battery, Morris (Virginia) Artillery, Capt. Richard C. M. Page
Four 12-pounder Napoleons
[114] (No losses reported) 0.0%
Fry's Battery, Orange (Virginia) Battery, Capt. Charles W. Fry
Two 3-inch ordnance rifles, two 10-pounder Parrott rifles
[82] (1k, 1w = 2) 2.4%

See also Albert G. Jenkins' brigade
(reported in the Second Winchester Order of Battle)

Union Surgeons and Chaplains Captured at Second Winchester and Confined to Libby Prison[1]

Surgeons

Dr. Lewis Applegate, 102nd New York (captured at Martinsburg)

Dr. W. F. Bowler, 12th Pennsylvania Cavalry

Dr. Josiah L. Brown, 116th Ohio, assistant surgeon

Dr. M. F. Bowen, 5th Maryland, assistant surgeon

Dr. Charles E. Goldsborough, 5th Maryland, assistant surgeon

Dr. Josiah B. Harrington, 18th Connecticut, first assistant surgeon

Dr. Lowell Holbrook, 18th Connecticut

Dr. William M. Houston, 122nd Ohio

Dr. H. L. Lewis, 6th Maryland (no one by that name listed on roster, however)

Dr. George B. Lummis, 13th Pennsylvania Cavalry (a.k.a. 117th Pennsylvania Volunteers)

Dr. Robert R. McCandliss, 110th Ohio

Dr. William Francis McCurdy, 87th Pennsylvania

Dr. Daniel Meeker, 2nd Division, 8th Corps, Medical Director

Dr. William B. North, 18th Connecticut, second assistant surgeon

Dr. Frederick Henry Patten, 12th West Virginia, assistant surgeon

Dr. Harvey Lindsley Pierce, 5th Maryland, 2nd assistant surgeon, died in prison of disease on Nov. 5, 1863

Dr. Thomas Curtis Smith, 116th Ohio, assistant surgeon

Dr. James H. Williams, 123rd Ohio, assistant surgeon (however, not in any lists of prisoners at Libby)

---

1 *Philadelphia Age*, Sept. 26, 1863, and *New York Times*, Nov. 6, 1863, with additions from other records.

Chaplains "The Winchester Eight"[2]

Rev. Edward C. Ambler, 67th Pennsylvania—returned to regiment in October and served out term (Baptist)

Rev. Ebenezer Walker Brady, 116th Ohio—returned to regiment in October and served out term (Methodist)

Rev. Joseph T. Brown, 6th Maryland—released in October, died of chronic diarrhea May 8, 1865 (Methodist)

Rev. David Christian Eberhart, 87th Pennsylvania—survived pneumonia and returned to regiment Oct. 7, 1863 (Methodist)

Rev. Charles Grandison Ferris, 123rd Ohio—held in Confederate hospital in Richmond, never returned to regiment; medical discharge (Methodist); brother Orris Ferris was the surgeon of the 123rd Ohio

Rev. George H. Hammer, 12th Pennsylvania Cavalry—released in October; hospitalized for a year afterward with prostate issues (Presbyterian)

Rev. James Augustus Harvey, 110th Ohio—held in Confederate hospital in Richmond, never returned to regiment, medical discharge after release in October (Baptist)

Rev. Charles Cardwell McCabe, 122nd Ohio—rejoined regiment after release late in 1863; health poor; resigned Jan. 8, 1864 (Methodist)

2   Pension Case Files, RG 15, Records of the Veterans Administration, NARA; Maryniak & Brinsfield, *The Spirit Divided*, 186; John W. Brinsfield, William C. Davis, Benedict Maryniak, James I. Robertson, Jr., *Faith in the Fight: Civil War Chaplains* (Mechanicsburg, PA: Stackpole Books, 2003), 129, 136, 138.

Resolution of the 123rd Ohio

Camp at Romney, [West] Virginia
Saturday, March 14, 1863

— As printed in the Tiffin (Ohio) *Weekly Tribune, April 3, 1863*

The following Preamble and Resolutions adopted by the 123rd Ohio, demonstrates the fact, that this entire gallant regiment are in for a vigorous prosecution on the war, and they advise traitors at home to read and ponder. The resolutions were drawn up by Major [A. Baldwin] Norton, a democrat, who voted for Breckinridge. A thrilling and enthusiastic speech was made to the regiment by Colonel [William T.] Wilson, but our limited space prevents its publication.

A vote was taken upon the resolutions, and they were adopted by the regiment with three rousing cheers. Three rousing cheers were then given for the Colonel and the old flag:

WHEREAS, Politicians in the Northern States are endeavoring by their insane clamor for peace, and denunciation of certain measures of the President to weaken the hands of the government and diminish our confidence in the justness of our cause, we deem it our duty as soldiers in the field—citizens at home, to express out unqualified disapprobation of all such acts. Therefore be it

Resolved, That we, officers and soldiers of the 123rd O. V. I., are still, and ever shall be loyal to the flag of our country, no matter whether it is assailed by Southern Rebels in arms; and we will carry it aloft with stout hearts and strong arms, ready to sacrifice our lives if need be in defense of the Union of which that flag, with its stars and stripes, is symbolical.

Resolved, That whilst we are sacrificing the prime of manhood, health and life in the defense of the Constitution and Union, in the suppression of this most infamous and wicked rebellion—we cannot but condemn, in the most unqualified terms, the conduct of those so-called patriots at home, who seek to bring disaster upon our arms, and disgrace to our cause, by their insane clamor for armistice, peace and compromise, when they know that the modes by which they purpose to bring about peace can only be accomplished by disgraceful submission on our part, the utter dismemberment of the Union and the overthrow of our Government.

Resolved, That decisive victory on our part and utter and complete defeat on the part of the Rebels, is the only way to peace, and to the permanent preservation of the Government and Union of the States.

Resolved, That although we may not, as many of us do not, fully approve of all of the acts of the Administration, yet we believe it to be the duty of every patriot in the land, regardless of policy, to do everything in his power, by thought, word and deed, to fight, bleed, and die, if necessary, in defense of this, the best Government which God in His infinite wisdom ever gave to man, which we received from our Fathers, and which we, if we are not degenerate sons of illustrious sires, will transmit to posterity.

Resolved, That so far as the matter of policy is concerned (if the people wish,) it can be changed, amended, or abrogated in the future; but as far as our National existence is concerned, it must be decided to day and forever. Not until the Union is saved should patriots disagree.

Resolved, That no citizen of the North, if he is a patriot, will refuse to give his hearty support to the present Administration in the prosecution of the war for the suppression of this rebellion; and if he does so refuse, he is a traitor far more dangerous than the armed rebel of the South, and should be pointed at with the finger of scorn, and followed by the derision of the world.

Resolved, That loyal citizens everywhere are determined not to suffer this Government to be overthrown, this rebellion to triumph—the loss of honor, country, everything we hold near and dear—and the military despotism of Jeff. Davis to be erected on the broken symbols and neglected emblems of American liberty, merely because they do not like the policy pursued by the Administration in power. But on the contrary, sacrificing the feelings of party and policy to the dire necessities of the hour, they will freely give their hearts and hands to the destruction of Treason, and to the maintenance of the Government in every vicissitude of fate and fortune.

Resolved, That the peace offerings of rebel sympathizers in the North, like the peace offerings of the Greeks to the Trojans, are filled with hypocrisy, deceit and trickery, and are only calculated and intended to aid and assist our enemies to overthrow our Government. They are either the pusillanimous teachings of a cowardly fear or of a dastardly treason.

Resolved, That we do not thank our friends at home for sending us letters and papers polluted with treason, which only tend to the field, and to encourage the rebels, but we would thank them to annihilate the last vestige of Treason in the North, whilst our armies are annihilating the armed traitors of the South.

Resolved, That we are in favor of using every beast of burden, every grade of intellect, every engine of power, all of God's creation and all of man's invention, known and recognized in civilized warfare, and within our power, for the overthrow of this hellish rebellion.

Resolved, That we hereby request the publication of these Resolutions in the *Ohio State Journal, Sandusky Register*, and in all the papers in Crawford, Seneca, Huron, and Wyandotte counties,

C. G. Ferris, Chaplain 123rd O. V. I.	H. L. McKee, 1st Lieut.
W. B. Hyatt, Asst. Sec'y.	J. W. Learnard, 2nd Lieut.
W. T. Wilson, Col. 123rd O. V. I.	Dwight Kellogg, 1st Lieut. Co. E.
H. B. Hunter, Lt. Col. 123rd O. V. I.	M. H. Smith, 2nd Lieut. Co. E.
A. C. Norton, Major 123rd O. V. I.	A. Robbins, 1st Lieut. Co. F.
O. Ferris, Sergeon [sic] 123rd O. V. I.	Jas. H. Gilliam, 2nd Lieut. Co. G.
W. McCracken, Adjt. 123rd O. V. I.	Chas. H. Riggs, Capt. Co. G.
J. W. Chamberlin, Capt. Co. A.	O. H. Rosenbaum, 1st Lieut. Co. G.
V. R. Davis, 1st Lieut. Co. A.	F. B. Colver, 2nd Lieut. Co. G.
Horace Kellogg, Capt. Co. B.	D. S. Caldwell, 1st Lieut. Co. H.
John T. Randolph, 1st Lieut. Co. B.	H. S. Bevington, 2nd Lieut. Co. H.
C. D. Williams, 2d Lt. Co. B.	W. H. Bender, 1st Lieut. Co. I.
Chas. O. Parmenter, Capt. Co. C.	G. F. Schuyler, 2nd Lieut. Co. I.
Abner Snyder, 2nd Lt. Co. C.	T. W. Boyce, 2nd Lieut. Co. K.
F. K. Shawhan, Capt. Co. D.	

Bibliography

Primary Sources

Newspapers

Adams Sentinel (Pa.) and General Advertiser
Alexandria (Va.) Gazette
Amite (La.) News Digest
Athens (Ohio) Messenger
Atlanta Daily Intelligencer
Atlanta Weekly Constitution
Augusta (Ga.) Chronicle and Sentinel
Baltimore American and Commercial Advertiser
Baltimore Sun
Bolivar (N.Y.) Breeze
Bryan (Ohio) Times
Bucyrus (Ohio) Journal
Buffalo Evening News
Cecil (Md.) Democrat
Cecil (Md.) Whig
Charleston (S.C.) Mercury
Cleveland Morning Leader
Clinch Valley (Va.) News
Columbia (Pa.) Democrat and Bloomsburg General Advertiser
Columbus (Ohio) Crisis
Cuthbert (Ga.) Appeal
Daily Illinois State Register
Dayton (Ohio) Daily Empire
Delphi (Ind.) Times
Early County (Blakely, Ga.) News
Fremont (Ohio) Journal
Franklin (Ohio) Chronicle
Franklin (Malone, N.Y.) Gazette
Gettysburg (Pa.) Compiler
Gettysburg (Pa.) Star & Sentinel

Grand Army Scout and Soldiers Mail
Harrisburg (Pa.) Evening Telegraph
Harrisburg (Pa.) Patriot and Union
Ironton (Ohio) Register
Lexington (Va.) Gazette and Citizen
Macon (Ga.) Telegraph
Mifflinburg (Pa.) Telegraph
Milwaukee Semi-Weekly Wisconsin
Morning Olympian (Olympia, Wa.)
National Tribune
New London (Ct.) The Day
New Orleans Picayune
New York Herald
New York Times
New York Tribune
North Carolina Standard (Raleigh)
Norwalk (Ohio) Experiment
Norwalk (Ohio) Reflector
Norwich (Ct.) Bulletin
Ohio State Journal
Philadelphia Age
Philadelphia Inquirer
Philadelphia Press
Philadelphia Public Ledger
Philadelphia Weekly Times
Portland (Me.) Weekly Advertiser
Raleigh (N.C.) Daily Progress
Raleigh (N.C.) Weekly State Journal
Richmond Dispatch
Richmond Enquirer
Richmond Examiner
Richmond Whig
Rochester Democrat and American
Rockingham (N.C.) Register
Rome (N.Y.) Daily Sentinel
Sandusky (Ohio) Register
Seneca (Ohio) Advertiser
Staunton (Va.) Spectator
Syracuse Daily Standard
The Spirit of Democracy (Woodsfield, Ohio)
The Spirit of the Age (Raleigh, N.C.)
The Times (London, England)
The Wellsburg (W.V.) Herald
Tiffin (Ohio) Weekly Tribune
Toledo (Ohio) Blade
Washington (D.C.) National Intelligencer

Washington (D.C.) Times
Western Democrat (Charlotte, N.C.)
Wheeling (W.V.) Intelligencer
Wheeling (W.V.) Sunday Register
Wilmington (N.C.) Northern Star
Winchester (Va.) Star
Wyandot (Ohio) Democratic Union
Wyandot (Ohio) Pioneer
Xenia (Ohio) Sentinel
York (Pa.) Daily Republican
York (Pa.) Gazette
Zanesville (Ohio) Courier

Manuscripts and letters

Adams County Historical Society, Gettysburg, PA:
   87th Pennsylvania File
Alabama Department of Archives and History, Montgomery:
   John Purifoy Memoirs
   Alan Crane Collection
   Julie A. Hawkins letter
Berkeley County Historical Society, Martinsburg, WV:
   Journal entries
   Vertical files on the town's history
Bowdoin College, Brunswick, ME:
   Albert M. Riddle Diary
Cecil County Historical Society, Elkton, MD:
   Joseph T. Brown Diary
George W. Hamilton Diary
   Holt Collection
   Charles Tilden Sempers Diary
Clark County Historical Society, Springfield, OH:
   Charles Berry Correspondence
J. Warren Keifer Papers
   Vertical files on the 110th Ohio Volunteer Infantry
Clarke County Historical Association, Berryville, VA:
   Various files and records on the town's history
College of William & Mary, Williamsburg, VA:
   Laura Lee Diary
Connecticut Historical Society, Hartford:
   Anonymous Diary, soldier in the 18th Connecticut
   George W. Cross Letter
   George Kies Letters
   Henry G. Tracy Diary
Connecticut State Library, Hartford:
   Henry Clinton Davis Letter

Davidson College Archives, Davidson, NC:
  William Erksine Ardrey Papers
Duke University, Durham, NC:
  Bedinger-Dandridge Family Papers
Emory University, Manuscript, Archives and Rare Book Library, Atlanta, GA:
  John D. Babb Family Papers
  George W. Nailer Papers
Franklin & Marshall College, Special Collections, Lancaster, PA:
  George W. Booth Personal Reminiscences
Franklin County Historical and Museum Society, Malone, NY:
  William Hubbard Diary
Fredericksburg-Spotsylvania National Military Park Library, Fredericksburg, VA:
  George D. Buswell Diary
Gettysburg College, Musselman Library, Gettysburg PA:
  Capt. Johannes (John) Sachs Narrative
Gettysburg National Military Park Library, Gettysburg, PA:
  Confederate Regimental Vertical Files
  William J. Seymour Diary
George Mason University, Fairfax, VA:
  Clark Barnes Letter
Greensboro Historical Museum, Greensboro, NC:
  Eli S. Coble Letters
Hancock County Museum, Findlay, OH:
  Diary of a Civil War Soldier in Company F, 126th Ohio, Stanley Scott Collection
Handley Regional Library, Stewart Bell Jr. Archives, Winchester, VA:
  Lewis Barton Manuscript
  James W. Beeler Diary
  Julia Chase Diary
  Richard Duncan Manuscript
  Mary Greenhow Lee (Mrs. Hugh Lee) Diary
  Matthella Page Harrison Diary
  J. M. Herr Diary
  Jacob Lemley Diary
  Kate McVicar Collection
  Ben Ritter Collection
  Abram Schultz Miller Letters
  Margaretta "Gettie" Sperry Miller Diary
  Kate Sperry Diary
  John H. Stone Diary
  J. William Thomas Diary
  J. Peter Williams Papers
Historical and Genealogical Society of Indiana County, Indiana, PA:
  White Family Collection
Historical Society of Pennsylvania, Philadelphia:
  James A. Congdon Papers
Huntington Library, San Marino, CA:

William Henry Mayo Diary
2nd Division, 8th Army Corps Orderly Book, 1863, June 8-13
Indiana University of Pennsylvania, Special Collections, Indiana, PA:
The Civil War Letters of Robert F. Templeton
Iowa Women's Archives at the University of Iowa Library, Ames:
Ellen Mowrer Miller Papers
Jasper County Public Library, Rensselaer, IN:
Robert H. Milroy Papers
John Herr Collection
Jacob M. Herr Diary
Library of Congress, Manuscript Division, Washington, DC:
Lorenzo D. Barnhart Reminiscences
Richard Stoddert Ewell Papers
John William Ford Hatton Papers
Jedediah Hotchkiss Papers
Joseph Warren Keifer Papers
Abraham Lincoln Papers
Henry McCullough Diary
Library of Virginia, Richmond:
Ted Barclay Papers
Samuel T. Buchanan, Clark-Buchanan Family Letters
Robert H. Depriest Letters
Henkel Family Letters
Ross Family Correspondence
Joseph L. Snider Journal
Kate Sperry Diary
Welsh Family Papers
W. H. Wheeler Letters
James P. Williams Letters
Maryland Historical Society, Baltimore:
August James Albert Papers
Baltimore Battery of Light Artillery Records, 1862-1865
Archibald T. Kirkwood Correspondence
William H. Lyons Diary
Moffett Papers
Miami University Archives, Oxford, OH:
Robert C. Schenck Papers
Middletown Valley Historical Society, Middletown, MD:
The Globe newspaper files
Daniel H. Mowen manuscript
National Archives and Records Administration, Washington, DC:
Civil War Pension Records
Jubal A. Early Papers
R. H. Milroy File M-952, Letters received by the office of the Adjutant General
Court of Inquiry Relative to the Evacuation of Martinsburg by the Command of Brig. Gen.
Daniel Tyler, Archives I, Record Group 153, Records of the Advocate General Office,
Court-Martial Files

Union Provost Marshals' File of Papers Relating to Individual Civilians, Publication M-345
New York Historical Society, New York, NY:
   Gilder-Lehrman Collection
New York State Military Museum, Saratoga Springs:
   New York Civil War Newspaper Clipping Files
North Carolina State Archives, Raleigh:
   John Futch Letters
   John C. Gorman Letters
Northwestern State University of Louisiana, Natchitoches:
   Edmund Stephens Collection
Ohio Historical Society, Columbus:
   J. Warren Keifer Papers
   Papers of Co. F, 122nd O.V.I.
   William T. Wilson Diary for 1863-1864
   William T. Wilson Letters
Ohio University, Athens:
   Josiah L. Brown Papers
Old Courthouse Civil War Museum, Winchester, VA:
   Robert Sherrard Bell Diary
Oregon Historical Society Research Library, Portland, OR:
   Robert Huston Milroy Papers
Private collections
   Jacob M. Herr Diary
   James Mason Smith Diary
   James T. Stepter Letter
Rutherford B. Hayes President Center, Fremont, OH:
   Arlington Dunn Papers
   John R. Rhoades Papers
Southern Historical Collection, University of North Carolina, Chapel Hill:
   W. R. Gwaltney Papers
   William Nelson Pendleton Papers
Tulane University, Howard-Tilton Memorial Library, New Orleans, LA:
   William Britton Bailey Memoirs
U. S. Army Heritage & Education Center, Carlisle, PA:
   S. Z. Ammen Papers
   Eugene Blackford Memoirs
   Samuel Pickens Diary
   W. H. Bruder Journal
   Thomas O. Crowl Letters
   George Greer Diary
   Jefferson O. McMillen Letters
   James David Michaels Letters
   David Powell Papers
   James A. Stahle Papers
United States National Library of Medicine, Bethesda, MD:
   Henkel Family Letters

University of Georgia Libraries, Hargrett Rare Book & Manuscript Library, Athens:
  John Brown Gordon Letters
University of Maryland, College Park:
  James F. Stepter Papers
University of North Carolina, Chapel Hill:
  John Paris/Jacob Pearch Diary
  William H. Proffit Letters
University of Texas, Dolf Briscoe Center for American History, Austin:
  William Adolphus Smith Papers, Littlefield Southern History Collection
University of Virginia, Alderman Library, Charlottesville:
  Blackford Family Letters
  Marcus Blakemore Buck Diary and Farm Journal
  John W. Daniel Collection
  Gilmer Family Letters
  Washington Hands Civil War Notebook
  Marthella Page Harrison Diary
  Jedediah Hotchkiss Papers
  Humphrey Memoirs
  Thomas McCullough Diary
  Alexander Neil Collection
  Samuel H. Pendleton Diary
  John M. Steptoe, Steptoe Family Papers
  George Williams Civil War Letters
Virginia Historical Society, Richmond:
  Jubal Anderson Early Papers
  Watkins Kearns Diary
  Phillip De Catesby Jones Papers
  Leonard K. Sparrow Letters
Virginia Military Institute Archives, Lexington:
  Henry H. Dedrick Papers
  John Garibaldi Letters
West Virginia State Archives, Charleston, WV:
  George M. Morehead Diary
  J. B. Willoughby Diary 1862-1865
Eric J. Wittenberg Collection, Columbus, OH:
  William H. Boyd, Jr. Papers
Yale University, Beinecke Rare Book and Manuscript Library, New Haven, CT:
  Edward Christopher James Papers
York County Heritage Trust, York, PA:
  Sam and George Blotcher Papers
  Dennis W. Brandt Collection, 87th Pennsylvania
  Dennis W. Brandt York and Adams County Civil War Soldiers Database
  William Brenneman Letters
  Charles E. Gotwalt Memoirs
  Alfred Jameson Letters
  John C. Keses Papers
  George W. Schriver Diary

Articles

"A Hand Made Comic," *Morning Olympian* (Olympia, WA), Feb. 14, 1904.

Ackerd, M. H., "Early's Brigade at Winchester," *Confederate Veteran*, Vol. 29, Feb. 1921.

"All Stand Up for Milroy. Comrades Tell of Their Experiences with Milroy at Winchester and While He Was in Alabama," *National Tribune*, March 31, 1901.

Averill, S. R. "About that Running," *National Tribune*, June 6, 1895.

———. "As to Milroy," *National Tribune*, September 16, 1909.

Baker, J. W. "War Reminiscences," *Clinch Valley News*, April 22, 1921.

Beach, Lt. William H. "Some Reminiscences of the First New York (Lincoln) Cavalry," in *War Papers Read Before the Commandery of the State of Wisconsin, Military Order of the Loyal Legion of the United States*. Milwaukee: Burdick, Armitage, & Allen, 1896.

Black, Wilfred W., ed. "Civil War Letters of George Washington McMillen and Jefferson McMillen 122nd Regiment O.V.I.," *West Virginia History*, Vol. 32, No. 3 (April 1972): 171-186.

Bliss, D. M. "With Milroy at Winchester," *National Tribune*, June 10, 1915.

Bond, Frank A., "Company A, First Maryland Cavalry," *Confederate Veteran*, Vol. 6, Feb. 1898.

Bradwell, Isaac G. "Capture of Winchester, Va. and Milroy's Army in June, 1863," *Confederate Veteran*, Vol. 30, Sept. 1922.

———. "The Burning of Wrightsville, Pa." *Confederate Veteran*, 27 (1919): 300-01.

Brown, Campbell, "General Ewell's Report on the Operations of the Second Army Corps," *The Southern Magazine*, Vol. 12, June 1873.

"Bullet Drops Out of His Breast," *Norwich* (CT) *Bulletin*, March 13, 1900.

"Captain William L. Rasin," *Confederate Veteran*, Vol. 24, Oct. 1919.

Chamberlain, J. W. "Scenes in Libby Prison," Robert Hunter, ed., *Sketches of War History, 1861-1865: Papers Read Before the Ohio Commandery of the Military Order of the Loyal Legion of the United States*. Cincinnati: Robert Clarke & Co., 1888. Vol. 2.

Chisolm, Samuel H., "Forward the Louisiana Brigade," *Confederate Veteran*, Vol. 27, Nov. 1919.

Clemens, Thomas G., ed. "The 'Diary' of John H. Stone, First Lieutenant, Company B, 2d Maryland Infantry, C.S.A.", *Maryland Historical Magazine*, Vol. 85 (Summer 1990).

Daniel, W. Harrison, ed. "H. H. Harris Civil War Diary, 1863-1865," *The Virginia Baptist Register*, 1996, No. 25.

Dalzell, James M. "A Lucky Blunder," *Lovell's Library*, Vol. 20, No. 967, May 9, 1887.

———. "Milroy Swore at Rebs from Box on Pole," *Winchester Evening Star*, January 2, 1922.

Dennis, C. Z. "What Milroy Did," *National Tribune*, June 5, 1884.

Early, John Cabell, "A Southern Boy's Experience at Gettysburg," *Journal of the Military Service Institution*, Vol. 43, Jan.-Feb. 1911.

Early, Jubal A., "A Review by General Early," *Southern Historical Society Papers*, Vol. 4, July 1887.

Erskine, Charles M., "The Battle of Winchester," *Grand Army Scout and Soldier's Mail*, March 14, 1885.

"Escape of One Hundred and Nine Commissioned Yankee Officers from the Libby Prison—A Scientific Tunnel—Their Underground Route to Liberty," *Richmond Examiner*, February 11, 1864.

Evril, S. L. "Gen. Milroy at Winchester," *National Tribune*, November 29, 1888.

Ewell, Richard S., "General Ewell's Report on the Operations of the Second Army Corps," *Southern Historical Society Papers*, Vol. 10, No. 7, July 1882.

"From Winchester," *The Daily Progress*, July 17, 1863.

"General Milroy and His Conduct at Winchester," *The Delphi Times*, September 18, 1868.

"General Milroy at Front Royal," *Alexandria Gazette*, November 1, 1867.

Goldsborough, Dr. Charles E., "Fighting Them Over: What Our Old Veterans Have to Say about Their Old Campaigns: Winchester," *National Tribune*, Dec. 18, 1884.

Grant, William J. "Letter from Lieut. W. J. Grant," *The Cecil Whig*, June 27, 1863.

Griffith, J. M. "Milroy at Winchester. The Commander was not Court-Martialed, but Given Another Command," *National Tribune*, February 11, 1909.

"H. C. H." "From the 12th Virginia," *The Wellsburg Herald*, July 3, 1863.

Hall, William D. "Milroy at Winchester. A Fight of Thirty Minutes That was One of the Most Desperate of the War," *Philadelphia Weekly Times*, March 5, 1881.

Hancock, R. J., "Singleton Got the Flag," *Confederate Veteran*, Vol. 15, July 1907.

Hardy, A. S., "Terrific Fighting at Winchester," *Confederate Veteran*, Vol. 9, March 1901.

Harrison, Mattella Page and Richard C. Plater, Jr., ed., "Civil War Diary of Miss Mattella Page Harrison of Clarke County, Virginia, 1835-1898," *Proceedings of the Clarke County Historical Association*, Vol. 22 (1982-1983).

"Heroic Defense of a Bridge at Stephenson's Depot, Va.," *Confederate Veteran*, Vol. 29, Feb. 1921.

Herzog, A. J., "Milroy at Close Range," *National Tribune*, March 31, 1910.

Hill, D. H., ed. "The Haversack," *The Land We Love*, Vol. 5, No.3, July 1886.

Howard, Oliver O., "Gen'l. O. O. Howard's Personal Reminiscences of the War of the Rebellion. Between Campaigns, Movements Preliminary to Lee's Second Invasion," *National Tribune*, June 19, 1884.

Hudgins, F. L. "With the 38th Georgia," *Confederate Veteran*, Vol. 26, 1918.

Hunter, Alexander, "Thirteenth Virginia Infantry Humor," *Confederate Veteran*, Vol. 16, No. 7, July 1908.

"Important from the Potomac," *Baltimore Sun*, June 19, 1863.

Jackson, J. Warren and Merl E. Reed, ed., "The Gettysburg Campaign: A Louisiana Lieutenant's Eye-witness Account," *Pennsylvania History*, Vol. 30, No. 2, April 1963.

Lauck, T. H., "The Little Corporal's Story," *Confederate Veteran*, Vol. 29, Feb. 1921.

"Leaves from a Diary Kept by a Lady," *Southern Bivouac*, Vol. 1, No. 12, August 1883.

"Lehigh." "From Captain Bennett's Company," *Syracuse Daily Standard*, May 17, 1863.

"Letter from an Officer in the Wheeling Battery," *New York Herald*, June 22, 1863.

"Letter from the 116th O.V.I.," *Athens Messenger*, July 16, 1863.

Linn, S. T., "The Cavalry at Winchester," *National Tribune*, March 31, 1910.

Lloyd, W. G., "Second Louisiana at Gettysburg," *Confederate Veteran*, Vol. 6, Feb. 1898.

Malone, Bartlett Y., "The Diary of Bartlett Y. Malone" *The James Sprunt Historical Publications*, vol. 16, no. 2, 1919, Chapel Hill, N.C.: The University of North Carolina.

McElhinny, R. H., "Milroy at Winchester: A Very Unsafe Place Generally," *National Tribune*, May 20, 1909.

McDonald, Cornelia Peake, "Battle at Winchester," *Southern Bivouac*, Vol. 2, No. 18, June 1884.

McGee, J. L. "Milroy at Winchester: Gen. Milroy Remained in Obedience to Orders and Against His Judgment," *National Tribune*, May 29, 1913.

McKellip, William A. "Gen. Milroy's Retreat," *Baltimore Sun*, April 19, 1904.

Manion, Richard. "Civil War Letters of Arlington Dunn, 123rd Ohio Volunteer Infantry," *Northwest Ohio Quarterly*, no. 63, issue 1, 2 (Winter/Spring 1991).

"M. E. K." "Border Land in War Time," *Toledo Blade*, October 4, 1894.

Metts, James I., "Jordan Springs Battle," *Confederate Veteran*, Vol. 29, Feb. 1921.

"Milroy," *New York Daily Tribune*, July 6, 1863.

"Milroy in Winchester—A Family Driven from Their Home," *Staunton Spectator*, April 21, 1863.

"Movements of Gen. Milroy," *New York Times*, June 20, 1863.

"Newspaper Reports; Winchester and Harpers Ferry," *New York Times*, June 19, 1863.

Northcott, Robert S. "Milroy at Winchester," *Philadelphia Weekly Times*, December 4, 1880.

"Ohio spelling," *Richmond Daily Dispatch*, June 30, 1863.

"Our Baltimore Letter," *Philadelphia Inquirer*, June 19, 1863.

"Our Winchester Campaigns," *Philadelphia Inquirer*, June 19, 1863.

Porter, Charles F., "Daring and Suffering: Three Chapters in the History of a Veteran," *The Old Guard*, Vol. 4, No. 1, Feb. 5, 1889.

Powell, D. "Shenandoah Valley. Milroy's Defense of Winchester in June, 1863," *National Tribune*, May 16, 1889.

Purifoy, John, "With Jackson in the Valley," *Confederate Veteran*, Vol. 30, Oct. 1922.

"Reports from Bedford," *New York Times*, June 24, 1863.

Rivera, John J., "Two Heroines of the Shenandoah Valley," *Confederate Veteran*, Vol. 8, Nov. 1900.

Sawyer, J. H. "Abandoned at Winchester. The Great Disaster Seen from the Rear by an 18th Conn. Boy," *National Tribune*, April 6, 1916.

———. "Captured at Winchester. A Day's March Down the Valley After the Disaster to Milroy's Forces," *National Tribune*, October 23, 1913.

———. "Memory of Carter's Farm: Humane Treatment of 1,500 Yankee Prisoners on Weary March from Winchester to Staunton, Va.," *The Bolivar Breeze*, June 25, 1914.

"Sixteen Years After: Why Lee Invaded the North," *The Cuthbert Appeal*, April 28, 1882.

"Southern Account of the Capture of Winchester," *The Cecil Democrat*, June 27, 1863.

Stevenson, James H. "The First Cavalry," in Alexander K. McClure, ed. Annals of the War. Philadelphia: *Weekly Times Publishing Co.*, 1887.

Stewart, Mrs. T. H. "Warring on Women. Experience of a Union Officer's Wife in a Confederate Prison," *Philadelphia Weekly Times*, August 22, 1885.

"Sunday's Fight at Winchester," *Daily National Intelligencer*, June 20, 1863.

Taylor, Michael, ed. "Ramseur's Brigade in the Gettysburg Campaign: A Newly Discovered Account by Capt. James I. Harris, Co. I, 30th Regt. N.C.T." *Gettysburg Magazine*, No. 17, Jan. 1997.

"The Battle at Winchester.; Official Dispatch from Gen. Milroy. His Outer Fortifications Carried by Storm. He Spikes His Guns and Cuts His Way out. Our Loss About 2,000 in Killed, Wounded and Prisoners," *New York Times*, June 17, 1863.

"The Battle of Winchester," *Columbia Democrat and Bloomsburg General Advertiser*, July 4, 1863.

"The Battle of Winchester: Authentic Details of the Contest," *New York Herald*, June 22, 1863.

"The Battle of Winchester. Milroy's Retreat," *New York Times*, June 19, 1863.

"The Defence and Evacuation of Winchester," *The Continental Monthly*, Vol. 4, No. 5, Nov. 1863.

"The Loss of Winchester: A Narrative of the Investment and Abandonment of the Place," *New York Times*, June 28, 1863.

"The Rebels at Hancock," *Philadelphia Inquirer*, June 19, 1863.

Valentine, Malden. "Saved Philadelphia. Milroy's Stubborn Resistance Gave Time for the Army of the Potomac to Get Up," *National Tribune*, November 19, 1908.

Waddell, J. N., "Milroy at Winchester: A Veteran of the 12th Va. Gives His Experiences," *National Tribune*, Jan. 14, 1909.

Williams, Frank B. "Our Army Correspondence. From the 50th (Engineer) Regiment," *Rochester Democrat and American*, June 29, 1863.

"Wives and Children of Yankees Captured at Winchester," *Confederate Veteran*, Vol. 30, Nov. 1922.

"Yankee Documents and Milroy's Departure," *Richmond Enquirer*, June 22, 1863.

Ziegler, W. T. "A Wartime Recollection of Hon. W. T. Ziegler at the Battle of Winchester," *Gettysburg Compiler*, July 2, 1913.

Books

Ashby, Thomas A. *The Valley Campaigns: Being the Reminiscences of a Non-Combatant While Between the Lines in the Shenandoah Valley During the War of the States*. New York: Neale Publishing Co., 1914.

Baer, Elizabeth R., ed. *Shadows on My Heart: The Civil War Diary of Lucy Rebecca Buck of Virginia*. Athens, Ga.: University of Georgia Press, 1997.

Bartlett, Napier. *A Soldier's Story of the War*. New Orleans: Clark and Hofeline, 1884.

Basler, Roy P., ed. *The Collected Works of Abraham Lincoln*. 8 vols. New Brunswick, NJ: Rutgers University Press, 1953.

Beach, William H. *The First New York (Lincoln) Cavalry*. New York: Lincoln Cavalry Association, 1902.

Bell, John W. *Memoirs of Governor William Smith of Virginia: His Political, Military and Personal History*. New York: Moss Engraving, 1891.

Black, Daniel P., ed. *A Lincoln Cavalryman: The Civil War Letters of Henry Suydam, 1st New York Lincoln Cavalry*. Hampstead, MD: Old Line Publishing, 2011.

Booth, Andrew B. *Records of Louisiana Confederate Soldiers and Louisiana Confederate Commands*, 3 vols. Spartanburg, S.C.: Reprint Co., 1984.

Borcke, Heros von and Justus Scheibert. *The Great Cavalry Battle of Brandy Station*. Trans. Stuart T. Wright and F.D. Bridgewater. 1893; reprint, Gaithersburg, MD: Olde Soldier Books, 1976.

Boyd, Belle. *Belle Boyd, In Camp and Prison*, 2 vols. London: Saunders, Otley, and Co., 1865.

Buck, Lucy. *Sad Earth, Sweet Heaven: The Diary of Lucy Rebecca Buck*, ed. William P. Buck. Birmingham, Al.: Cornerstone, 1973.

Buck, S. D. *With the Old Confeds. Actual Experiences of a Captain in the Line*. Baltimore: H. E. Houck and Co., 1925.

Burlingame, Michael and John R. Turner Ettlinger, eds. *Inside Lincoln's White House: The Complete Civil War Diary of John Hay*. Carbondale: Southern Illinois University Press, 1997.

Bush, Lt. James C. and Theophilus F. Rodenbough, ed. "The Fifth Regiment of Artillery," in *The Army of the United States: Historical Sketches of Staff and Line with Portraits of Generals-in-Chief*. New York: Maynard, Merrill, and Co., 1896.

Caldwell, D. S. *Incidents of War, and Southern Prison Life*. Dayton, OH: United Brethren Printing Establishment, 1864.

Carmean, Edna J., ed. *Uncle Phil and the Rebbles*. Annville, PA: Lebanon Valley College Press, 1989.

Casler, John O. *Four Years in the Stonewall Brigade*. Girard, Kansas: Appeal Publishing Co., 1906.

Clapp, Henry S. "123rd Ohio: Recollections of a Private, 1863," in E. R. Hutchins, ed., *The War of the Sixties*. New York: Neale Publishing Co., 1912.

———. "With Milroy at Winchester: The Reminiscences of a Private," in *The National Tribune Repository: Good Stories of Experience and Adventure*. Vol. 1, No. 4. Washington, D. C., *National Tribune*, 1908.

Coles, David J. and Stephen D. Engle, eds. *A Yankee Horseman in the Shenandoah Valley: The Civil War Letters of John H. Black, Twelfth Pennsylvania Cavalry*. Knoxville: University of Tennessee Press, 2012.

Cornwall, Robert T. and Thomas M. Boaz. *Libby Prison & Beyond: A Union Staff Officer in the East, 1862-1865*. Shippensburg, Pa.: Burd Street Press, 2000.

Cox, Jacob Dolson. *Military Reminiscences of the Civil War*. 2 vols. New York: Charles Scribner's Sons, 1900.

Davidson, Garber A., ed. *The Civil War Letters of the Late Lieut. James J. Hartley, 122nd Ohio Infantry Regiment*. Jefferson, N. C.: McFarland & Co., 1998.

Davis, Jefferson. *Rise and Fall of the Confederate Government*. 2 vols. New York: D. Appleton & Co., 1881.

Dear Transcript: Letters home from the boys and regiments of Windham County written to the editor of their hometown newspaper, 'The Windham County Transcript.' Danielson, CT: Killingly Historical & Genealogical Society, 2009.

Douglas, Henry Kyd. *I Rode with Stonewall*. Chapel Hill: University of North Carolina Press, 1948.

Durkin, Joseph T., ed. *Confederate Chaplain: A War Journal of Rev. James B. Sheeran, c.ss.r., 14th Louisiana, C.S.A.* Milwaukee: Bruce Publishing Co., 1960.

Early, Jubal A. *Autobiographical Sketch and Narrative of the War Between the States*. Philadelphia: J. B. Lippincott Co., 1912.

Eby, Cecil D., Jr., ed. *A Virginia Yankee in the Civil War: The Diaries of David Hunter Strother*. Chapel Hill: University of North Carolina Press, 1961.

Edgar, Alfred Mallory. *My Reminiscences of the Civil War with the Stonewall Brigade and the Immortal 600*. Charleston, WV: 35th Star Publishing, 2011.

Edmondston, Catherine Ann Devereux, Beth G. Crabtree and James W. Patton, eds. *Journal of a Secesh Lady: The Diary of Catherine Ann Devereux Edmondston 1860-1866*. Raleigh: North Carolina Division of Archives and History, 1979.

Fluharty, Linda Cunningham, ed. *Civil War Letters of Lt. Milton B. Campbell, 12th West Virginia Infantry*. Baton Rouge, LA: self-published, 2004.

Fonerden, C. A. *A Brief History of Carpenter's Battery*. New Market, Va.: Henkel & Company, 1911.

Gallagher, Gary W., ed. *Fighting for the Confederacy: The Personal Recollections of General Edward Porter Alexander*. Chapel Hill: University of North Carolina Press, 1989.

Gill, John. *Courier for Lee and Jackson: 1861-1865 Memoirs*. Ed. by Walbrook D. Swank. Shippensburg, PA: Burd Street Press, 1993.

Gilmor, Harry. *Four Years in the Saddle*. New York: Harper & Brothers, 1866.

Gilson, J. H. *Concise History of the One Hundred and Twenty-Sixth Regiment, Ohio Volunteer Infantry*. Salem, Ohio: Walton, 1883.

Goldsborough, Dr. C. E. "Reminiscences from an Army Surgeon," in *The National Tribune Scrapbook: Stories of the Camp, March, Battle, Hospital and Prison Told by Comrades*. Washington, D. C.: National Tribune.

Goldsborough, William W. *The Maryland Line in the Confederate Army, 1861-1865*. Baltimore: Guggenheimer, Weil, and Co., 1900.

Gordon, John B. *Reminiscences of the Civil War*. New York: Charles Scribner's Sons, 1905.

Gotwald, Charles E. *The Adventures of a Private in the American Civil War*. York, PA: privately printed, n.d.

Granger, Moses Moorhead. *The Official War Record of the 122nd Regiment of Ohio Volunteer Infantry from October 8, 1862, to June 26, 1865*. Zanesville, OH: George Lilienthal, 1912.

Green, Wharton J. *Recollections and Reflections: An Auto of Half a Century and More.* Raleigh, NC: Edwards and Broughton, 1906.

Hall, James Edmond and Ruth Dayton Woods, eds. *The Diary of a Confederate Soldier.* Lewisburg, WV: n. p., 1961.

Hewitt, Janet B., Noah Andre Trudeau, and Bryce A. Suderow, eds. *Supplement to the Official Records of the Union and Confederate Armies.* 100 vols. Wilmington, NC: Broadfoot Publishing, 1994.

Hewitt, William. *The History of the 12th West Virginia Volunteer Infantry: The Part It Took in the War of the Rebellion, 1861-1865.* Steubenville, OH: H. C. Cook & Co., 1892.

Hodam, Robert P., ed. *The Journal of James H. Hodam: Sketches and Personal Reminiscences of the Civil War as Experienced by a Confederate Soldier.* Eugene, OR: privately published, 1995.

Hoke, Jacob. *The Great Invasion of 1863, or General Lee in Pennsylvania.* Dayton, OH: W. J. Shuey, 1887.

Horner, John B., ed. *Captain John M. Sachs: His Long Road Back to Gettysburg.* Gettysburg, PA: Horner Enterprises, 1994.

Hotchkiss, Jedediah. *Make Me a Map of the Valley: The Civil War Journal of Stonewall Jackson's Topographer.* Ed. by Archie P. McDonald. Dallas: Southern Methodist University Press, 1973.

Hubbs, G. Ward. *Voices from Company D: Diaries by the Greensboro Guards, Fifth Alabama Infantry Regiment, Army of Northern Virginia.* Athens: University of Georgia Press, 2003.

Jones, John B. *A Rebel War Clerk's Diary at the Confederate States Capitol.* 2 vols. Philadelphia: J. B. Lippincott, 1866.

Jones, Terry L., ed. *Campbell Brown's Civil War: With Ewell and the Army of Northern Virginia.* Baton Rouge: Louisiana State University Press, 2001.

———. *The Civil War Memoirs of William J. Seymour.* Baton Rouge: Louisiana State University Press, 1991.

Johnson, Pharris Deloach, ed. *Under the Southern Cross: Soldier Life with Gordon Bradwell and the Army of Northern Virginia.* Macon, GA: Mercer University Press, 2002.

Johnson, Robert Underwood and Clarence C. Buel, eds. *Battles and Leaders of the Civil War.* 4 vols. New York: The Century Co., 1887-1888.

Keifer, J. Warren. *Official Reports of J. Warren Keifer, Major General of Volunteers.* Springfield, OH: Daily Republic Steam Job Office, 1866.

———. *Slavery and Four Years of War.* New York: G. P. Putnam's Sons, 1900.

Kelley, Tom, ed. *The Personal Memoirs of Jonathan Thomas Scharf of the First Maryland Artillery.* Baltimore: Butternut & Blue, 1992.

Keyes, C. M. *The Military History of the 123rd Ohio Volunteer Infantry.* Sandusky, OH: Sandusky Steam Press, 1874.

Kimber, Thomas A. *Construction of Vauban's First System, Consisting of Six Drawings as Executed at Sandhurst and Addiscombe.* London: Parker, Furnival, and Parker, 1851.

King, John R. *My Experience in the Confederate Army and in Northern Prisons.* Clarksburg, WV: United Daughters of the Confederacy, 1917.

Lee, Susan P., ed. *Memoirs of William Nelson Pendleton, D.D., Rector of Latimer Parish, Lexington, Virginia, Brigadier-General C.S.A.; Chief of Artillery, Army of Northern Virginia.* Philadelphia: J. B. Lippincott, 1893.

Leon, Louis. *Diary of a Tar Heel Confederate Soldier.* Charlotte, NC: Stone Publishing, 1911.

Long, Armistead L. *Memoirs of Robert E. Lee.* New York: J. M. Stoddart & Co., 1886.

Lynch, Charles H. *The Civil War Diary, 1862-1865, of Charles H. Lynch, 18th Connecticut Volunteers.* Hartford, Conn.: private printing, 1915.

Macon, Emma Cassandra Riely. *Reminiscences of the Civil War.* Cedar Rapids, IA: The Torch Press, 1911.

Magill, Mary Tucker. "The Old Red House on Fort Hill," in "Our Women in the War": *The Lives They Lived, The Deaths They Died.* Charleston, SC: The Weekly News and Courier, 1885.

Mahon, Michael G., ed. *Winchester Divided: The Civil War Diaries of Julia Chase and Laura Lee.* Mechanicsburg, PA: Stackpole Books, 2002.

Malone, Barrett Y. *Whipt 'Em Everytime: The Diary of Bartlett Yancey Malone.* Jackson, TN: McCowat-Mercer Press, 1960.

"Mary J. Milroy: Report to Accompany S. 3348," Report No. 1891, House of Representatives, 51st Congress, 1st Session, May 5, 1890. Washington, DC: U.S. Government Printing Office, 1890.

Maurice, Sir Frederick, ed. *An Aide-de-Camp of Lee, Being the Papers of Colonel Charles Marshall, Sometime Aide-de-Camp, Military Secretary, and Assistant Adjutant General on the Staff of Robert E. Lee, 1862-1865.* Boston: Little, Brown & Co., 1927.

McCordick, David, ed. *The Civil War Letters of Private Henry Kauffman: The Harmony Boys are All Well.* Lewiston, NY: E. Mellen Press, 1991.

McDonald, Archie P., ed. *Make Me a Map of the Valley: The Civil War Journal of Stonewall Jackson's Topographer.* Dallas: Southern Methodist University Press, 1973.

McDonald, Cornelia Peake. *A Woman's Civil War: A Diary with Reminiscences of the War, from March 1862.* Ed. by Minrose C. Gwin. Madison: University of Wisconsin Press, 1992.

McKim, Randolph H. *A Soldier's Recollections: Leaves from the Diary of a Young Confederate.* New York: Longman, Green, and Co., 1910.

Miller, Margaretta. *The Diary of Margaretta "Gettie" Sperry Miller, March 23, 1863-September 19, 1863.* Winchester, VA: Godfrey Miller Historic Home and Fellowship Center Board of Directors, 2008.

Moore, Edward A. *The Story of a Cannoneer under Stonewall Jackson.* New York: Neale Publishing Company, 1907.

Myers, Frank M. *The Comanches: A History of White's Battalion, Virginia Cavalry.* Baltimore: Kelly, Piet & Co., 1871.

Official Army Register of the Volunteer Force of the United States Army for the Years 1861, '62, '63, '64, '65. Washington, DC: Adjutant General's Office, 1865.

Navary, James T., ed. *The Prison Diary of Michael Dougherty: Union Survivor of Two Years Confinement in Confederate Prisons.* Create Space, 2009.

Newcomer, C. Armour. *Cole's Cavalry; or Three Years in the Saddle in the Shenandoah Valley.* Baltimore: Cushing & Co., 1895.

Nichols, G. W. *A Soldier's Story of His Regiment (61st Georgia) and Incidentally of the Lawton-Gordon-Evans Brigade, Army of Northern Virginia.* Jesup, GA: privately published, 1898.

Ohio Roster Commission. *Official Roster of the Soldiers of the State of Ohio in the War of the Rebellion, 1861-1866.* 12 vols. Akron: Werner Company and Cincinnati: The Ohio Valley Press, 1886-95.

Paulus, Margaret B., comp. *Papers of General Robert Houston Milroy.* 2 vols. n.p., n.d.

Pearson, Johnnie Perry, ed. *Lee and Jackson's Bloody Twelfth: The Letters of Irby Goodwin Scott, First Lieutenant, Company G, Putnam Light Infantry, Twelfth Georgia Volunteer Infantry.* Knoxville: University of Tennessee Press, 2010.

Pfanz, Donald C., ed. *The Letters of General Richard S. Ewell: Stonewall's Successor.* Knoxville: University of Tennessee Press, 2012.

Piatt, Donn. *Memories of the Men Who Saved the Union.* New York: Belford, Clarke & Co., 1887.

Prowell, George R. *History of the Eighty-seventh Regiment, Pennsylvania Volunteers.* York, Pa.: Press of the Daily Record, 1903.

Racine, J. Polk. *Recollections of a Veteran: or, Four Years in Dixie.* Elkton, MD: Appeal Printing Office, 1894.

Reed, Thomas Benton. *A Private in Gray.* Camden, AR: s.n., 1902.

Report on the Treatment of Prisoners of War, by the Rebel Authorities, during the War of the Rebellion; To which Are Appended the Testimony Taken by the Committee, and Official Documents and Statistics, etc. Report No. 45, 40th Congress, 3d Session, House of Representatives. Washington, D.C.: U.S. Government Printing Office, 1869.

Report No. 1480, 59th Congress, 1st Session. *Thomas A. Maulsby Report to Accompany S. 4775. U.S. Senate Committee on Pensions.* Washington, DC: U.S. Government Printing Office, 1906.

Roe, Alfred Seelye. *History of the First Regiment of Heavy Artillery Massachusetts Volunteers, Formerly the Fourteenth Regiment of Infantry.* Worcester, MA: The Regimental Association, 1917.

Roper, John Herbert, ed. *Repairing the "March of Mars": The Civil War Diaries of John Samuel Apperson.* Macon, GA: Mercer University Press, 2001.

Runge, William H., ed. *Four Years in the Confederate Artillery: The Diary of Pvt. Henry Robinson Berkeley.* Chapel Hill: University of North Carolina Press, 1961.

Sauers, Richard A., ed. *Fighting Them Over: How the Veterans Remembered Gettysburg in the Pages of the National Tribune.* Baltimore: Butternut & Blue, 1998.

Schurz, Carl. *The Reminiscences of Carl Schurz.* 3 vols. New York: Doubleday, Page & Co., 1907-1908.

Simon, John Y., ed. *The Papers of Ulysses S. Grant.* 18 vols. Carbondale: Southern Illinois University Press, 1979-1991.

Smith, William Alexander, *The Anson Guards: Company C, Fourteenth Regiment North Carolina Volunteers 1861-1865* (Charlotte: Stone Publishing, 1914).

Souvenir. First Regiment of Heavy Artillery Massachusetts Volunteers. Dedication of Monument, May 19, 1901. Boston: First Massachusetts Heavy Artillery Association, 1901.

Snyder, Edmund P. *Autobiography of a Soldier of the Civil War.* Privately published, 1915.

Stephens, Robert Grier, Jr., ed. *Intrepid Warrior: Clement Anselm Evans.* Dayton, OH: Morningside Press, 1992.

Stiles, Robert. *Four Years Under Marse Robert.* New York: The Neale Publishing Co., 1904.

Stevenson, James H. *Boots and Saddles: A History of the First Volunteer Cavalry of the War, Known as the First New York (Lincoln) Cavalry.* Harrisburg, PA: Patriot Publishing, 1879.

Stout, Nancy K., ed. *The Blue Soldier: Letters of the Civil War.* Brush Prairie, WA: privately published, 1998.

Strader, Eloise, ed. *The Civil War Journal of Mary Greenhow Lee (Mrs. Hugh Holmes Lee) of Winchester, Virginia.* Winchester, VA: Winchester-Frederick County Historical Society, 2012.

Swinton, William. *Campaigns of the Army of the Potomac: A Critical History of Operations in Virginia, Maryland, and Pennsylvania from the Commencement to the Close of the War 1861-5.* New York: Charles B. Richardson, 1866.

Taylor, James E. *The James E. Taylor Sketchbook: With Sheridan Up the Shenandoah Valley in 1864.* Dayton, OH: Morningside, 1989.

Thomas, Henry W. *History of the Doles-Cook Brigade, Army of Northern Virginia.* Atlanta: Franklin Printing and Publishing Co., 1903.

Turner, Charles W., ed. Ted Barclay, *Liberty Hall Volunteers: Letters from the Stonewall Brigade (1861-1864).* Berryville, Va.: Rockbridge Publishing Co., 1992.

———. *The Allen Family of Amherst County, Virginia: Civil War Letters.* Berryville, VA: Rockbridge Publishing Co., 1995.

United States War Department. *Atlas to Accompany the Official Records of the Union and Confederate Armies*. 4 vols. Washington, D.C.: 1891-1895.

——. *The War of the Rebellion: A Compilation of the Official Records of the Union and Confederate Armies*. 128 vols. in 3 series. Washington, DC: 1880-1901.

Vaughan, B. F., ed. *Life and Writings of Rev. Henry Y. Rush, D. D.* Dayton, OH: The Christian Publishing Association, 1911.

Waddell, Joseph A. *Annals of Augusta County, Virginia, from 1726 to 1871*. Staunton, VA: C. Russell Caldwell, 1902.

Walcott, Charles F. *History of the Twenty-First Regiment Massachusetts Volunteers*. Boston: Houghton-Mifflin, 1882.

Walker, Chaplain William C. *History of the Eighteenth Regiment Conn. Volunteers in the War for the Union*. Norwich, CT: Regimental Committee, 1885.

Welles, Gideon. *Diary of Gideon Welles: Secretary of the Navy under Lincoln and Johnson*. 2 vols. Boston: Houghton-Mifflin, 1909.

White, William S. "A Diary of the War: What I Saw of It," in Carlton McCarthy, ed., *Contributions to a History of the Richmond Howitzers, Pamphlet No. 2*. Richmond, VA: Carlton McCarthy and Co., 1883.

Wild, Frederick W. *Memoirs and History of Capt. F. W. Alexander's Baltimore Battery of Light Artillery, U. S. V.* Loch Raven, MD: Press of the Maryland School for Boys, 1912.

Wildes, Thomas F. *Record of the 116th Regiment Ohio Infantry Volunteers*. Sandusky, OH: I. F. Mack, 1884.

Worsham, John H. *One of Jackson's Foot Cavalry*. New York: Neale Publishing Co., 1912.

Electronic Sources

Ted Barclay Letters, Washington and Lee University,
https://repository.wlu.edu/handle/11021/5668

Lorenzo D. Barnhart Reminiscences, 110th Ohio Volunteer Infantry,
http://www.frontierfamilies.net/family/2ndwintr.htm

David Close Letters, 126th Ohio Volunteer Infantry,
http://frontierfamilies.net/family/DCletters.htm#mberg

Jim Fisher's Sixth Regiment of Maryland Infantry Descendants Association website,
http://www.6thmarylandinfantry.org/DescriptiveCoH.htm

Charles M. Gross, "Sketch of Army and Prison Life from the Diary of Charles Milford Gross 1823-1909," Cathy Coplen collection,
http://www.latinamericanstudies.org/cavada/charles-gross.htm

Jedediah Hotchkiss Letters to his Wife, Valley of the Shadow,
http://valley.lib.virginia.edu/

Abraham Lincoln note of October 19, 1863 (with Milroy's commentary on back),
http://www.shapell.org/manuscript.aspx?abraham-lincoln-avoids-general-milroy

Gregory Lepore's Russell County, Va., Civil War Website,
http://russellvets.org/letters/ckelly.html

Charles H. Lynch Diary, Soldier Studies,
http://www.soldierstudies.org/index.php?action=view_letter&Letter=884 and
http://www.soldierstudies.org/index.php?action=view_letter&Letter=885

Arch Rowand Letters Home, Jessie Scouts,
http://www.jessiescouts.com/JS_Letters_1863_June_21.html

Civil War Letters of Thomas S. Taylor,
http://www.usgennet.org/usa/al/state1/military/6th/letters/taylor6.htm
"Veritas," letter of July 24, 1863, 1st Regiment Cavalry, N.Y. Volunteers Civil War Newspaper Clippings,
http://dmna.ny.gov/historic/reghist/civil/cavalry/1stCav/1stCavCWN.htm.

Maps

Blythe, M. "Map of Homespun The Property of John N. Bell, Esq., Frederick County, Virginia; Surveyed and Drawn by C. Engineer 1858," Handley Regional Library Archives, Winchester, Va.

"Frederick County Wall Map," 1860s, www.historicmapworks.com.

Gillespie, G. L. "Battle field of Winchester, Va. (Opequon) [19 September, 1864]," United States Army, 1873, Library of Congress.

Hotchkiss, Jedediah. "Sketch of the Second Battle of Winchester, June 13th, 14th, and 15th, 1863," Library of Congress.

Lake, D. J. "Map of Frederick County, Virginia," D. J. Lake & Co., 1885, Handley Library, Winchester, Va.;

"Map of the Winchester battlefield," *New York Herald*, June 22, 1863.

Secondary Sources

Articles

Bean, William G., "A House Divided: The Civil War Letters of A Virginia Family," *Virginia Magazine of History and Biography*, Vol. 59, No. 4, Oct. 1951.

Beck, Brandon H., "The Second Battle of Winchester," *Potomac Magazine*, Spring 1994.

Chance, Mark A., "Prelude to Invasion: Lee's Preparations and the Second Battle of Winchester," *Gettysburg Magazine*, No. 19, Jan. 1999.

Collins, Cary C., "Grey Eagle: Major General Robert Huston Milroy and the Civil War," *Indiana Magazine of History*, No. 90, March 1994.

Droegemeyer, James R., "The Battle of Martinsburg, June 14, 1863," *The Berkeley Journal*, No. 27, 2001.

Fordney, Chris, "A Town Embattled," *Civil War Times Illustrated*, Vol. 34, No. 6, Feb. 1996.

French, Steve, "Battle Depended upon Delay," *Washington Times*, Nov. 23, 2002.

———, "Federals on 'Safe' Road to Trouble," *Washington Times*, Dec. 2, 2005.

———, "The Battle of Martinsburg," *Gettysburg Magazine*, No. 34, Jan. 2006.

Harter, Dale, "John B. Sheets Diary," *Harrisonburg-Rockingham Historical Society Newsletter*, Vol. 31, No. 1, Winter 2009.

Holsworth, Jerry W., "Quiet Courage: Winchester, Va., in the Civil War," *Blue & Gray*, Vol. 15, No. 2, Dec. 1997.

Jones, Terry L., "Going Back in the Union at Last: A Louisiana Tiger's account of the Gettysburg Campaign," *Civil War Times Illustrated*, vol. 29, no. 6, Jan./Feb. 1991.

Longacre, Edward G., "Target: Winchester, Virginia," *Civil War Times Illustrated*, June 1976.

Miller, William J., "Grey Eagle on a Tether," *America's Civil War*, No. 5, 2002.

Miner, Mark A., "First Fight, First Blood: The 12th West Virginia Infantry at the Second Battle of Winchester," *Journal of the Winchester-Frederick County Historical Society*, Vol. 4, 1989.

Moore, Maj. Samuel J. C., "Milroy at Winchester," *Journal of the Winchester-Frederick County Historical Society*, No. 11.

Noyalas, Jonathan A., "The Most Hated Man in Winchester," *America's Civil War*, Vol. 17, No. 1, 2004.

Scott, W. W., ed., "Two Confederate Items," *Bulletin of the Virginia State Library* (Richmond, Va.: David Bottom, Superintendent of Public Printing, 1927).

Wells, Dean M., "Ewell Seizes the Day at Winchester," *America's Civil War*, March 1997.

Books

Ackinclose, Timothy R., *Sabres & Pistols: The Civil War Career of Col. Harry Gilmor*. Gettysburg, PA: Stan Clark Military Books, 1997.

Armstrong, Richard L. *25th Virginia Infantry and 9th Battalion Virginia Infantry*. Lynchburg, VA: H. E. Howard, 1990.

Ashcraft, John M. *31st Virginia Infantry*. Lynchburg, VA: H.E. Howard, 1988.

Bates, Samuel P. *History of Pennsylvania Volunteers, 1861-5*. 5 vols. Harrisburg: B. Singerly, 1869-71.

Beck, Brandon H. and Charles S. Grunder. *The First Battle of Winchester*. Lynchburg, VA: H. E. Howard, 1992.

——. *The Second Battle of Winchester, June 12-15, 1863*. Lynchburg, VA: H. E. Howard, 1989.

——. *Three Battles of Winchester: A History and Guided Tour*. Berryville, VA: Country Publishers, 1988.

Berkey, Jonathan M. "War in the Borderland: The Civilians' Civil War in Virginia's Lower Shenandoah Valley." PhD diss., Pennsylvania State University, 2003.

Bittinger, Emmert F., ed., with David S. Rodes and Norman R. Wenger, comps. *Unionists and the Civil War Experience in the Shenandoah Valley*. 6 vols. Camden, ME: Penobscot Press, 2008.

Boatner, Mark M. *The Civil War Dictionary*. New York: David McKay Co., 1959.

Boaz, Thomas M. *Libby Prison and Beyond: A Union Staff Officer in the East, 1862-1865*. Shippensburg, PA: Burd Street Press, 1999.

Bohannon, Keith S. *The Giles, Alleghany and Jackson Artillery*. Lynchburg, VA: H.E. Howard, 1990.

Brandt, Dennis W. *From Home Guards to Heroes: The 87th Pennsylvania and Its Civil War Community*. Columbia, MO: University of Missouri Press, 2006.

Bridges, Peter. *Donn Piatt: Gadfly of the Gilded Age*. Kent, OH: Kent State University Press, 2012.

Brinsfield, John W., William C. Davis, Benedict Maryniak, and James I Robertson Jr. *Faith in the Fight: Civil War Chaplains*. Mechanicsburg PA: Stackpole Books, 2003.

Broadwater, Robert P. *Civil War Medal of Honor Recipients: A Complete Record*. Jefferson, NC: McFarland, 2007.

Cartmell, T. K. *Shenandoah Valley Pioneers and Their Descendants*. Privately printed, 1908.

Chapla, John D. *42nd Virginia Infantry*. Lynchburg, VA: H.E. Howard, 1983.

——. *48th Virginia Infantry*. Lynchburg, VA: H.E. Howard, 1989.

——. *50th Virginia Infantry*. Lynchburg, VA: H.E. Howard, 1997.

Clark, Walter, ed. *Histories of the Several Regiments and Battalions from North Carolina in the Great War 1861-1865*. 5 vols. Goldsboro, NC: n.p., 1901.

Clemmer, Gregg S. *Old Alleghany: The Life and Wars of General Ed Johnson*. North Potomac, MD: Hearthside Publishing Co., 2004.

Coddington, Edwin B. *The Gettysburg Campaign: A Study in Command*. New York: Macmillan, 1968.

Collins, Darrell L. *Major General Robert E. Rodes of the Army of Northern Virginia: A Biography*. El Dorado Hills, CA: Savas-Beatie, 2008.

Colt, Margaretta Barton, ed. *Defend the Valley: A Shenandoah Family in the Civil War*. New York: Oxford University Press, 1999.

Croffut, W. A. and John M. Morris. *The Military and Civil History of Connecticut During the War of 1861-65*. New York: Ledyard Bill, 1868.

Davis, William C. and Julie Hoffman, eds. *The Confederate General*. 5 vols. New York: National Historical Society, 1991.

Dawson, John Harper. *Wildcat Cavalry: A Synoptic History of the Seventeenth Virginia Cavalry Regiment of the Jenkins-McCausland Brigade in the War Between the States*. Dayton, OH: Morningside, 1982.

Delauter, Roger U. *McNeill's Rangers*. Lynchburg, VA: H.E. Howard, 1986.

———. *Winchester in the Civil War*. Lynchburg, VA: H. E. Howard, 1992.

Dickinson, Jack L. *16th Virginia Cavalry*. Lynchburg, VA: H.E. Howard, 1989.

Driver, Robert J., Jr. *First and Second Maryland Infantry C.S.A.* Westminster, MD: Willow Bend Books, 2003.

———. *14th Virginia Cavalry*. Lynchburg, VA: H.E. Howard, 1988.

———. *52nd Virginia Infantry*. Lynchburg, VA: H.E. Howard, 1986.

———. *58th Virginia Infantry*. Lynchburg, VA: H.E. Howard, 1990.

Droegemeyer, James R. *"He is Our Colonel and We are His Soldiers": When the 106th New York Volunteer Infantry Came to Virginia (West Virginia)*. Seattle: Amazon Digital Services, 2007.

Duncan, Richard R. *Beleaguered Winchester: A Virginia Community at War, 1861-1865*. Baton Rouge: Louisiana State University Press, 2007.

Earley, Gerald L. *I Belonged to the 116th: A Narrative of the 116th Ohio Volunteer Infantry in the Civil War*. Berwyn Heights, MD: Heritage Books, 2004.

Fishel, Edwin C. *The Secret War for the Union: The Untold Story of Military Intelligence in the Civil War*. Boston: Houghton-Mifflin, 1996.

Fisher, James R. *Manly Deeds—Womanly Words. History of the 6th Regiment Maryland Infantry*. Westminster, MD: Willow Bend Books, 2003.

Flaherty, Linda Cunningham and Edward L. Phillips. *Carlin's Wheeling Battery: A History of Battery D, First West Virginia Light Artillery*. Baton Rouge, LA: Linda Cunningham Fluharty, 2005.

Freeman, Douglas Southall. *Lee's Lieutenants: A Study in Command*. 3 vols. New York: Charles Scribner's Sons, 1942.

French, Steve. *Imboden's Brigade in the Gettysburg Campaign*. Berkeley Springs, WV: Morgan Messenger, 2008.

Frye, Dennis E. *2nd Virginia Infantry*. Lynchburg, VA: H. E. Howard, 1984.

Gallagher, Gary W. *Stephen Dodson Ramseur: Lee's Gallant General*. Chapel Hill: University of North Carolina Press, 1985.

Gannon, James. *Irish Rebels, Confederate Tigers: A History of the 6th Louisiana Volunteers, 1861-1865*. Campbell, CA: Savas Publishing Co., 1998.

Gottfried, Bradley M. *The Maps of Gettysburg: An Atlas of the Gettysburg Campaign, June 3-July 13, 1863*. New York: Savas Beatie, 2007.

———. *Roads to Gettysburg: Lee's Invasion of the North, 1863*. Shippensburg, PA: White Mane, 2001.

Hale, Laura Virginia. *Four Valiant Years in the Lower Shenandoah Valley, 1861-1865*. Front Royal, VA: Hathaway Publishing, 1968.

Hale, Laura V. and Stanley S. Phillips. *History of the Forty-Ninth Virginia Infantry, C.S.A.: "Extra Billy Smith's Boys"*. Lanham, MD: S. S. Phillips, 1981.

Hall, Susan G. *Appalachian Ohio and the Civil War, 1862-1863.* Jefferson, NC: McFarland, 2008.

Hamilton, Louis H. and William Darroch, eds. *A Standard History of Jasper and Newton Counties Indiana. An Authentic Narrative of the Past, with an Extended Survey of Modern Developments in the Progress of Town and County.* 2 vols. Chicago: The Lewis Publishing Co., 1918.

Hand, Harold, Jr. *One Good Regiment: The 13th Pennsylvania Cavalry in the Civil War 1861-1865.* Victoria, BC: Trafford, 2000.

Harris, Nelson. *17th Virginia Cavalry.* Lynchburg, VA: H.E. Howard, 1994.

Hazlett, James C., Edwin Olmstead and M. Hume Parks. *Field Artillery Weapons of the Civil War.* Champaign: University of Illinois Press, 2004.

Hofe, Michael W. *That There Be No Stain Upon My Stones: Lieutenant Colonel William L. McLeod, 38th Georgia Regiment, 1842-1863.* Gettysburg, PA: Thomas Publications, 1995.

Hollingshead, Steve and Jeffrey Whetstone. *From Winchester to Bloody Run: Border Raids and Skirmishes in Western Pennsylvania During the Gettysburg Campaign.* Everett, PA: privately published, 2004.

Holsworth, Jerry W. *Civil War Winchester.* Charleston, SC: The History Press, 2011.

Hunt, Roger D. *Colonels in Blue: Union Army Colonels of the Civil War.* New York. Atglen, PA: Schiffer Military History, 2003.

———. *Colonels in Blue: Union Army Colonels of the Civil War. The Mid-Atlantic States: Pennsylvania, New Jersey, Maryland, Delaware, and the District of Columbia.* Mechanicsburg, PA: Stackpole Books, 2007.

Kellogg, Sanford C. *The Shenandoah Valley and Virginia, 1861-1865: A War Study.* New York: Neale Publishing, 1903.

Kesterson, Brian S. *Campaigning with the 17th Virginia Cavalry: Night Hawks at Monocacy.* Washington, WV: Night Hawk Press, 2005.

Lowe, David. *Study of Civil War Sites in the Shenandoah Valley of Virginia.* Washington, DC: U. S. Department of the Interior, National Park Service, 1992.

Macaluso, Gregory J. *Morris, Orange, and King William Artillery.* Lynchburg, VA: H. E. Howard, 1991.

Maier, Larry B. *Gateway to Gettysburg: The Second Battle of Winchester.* Shippensburg, PA: Burd Street Press, 2002.

———. *Leather & Steel: The 12th Pennsylvania Cavalry in the Civil War.* Shippensburg, PA: Burd Street Press, 2002.

Maryniak, Benedict R. and John Wesley Brinsfield, eds. *The Spirit Divided: Memoirs of Civil War Chaplains: The Union.* Macon, GA: Mercer University Press, 2007.

Mingus, Scott L., *Confederate General William "Extra Billy" Smith: From Virginia's Statehouse to Gettysburg Scapegoat.* El Dorado Hills, CA: Savas Beatie, 2013.

———. *The Louisiana Tigers in the Gettysburg Campaign.* Baton Rouge: Louisiana State University Press, 2009.

Moore, Robert H., II. *The Charlottesville, Lee Lynchburg and Johnson's Bedford Artillery.* Lynchburg, VA: H.E. Howard, 1990.

Morton, Frederic. *The Story of Winchester in Virginia: The Oldest Town in the Shenandoah Valley.* Westminster, MD: Heritage Books, 2007.

Murphy, Terrence V. *10th Virginia Infantry.* Lynchburg, VA: H.E. Howard, 1989.

Murray, Alton J. *South Georgia Rebels: The True Wartime Experiences of the 26th Regiment, Georgia Volunteer Infantry.* St. Mary's, Ga.: Self-published, 1976.

Nicholas, Richard L. and Joseph Servis. *Powhatan, Salem and Courtney Henrico Artillery.* Lynchburg, VA: H. E. Howard, 1997.

Noyalas, Jonathan A. *"My Will is Absolute Law": A Biography of Union General Robert H. Milroy.* Jefferson, NC: McFarland, 2006.

————. *Plagued by War: Winchester, Virginia during the Civil War.* Leesburg, VA: Gauley Mount Press, 2003.

Nye, Wilbur S., *Here Come the Rebels!* Baton Rouge: Louisiana State University Press, 1965.

Patchan, Scott C. *Second Manassas: Longstreet's Attack and the Struggle for Chinn Ridge.* Dulles, VA: Potomac Books, 2011.

————. *The Last Battle of Winchester: Phil Sheridan, Jubal Early, and the Shenandoah Valley Campaign, August 7 - September 19, 1864.* El Dorado Hills, CA: Savas-Beatie, 2013.

Petruzzi, J. David and Steven A. Stanley. *The Gettysburg Campaign in Numbers and Losses.* El Dorado Hills, CA: Savas Beatie, 2012.

Pfanz, Donald C. *Richard S. Ewell: A Soldier's Life.* Chapel Hill: University of North Carolina Press, 1998.

Phillips, Edward H. *The Lower Shenandoah Valley in the Civil War.* Lynchburg, VA: H. E. Howard, 1993.

Phipps, Sheila R. *Genteel Rebel: The Life of Mary Greenhow Lee.* Baton Rouge: Louisiana State University Press, 2004.

Ping, Laura J. *Life in an Occupied City: Women in Winchester, Virginia during the Civil War.* Richmond: Master's Thesis, Virginia Commonwealth University, 2007.

Poirier, Robert G. *By the Blood of Our Alumni: Norwich University Citizen Soldiers in the Army of the Potomac, 1861-1865.* Mason City, IA: Savas Publishing, 1999.

Pope, Thomas E., ed. *The Weary Boys: Col. J. Warren Keifer and the 110th Ohio Volunteer Infantry.* Kent, Ohio, Kent State University Press, 2002.

Quarles, Garland. *Civil War Battles in Winchester and Frederick County.* Winchester, VA: Civil War Centennial Commission, 1960.

————. *Diaries, Letters, and Recollections of the War Between the States.* Winchester, VA: Winchester-Frederick County Historical Society, 1955.

————. *Occupied Winchester.* Winchester, VA: Farmers and Merchants National Bank, 1976.

Rankin, Thomas M. *23rd Virginia Infantry.* Lynchburg, VA: H.E. Howard, 1985.

————. *37th Virginia Infantry.* Lynchburg, VA: H.E. Howard, 1987.

Reid, Whitelaw. *Ohio in the War: Her Statesmen, Her Generals and Soldiers.* 2 vols. Cincinnati: Moore, Wilstack and Baldwin, 1868.

Reidenbaugh, Lowell. *27th Virginia Infantry.* Lynchburg, VA: H.E. Howard, 1993.

————. *33rd Virginia Infantry.* Lynchburg, VA: H.E. Howard, 1987.

Rhodes, Robert M. "Fortifications in Frederick County," in Sam Lehman, ed. *The Story of Frederick County.* Winchester, VA: Frederick County Board of Supervisors, 1984.

Riggs, David F. *13th Virginia Infantry.* Lynchburg, VA: H.E. Howard, 1988.

Riggs, Susan A. *21st Virginia Infantry.* Lynchburg, VA: H.E. Howard, 1991.

Robertson, James I. *4th Virginia Infantry.* Lynchburg, VA: H.E. Howard, 1982.

Ruffner, Kevin C. *44th Virginia Infantry.* Lynchburg, VA: H.E. Howard, 1987.

Sauers, Richard A. *Advance the Colors! Pennsylvania Civil War Battle Flags.* 2 vols. Harrisburg: Capitol Preservation Committee, 1987.

Schildt, John W. *Roads to Gettysburg.* Parsons, WV: McClain Printing Co., 1978.

Scott, J. L. *36th and 37th Battalions Virginia Infantry.* Lynchburg, VA: H.E. Howard, 1986.

Smith, Tunstall, ed. *Richard Snowden Andrews: Lieutenant Colonel Commanding the First Maryland Artillery.* Baltimore: The Sun Job Printing Office, 1910.

Summers, Festus P. *The Baltimore and Ohio in the Civil War*. Gettysburg, PA: Stan Clark Military Books, 1993.

Swisher, James K. *Warrior in Gray: General Robert Rodes of Lee's Army*. Shippensburg, PA: White Mane, 2000.

Valuska, David L. and Christian B. Keller. *Damn Dutch: Pennsylvania Germans at Gettysburg*. Mechanicsburg, PA: Stackpole Books, 2004.

Wallace, Lee A., Jr. *5th Virginia Infantry*. Lynchburg, VA: H.E. Howard, 1988.

Warner, Ezra J. *Generals in Blue: Lives of the Union Commanders*. Baton Rouge: Louisiana State University Press, 1964.

————. *Generals in Gray: Lives of the Confederate Commanders*. Baton Rouge: Louisiana State University Press, 1959.

Wellman, Manly Wade. *Rebel Boast: First at Bethel-Last at Appomattox*. New York: Henry Holt & Co., 1974.

Wert, Jeffry D. *Cavalryman of the Lost Cause: A Biography of J.E.B. Stuart*. New York: Simon & Schuster, 2008.

Wheelan, Joseph. *Libby Prison Breakout: The Daring Escape from the Notorious Civil War Prison*. New York: Public Affairs, 2010.

Wilmer, L. Allison, J. H. Jarrett, and George W. F. Vernon. *History and Roster of Maryland Volunteers, War of 1861-5*. 2 vols. Baltimore: Press of Guggenheim, Weil & Co., 1898.

Wise, Jennings Cropper. *The Long Arm of Lee, of the History of the Artillery of the Army of Northern Virginia*. 2 vols. Lynchburg, VA: J. P. Bell Co., 1915.

Wittenberg, Eric J. T*he Battle of Brandy Station: North America's Largest Cavalry Battle*. Charleston, SC: The History Press, 2010.

Wittenberg, Eric J., J. David Petruzzi and Michael F. Nugent. *One Continuous Fight: The Retreat from Gettysburg and the Pursuit of Lee's Army of Northern Virginia, July 4-14, 1863*. El Dorado Hills, CA: Savas Beatie, 2008.

Wynstra, Robert J. *The Rashness of That Hour: Politics, Gettysburg, and the Downfall of Confederate Brigadier General Alfred Iverson*. El Dorado Hills, CA: Savas Beatie, 2010.

Electronic Sources

"First Fight, First Blood: The Twelfth West Virginia Infantry at the Second Battle of Winchester," by Mark A. Miner,
http://www.markminer.com/12wv.htm.

"Northwest Ohio in the Civil War," Bowling Green University
http://www.bgsu.edu/colleges/library/cac/cwar/123ovib.html.

"Second Winchester (13-15 June 1863)," National Park Service,
http://www.nps.gov/hps/abpp/shenandoah/svs3-7.html.

Wittenberg, Eric J. "Col. William H. Boyd, Part 2,"
http://civilwarcavalry.com/?p=3849.

Index

About the Author

Scott L. Mingus Sr. is a scientist, executive in the global paper industry, and an award-winning author.

In addition to a wide variety of published articles for magazines and blogs, Scott has penned eighteen Civil War books, including the best-selling *Flames Beyond Gettysburg: The Confederate Expedition to the Susquehanna River, June 1863* (Savas Beatie, 2011), and *Confederate General William "Extra Billy" Smith: From Virginia's Statehouse to Gettysburg Scapegoat* (Savas Beatie, 2013), which won the Nathan Bedford Forrest Southern History Award and the Dr. James I. Robertson, Jr. Literary Prize, and was nominated for the Virginia Literary Award for Non-Fiction. His most recent book with Savas Beatie, co-authored with David Shultz, is *The Second Day at Gettysburg: The Attack and Defense of Cemetery Ridge, July 2, 1863* (2016). Scott is currently finishing, with co-author Walter Westcote, *Books on the American Civil War Era: A Critical Bibliography* (Savas Beatie, 2016).

Scott maintains a blog on the Civil War history of York County (www.yorkblog.com/cannonball) and resides in York, Pennsylvania, with his wife Debi.

Author

About the Author

Eric J. Wittenberg is an attorney, accomplished American Civil War cavalry historian, and an award-winning author.

In addition to penning articles for a variety of different magazines, Eric is also the author, co-author, or editor of more than a dozen books on Civil War cavalry subjects, including *The Battle of Monroe's Crossroads: The Civil War's Final Campaign* (Savas Beatie, 2006), *Plenty of Blame to Go Around: Jeb Stuart's Controversial Ride to Gettysburg* (Savas Beatie, 2006), and *One Continuous Fight: The Retreat from Gettysburg and the Pursuit of Lee's Army of Northern Virginia, July 4-14, 1863* (Savas Beatie, 2008). His *Gettysburg's Forgotten Cavalry Actions: Farnsworth's Charge, South Cavalry Field, and the Battle of Fairfield, July 3, 1863* (Thomas, 1998; revised and expanded by Savas Beatie, 2011), was the recipient of the prestigious Bachelder-Coddington Literary Award. His latest bestseller is *"The Devil's to Pay": John Buford at Gettysburg. A History and Walking Tour* (Savas Beatie, 2014), which won the Gettysburg CWRT's 2015 Book Award.

Eric, who regularly leads battlefield tours and speaks widely on the war, lives and works in Columbus, Ohio, with his wife Susan.